Wealth
by Virtue

———

CHAD GORDON

Cover designed by Juan Fuentes juanitofu@gmail.com
Interior graphic design by Gabi Hill gabihill.co.za

ISBN: 978-0-692-76915-7
Library of Congress Control Number: 2017952083
Classification: LCC HG179 .G67 2017 | DDC 332.024—dc23

Publisher: GreenStar Press
Copyright © Chad Gordon, 2017

Printed and bound in Canada by Friesens. All materials in this book are Forest Stewardship Council certified which ensures the trees came from well-managed sustainable forests. All inks are soy based.

Wealth
by Virtue

—

CHAD GORDON

GreenStar
PRESS
2017

Contents

AREAS

OF FINANCE

What could happen

NEGATIVE POSSIBILITIES

WHAT COULD

WHAT IS

Introduction

Most people share a central fear: that at some point in their lives, they will need money and not have it. Not just that. We fear finding ourselves in the horrifying position of *desperately needing money and not having it*. Throughout my career in financial services, I've found that people are hungry for direction. The vast torrent of available knowledge seems to cause as much confusion as clarity. As the flood of information rises, bad advice has become harder to filter out.

The internet has brought us the gift of information, but we still have to apply it to our own lives. It's one thing to use the internet to learn how to unclog your sink; it's another to YouTube your family's financial planning.

In the journey to financial security, many of us sail our metaphorical boats without navigational tools. Sometimes luck gets us further than it should. We sail smooth waters hoping they stay calm, and react to the frightful storms with short-term thinking. In the pouring rain and turbulent sea, all of our hopes collapse to the single concern of staying afloat. We forget our lifelong goals and jettison the tools we'll need to survive beyond the storm. Wise financial decisions chart a longer-term course where luck is not a factor, hope is never a strategy, and fear is not an option.

Great accomplishments begin with a courageous and honest assessment of the facts. If you are fighting a war, you must know the strength of your enemy. If you are building a bridge, you must know the span length. If you want to maximize your wealth, you must face the *brutal facts* about who you are, where you are, and what you need. Recognize the facts about your assets, debt, and income, but also know who you are as a psychological and biological creature you are prone to getting in your own way. It is not just investing, but behavior during the voyage, that creates wealth.

This book is about *how* to think about money in a constructive and cohesive way. If you are looking for something in the get-rich-quick genre, look elsewhere. Then set it on fire. I have known many wealthy people. Not one of them keeps a shelf of get-rich-quick books. But many possess libraries about principles, wisdom, and approaching the world with a balance of caution and boldness.

If you are like most people, you can identify with the fear that at some point in your life, you will need money and not have it. The answer to this fear is within these pages. It is a balance of strengthening your finances, protecting your assets, and recognizing the system in which you live. It is not just a game of numbers, but a game of psychology—especially *your* psychology and the psychology of your advisors.

My goal is to provide you a basis on which to become a discerning consumer of financial information. Just as it would be foolhardy for me to try to make this book encyclopedic, it would be foolish to believe that you can learn enough in a single book to not need professionals. This book will empower you to make decisions about how to structure your finances and give you the foundation to choose the right professionals to advise you. It will also help you make educated decisions when you find yourself in a position where you are being *sold* to, rather than *advised*. This book exists to empower you as someone who makes *investments* rather than a buyer of *financial products*.

Education is power. Uninformed people are vulnerable. Ignorance hinders freedom, and freedom and independence are among the most important sources of human joy.

And joy is where it gets tricky. Years ago I began advising a lovely couple. They were very kind, and the most frugal people I had ever met in my life (this is saying a lot; I come from a Scottish family). They lived in a trailer home located in a less-than-desirable part of town. They rarely splurged on eating out or traveling. They shopped at thrift stores when they occasionally updated their clothing. And ... their net worth was well over a million dollars. They were—literally—trailer park millionaires.

When I first met with them, their needs were a mix of issues ranging from optimizing their investments, legal planning, and using insurance to prevent their heirs from being excessively taxed. After we had established our mutual game plan, I asked them rather bluntly, "What's the point?" They looked at me funny and I clarified, "Let's say we get everything optimized, let's say your portfolio doubles or triples ... so what? What would it do for your lives, what would change?"

This question visibly made them uncomfortable. As they squirmed I said, "Let me tell you a story."

Early in my career I worked at an old fashioned savings and loan bank. We offered the best rates in town, and this attracted a certain kind of customer. One emblematic individual was Mr. Tonlin. He was meticulous in his management of his $4,000,000, which was divided among *fifty* or so accounts with different maturity dates. He would come in every week with his list on a clipboard held proudly to his chest and carefully make decisions about which ones to get, haggling with management for better rates. He carried the air of a business magnate from the Industrial Revolution. This was his pride and joy. Then, after years of this routine, his wife passed away.

Mr. Tonlin came in the afternoon after the funeral—perhaps to get some grounding in his routines. He seemed like he had lost six inches of height. He came into the bank lobby expressionless, posture limp, disoriented. Various staff came up to him, expressing their condolences. He ambled to the counter holding his clipboard, which now seemed to be very heavy to him. We waited for him to say something as he looked at the list. Then quietly, looking down at his clipboard, his chin quivered and his eyes welled up, "I should have spent this money with her. What am I going to do with it?"

It's been over a decade since this happened. I would bet that a week hasn't gone by that I haven't thought of that man and this single phrase.

After telling my clients this story, I repeated the question to these trailer park millionaires, "What's the point?"

I believe that those who have saved up deserve the reward of minimizing their fears about money while maximizing their energy for the real things of life. Ask yourself: what is the point? This is not a rhetorical question. If you and I optimize your financial life, leaving no stone unturned, what's the point? What would change? What *should* change?

To me, the point is this: you should have the luxury of diverting your emotional energy away from worrying about money. Spend that same energy on more important things like family and friends, pursuing goals and experiences, enjoying life, or giving back to the world. The emotional cost of financial chaos is profoundly impoverishing. Bringing order to chaos will enable you to divert your energy to the things that enrich your life.

Financial strength is not about having a lot of money. The ancient Romans had a saying, "Money is like seawater. The more you drink, the thirstier you become." As you grow in wealth, you must also grow in wisdom.

"Wealth" is not a certain amount of accumulation, or the territory beyond a numerical line in the sand. Wealth is the absence of financial worry. Wealth is an internal sense of freedom. When you retire, your financial life collapses down to one core binary question:

Will your money outlive you, or will you outlive your money?

If you want to build a tall tower you have to lay every brick correctly, especially the ones you lay down first. To begin constructing your financial tower, let us first look at our blueprint. It is here where we will establish the three "Pool Rules" of growing your money and outline everything you will learn. These rules will give you the foundation for financial self-empowerment. Learn these rules first, and let the understanding settle in your mind before moving on.

I wish you all the best in growing in your understanding, wisdom, and wealth.

This book exists
to empower you as
someone who makes
investments
rather than a buyer of
financial products.

Blueprint

Your finances are like a car: if all the parts don't work together, the whole system can break. There's no point in having a powerful engine if the gas tank only carries four gallons. There's no point in having top of the line tires attached to a bent axle.

I have meticulously arranged information in this book. Each chapter builds on the previous chapter. It may be tempting to skip ahead. However, I encourage you to read it in order from cover to cover. Before you learn about *real estate*, you must first ground yourself in *investments*, because I will talk about real estate as an investment—that is, something that has the ability to vastly increase or decrease your net worth. I will also talk about cash flow as it relates to *real estate*, but I will speak of it assuming you've gone through the information on cash flow in the *banking* section.

Here is the reasoning for the order of the chapters:

1. **Banking** – We start here because we must fully understand where we live in the financial universe. This is not about banks, this is about the implications of one breathtaking truth: money is to buy stuff. It may be food, material goods, experiences, services, but we can generalize it all as "stuff." It seems stupidly simple to point out that money is to buy stuff, but if you hold this in your mind, everything else falls into place. The cost of stuff tends to rise. The biggest long-term headwind of your financial world is inflation. It's the most probable and destructive financial risk you will face over your lifetime.

2. **Investments** – It is my assumption that your broad goal is to increase your ability to buy stuff. To increase that ability, you have to grow your money.

3. **Real Estate** – Housing is a unique form of investment in that people (generally) live inside of this investment. In this section, we'll talk about the math of homeownership and how to put yourself in the strongest position to use real estate as a springboard. With real estate, you have the ability to get yourself on the right side of the inflation problem, and using inflation as a tailwind instead of a headwind.

4. **Insurance** – We'll look at insurance from a financial planning perspective. A financial plan can plot out an ideal "perfect world" course for you, but what if you get sued just before retirement? What if you or your spouse end up in long-term care hemorrhaging thousands of dollars per month? What if the main income earner dies or becomes disabled? What if ...? Insurance is about looking at your life and protecting yourself from accidents that could derail the financial plan.

5. **Legal Planning** – Legal planning is a mental extension of insurance. If you end up in a coma, how do you make sure your mortgage payment gets paid and you don't wake up six months later in foreclosure? If you and your spouse pass away, how do you make sure your kids are raised by the people of your choosing? Legal planning is about protecting yourself from threats outside your control and extending your control to situations it won't normally reach. Think death, divorce, and incapacity.

6. **Tax Planning** – Tax planning is about working with the current tax environment and making wise decisions. In this section we'll go over different options that are available to reduce and optimize taxation.

All of your financial life will fit under one of these categories. These are *The Six Areas of Finance*. Keeping this organized structure in your mind will help you make them all work together. And now for the fun part: the three "Pool Rules" of growing money. But first, story time to help these rules sink in.

Horror Stories to Read Under the Sheets

All of the stories I will tell you are true and from my own direct experience. I have disguised identities to protect the innocent, but the details are factual. Whenever I'm roasting marshmallows with my children, I remind them of the boy I knew in elementary school who had a huge circular burn scar on front of his neck. While camping, the boy's brother was trying to put out his flaming marshmallow by shaking his roasting stick. The marshmallow flung off the stick, right onto the boy's neck. This story makes the point better than, "Kids, when your marshmallow catches fire, don't freak out and shake the stick."

It is in the same spirit that I share the following. It is crucial that the six areas of your finances work *together*. When they don't, you are shaking a stick with a flaming marshmallow. Behold the burn scars of working in financial services.

- I once had a client die. Shortly after his death, I learned that his wife was actually his second wife. When they got married, they each had two kids. When his second wife inherited his sizable accounts, she put the money solely in her name with her two biological kids as her beneficiaries. She explained to me that she always hated his kids and they weren't getting a dime. His own kids got nothing.

- Once I had a situation where a client's mother hadn't updated her trust documents after her husband passed away 20 years prior. The result was that real estate was still titled in her husband's name and the family unnecessarily had to pay capital gains amounting to $500,000. They missed a crucial step: filing a $6.00 document with the county that would have prevented this.

- Years ago, I had a client pass away and then I watched his kids sue each other for more inheritance. The client had invested and saved wisely, but had no legal planning and much of the estate (roughly half) went to taxes and lawyers.

- About twelve years ago, I was working in a bank when a woman came in who had just inherited $150,000. We set a time to review her options one week out. When she came in for her appointment, she proudly told me that her friend said that she would be smart to start up an IRA (Individual Retirement Account) with the money, so she put the whole $150,000 into one. Like finding your toddler with a knife, I tried to stifle the panic on my face when I explained to her that this was a big mistake because the IRS only allowed her (at the time) to put $5,000 into an IRA and that they were going to penalize her about $8,700 every year until she took it out. Her face went white and she left without discussing it further. One week later she happily came back to the bank feeling proud of herself saying that she fixed it. "What do you mean?" "I closed down the IRA, so it's all okay now." Her face went white again when I explained to her that the way she closed it down is considered "early withdrawal," which was subject to another 10% penalty ($15,000)—and the entire amount was taxable (roughly $45,000). Total tab: $68,700. I would like to believe the IRS was understanding and didn't make her pay all of this, but I never saw her again.

- I once had a client whom I told about an insurance option that would allow her to take $100,000 she had sitting in the bank and immediately convert it into a $250,000 spending account for long-term care. Whatever she didn't use became a tax free death benefit. As a bonus, she would be able to get back every dime of the original $100,000 at any time if she needed the money for something else. She was healthy and said that because of her excellent health, she didn't want to let the insurance company make money off of her. Six months later she called me crying because she had just found out she had a cancerous growth wrapped around her spine. The next week she was going into surgery, and there was a 50% chance she'd wake up paralyzed (and needing long-term care) and about the same chance she wouldn't live longer than two years. She wanted to know, "Is it too late for me to get the insurance?" Sadly, you know the answer.

What pains me is that most of these flaming marshmallows could have been prevented with planning—or more precisely, that a professional could have seen these holes before families fell into them. Experiences like these caused me to probe deeply, looking at things comprehensively. We'll revisit some of them later on.

Thankfully, my list of happy stories is longer than my list of horror stories. I'm not telling you the happy stories for now. Even though the core of my job is in managing investments, often I make people more money by mentioning red flags. Over and over again, I earn my keep with eight simple words, "Ummm, you *really* don't want to do that." It's important to have professionals looking over your shoulder. Everyone's situation is unique. The probability and expense of mistakes is far too great.

You must have good professionals helping you through a financial plan, acting as a sounding board along the way, and performing stress tests on your plan. Life constantly changes and the right choice is not necessarily obvious. In my experience, good advice is always worth its cost. Pinching pennies on advisors can end up costing you dollars. Excellent advice at a fair price is always better than terrible advice at an excellent price.

First "Pool Rule" of Growing Money: Understand the Six Areas of Finance

For years I've tried hard to challenge my observation that there are six key areas of finance. Why six? Could any be consolidated to make it five? Is there a seventh one I'm not thinking of? I think you'll find, like I did, that every financial topic will fit into one of these six areas.

So the first rule is that you must have a solid mental framework for the Six Areas of Finance. We will look at their functions and establish them as the conceptual pillars of your financial life. In a moment, we will color coordinate them to help us keep them straight.

Your entire financial life will fit into one of these six areas. Recognizing this structure will help identify the weak spots in your finances. You may have rock solid investments but haven't done legal planning. Improper tax planning may be causing you to invest inefficiently. Or if you've focused on paying off your house, you may be strong on the real estate side, but weak on other investments.

Let's look at them by function:

What *Should* **Happen**

Investments and real estate are based on **positive** probabilities, or *what should* happen. They're positive in the sense that what you would normally expect from them—the reality that is most *probable*—is a good thing. The stock market *normally* goes up. Your home *normally* increases in value.

Yes it's *possible* that the stock market may crash forever or the world economy may dissolve. It's *possible*, but it's not *probable*. Keep in mind that while anything is possible, only a few outcomes are probable. Later we'll talk about your investing presuppositions, your worldview, and how it is that you view the global landscape.

What *Could* **Happen**

Insurance and legal planning are based on **negative** possibilities—or the *what ifs*. What if the proverbial doo-doo hits the fan? It's about having a trash bag behind the fan to minimize the mess.

The odds are your house *isn't* going to catch fire. But just in case that happens, you get homeowner's insurance for protection. The odds are that you aren't going to crash your car, but you get auto insurance just in case. All insurance has the same concept: protecting you against the "what ifs" or "what coulds." These events will *probably* not happen, but *possibly* could.

Legal planning can be framed the same way. The odds are that you aren't going to end up in a coma for six months, but just in case, you assign powers of attorney and make a living will.

While investments harness probabilities, legal planning and insurance cover possibilities. You construct your life and financial plan upon probabilities, while protecting yourself against negative (and usually unlikely) possibilities.

What *Is*

Lastly, we arrive at banking and tax planning. While the other areas are about "what should" happen or "what could" happen, banking and tax planning are about "what is." Tax laws just *are*. You will never have control over them. You can only control how you co-exist with them and strategically minimize their pain.

Banking is similar. Interest rates change and you have zero control over them. You need emergency funds—and emergencies are by definition unexpected. Banking is also cash flow management. It's making sure you have enough cash to avoid undue stress, while knowing that it's bad to have too much of your money in an area that traditionally doesn't grow much. When it comes to banking and taxes, it is what it is. Like a donkey in the rain, you just have to stand there and take it.

6 Think of the Six Areas of Finance as the "what shoulds," the "what coulds," and "what is."

Not everything will fit into these tidy categories. If you have a big stamp collection, I'm going to put it in the insurance section because it is an insurable asset like a car or boat. If you own a mutual fund that invests in real estate, is this in the investments section or the real estate section? I say investment section. However, if you are a landlord, you probably should diversify away from real estate-oriented investments in your portfolio. Splitting hairs over categorizing fringe assets normally doesn't change anything. It's more important that you see the big picture: how the bulk of your assets are meant to function as one unit for a common goal.

We will spend a chapter each on these six areas, starting with banking and moving clockwise around the wheel. Poetically, the content is book-ended by reality: that which *is*.

Between chapters, we'll take a short break with the wealth-relevant topics of the time value of money, optimism, minimalism, finding purpose in life, and philanthropy.

Second "Pool Rule" of Growing Money: Embrace the Things You Can't Control

Direct your effort and energy away from what you can't change, and instead focus on what is *probably* going to grow your financial power. Remember: *money is for buying stuff.*

It's easy to skip over the depth of this point. Your money is for buying stuff. In fact, take a moment and visualize your money. Visualize where it is. It may be in the stock market or your bank or as equity in your house. It may be a grand piano, or art. Every penny of it, someday, will be converted into usable currency and then converted again into goods and services. This will happen, done by you or by someone else, eventually.

All the components of your net worth are holding vessels waiting to be converted into stuff. It may be 100 years from now, but someday it will be used as designed: *to buy stuff*. It may be you when you go into long-term care in 20 years. If you give it away, someone else will use it. At some point, every brass farthing of your net worth will exit from you as a good or service. Or you will pass away and someone else will inherit the same reality.

Imagine the rest of your life as an endless set of train tracks extending in front of you. You are the conductor of a train pulling cars with piles of coal in them. To keep the train going, you have to keep shoveling that coal into the engine. The coal represents the money you have available to keep your train running. If you have a lot of money, you have more of these train cars. If you are living paycheck to paycheck, coal appears in your shovel and you immediately throw it in the engine.

However, not all train cars are created equal and you can decide which cars should hold your coal. Some train cars have a magic ability to help your coal pile grow. Other train cars shrink the coal inside of them without ever using it as fuel. The key thing is that, regardless of which type of train car you choose to store your coal, you eventually *have* to throw that coal in the engine to keep it going.

The coal you throw into the engine represents "buying stuff." At some point, every piece of coal will be thrown into the fire. If you don't imminently need it to keep the train going, it needs to replenish in the magical cars to create more fuel for future needs. At some point along those train tracks, you will die and the train will be run by someone else who faces the same decisions.

In this scenario, there are several things you can't control:

Number one: the speed of the train. Time only goes one speed. The relentless ride of time just *is*. You can embrace the power of time or dread it. Dread is never a financial strategy.

Number two: your need for income. You need to burn money to keep going. Worse, the amount of money needed will *increase* over time. The price of goods and services always goes up. You can't control this. Inflation is a reality beyond your influence. It is no cause for anger, it just is: don't waste energy on the uncontrollable. Let the brutal fact of inflation inform your planning.

Number three: neither you nor I have any idea how the financial markets will do. Nobody has any idea, and there is no shame in this. All we can do is look at the past and infer the future. If you organize your finances well, it won't matter what the stock market does this year.

This is the takeaway: *embrace* (not just acknowledge) the things you can't control. This is great news because we've just eliminated some things you don't need to worry about. You don't need to worry about time. Time is moving. You don't need to worry about rising costs. Costs are rising. You don't need to worry about what the stock market is going to do this year, you simply need to plan for its volatility.

Third "Pool Rule" of Growing Money: Control the Things You Can Control

As you release your focus away from the things you have *no ability* to control, focus instead on what you *can* control. I sometimes joke that the absolute worst financial advisor that you'll ever come across is *yourself*. Your emotions, regardless of your education level, background, IQ level, or career status will constantly whisper self-destructive advice. When you are scared, your "gut instinct" is the voice of your emotions, not the voice of your rational mind. Rationality and evidence are shockingly unpersuasive against fear.

When your emotions see the stock market setting records, getting higher and higher, you will *feel* completely comfortable with investing. You will see the market as safe and investing as easy, and your emotions will guide you into buying in at the *peak* of the market. Emotionally, the peak of the market always *feels* the safest, when in reality it's the most precarious.

It is this reality that drives asset price bubbles. Humankind's emotional tyranny is why most investors underperform.

On the other hand, when is the best time to buy?

When the market has taken a beating, when it has fallen a lot, and when everyone is talking about the end of the world.

However, when the market is falling like a rock, what do your emotions tell you?

"Sell, sell, sell! Get out! It's not safe!"

Again, your emotions are the *worst* financial advisor you'll ever come across. I suspect that each year, emotions cost investors *multiples* more than unethical advisors, high commissions, or bad advice.

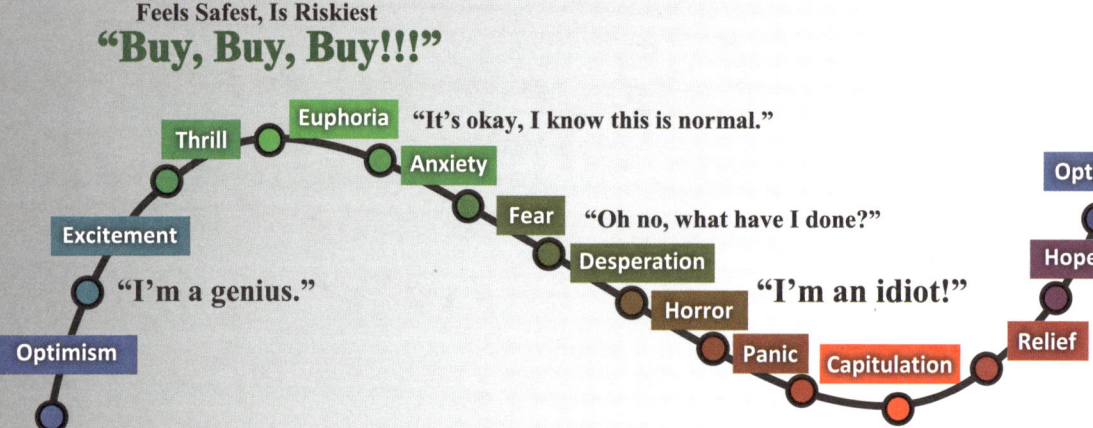

Often, emotional investing is merely investing with a pessimistic worldview. It is a view that will cause you to be skeptical of seasons of growth and a sense of vindication during periods of decline.

The pessimistic worldview encourages total disengagement, which will cost far more in the long term than even the most dramatic stock market decline.

This is the perpetual monologue of the pessimist:

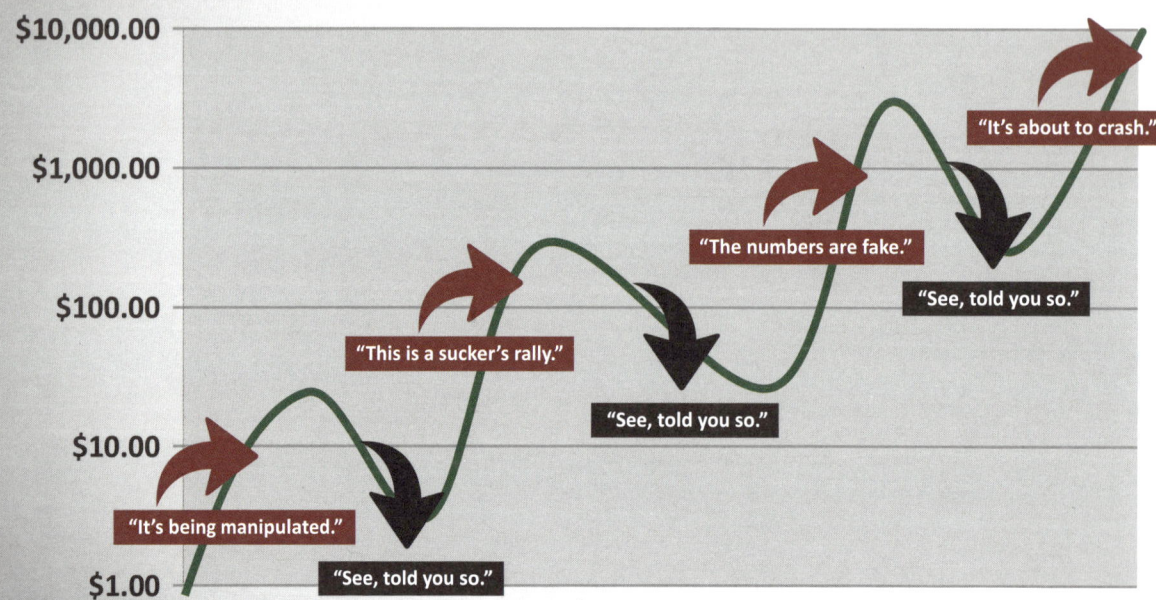

Your Investing Behavior

The most influential factor in your entire investing world is thankfully the one thing that only you can control: *your investing behavior.* You must control how you behave during market ups and downs. Behaving with a long-term focus is absolute financial *power.*

Evidence shows that a minority of the population does this. Most people have a really hard time not making impulsive short-sighted mistakes when the stock market gets crazy. People are generally naïve about their emotions. Emotional decisions feel rational in the moment. When new clients come to me, I always go over these principles. They nod happily. But emotions still take over during market swings, causing temporary insanity and converting temporary market pullbacks into permanent financial losses—which could have been averted with patience.

Your Long-Term Perspective

To twist the NRA slogan: stocks don't kill portfolios, people kill their own portfolios. Which leads us to the second thing you can control: maintaining a *long-term perspective.* A good financial advisor cultivates this perspective. Long-term perspective is indispensable when things get scary. *Control* your long-term perspective, by tuning out your short-term worries. Another day, another apocalypse. We have to use discernment in order to starve our natural tendency to panic. The media (particularly the financial media) thrives off humankind's instinctive attraction to the feeding frenzy of worry. If you are prone to panic and stress, obsessing over the stock market helps with all the productivity of a hypochondriac studying a medical dictionary.

The solution is to steadfastly *reinforce a long-term perspective.* We will talk about this later, but you need to take long looks at things that reinforce an optimistic worldview. Controlling your long-term perspective is largely about adopting a personal creed and faith in how you view the world, particularly the financial world.

Your Financial Planning

You must control your own financial planning. The primary role of a financial plan is to keep a long-term perspective that can inform present-day decisions. You can *control* your plans and be mindful of your goals. You can study the past to make informed decisions with realistic expectations. When it comes to getting yourself to behave properly, your plan can be your best friend—it helps you think clearly, maintain a long-term perspective, and engage in good behaviors.

Please note, this is not a how-to manual on financial planning. I will tell you all the ingredients that go into a plan, but it's up to you whether you cook it yourself or hire a professional. My bias: hire a pro. It's too important.

Your Investment Choices

You can control what you invest in. Invest only in things suitable to you and to your life plan. Abstain from investments that do not support this. What will help you psychologically keep you from panicking? What will outpace the rising cost of buying stuff? Some investments are programmed for self-destruction, others are not.

I have listed this controllable aspect, what to invest in, last because it is the *least* important factor in your control. Your lifetime rate of return will be determined *mostly* by your attitudes and the choices they inspire.

This may come as a surprise since a great deal of literature on wealth focuses *solely* on selecting investments. Your lifelong rate of return is rather like the mass of the universe: only 4.6% of it is "observable" and the rest consists of abstractions—dark energy and dark matter. By analogy, the bulk of your return will be driven by abstractions such as behavior and perspective.

Summary

Let's review the pool rules:

1. Understand the Six Areas of Finance. Be mindful of them.
2. Embrace what you can't control. We listed three things: time, inflation, and short-term movements of the capital markets.
3. Control what you can control. We talked about four things: deciding how you behave, keeping a long-term perspective, maintaining a financial plan, and choosing the appropriate investments.

Keep these founding principles in your mind at all times. They are the "pool rules." If you are going to swim in this pool, you have to obey these rules or you will get hurt. There is no lifeguard on duty. If you do your own investments, you watch yourself. If you work with a financial advisor, they should blow the whistle when you get reckless.

Each of these Six Areas of Finance will be thoroughly discussed. The next chapter will be on banking and cash management. It is *crucial* that we are rooted in this primary "what is" and the things we can't control about banking.

When we see the uncontrollable, the response must be to focus energy on the things we *do* have control over.

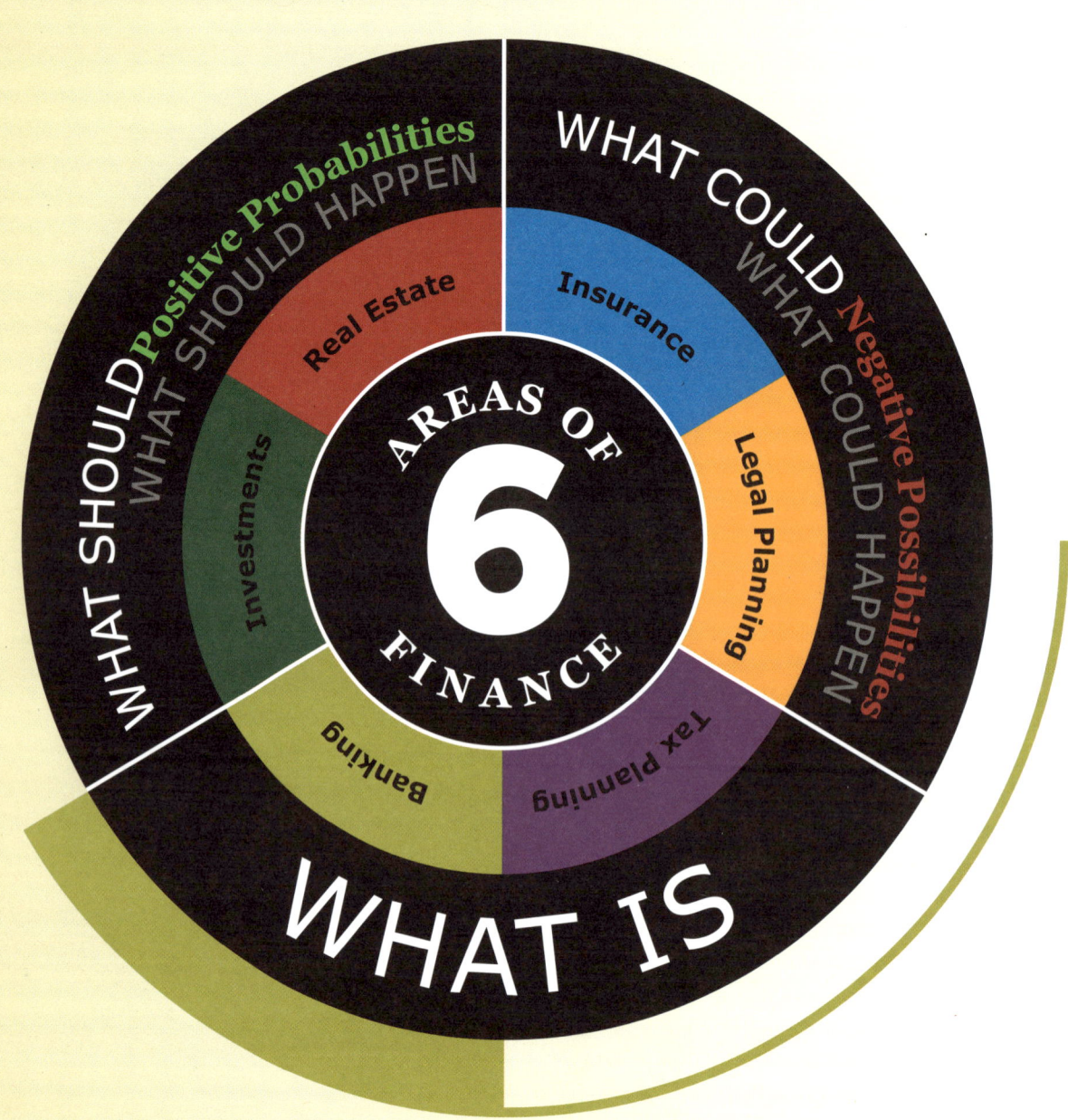

A gowk kin earn dosh,
but it steals a wise jimmy tae keep it.

Scottish Proverb

Banking

The area of banking can be thought of as cash and cash management. Cash management generally happens through bank accounts and credit cards, so it's preferable to consider this area "banking" instead of "cash."

We start our comprehensive financial conversation here for two key reasons. First, growing money starts with saving money. Consider saving a decision about cash flow allocation. The second reason we start here is because money is to buy stuff. Whenever you buy stuff, it is after money comes into your bank from your income or from your savings. Your bank account functions as a transitional and transactional account. It is the place money passes through just before you buy stuff, and it should not be used as or thought of as something beyond this. Long-term investing should not happen here, and I will show you why.

The money in your bank should be there for two reasons:

- Because you will buy stuff with it soon
- Because you want it readily available in case you need to buy stuff (i.e. emergencies)

And that's it, folks. A word of warning, this chapter is a bit of a downer. The realities of "what is" with banking may surprise (if not depress) you. This is part of facing the brutal facts of our financial world. The better you understand banking, the more you'll benefit from the chapter on investments. To build our foundation, in this chapter we will lay down eight basic concepts on which to construct your understanding of finances. We'll call them stones.

The Cornerstone: Money is to Buy Stuff

We need to revisit this concept. Money is meant to buy stuff—and whether you use it, lose it, give it away, or see it stolen, it always *eventually* buys stuff. Accept this and your financial plan tends to create itself. The value of your assets represents a particular amount of power to purchase goods and services.

To visualize this, imagine everything that you have. Add up the value of your investments, your house, your bank account—even that pinball machine in your garage collecting dust. Each of those dollars has a unknown, yet specific date for when they will buy stuff.

Some date in the future, every dollar of your net worth will become stuff. The only variable is *time*. Namely, how much time between now and that mysterious date on every single dollar of your net worth. This is the most relevant piece of reality to your financial plan.

Because money is to buy stuff, financial power can be defined as how much stuff you are able to buy. Increasing wealth can *only* be defined as growing in your ability to buy stuff.

Stone #2: The Permanent Rising Cost of Stuff

Here's the catch. The price of everything in your life, the price of the stuff you will buy, always goes up. **Let me ask you another question:**

What on earth is this?

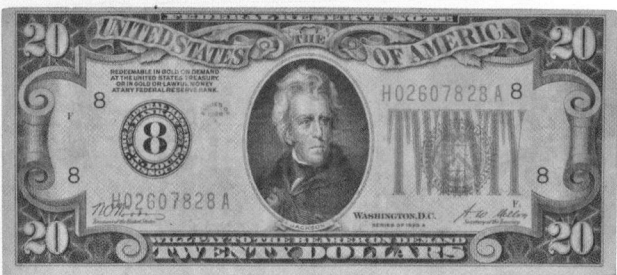

If your answer is "money," I'll give you partial credit. The best answer is "currency." It's not just for nostalgia that I used an older tiny numbers and portrait version of the bill. You must think of this as *currency* because all it represents is a certain amount of stuff that this bill could be exchanged for *today*. When the bill was printed in 1928, it could buy much more stuff.

Let's use a bigger number. Imagine today you had $100,000 in cash and you had to spend every penny in the next 24 hours. It would create a massive pile of stuff. If we were to do the experiment one year from now, the pile would be slightly smaller. The amount of stuff that this $100,000 of currency could be exchanged for will likely be smaller every year for the rest of your life. The term for this is *inflation*. It is the constant loss of purchasing power.

We'll use our currency amount of $100,000. Let's look at its purchasing power in 25-year increments on the nice round years of 1965, 1990, 2015. Imagine you had that $100,000 in a coffee can buried in the backyard. Starting in 1965, you shop around to see what you can buy, get angry at the high prices, bury it for 25 years and then see what you can buy again. The money in the coffee can obviously isn't earning interest, so the currency amount of $100,000 is always the same, but what it can buy *radically* changes. Here is a chart of average prices from those years and a shrinking "pile of stuff" that you could have bought in each year for $100,000.[1]

	1965	1990	2015
AVERAGE COST OF THINGS			
New Home	$18,075	$123,000	$289,500
New Car	$3,025	$16,950	$31,352
Gallon of Gas	$0.30	$1.34	$3.80
Loaf of Bread	$0.24	$0.70	$1.98
PILE OF STUFF FOR $100,000			
How much **$100,000** could Buy	4 Houses ($72,300)	0 Houses	0 Houses
	5 Cars ($15,125)	5 Cars ($84,750)	3 Cars ($94,056)
	25,000 Gallons of Gas ($7,500)	7,000 Gallons of Gas ($9,380)	782 Gallons of Gas ($2,971.60)
	21,125 Loaves of Bread ($5,075)	8,385 Loaves of Bread ($5,870)	1,501 Loaves of Bread ($2,972.40)

It's astounding, but it's not very strange. If we follow a long-term average, the prices of everything go up each year by about 3%—we'll nail down this inflation number down the road. This means that we can add a fourth column to our chart and have a pretty good guess at what prices will be in 2040.

	1965	1990	2015	2040 (Projected)
	AVERAGE COST OF THINGS			
New Home	$18,075	$123,000	$289,500	$606,149
New Car	$3,025	$16,950	$31,352	$65,644
Gallon of Gas	$0.30	$1.34	$3.80	$7.96
Loaf of Bread	$0.24	$0.70	$1.98	$4.15

Do these prices sound absurd? So would 2015 prices to most people only a generation ago.

Let's bring this home. The average retirement length is *more than* 25 years. This means that from the date of your retirement to the date of your death, prices of everything will increase two to three times. Or, *over the course* of your retirement the dollar will lose around **60%** of its ability to buy stuff. $1.00 of income at the beginning of your retirement will require $2.50 at the "end" of your retirement—less euphemistically known as your death. Don't shoot the messenger—just remember: embrace the Things You Can't Control. You must recognize the permanent rising cost of stuff.

The pesky nature of the future is that it is unknowable. Maybe you'll get lucky and inflation will be less than 3%, with prices "only" doubling to $2.00. Or, maybe you'll have bad luck and something that cost $1.00 at your retirement will be $4.00 at your death. None of us know this inflation rate, but life experience has taught us that prices keep rising and we should assume they will keep rising. In the words of Joe Friday, "It's just the facts, ma'am."

Because our $100,000 is in a coffee can the number—the currency amount—stays the same. Since money is to buy stuff and the price of stuff typically goes up by about 3% each year, this means that $100,000 at the beginning of the year needs to become $103,000 at the end of the year *just to be worth the same*. If your currency amount is any number less than this, then *you have lost some ability to buy stuff*. You've lost money.

Let's test the concept. You start the year with $100,000 and it is earning **2%** in interest. At end of the year it is worth $102,000. During the year prices go up by 3%. Prices are now $103,000 on what cost $100,000 just last year. In this scenario, have you gotten richer or poorer?

Poorer.

Inflation tells us how to define growing money. Money is to buy stuff and growing money is only defined by growing your ability to buy stuff. Ladies and gentlemen, behold, public enemy number one: rising prices. You must understand this as your greatest, most certain, most unavoidable risk. Prices will go up and there's nothing you can do about it. Growing your money means facing rising costs and your diminishing ability to generate income to pay them.

Prices virtually never go down. There are only a few exceptions to this. We'll play a game: I'll name an exception, and then it's your turn. Me first: technology gets cheaper over time. Now your turn...

Yeah, I can't think of anything else either—at least anything where the price isn't correlated to technology improvements. Everything is getting more expensive and you need to plan for it.

Stone #3: The Wealth Headwinds of Saving Money into a Bank

The place *where* you keep your money between now and the date it buys stuff is vitally important. The coffee can option is untenable. You may deposit it in a bank, invest it, or it may buy something of value. You have to put it *somewhere*.

Let's confront the mathematical reality of what happens to money held in a bank account or other cash-like instruments (like a short-term U.S. government bond) over an extended period of time.

Any amount of bank interest you earn mitigates your buying power loss to inflation. In the best-case scenario, the interest you earn outpaces the rate of inflation. However, the normal-case scenario is that the choice to store money conservatively erodes your wealth.

Another component we didn't mention is taxation. When you earn interest at a bank, it is taxed as ordinary income at *both* the federal level and (usually) the state level. There are only seven states that don't have taxes on interest. **This means the simple math of each year you have money in a bank looks like this:**

Interest Rate minus Taxes Paid minus Inflation Rate = Net Result

If this number is positive, you got richer in *real money*; if it's not, you got poorer. So let's put some numbers to this. Assume that you are earning **5%** in interest, that you pay **20%** in taxes (**20%** *of* your **5%** earned in interest is 1%) and inflation is 3%.

Here's your math: 5% - 1% - 3% = 1%

5% (interest rate) - **1%** (paid in taxes) - **3%** (lost to inflation)

= 1% (your net gain in purchasing power)

On $100,000, this is what it would look like at the end of the year:

Real Rate of Return

$100,000	Prices of stuff at the beginning of the year
$105,000	Year end balance after $5,000 in interest earned (before taxes)
$104,000	Year end balance after $1,000 in taxes are paid (after taxes)
$103,000	Price of stuff one year later
$1,000	Amount of wealth (ability to buy stuff) created

Slightly depressing. Well, it's about to get worse. Now that the math is established, let's look at some actual numbers. The days of a **5%** banking interest rate are long gone. The good news is that inflation is lower too. Taxes, unsurprisingly, are largely unchanged.

At the end of 2016, these were the national averages for bank interest rates on deposits:[2]

Average Interest Rates

	DEPOSIT SIZE	
	< $100,000 (Non-Jumbo)	> $100,000 (Jumbo)
Savings	0.06%	0.06%
Interest Checking	0.04%	0.04%
Money Market	0.08%	0.11%
1 month CD	0.06%	0.07%
3 month CD	0.08%	0.10%
6 month CD	0.13%	0.15%
12 month CD	0.22%	0.24%
24 month CD	0.36%	0.39%
36 month CD	0.49%	0.54%
48 month CD	0.61%	0.65%
60 month CD	0.78%	0.80%

Before you get too excited about those rates, keep in mind that you have to pay taxes on them. Inflation last year was 2.50%[3]. Using the 12-month jumbo-rate CD, here's the math after **20%** in taxes and 2.50% in inflation:

0.24% - 0.048% - 2.50% = -2.308%

Yes, that's a *negative* interest rate in real money. In real money, if you bought the 12-month CD, you are going *backward* in your ability to buy stuff. On $100,000, this is what it would look like at the end of the year:

Real Rate of Return

$100,000	Prices of stuff at the beginning of the year
$100,240	Year end balance after $240 in interest earned
$100,192	Year end balance after $48 in taxes are paid
$102,500	Prices of stuff one year later
-$2,308	**Amount of wealth (ability to buy stuff) created**

In the situation above, the person has *lost money*. Again, money is to buy stuff. Even though they have $192 more *currency* at the end of the year (after taxes are paid), they have effectively lost $2,308 because their money was parked in a CD. Again, this punctuates the importance of *where* money is. It's the same challenge with all cash-like investments right now. In real money, you are virtually guaranteed to lose. Here is the previous interest rate chart expanded. We can see that *none* of the interest rates produced a positive real rate of return:

Average Interest Rates

	DEPOSIT SIZE					
	< $100,000 (Non-Jumbo)			> $100,000 (Jumbo)		
	Interest Rate	After 20% in Taxes	After 2.50% in Inflation	Interest Rate	After 20% in Taxes	After 2.50% in Inflation
Savings	0.06%	0.05%	-2.45%	0.06%	0.05%	-2.45%
Interest Checking	0.04%	0.03%	-2.47%	0.04%	0.03%	-2.47%
Money Market	0.08%	0.06%	-2.44%	0.11%	0.09%	-2.41%
1 month CD	0.06%	0.05%	-2.45%	0.07%	0.06%	-2.44%
3 month CD	0.08%	0.06%	-2.44%	0.10%	0.08%	-2.42%
6 month CD	0.13%	0.10%	-2.40%	0.15%	0.12%	-2.38%
12 month CD	0.22%	0.18%	-2.32%	0.24%	0.19%	-2.31%
24 month CD	0.36%	0.29%	-2.21%	0.39%	0.31%	-2.19%
36 month CD	0.49%	0.39%	-2.11%	0.54%	0.43%	-2.07%
48 month CD	0.61%	0.49%	-2.01%	0.65%	0.52%	-1.98%
60 month CD	0.78%	0.62%	-1.88%	0.80%	0.64%	-1.86%

Folks, I hope that you are catching the resounding gong that you *cannot* get hung up on the currency number. The currency number may give you the false impression that you are growing your wealth, when silently and slowly, you are getting poorer. Your interest rate only matters in the context of taxes and inflation.

Inflation is an *invisible* risk. It's not obvious until you look down and notice how expensive candy is at the gas station, and wistfully mumble to yourself the prices when you were a kid.

It almost makes one yearn for the good ol' days when CDs paid much more. My first CD in the early '80s earned **9.5%**. Before you get too nostalgic, here's the cruelty of it: the math that I'm describing is ugly in nearly *every* single year, even back when CDs paid better rates. I showed you the 2016 math of a one-year CD, but what if we looked at 50 years to see this math each and every year?

We'll give our scenario a little boost by using one-year U.S. government bonds as the interest rate. The interest rate is historically slightly higher on one-year government bonds over one-year CDs—in 2016, the one-year CD rate was **0.24%**, the bond rate was **0.61%**.

We just need to know three numbers for each year:

1. Interest rate for one-year U.S. Treasury Securities[4]
2. Average taxation rate at both the state and federal level[5]
3. The inflation rate[6]

State income tax is going to vary greatly depending on which state you live in. Federal taxes depend on your income. The more you make, the worse your net results for saving. Let's look at someone who started in 1967 with $100,000, investing in one-year interest rates.

The key figures are in the graph below and the details in the table on the opposite page:

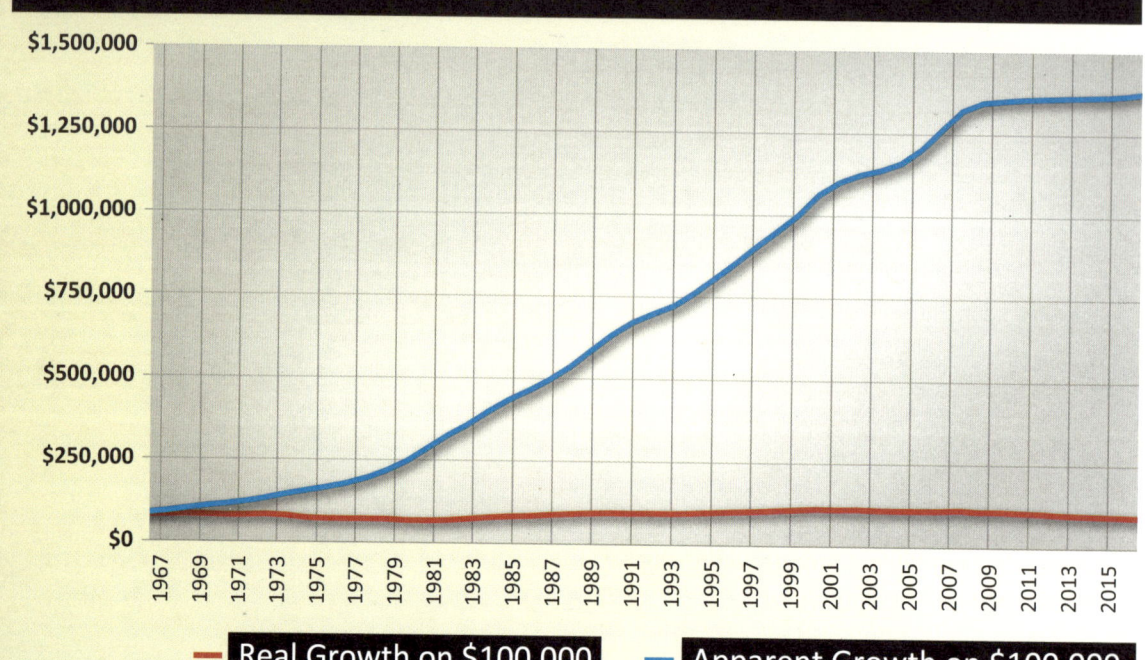

— Real Growth on $100,000   — Apparent Growth on $100,000

Year	One-Year Interest Rate	Average Federal Tax Rate	Average State Tax Rate	Inflation Rate	Ignoring Inflation	Ignoring Inflation and Taxes	Net Rate of Return	Real Growth on $100,000
1967	4.89%	16.64%	3.17%	3.46%	$103,918	$104,885	0.46%	$100,458
1968	5.69%	16.82%	3.20%	3.65%	$108,647	$110,854	0.90%	$101,363
1969	7.12%	17.00%	3.24%	4.40%	$114,819	$118,749	1.28%	$102,661
1970	6.90%	17.09%	3.25%	6.18%	$121,127	$126,940	-0.69%	$101,957
1971	4.88%	17.15%	3.27%	5.29%	$125,832	$133,135	-1.41%	$100,523
1972	4.96%	17.37%	3.31%	3.27%	$130,782	$139,738	0.66%	$101,191
1973	7.31%	17.73%	3.38%	3.65%	$138,327	$149,955	2.12%	$103,335
1974	8.18%	18.03%	3.43%	9.39%	$147,215	$162,224	-2.96%	$100,272
1975	6.76%	18.25%	3.47%	11.80%	$155,003	$173,188	-6.51%	$93,744
1976	5.87%	18.51%	3.52%	6.72%	$162,103	$183,361	-2.14%	$91,738
1977	6.09%	12.80%	2.76%	5.22%	$170,436	$194,525	-0.08%	$91,666
1978	8.34%	13.76%	2.75%	6.84%	$182,303	$210,748	0.12%	$91,778
1979	10.67%	13.51%	2.65%	9.28%	$198,604	$233,225	-0.34%	$91,468
1980	12.05%	14.21%	2.59%	13.91%	$218,512	$261,324	-3.89%	$87,913
1981	14.78%	14.96%	2.55%	11.83%	$245,149	$299,944	0.36%	$88,230
1982	12.28%	13.84%	2.59%	8.39%	$270,295	$336,762	1.87%	$89,878
1983	9.57%	12.69%	2.79%	3.71%	$292,163	$368,998	4.38%	$93,815
1984	10.89%	12.43%	2.77%	4.19%	$319,139	$409,173	5.04%	$98,546
1985	8.43%	12.57%	2.69%	3.53%	$341,927	$443,649	3.61%	$102,104
1986	6.46%	12.72%	2.63%	3.89%	$360,633	$472,320	1.58%	$103,718
1987	6.76%	14.47%	2.53%	1.46%	$380,880	$504,269	4.15%	$108,027
1988	7.65%	14.97%	2.47%	4.05%	$404,944	$542,858	2.27%	$110,477
1989	8.54%	14.97%	2.48%	4.67%	$433,476	$589,191	2.38%	$113,101
1990	7.88%	14.97%	2.51%	5.20%	$461,672	$635,634	1.30%	$114,577
1991	5.86%	14.97%	2.69%	5.65%	$483,941	$672,871	-0.83%	$113,630
1992	3.89%	14.97%	2.77%	2.60%	$499,424	$699,040	0.60%	$114,311
1993	3.43%	14.97%	2.78%	3.26%	$513,531	$723,047	-0.44%	$113,813
1994	5.31%	14.97%	2.76%	2.52%	$535,964	$761,440	1.85%	$115,917
1995	5.95%	14.97%	2.73%	2.80%	$562,200	$806,734	2.10%	$118,346
1996	5.51%	14.97%	2.70%	2.73%	$587,716	$851,205	1.81%	$120,486
1997	5.63%	14.97%	2.69%	3.04%	$614,960	$899,128	1.60%	$122,409
1998	5.05%	14.97%	2.67%	1.57%	$640,544	$944,548	2.59%	$125,579
1999	5.08%	14.97%	2.65%	1.67%	$667,336	$992,508	2.51%	$128,735
2000	6.11%	14.97%	2.63%	2.74%	$700,923	$1,053,134	2.29%	$131,687
2001	3.48%	14.97%	2.63%	3.73%	$721,027	$1,089,791	-0.86%	$130,552
2002	2.00%	13.50%	2.62%	1.14%	$733,134	$1,111,605	0.54%	$131,256
2003	1.24%	13.29%	2.65%	2.60%	$740,802	$1,125,436	-1.55%	$129,216
2004	1.89%	13.29%	2.67%	1.93%	$752,548	$1,146,669	-0.34%	$128,771
2005	3.62%	13.33%	2.65%	2.97%	$775,426	$1,188,159	0.07%	$128,861
2006	4.93%	13.34%	2.62%	3.99%	$807,571	$1,246,765	0.16%	$129,061
2007	4.52%	13.35%	2.58%	2.08%	$838,270	$1,303,140	1.72%	$131,283
2008	1.82%	13.31%	2.55%	4.28%	$851,125	$1,326,889	-2.75%	$127,677
2009	0.47%	13.22%	2.63%	0.03%	$854,497	$1,333,137	0.37%	$128,145
2010	0.32%	13.20%	2.60%	2.63%	$856,788	$1,337,381	-2.36%	$125,118
2011	0.18%	13.20%	2.62%	1.63%	$858,098	$1,339,810	-1.48%	$123,270
2012	0.18%	13.19%	2.61%	2.93%	$859,362	$1,342,155	-2.78%	$119,840
2013	0.13%	13.18%	2.63%	1.59%	$860,315	$1,343,922	-1.48%	$118,067
2014	0.12%	13.18%	2.60%	1.58%	$861,190	$1,345,546	-1.48%	$116,322
2015	0.32%	13.19%	2.51%	1.37%	$863,526	$1,349,874	-1.10%	$115,044
2016	0.61%	13.21%	2.52%	2.50%	$867,995	$1,358,165	-1.98%	$112,763

In this, we see all of our key numbers in every year for interest rate, taxes, and inflation. The two white columns show what your bank statement balance would show—your currency amount. If you paid the taxes every year from the account itself, then your numbers would look like the left white column. If you paid them outside the account, then it would look like the right white column.

The far right two columns are the numbers we're after. We can see the actual real rate of return after taxes and inflation. The far right column starts you out with $100,000 and shows the value of it in real money at the end of each year.

After half a century of patiently leaving your money alone, your $100,000 *barely grew* in real money. Over 50 years your average real rate of return was **0.26%**.

What's interesting to me is the era in the late '70s and early '80s when interest rates were double-digit. Even then, in most of those years—if you factor in taxes and inflation—you still weren't notably getting richer in your ability to buy stuff. 50 years is a very long time. Normally that should be *plenty of time* to make any investment work.

Another thing you can observe is how much time can obscure numbers. In this chart I've adjusted the number for inflation to make the point that your ability to buy stuff barely changes over a tremendous amount of time. However, in practice you would never see this number—it is "invisible." What you would see are those balances in the white columns and it would be easy to tell yourself that you are doing quite well.

The bottom line is this: there is no historical precedent for bank interest making any significant amount of money in real terms. The illusion of watching your account grow was, on average, only maintaining the purchasing power. In real terms, you weren't getting any wealthier over those 50 years.

Does this change because we are currently in an environment with below average inflation? No, because with lower inflation comes lower interest rates that are *still taxed*. Since the year 2000, while your average interest rate was only **1.88%**, your average *real* rate was **-0.77%**. Thus the headwinds of trying to get wealthier by saving money in a bank account.

Does this change if interest rates go up? Possibly. If history is our guide (and it's our only guide) high interest is normally paired with high inflation and your net gains are about the same. Besides, we've had extremely low interest rates since 2009, so you may be waiting awhile.

An investment commonly thought of as "safe" slowly loses money over time. This culminates in dramatic financial loss over a lifetime. The certain loss of your ability to buy stuff should never be considered safe or comfortable.

Stone #4: Longevity Risk

Let's step back for a minute to remind ourselves that this entire chapter on banking is about "what is." Banking and taxation just "are." We must embrace and deal with that reality. So far the brutal banking "what is"es have been:

1. Money is to buy stuff
2. Prices of stuff always go up
3. Saving money into cash-like investments does not normally enhance your ability to buy stuff

Now we'll shift gears away from money and talk about your longevity, or how long it should be until you bite the dust. This may not seem relevant to banking, but the key concept here is *time*. How much time do you have to work with these realities of rising costs? In our examples earlier, we were working with 50 year time spans—but how long will you live?

I've made clients cry. Thankfully never from market performance, but because I put their life expectancies right under their noses. I do this with love; it should be part of your financial plan to brutally contemplate your (and possibly your spouse's) life expectancy. As a rule of thumb, most people like living. Let's put emotions about death on the shelf and think of it in a more impersonal way. There's no reason to get all worked up about something as routine as dying.

Death is a question of probability. Thankfully for us, groups of people (namely insurance companies and the Social Security Administration) have a vested interest to grind out those stats. We'll start with the easy part and list out current life expectancy. On the next page are the results from the last census.[7]

So, how do you read this morbid thing? Look up your age and gender on the chart and you'll see a row of numbers. Let's say that you are a sixty-five-year-old female. The numbers mean:

- 1.00%—You have a 1.00% chance of dying this year
- 88,050—Of 100,000 females born when you were, 88,050 are still alive (i.e. 88% of your peers)
- 20.22—On average, you should expect to live another 20.22 years
- 85.22—On average, you will pass away at 85.22 years of age.

Perhaps you've heard a different life expectancy number and know that men live to 76 and women 81. This is the life expectancy of someone born today, and you can see these numbers under Age 0. Brand new people have a different life expectancy than people who are older. Knowing the life expectancy of someone born today

AGE	MALE Death Probability	MALE Number of Lives	MALE Additional Life Expectancy	MALE Life Expectancy	FEMALE Death Probability	FEMALE Number of Lives	FEMALE Additional Life Expectancy	FEMALE Life Expectancy	AGE	MALE Death Probability	MALE Number of Lives	MALE Additional Life Expectancy	MALE Life Expectancy	FEMALE Death Probability	FEMALE Number of Lives	FEMALE Additional Life Expectancy	FEMALE Life Expectancy
0	0.66%	100,000	76.18	76.18	0.55%	100,000	80.95	80.95	60	1.09%	85,995	21.44	81.44	0.65%	91,516	24.37	84.37
1	0.04%	99,343	75.69	76.69	0.04%	99,449	80.39	81.39	61	1.16%	85,060	20.67	81.67	0.70%	90,923	23.52	84.52
2	0.03%	99,299	74.72	76.72	0.02%	99,411	79.42	81.42	62	1.24%	84,075	19.90	81.90	0.76%	90,287	22.68	84.68
3	0.02%	99,270	73.74	76.74	0.02%	99,389	78.44	81.44	63	1.33%	83,032	19.15	82.15	0.83%	89,600	21.85	84.85
4	0.02%	99,248	72.76	76.76	0.01%	99,373	77.45	81.45	64	1.44%	81,925	18.40	82.40	0.91%	88,857	21.03	85.03
5	0.02%	99,230	71.77	76.77	0.01%	99,358	76.47	81.47	65	1.56%	80,748	17.66	82.66	1.00%	88,050	20.22	85.22
6	0.01%	99,215	70.78	76.78	0.01%	99,346	75.48	81.48	66	1.69%	79,492	16.93	82.93	1.10%	87,171	19.42	85.42
7	0.01%	99,200	69.79	76.79	0.01%	99,334	74.48	81.48	67	1.83%	78,151	16.21	83.21	1.21%	86,211	18.63	85.63
8	0.01%	99,187	68.80	76.80	0.01%	99,324	73.49	81.49	68	2.00%	76,717	15.51	83.51	1.33%	85,168	17.85	85.85
9	0.01%	99,175	67.81	76.81	0.01%	99,314	72.50	81.50	69	2.18%	75,185	14.81	83.81	1.45%	84,039	17.09	86.09
10	0.01%	99,164	66.82	76.82	0.01%	99,305	71.51	81.51	70	2.38%	73,548	14.13	84.13	1.60%	82,818	16.33	86.33
11	0.01%	99,155	65.82	76.82	0.01%	99,296	70.51	81.51	71	2.62%	71,795	13.47	84.47	1.77%	81,494	15.59	86.59
12	0.01%	99,146	64.83	76.83	0.01%	99,288	69.52	81.52	72	2.86%	69,917	12.81	84.81	1.95%	80,054	14.86	86.86
13	0.02%	99,132	63.84	76.84	0.01%	99,277	68.52	81.52	73	3.12%	67,915	12.18	85.18	2.15%	78,494	14.14	87.14
14	0.03%	99,112	62.85	76.85	0.02%	99,265	67.53	81.53	74	3.40%	65,796	11.55	85.55	2.37%	76,809	13.44	87.44
15	0.04%	99,080	61.87	76.87	0.02%	99,248	66.54	81.54	75	3.72%	63,559	10.94	85.94	2.62%	74,992	12.76	87.76
16	0.05%	99,037	60.90	76.90	0.02%	99,228	65.56	81.56	76	4.09%	61,195	10.34	86.34	2.92%	73,026	12.09	88.09
17	0.07%	98,983	59.93	76.93	0.03%	99,204	64.57	81.57	77	4.50%	58,692	9.76	86.76	3.23%	70,896	11.44	88.44
18	0.08%	98,917	58.97	76.97	0.03%	99,175	63.59	81.59	78	4.97%	56,048	9.20	87.20	3.57%	68,604	10.80	88.80
19	0.09%	98,837	58.02	77.02	0.04%	99,144	62.61	81.61	79	5.48%	53,265	8.66	87.66	3.95%	66,153	10.18	89.18
20	0.11%	98,744	57.07	77.07	0.04%	99,109	61.63	81.63	80	6.08%	50,344	8.13	88.13	4.38%	63,542	9.58	89.58
21	0.12%	98,637	56.13	77.13	0.04%	99,071	60.66	81.66	81	6.75%	47,283	7.62	88.62	4.89%	60,757	9.00	90.00
22	0.13%	98,517	55.20	77.20	0.04%	99,030	59.68	81.68	82	7.48%	44,091	7.14	89.14	5.46%	57,786	8.43	90.43
23	0.14%	98,387	54.27	77.27	0.05%	98,986	58.71	81.71	83	8.26%	40,794	6.68	89.68	6.09%	54,633	7.89	90.89
24	0.14%	98,254	53.35	77.35	0.05%	98,939	57.74	81.74	84	9.11%	37,424	6.23	90.23	6.80%	51,305	7.37	91.37
25	0.14%	98,120	52.42	77.42	0.05%	98,891	56.76	81.76	85	10.07%	34,014	5.81	90.81	7.61%	47,815	6.87	91.87
26	0.14%	97,987	51.49	77.49	0.05%	98,841	55.79	81.79	86	11.14%	30,589	5.40	91.40	8.51%	44,179	6.40	92.40
27	0.14%	97,855	50.56	77.56	0.06%	98,789	54.82	81.82	87	12.36%	27,180	5.02	92.02	9.54%	40,417	5.94	92.94
28	0.14%	97,722	49.63	77.63	0.06%	98,735	53.85	81.85	88	13.71%	23,822	4.65	92.65	10.69%	36,561	5.52	93.52
29	0.14%	97,588	48.69	77.69	0.06%	98,677	52.88	81.88	89	15.21%	20,555	4.31	93.31	11.96%	32,655	5.12	94.12
30	0.14%	97,452	47.76	77.76	0.07%	98,615	51.92	81.92	90	16.84%	17,429	4.00	94.00	13.35%	28,751	4.75	94.75
31	0.15%	97,312	46.83	77.83	0.07%	98,549	50.95	81.95	91	18.61%	14,493	3.70	94.70	14.87%	24,912	4.40	95.40
32	0.15%	97,170	45.90	77.90	0.08%	98,478	49.99	81.99	92	20.49%	11,797	3.44	95.44	16.51%	21,208	4.08	96.08
33	0.15%	97,024	44.96	77.96	0.08%	98,403	49.02	82.02	93	22.49%	9,379	3.19	96.19	18.27%	17,707	3.79	96.79
34	0.16%	96,876	44.03	78.03	0.08%	98,323	48.06	82.06	94	24.60%	7,270	2.97	96.97	20.14%	14,472	3.53	97.53
35	0.16%	96,724	43.10	78.10	0.09%	98,240	47.10	82.10	95	26.69%	5,481	2.78	97.78	22.04%	11,557	3.29	98.29
36	0.17%	96,568	42.17	78.17	0.09%	98,153	46.15	82.15	96	28.72%	4,018	2.61	98.61	23.93%	9,010	3.08	99.08
37	0.18%	96,405	41.24	78.24	0.10%	98,060	45.19	82.19	97	30.66%	2,864	2.46	99.46	25.77%	6,854	2.89	99.89
38	0.19%	96,236	40.31	78.31	0.11%	97,960	44.23	82.23	98	32.46%	1,986	2.33	100.33	27.54%	5,088	2.72	100.72
39	0.20%	96,057	39.39	78.39	0.12%	97,853	43.28	82.28	99	34.08%	1,341	2.21	101.21	29.19%	3,687	2.56	101.56
40	0.21%	95,869	38.46	78.46	0.13%	97,737	42.33	82.33	100	35.79%	884	2.09	102.09	30.94%	2,610	2.41	102.41
41	0.22%	95,668	37.54	78.54	0.14%	97,610	41.39	82.39	101	37.58%	568	1.98	102.98	32.80%	1,803	2.27	103.27
42	0.24%	95,453	36.62	78.62	0.15%	97,472	40.45	82.45	102	39.46%	354	1.88	103.88	34.77%	1,211	2.13	104.13
43	0.27%	95,221	35.71	78.71	0.17%	97,321	39.51	82.51	103	41.43%	215	1.77	104.77	36.85%	790	2.00	105.00
44	0.29%	94,967	34.81	78.81	0.19%	97,155	38.57	82.57	104	43.50%	126	1.68	105.68	39.06%	499	1.87	105.87
45	0.32%	94,687	33.91	78.91	0.21%	96,972	37.65	82.65	105	45.67%	71	1.58	106.58	41.41%	304	1.75	106.75
46	0.36%	94,380	33.02	79.02	0.23%	96,772	36.72	82.72	106	47.96%	39	1.49	107.49	43.89%	178	1.64	107.64
47	0.39%	94,043	32.13	79.13	0.25%	96,552	35.81	82.81	107	50.36%	20	1.40	108.40	46.52%	100	1.53	108.53
48	0.43%	93,674	31.26	79.26	0.27%	96,312	34.89	82.89	108	52.87%	10	1.32	109.32	49.32%	53	1.43	109.43
49	0.47%	93,270	30.39	79.39	0.30%	96,050	33.99	82.99	109	55.52%	5	1.24	110.24	52.27%	27	1.33	110.33
50	0.52%	92,830	29.53	79.53	0.32%	95,766	33.09	83.09	110	58.29%	2	1.16	111.16	55.41%	13	1.23	111.23
51	0.56%	92,352	28.68	79.68	0.35%	95,457	32.19	83.19	111	61.21%	1	1.09	112.09	58.74%	6	1.14	112.14
52	0.61%	91,832	27.84	79.84	0.38%	95,123	31.30	83.30	112	64.27%	0	1.02	113.02	62.26%	2	1.06	113.06
53	0.67%	91,270	27.01	80.01	0.40%	94,763	30.42	83.42	113	67.48%	0	0.95	113.95	66.00%	1	0.98	113.98
54	0.72%	90,663	26.19	80.19	0.43%	94,380	29.54	83.54	114	70.86%	0	0.89	114.89	69.96%	0	0.90	114.90
55	0.78%	90,008	25.38	80.38	0.46%	93,974	28.67	83.67	115	74.40%	0	0.82	115.82	74.15%	0	0.83	115.83
56	0.85%	89,302	24.57	80.57	0.49%	93,543	27.80	83.80	116	78.12%	0	0.76	116.76	78.12%	0	0.76	116.76
57	0.91%	88,544	23.78	80.78	0.53%	93,083	26.93	83.93	117	82.02%	0	0.71	117.71	82.02%	0	0.71	117.71
58	0.97%	87,736	22.99	80.99	0.56%	92,592	26.07	84.07	118	86.13%	0	0.65	118.65	86.13%	0	0.65	118.65
59	1.03%	86,886	22.21	81.21	0.60%	92,071	25.22	84.22	119	90.43%	0	0.60	119.60	90.43%	0	0.60	119.60

AGE	MALE Life Expectancy	FEMALE Life Expectancy	JOINT Life Expectancy
50	79.53	83.09	91.40
51	79.68	83.19	91.40
52	79.84	83.30	91.50
53	80.01	83.42	91.50
54	80.19	83.54	91.50
55	80.38	83.67	91.60
56	80.57	83.80	91.60
57	80.78	83.93	91.60
58	80.99	84.07	91.70
59	81.21	84.22	91.70
60	81.44	84.37	91.80
61	81.67	84.52	91.90
62	81.90	84.68	91.90
63	82.15	84.85	92.00
64	82.40	85.03	92.00
65	82.66	85.22	92.10
66	82.93	85.42	92.20
67	83.21	85.63	92.30
68	83.51	85.85	92.40
69	83.81	86.09	92.50
70	84.13	86.33	92.60
71	84.47	86.59	92.70
72	84.81	86.86	92.90
73	85.18	87.14	93.00
74	85.55	87.44	93.20
75	85.94	87.76	93.40
76	86.34	88.09	93.50
77	86.76	88.44	93.70
78	87.20	88.80	94.00
79	87.66	89.18	94.20
80	88.13	89.58	94.50
81	88.62	90.00	94.80
82	89.14	90.43	95.10
83	89.68	90.89	95.40
84	90.23	91.37	95.70
85	90.81	91.87	96.10
86	91.40	92.40	96.50
87	92.02	92.94	96.90
88	92.65	93.52	97.40
89	93.31	94.12	97.90
90	94.00	94.75	98.40

isn't helpful in planning the retirement of someone who is 65.

Let's say that 20 years ago, as a sixty-five-year-old female, you looked up your life expectancy and it told you on average you'd cash in your chips at 85. Yet here you are kicking around *at* your life expectancy; does this mean you should stop buying green bananas and expect to die any day now? No, you are now on a different row of this chart. You could then look up your age as an eighty-five-year-old female and see:

• There's a 7.61% chance you'll kick the bucket this year
• 47,815 of the 100,000 females born when you were are still alive
• You should expect to live another 6.87 years and pass away at 91.87.

Let's say you pass up your life expectancy again and are now 92 years old. Now you are on the age 92 row. You get the idea.

One more nuance of this before we finish off with some things that may sound like science fiction. You should think of financial planning "by household" rather than solely by individual. If you are married, you should think about your life in terms of *joint* life expectancy—planning through the life of the *second* person to die. Joint life expectancy is *always* longer because you have two "rolls of the dice" to beat the average. This is less true if a big age gap separates you and your spouse. To the left is a simplified table of the life expectancies assuming both spouses are the same age.[8]

The way you read this is that if you have a heterosexual couple that are both 65, the man on average will pass away at 82.66 years of age and the woman at 85.22.

However, since you have two rolls of the dice, there is now a third purple column on this chart. For a sixty-five-year-old couple, on average, the second person to die will be 92.10 years old. Those planning for a life expectancy of 80 will undershoot their income need.

And lastly, exponential advances in medical technology are increasing these numbers very quickly. The things that routinely killed people in the past are quickly becoming preventable, treatable, and curable. Diseases which were a death sentence only 10 years ago are now manageable. Present day medical death sentences won't be in 10 years. In the not-too-distant future, technology within our bodies will warn us of life-threatening ailments.

Where this becomes vitally relevant to financial planning is asking, "How much is life expectancy going up between now and when you *expect* to pass away?" Life expectancy is increasing by about 0.2 years every year. The above tables come from the 2010 U.S. Census, so you can already add a year to these numbers.

If you are this sixty-five-year-old couple, you are wise to financially plan that one of you will make it to 92.10. But the truth is that over the next 27.10 years, life expectancy will likely go up by more than five years and second-to-die life expectancy is more than 97 years old. At the current rate of 0.2 more years of life expectancy each year, every five years you manage to stick around, you get a bonus year of life.

Currently this rate is *increasing* with time. Eventually this number may be 0.3, then 0.4, etc. Eventually when it is 0.5, for every year you continue to live, you get a "bonus" six months *more* to live.

When a rocket shoots into space, it must accelerate to escape velocity—the speed at which the rocket can "break free" from earth's gravitational pull and continue under its own momentum. The human race is charging toward a *longevity* escape velocity. It will be the point at which every year we are adding a year or more to life expectancy.

We are entering into a very bizarre era of human history where the things that ordinarily kill us or incapacitate us simply won't. In the coming decades most of your internal organs and body parts will be able to be replaced by brand new ones generated by your own stem cells. There are already thousands of people walking around with replacement tissues generated from stem cells. In time, microscopic robots will be floating through your blood-stream fighting off infections, viruses, and cancer. We are making progress with diseases of the mind and being able to heal people at the genetic level.

The ability to link our minds to computers could open up options to supplement our intelligence and experience. Research is currently confirming that aging itself is not an inevitable part of being a human, but is a curable disease that will likely someday be reversed.

Over the years my message has been the same: you need to do your financial planning with the possibility of *extreme* longevity. I've shared this with people since the early 2000s. I had more hair and less wrinkles in those days, so perhaps the condescending smirks were well deserved. As we've all experienced rapid technological progression, it doesn't sound quite as far-fetched. In 20 years, extreme longevity may feel rather inevitable.

Naturally, none of this is certain. But current research suggests that at some point death itself may be "cured." Personally, I have mixed feelings about this. Professionally, I have a *strong* feeling about this: in financial planning, people need to be ready to live *way* longer than they think is possible.

The ridiculous amount of time on your side will be a powerful point to consider in the next chapter on the time value of money. For now, keep this bug in your ear: even if you are at retirement age, statistically you *still* have a long investing time horizon even at today's life expectancy, let alone with technology.

This tremendous amount of time is your biggest tool for creating wealth, or a tremendous challenge because of rising prices. Mistakes now will make things really challenging when you are 142 years old. At a 3% inflation rate, the prices of everything will double every 24 years. **This is what it looks like if you retire at 65:**

Nobody has ever lived as long as half the ages in this table (the record is 122), but I believe that will soon change and the retiring public will face retirements longer than their pre-retirement work life.

Inflation Over a Really Long Life

Price	Years from Now	Age
$1,000	0.00	65.00
$2,000	23.45	88.45
$3,000	37.17	102.17
$4,000	46.90	111.90
$5,000	54.45	119.45
$6,000	60.62	125.62
$7,000	65.83	130.83
$8,000	70.35	135.35
$9,000	74.33	139.33
$10,000	77.90	142.90

Extreme longevity does not give you the luxury of having your money parked in cash while prices rapidly rise. Ultimately, if money is to buy stuff, you must have a long-term plan that looks realistically at what stuff will cost for as long as you may live—however long that might be.

Does it sound crazy that prices would multiply 10 times? 50 years ago the price of a stamp was five cents. Then, a (nearly) $0.50 stamp would have sounded about as absurd as a $5.00 stamp sounds to us today. If your retirement lasts 50 years, your entire budget will feel like price absurdities. I think that people subconsciously assume their life expectancy will be that of their parents and grandparents. This is a mistake.

Stone #5: Emergency Funds and the Cost of Liquidity

Pause for a moment and consider the money in your bank account. Based on what we've learned about how money earning a low interest amount loses purchasing power, what does that tell you about your balance? For the rest of your life, no matter how unusually long, the money in your bank is nearly guaranteed to get weaker in its ability to buy stuff. Yet everybody *must* have money that can be gotten to quickly and easily. That's called **liquidity**. The name of the game is keeping *only what you need* in the bank and not a penny more ... no matter what your emotions tell you.

I've worked with a lot of people on this. I mentioned Mr. Tonlin in the introduction, who had $4,000,000 in the bank. When I worked at that bank, he certainly wasn't the only customer who had multiple millions in the bank. We all have a certain number that we get used to seeing, and we feel nervous with less. There are some people who live paycheck-to-paycheck and don't feel poor until their account has more or less flatlined. For others, it's $10,000 or $20,000 or $50,000—whatever (usually) arbitrary number they've grown accustomed to seeing.

Let's say your arbitrary number happens to be $100,000. As we learned earlier, using today's average interest rate and inflation numbers, someone holding an average one-year CD is losing buying power at a rate of **-2.308%**. For $100,000, this is $2,308. I suspect that if every year the Inflation Fairy left a bill under your pillow and you had to write a check to the financial universe for $2,308 as a fee, you would do something about it.

We need to move our liquidity away from being an arbitrary number, and towards being the right and specific number unique to you and your needs.

When I come across new clients with a lot of money unnecessarily tied up in cash, I like to start the conversation with, "What are some things in your life that may happen, that you will suddenly need $100,000 for?" Usually, the answer is some version of "Not much." Sometimes (rarely) these people are saving for a car, a home, a major improvement on their home, big vacation, college, or a wedding. There's a difference between planning a very specific need and hoarding cash. A narrower way to ask the question is, "What emergencies do you see costing you $100,000?"

Here are the usual suspects:

- Your house—Hail or water damage is normally insured and most people only have to pony up around $1,000. Major plumbing or repairs can come up (like replacing a sewer line), but for an average house this will be less than $10,000. Even roof replacement for most houses costs less than $20,000. A furnace is usually around $5,000 and water heater less than that. These expenses happen every 15–20 years. Upgrades and remodels are not emergencies.
- Your car—Most states require you to be fully insured and if you get in a car wreck you only pay a deductible. You may be driving a clunker waiting for it to give up its ghost, but this is closer to a planned emergency.

Maybe there's a medical emergency. Maybe you have multiple houses, or a boat. In my experience, most people have just gotten used to seeing a certain cash balance.

This is the formula I use for someone who is retired:

1. Three months of budget (minus income from guaranteed sources)
2. If married, 12 months of Negative Cash Flow that would be lost if income changes due to a job loss, disability or death. For example, if you spend $2,000 per month and unemployment benefits would give you $1,500, then you need to plan to fill in that $500. You anticipate that same gap if your spouse's income goes away or if you become disabled.
3. Deductible on homeowner's insurance
4. 50% of the replacement value of your car
5. 5% of the value of your home

For a typical household, this usually results in still too much liquidity. It's unlikely that *all* of these things would happen within a short time-frame.

1. If your income is guaranteed and is more than your spending, it means that #1 is $0.00.
2. If income is guaranteed for both you and your spouse or if you are single, then #2 is $0.00.
3. #3 is usually about $1,000.
4. If you would replace your car with one costing $30,000, then #4 is $15,000.
5. If your house is worth $300,000, then #5 is $15,000.

Total amount recommended to keep liquid ... $31,000. I think you could also reduce this number if you have access to a low interest credit line such as a home equity line of credit (we'll talk about this in the chapter on real estate).

An alternative, simpler way to come up with a liquidity need figure is to just keep 6 months of expenses in cash. If you spend $4,000 per month, then 6 months is $24,000.

When I plan someone's cash reserves, I consider how certain their income is. I also consider their overall ability to access money. If your house has equity (and if you are very disciplined about *not* spending money), I'm a fan of opening up a home equity line of credit even if you don't need it. Banks and credit unions often do this for no upfront cost. Some may charge you an annual fee of less than $100 per year—nothing a civilized tantrum in your bank lobby won't be able to remove. Even if you pay some money to get the line of credit, the cost is likely worth the ability to maintain less money in cash. It's very important to set these up *especially* if you don't need the funds.

This is an old rule for credit: get it when you don't need it because you can't when you do.

If you feel like you need access to $100,000 in cash, but that cash is costing you $2,308 in purchasing power every year, it is better to pay a small annual fee every year to have access to money, but get that $100,000 working harder for you outside of a bank.

We're painting in very broad strokes here. Everyone's situation is unique. Still, minimize how much money you keep liquid.

Stone #6: The Availability and Unavailability of Money

Here's a profound truth: *the secret to saving money is not spending money.* I believe that subconsciously many people think that the secret to saving more is *making* more. This is only partially true. To save money, you have to actively chose *not* to spend it.

Normally if you're reading a book like this, you've achieved at least some amount of financial solidity. This is not information aimed for absolute beginners. However, I want to address those who feel they don't have any extra money to save, as well as those in retirement going through their savings at an uncomfortable rate.

Truth be told, some people have a lower income and feel that they can't get ahead. Getting ahead financially begins with not having junk debt (the next stone) and regularly saving money into investments. Both of these can only happen if you free up some money each month. Here are some ideas on pinching pennies:

- Cut your cable TV and entertain yourself with much cheaper viewing over the internet. Eventually you won't miss it. For less than $10.00 per month you can entertain yourself just as effectively.
- You don't always have to upgrade technology. If your computer is getting slow, take it to a professional. Often for less than $100 they can get it running much faster. You don't have to get the newest cell phone; get last year's model. You don't need to upgrade your TV to 4K or 8K when HD does the job.
- Resist upgrading your car. If your car is having problems, remember that paying $1,000 to fix it is much less than $30,000 to replace it. Getting a loan for $30,000 is *worse than* blowing $30,000 in cash. Never buy a new car. And buy a brand that is reliable—come on, we *all* know which car brands last. If you aren't certain, the next time you get your oil changed, ask the mechanic which cars are built the best.
- Vacation in your own state. There's so much you haven't explored right in your own backyard. Engage in cheap travel. You can see so much with very little money and some creativity.
- Get rid of stuff. Sell the things you never use. Don't buy things you won't use. Live simply. Later in the book we will have a chapter on minimalism (which is, predictably, short).
- Use the 30 day rule. Think about a purchase for at least 30 days before you buy. You'll be surprised how often you change your mind.
- When shopping, use the 10 second rule. Before you put something in your cart, pause for 10 seconds and ask yourself why you are buying it and if you really need it.
- Have potlucks with friends instead of meeting at restaurants. You'll feel more relaxed in a home.
- Don't put up with any petty fee or monthly cost that doesn't have justified value. *Always* ask for a valueless fee to be waived.
- If you buy something you don't end up liking, take it or send it back *right away*. The more time you wait, the less likely it is you'll return it.
- Cancel subscriptions you aren't getting value for.
- Drink water instead of buying drinks.
- Rent or borrow books, eBooks, audiobooks, movies, and music. Don't buy these things. Most are available through your library. Of course, I waited until *after* you've bought my book to tell you this.
- Be reasonable with your giving. Be creative and thoughtful. For many people, the gifts they remember years later are handmade, shared experiences, and anything creative.
- Never pay retail. Shop sales in opposite buying times (buy winter clothes during the springtime and summer clothes in the fall).

- Take care of your expensive things (get routine maintenance and tune up work on your car, furnace, and major appliances).
- Travel during the shoulder seasons (Fall and Spring).
- Buy used (eBay and Craigslist), especially items that people buy impulsively, like sports equipment and musical instruments. If you don't end up using it, sell it back right away.
- Learn to be handy. YouTube has videos on how to do anything.
- Shop in bulk.
- Take up cooking as a hobby. The skill will save you money and earn you hungry friends.
- Become a connoisseur of free and cheap things. Go to high school football games instead of NFL. Go to free concerts in the park. Go to summertime community outdoor movie screenings. You might find it fills the same need.

Lastly, know that every time you spend $100 on something you don't need, this portrait of Benjamin Franklin will frown upon you in judgment:

I'm not saying *everyone* needs to do these things, but if you need to make room, you have options. With any of these, you won't get ahead financially unless you utilize the "save and save" method. Once you "save" yourself from the monthly expense, *immediately* set up an automatic transfer to "save" into your investment account. You were already getting by with this expense; you can get by forcing yourself to save. If you talk yourself out of buying something you don't need, instead transfer that money to your savings to celebrate.

What I've found is that unless you do this, the extra money just becomes part of the financial ether of your life. I would suggest the same for when you get a pay raise.

Your personal battle is to *fight* until you've saved enough that your investments become self-propagating through compounding interest.

Stone #7: Debt and Seeing the Other Side of Your Balance Sheet

There are three kinds of debt: smart debt, stupid debt, and "dang, I guess I gotta get a loan" debt. If you are up to your ears in debt right now, I'm surprised you've made it this far. There are other resources for getting out of debt, and this book is not that. I will only discuss how to view debt. I will then expand on it when we go into the chapter on real estate and touch on insurmountable debt in the legal planning chapter.

Debt is either *secured* or *unsecured*. Secured debt is tied to an asset (such as a car loan—if you don't pay the loan, they take the car). Unsecured debt isn't tied to an asset (such as a credit card—if you don't pay, there isn't an asset to repossess). The interest rates on unsecured debt are nearly always much higher than on secured debt.

Generally, credit card debt is junk debt, meaning you have nothing to show for it. I have seen interest rates on credit cards as high as 29.99% (and I've heard of even higher). Have you ever noticed that there aren't any loan sharks anymore in our culture? Loan sharks are common in developing countries. These financial predators bury people under insurmountable debt, and rather than expect them to repay the principal, the intention is to collect absurdly high interest indefinitely. That sounds like a really familiar scenario in our culture, but I can't quite put my finger on it ...

Avoid credit card debt like the plague. I know that some people make a game of earning airline points or cash back. I suspect many people would be better off financially to pretend that these points programs don't exist. When big companies bait you into a game, expect to lose.

Let's say that five years ago you put a $5.00 hamburger on your credit card. It's obviously unsecured because nobody is going to try to repo your hamburger. Let's then say that you just pay interest on it over the next five years and then pay off the $5.00 balance after the 5th year. Here is your situation:

Time Value Cost of a Burger	BALANCE	29.99% INTEREST
Year 1	$5.00	$1.50
Year 2	$5.00	$1.50
Year 3	$5.00	$1.50
Year 4	$5.00	$1.50
Year 5 *(Pay Off)*	$5.00	$1.50
TOTAL COST OF THE BURGER		$12.50

I hope it was delicious. Nobody gets ahead with the financial mindset of Wimpy from Popeye: "I will gladly pay you Tuesday for a hamburger today." It is stupid to pay interest on something you digested five years ago.

The same goes for clothes you wear in the first two years and give to Goodwill in the third, or for seeing movies at the theater you wouldn't bother renting for free a few months later at the library.

The biggest deciding question to ask is, "What will happen to the value of the asset after I buy it using a loan?" For nearly everything you buy in life, the value drops once you buy it. Not all debt is created equal. There is a massive difference between:

1. Buying a house with a mortgage when the house value normally goes *up* **4%** each year
2. Buying a car with a loan when the car goes *down* in value by **15%** every year
3. Buying a cheeseburger with a 29.99% credit card when in about 24 hours that cheeseburger literally ain't worth … anything.

Try to see your whole financial picture as a balance sheet. What asset on the other side justifies the debt?

Granted, there are times where people haven't established an emergency fund. Perhaps your furnace goes out in the middle of winter and you realistically have no option but to go into debt. This is what can be categorized as, "dang, I guess I gotta get a loan" debt. The purchase is justified, though less than ideal financially because of a lack of liquidity.

I have found that people will fight *ten times* harder to get themselves out of a bad place than they will to actively *put* themselves into a good place. You must take on that fight to *actively* put yourself in a good place. Have that emergency money so that you don't end up in a bad place.

Much of what we'll later discuss regarding investments will assume that you aren't servicing high interest debt. Even if the general stock market averages **10%**, it wouldn't make sense to invest in that while holding credit card debt at a 29.99% interest rate.

I should say a word on student loans. There is a cloud moving through America right now that I really don't like. After the Financial Crisis, some regulation was rightly handed down and banks couldn't make money in the same ways. Many of them shifted their emphasis to student loans. It is brilliant in a way; from a PR perspective, student loans sound so positive, and from a bank's perspective they're very low risk, because student loans are one of the few things you can't purge away in a bankruptcy.

I think that these features of student loans are part of what's fueling a growing epidemic of education-related debt. And I will add that while it may seem like a necessary evil, these student loans are not always buying education and training that is marketable. I have seen many young people take on $20,000 in federal student loans to get a certificate that gets them a job paying minimum wage.

The Financial Crisis was caused in part by an age of "easy money." Student loans are a new era of "easy money." The key difference is that the Financial Crisis resulted in financial institutions taking crippling write-downs from the defaulting loans. Since student loans can't be discharged, you won't see that. They remain an ongoing burden to that generation.

Adults, I urge you to be nosy and assert yourself when the young people of your life explore these options.

Stone #8: The Psychology of Money

I have a multi-millionaire client who, several times per year, ends up having the utility company turn his electricity off, cut his water, or disconnect his phone. He intentionally doesn't pay the bill until they make him. He also keeps his house thermostat in the low 50s through the winter. Years ago I heard of a man also worth millions who died in his Midwest home for not turning the heat on when it was cold because he was pinching pennies.

What causes this irrational frugality? An outsider would think that these people realize they've made it, relax, and, heck, set their thermostats at a cozy level. What causes some people to hoard money? What causes other people to burn through money? Much of it has to do with psychology. Some people's psychology puts them on an inevitable path to wealth. Other types of psychology hobble their pursuit.

The final stone of our foundation is recognizing that the psychology of money is deeply rooted and sometimes you need to consciously change those roots to maximize your potential for wealth.

None of these strategies will work without discipline and focus. Your psychology may sabotage these virtues. I often tell people that there is the mathematical answer and the real world answer.

In a perfect world, we would stick to what the math tells us, but in reality, we commonly get in our own way. We make decisions and immediately question them. We become convinced of a view and then quickly seek out opposing viewpoints, doing things that confuse us and cloud our decision-making.

At some point, you have to come to a conclusion about your strategy and stick with it. You must have faith—much like a religious faith—in the numbers, no matter how you feel each moment.

Feelings don't change truth. This means that you must actively change your psychology and emotions to avoid self-destructive behavior. That change will look different for everyone. Spenders must learn to tell themselves, "No." A cash hoarder must learn to relax and focus on growing their money's ability to buy stuff.

Make no mistake, although you will see lots of numbers in the next chapter on investments, psychology is 90% of the game. Investing can only reliably increase your wealth if your investments are married to your ability to ignore emotion and focus on optimistic creed.

Summary

These are the financial foundation stones of growing wealth:

1. Money is to buy stuff
2. The permanent rising cost of stuff—prices always mercilessly increase over your lifetime
3. When you factor in taxes and inflation, money in banks does not notably grow in its ability to buy stuff
4. Longevity risk—you will live a long time, possibly a *really* long time, and because of this your focus needs to be on the long term

5. Emergency funds and the cost of liquidity—having cash is like oxygen. You need enough to breathe, but having more than what you need doesn't help you.
6. The secret to saving money is not spending it.
7. Debt is dangerous. Not all debt is created equal.
8. Psychology has a profound impact on the financial habits that keep you financially healthy. Actively cultivate a healthy attitude.

Now that we have the blueprint and the foundation firmly in our minds, we will be leaving our "building a house" analogy behind. As we pivot into investments and investing, we explore how to grow purchasing power over time even as prices continually rise. That is our sole objective.

This chapter has been a doozy of generally bad news. It is crucial that we look at the facts and not fear them. Banking was a downer, but the section on investments is full of good news. First, to whet our appetites: the time value of money.

Endnotes

1. Source: http://www.thepeoplehistory.com/70yearsofpricechange.html

2. Source: https://www.fdic.gov/regulations/resources/rates/historical/2016-12-27.html.

3. U.S. Bureau of Labor Statistics Consumer Price Index

4. Source: http://www.federalreserve.gov/releases/h15/data.htm, Market yield on U.S. Treasury securities at 1-year constant maturity, quoted on investment basis.

5. Source: U.S. Internal Revenue Service. Taxation is the most subjective of these numbers because everyone pays a different rate depending on your income, marital status, and what state you live in. For federal taxes, what I've done is taken the historical median household income and run this through the historical tax bracket for that year as a married couple filing jointly. This is supremely better and more accurate than the highly annoying practice of using the *top* tax bracket. In 1965 the top bracket was 70%, but it was only on income greater than $200,000. In 1965 median income was $4,916 which meant that the median (married) *top* tax bracket was 19% and your effective tax rate 16.14%. State taxes are much trickier because the data is harder to come by. For the years 1977–2014, the data comes from http://users.nber.org/~taxsim/state-rates/ which has the maximum tax rate for all the states. I took each year's numbers and averaged the tax rate across all the states and then divided that number in two. For the years 1965–1976 and 2015–2016, I artificially imputed them using recent data. My method was to take the 1977–2014 average state to federal income tax ratio (19.04%) and multiply it by that year's federal tax rate. This isn't scientific, but it is fair and doesn't radically change the point.

6. Source: U.S. Bureau of Labor Statistics.

7. Source: Social Security Administration http://www.ssa.gov/oact/STATS/table4c6.html#fn2

8. Source: http://www.pgcalc.com/pdf/twolife.pdf

It does not matter how slowly you go as long as you do not stop.

Confucius

The Time Value of Money

Exponential thinking doesn't come naturally to humans. We can run the numbers, but rarely conceive the real world results. Let's take a non-financial example: the Human Genome Project. This ambitious project began in 1990 with the goal of decoding the three billion chemical base pairs that make up the human genome. It was funded for 15 years with a grand total budget of $3.0 billion—which comes out to a $1.00 per chemical pair.

In 1997, seven and a half years in, results seemed discouraging. The project announced that the various teams involved had thus far decoded a dismal 1% of the human genome. Politicians called for the project to be shut down because at that rate, it would take over 700 years to finish it—from a linear perspective. The exponential truth is that as they were working, the amount of information they could decode doubled every year.

When they were 1% finished, they were actually *half* way done in terms of time.

Human Genome Project

YEAR	% COMPLETE
1990	0.01%
1991	0.02%
1992	0.03%
1993	0.06%
1994	0.13%
1995	0.25%
1996	0.50%
1997	1%
1998	2%
1999	4%
2000	8%
2001	16%
2002	32%
2003	64%
April 2003	100%

This was roughly their progress:

In 1997, you could have projected that they would be done somewhere in the middle of 2003, which is exactly what happened. The project announced its completion in April 2003, nearly two years ahead of schedule at a total cost of $2.7 billion. To be clear: ahead of schedule and under budget.[1]

The scientists celebrated how this would change medicine, but skeptics weren't silenced. At a cost of $2.7 billion dollars and 13 years per genome, how could this technology possibly be useful? Again, the concern assumed a linear world.

Below is a chart of the historical cost of sequencing one human genome.

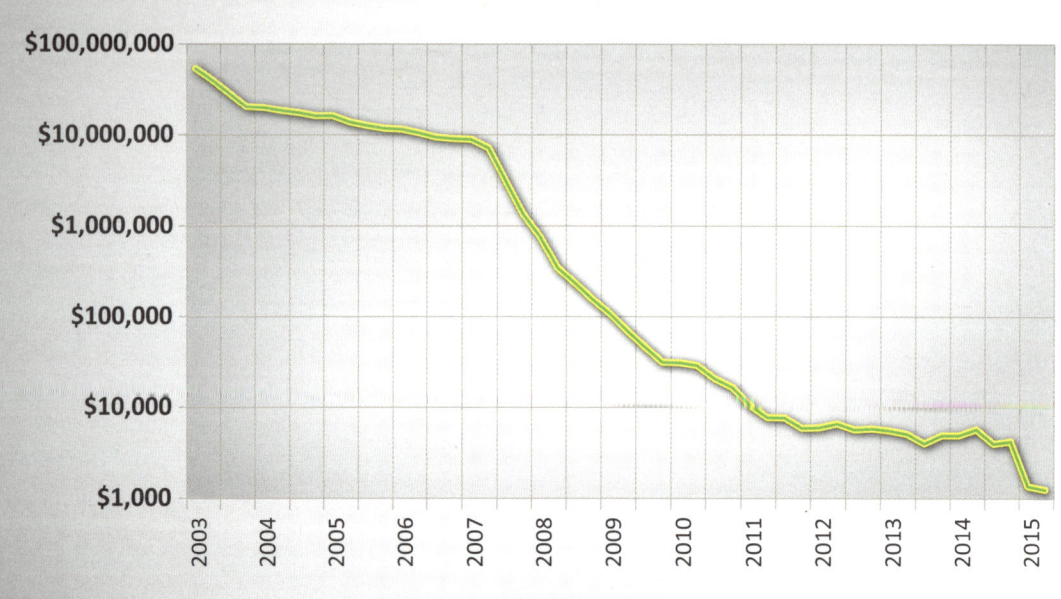

Cost to Sequence One Human Genome

As I write this in 2017, the cost to sequence your DNA is less than $1,000. In a few years, the cost to sequence your DNA will be less than $100. In time, the cost will be less than a cup of coffee. To note, the same thing that cost *three billion* dollars at one point will cost $3.00 within about a forty year time-frame.

Exponential improvements look obvious in hindsight. When DNA sequencing is a billion times cheaper, it will be impressive, but not as impressive as it sounded in 1990. Soon, sequencing your DNA will be a standard and affordable aspect of monitoring your health.

We see the same pattern with renewable energy. Right now, it probably seems impossible that the world will get a majority of our electrical energy from the sun and that fossil fuels would be economically obsolete for most people. But scales are tilting because of similar factors.

The key economic driver of this is the cost per watt of energy. When you look at your utility bill, it will tell you the cost per kilowatt-hour of electricity ($0.12 is average). On a cost per kilowatt-hour basis, solar energy is rapidly getting cheaper. The economic turning point occurs when it is *cheaper* to get energy from solar panels on your roof than it would be to buy it from a utility company. This is what's called *price parity*.

Solar price parity is happening faster than anyone predicted five years ago. In fact, right now, for large areas of the country, it is already cheaper to get energy from solar than from traditional sources.

By the year 2021, over 100 million Americans will be at price parity for solar.[2] The 2020s will be marked by a massive shift of consumers over to solar energy. This will be the case *even as* tax incentives go away.

By 2030, it will be far less expensive for all Americans to get their energy from solar panels than from their utility company. Beyond this, it will *continue* to get cheaper.

Naturally, various forces will slow this down—such as existing disinterested forces, politics, and utility companies who may be less than eager for their inevitable displacement. But economic forces are rarely held back over the long run. The entire energy industry will be turned on its head.

So ... what does this have to do with money?

Regrettably, the exponential rate on technology is far more impressive than your rate of return ever will be. The Rule of 72 approximates how fast your principal will double based on your interest rate. If you take your rate of return and divide 72 by this rate, then it will tell you how many years it would take to double.

For example, something growing at **10%** would take 7.2 years to double (i.e. 72/10 = 7.2).

Here would be some sample interest rates[3]:

Rule of 72	
Interest Rate	Years to Double
20.0%	3.6
15.0%	4.8
10.0%	7.2
9.0%	8.0
7.2%	10.0
5.0%	14.4
2.5%	28.8
1.0%	72.0

I've noted the two interest rates: **9%** and **10%**. A mere 1% may not sound like a big difference, but over a lifetime, the difference is *radical*. Let's say you had two people who at 20 years old had $100,000. One person is earning **9%**, the other **10%**. This is what their balance would look like over a lifetime:

Investing Results of a Lifetime

Age	Balance with 9%	Balance with 10%	Difference
20	$100,000	$100,000	$0
30	$236,736	$259,374	$22,638
40	$560,441	$672,750	$112,309
50	$1,326,768	$1,744,940	$418,172
60	$3,140,942	$4,525,926	$1,384,984
70	$7,435,752	$11,739,085	$4,303,333
80	$17,603,129	$30,448,164	$12,845,035
90	$41,673,009	$78,974,696	$37,301,687
100	$98,655,167	$204,840,021	$106,184,855

As we will learn in the next chapter on investments, it is common to lose 1% on wrong investment choices, valueless fees, foolishly trying to time the market, being unnecessarily conservative, or worse yet, panicking and selling out of your investments during a market downturn. For now, let us take a deep breath and observe the powerful *time value of money*. Much like the Human Genome Project, a strong compounding rate over time catapults your wealth into *counterintuitive* results. Given enough time, any amount of money is a fortune in a chrysalis.

Let's look at this from another angle to punctuate the time power of money. We'll imagine two twins named Mary and Terry. Mary begins saving $100 per month on the day they both turn 21 years old. She puts it into an account with a **10%** return. Nine years later, on their 30th birthday, Mary stops saving and never adds another penny to her investments.

Mary's twin brother Terry doesn't start saving *until* their 30th birthday. His *first* $100 into savings begins the month after Mary's *last* savings deposit. Everything else is identical, most notably the **10%** rate of return, their ages, and the $100 savings rate. The results are on the next page.

If we look at their 65th birthday, Mary—who hasn't saved *a penny* the past 35 years—has a balance of $538,047, while Terry only has $420,676. In fact, on the twins' 100th birthday, even though Terry has been *rigorously* saving most of his life, his account balance *never* catches up with Mary's. Mary's early nine years had more power than Terry's late 70 years of saving. Eventually when the twins are 116 years old Terry's balance catches up to Mary's. An early nine years is the same as a late 86 years.

There is another lesson available in this example. I have used a modest, even-dollar savings amount and fixed interest rate to make a simplified point, but there is a similar element to the Human Genome Project. Some people retiring at 65 with these balances may feel that they've fallen short on their savings. But if they left it alone, by the time they reached their life expectancy, their balance would become more than five times what it was at retirement. Time heals financial wounds.

For the time being, we don't live forever and there is no substitute for front loading your savings accounts as early in life as possible. Lost time cannot be redeemed. On the other hand, if we do enter into an era of indefinite longevity, there is an exciting possibility to leverage massive time to create massive wealth. I believe that in the future, those who follow what I say in the next chapter on investments and notably the chapter after that on optimism, will be more than the millionaires next door. In time they will be *barons* next door. The Methuselah class of patient high rollers.

Mary and Terry

THE TIME VALUE OF MONEY

Mary begins saving $100 per month on the day they both turn 21 years old. She puts it into an account with a 10% return. Nine years later, on their 30th birthday, Mary stops saving and never adds another penny to her investments.

Age	Mary Saving Ages 20-29		Terry Saving Ages 30-100		Difference
	Monthly Savings	Investment Balance	Monthly Savings	Investment Balance	
21	$100	$1,257	$0	$0	$1,257
22	$100	$2,645	$0	$0	$2,645
23	$100	$4,178	$0	$0	$4,178
24	$100	$5,872	$0	$0	$5,872
25	$100	$7,744	$0	$0	$7,744
26	$100	$9,811	$0	$0	$9,811
27	$100	$12,095	$0	$0	$12,095
28	$100	$14,618	$0	$0	$14,618
29	$100	$17,405	$0	$0	$17,405
30	$0	$19,146	$100	$1,257	$17,889
31	$0	$21,060	$100	$2,645	$18,416
32	$0	$23,167	$100	$4,178	$18,988
33	$0	$25,483	$100	$5,872	$19,611
34	$0	$28,032	$100	$7,744	$20,288
35	$0	$30,835	$100	$9,811	$21,024
36	$0	$33,918	$100	$12,095	$21,823
37	$0	$37,310	$100	$14,618	$22,692
38	$0	$41,041	$100	$17,405	$23,636
39	$0	$45,145	$100	$20,484	$24,661
40	$0	$49,660	$100	$23,886	$25,774
41	$0	$54,626	$100	$27,644	$26,982
42	$0	$60,088	$100	$31,795	$28,293
43	$0	$66,097	$100	$36,381	$29,716
44	$0	$72,707	$100	$41,447	$31,260
45	$0	$79,977	$100	$47,044	$32,934
46	$0	$87,975	$100	$53,226	$34,749
47	$0	$96,772	$100	$60,056	$36,716
48	$0	$106,450	$100	$67,602	$38,848
49	$0	$117,095	$100	$75,937	$41,158
50	$0	$128,804	$100	$85,145	$43,659
51	$0	$141,685	$100	$95,317	$46,367
52	$0	$155,050	$100	$106,555	$49,298
53	$0	$171,438	$100	$118,969	$52,469
54	$0	$188,582	$100	$132,683	$55,899
55	$0	$207,440	$100	$147,834	$59,607
56	$0	$228,184	$100	$164,570	$63,614
57	$0	$251,003	$100	$183,059	$67,943
58	$0	$276,103	$100	$203,485	$72,618
59	$0	$303,713	$100	$226,049	$77,665
60	$0	$334,085	$100	$250,976	$83,109

Monthly Savings Account Results: 61 to 100

Age	Mary Saving Ages 20-29		Terry Saving Ages 30-100		
	Monthly Savings	Investment Balance	Monthly Savings	Investment Balance	Difference
61	$0	$367,493	$100	$278,513	$88,981
62	$0	$404,242	$100	$308,933	$95,309
63	$0	$444,667	$100	$342,539	$102,128
64	$0	$489,133	$100	$379,664	$109,470
65	$0	$538,047	$100	$420,676	$117,371
66	$0	$591,851	$100	$465,983	$125,868
67	$0	$651,036	$100	$516,034	$135,002
68	$0	$716,140	$100	$571,326	$144,814
69	$0	$787,754	$100	$632,408	$155,346
70	$0	$866,530	$100	$699,886	$166,644
71	$0	$953,183	$100	$774,430	$178,753
72	$0	$1,048,501	$100	$856,779	$191,722
73	$0	$1,153,351	$100	$947,752	$205,599
74	$0	$1,268,686	$100	$1,048,250	$220,436
75	$0	$1,395,555	$100	$1,159,272	$236,282
76	$0	$1,535,110	$100	$1,281,920	$253,190
77	$0	$1,688,621	$100	$1,417,410	$271,211
78	$0	$1,857,483	$100	$1,567,088	$290,395
79	$0	$2,043,231	$100	$1,732,439	$310,792
80	$0	$2,247,555	$100	$1,915,105	$332,450
81	$0	$2,472,310	$100	$2,116,898	$355,412
82	$0	$2,719,541	$100	$2,339,821	$379,720
83	$0	$2,991,495	$100	$2,586,087	$405,408
84	$0	$3,290,645	$100	$2,858,141	$432,503
85	$0	$3,619,709	$100	$3,158,682	$461,027
86	$0	$3,981,680	$100	$3,490,694	$490,986
87	$0	$4,379,848	$100	$3,857,472	$522,376
88	$0	$4,817,833	$100	$4,262,657	$555,176
89	$0	$5,299,616	$100	$4,710,269	$589,347
90	$0	$5,829,578	$100	$5,204,752	$624,825
91	$0	$6,412,535	$100	$5,751,014	$661,521
92	$0	$7,053,789	$100	$6,354,477	$699,312
93	$0	$7,759,168	$100	$7,021,131	$738,037
94	$0	$8,535,085	$100	$7,757,591	$777,493
95	$0	$9,388,593	$100	$8,571,169	$817,424
96	$0	$10,327,452	$100	$9,469,939	$857,513
97	$0	$11,360,198	$100	$10,462,822	$897,376
98	$0	$12,496,217	$100	$11,559,673	$936,545
99	$0	$13,745,839	$100	$12,771,378	$974,461
100	$0	$15,120,423	$100	$14,109,965	$1,010,458

If we look at their 65th birthday, Mary—who hasn't saved a penny the past 35 years—has a balance of $538,047, while Terry only has $420,676. In fact, on the twins' 100th birthday, even though Terry has been rigorously saving most of his life, his account balance never catches up with Mary's.

The Smoker's Challenge

Saving doesn't come naturally to Americans. Our savings rate is about a third of many of our peers in the world. Spending money is part of our culture. It's as American as apple pie, baseball, and liposuction. It also seems to be natural and common to feel like you don't have any money to save every month. I submit to you what we'll call The Smoker's Challenge.

When I was in middle school I remember a rather terse exchange between my friend Matt who smoked cigarettes and an older teacher who did not. She chided him, "Did you know that with the money you'd save *not* buying cigarettes you could have a Ferrari when you retire?" He smiled with premature confidence and asked, "Where's your Ferrari?" Both people were entirely right. Let's start with the teacher. We'll begin our scenario in 1970 when a pack of cigarettes was $0.38. We'll assume our smoker consumes two packs per day and his account is growing at **10%**. In the first year, he is saving $23.18 per month from *not* spending the money on cigarettes.[4] Over time, as the price of cigarettes goes up, so does his monthly savings amount.

By the time he retires, he has $536,884 in savings—plenty of money for a top of the line Ferrari, second home, or epic Hummel collection. A household with two smokers could double this number.

But my friend Matt was also right: where was our teacher's Ferrari?

There is always the mathematical answer and the real world answer. The math suggests modest savings can build a sizable nest egg. In the real world, few set up automatic savings.

The same case applies to chai lattes, eating out, or entertainment—these are choices that forgo future Ferraris. Many people have more "extra money" than they think they do. They spend it.

Look around at your peers. Do they have a big gas guzzling car and you don't? That's a couple hundred dollars. Do they have a car payment and you don't? Do they have newer and nicer furniture? It's important to change your mindset from "Keeping up with the Joneses" to observing the Joneses while humbly making better lifelong decisions.

Smoker's Challenge

Year	Age	Cost of Pack of Cigarettes	Monthly Cost for Two Packs Per Day	Investment Balance
1970	21	$0.38	$23.18	$291
1971	22	$0.39	$24.01	$623
1972	23	$0.40	$24.33	$994
1973	24	$0.41	$25.13	$1,414
1974	25	$0.44	$26.86	$1,900
1975	26	$0.48	$28.93	$2,463
1976	27	$0.49	$29.72	$3,094
1977	28	$0.54	$33.09	$3,834
1978	29	$0.57	$34.44	$4,668
1979	30	$0.60	$36.33	$5,613
1980	31	$0.63	$38.27	$6,682
1981	32	$0.70	$42.41	$7,914
1982	33	$0.81	$49.48	$9,365
1983	34	$0.93	$56.31	$11,053
1984	35	$0.98	$59.57	$12,959
1985	36	$1.04	$63.49	$15,114
1986	37	$1.11	$67.77	$17,548
1987	38	$1.20	$73.09	$20,304
1988	39	$1.31	$79.75	$23,432
1989	40	$1.45	$88.08	$26,993
1990	41	$1.53	$93.30	$30,991
1991	42	$1.74	$105.63	$35,564
1992	43	$1.84	$111.79	$40,693
1993	44	$1.68	$102.52	$46,242
1994	45	$1.75	$106.36	$52,421
1995	46	$1.81	$110.45	$59,298
1996	47	$1.88	$114.52	$66,946
1997	48	$2.01	$122.14	$75,491
1998	49	$2.23	$135.97	$85,104
1999	50	$2.96	$180.31	$96,282
2000	51	$3.16	$192.34	$108,781
2001	52	$3.40	$206.97	$122,772
2002	53	$3.70	$225.49	$138,461
2003	54	$3.82	$232.71	$155,884
2004	55	$3.87	$235.31	$175,164
2005	56	$4.04	$245.76	$196,594
2006	57	$4.10	$249.67	$220,317
2007	58	$4.37	$265.82	$246,727
2008	59	$4.55	$276.82	$276,041
2009	60	$5.53	$336.57	$309,176
2010	61	$5.81	$353.72	$345,995
2011	62	$5.93	$361.06	$386,762
2012	63	$5.97	$363.17	$431,825
2013	64	$6.10	$371.30	$481,708
2014	65	$6.19	$376.77	$536,884

Thus The Smoker's Challenge:

If you don't have automatic savings, invest each month what a smoker would pay for two packs of daily cigarettes.

The Escape Velocity of Money

The final concept is what I call the escape velocity of money. I used this same term when talking about longevity. When you save up money, as you apply force (i.e. adding money to your investments), eventually it soars on its own (i.e. you don't necessarily need to add money to it for it to keep going). This is what we saw with Mary and Terry. Mary's account was soaring even though she turned the engines off fairly early.

When your account self-propels, your savings have reached escape velocity. However, reaching that point requires mindful force and commitment. To be sure we don't miss our analogy here, what's holding our rocket down to the earth? What is our metaphorical "gravity"? Low interest rates, taxation, and worst of all, inflation.

So what does this look like? I'm going to simplify things so that the numbers are clearer. Let's say you save $1,000 per year earning **10%**.

Year	Balance before Addition	Addition	Balance after Addition	Interest Earned That Year	Total Additions	Total Interest Earned
0	$0	$1,000	$1,000	$100	$1,000	$0
1	$1,100	$1,000	$2,100	$210	$2,000	$100
2	$2,310	$1,000	$3,310	$331	$3,000	$310
3	$3,641	$1,000	$4,641	$464	$4,000	$641
4	$5,105	$1,000	$6,105	$611	$5,000	$1,105
5	$6,716	$1,000	$7,716	$772	$6,000	$1,716
6	$8,487	$1,000	$9,487	$949	$7,000	$2,487
7	$10,436	$1,000	$11,436	$1,144	$8,000	$3,436

A magical thing happens in the seventh year. You have saved up enough money that the amount of interest you earned ($1,144) is *greater* than your regular deposit. It is absolute financial wizardry. After seven years of working hard, you reached your financial escape velocity. If you don't add money to it anymore, the account continues to have a life of its own.

Here's the truly exciting thing: what happens if you keep pushing that rocket?

8	$12,579	$1,000	$13,579	$1,358	$9,000	$4,579
9	$14,937	$1,000	$15,937	$1,594	$10,000	$5,937
10	$17,531	$1,000	$18,531	$1,853	$11,000	$7,531
11	$20,384	$1,000	$21,384	$2,138	$12,000	$9,384
12	$23,523	$1,000	$24,523	$2,452	$13,000	$11,523
13	$26,975	$1,000	$27,975	$2,797	$14,000	$13,975
14	$30,772	$1,000	$31,772	$3,177	$15,000	$16,772
15	$34,950	$1,000	$35,950	$3,595	$16,000	$19,950
16	$39,545	$1,000	$40,545	$4,054	$17,000	$23,545

Only four years later you reach twice your escape velocity. Now, each year you are earning *twice* in interest what you are adding to it from your own money. Only *three* years after that, in the 14th year, you are earning *three times* your contribution amount and only two years later *four times* the contribution amount. It's nothing short of financial witchcraft.

Call me indulgent, but this is just too much fun. Let's go all the way through 21 years.

17	$44,599	$1,000	$45,599	$4,560	$18,000	$27,599
18	$50,159	$1,000	$51,159	$5,116	$19,000	$32,159
19	$56,275	$1,000	$57,275	$5,727	$20,000	$37,275
20	$63,002	$1,000	$64,002	$6,400	$21,000	$43,002
21	$70,403	$1,000	$71,403	$7,140	$22,000	$49,403

After twenty-one years of this you are earning *seven times* more in interest than your contribution. If we look at your final contributions, you would have only added $22,000 of your money yet earned more than twice that in interest. And it only keeps getting better beyond this. This is what is known as **compounding interest** or the **time value of money**. Folks, this must be the goal for those starting out. You have to push to reach this point of escape velocity.

Saving Money into a Bank Revisited

I used the **10%** number to expedite my point, but let's revisit dismal bank interest. We can imagine someone trying to do the same thing, but saving money into a bank. They would diligently save $1,000 per year. However, instead of reaching an escape velocity, at some point the account balance would not grow in real money. It would be when their $1,000 addition is *less than* what the account balance lost to inflation that year.

Using the 2016 numbers, if the real rate of return was **-2.308%**, any balance more than $43,328 means that a $1,000 addition doesn't even maintain the purchasing power of the account. Somebody regularly saving money into a bank should expect to reach a glass ceiling at some point—it is the level where nominal growth is actually meandering deeper into futility.

We can also imagine an analogy of someone blowing up a balloon with a hole in it. At first, for each breath they blow into the balloon, *most* of it stays in. As the balloon grows, the hole size stretches along with it, and for every breath added, the balloon loses two breaths of air. Because of the hole, the balloon has very little chance of growing past a certain size.

In real money, even though you are *adding* money to a bank account, it may not be growing in its ability to buy stuff. It is not enough just to save money. It must be invested in the right place.

A True Story of 200 Years of Compounding Interest

Toward the end of his life Benjamin Franklin was mulling compounding interest and wanted to do a postmortem experiment. In his will, he gave 2,000 pounds (about $9,100) to the cities of Philadelphia and Boston. The will said that in 100 years they could take out some of the money, but that the rest had to stay invested at about a **5%** return for *another* 100 years. Franklin died in 1790. By 1990, despite some withdrawals along the way, the two funds were worth $6,500,000.

Benjamin Franklin famously said, "A penny saved is a penny earned." My version of this is somewhat less catchy, "A penny saved is a penny earned ... but subject to inflation which is overcome by your rate of return."

I suppose that nuance and catchiness are arch-enemies.

Franklin's endowment fell massively short of its potential when he missed a nuance. His bequest is astounding, but measly compared to if Franklin had appreciated the devastating power of inflation, which also compounds over time. Franklin estimated that the money would earn **5%** over those 200 years, but the *real* rate of return for these separately managed funds ended up being only **2.0%** for Boston and **2.36%** for Philadelphia.[5]

The reason for this dismal rate was because of *where* Franklin wanted the money invested—the key point of Stone #3: *where*. Had Franklin invested in the general stock market, by 1990 these cities would *each* have had well over 12 billion dollars.[6] Ahem ... 12 b-b-*billion*. To put this figure in relative perspective, here are some mega-projects from just after 1990:

- In 1994 the Channel Tunnel was completed as a 31.4 mile tunnel beneath the English Channel. The project cost was $15.4 billion.
- In 1995 Denver International Airport was built for $4.8 billion. It is the largest airport as measured by land area and the 6th busiest in the United States.
- In 1998 the Akashi Kaikyō Bridge was completed as the longest suspension bridge in the world for a project cost of $5 billion.

Franklin was spot on in his 200 year homage to the time value of money, but made a rather regrettable *where* error. For my fellow numberphiles, I've estimated what Franklin's endowments would have experienced if invested in the stock market. The stock market returns from 1824–1990 are accurate, but because of a lack of data I had to fill in a return for the years 1790–1823. I chose to use the same rate that Boston was able to achieve for those years, which was likely less than actual stock market returns.

Endnotes

1   Source: National Human Genome Research Institute (NHGRI) https://www.genome.gov/sequencingcosts/

2   Source: http://cleantechnica.com/2015/05/22/solar-parity-coming-faster-expected/

3   Again, this is an approximation. The real times are 20% = 3.80 years, 15% = 4.96 years, 10% = 7.27 years, 9% = 8.04 years, 7.2% = 9.97 years, 5% = 14.21 years, 2.5% = 28.07 years, and 1% = 69.66 years.

4   The overly observant may notice that these numbers don't quite add up. The average cost for a pack of cigarettes in 1970 was actually $0.380745098. Our monthly number is the average cost *times* two packs per day *times* 365.25 days *divided* by 12 months.

5   Source: *Inflation Conversion Factors for years 1774 to estimated 2025*, in dollars of recent years by Robert Sahr

6   Market data from 1824–1990 is from 2015 Ibbotson SBBI Classic Yearbook Table 13-3: Large Cap Stocks. For years 1790–1823, the return figure used was a fixed rate of 4.55% which was the average rate of return of the Boston fund during this time.

Benjamin Franklin's 200 Year Experiment

		Boston				Philadelphia				Using the Stock Market			
Year	Inflation	Estimated Balance	In Today's Money	Implied Return	Real Return	Estimated Balance	In Today's Money	Implied Return	Real Return	Total Market Return	Real Rate	Boston Balance	Philadelphia Balance
1790	4.50%	$4,550	$116,667	4.55%	0.05%	$4,550	$116,667	2.94%	-1.56%	4.55%	0.05%	$4,550	$4,550
1791	2.20%	$4,757	$118,930	4.55%	2.35%	$4,684	$117,094	2.94%	0.74%	4.55%	2.35%	$4,757	$4,757
1792	2.10%	$4,974	$121,314	4.55%	2.45%	$4,821	$117,597	2.94%	0.84%	4.55%	2.45%	$4,974	$4,974
1793	3.10%	$5,200	$123,819	4.55%	1.45%	$4,963	$118,172	2.94%	-0.16%	4.55%	1.45%	$5,200	$5,200
1794	11.10%	$5,437	$118,201	4.55%	-6.55%	$5,109	$111,069	2.94%	-8.16%	4.55%	-6.55%	$5,437	$5,437
1795	14.50%	$5,685	$107,261	4.55%	-9.95%	$5,259	$99,234	2.94%	-11.56%	4.55%	-9.95%	$5,685	$5,685
1796	4.80%	$5,944	$106,139	4.55%	-0.25%	$5,414	$96,679	2.94%	-1.86%	4.55%	-0.25%	$5,944	$5,944
1797	-3.80%	$6,214	$115,082	4.55%	8.35%	$5,573	$103,207	2.94%	6.74%	4.55%	8.35%	$6,214	$6,214
1798	-3.10%	$6,497	$124,951	4.55%	7.65%	$5,737	$110,328	2.94%	6.04%	4.55%	7.65%	$6,497	$6,497
1799	0.00%	$6,793	$130,642	4.55%	4.55%	$5,906	$113,572	2.94%	2.94%	4.55%	4.55%	$6,793	$6,793
1800	2.40%	$7,103	$134,015	4.55%	2.15%	$6,079	$114,705	2.94%	0.54%	4.55%	2.15%	$7,103	$7,103
1801	0.80%	$7,426	$137,523	4.55%	3.75%	$6,258	$115,891	2.94%	2.14%	4.55%	3.75%	$7,426	$7,426
1802	-15.70%	$7,764	$172,544	4.55%	20.25%	$6,442	$143,158	2.94%	18.64%	4.55%	20.25%	$7,764	$7,764
1803	5.60%	$8,118	$169,126	4.55%	-1.05%	$6,632	$138,157	2.94%	-2.66%	4.55%	-1.05%	$8,118	$8,118
1804	4.40%	$8,488	$169,756	4.55%	0.15%	$6,827	$136,530	2.94%	-1.46%	4.55%	0.15%	$8,488	$8,488
1805	-0.80%	$8,874	$181,109	4.55%	5.35%	$7,027	$143,412	2.94%	3.74%	4.55%	5.35%	$8,874	$8,874
1806	4.30%	$9,279	$178,433	4.55%	0.25%	$7,234	$139,112	2.94%	-1.36%	4.55%	0.25%	$9,279	$9,279
1807	-4.90%	$9,701	$197,981	4.55%	9.45%	$7,447	$151,969	2.94%	7.84%	4.55%	9.45%	$9,701	$9,701
1808	8.60%	$10,143	$191,375	4.55%	-4.05%	$7,665	$144,631	2.94%	-5.66%	4.55%	-4.05%	$10,143	$10,143
1809	-2.40%	$10,605	$203,939	4.55%	6.95%	$7,891	$151,746	2.94%	5.34%	4.55%	6.95%	$10,605	$10,605
1810	0.00%	$11,088	$213,226	4.55%	4.55%	$8,123	$156,208	2.94%	2.94%	4.55%	4.55%	$11,088	$11,088
1811	6.50%	$11,593	$210,777	4.55%	-1.95%	$8,362	$152,030	2.94%	-3.56%	4.55%	-1.95%	$11,593	$11,593
1812	1.50%	$12,121	$216,441	4.55%	3.05%	$8,607	$153,705	2.94%	1.44%	4.55%	3.05%	$12,121	$12,121
1813	20.30%	$12,673	$186,363	4.55%	-15.75%	$8,861	$130,302	2.94%	-17.36%	4.55%	-15.75%	$12,673	$12,673
1814	10.00%	$13,250	$179,052	4.55%	-5.45%	$9,121	$123,258	2.94%	-7.06%	4.55%	-5.45%	$13,250	$13,250
1815	-12.50%	$13,853	$213,127	4.55%	17.05%	$9,389	$144,450	2.94%	15.44%	4.55%	17.05%	$13,853	$13,853
1816	-8.40%	$14,484	$241,403	4.55%	12.95%	$9,665	$161,088	2.94%	11.34%	4.55%	12.95%	$14,484	$14,484
1817	-5.70%	$15,144	$270,426	4.55%	10.25%	$9,949	$177,669	2.94%	8.64%	4.55%	10.25%	$15,144	$15,144
1818	-4.50%	$15,834	$293,213	4.55%	9.05%	$10,242	$189,667	2.94%	7.44%	4.55%	9.05%	$15,834	$15,834
1819	0.00%	$16,555	$306,567	4.55%	4.55%	$10,543	$195,243	2.94%	2.94%	4.55%	4.55%	$16,555	$16,555
1820	-7.90%	$17,309	$353,236	4.55%	12.45%	$10,853	$221,492	2.94%	10.84%	4.55%	12.45%	$17,309	$17,309
1821	-3.40%	$18,097	$377,017	4.55%	7.95%	$11,172	$232,754	2.94%	6.34%	4.55%	7.95%	$18,097	$18,097
1822	3.50%	$18,921	$386,143	4.55%	1.05%	$11,501	$234,708	2.94%	-0.56%	4.55%	1.05%	$18,921	$18,921
1823	-10.30%	$19,783	$449,607	4.55%	14.85%	$11,839	$269,064	2.94%	13.24%	4.55%	14.85%	$19,783	$19,783
1824	-7.60%	$20,684	$504,480	4.55%	12.15%	$12,187	$297,242	2.94%	10.54%	4.55%	12.15%	$20,684	$20,684
1825	2.10%	$21,626	$514,897	4.55%	2.45%	$12,545	$298,696	2.94%	0.84%	-9.00%	-11.10%	$18,822	$18,822
1826	0.00%	$22,611	$538,346	4.55%	4.55%	$12,914	$307,478	2.94%	2.94%	2.20%	2.20%	$19,236	$19,236
1827	1.00%	$23,640	$562,864	4.55%	3.55%	$13,294	$316,518	2.94%	1.94%	-2.15%	-3.15%	$18,822	$18,822
1828	-5.00%	$24,717	$617,923	4.55%	9.55%	$13,685	$342,115	2.94%	7.94%	-13.19%	-8.19%	$16,340	$16,340
1829	-2.10%	$25,843	$662,630	4.55%	6.65%	$14,087	$361,204	2.94%	5.04%	15.19%	17.29%	$18,822	$18,822
1830	-1.10%	$27,020	$692,808	4.55%	5.65%	$14,501	$371,824	2.94%	4.04%	31.87%	32.97%	$24,820	$24,820
1831	-5.40%	$28,250	$763,515	4.55%	9.95%	$14,927	$403,446	2.94%	8.34%	-14.17%	-8.77%	$21,304	$21,304
1832	-1.10%	$29,537	$820,462	4.55%	5.65%	$15,366	$426,844	2.94%	4.04%	12.62%	13.72%	$23,993	$23,993
1833	-2.30%	$30,882	$882,337	4.55%	6.85%	$15,818	$451,948	2.94%	5.24%	-1.72%	0.58%	$23,579	$23,579
1834	2.40%	$32,288	$896,895	4.55%	2.15%	$16,283	$452,313	2.94%	0.54%	13.16%	10.76%	$26,682	$26,682
1835	2.30%	$33,759	$912,397	4.55%	2.25%	$16,762	$453,027	2.94%	0.64%	-2.33%	-4.63%	$26,061	$26,061
1836	5.70%	$35,296	$905,030	4.55%	-1.15%	$17,255	$442,432	2.94%	-2.76%	12.70%	7.00%	$29,371	$29,371
1837	3.20%	$36,904	$900,089	4.55%	1.35%	$17,762	$433,223	2.94%	-0.26%	-13.38%	-16.58%	$25,441	$25,441
1838	-3.10%	$38,584	$989,341	4.55%	7.65%	$18,284	$468,830	2.94%	6.04%	21.14%	24.24%	$30,819	$30,819
1839	0.00%	$40,342	$1,034,390	4.55%	4.55%	$18,822	$492,616	2.94%	2.94%	19.40%	19.40%	$24,820	$24,820
1840	-6.50%	$42,179	$1,139,967	4.55%	11.05%	$19,375	$523,658	2.94%	9.44%	9.17%	15.67%	$27,096	$27,096
1841	0.00%	$44,100	$1,191,884	4.55%	4.55%	$19,945	$539,055	2.94%	2.94%	-16.03%	-16.03%	$22,752	$22,752
1842	-5.70%	$46,108	$1,317,375	4.55%	10.25%	$20,531	$586,612	2.94%	8.64%	10.91%	16.61%	$25,234	$25,234
1843	-9.80%	$48,208	$1,555,097	4.55%	14.35%	$21,135	$681,777	2.94%	12.74%	55.74%	65.54%	$39,299	$39,299
1844	1.40%	$50,403	$1,575,109	4.55%	3.15%	$21,756	$679,890	2.94%	1.54%	12.63%	11.23%	$44,263	$44,263
1845	1.30%	$52,699	$1,646,844	4.55%	3.25%	$22,396	$699,880	2.94%	1.64%	-6.07%	-7.37%	$41,574	$41,574
1846	1.30%	$55,099	$1,669,668	4.55%	3.25%	$23,055	$698,626	2.94%	1.64%	28.86%	27.56%	$53,571	$53,571
1847	6.50%	$57,608	$1,645,954	4.55%	-1.95%	$23,732	$678,071	2.94%	-3.56%	15.83%	9.33%	$62,051	$62,051
1848	-3.70%	$60,232	$1,825,212	4.55%	8.25%	$24,430	$740,311	2.94%	6.64%	13.00%	16.70%	$70,118	$70,118
1849	-2.50%	$62,975	$1,908,337	4.55%	7.05%	$25,149	$762,077	2.94%	5.44%	18.29%	20.79%	$82,942	$82,942
1850	1.30%	$65,843	$1,995,247	4.55%	3.25%	$25,888	$784,483	2.94%	1.64%	16.96%	15.66%	$97,006	$97,006
1851	-1.30%	$68,842	$2,086,115	4.55%	5.85%	$26,649	$807,548	2.94%	4.24%	1.92%	3.22%	$98,868	$98,868

Year	%			%	%			%	%	%	%		
1852	0.00%	$71,977	$2,181,122	4.55%	4.55%	$27,433	$831,291	2.94%	2.94%	25.52%	25.52%	$124,102	$124,102
1853	0.00%	$75,255	$2,280,456	4.55%	4.55%	$28,239	$855,732	2.94%	2.94%	-1.17%	-1.17%	$122,654	$122,654
1854	9.10%	$78,682	$2,248,067	4.55%	-4.55%	$29,069	$830,555	2.94%	-6.16%	-10.62%	-19.72%	$109,623	$109,623
1855	3.60%	$82,266	$2,223,398	4.55%	0.95%	$29,924	$808,760	2.94%	-0.66%	21.70%	18.10%	$133,410	$133,410
1856	-2.30%	$86,012	$2,389,230	4.55%	6.85%	$30,804	$855,665	2.94%	5.24%	8.84%	11.14%	$145,199	$145,199
1857	2.40%	$89,930	$2,430,527	4.55%	2.15%	$31,710	$857,016	2.94%	0.54%	-13.25%	-15.65%	$125,964	$125,964
1858	-5.70%	$94,025	$2,686,432	4.55%	10.25%	$32,642	$932,626	2.94%	8.64%	17.08%	22.78%	$147,475	$147,475
1859	1.20%	$98,307	$2,808,778	4.55%	3.35%	$33,602	$960,047	2.94%	1.74%	7.01%	5.81%	$157,816	$157,816
1860	0.00%	$102,784	$2,936,697	4.55%	4.55%	$34,590	$988,273	2.94%	2.94%	-0.13%	-0.13%	$157,610	$157,610
1861	6.00%	$107,465	$2,904,471	4.55%	-1.45%	$35,607	$962,339	2.94%	-3.06%	1.57%	-4.43%	$160,092	$160,092
1862	14.80%	$112,360	$2,613,016	4.55%	-10.25%	$36,653	$852,405	2.94%	-11.86%	55.04%	40.24%	$248,204	$248,204
1863	24.80%	$117,477	$2,216,543	4.55%	-20.25%	$37,731	$711,908	2.94%	-21.86%	46.33%	21.53%	$363,205	$363,205
1864	24.60%	$122,827	$1,861,015	4.55%	-20.05%	$38,840	$588,492	2.94%	-21.66%	16.63%	-7.97%	$423,602	$423,602
1865	3.80%	$128,421	$1,861,171	4.55%	0.75%	$39,982	$579,455	2.94%	-0.86%	4.74%	0.94%	$443,665	$443,665
1866	-2.50%	$134,269	$2,004,021	4.55%	7.05%	$41,158	$614,298	2.94%	5.44%	7.32%	9.82%	$476,138	$476,138
1867	-6.90%	$140,384	$2,228,323	4.55%	11.45%	$42,368	$672,509	2.94%	9.84%	3.87%	10.77%	$494,547	$494,547
1868	-4.10%	$146,778	$2,446,297	4.55%	8.65%	$43,614	$726,896	2.94%	7.04%	8.07%	12.17%	$534,466	$534,466
1869	-4.20%	$153,462	$2,692,323	4.55%	8.75%	$44,896	$787,650	2.94%	7.14%	3.68%	7.88%	$554,116	$554,116
1870	-3.70%	$160,451	$2,917,299	4.55%	8.25%	$46,216	$840,292	2.94%	6.64%	5.23%	8.93%	$583,073	$583,073
1871	-6.90%	$167,759	$3,226,131	4.55%	11.45%	$47,575	$914,901	2.94%	9.84%	9.19%	16.09%	$636,643	$636,643
1872	0.00%	$175,399	$3,373,057	4.55%	4.55%	$48,974	$941,801	2.94%	2.94%	6.86%	6.86%	$680,286	$680,286
1873	-1.60%	$183,387	$3,595,824	4.55%	6.15%	$50,414	$988,501	2.94%	4.54%	-11.19%	-9.59%	$604,170	$604,170
1874	-5.00%	$191,739	$3,994,561	4.55%	9.55%	$51,896	$1,081,162	2.94%	7.94%	1.68%	6.68%	$614,305	$614,305
1875	-3.50%	$200,471	$4,358,069	4.55%	8.05%	$53,422	$1,161,339	2.94%	6.44%	1.89%	5.39%	$625,888	$625,888
1876	-2.70%	$209,601	$4,657,803	4.55%	7.25%	$54,992	$1,222,050	2.94%	5.64%	-6.44%	-3.74%	$585,555	$585,555
1877	-1.90%	$219,147	$4,980,611	4.55%	6.45%	$56,609	$1,286,570	2.94%	4.84%	7.06%	8.96%	$626,922	$626,922
1878	-4.80%	$229,127	$5,455,413	4.55%	9.35%	$58,273	$1,387,464	2.94%	7.74%	16.03%	20.83%	$727,445	$727,445
1879	0.00%	$239,562	$5,703,866	4.55%	4.55%	$59,987	$1,428,257	2.94%	2.94%	57.09%	57.09%	$1,142,773	$1,142,773
1880	2.00%	$250,473	$5,824,944	4.55%	2.55%	$61,751	$1,436,058	2.94%	0.94%	25.12%	23.12%	$1,429,862	$1,429,862
1881	0.00%	$261,880	$6,090,226	4.55%	4.55%	$63,566	$1,478,280	2.94%	2.94%	7.36%	7.36%	$1,535,142	$1,535,142
1882	0.00%	$273,806	$6,367,590	4.55%	4.55%	$65,435	$1,521,744	2.94%	2.94%	-4.22%	-4.22%	$1,470,402	$1,470,402
1883	-1.00%	$286,276	$6,657,585	4.55%	5.55%	$67,359	$1,566,485	2.94%	3.94%	-9.40%	-8.40%	$1,332,235	$1,332,235
1884	-3.00%	$299,314	$7,300,338	4.55%	7.55%	$69,339	$1,691,203	2.94%	5.94%	-18.48%	-15.48%	$1,086,100	$1,086,100
1885	-1.00%	$312,945	$7,632,813	4.55%	5.55%	$71,378	$1,740,927	2.94%	3.94%	50.85%	51.85%	$1,638,354	$1,638,354
1886	-3.10%	$327,198	$8,179,941	4.55%	7.65%	$73,477	$1,836,915	2.94%	6.04%	16.70%	19.80%	$1,911,999	$1,911,999
1887	1.10%	$342,099	$8,552,475	4.55%	3.45%	$75,637	$1,890,923	2.94%	1.84%	-7.70%	-8.80%	$1,764,731	$1,764,731
1888	0.00%	$357,679	$8,941,975	4.55%	4.55%	$77,861	$1,946,519	2.94%	2.94%	6.46%	6.46%	$1,878,698	$1,878,698
1889	-3.20%	$373,969	$9,588,938	4.55%	7.75%	$80,150	$2,055,128	2.94%	6.14%	8.76%	11.96%	$2,043,340	$2,043,340
1890	-1.10%	$391,000	$10,289,474	4.55%	5.65%	$82,507	$2,171,224	2.94%	4.04%	-6.59%	-5.49%	$1,908,689	$1,908,689
1891	0.00%	$402,002	$10,579,013	2.81%	2.81%	$84,932	$2,235,061	2.94%	2.94%	7.74%	7.74%	$2,056,371	$2,056,371
1892	0.00%	$413,315	$10,876,700	2.81%	2.81%	$87,429	$2,300,775	2.94%	2.94%	14.79%	14.79%	$2,360,421	$2,360,421
1893	-1.10%	$424,945	$11,182,763	2.81%	3.91%	$90,000	$2,368,421	2.94%	4.04%	-12.32%	-11.22%	$2,069,608	$2,069,608
1894	-4.40%	$435,410	$12,094,725	2.46%	6.86%	$94,275	$2,618,755	4.75%	9.15%	1.94%	6.34%	$2,109,734	$2,109,734
1895	-2.30%	$446,133	$12,746,655	2.46%	4.76%	$98,753	$2,821,528	4.75%	7.05%	6.56%	8.86%	$2,248,108	$2,248,108
1896	0.00%	$457,120	$13,060,566	2.46%	2.46%	$103,444	$2,955,556	4.75%	4.75%	4.86%	4.86%	$2,357,318	$2,357,318
1897	-1.20%	$468,377	$13,382,208	2.46%	3.66%	$108,358	$3,095,951	4.75%	5.95%	18.42%	19.62%	$2,791,468	$2,791,468
1898	0.00%	$479,912	$13,711,770	2.46%	2.46%	$113,506	$3,243,016	4.75%	4.75%	16.38%	16.38%	$3,248,784	$3,248,784
1899	0.00%	$491,731	$14,049,449	2.46%	2.46%	$118,897	$3,397,066	4.75%	4.75%	7.88%	7.88%	$3,504,848	$3,504,848
1900	1.20%	$503,841	$14,395,444	2.46%	1.26%	$124,545	$3,558,434	4.75%	3.55%	22.97%	21.77%	$4,310,063	$4,310,063
1901	1.20%	$516,249	$14,340,239	2.46%	1.26%	$130,461	$3,623,926	4.75%	3.55%	29.25%	28.05%	$5,570,940	$5,570,940
1902	1.20%	$528,962	$14,693,395	2.46%	1.26%	$136,659	$3,796,070	4.75%	3.55%	9.44%	8.24%	$6,096,926	$6,096,926
1903	2.30%	$541,989	$14,648,350	2.46%	0.16%	$143,150	$3,868,921	4.75%	2.45%	-8.53%	-10.83%	$5,576,938	$5,576,938
1904	1.10%	$555,336	$14,614,118	2.46%	1.36%	$149,950	$3,946,053	4.75%	3.65%	19.66%	18.56%	$6,673,586	$6,673,586
1905	-1.10%	$569,013	$15,378,722	2.46%	3.56%	$157,073	$4,245,215	4.75%	5.85%	10.67%	11.77%	$7,385,518	$7,385,518
1906	2.30%	$583,026	$15,342,783	2.46%	0.16%	$164,534	$4,329,849	4.75%	2.45%	3.10%	0.80%	$7,614,487	$7,614,487
1907	4.40%	$597,384	$14,934,598	2.46%	-1.94%	$172,350	$4,308,750	4.75%	0.35%	-21.79%	-26.19%	$5,955,243	$5,955,243
1908	-2.10%	$612,096	$15,694,760	2.46%	4.56%	$39,274	$1,007,026	4.91%	7.01%	34.56%	36.66%	$8,013,268	$7,880,192
1909	-1.10%	$627,170	$16,504,465	2.46%	3.56%	$41,202	$1,084,271	4.91%	6.01%	23.76%	24.86%	$9,917,613	$9,752,912
1910	4.40%	$642,615	$16,065,374	2.46%	-1.94%	$43,225	$1,080,631	4.91%	0.51%	-11.50%	-15.90%	$8,777,529	$8,631,761
1911	0.00%	$658,441	$16,461,015	2.46%	2.46%	$45,348	$1,133,688	4.91%	4.91%	7.37%	7.37%	$9,424,101	$9,267,595
1912	2.10%	$674,656	$16,455,024	2.46%	0.36%	$47,574	$1,160,342	4.91%	2.81%	5.24%	3.14%	$9,917,613	$9,752,912
1913	2.10%	$691,271	$16,458,826	2.46%	0.36%	$49,910	$1,188,329	4.91%	2.81%	-9.27%	-11.37%	$8,998,224	$8,848,791
1914	1.00%	$708,295	$16,864,157	2.46%	1.46%	$52,360	$1,246,674	4.91%	3.91%	-3.25%	-4.25%	$8,705,757	$8,561,181
1915	1.00%	$725,738	$16,877,621	2.46%	1.46%	$54,931	$1,277,467	4.91%	3.91%	21.73%	20.73%	$10,597,899	$10,421,900
1916	7.90%	$743,610	$16,165,444	2.46%	-5.44%	$57,628	$1,252,785	4.91%	-2.99%	7.19%	-0.71%	$11,360,299	$11,171,639
1917	17.40%	$761,923	$14,109,690	2.46%	-14.94%	$60,458	$1,119,584	4.91%	-12.49%	-16.44%	-33.84%	$9,492,978	$9,335,328
1918	18.00%	$780,687	$12,198,236	2.46%	-15.54%	$63,426	$991,030	4.91%	-13.09%	11.26%	-6.74%	$10,562,323	$10,386,915
1919	14.60%	$799,913	$10,957,713	2.46%	-12.14%	$66,540	$911,507	4.91%	-9.69%	16.09%	1.49%	$12,262,107	$12,058,471
1920	15.60%	$819,612	$9,757,291	2.46%	-13.14%	$69,807	$831,036	4.91%	-10.69%	-15.02%	-30.62%	$10,420,020	$10,246,975
1921	-10.50%	$839,797	$11,049,960	2.46%	12.96%	$73,234	$963,611	4.91%	15.41%	11.01%	21.51%	$11,567,757	$11,375,651

Year													
1922	-6.10%	$860,479	$12,119,417	2.46%	8.56%	$76,830	$1,082,114	4.91%	11.01%	26.72%	32.82%	$14,658,104	$14,414,677
1923	1.80%	$881,670	$12,245,411	2.46%	0.66%	$80,602	$1,119,477	4.91%	3.11%	3.90%	2.10%	$15,230,214	$14,977,287
1924	0.00%	$903,382	$12,546,978	2.46%	2.46%	$84,560	$1,174,441	4.91%	4.91%	26.18%	26.18%	$19,216,992	$18,897,856
1925	2.30%	$925,630	$12,508,513	2.46%	0.16%	$88,711	$1,198,804	4.91%	2.61%	28.71%	26.41%	$24,733,327	$24,322,582
1926	1.10%	$948,425	$12,645,672	2.46%	1.36%	$93,067	$1,240,894	4.91%	3.81%	11.62%	10.52%	$27,608,357	$27,149,866
1927	-1.70%	$971,782	$13,312,085	2.46%	4.16%	$97,636	$1,337,486	4.91%	6.61%	37.49%	39.19%	$37,958,259	$37,327,888
1928	-1.70%	$995,714	$13,829,364	2.46%	4.16%	$102,430	$1,422,642	4.91%	6.61%	43.61%	45.31%	$54,511,194	$53,605,929
1929	0.00%	$1,020,236	$14,169,939	2.46%	2.46%	$107,459	$1,492,492	4.91%	4.91%	-8.42%	-8.42%	$49,923,970	$49,094,884
1930	-2.30%	$1,045,361	$14,723,393	2.46%	4.76%	$112,735	$1,587,824	4.91%	7.21%	-24.90%	-22.60%	$37,494,324	$36,871,658
1931	-9.00%	$1,071,105	$16,736,015	2.46%	11.46%	$118,271	$1,847,978	4.91%	13.91%	-43.34%	-34.34%	$21,245,646	$20,892,821
1932	-9.90%	$1,097,483	$18,922,120	2.46%	12.36%	$124,077	$2,139,267	4.91%	14.81%	-8.19%	1.71%	$19,504,909	$19,180,991
1933	-5.10%	$1,124,511	$20,445,648	2.46%	7.56%	$130,169	$2,366,717	4.91%	10.01%	53.99%	59.09%	$30,035,793	$29,536,990
1934	3.10%	$1,152,204	$20,214,103	2.46%	-0.64%	$136,561	$2,395,799	4.91%	1.81%	-1.44%	-4.54%	$29,602,470	$29,110,863
1935	2.20%	$1,180,579	$20,354,813	2.46%	0.26%	$143,265	$2,470,093	4.91%	2.71%	47.67%	45.47%	$43,713,491	$42,987,543
1936	1.50%	$1,209,653	$20,502,597	2.46%	0.96%	$150,299	$2,547,449	4.91%	3.41%	33.92%	32.42%	$58,541,821	$57,569,620
1937	3.60%	$1,239,443	$20,318,742	2.46%	-1.14%	$157,679	$2,584,901	4.91%	1.31%	-35.03%	-38.63%	$38,036,650	$37,404,977
1938	-2.10%	$1,269,967	$21,166,116	2.46%	4.56%	$165,421	$2,757,012	4.91%	7.01%	31.12%	33.22%	$49,874,122	$49,045,865
1939	-1.40%	$1,301,242	$22,054,955	2.46%	3.86%	$173,543	$2,941,399	4.91%	6.31%	-0.41%	0.99%	$49,669,354	$48,844,497
1940	0.70%	$1,333,288	$22,598,101	2.46%	1.76%	$182,063	$3,085,817	4.91%	4.21%	-9.78%	-10.48%	$44,809,518	$44,065,369
1941	5.00%	$1,366,123	$22,034,238	2.46%	-2.54%	$191,002	$3,080,680	4.91%	-0.09%	-11.59%	-16.59%	$39,615,021	$38,957,136
1942	10.90%	$1,399,766	$20,286,467	2.46%	-8.44%	$200,380	$2,904,059	4.91%	-5.99%	20.34%	9.44%	$47,672,966	$46,881,263
1943	6.10%	$1,434,238	$19,647,098	2.46%	-3.64%	$210,218	$2,879,703	4.91%	-1.19%	25.90%	19.80%	$60,020,083	$59,023,332
1944	1.70%	$1,469,559	$19,858,906	2.46%	0.76%	$220,540	$2,980,266	4.91%	3.21%	19.75%	18.05%	$71,875,550	$70,681,915
1945	2.30%	$1,505,750	$19,812,498	2.46%	0.16%	$231,368	$3,044,313	4.91%	2.61%	36.44%	34.14%	$98,064,386	$96,435,835
1946	8.30%	$1,542,832	$18,815,022	2.46%	-5.84%	$242,728	$2,960,092	4.91%	-3.39%	-8.07%	-16.37%	$90,149,159	$88,652,056
1947	14.40%	$1,580,827	$16,817,309	2.46%	-11.94%	$254,645	$2,708,990	4.91%	-9.49%	5.71%	-8.69%	$95,294,843	$93,712,285
1948	8.10%	$1,619,758	$15,879,980	2.46%	-5.64%	$267,148	$2,619,095	4.91%	-3.19%	5.50%	-2.60%	$100,537,326	$98,867,707
1949	-1.20%	$1,659,648	$16,432,155	2.46%	3.66%	$280,264	$2,774,893	4.91%	6.11%	18.79%	19.99%	$119,430,825	$117,447,443
1950	1.30%	$1,700,520	$16,671,762	2.46%	1.16%	$294,025	$2,882,594	4.91%	3.61%	31.71%	30.41%	$157,305,729	$154,693,360
1951	7.90%	$1,742,398	$15,839,985	2.46%	-5.44%	$308,461	$2,804,188	4.91%	-2.99%	24.02%	16.12%	$195,084,868	$191,845,102
1952	1.90%	$1,785,308	$15,940,252	2.46%	0.56%	$323,606	$2,889,336	4.91%	3.01%	18.37%	16.47%	$230,917,052	$227,082,223
1953	0.80%	$1,829,275	$16,188,274	2.46%	1.66%	$339,494	$3,004,372	4.91%	4.11%	-0.99%	-1.79%	$228,632,955	$224,836,057
1954	0.70%	$1,874,324	$16,441,442	2.46%	1.76%	$356,163	$3,124,234	4.91%	4.21%	52.62%	51.92%	$348,947,800	$343,152,839
1955	-0.40%	$1,920,483	$16,995,427	2.46%	2.86%	$373,650	$3,306,634	4.91%	5.31%	31.56%	31.96%	$459,085,245	$451,461,236
1956	1.50%	$1,967,779	$17,111,121	2.46%	0.96%	$391,995	$3,408,653	4.91%	3.41%	6.56%	5.06%	$489,182,468	$481,058,636
1957	3.30%	$2,016,239	$16,943,187	2.46%	-0.84%	$411,241	$3,455,810	4.91%	1.61%	-10.78%	-14.08%	$436,436,625	$429,188,741
1958	2.80%	$2,065,893	$16,933,550	2.46%	-0.34%	$431,433	$3,536,333	4.91%	2.11%	43.36%	40.56%	$625,691,594	$615,300,760
1959	0.70%	$2,116,770	$17,209,510	2.46%	1.76%	$452,615	$3,679,798	4.91%	4.21%	11.96%	11.26%	$700,493,676	$688,860,607
1960	1.70%	$2,168,899	$17,351,194	2.46%	0.76%	$474,838	$3,798,702	4.91%	3.21%	0.47%	-1.23%	$703,783,414	$692,095,712
1961	1.00%	$2,222,313	$17,637,402	2.46%	1.46%	$498,152	$3,953,583	4.91%	3.91%	26.89%	25.89%	$893,019,974	$878,189,629
1962	1.00%	$2,277,041	$17,789,386	2.46%	1.46%	$522,610	$4,082,890	4.91%	3.91%	-8.73%	-9.73%	$815,072,732	$801,536,854
1963	1.30%	$2,333,118	$18,086,186	2.46%	1.16%	$548,269	$4,250,148	4.91%	3.61%	22.80%	21.50%	$1,000,919,032	$984,296,812
1964	1.30%	$2,390,576	$18,248,668	2.46%	1.16%	$575,188	$4,390,749	4.91%	3.61%	16.48%	15.18%	$1,165,897,576	$1,146,535,564
1965	1.60%	$2,449,448	$18,416,903	2.46%	0.86%	$603,429	$4,537,059	4.91%	3.31%	12.45%	10.85%	$1,311,063,852	$1,289,291,070
1966	2.90%	$2,509,770	$18,319,493	2.46%	-0.44%	$633,056	$4,620,848	4.91%	2.01%	-10.06%	-12.96%	$1,179,127,886	$1,159,546,159
1967	3.10%	$2,571,578	$18,238,145	2.46%	-0.64%	$664,138	$4,710,199	4.91%	1.81%	23.98%	20.88%	$1,461,831,679	$1,437,555,102
1968	4.20%	$2,634,909	$17,924,548	2.46%	-1.74%	$696,746	$4,739,769	4.91%	0.71%	11.06%	6.86%	$1,623,530,827	$1,596,568,919
1969	5.50%	$2,699,798	$17,418,054	2.46%	-3.04%	$730,955	$4,715,839	4.91%	-0.59%	-8.50%	-14.00%	$1,485,456,775	$1,460,787,857
1970	5.70%	$2,766,286	$16,867,598	2.46%	-3.24%	$766,844	$4,675,876	4.91%	-0.79%	3.86%	-1.84%	$1,542,749,096	$1,517,128,726
1971	4.40%	$2,834,411	$16,575,504	2.46%	-1.94%	$804,494	$4,704,646	4.91%	0.51%	14.30%	9.90%	$1,763,367,541	$1,734,083,371
1972	3.20%	$2,904,214	$16,407,989	2.46%	-0.74%	$843,994	$4,768,326	4.91%	1.71%	18.99%	15.79%	$2,098,318,288	$2,063,471,604
1973	6.20%	$2,975,736	$15,828,383	2.46%	-3.74%	$885,432	$4,709,746	4.91%	-1.29%	-14.69%	-20.89%	$1,790,100,566	$1,760,372,441
1974	11.00%	$3,049,019	$14,658,747	2.46%	-8.54%	$928,905	$4,465,891	4.91%	-6.09%	-26.47%	-37.47%	$1,316,310,265	$1,294,450,356
1975	9.10%	$3,124,107	$13,762,587	2.46%	-6.64%	$974,513	$4,293,009	4.91%	-4.19%	37.23%	28.13%	$1,806,353,381	$1,776,355,346
1976	5.80%	$3,201,045	$13,337,686	2.46%	-3.34%	$1,022,360	$4,259,833	4.91%	-0.89%	23.93%	18.13%	$2,238,560,816	$2,201,385,131
1977	6.50%	$3,279,876	$12,812,018	2.46%	-4.04%	$1,072,556	$4,189,672	4.91%	-1.59%	-7.16%	-13.66%	$2,078,325,038	$2,043,810,382
1978	7.60%	$3,360,650	$12,220,545	2.46%	-5.14%	$1,125,217	$4,091,697	4.91%	-2.69%	6.57%	-1.03%	$2,214,892,077	$2,178,109,458
1979	11.30%	$3,443,412	$11,216,327	2.46%	-8.84%	$1,180,463	$3,845,155	4.91%	-6.39%	18.61%	7.31%	$2,627,074,410	$2,583,446,696
1980	13.50%	$3,528,213	$10,138,543	2.46%	-11.04%	$1,238,421	$3,558,682	4.91%	-8.59%	32.50%	19.00%	$3,480,977,218	$3,423,168,777
1981	10.30%	$3,615,102	$9,414,329	2.46%	-7.84%	$1,299,226	$3,383,400	4.91%	-5.39%	-4.92%	-15.22%	$3,309,599,767	$3,254,637,384
1982	6.20%	$3,704,131	$9,078,753	2.46%	-3.74%	$1,363,015	$3,340,724	4.91%	-1.29%	21.55%	15.35%	$4,022,696,211	$3,955,891,464
1983	3.20%	$3,795,352	$9,015,089	2.46%	-0.74%	$1,429,937	$3,396,525	4.91%	1.71%	22.56%	19.36%	$4,930,032,594	$4,848,159,751
1984	4.30%	$3,888,820	$8,858,361	2.46%	-1.84%	$1,500,144	$3,417,185	4.91%	0.61%	6.27%	1.97%	$5,239,329,797	$5,152,320,468
1985	3.60%	$3,984,590	$8,776,630	2.46%	-1.14%	$1,573,799	$3,466,517	4.91%	1.31%	31.73%	28.13%	$6,901,602,174	$6,786,987,558
1986	1.90%	$4,082,718	$8,817,966	2.46%	0.56%	$1,651,070	$3,566,025	4.91%	3.01%	18.67%	16.77%	$8,189,792,574	$8,053,785,034
1987	3.60%	$4,183,263	$8,715,132	2.46%	-1.14%	$1,732,134	$3,608,613	4.91%	1.31%	5.25%	1.65%	$8,619,808,161	$8,476,659,370
1988	4.10%	$4,286,284	$8,572,569	2.46%	-1.64%	$1,817,179	$3,634,358	4.91%	0.81%	16.61%	12.51%	$10,051,410,241	$9,884,486,896
1989	4.80%	$4,391,842	$8,381,379	2.46%	-2.34%	$1,906,399	$3,638,166	4.91%	0.11%	31.69%	26.89%	$13,236,319,946	$13,016,504,940
1990	5.40%	$4,500,000	$8,152,174	2.46%	-2.94%	$2,000,000	$3,623,188	4.91%	-0.49%	-3.10%	-8.50%	$12,825,436,755	$12,612,445,268
Average	1.52%			3.52%	2.00%			3.88%	2.36%	8.96%	7.44%		

It is not enough just to save money.
It must be **invested** in the right place.

If you know the enemy and know yourself,
you need not fear the result of a hundred battles.

If you know yourself but not the enemy,
for every victory gained you will also suffer a defeat.

If you know neither the enemy nor yourself,
you will succumb in every battle.

Sun Tzu

Investments

Let's review:

1. Money is to buy stuff
2. The price of "stuff" is always rising
3. You are likely to live longer than you think you will
4. Your money may not buy stuff for a long time, even beyond your very long life expectancy
5. Cash-like investments (CDs, government bonds, etc.) do not make you notably wealthier in real dollars

We cannot emphasize enough that the only sane measurement of "wealth" is the power to buy stuff. Getting wealthier only happens when your ability to buy stuff is *growing*. If it is not, then you are getting poorer.

The way you grow wealth is profoundly simple: *actively* place and keep yourself on the *other* side of rising prices, so that inflation becomes a tailwind instead of a headwind. There are two ways that you put yourself on the other side of rising prices:

1. By *owning the income* from things going up in price
2. By *owning assets* that generally go up in value

When I say "owning the income," I mean owning the dividends from profitable companies, or income from real estate property that you own—or at a minimum *not* paying this income to someone else who owns it. "Owning assets" happens in two key ways: (1) owning parts of companies, otherwise known as owning stocks or equities, and (2) owning real estate. And that's all, folks.

This chapter will be on owning equities. In the next area of finance, I will show you how owning real estate fits into our discussion. First we need to lay some groundwork and define terms.

Getting our Heads Around Equities

Thus far, I've resisted comprehensively defining words. You have access to definitions online. However, financial terms have slippery meanings depending on the context. We need to agree on a specific understanding for some terms.

When I say *"equity investments,"* or *"equities,"* I mean ownership of stock. Stocks = equities. Sometimes I'll say "stock" for variety's sake. However, "ownership of stock," in this context doesn't *necessarily* mean ownership of *individual* stock in ABC Company or XYZ Company. Stock can be owned in many different ways, individually or through funds. We'll return later to *how* to go about owning them.

The important thing is that I mean owning a diversified mix of stocks representative of companies from a variety of industries, sizes, and located in different parts of the globe. All of this boils down into a single term: **equities**.

Walt's Auto Shop

If the gods made me emperor of the free world, I would make everyone replace the words stock and equities with the phrase "ownership of the largest and most profitable companies of the world." I believe that people are financially worse off in our society because at our core, we are operating under a false conception of "equities" (or stock). People have less wealth because our culture has falsely equated the stock market with gambling, i.e., "The stock market is a gamble." This statement feels like getting tin foil on your tooth filling.

Let's paint a picture of the stock universe. I want you to imagine a quaint small town auto shop where you get your oil changed. Let's say the owner's name is Walt. Walt is the third generation owner. He has thousands of loyal customers who are multi-generational. His grandfather fixed your grandfather's car. Walt has a solid reputation as the most trustworthy repairman around. People will have their cars towed hundreds of miles because they wouldn't dream of letting anyone but Walt touch their cars. Because of this, Walt has quietly created a multi-million dollar business, with no meaningful debt, and a constant stream of profit from those loyal customers.

Walt decides he wants to sell his business, but instead of selling it to one person, he wants to sell it to the community that he serves. Walt will still run the business and actually maintain ownership of half of it, but the community will own the other half of it. The community gets together and agrees that the fair value of the Walt's Auto Shop is $3,000,000. Walt is selling half, which means he'll pocket $1,500,000 when he sells it to the community. To make it easier, the community decides to chop up this $1,500,000 into $20.00 shares of ownership. Here is what this looks like:

$\dfrac{\text{Value of Walt's Auto Shop: \$3,000,000}}{\text{Value of Each Share: \$20.00}}$ =	Total Number of Shares: 150,000
Walt's Half … 75,000 shares worth $1,500,000	
The Community's Half … 75,000 shares worth $1,500,000	

The company's value is split up into 150,000 shares of stock ownership split evenly between Walt and everybody else. When you own something you have equity in it. If you own lots of little pieces, one would awkwardly pluralize this as equities—one of those words where if you think about it too much, it starts to sound incorrect.

Walt is keeping 75,000 shares and publicly offering 75,000 shares of equity in the business to whoever wants to buy them. One may call this transaction an ***initial public offering***, more commonly abbreviated as ***IPO***. If somebody wants to own $100,000 of Walt's business then they would buy 5,000 shares worth $20.00 each. Anyone has the right to own shares.

When only Walt owned the company, he collected all the profit and paid himself. But now as partial owners of Walt's store, the equity owners get paid some of the income based on how many shares they own. Let's say there was $150,000 in profit in a year that pays out to shareholders. Each share gets $1.00. If you have 5,000 shares you get $5,000. As an owner of the business, you own the rights to this income.

Also, when only Walt owned it, as the business expanded and eventually became worth $3,000,000, Walt was the only one who got richer. Let's say Walt's business keeps growing—maybe they open additional locations and the business becomes worth $6,000,000. This means that the price of the shares of equity, those little slices of ownership, goes up. A $20.00 share increases in value to $40.00. The person who owned 5,000 shares still owns the same number of shares, but now they are worth $200,000. Naturally, the opposite of this is also true if the business goes down in value.

As a mutual business owner along with Walt, you get to participate (based on however many shares you bought) in his business acumen, unparalleled reputation, and multi-generational customer loyalty, *just as much* as Walt himself benefits. But, you do zero work. You just sit there and enjoy it. Walt does all the work and transparently reports to you every quarter how the business is going. At any point you can sell your part of the business for whatever price someone else is willing to pay for it.

Let's take a few steps back to the banking chapter where we greatly emphasized the destructive power of inflation and the eternal likelihood of *rising prices*. I want you to take a few breaths because I'm going to ask you yet another seemingly obvious, but profound question: **the prices of what?**

It's a question we've already answered, but not followed through. The prices of what? The esoteric term we've been using is "stuff." The reality is that the act of you spending more money means that someone or some business is getting more money (**revenue** would be the business word).

This is one of the primary springboards of all economies. My spending is your income ... and your spending is someone else's income ... and their spending is my income. Around and around it goes.

If you get your oil changed at Walt's shop, your spending becomes his income. Walt spends this income on employees, rent, and, among other things, oil. What will Walt do if the cost of oil goes up? He will raise the price of changing your oil. When you own shares of Walt's shop you are enjoying an inherent protection from rising prices. A good business isn't going to just sit idly by and watch inflation eat up their profits. They will raise prices right along with inflation. As an owner of that business, you should see your earnings rise too.

This open offer to buy parts of businesses is an amazing invention. We call owning these tiny pieces, or shares of a business, **stock**. I prefer the term "owning equities" because you are owning equity in a business, including everything inside the business. You are, as we said earlier, owning the assets. Let's say Walt's business owns the actual building of the auto shop. If the real estate value appreciates, the value of the stock should go up too. When Walt gives you some of the profit left over at the end of the year, he is paying you a **dividend**, and in getting this dividend you are owning the income.

While you love owning part of Walt's Auto Shop, in the back of your mind may be some concerns. What if Walt retires and the business goes downhill? What if electric cars take off and people don't need their oil changed? You don't want to put all your eggs in one basket, so you buy part of other businesses in your community. These businesses also enjoy a great reputation. You buy little pieces of Susie's Dental Practice, John's Barber Shop, Mary's Home Decorating Store, Bill's Plumbing Service, Kathy's Home Building, etc. You know that there is a risk that something could happen to any of these businesses. The economy of your community may take a few steps back, but the odds that *everybody* would go out of business is highly unlikely.

However, maybe you want to spread it out even more and go into other communities, perhaps even in other states, or in other countries. At that point you know that outside of an apocalyptic scenario, it's simply not possible for all businesses to go belly up. This spreading out of exposure is **diversification**. A closely related strategy, balancing out what types of businesses you own (whether by sector, size, location), is called **asset allocation.**

A Proxy for the Stock Universe

Our final definition is more subjective. Many of you will be familiar with the **S&P 500 Index** at some level or another—perhaps hearing it quoted along with the Dow Jones or Nasdaq indices. This is a book of broad strokes, so we need a reference point to gauge the universe of stocks. I am choosing the S&P 500 because it is famous, accessible, constantly referenced, and, best of all, has plenty of historical data for us to sink our teeth into. Delicious. When people ask, "how the stock market is doing," they are nearly always consciously or unconsciously referring to either the S&P 500 or the Dow Jones.

What you need to know about the S&P 500 is that it represents 500 of the largest and most profitable great companies in America and the world (but mostly America). This happens to be about 75–80% of the total U.S. stock market. Think of an American car company ... their stock is probably in there. What brand is your computer? Probably in there. Think of a major fast food restaurant. Probably in there. Think of your cell phone company. You get the idea. The 500 stocks are mostly companies in the United States, so it gives a rough idea on how the U.S. economy is doing. Or to split hairs, how U.S. *companies* are doing. Though closely related, the economy and the stock market are two different things. Henceforth, when I say "the stock market" (unless I specify otherwise), you can assume that I mean the S&P 500. Using other measurements (such as the Dow Jones Industrial Average) doesn't radically change what we're talking about.

A Diversified, Passive Assumption

Although our data will be exclusively focused on the S&P 500, this is not meant to suggest you put all your equity holdings in just this one index. You can, and you'd likely be fine, but I suggest spreading it out more. At the end of the chapter I will give you a basic "secret sauce" portfolio that I recommend—which is hardly a "secret" and only in nuance my own creation.

Passive vs. Active Portfolio Management

I'll mention, not open, this can of worms. My objective with this chapter is to foster a faith in the stock market. It is to show that in the long run, stocks are the most probable way to protect yourself from rising prices and increase your net worth. Because of this, partly for simplicity's sake, I will be advocating a buy and hold approach otherwise known as **passive investing using an index**. **Active investing** is any other approach—where investments are changed around.

For the purposes of this book, we can be agnostic on this issue. This is written for a simple path to wealth. We can imagine a world where there is only the option of buying and holding. I would argue that anyone's financial goals can be met reliably using only buy and hold. Also, I strongly believe that the *more* frequently you trade, the *less* likely you are to keep up with an otherwise passive rate of return.

However, as an asset manager, I fully recognize that in the real world, people need to take income from their investments. Or, they may utterly lack the stomach for volatility. I have found that money management is the marriage of ideal mathematical numbers to the real world of human needs and emotions.

I do not see passive vs. active investing as contradictory choices. They are two sides of the same coin, but you have to believe in the coin in the first place.

This chapter solely advocates passive investing because at a minimum if this is all you do, and you take the lessons here very literally, you'll be fine.

My objective in this chapter is to help readers see that equities are their friends. This is the only dragon I wish to slay here. The far more important issue is *that* you invest rather than *how* you invest.

Investing in Individual Stock

The S&P 500 is a useful proxy for us because it represents a diversity of stocks. Although I may use the word "stock" (in the singular sense), in practice I never actually mean individual stock. I don't believe that the average investors should own individual stock, even in a great business like Walt's Auto Shop. Sometimes I find that people end up with individual stocks for various reasons, but my bias is that these holdings should be unwound and diversified as quickly as possible.

In the next section, we'll see that history shows us that all declines in the general stock market go away with in time. However, history also teaches us that *individual* stocks often never recover. Enron, Pan Am, Blockbuster, Lehman Brothers, Washington Mutual, WorldCom, Woolworth's, Polaroid, Kodak, RCA, etc.—all high fliers that ended up in the mud. As technology develops, large companies are increasingly vulnerable to sudden derailment.

Excellent businesses *normally* don't stay excellent the length of your longevity. I don't think that the average person should wager their future on individual stocks— their precarious nature necessitates investors to constantly discern a downturn from a downfall. It's an unnecessary risk that is easily and cheaply mitigated with diversification.

As we shift into a purely mathematical world, these are the key things I want you to keep in the back of your mind:

1. Owning a diversity of businesses like Walt's Auto Shop is wholly different than gambling. It is far from a "gamble" to own equity in companies that are well-managed, expanding their earnings ability and productivity. Stocks normally—not sometimes, *normally*—outpace inflation.

2. Money is to buy stuff. This turns the economic engine. When you, and everyone around you, buy stuff, that spending becomes someone else's income or, more commonly, a company's. When you limit your position to that of a spender, then inflation is nothing but destructive headwind to growing wealth. When you own equities, rising prices are a tailwind to growing wealth—or at a minimum, make inflation irrelevant—for *you* are the one raising prices via the companies you own.

You will hear me say several times that the particulars of *how* you invest in equities isn't nearly as important as *whether* you invest in equities and hold onto them when you feel pressured to sell. Whether you invest in ABC Fund versus XYZ Fund, or whether you are doing this through a retirement account or outside of one, isn't going to matter nearly as much as whether or not you choose to invest in equities and commit to stay in equities as a lifelong choice.

The Behavior of The Stock Market

Wealth requires growing in your ability to buy stuff. Think of a **risk** as anything that would permanently harm your ability to buy stuff.

If you invest money in an individual stock that goes out of business, you *permanently* lose your ability to buy stuff with that money. This possibility is *risk*. If you invest in stock that dips then fully recovers, you *temporarily* had a reduced ability to buy stuff. As long as you didn't sell it, your suffering was in your blood pressure. To me, it is absurd to refer to such a situation as a "loss." Humor me in calling this a temporary *decline*.

Temporary price declines are never pleasant, but so long as they are temporary, they are not risky. In investing, you have two types of unpleasant possibilities:

A. PERMANENT LOSS   OR   **B.** TEMPORARY DECLINE

Although this book sweeps over many topics, my highest ambition is that you'd walk away with this one distinction. I believe that it is very easy to avoid permanent losses. This is mostly by not mistaking a temporary decline for a permanent loss.

Because it's likely *the most* important concept of this book, we're going to have a pop quiz:

Scenario #1: You invest in Walt's Auto Shop with one share of stock. The stock price is $20.00 when you buy it. His shop goes bankrupt and the shop is converted into a parking lot. This makes the share price $0.00. Which type of loss is this?

A. PERMANENT LOSS   OR   **B.** TEMPORARY DECLINE

How much loss did you experience?
- A. $0.00
- B. $5.00
- C. $20.00
- D. $100.00

Scenario #2: You invest in Walt's Auto Shop with one share of stock. The stock price is $20.00 when you buy it. Right after you buy it, his shop goes through a rough couple of years and Walt's revenue goes down for a while. One year after you buy it, the stock is worth $18.00. Two years after, it is worth $12.00. Three years after you buy it, the price returns to $15.00 and on the fourth year it is even at $20.00. Which type of loss is this?

A. PERMANENT LOSS   OR   **B.** TEMPORARY DECLINE

How much loss did you experience?
- A. $0.00
- B. $2.00
- C. $5.00
- D. $8.00

Scenario #3: You invest in Walt's Auto Shop with one share of stock. The stock price is $20.00 when you buy it. Right after you buy it, his shop goes through a rough couple of years and Walt's revenue goes down for a while. One year after you buy it, the stock is worth $18.00. Two years after, it is worth $12.00 ... and it is at this moment that you get scared, you *panic* and decide that the wise thing would be to "cut your losses" and sell the stock at $12.00. After you sell it (just like in Scenario #2), three years after your purchase, the price goes back up to $15.00 and on the fourth year it is worth $20.00. Which type of loss is this?

A. PERMANENT LOSS   OR   **B.** TEMPORARY DECLINE

How much loss did you experience?
- A. $0.00
- B. $2.00
- C. $5.00
- D. $8.00

Here are the answers:

1. **Scenario #1**—A. Permanent loss C. $20.00
2. **Scenario #2**—B. Temporary decline A. $0.00
3. **Scenario #3**—A. Permanent loss D. $8.00

The key thing to point out is that the external events of Walt's Shop in Scenario #2 and Scenario #3 are *identical*. The only difference is how <u>you</u>, the owner of the stock, *behaved*. The difference in risk was the *investor*, not the *investment*. This is a point that fools even the wisest among us.

Thankfully, when it comes to the S&P 500 we can say that all declines have been temporary. There is simply no precedent for permanent losses except for those who sold—sometimes out of fear, sometimes out of need.

The bulk of this chapter will focus on two behaviors: (1) how the S&P 500 has historically behaved (2) how your behavior will drive your return. We will quantify how much the stock market performs (its **rate of return**) versus how much it goes up and down (its **volatility**) and whether or not this volatility is an ultimate and permanent purchasing power risk for you and your family. Or to put it as one singular question: is volatility itself risk? Spoiler alert: it's not a risk and I will show you why.

After we retire this seeming threat, we'll turn the spotlight on the true enemy to your financial success: you. We will drive home the point that for the average investor, stocks aren't the problem, you are the problem. Investing success is a question of *how stocks behave* versus *how the investor behaves*. In the same way that our society has muddied the waters by equating investing in stock with gambling, we have also falsely conflated volatility with risk. Volatility goes away and doesn't change the long-term outcome.

It is crucial that you *embrace and expect* volatility as "the price of admission" in the pursuit of wealth. It is also crucial that you see that when stocks are volatile, the risk is not that the price went down, but the risk is that *you* will react wrongly by selling. The stock market isn't risky, *you* are risky. Let's dig into the S&P 500 to see how it behaves.

A Review of Historical Performance and Volatility

Investment advertising always includes the anti-litigation blurb "past performance doesn't guarantee future results." This is true, just as it's true in all of life. However, the past is all we've got as a reference. Every decision in your life is informed by your past experiences. When we choose, we anticipate outcomes based on experience. Certainty is a rare luxury.

Records of the daily price data for the S&P 500 stretch over the 89 year period from 1928–2016. This data incorporates virtually all types of events, from wars and threats of war, economic and monetary crisis, high inflation and deflation. It includes times of peace, innovations, breakthroughs, and new efficiencies. The next 89 years will likely comprise of a similar mix of the dreadful and inspirational.

Before I unload decades of data upon you, I must caution that fear compels human action more powerfully than facts, or even life experience.

I do not want you to get the impression that evidence alone will inculcate an enduring faith in the future. That I believe comes only by adopting a creed of optimism—the topic for the next chapter.

A quick word on pessimists. There is always and forever a group of people who believe that we are on the brink of collapse. I concede that it is possible that the economic engine that created our current prosperity may permanently and irrecoverably break. There are plenty of examples from history to illustrate this possibility. Also, there will always be plenty of present day realities that seem to ominously echo these examples.

Pessimists virtually never self-identify as pessimists, but instead think of themselves as *realists*. They've always had their reasons, many logical, yet hindsight shows that their hawkish dispositions were dead wrong in the long run. Anyone who had followed them would have been far worse off financially than those who ignored them. I suspect I will be able to say the same thing many years from now.

I'm constantly hearing warnings about the latest danger that will crash the financial markets. Pull up any financial website, open any financial publication, or turn on any financial news channel and you will inevitably encounter predictions of apocalypse. Perhaps it's the U.S. dollar that's about to crash. Maybe it's cyberwarfare or terrorism. Maybe it's problems in the Middle East. Maybe it's the wrong political party in control. Maybe it's some kind of major legislation. Maybe sun flares will take out our satellite communications. Maybe the Yellowstone supervolcano is going to destroy us.

We stand at the end of a long line of false alarms. Going forward, I have an exercise that will help you shake off these prophesies of doom. The next time one rattles you, go to a mirror and tell yourself, "Self, all of the thousands of past apocalyptic predictions were wrong up to this point ... but *finally* this latest one I just heard is true." See if you can keep a straight face.

Over the years, I've concluded the following: pessimists are *always* right ... eventually, but only temporarily.

There are two key components to investing in equities: performance and volatility. Performance is your reward for patiently sitting through the wild ride of volatility. Let's get a historical quantification of what has come before us.

Performance

I like to explain performance with a weather analogy. I'm going to use my hometown of Denver, Colorado. If you were to plan a trip to Denver months in advance and ask me, "What is normal weather in Denver during April?" I could say that looking back to 1948 (when the daily data started), the average of all temperatures, during the month of April, throughout the night and day is 47.87 °F. It would also help to hear of normal ranges. About 2/3rds of the time the average temperature falls between 38.47–57.26 °F.

However, weather tends to affect us the most during the daytime. You could split up the data and focus on the daytime highs and nighttime lows. While 47.87 °F is the average for *both* the night and day, the average high during the day is 61.36 °F and the average low during the night is 34.39 °F. If we are looking at just the highs, you could say that the average daytime high temperature falls between 48.75–73.96°F for 2/3rds of the time.

Maybe it helps to look at extremes. As far as records in the month of April, it has been as hot as 90 °F during the day and as cold as -2 °F during the night. We hear this and understand that these were just the extreme moments during single days. They don't represent a typical experience.

If you visit Denver for a single day in April, what is your experience going to be? We would just be guessing because it's *too short* of a time period. You might experience a temperature of 20 °F or 70 °F. However, if you were coming for a week, or even the whole month, the more likely it is that your long-term experience will be *about* the historical average, while experiencing extremes along the way.

Here's the point: the *longer* you are in Denver, the *more likely* your experience will revert to the mean (or average) temperature of 47.87 °F. Short time periods give a random experience. Long time periods give a predictable experience.

For the right-brained folks, we could take the historical average of both daytime and nighttime temperatures, every day from 1948–2016 in April and make a bar graph of it. A graph that looks like this is sometimes called a "bell curve" because the bars form a curve that resembles a ... you guessed it:

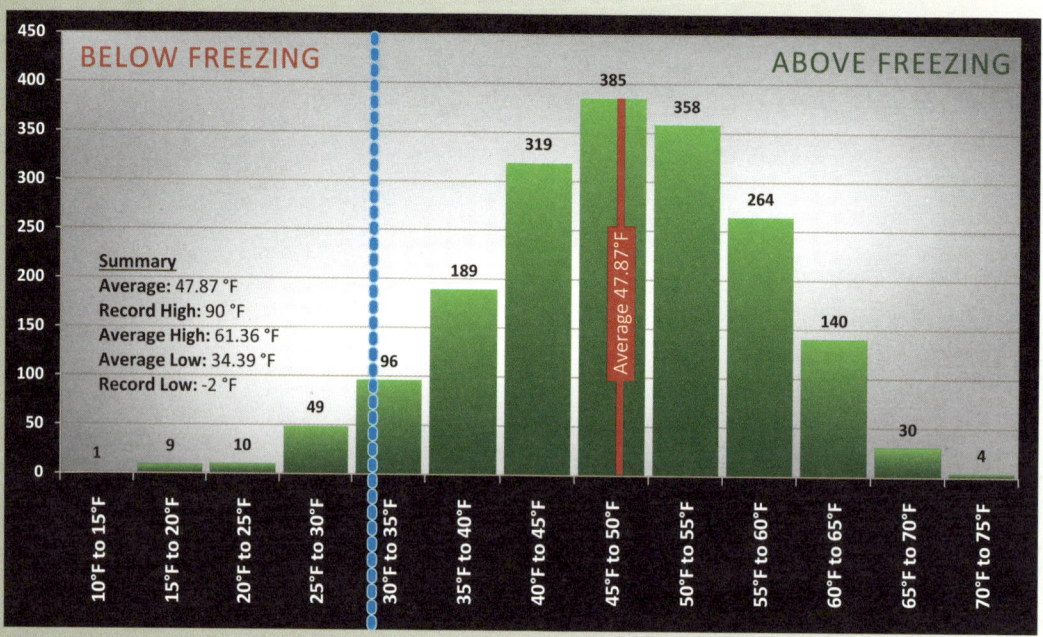

We are looking at the 69 years from 1948–2016. That's 2,070 days of temperature data. The numbers along the bottom of the graph tell temperature ranges. The total number of days is on the left and the specific number of days in each range is on top of the column. The higher the column, the more days in that temperature range. I drew a blue line to show the freezing mark.

In your personal experience, the information from this chart should (quite literally) *feel* about right. There is a normal range. We can visually see that normal temperature is the fat middle part of the bell curve. In this case somewhere around 35–65 °F. We could then say that abnormal temperatures are outside this range. You could also observe that in April, the average temperature is above freezing 94.06% of the time.

To get a realistic expectation for a week-long visit to Denver in April, your best bet would be to describe a range and to note the extremes. In a short time-frame, you couldn't know what *will* happen, although you could guess what *should* happen.

One final observation on the weather data is that we don't have what's called "long tails." The "tails" of the curve are the extremes of weather on the far left or far right. The 73 °F average or the 12 °F average were the extremes. But you don't have 180 °F instances, or -200 °F instances.

Hopefully you see where I'm leading you with this. Using the S&P 500 as our proxy, the stock market *more or less* behaves in a similar way—key phrase "more or less." If you are looking at short periods of time (such as one year, one month, or even one day), what you are going to experience is harder to predict and the past is less helpful. However, when you invest over a lifetime, you are more likely to have an experience that follows averages. Let's explore what to expect in terms of performance.

There are two key nuances to our performance data which bring it closer to a realistic expectation:

1. If we're looking at a chart of one-year performance, I've taken *all* one-year periods going back to 1928 (the same is true for the 5, 10, 15, 20, and 30-year charts). The financial services industry has an unhelpful obsession with calendar year performance. Calendar year performance has very little practical relevance to individual investors. At a minimum, looking at only calendar years limits your data substantially. Because of this, when I talk about historical one-year periods (or other longer periods), I'm not just looking at the one-year *calendar* period of January 1–December 31, but I'm looking at *all* one-year periods, such as June 5, 1973–June 4, 1974. Counting it this way means that there were 22,953 one-year periods of time from 1928–2016. There is obviously tons of overlap in the data when counting it this way. This lets our calculations show a *random one-year experience* along the 89 year stretch, which mirrors the reality that people don't enter the market solely on January 1st each year.

2. I am also including dividends. After our explanation of Walt's Auto Shop, this may seem obvious. The income you receive along the way is obviously part of your rate of return as an owner. However, the fine print of a lot of stock market performance charts will say that they show "price only" performance and do not include the reinvesting of dividends. I don't know why analysts don't include them. It's part of your investment. I can't help but think that there's a tinge of laziness in this. It is much more work to run numbers to include the dividends, but I've included them here.

All returns you will hear from me are what are called **total returns** which is simply a combination of the price growth plus the dividend. The dividends are calculated on a monthly basis by spreading out the quarterly dividend. Most mutual fund and ETF investments pay dividends monthly and my goal is to make my numbers as close to real life experience as I can. This also means that if you compare my annual return numbers with someone else's, they may be slightly different—but not by much.

To start off with, let's talk about how the market performs over a one-year period. Shorter periods of time do not behave *as much* along a predictable pattern as longer periods of time. So here it is: the average total return of all *rolling* one-year periods in the S&P 500 from 1928–2016 is **11.62%**.

Now, before you call your mother about this exciting news, we need to tame this number down some. This number represents the average for any given *one* year. Let's imagine the game show Wheel of Fortune. Instead of three contestants, we have a thousand. Instead of the normal wheel, our wheel has lots of little slices with all 22,953 one-year periods of stock performance. When Pat Sajak has everyone spin, the thousand spins would average out to around **11.62%**. It is a one spin average.

But let's say our spinners added a real world element. Pat Sajak gives all the spinners $100. Each spin is how much your $100 changes in value. A **11.62%** spin would make your $100 become $111.62. If you keep doing round after round of spinning, you'd likely see that average return number slowly drift down a little because of how compounding volatile percentages work.

Before we move on, we need to note the difference between what's called "arithmetic return" and "geometric return." The longer you go out in time, the more this is important. Let's exit this Wheel of Fortune world and imagine one with extreme volatility. You start out with $100. In the first year it grows **100%** (the balance goes to $200) and in the second year it falls **50%** (it goes back down to $100). This was the path of your account balance:

Path of Return

	Rate of Return	Balance
Starting Amount		$100
Year 1	100%	$200
Year 2	-50%	$100
Ending Amount		$100

You and I can both agree that you experienced a **0.00%** return. You have exactly what you started with. However, if you were to mathematically calculate the *arithmetic* average, this is what it would look like:

$$\text{Arithmetic Return} \quad \frac{100\% + \text{-}50\%}{2} = 25\%$$

You *averaged* **25%**! Yay! Come on, what are you complaining about? Yes, you had an *average* return of **25%** and yet you have the exact same amount of money you started with. Weird. You can see why in the task of setting expectations, it's important to make this distinction. *Geometric* return calculates it as a *real world* number. In this case, your geometric return would be: **0.00%**. Which is how everyone would measure their own rate of return. Arithmetic return has very little financial relevance. There are four key things to know about this when it comes to investing:

1. The geometric return is normally less than the arithmetic return.
2. The more volatile the investment, the greater the difference between these two numbers. In the example above the difference was 25%.
3. Normally in the stock market, there is going to be about a 1–2% difference. This means that, practically speaking, your *real* rate of return is about 1–2% less than your average.
4. The good news is that the longer the time-frame, the more compounding makes your real rate converge with your average rate. You will see that the real rate drops for five-year periods of time and then drifts closer to the **11.62%** number as we approach 30-year averages.
5. You will almost never hear of this distinction in financial discussions.

Geometric vs. arithmetic returns become *vitally* relevant when you expect to take regular withdrawals from your investments, such as in retirement. You must factor in the possibility of an adverse sequence of returns if bad luck strikes and your first few years are negative years.

All the more reason to create a financial plan that takes this into consideration. Conversely, if you are saving up money, there is no greater financial boon than to invest money when the stock market's in the toilet. For now, let us take a deep breath and note that we have no use here for arithmetic returns.

All returns you see are geometric "real world" returns. However, before I throw the one-year numbers at you, it was important that you know this difference, otherwise taking these percentages at face value can be misleading—notably if you plan on them being fixed versus volatile. Let's get a picture of this single one-year Wheel of Fortune. The average single one-year rate of return is **11.62%**. The range of return on any given year was *normally* plus or minus this number by *about* 20%.

Or, to do the math, the return was normally in the range of **-10%** to **33%**. By normal I mean that about two-thirds of the time, it was in that range. We could put this visually:

One-Year Summary
Average: 11.62%
Worst 1-Year Period: -68.34%
Best 1-Year Period: 190.73%
Positive Return: 74.24%
% Positive Return Follows
Negative Return: 69.47%

This is similar to the weather graph. If a certain year's return was **5%**, then it would add to the height of the column in the "**0%** to **10%**" range of return. Along the left and on top of each column you can see how many rolling one-year periods fell into that range. From 1928–2016 there were 22,953 one-year periods of time. Our bell curve is not perfectly symmetrical, but "sort of" symmetrical.[1]

The blue line at the 0% mark shows a boundary between positive and negative returns. The average falls in the chart with a labeled rose line. In a rose colored box, I summarized all the key data. All the subsequent charts take the same format. You may notice that a majority of one-year periods are positive, but certainly not all of them. To put a number to this, on a year over year basis, the stock market is positive 74.24% of the time and negative the rest. Going forward, a normal *expectation* based on the past would be that 1 out of 4 years will be negative and the other three positive. Actual *experience* tends to differ, putting multiple lean years in a row, but that's a rough expectation. You can also observe that 69.47% of the time, a positive return year follows a negative return year.

One crucial question is, "How negative can it be?" And perhaps the opposite question, "How positive?" Like record temperatures in Denver during April, let's talk about extremes:

> **Worst Year = -68.34% from June 26, 1931–June 27, 1932[2]**
> **Best Year = 190.73% from July 8, 1932–July 7, 1933**

It's not surprising that these extremes happened during the Great Depression. Two observations jump out. The best year is about three times better than the worst decline, a number parallel to the market historically being positive three times more often than it is negative. This is just a poetic coincidence. The second interesting thing is that about a week after the worst year ended, the best year began.

The same thing happened more recently with the extreme declines of the Financial Crisis:

Worst Year = -46.23% from March 6, 2008–March 5, 2009
Best Year = 72.38% from March 9, 2009–March 8, 2010

Four days after the worst year of modern times ended, the best year began. This is what's called ***reverting to mean*** (or average) return. Another observation is that the one-year graph has "long tails." The extremes are quite distant from the average. So then, let's talk about frequency. What percent of the time has the return fallen between different ranges of return? Let's take the same chart from above and expand different levels of "normal" visually:

Again, looking at these one-year periods is analogous to visiting Denver in April and trying to predict the weather. Actual experience is more likely to behave along a range, but it's anyone's guess where in that range you will land. The shorter the time period, the less averages mean anything. Although the financial industry has an obsession with single year returns, for practical reasons nobody should ever consider investing in equities for such a short period of time.

increments, the 5-year in 5% increments, and the rest in 1% increments. I will let the charts speak for themselves and summarize all of them in one chart at the end.

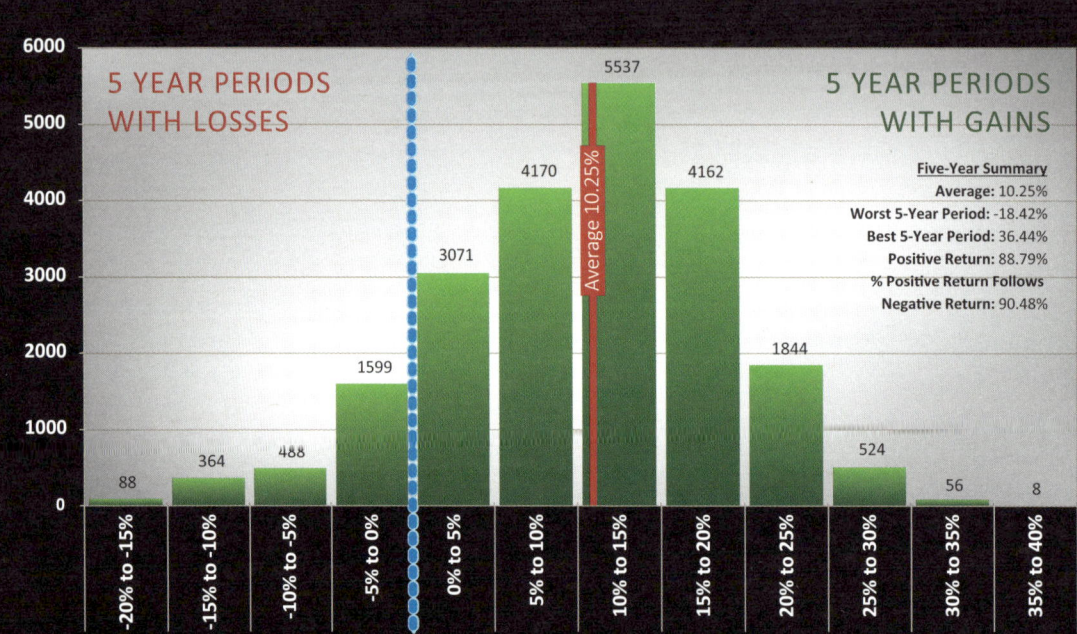

5 YEAR PERIODS WITH LOSSES

5 YEAR PERIODS WITH GAINS

Five-Year Summary
Average: 10.25%
Worst 5-Year Period: -18.42%
Best 5-Year Period: 36.44%
Positive Return: 88.79%
% Positive Return Follows
Negative Return: 90.48%

Average 10.25%

-20% to -15%	-15% to -10%	-10% to -5%	-5% to 0%	0% to 5%	5% to 10%	10% to 15%	15% to 20%	20% to 25%	25% to 30%	30% to 35%	35% to 40%
88	364	488	1599	3071	4170	5537	4162	1844	524	56	8

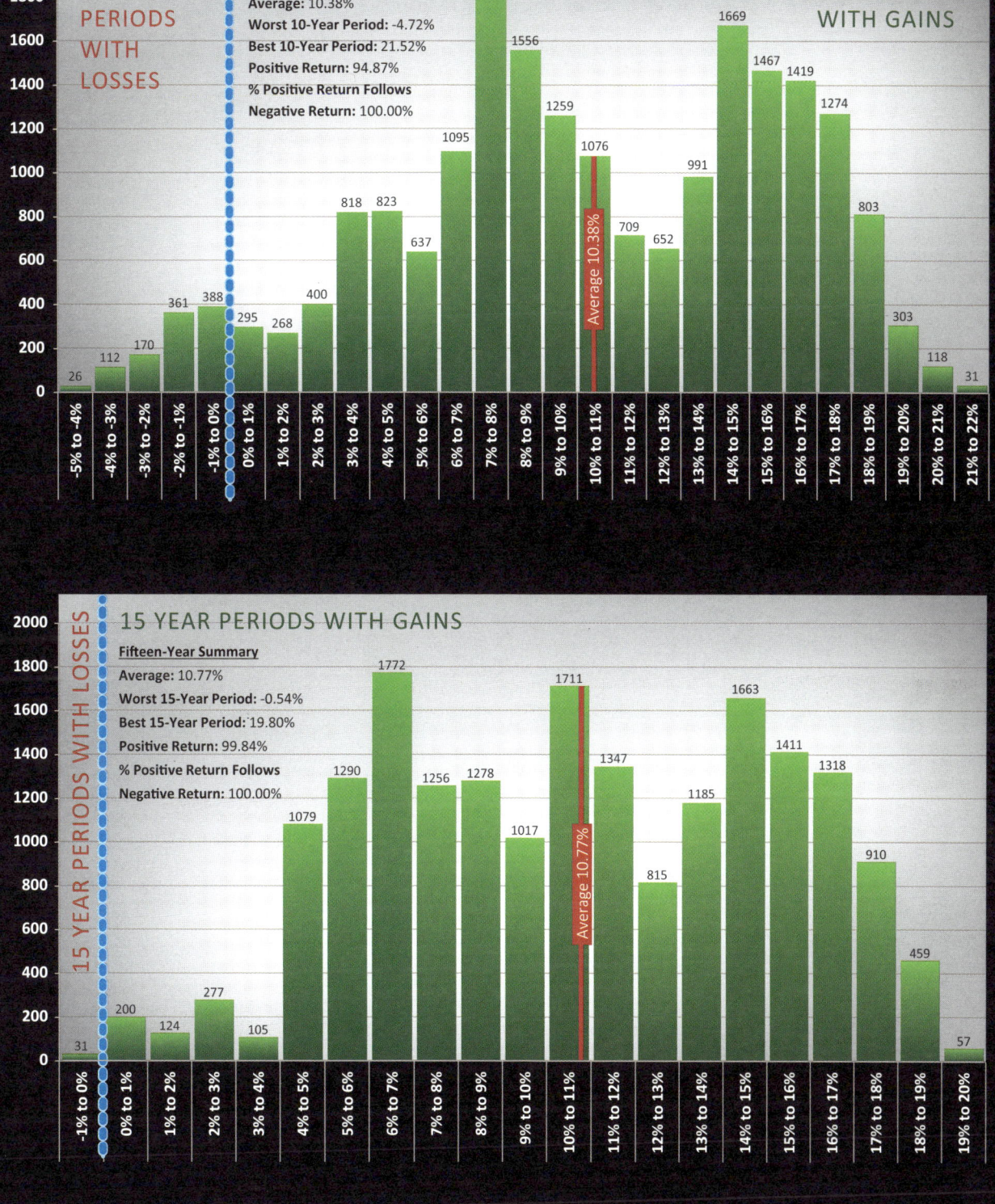

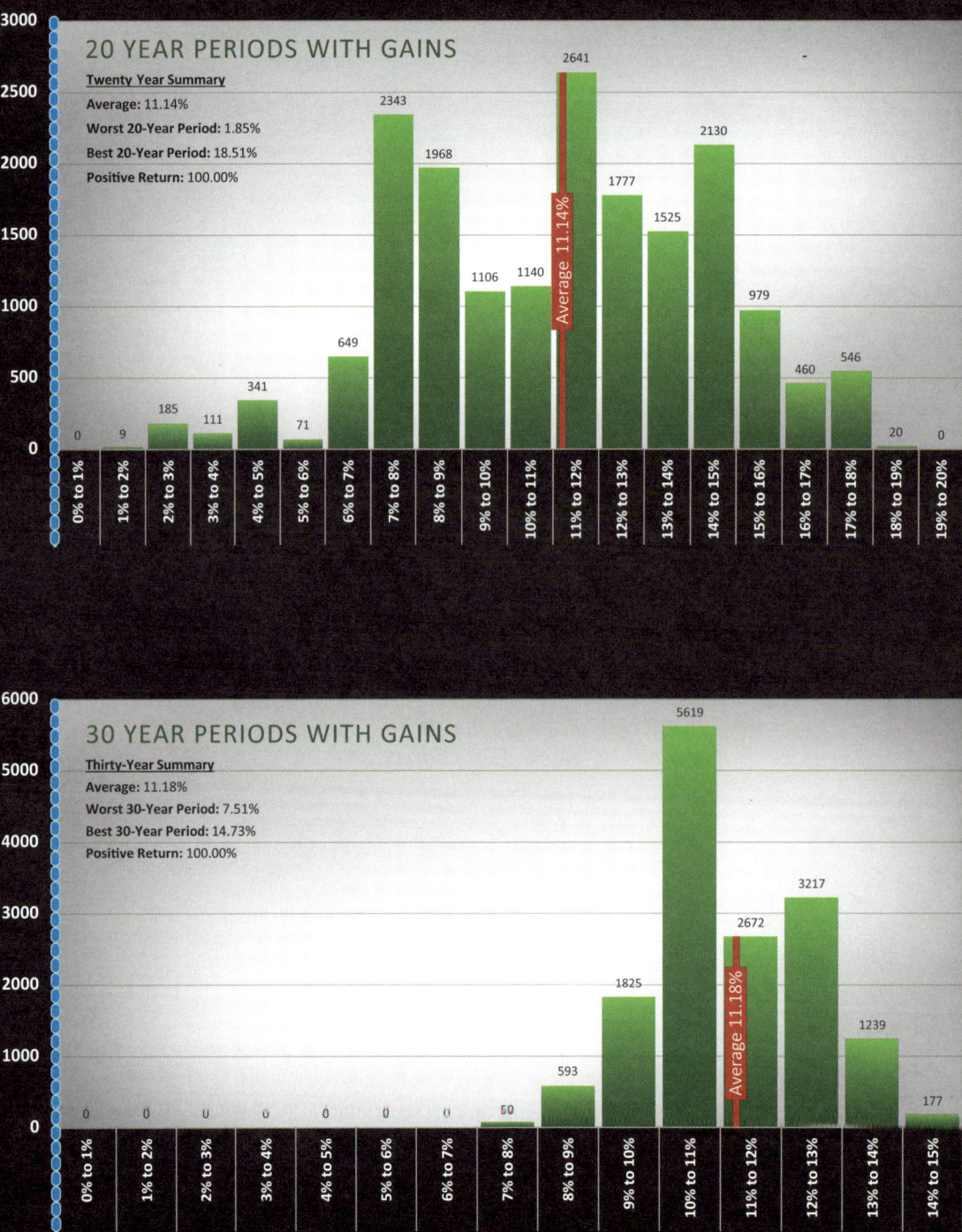

As you compare these charts with each other, you will see that as we go further out in investing time period:

- The average return stays azbout the same. We are looking at real world geometric returns.
- We progressively lose our "long tails" until they are completely gone. The best and worst periods are much closer to the average. Even at 5 years, it begins to look a lot like April temperatures in Denver.
- As we measure wider swaths of time, we eventually reach the point where the stock market has been positive 100% of the time. The only 15-year stretch with a negative return was during the Great Depression.
- Since 1928, there has *never* been a 20-year or 30-year stretch that didn't produce a positive return.

Behold the sweep of stock market return history:

Summary of Rolling Total Return Performance of the S&P 500 1928-2016					
Period	**Worst**	**Average**	**Best**	**% Positive**	**% of the Time a Positive Return Period Follows a Negative Return Period**
1 Year	-68.34%	11.62%	190.73%	73.96%	69.47%
5 Years	-18.42%	10.25%	36.44%	88.79%	90.48%
10 Years	-4.72%	10.38%	21.52%	94.87%	100.00%
15 Years	-0.54%	10.77%	19.80%	99.84%	100.00%
20 Years	1.85%	11.14%	18.51%	100.00%	N/A
30 Years	7.51%	11.18%	14.73%	100.00%	N/A

If you're a right-brained person, we could make a graph of these numbers. A graph that looks like this is sometimes called a "trumpet curve" because the curves resembles a ... you guessed it:

Graph of S&P 500 Performance Over Time

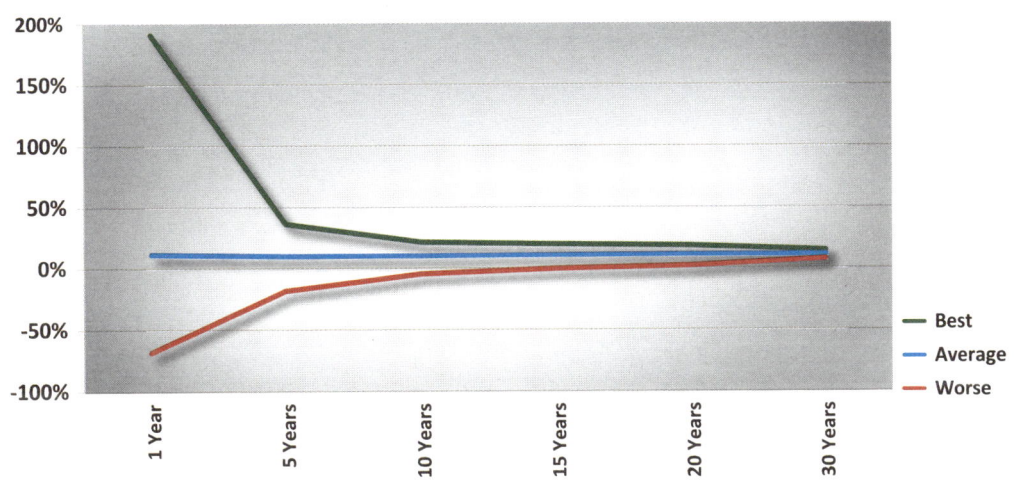

Contrary to popular notions, stock market returns are fairly predictable—on a long investment horizon. Historically speaking, time heals all wounds in the stock market. There has never been a decline that time hasn't restored. The longer equities are held, the more likely the rate of return will be *about* the average.

You can also see that the longer you own equities, the more likely it is that you will experience a positive return. The worst luck scenario you could have experienced was the 15-year, 3-month, and 27-day period from August 29, 1929 to December 26, 1944. This period encompassed both the Great Depression and World War II. Over this span the market produced a **0.00%** return (that's the longest you would have ever had to wait). As unpleasant as this may have been, the next 15 years, 3 months, and 27 days would have rewarded you with an average return of **15.48%**.

Stock market declines are rarely brief and never enjoyable. But over long periods of time, only the impatient lose. The two main exceptions are those who end up needing money from their investments when they didn't plan to and those who had bad luck and retired at the beginning of a long period of poor stock market performance. We'll discuss these situations later down the road.

These charts are the clearest way that I know to quantify a realistic expectation of stock market returns. I have no idea what the market will return in the next 12 months (and neither does anyone else) and frankly I don't care. The next 12 months of market performance are not nearly as important as your personal need to keep up with the rising cost of living. I believe that the stock market is your best shot at stable wealth, *especially* in retirement.

The average retirement is 30 years long. Yours may last *much* longer. Now look at the 30-year chart of returns. Even the worst case 30-year return is more than double the historical rate of inflation. Am I saying that you are *guaranteed* not to lose money over 30 years? No one can make that guarantee. What I can say is that there is simply no historical precedent for the market returning less than **7.51%** over a 30-year period of time (all the while averaging much more than that).

The market has always recovered from all declines. However, when you interpret a temporary decline as a permanent loss, you lose.

In this next section, I have one goal: to give you a realistic *expectation* for market volatility. This is to help you maintain long-term faith in the face of short-term, horrific price declines—by seeing that they are *normal*.

Volatility

When people say "stocks are risky" they usually mean "stocks are *volatile*." "Risk" is not "volatility." Over the long run, stocks aren't risky, *you* are risky.

You may have heard the saying, "Higher return, higher risk." My version is much less tidy and symmetrical, "The stock market *usually* produces high returns in short periods of time, but *always* in long periods of time. So price movements are not risky; what *is* risky is (1) to not have your money grow with rising costs, or (2) that you react self-destructively to a price dip."

I think we could cram that on a bumper sticker.

For those keeping score, we now have two false equivalences:

1. Stock Market = A Gamble
2. Volatility = Risk

So what is risk? What would be a *risk* to the accumulation of wealth? Risk is anything that *permanently* threatens purchasing power. And, what is financial safety? Anything that protects or even increases purchasing power.

When I worked in banks, people constantly, grossly misassessed risk. I remember one man who would wrap his wallet in tin foil because he didn't want the government to know his bank balance. At times he would come into the bank wearing a baseball hat lined with tin foil. He didn't wear the hat every day, and I always wondered what he was thinking about on hat days. I didn't have the heart to tell him that based on my memory of rabbit ears TVs, wrapping stuff in tin foil actually *helped* transmit signals. I may be a bit hard-nosed, but I strongly feel that this man spent a lot of energy (and tin foil) fending off a completely invented risk. (It's worth reiterating: all the stories in this book are true.)

It's easy to pick on the man with the tin foil hat, but to me the fear of the market permanently decreasing is equally as unreasonable. When stock market prices drop, it will be uncomfortable, it will be unsettling, but a long-term risk it is not. "Losing money in the stock market" is a risk of the imagination, so long as you are investing in a normal way and don't sell when it goes down.

Another pet peeve I have is when people say, "I lost a bunch of money in the stock market during the Financial Crisis."

My first question is always, "Did you sell out of your investments when the market went down?"

"Oh no, I didn't sell, but I lost a bunch of money." At this point my brain starts short-circuiting and sparks fly out of my ears. If you didn't sell out, you didn't lose money. Your portfolio value temporarily declined just before it spectacularly rebounded faster than anyone expected. If you own a house, unbeknownst to you, every day the selling price of your home constantly fluctuates along its upward price trend. Sometimes you do know about it when you hear that your neighbor sold their house at a reduced price. But nobody ever says, "The neighbor just sold their house under market, we lost a bunch of money in *our* house." Why? Because you didn't sell your house.

Alright, one more pet peeve. There is no such thing as no risk. One more time: there is no such thing as *no risk*. As we discussed in banking, investments that purport to have a "riskless return" *normally* perform at a loss in real money. They are quite safely and slowly losing money. That's not riskless. Every strategy has risk—whether that is a risk inherent in the investment or in you as the investor. You must decide which one you can handle. Keep your eye on acceptable risk, true risk, and imagined risk. I think it is a colossal risk to put your money in investments that have no historical basis for real money growth.

I know I said only one more, but let's pick on the gold bugs while we're at it. In another bank where I worked, there was an impressively stern customer. He had spent seven years in Vietnam. *Seven*. He had a healthy, erm … unhealthy perhaps, hatred of the government. He felt that we were constantly on the brink of our guns being seized and paper currency having no value. To cope with this, he stowed away copious amounts of physical gold. Who knows how much he had. The tellers told me his multiple safe deposit boxes were all unbearably heavy. I always enjoyed talking to him and hearing about his past experiences and current paranoia. His thought was that when the doo doo hit the fan, he could barter with his gold and defend himself with his arsenal. After hearing him brag on his plan several times, I said to him, "So let me ask you something. Let's say everything does collapse and gold is the only currency. We, here in the suburbs of Denver, are all living in some sort of apocalyptic mix of *The Wonder Years* and *Road Warrior*. You are one of the few guys in town who has gold and the rest of us don't. Wouldn't you suppose that the moment you bought something with a piece of gold, it's going cue everyone that this guy has gold? And don't you think it wouldn't be terribly difficult for a group of starving people to follow you home and overpower you? I mean it's just you and your wife right?" His expression led me to believe he hadn't thought of that. The apocalypse may not be the peaceful bartering utopia we'd all like it to be.

Do not mistake the cozy warm familiar fire of long held paranoias with level-headed assessment. Historically speaking, the permanently paranoid have fared far worse than the naïvely optimistic. Hatred of the government is not an investing strategy. The real danger is your human tendency toward self-destructive behavior.

I will repeat one highly important warning: do not underestimate the capacity of your emotions to override your reason. If the market is setting records, then it's easy for you to tell yourself, "Don't panic out of the market … got it." But when you see your portfolio drop by *half*, your emotions usurp your mind's capacity to steer the ship. The coup will begin when you think it is *logical* to cut your losses and sell out. Your inner mutineer will whisper that it is better to sell out and "play it safe." You will tell yourself that based on your life experience you'll sell out and go back in when things have settled down or perhaps at the bottom of the decline. I'm telling you this as a friend ... that is the devil in you talkin'. I know I keep harping on this and my guess is that you don't think this applies to you and you're sick of being lectured. Folks, this is the most important point I can make.

Although emotions are more likely to compel decisions than facts, let us give some love to the facts. We will examine volatility. Before we study 1928–2016, let's look at one year: 2011.

It was the year that the S&P 500 (on a price-only basis) returned exactly **0.00%**. It's the only time this has happened. The opening price for 2011 was 1,257.62 and the closing price for the year was 1,257.60. A very slight and unnoticeable two cent loss for the year. If you include dividends, the year experienced a slight gain of **0.67%**. On the surface it sounds like an unexciting year. However, this would have been your experience for that "dead year":

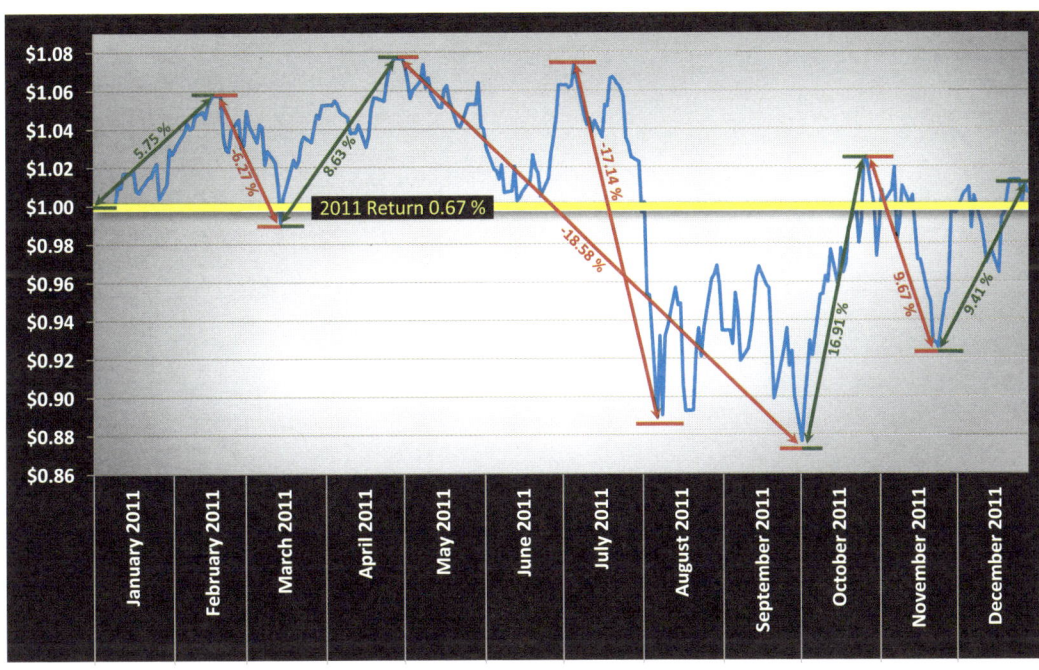

The journey to a **0.67%** year was a breathtaking tour of ups and downs. There were so many opportunities to succumb to emotions. In 2011, you would have celebrated Thanksgiving glad your price decline was only **-7.19%**. You would have consoled yourself with an extra piece of pumpkin pie, not knowing that December would erase all of your decline for the year. While **0.67%** is no reward to write home about, your delayed reward was a **15.59%** return in 2012 and a **32.05%** return in 2013.

I hope this section on volatility sets a historical, long-term perspective on how the market behaves, and that this perspective translates to you as *anticipation*. You'll find that even times of extreme volatility are within normal stock market price movement. Short-term volatility is largely driven by randomness, and because it's random, only a fool would try to outsmart it. It's a losing battle, particularly in the long run. Just as time heals all market wounds, time also kills all winning streaks.

Let's boil 2011 down into three pieces of information:

- Deepest intra-year decline: **-18.58%**
- Greatest intra-year gain: **16.91%**
- Year end return: **0.67%**

Intra-year means price movements within the year 2011. Admittedly 2011 was extreme. So let's look at a more typical year: 2010. The three key numbers were:

- Deepest intra-year decline: **-15.57%**
- Greatest intra-year gain: **24.19%**
- Year end return: **14.82%**

Graphically, the experience for 2010 is shown below:

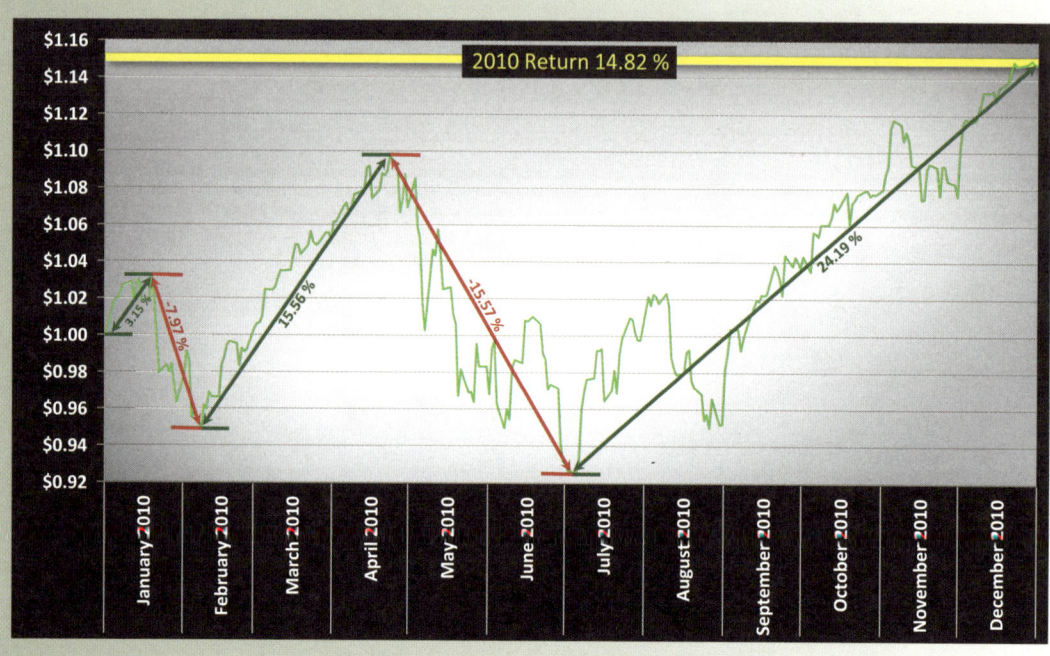

In the late summer of 2010 you would have started the NFL season negative for the year. While you divert energy to your fantasy football team, your portfolio not only quietly reverses the decline, but ends up **14.82%** positive for the year.

We could represent these two years as a graph called a "candlestick chart" because the each column resembles a … you guessed it.

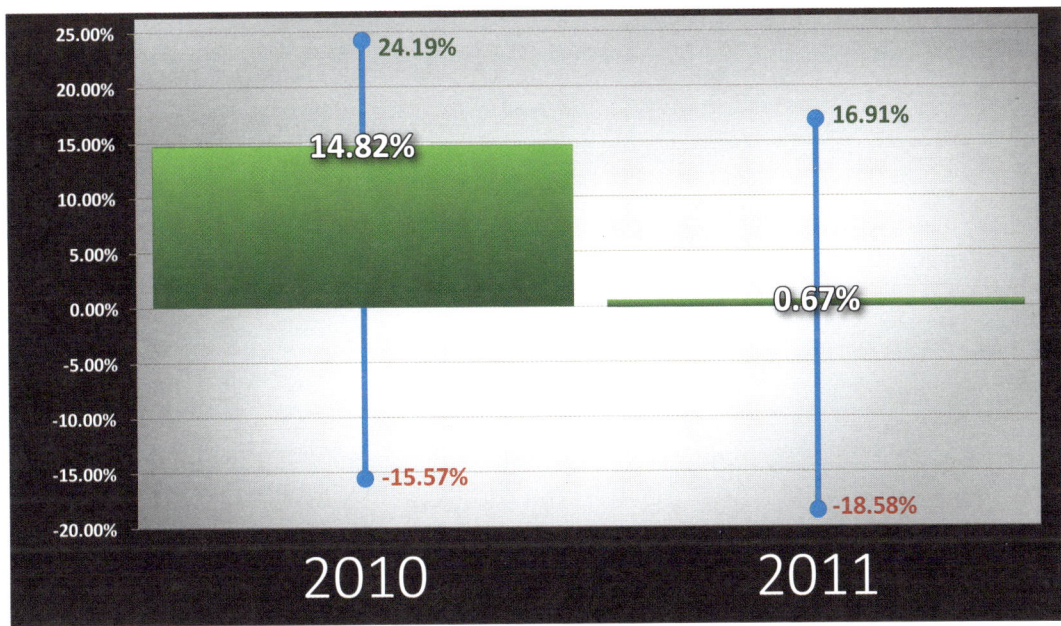

The thick, filled-in green parts shows the year-end return—what you actually ended up with after all the year's price movement. The blue line going down the middle has dots on the ends to show you the extremes you would have experienced through the year.

If we study 1928–2016, this shows what each of those years would have looked like. The specific numbers are to the right.

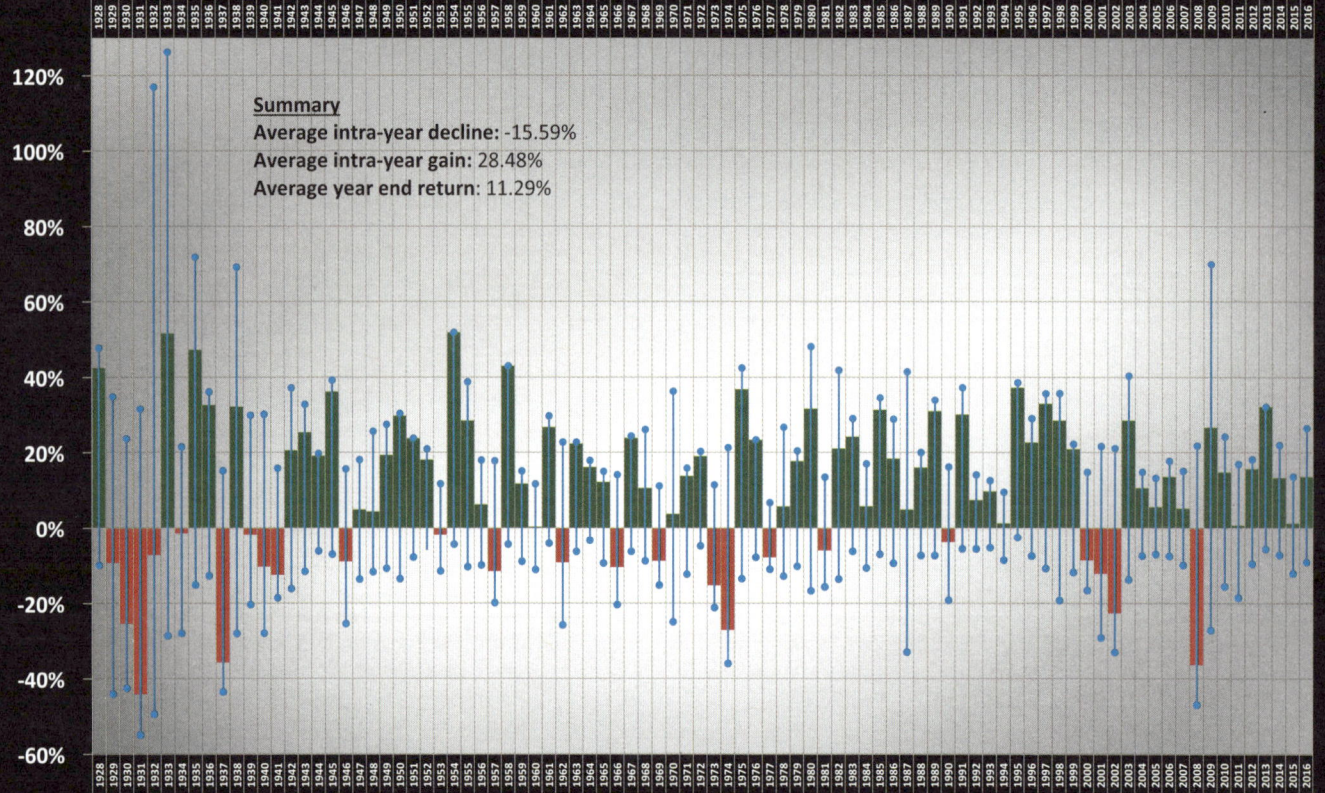

Summary
Average intra-year decline: -15.59%
Average intra-year gain: 28.48%
Average year end return: 11.29%

S&P 500 Extremes by Year

Year	Year End Return	Deepest Intra-Year Decline	Greatest Intra-Year Gain	Year	Year End Return	Deepest Intra-Year Decline	Greatest Intra-Year Gain
1928	42.37%	-9.97%	47.74%	1973	-15.00%	-21.16%	11.43%
1929	-9.04%	-44.24%	34.79%	1974	-26.85%	-35.95%	21.25%
1930	-25.41%	-42.48%	23.63%	1975	36.78%	-13.53%	42.44%
1931	-43.66%	-55.00%	31.47%	1976	23.30%	-7.78%	22.63%
1932	-6.85%	-49.46%	116.89%	1977	-7.39%	-11.04%	6.70%
1933	51.46%	-28.65%	126.21%	1978	5.91%	-12.84%	26.66%
1934	-0.61%	-27.97%	21.49%	1979	17.84%	-10.13%	20.39%
1935	47.14%	-15.16%	71.82%	1980	31.78%	-16.71%	48.06%
1936	32.39%	-12.77%	36.15%	1981	-5.48%	-15.71%	13.47%
1937	-35.58%	-43.59%	15.16%	1982	20.96%	-13.59%	41.84%
1938	32.14%	-28.05%	69.09%	1983	24.08%	-6.25%	28.96%
1939	-1.06%	-20.39%	29.80%	1984	5.72%	-10.66%	17.03%
1940	-10.27%	-27.92%	30.08%	1985	31.21%	-7.03%	34.54%
1941	-12.34%	-18.58%	15.82%	1986	18.27%	-9.42%	28.80%
1942	20.46%	-16.13%	37.17%	1987	4.85%	-32.94%	41.43%
1943	25.19%	-11.56%	32.71%	1988	16.05%	-7.37%	20.00%
1944	19.29%	-6.16%	19.71%	1989	31.06%	-7.31%	33.89%
1945	35.97%	-6.88%	39.21%	1990	-3.53%	-19.20%	16.16%
1946	-8.55%	-25.43%	15.60%	1991	30.07%	-5.58%	37.24%
1947	4.73%	-13.65%	18.07%	1992	7.33%	-5.54%	14.07%
1948	4.50%	-11.68%	25.59%	1993	9.79%	-4.77%	12.57%
1949	19.52%	-10.74%	27.40%	1994	1.24%	-8.51%	9.49%
1950	29.60%	-13.51%	30.29%	1995	37.21%	-2.53%	38.55%
1951	23.76%	-7.80%	23.35%	1996	22.65%	-7.47%	28.96%
1952	17.94%	-5.94%	20.92%	1997	33.12%	-10.80%	35.64%
1953	-1.58%	-11.53%	11.67%	1998	28.39%	-19.24%	35.68%
1954	51.84%	-4.42%	50.88%	1999	20.89%	-11.80%	22.19%
1955	28.33%	-10.29%	38.75%	2000	-8.32%	-16.59%	14.81%
1956	6.25%	-9.90%	17.94%	2001	-11.98%	-29.15%	21.62%
1957	-11.17%	-19.89%	17.74%	2002	-22.23%	-32.99%	21.05%
1958	42.94%	-4.36%	42.22%	2003	28.39%	-13.78%	40.34%
1959	11.61%	-8.94%	15.06%	2004	10.65%	-7.46%	14.78%
1960	0.19%	-11.10%	11.65%	2005	5.51%	-7.03%	13.21%
1961	26.50%	-4.10%	29.63%	2006	13.65%	-7.56%	17.69%
1962	-9.05%	-25.78%	22.72%	2007	5.24%	-9.95%	15.08%
1963	22.38%	-6.30%	22.72%	2008	-36.21%	-47.03%	21.75%
1964	16.06%	-3.30%	17.86%	2009	26.61%	-27.17%	69.91%
1965	12.08%	-9.38%	14.96%	2010	14.82%	-15.57%	24.19%
1966	-10.11%	-20.40%	14.06%	2011	0.67%	-18.58%	16.91%
1967	23.62%	-6.28%	24.31%	2012	15.59%	-9.62%	18.17%
1968	10.71%	-8.81%	26.07%	2013	32.05%	-5.60%	31.60%
1969	-8.73%	-15.27%	11.11%	2014	13.41%	-7.25%	21.98%
1970	3.68%	-24.96%	36.26%	2015	1.14%	-12.10%	13.58%
1971	13.87%	-12.36%	15.86%	2016	13.42%	-9.13%	26.40%
1972	19.15%	-4.71%	20.23%				

In every year, the ups and downs you experience are always *much more* than where you end up. In other words, extreme experiences settle out. According to averages, this is normal:

Average intra-year decline: -15.59%

Average intra-year gain: 28.48%

Average *calendar* year end return: 11.29%[3]

These statistics could easily become abstract. It is *crucial* that you let that **-15.59%** intra-year decline number sink into your soul for a moment. Don't just *know* how volatile the market is, *embrace* it. You must welcome volatility into your financial home as a pungent guest. Every year, you should *expect* your all equity portfolio to drop *on average* **-15.59%** at some point. A **10%** decline is, in fact, *on the low side of normal*. The odd thing is that every time the market goes down **10%**, the media reports it as, perhaps, the end of all humanity. No, I'm not above hyperbole.

Interestingly, if we split these 89 calendar year returns into positive years and negative ones, we still see double-digit declines *during* positive years.

S&P Extremes Split by Positive vs. Negative Years	Negative Years	Positive Years
Number of Years	24	65
Average Year End Return	-13.79%	20.54%
Average Deepest Intra-Year Decline	-28.20%	-10.93%
Average Greatest Intra-Year Gain	23.34%	30.38%

Again, you already know my pet peeve with the financial industry's obsession with calendar year returns, but I'm doing this by calendar year specifically to inoculate you *when* the media obsesses about "year to date" performance.

This isn't about the reality that some eras are better for the market than others. And it's *not* about the reality that the market goes up and down. It is about the reality that the good years and bad both experience considerable volatility. In 2009, the best time to invest was when unemployment was marching up to 10%, we had a 1.5 trillion dollar deficit, and the price-earnings ratio of the market was twice what it was at the dot com peak. It seemed like a terrible time to buy, but it was the deal of our lifetimes. It was the chance to buy at prices we'll likely never see again.

With this survey of volatility, we begin to quantify the "price of admission" for superior returns. To enjoy the excellent performance returns we saw in the long-term historical graphs, you have to *not just tolerate*, but *expect* to see your portfolio pass through horrific declines. The reward of the patient is a return that isn't *reliably* found elsewhere. It's possible to find it elsewhere, but not so reliably.

We can stretch out our candlestick line of thought by looking at five-year periods of time. The first period (to the left of the dotted orange line) is only four years long, since five doesn't evenly divide into 89. Feel free to ignore it as an incomplete period.

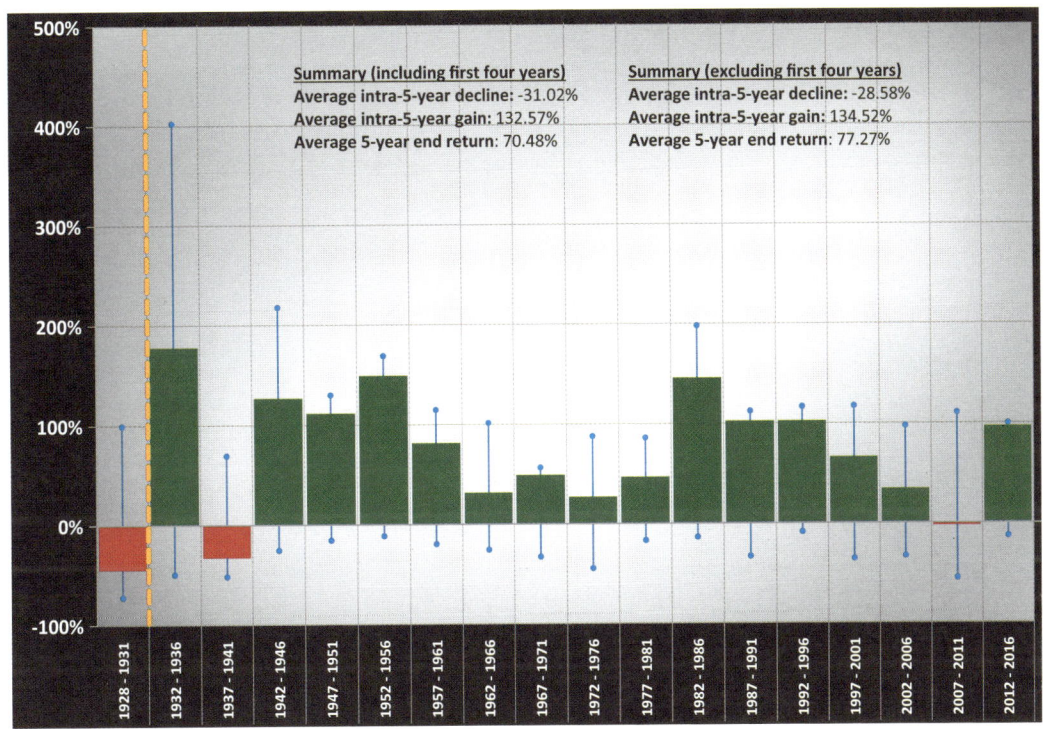

We know from before that 88.79% of all 5-year periods were positive (or 8 out of 9). This means you'd expect two of these columns to be red (negative). This is essentially what we have with two solidly negative periods and one thinly negative one.

What you notice is the positivity of the returns and the five-year average return of **70.48%** (the return for the *full* five years). Earning this reward required you to endure an average decline of **-31.02%** within those five years.

Lest you think I am cherry picking the data, here is the same scenario, but I've shifted the data forward one year. Now the incomplete period is on the end of the chart from 2013–2016. This means that all of the five-year periods are different than the previous chart:

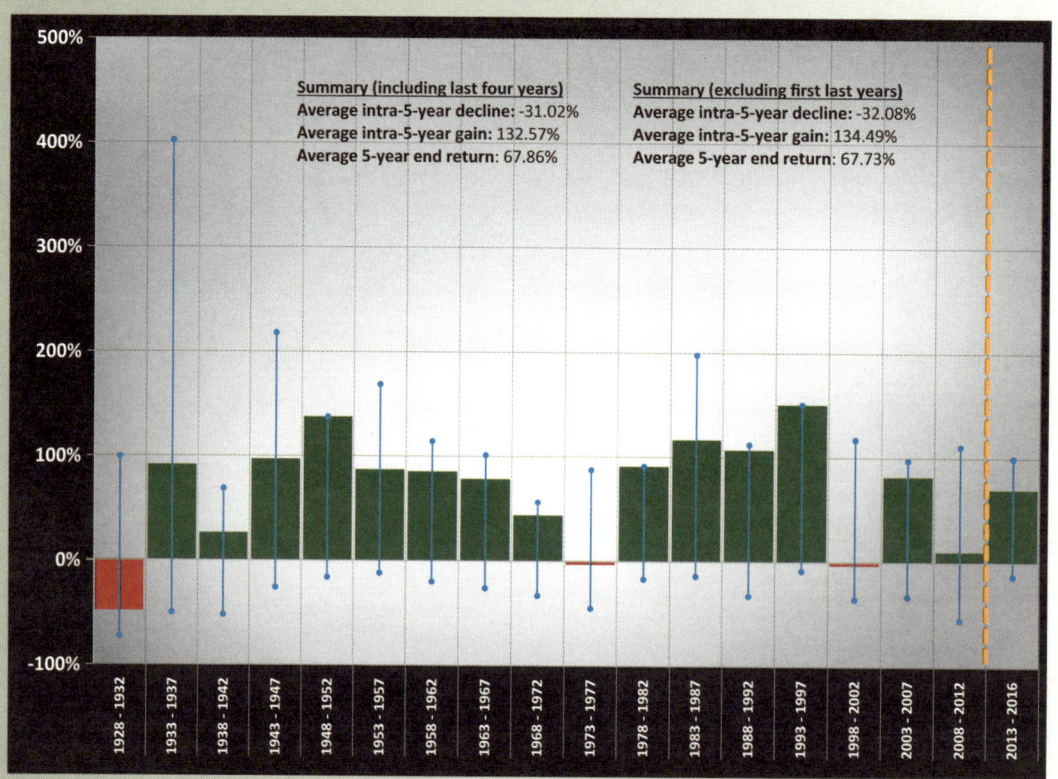

Alas we have three negative five-year periods—one more than you'd expect. About half of the intra-five-year declines flirted with a **-50%** loss at some point, yet, nearly all were positive or tolerably negative, with the big exception of the Great Depression. The patient shall inherit the earth and the children of the patient inherit the money built from superior returns earned via waiting through dark times. On the top of the opposite page is a chart of the numbers from these graphs.

S&P 500 Five-Year Extremes

Year Range	Five-Year Return	Deepest Intra-Five-Year Decline	Greatest Intra-Five-Year Gain	Year Range	Five-Year Return	Deepest Intra-Five-Year Decline	Greatest Intra-Five-Year Gain
1928 - 1931	-44.92%	-72.59%	99.42%	1928 - 1932	-48.28%	-83.51%	269.42%
1932 - 1936	177.71%	-49.46%	402.29%	1933 - 1937	91.60%	-51.71%	177.51%
1937 - 1941	-32.68%	-51.71%	69.09%	1938 - 1942	26.30%	-33.45%	69.09%
1942 - 1946	127.26%	-25.43%	218.01%	1943 - 1947	97.34%	-25.43%	108.36%
1947 - 1951	110.87%	-15.69%	130.62%	1948 - 1952	137.57%	-15.69%	76.98%
1952 - 1956	149.36%	-11.53%	168.81%	1953 - 1957	87.56%	-19.89%	126.36%
1957 - 1961	81.73%	-19.89%	114.66%	1958 - 1962	85.83%	-26.87%	61.72%
1962 - 1966	31.14%	-25.78%	101.52%	1963 - 1967	78.28%	-22.84%	61.05%
1967 - 1971	49.06%	-32.85%	56.39%	1968 - 1972	43.27%	-44.21%	36.26%
1972 - 1976	26.57%	-44.85%	88.71%	1973 - 1977	-1.94%	-44.85%	58.85%
1977 - 1981	46.39%	-16.71%	86.11%	1978 - 1982	91.28%	-20.01%	86.11%
1982 - 1986	145.80%	-13.59%	197.90%	1983 - 1987	116.30%	-32.94%	74.00%
1987 - 1991	102.43%	-32.94%	113.43%	1988 - 1992	107.12%	-19.20%	65.34%
1992 - 1996	102.14%	-8.51%	116.72%	1993 - 1997	150.54%	-15.75%	56.73%
1997 - 2001	65.89%	-35.69%	117.32%	1998 - 2002	-3.11%	-47.41%	72.59%
2002 - 2006	34.33%	-32.99%	97.42%	2003 - 2007	81.76%	-55.22%	66.48%
2007 - 2011	-1.34%	-55.22%	110.75%	2008 - 2012	9.97%	-51.80%	93.55%
2012 - 2016	96.91%	-12.97%	99.80%	2013 - 2016	51.96%	-12.10%	56.84%

To further build your expectation of the volatility of the stock market, let's talk about *how often* and *how much* the market drops, and *how long* it takes to recover. It's worth repeating that in true statistical terms we cannot speak of how *likely* the market is to go down. The market doesn't behave that way. However, I think it is helpful to simply quantify all past market declines because it *sort of* follows the same pattern.

If we look at our period of 1928–2016, we can observe two different types of long-term eras:

1. Upward bull markets where declines are erased relatively quickly. A good example of this is the 1982–2000 bull market. Even a decline like the Black Monday crash of 1987 was erased in only 263 days.
2. Horizontal markets that are often characterized by *deep* and *multiple* declines and overall zero market growth for a prolonged period of time. In these epochs, the market is highly volatile without ever seeming to gain traction.

Graphically, this looks like:

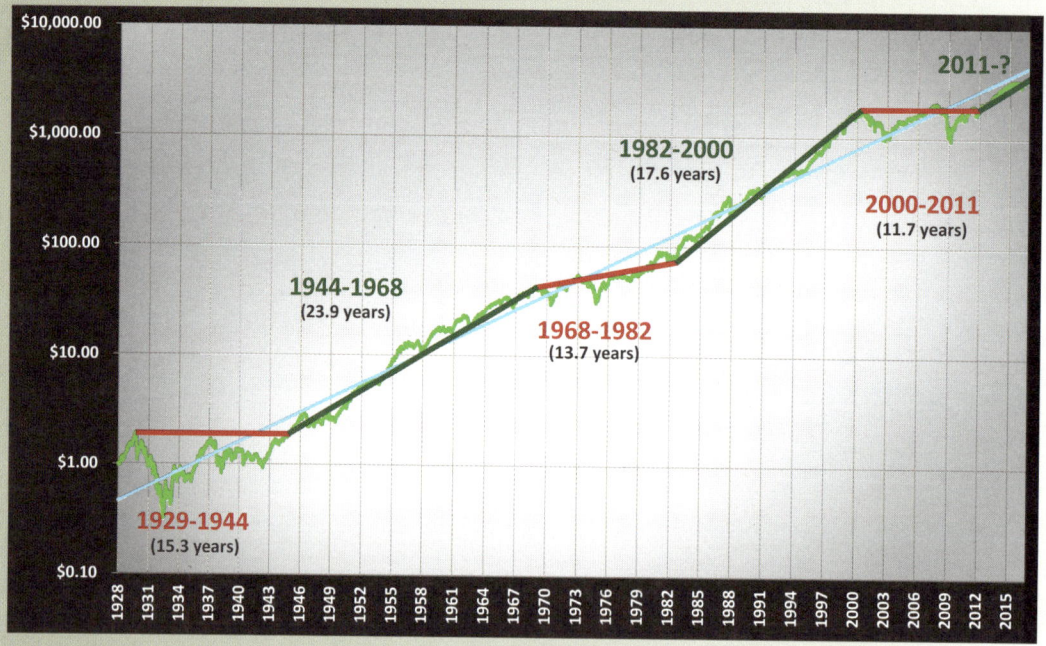

The number-friendly and anal may like the specific numbers and dates of these long seasons:

The Long Seasons of the S&P 500

Beginning	End	Days	Years	Return
September 16, 1929	December 29, 1944	5,583 days	15.3 years	-0.39%
January 1, 1945	December 2, 1968	8,736 days	23.9 years	2172.0%
December 3, 1968	August 12, 1982	5,000 days	13.7 years	68.03%
August 13, 1982	March 24, 2000	6,433 days	17.6 years	2392.78%
March 27, 2000	December 20, 2011	4,285 days	11.7 years	0.97%
December 21, 2011	December 31, 2016	1,836 days	5.0 years	99.46%

Granted, this is a subjective observation and three horizontal periods isn't enough data to declare it a cycle. At a minimum we can learn that there is certainly precedent for long-term faith in the market. You will notice that I have added a straight thin blue line to show the trendline going through the middle of the thicker lime-green growth line (the bumpy line). Think of this middle line as what the price *should* be if the stock market were a perfectly efficient well-oiled machine. The market is constantly finding its way back to that blue line.

The history of the stock market shows a strong tendency to revert to the mean (or average) growth rate. We have too little information to say with certainty that it is normal for the market to plateau for extended periods. But we know this: herd mentality triggers stocks to become over-bought, making them over-priced.

You can see this at each of the beginnings of the red lines. The price of the market is well above the blue line, particularly in 1929 and in 2000 where the stock prices were *way* above the blue line and hence over-priced. On this chart you can see that when the price gets too far above the straight blue line, that it leads into an era of price correction as the price works its way back to normal.

However, herd mentality stampedes downhill too. The price typically *overcorrects* and then becomes *underpriced*—causing the horizontal market to last even *longer* when the masses lose faith in stocks altogether. Then the price falls well *below* the blue line. In time, the market snaps up and overshoots what the value "should be" and becomes overpriced again.

History tells us that while it's not predictable when or how long these horizontal periods occur, at times the market will "chill out" after being overbought. It's key to not lose faith during these prolonged winters of no returns and high volatility. You should expect to see a few of these winters in your lifetime and at least one during your retirement.

As always, patience and survival are rewarded. Growth happens rapidly and suddenly *just when* it feels that winter will never end. If you are still in a time of life where you are adding money to your investments or at a minimum, reinvesting your dividends, there is no greater blessing than a really long period of no returns when John Q. Public has lost faith in the stock market. To be clear, if you are saving up money, you should be *ecstatic* to find yourself in a really long horizontal market. This does become a problem in retirement, when you are taking income from your investments.

Now is a perfect time for me to plug the necessity of a financial plan to anticipate this risk. Make a financial plan.

The whole objective here is to get an expectation of volatility. We can see these long seasons of the stock market, but what about shorter periods? You may ask:

- How often does the market go down **10%** or **20%**?
- If the market goes down **5%**, you may start to get uncomfortable. What percent of the time does a **5%** decline grow to become a **10%** decline?
- If it stays at a **5%** decline, how long does it usually last?

There is some subjectivity with how declines are calculated, so I'll explain how I chose to calculate it. First of all, I will be categorizing decline amounts by ranges. I will use the industry term of a **bear market** to describe declines of **20%** or more. There's nothing magical about the **20%** number.

Much like calendar year returns, it's just another financial industry artificial peg. However, to aid our discussion, we could create our own artificial pegs and call the ranges:

Normal Declines		
1.0 - 2.5%	Routine Declines	
2.5 - 5%	Mild Declines	
5 - 10%	Moderate Declines	
10 - 20%	Severe Declines	

Bear Markets		
20 - 30%	Mild Bear Markets	
30 - 40%	Moderate Bear Markets	
40 - 50%	Severe Bear Markets	
50%+	Extreme Bear Markets	

We will examine how often these various decline amounts happen and how long they last. When counting past declines, we'll add a tally mark to each decline range. To illustrate how this can be subjective, let's say this is your return over 10 days:

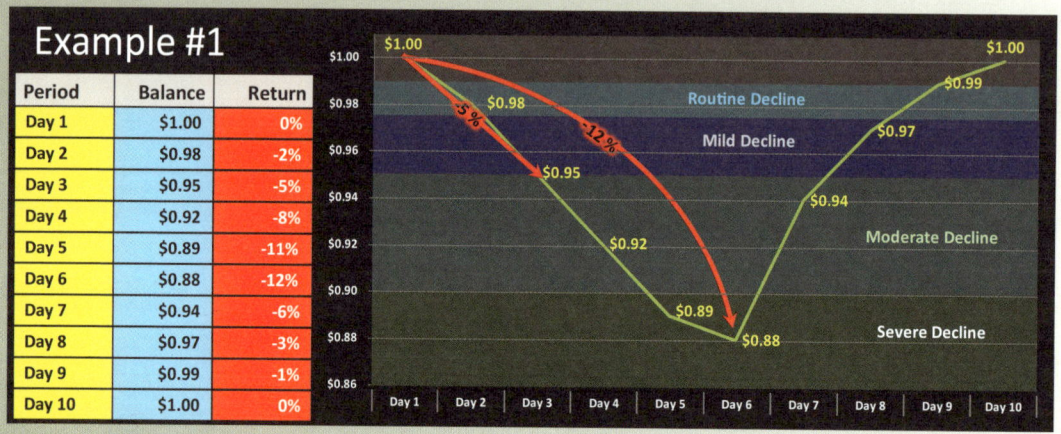

Example #1

Period	Balance	Return
Day 1	$1.00	0%
Day 2	$0.98	-2%
Day 3	$0.95	-5%
Day 4	$0.92	-8%
Day 5	$0.89	-11%
Day 6	$0.88	-12%
Day 7	$0.94	-6%
Day 8	$0.97	-3%
Day 9	$0.99	-1%
Day 10	$1.00	0%

Over the 10 days, the balance went from $1.00 to $1.00. In that path, we saw a decline that passed through each of these zones. In counting this path, I put one tally in each of the four zones. Ultimately the decline ended up being a Severe Decline in the **10–20%** range, but we didn't know that as we went along.

The decline started small and escalated—which is how all crashes begin. By including the initial small decline in our tally marks, we can collect useful statistics such as, "Historically, following a Moderate Decline of **5–10%**, 21.50% of the time the decline escalates to at least a Severe Decline of more than **10%**." On the other hand, this technique counts the same decline twice, at multiple levels. That's because I want to give you an *expectation mentality*. On the way to a **12%** decline, you will experience a **5%** decline and I want you to have an expectation of normal against which to judge the current situation. Historically, *how often* has this sort of situation gotten worse? In the spirit of giving you the clearest expectation *looking forward*, here's a trickier path:

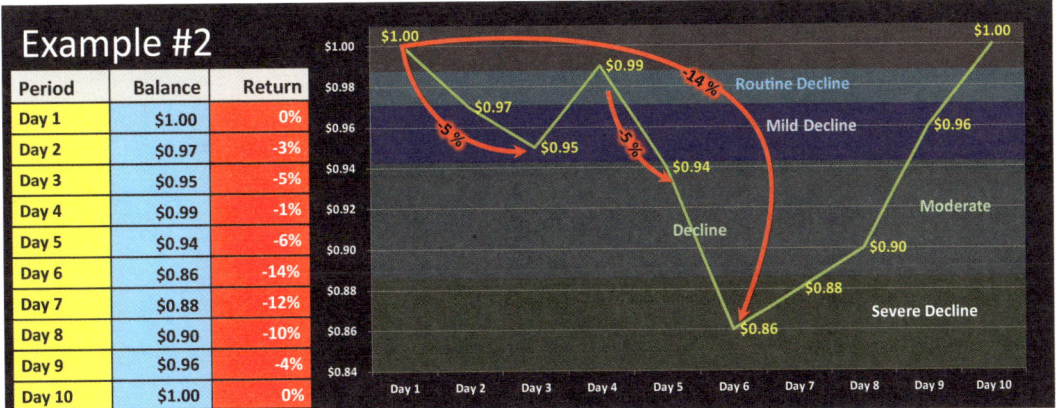

Period	Balance	Return
Day 1	$1.00	0%
Day 2	$0.97	-3%
Day 3	$0.95	-5%
Day 4	$0.99	-1%
Day 5	$0.94	-6%
Day 6	$0.86	-14%
Day 7	$0.88	-12%
Day 8	$0.90	-10%
Day 9	$0.96	-4%
Day 10	$1.00	0%

It declines **5%**, recovers up and out of the range, then declines **5%** again before bottoming out at a decline of **14%**. So how do you count this? Would you count the two **5%** declines as one or as two? I count it as two. I see it as a "**14%** decline era" and as an initial **5%** with a fake recovery that escalated to a **14%** decline. Some may call it one. I'm considering the experience of watching your account balance go up and down, which *feels* like two, although you are a bit more numb for the second one.

My methodology stems from the aspiration for a useful expectation. If you see your portfolio decline to the Mild Decline **2.5–5%** range, you can look back and see that in about two-thirds of all cases, this was as bad as it got. One-third of the time, it got worse and crossed the **5%** mark.

I've found that my clients (and my assumption is most everyone else too) tend to think about their accounts in terms of recent record values.

If the account is worth $1.00 and experiences a **5%** decline to $0.95, your thought is, "Is this normal? In the past, how often does this situation get worse? How long would it normally take to recover back to $1.00?" We could call the vantage point I'm describing as: looking at things *from the perspective of decline*. Mentally, you are thinking of your account as setting record values and then experiencing periods, sometimes long periods of time, before it sets records again. The centerpiece of your mindset is on the $1.00 record value figure and feeling antsy on getting back to the $1.00 value.

The other vantage point is from the bottom end of the decline. If it is Example #2, the centerpiece of our mindset is on the $0.86 figure. We could call this vantage point as: looking at things *from the perspective of recovery*. In my experience, clients tend to remember their *recent* low point, particularly if it was deep. As I write this in 2017, many people remember their lowest account value during the 2008–2009 Financial Crisis, but not their low point in 2002.) As investors, we tend to hold *both* of these perspectives, decline and recovery, in mind.

In both cases, we ask, "Is this normal?" During declines, people want to predict the likelihood of further decline. During recoveries, one wonders how long to expect before full recovery. Without further ado, here are the numbers for all historical declines from 1928–2016 that are greater than **1.00%**.

	Decline Range	Name	Amount of All Declines in Range	PERSPECTIVE OF DECLINE			PERSPECTIVE OF RECOVERY
				Amount of Declines this Bad or Worse	Amount of Declines that Escalate to Next Range	How Often Declines in this Range Happen	Average Length of Declines that Don't Escalate
Normal Declines	1.0 - 2.5%	Routine Declines	58.36%	100.00%	41.67%	11.42 days	10.46 days
	2.5 - 5%	Mild Declines	28.40%	41.67%	32.04%	27.42 days	26.36 days
	5 - 10%	Moderate Declines	10.36%	13.35%	21.50%	2.83 months	2.20 months
	10 - 20%	Severe Declines	2.20%	2.87%	23.69%	1.08 years	6.15 months
Bear Markets	20 - 30%	Mild Bear Markets	0.36%	0.68%	47.06%	4.62 years	1.96 years
	30 - 40%	Moderate Bear Markets	0.14%	0.32%	56.25%	9.76 years	2.23 years
	40 - 50%	Severe Bear Markets	0.07%	0.18%	61.11%	17.57 years	4.82 years
	50%+	Extreme Bear Markets	0.11%	0.11%	N/A	29.28 years	6.59 years

(Normal Declines total: 99.32%; Bear Markets total: 0.68%)

There is a great deal to glean from this. The cold brutal facts:

1. Declines happen *all the time*. On average, every two weeks or so (11.42 calendar days is the average) you should expect to see the stock market drop at least **1.0–2.5%**.
2. On average, you should expect to see the stock market go down **10–20%** each and every year. It's completely normal.
3. Bear markets happen on average 4.62 years. They are just as normal and cyclical as presidential elections. And just like elections, nobody likes them. They are just something we all have to endure.
4. In a typical 30-year retirement, you should expect to see more than six bear markets. Six times you will see the stock market take a breathtaking drop of more than **20%**. You will either make a terrible mistake and panic out, or you won't.

The good news:

1. Most declines (58.36%) are Routine Declines and never get worse than **-2.5%**.

2. 99.32% of declines never cross the **20%** bear market mark and recover in less than six months on average.

3. Even declines in the **20–40%** range require of you, on average, only two years of patience.

4. Even the nastiest of Extreme Bear Markets, on average, go away within what most people would describe as a "short investing time-frame" (6.59 years).

Again, this is all looking at the past. The probability of the future resembling what we've seen is far greater than the odds of it carving a new path.

Think about it like weather. You can't prevent the weather, but you can prepare for it. How often do you expect to see a big market decline? How long does it usually last? What is the range? What are the extremes? The above chart is a "weather guide" on the stock market. Although the stock market doesn't exactly follow its own *odds*, we can at least say that the longer the time, the more the market follows its own *patterns*. The more you can incorporate this weather guide into your financial consciousness, the better you will invest.

Imagine someone spending a winter in a remote cabin in the woods. He chops wood, melts snow, plays solitaire. He may start to lose his mind as the season suffocates him. Keeping a proactive awareness that the winter has an end is his greatest psychological safeguard. Without the anticipation of spring, he'll go cuckoo for Cocoa Puffs and run naked into a snow storm. Use history to maintain long-term perspective.

Performance and Volatility Epilogue

A coin has a 50% chance of landing heads or tails. Those are the odds. You may luck out and flip heads ten times in a row. It doesn't mean the odds changed, but your experience was one of the more rare possibilities within them. With the stock market, you can't fully use a concept like "odds."

There are limits to the usefulness of statistics. Earlier we discussed average temperatures during April in Denver. This is an example of an experience that follows a normal distribution. The data creates a lovely symmetrical bell curve shape. Other data will do this too. If a salmon fisherman recorded the length of all of the adult fish he caught, it would probably look like a symmetrical bell. He'd brag about a few big ones, but most of his experience would be plus or minus the average size. You could do the same with height, IQ, or how far you can throw a baseball.

Most of the time the market behaves around the average … that is, until it distressingly doesn't. The wild deviations from the average are what we call *long tails* on our bell curve. I'll give you the best example I know of: October 19, 1987. On that day, commonly called Black Monday, the S&P 500 fell **-20.47%** *in one day*. A fall of this much over *a year* is certainly within normal 12 month experience, but not in *one day*.

If we were to assume for a moment that the market behaved on "odds" alone, you could observe that the average daily movement of the S&P 500 is **0.0423%**. Each day the market may swing a lot, but the average daily price movement is an incremental rise. You could then say that 99% of the time, the daily movement has been in between **-3%** and **3%**. We could also calculate that the odds of it falling **-20.47%** in a single day are about 1 in 3.0146 duovigintillion and some change.

Now I know what you're thinking, "Chad, duovigintillion isn't a word." To which I say, "Oh yes it is, boys and girls. It's what you call a 1 with 69 zeros after it." To put it in some perspective on a really big number you know, a trillion is a 1 with 12 zeros after it. Adding one more zero makes it 13 zeros and *10x* bigger. Adding the 14th zero makes it *100x* bigger.

So either we don't need to worry about this happening again for another three duovigintillion trading days or so … or the stock market doesn't behave along a normal distribution of data and probabilities don't fully apply to it over *short* periods of time.

1987's Black Monday was undoubtedly a crazy event beyond calculable "odds." However when you zoom out and look at that year, the 12-month returns absolutely fit inside the normal expectation that 68.3% of the time your 12 month return should be between **-9.59%** and **33.02%**:

- October 16, 1987–October 17, 1988[4] = **+1.26%** (this is buying in the trading day just *before* the crash)
- October 19, 1987–October 18, 1988 = **+28.69%** (this is buying in just *after* the crash)
- January 1, 1987–December 31, 1987 = **+4.85%** (this is simply *buying and holding* through 1987)

So why have I gone into this?

I want to emphasize that the stock market is not predictable over the short term (i.e. one day such as Black Monday). The longer the timeframe we work with, the more reliable the experience.

The good news is that next to nobody invests for short periods, let alone for individual days.

You may remember my earlier rant about people falsely equating gambling to the stock market. I concede that on the short term, this is *closer* to a fair comparison. On individual days, the market behaves like a roulette wheel. However, in the long term, the stock market is a value *weighing* machine. Like an old-fashioned scale, it wobbles, while measuring fair market value for Walt's Auto Shop (or whatever company). The value of a company is subjective. Its value is only as high as someone is willing to pay for it.

You could also consider the stock market a value *voting* machine. Individuals, institutions, and computers all have different opinions on that value. They will "vote" via their buying and selling. This valuation voting machine is at times *very* poorly lubricated for or against the investor. However, in the end, the machine oscillates around the underlying value and in time will always find (or cross through would be more accurate) that value. There is always *some* underlying value the market is seeking to find. The stock market is composed of many "Walt's Auto Shops" that have actual revenue and actual assets.

Like a school of fish jerking away from a shadow, masses will always react to short-term news, vote for pessimism, and sell. This is how the slowly tilting value-weighing machine massages out the long tails found in short timeframes. The statistical lesson from Black Monday is not some esoteric academic point. You may be a long-term investor, but every day you are a short-term participant. You may know that you are investing for life, but inevitably a good day pleases you and a bad day causes stress.

As a person utilizing the stock market, you must pin some *faith* that short-term price extremes go away in time. Multiple times a year, the stock market will scare the snot out of you. Keep focus. Your investments don't represent ownership in the daily inefficiencies of the poorly oiled voting machine. Have faith in the underlying value of your businesses.

The Zeitgeist of the Voting Machine: It Takes a Village to Make a Bad Decision

There was a time where if you wanted to panic out of the stock market you had to call up or telegraph your broker to make a sale, at which point you got kicked in the tush with a steep *fixed* commission. There was a respectable barrier between an investor's emotions and ultimately voting through a buy or a sell transaction. As humanity has marched headlong into technology, that barrier has shrunk. Millions of people are mere clicks away from voting the market downward. Time and technology will only bring stock prices closer to this raw emotional nerve. This is why it's essential to understand these "long tail" events as mass voting, regardless of underlying value. There's no use dreading them because you can't anticipate or predict where the ball will land on the daily roulette wheel. Instead, embrace, if not quietly *scoff at* these foolish short-term, short-sighted voting maneuvers by your peers. You can expect them right on through your retirement. Now that you know, you don't have to worry about it anymore.

To finish this out, I have two final nuances to build your psychological seawall against the storms. Periodic declines are merely the wind and the rain of the hurricane. However, a turbulent tide also threatens to sink you: general pessimistic consensus. This consensus usually starts in the news (the first nuance), and ends in your community (the second nuance).

Bashing the media's propensity for hype is whacking an easy target. I won't pile on here. The media is part of "what is." You must anticipate that when the doo-doo hits the fan, or even when a mild fart hits the fan, someone will report it as the end of the world.

We know that it is normal each and every year for the stock market to experience a **10%** decline. Just as sure as Christmas, you can expect an annual financial media circus. This annual Chicken Little tradition costs the public millions of dollars by getting them worked up about very normal stock market volatility.

This will never be any different in our lifetimes. As members of society, we are shackled to this pessimistic bedfellow, so it's best to get used to responding in either of the following ways (1) rolling your eyes (2) laughing at whatever volume suits you.

The second nuance threatening your psychological seawall is your community. This can mean a lot of things. Your community may be your co-workers, family, friends, people in your church, Irish lawn bowling league and yes, your *financial advisor*. We'll pick on financial advisors in a moment, but when prices are going up in the stock market, everyone around you becomes optimistic.

Conversely, when things start plummeting, you hear these moronic things like, "It went down so I sold out because I didn't want to lose any more." My forehead is furrowed with scars from slapping it so many times. I beg you, don't invest how your community is investing. We will soon learn that community performance (i.e. the average investor) is *substantially* less than the general stock market.

We have talked about the importance of holding stocks, now we'll delve into the importance of your discipline while holding them.

Our historical data tells us that thus far, all stock market declines have been temporary. It's *possible* that any current decline is permanent, but it's not *probable*. Bear markets happen on average every 4.62 years. You will need to ignore the panic around you and patiently wait through the two years on average that it takes to erase it. Once it's erased, start the clock again *expecting* another one to happen within a few more years.

I remember during the bottom of The Great Recession how you *commonly* heard well-respected people say that the recovery would take a decade and we wouldn't pull even until the 2020s. In the late '90s tech boom, I remember the constant explanation that a new technological global economy supported valuations higher than what we've seen in the past. Pundits will always justify the present in disrespect of the past with some nuance of "this time is different." This time is *never* different, in both good ways and bad. Everything reverts to the mean ... eventually, and later than it should.

Discipline isn't easy. Do not be naïve about the power of fear to muscle out your mind. If you think you aren't susceptible to the power of your emotions to override your intellect, I beg you to review your thoughts versus your heart when you watch a three act story (pretty much every mainstream movie). When I was a teenager I had a game of making fun of how predictable movies were. When we were waiting in line, I'd challenge my friends to guess the entire plot of the movie just off the poster. It was never difficult, yet when I inevitably saw thc movie, there I was on the edge of my seat, all along knowing the guy gets the girl and the bad guy gets it in the end. When it comes to investing, you *know* how the movie ends, yet you *feel* every zig and zag.

Despite all anyone intellectually *knows* about buy and hold investing, your knowledge always *feels* different when things are volatile. No amount of robust stock market growth will ever offset how horrifying it is to see even a modest decline in your portfolio.

Stock market declines feel terrible *even if* you hadn't expected the level of growth in the first place. In 2009, hardly anyone thought the stock market would be where it is today. Most would have been happy with half the growth, but a mere **10%** decline would now induce panic.

Much like in wars of aggression, humans are far more willing to fight to keep what they perceive as theirs rather than to fight to seize what isn't. It is an asymmetric sense of possession. Once you have seen those dollar signs in your account, it feels 100% yours.

Another key principle and personal observation is that investing is primarily a game of percentages, not a game of dollars. I have found that the larger a portfolio gets, the more investors' minds tend to drift to the dollar amount rather than the percentage amount. With my clients, I have found this especially true with the mul-timillionaires. Let's say the market falls **10%**. If you have a $10,000 account, this is $1,000. If you have a $10,000,000 account, this is $1,000,000. Mentally, you didn't decline **10%**, you "lost a million dollars." Which, as we learned, happens on an annual basis. If your psychology is (1) temporary market declines are "losses" (2) looking at declines as a dollar amount versus a percent, then you are all but doomed to the annual emotional experience of "losing a million dollars."

The same "**10%** decline" event has happened, but the psychology of higher balances can irrationally and mistakenly drive people to invest with lower volatility which is not necessarily lower long-term risk in terms of wealth.

Rather than feeling consciously or subconsciously that you can avoid stock market declines by selling, it is far wiser to embrace volatility as your price of admission for a higher return. It's interesting to me that people don't seem terribly upset that their cars constantly decline in value. It is an assumed reality of owning a car. Let volatility be the assumed reality of the path to higher long-term wealth. As we learned in our chapter on banking, there is only one direction for the real value of money invested in things without volatility: down.

The Inflation Layer

I thought it best to put inflation on the shelf for a while. Inflation is always an invisible risk. If someone gets a statement that says their balance went down **10%**, they aren't thinking about inflation. Being aware of inflation does very little to help people psychologically cope with surprising market declines. When you get your statement, the numbers should reflect what you now expect: volatility. But let's talk about this in terms of real money. Since money is to buy stuff and we are defining wealth as growing in your power to buy stuff, we must look at how stocks do that.

The Stock Market and Inflation (and Deflation)

Inflation and deflation skew the stock market in surprising ways. To be clear, deflation is the opposite of inflation—that is, when prices go *down*. Wait, I thought prices always went up? They nearly always do. The few exceptions are during extreme economic times, when money isn't out there buying much stuff. The only recent extended period of deflation in America was the Great Depression. Earlier we talked about the sometimes long horizontal seasons of the stock market. Take note of that first red era of the Great Depression.

The Long Seasons of the S&P 500

Beginning	End	Days	Years	Return
September 16, 1929	December 29, 1944	5,583 days	15.3 years	-0.39%
January 1, 1945	December 2, 1968	8,736 days	23.9 years	2172.0%
December 3, 1968	August 12, 1982	5,000 days	13.7 years	68.03%
August 13, 1982	March 24, 2000	6,433 days	17.6 years	2392.78%
March 27, 2000	December 20, 2011	4,285 days	11.7 years	0.97%
December 21, 2011	December 31, 2016	1,836 days	5.0 years	99.46%

Earlier we learned that in the past century, the Great Depression was the longest stretch that the market produced a **0.00%** return. It was an era 15 years 3 months and 27 days in length. What I didn't mention is that it was an era marked by *deflation*. The severe economic downturn made prices actually go *down*. Starting with an item priced at $1.00, this is what the price would have looked like over those 15 years.

Something that would have cost $1.00 in September of 1929, would have only cost $0.73 by February of 1933. If you were lucky enough to hold cash during this terrible time, it meant that your dollars were able to buy *more* stuff.

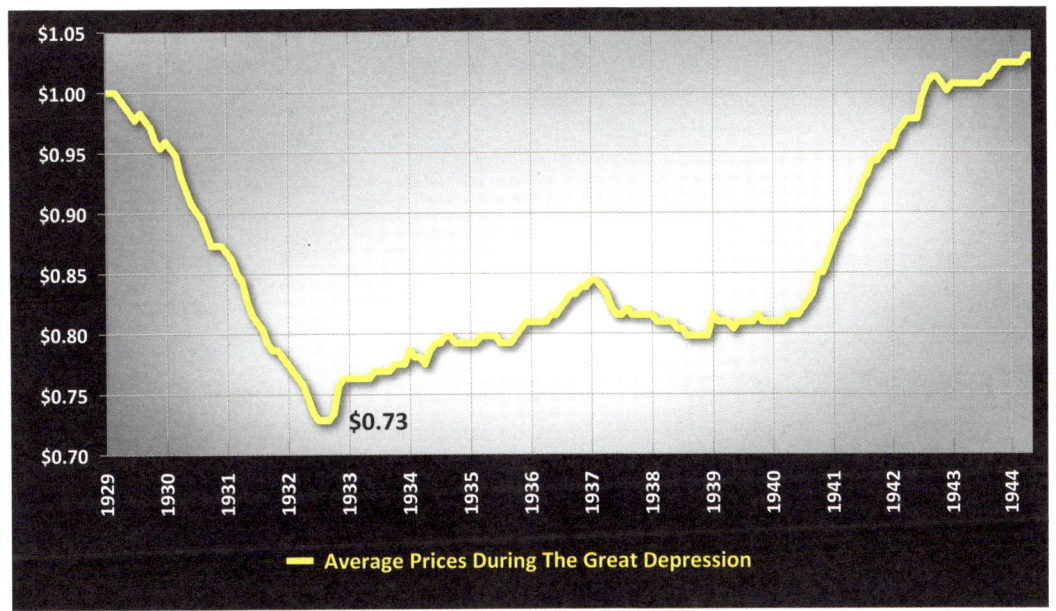

The stock market famously crashed on October 29, 1929, which was a Tuesday, so they called it ... Black Tuesday. It then began a precipitous decline that culminated in the middle of 1932. Our analysis begins two months before this, on September 1, 1929. Black Tuesday is that initial sharp cliff on the graph on the next page.

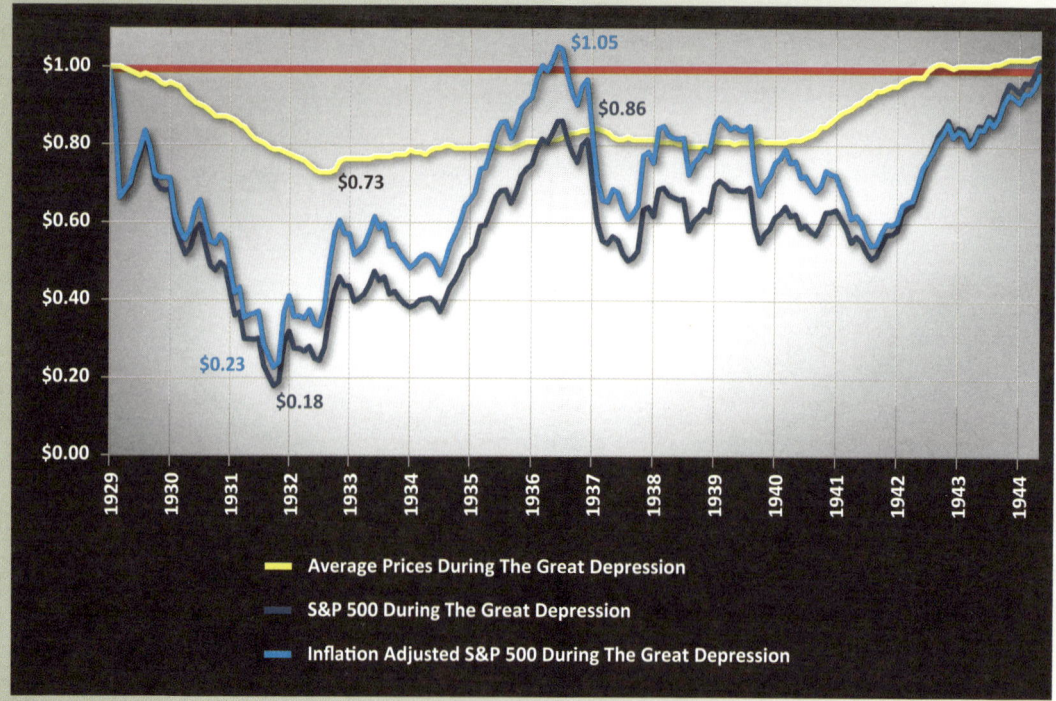

The yellow line is the same inflation line on the previous graph, but squeezed down on this broader scale. The dark blue line is the nominal value of the S&P 500 starting with $1.00. We can see it bottoming out at $0.18. However, when we adjust for *deflation* with the lighter blue line, in real money this bottoming out figure was $0.23. Hardly something to get jolly about, but not quite as bad. Ignoring inflation/deflation, it took more than 15 years to see your account balance break even during the Battle of the Bulge late in 1944.

The interesting thing is where the dark blue S&P 500 line crosses the yellow line—or, the light blue line crosses the red line, which is the same thing. This crosspoint represents the moment you were in the same real dollar position as you were just before Black Tuesday. Factoring in inflation/deflation, your account briefly broke even in 1936, when Jesse Owens was stickin' it to Nazis through his non-Aryan athleticism. If you were to ignore how deflation changed the buying power of your currency, it would seem that you were still underwater. If you were waiting for your account to break even, instead of 15 years, in real money, it was only 7 years. While you were lifting your newly legalized whiskey in the air and singing *Happy Days Are Here Again*, financially speaking, they had already arrived.

The years just before World War II were not kind to investors. From 1936 until the Pearl Harbor attack, the market sank. Once the war started, the market was uplifted by massive government war spending. Look at our lines. There was a moment during the Great Depression where even the toxic wasteland of the stock market delivered greater buying power than having cash buried in the backyard—even when your nominal balance was still sitting on a decline, prices had declined along with it to some extent and in real money softened the blow.

Let's contrast this era of deflation with an era of high inflation. This is the second horizontal period from December 3, 1968 – August 12, 1982 which was modestly uphill by **68.02%**. When we factor in the high inflation during this time, the period return drops to **-39.26%** in real money. Our new color is green—the dark green is what your account balance would have shown, and the light green line shows the inflation adjusted numbers.

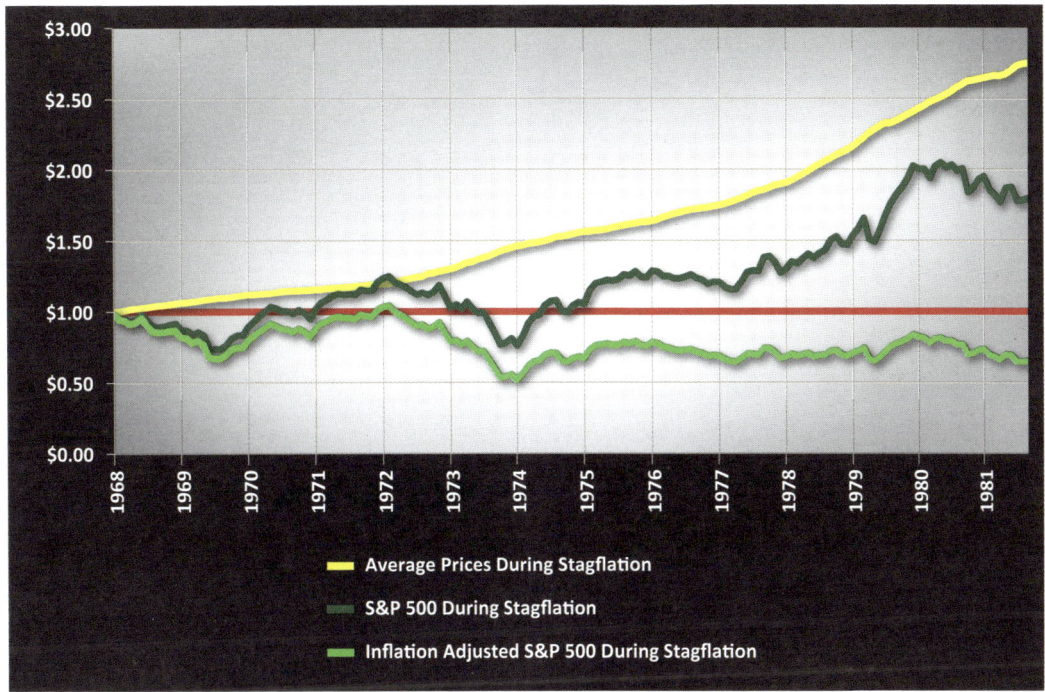

During this era sometimes referred to as stagflation (<u>stag</u>nant economy + high in<u>flation</u>), prices nearly tripled. This is a great illustration of how inflation is an invisible risk. While you would have seen your investment balance go up **68%**, in real money it lost nearly half its value. Yet, most people don't think of the 1970s as having had worst stock market performance than the Great Depression—principally because inflation obscures the numbers. Although Chic's *Good Times* was trying to have you believe that "happy days are here again," the inflation adjusted reality was that your performance was more or less what you would have endured at the same point during the Great Depression.

Let's get down to the nitty-gritty and look at the inflation-adjusted stock market performance during these two eras. We can see this at the top of the next page. I've extended the stagflation era another two years to make them equal length—the extension is noted by changing the line color to orange, which includes a smidgen of the early '80s Paul Volcker boom. Green and orange, in honor of your decor at the time.

As a first note, the market decline during the initial part of the Great Depression was a far deeper gouge and for that alone, stagflation looks like a junior varsity horror in comparison. Six years into the eras, so far as stock market performance is concerned, real dollar life wasn't radically different, though slightly worse for stagflation.

These are wonderful extremes we have to play with, but let's talk about this in practice. Inflation just *is*. There's no avoiding it. Ultimately, money is to buy stuff and you have no control over what those prices are and whether those prices are going up or (rarely) going down. What you do have control over is your effort to outpace it. This may be an unusual segue into bonds, but hang in here with me.

Bonds

We can think of understanding stocks as a prerequisite for understanding bonds. I'm going to tell you the ending of the movie: if you passed Stocks and Risk 101, you will see that most people have little use for bonds. The discussion of bonds is like having "the talk" with your prepubescent son—you don't want to talk about it, he doesn't want to hear it, but it needs to be said. Let's get this over with and we'll go out for ice cream afterwards.

A Brief Picture of the Bond Universe

Earlier we described stock in terms of partial ownership of Walt's Auto Shop. Instead of selling the business to one person, he divides up the ownership into small shares. Let's say Walt wants to open another location and he needs to raise $800,000. He could go to the bank for a loan, or he could issue $800,000 in debt and divide it into many small loans that individuals could grant him. These little pieces of debt are called **bonds**. It is money that you are lending to Walt's Auto Shop in exchange for interest that he is paying you (the interest is confusingly called **dividends**, just like stock). There are three main types of bonds:

1. Government
2. Mortgage
3. Corporate

We could further segment these three categories. Bonds issued by the government at the federal level are issued through the U.S. Treasury Department and are called **treasury bonds**. You may also hear of treasury notes, treasury bills (or as "T-bills") and other types. It's all the same idea, but the name tells you the maturity length. With these, you are lending the U.S. Government money. During World War II, famous people were going around the country peddling war bonds. This was to lend the government money to bankroll the war effort. Whenever the government runs a deficit (i.e. spends more money than it's getting from taxes and other revenues), it has to get additional money by issuing bonds.

Another type of government bonds are municipal bonds, which are issued by smaller government entities and pay dividends that are tax free at the federal level. They can be issued for specific projects such as building a convention center, water treatment facility, airport, and anything government-related you can imagine. If you live in the district then generally you don't have to pay local taxes on the dividends. If you live in Colorado and buy Colorado state municipal bonds, they are federally *and* state tax exempt, or "double tax exempt." If you live in Denver and buy Denver municipal bonds, they are free from federal, state, and city taxes, or "triple tax exempt." We'll discuss this again in the chapter on taxes.

There are also mortgage bonds. Someone buys a house, their mortgage is divided up into small bonds that people can buy. Investors have a sense of safety, sometimes a false sense of safety, with mortgage bonds because they represent a loan on a house than can be sold off if the homeowner defaults. Some mortgage bonds have an *implicit* government guarantee, which we saw activated during the recent financial crisis. That means the government isn't required to cover losses, but everyone assumes they will. At the time, Congress decided not to clarify the government's relationship with mortgage bonds.

Lastly, corporate bonds are like the loan to Walt's Auto Shop. It's a company needing to raise money for whatever reason. Those reasons can range from expansion to escaping insolvency. The reason for needing the money, the financial strength of the entity needing the money, along with various other factors make some bonds riskier than others. If you are buying bonds from a company on the verge of bankruptcy, you are at an elevated risk of permanent loss of principal. This higher risk is normally answered with the company paying a much higher dividend rate. In an attempt to make this relative evaluation of bonds easier, there are companies who will rate the bonds. You will hear of bonds being AAA (" triple A"), AA ("double A"), B+, or the less intuitive Baa3.

A Tricky Proxy

Using the S&P 500 is the standard way of talking generally about stocks, but it's not quite as easy to generalize the health of bonds. One of the more popular indices used to broadly talk about general bond performance is the Barclays Capital Aggregate Bond Index, which counts most types of bonds. It *excludes* bonds with special tax treatment because it wouldn't be an apples-for-apples representation. Also, quite punishingly, 70% of it is in U.S. Securities that have a lower yield (and lower volatility) than corporate bonds. Having 70% of your bond portfolio in U.S. Securities, is not reflective of the average bond investor. There are other new bond indices that are more representative of how people *actually* tend to invest. Because of their newness there is lack of long-term data, making them useless for setting up long-term expectations.

With the Barclays Capital Aggregate Bond Index we have the oldest *daily* data publicly available. It goes back to December 1986, so we have a mere 29 years of good data. Sort of. Raw historical data is not publicly available, so even if we are happy with this time-frame, we'd have to try to recreate the index by taking an index fund and adding the expense ratio back into the return. But … it's not likely that the expense ratio has always been the same, so this would be just an approximation—not my style. It's also not helpful that this time period from 1986 to now represents most of the greatest bond rally in American history and thus is not excellent in terms of setting realistic expectations. Again, a tricky proxy.

Yearly data is handily available for several bond categories going back to 1928. Yearly data is very useful for long-term growth expectations. On the other hand, only having the yearly return numbers on artificial calendar years means we don't have the data to talk about rolling one-year periods and intra-year declines as we did with stocks. My heart bleeds along with yours. We'll work with what we've got.

Performance and Volatility of Bonds

We will use four proxies for bonds[5]:

1. Long-term Corporate Bonds
2. Long-term Government Bonds
3. Intermediate-term Government Bonds
4. U.S. Treasury Bills

From 1928–2016, this has been the return of these four asset classes along with the familiar S&P 500 and inflation.

Asset Class Performance 1928-2016

Asset Class	Return	Beginning Balance	Ending Balance
S&P 500	9.63%	$1.00	$3,269.24
Long-Term Corporate Bonds	5.96%	$1.00	$162.79
Long-Term Government Bonds	5.51%	$1.00	$112.48
Intermediate-Term Government Bonds	5.18%	$1.00	$85.33
U.S. Treasury Bills	3.42%	$1.00	$19.33
Inflation	3.04%	$1.00	$13.69

Visually, this is what the past 89 years has looked like.

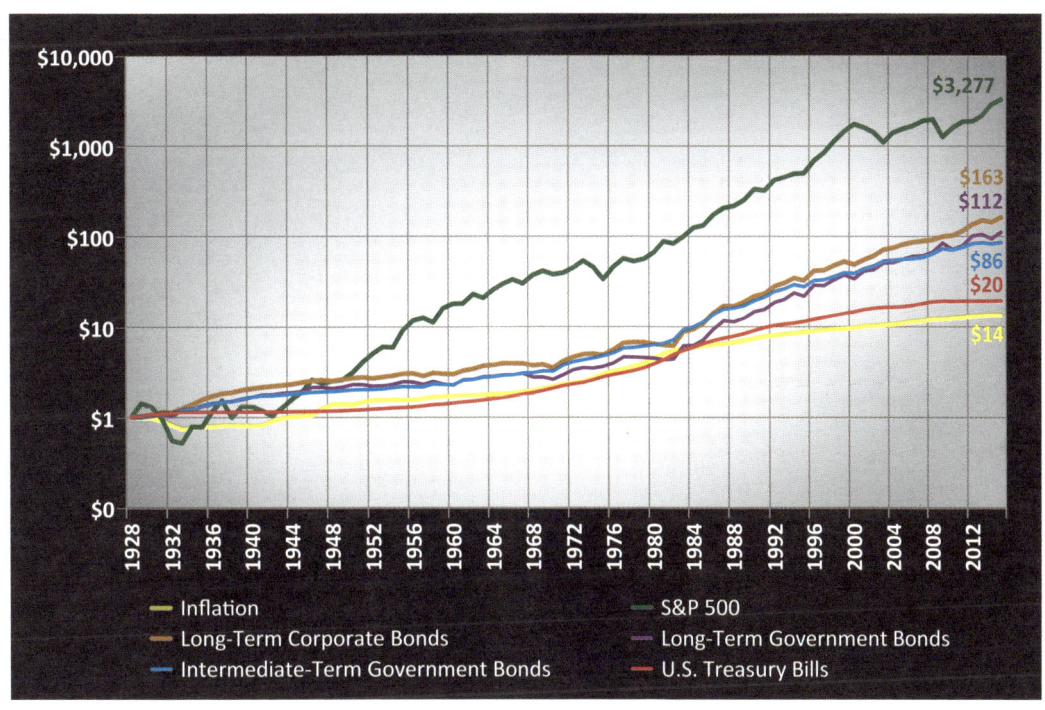

Do strongly note the scale on the left side as it tends to visually understate the radical outperformance of stocks. All classes of bonds have historically performed *much* worse than stocks. On the plus side, bonds have enjoyed lower volatility—if that's your cup of tea.

The Nature of Bonds is to Underperform Stocks

The underperformance of bonds versus stocks should not be surprising. It is the *nature* of bonds to deliver a return *significantly* less than stocks. It is the essence of lending versus owning.

A lender has a contractual agreement to receive payment, an owner does not. If a company struggles with earnings, payment on debt gets higher priority than payments of dividends to owners. On the other hand, the expected return upside of bonds is generally limited to the interest.

Bonds naturally return less than stocks. Knowing what we know about rising prices, the use of bonds in a long-term portfolio nudges you back toward inflation risk.

What Do You Want?

This is the first question that must be asked before any investment. If your goal is to never see your currency amount go down, then the coffee can in the backyard is your answer. If your goal is to put yourself in a position that has the highest and strongest historical precedent for wealth creation, then avoid bonds.

Let's adjust these asset class returns for inflation. These are the real dollar results:

Asset Class Performance 1928-2016 (Inflation Adjusted)			
Asset Class	Return	Beginning Balance	Ending Balance
S&P 500	6.17%	$1.00	$193.53
Long-Term Corporate Bonds	2.71%	$1.00	$10.54
Long-Term Government Bonds	2.27%	$1.00	$7.20
Intermediate-Term Government Bonds	2.00%	$1.00	$5.72
U.S. Treasury Bills	0.29%	$1.00	$1.29
Inflation	0.00%	$1.00	$1.00

When we discussed the time value of money, we looked at how the mere *1% difference* between a **9%** return versus a **10%** return meant having *half* the amount of money over a lifetime. Well, stocks give you around *two to three times* the real return on bonds.

Lifetime Results of Investing Choice

Age	Not Inflation Adjusted						Inflation Adjusted					
	S&P 500	Long-Term Corporate Bonds	Long-Term Government Bonds	Intermediate-Term Government Bonds	U.S. Treasury Bills	Inflation	S&P 500	Long-Term Corporate Bonds	Long-Term Government Bonds	Intermediate-Term Government Bonds	U.S. Treasury Bills	Inflation
	9.63%	5.96%	5.51%	5.18%	3.42%	3.04%	6.17%	2.71%	2.27%	2.00%	0.29%	0.00%
20	$100,000	$100,000	$100,000	$100,000	$100,000	$100,000	$100,000	$100,000	$100,000	$100,000	$100,000	$100,000
30	$250,824	$178,370	$171,032	$165,747	$140,013	$134,883	$181,911	$130,685	$125,149	$121,925	$102,979	$100,000
40	$629,126	$318,157	$292,519	$274,719	$196,037	$181,934	$330,915	$170,787	$156,622	$148,656	$106,046	$100,000
50	$1,577,999	$567,497	$500,301	$455,338	$274,478	$245,398	$601,969	$223,193	$196,010	$181,248	$109,205	$100,000
60	$3,957,998	$1,012,242	$855,674	$754,707	$384,305	$331,000	$1,095,046	$291,681	$245,304	$220,986	$112,458	$100,000
70	$9,927,604	$1,805,533	$1,463,475	$1,250,901	$538,078	$446,462	$1,992,004	$381,185	$306,994	$269,436	$115,808	$100,000
80	$24,900,802	$3,220,523	$2,503,008	$2,073,326	$753,380	$602,201	$3,623,668	$498,152	$384,199	$328,508	$119,258	$100,000
90	$62,457,158	$5,744,438	$4,280,942	$3,436,467	$1,054,831	$812,267	$6,591,837	$651,013	$480,820	$400,532	$122,811	$100,000
100	$156,657,469	$10,246,337	$7,321,775	$5,695,827	$1,476,902	$1,095,609	$11,991,251	$850,778	$601,739	$488,346	$126,469	$100,000

We can revisit the **9%** versus **10%** scenario, but add real numbers and adjust it all for inflation. The choice of stocks versus any of the kinds of bonds is an excellent real world illustration of the benefit of committing to stocks as a lifetime decision.

I would encourage you to absorb the right side of this chart, which are the results in *real money*, using *real returns*. In this illustration, the choice of stock made the investor about *20 times* wealthier than the choice of bonds (depending on which kind the investor chose). What did the enjoyment of lower volatility of bonds ultimately give the bond investors? Less stress along the way. What was the cost of this lower stress? Having their wealth be 5% of what it could have been.

Oddly, I have found that when the stock market goes into a sharp decline, this stresses out bondholders just as much as stockholders. I've had clients who *didn't have a penny* in the stock market call because they were worried about the stock market dropping. While the stockholder in our example ended up with 20 times the wealth, I doubt the bondholder enjoyed 95% less stress.

The key takeaway with this chart is this: ***in dollars and cents, how much are you willing to pay for the comfort of lower volatility?***

In our example, the lifetime cost was considerable: over $11,000,000 in 1928 money (or over $150,000,000 in today's money). That seems rather pricey to me. Risk is the possibility of permanent loss of purchasing power. If in nominal returns, bonds historically deliver around **6%** and stocks deliver around **10%**, then the choice of bonds is to willfully adopt another **-4%** headwind.

Knowing it's less is all you need to know—particularly knowing that the *slightest* difference in your rate of return makes a *radical* difference to your long-term wealth.

The Use and Inappropriate Use of Bonds

Does this mean that no one should *ever* own bonds? No. Of course not. But if you own bonds, don't run around telling the world that you are positioning yourself for wealth creation and maximizing *long-term* real dollar preservation.

The inappropriate use of bonds can be summed up in one word: psychology. If you are uncomfortable with volatility and you are using bonds to make yourself feel better, don't. Spend your energy getting more comfortable with volatility.

Bonds do have some use. Municipal bonds are tax free. For various reasons, some people have to be highly careful to minimize taxes. Some may create a bond ladder to create an income stream. Some people have a very short time-frame and are trying to earn a little return within only a few years. Others may be in a position, perhaps for medical reasons, where they have to take an aggressive amount of money from their savings.

There is a place for bonds, but truth be told, most bonds are a short-term psychological balm bought with the sacrifice of long-term financial health.

Conclusion

Most people's money is for the long term, so *most* people don't have a significant place for bonds. Your comfort with volatility has nothing to do with the best portfolio for you.

There is no rational case for including *any* bonds in a *long-term* portfolio ... if you are able to manage your emotions and behavior.

Getting Our Heads Around Our Hearts

Thus far, we have established the behavior of the stock market, now we will look at your behavior as an owner in the stock market. As we spoke of how the stock market behaved, I emphasized the importance of behaving well when the stock market doesn't. Like parenting a volatile child, calmness and consistency is the best route. Getting frustrated, angry, or scared just makes the situation worse. This is about one issue: your discipline in holding onto stocks when you don't want to.

Time Heals All Wounds

The discussion on stock market behavior was unapologetically given with a lot of detail, numbers, and nuance. All of this is meant to deliver to you a single takeaway, that the grand lesson, the resounding message of financial history is this: **time heals even the *deepest* of wounds—except for the wounds you inflict on yourself.**

In a diversified portfolio, only the investor can create a permanent loss. Avoiding permanent loss is as simple as not choosing it. All market declines must be seen as temporary wounds that time, and sometimes a lot of time, eventually heals.

The probability that you will lose money investing in diversified equities declines directly with time until it virtually disappears. On the way, panic flares up very intensely. It is a threat only vanquished by old fashioned virtues.

Faith

Faith builds as you internalize what you know about the stock market. When the market goes down, you know, in faith, that it isn't because of some fundamental problem. This faith calms you that all declines are temporary and go away. At times, this may feel irrational. It may even seem irrational to those around you, but creeds don't look for ongoing justification. They are part of your identity and character.

An investor must have an inherent child-like faith in the capital markets. Are there ever times when the markets are fundamentally flawed? Certainly, but the flaws are temporary and highly difficult to identify. The best approach is to avoid this vain pursuit and answer it with diversification and patience.

Preparedness

Practice ongoing psychological self-strengthening against the possible *surprise* of stock market declines. Surprise leaves one highly susceptible to fear.

It is healthy to create mental war games with yourself. "If the market goes down **50%**, I will _____." Know ahead of time what you will do when the inevitable comes.

Courage

Preparation is the mother of courage. You must let faith ferment within you and mix it with preparation until it becomes courage. Bravery is the byproduct of internalized creed.

Hope

When you have faith that the earth warms after a winter, that's hope. The nature of your hope should be to look past the frightening present.

Peace

Hope invites peace, as you learn not to worry. Faith in the markets manifests in a monk-like peace, where the external world does not derail your resolve.

Humility

You cannot time the market. You cannot outsmart the market. The average person would do better doing literally nothing. On average, someone in a coma is a better portfolio manager than you are.

The return of the index is all you will ever need to accomplish your financial goals. Stop trying to look elsewhere when you have the solution in your hands.

Remind yourself of this the next time you feel that ubiquitous, natural notion that you know something special about the capital markets, the economy, an industry, or any individual stock.

If you are honest with yourself, your track record is likely to be far more abysmal than you realize. Gamblers only talk about their wins, giving them a false sense of luck, if not talent. In the end, the house beats them. Be humble and truthful by regularly acknowledging without hesitation: I don't know.

Steadfastness

Steadfastness is maintaining habits even in discomfort. With human health, it is important to eat right and exercise. In investing, it is having the foot on the equities gas pedal and not taking it off no matter what insanity ensues out the window.

Patience

There is wisdom in not obsessing over your monthly statement or reflexively checking your performance online. I call it *responsible neglect*. If you were to invest today and fall asleep for 20 years like Rip Van Winkle, you would wake up to find you had miraculously outperformed nearly everyone you knew. To use a shorter and more contemporary time-frame, if you fell asleep on October 9, 2007 (the record stock market price before the Financial Crisis) and woke up a mere *5 ½ years* later on March 28, 2013, you would have peacefully slept through the greatest downturn of our lifetime. You may have been mildly disappointed that the value of your portfolio was the same, but comforted that you weren't like your neighbor Bob, who "protected" his savings by selling out when his portfolio was down by half. You may also be disappointed that he still hasn't returned your leaf blower and extension cords.

Patience comes with having a firm commitment to the realities of time. Become a self-imposed Rip Van Winkle. With time on your side, the biggest risk you face is discipline risk.

A Case Study of Time

Maintaining patience in the face of unsettling fear comes with firmly knowing the reality of your time-frame. That is, know the reality of your *very long time horizon*. The key to defining your time horizon is to focus, not on your age or anything else, but on when your money is going to be converted into stuff. It is with this that we can begin to bring these things back down to earth and select a portfolio. I will use a personal example.

My grandparents were exceedingly frugal—the epitome of Scottish thrift. They retired at the age of 62 in 1985. The rule of thumb in those days was to go 100% to bonds *because you are retired*. This is an example of how generalizations are generally wrong, and thankfully. The reality of my grandparents' situation was that a lifetime of frugal habits, influenced by growing up during the (not so) Great Depression, did not suddenly end at retirement.

For the most part, they lived off their retirement income and rarely tapped into their investments. The carpet in their living room dated from the Kennedy administration. My grandmother passed away in 2001 from an aneurysm. Eight years later, my grandfather succumbed to advanced dementia on July 11, 2009 with most of their savings intact. Their savings was passed along to their six children, who inherited their frugal habits. To my knowledge, none of them have spent the money, and will likely hold onto it to *their* deaths. If frugality holds steadfast, this money will go to the next generation in about 20–30 years *from now*.

If you were my grandparents' financial advisor in 1985, your best advice would come after you established, through a financial plan, the likely fate of their savings. The key determination of the plan should be *when* their retirement savings would be spent on goods and services. It may initially sound insane to suggest to a retiree that they invest 100% in stock. However, by every definition, their money had a *very* long time before it was going to buy stuff. To put a number on it, at their retirement, a majority of their savings wasn't going to buy stuff for more than *half a century*.

To be clear, I have no knowledge of the details of their investments or their account balance—they did own stock and weren't entirely in bonds. But I do know the dates of their retirement and the date of their "second to die." As good luck would have it, my grandfather retired at the beginning of the greatest bond bull market in modern times. As bad luck would have it, my grandfather passed away just after the bottom of the greatest market down turn since his boyhood. If there was any time in recent history that there would have been an exception to my rule, it would have been these two dates for my grandfather.

On the top of the next page is what his results would have been if we imagine a starting balance of $100,000.

PAPA'S RETIREMENT

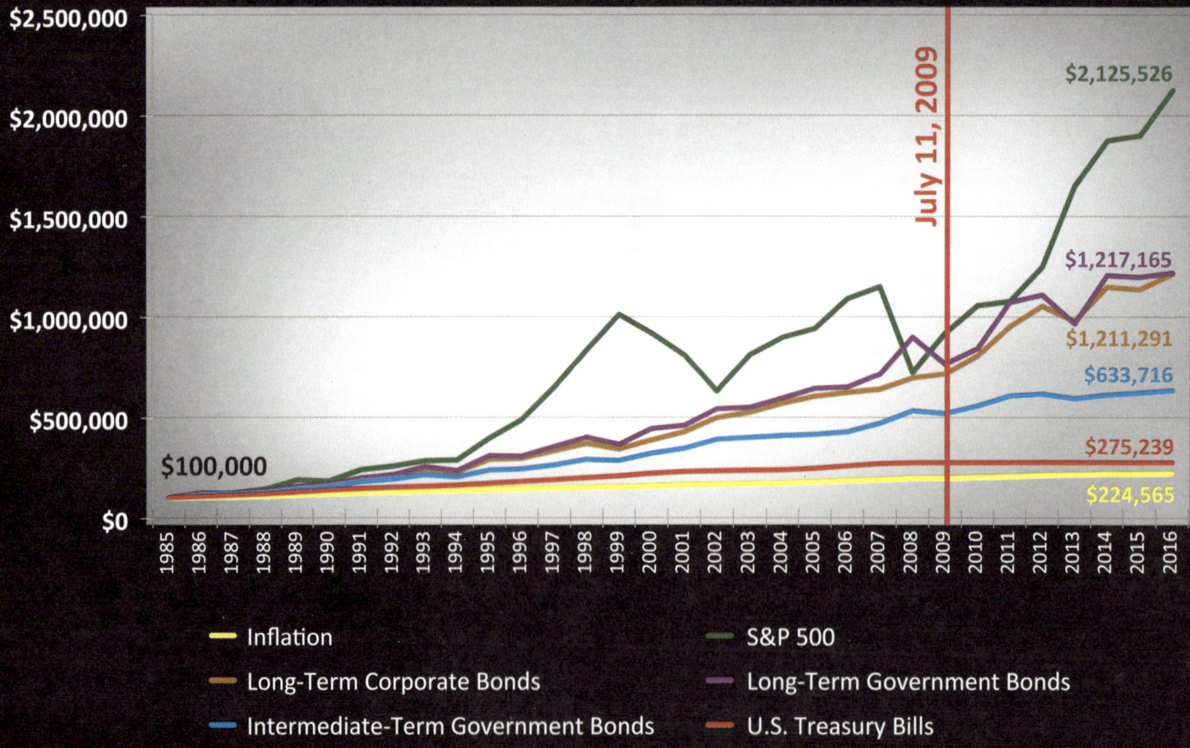
$2,500,000
$2,000,000
$1,500,000
$1,000,000
$500,000
$0
July 11, 2009
$2,125,526
$1,217,165
$1,211,291
$633,716
$275,239
$224,565
$100,000
1985 1986 1987 1988 1989 1990 1991 1992 1993 1994 1995 1996 1997 1998 1999 2000 2001 2002 2003 2004 2005 2006 2007 2008 2009 2010 2011 2012 2013 2014 2015 2016
Inflation
S&P 500
Long-Term Corporate Bonds
Long-Term Government Bonds
Intermediate-Term Government Bonds
U.S. Treasury Bills

PAPA'S RETIREMENT PROJECTED

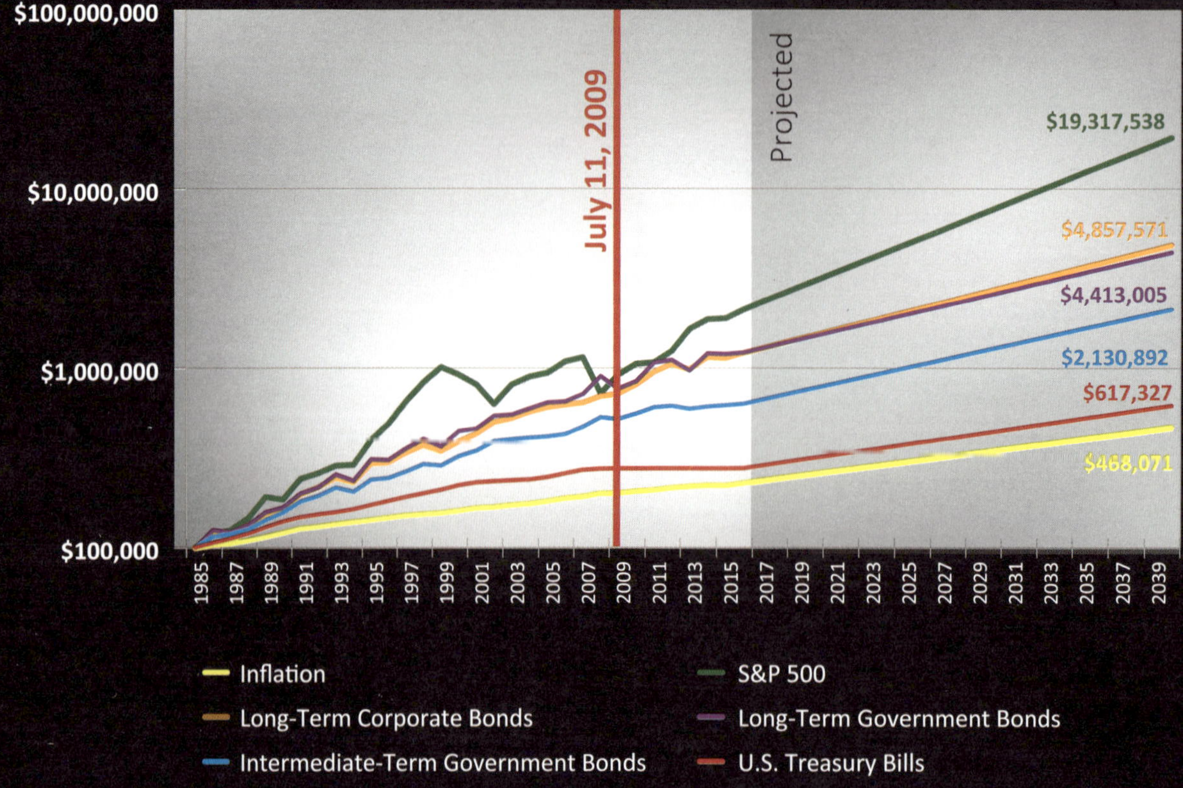
$100,000,000
$10,000,000
$1,000,000
$100,000
July 11, 2009
Projected
$19,317,538
$4,857,571
$4,413,005
$2,130,892
$617,327
$468,071
1985 1987 1989 1991 1993 1995 1997 1999 2001 2003 2005 2007 2009 2011 2013 2015 2017 2019 2021 2023 2025 2027 2029 2031 2033 2035 2037 2039
Inflation
S&P 500
Long-Term Corporate Bonds
Long-Term Government Bonds
Intermediate-Term Government Bonds
U.S. Treasury Bills

On the face of it, it would seem that on the date of his death, my method of weighing investing decisions proved wrong. At the time of his death, he would have been in the same position if he had invested in long-term bonds. Keep in mind that at the time of his death, his money still wasn't going to buy stuff for a very long time, so my method would say to keep it in stocks.

As we look past his life and onto the first six years of the next generation, the severe downturn was erased and the superior returns resumed, leaving bonds in the dust, likely for good. In the same way that his age or even retirement itself had nothing to do with how he should invest, ultimately neither did the timing of his death. If money won't be buying stuff anytime soon, it must be 100% in equities. If we use the historical numbers to project this forward another 25 years, the bottom of the last page shows how the balance continues with the next generation, growing and awaiting its time to buy stuff.

Deciding what to invest in when you retire is not about your age; it's about when is your money going to be spent. If you are investing for more than 15 years (and 3 months, and 27 days), there is simply no historical precedent for the stock market not delivering a positive return.

Nearly everyone has a long-term investing objective and *nearly everyone* has the heart of a short-term investor. Because of this inner demon, there must be an ongoing effort to tame your own behavior.

Investor Behavior

There is no magic pill to help investors behave their way to wealth. It is analogous to alcoholism. You treat it with mindfulness, abstinence, and the daily admission that you are an alcoholic even if you've been off the sauce for decades. In our analogy, panicking out of the market and emotional investing is alcohol. Not engaging in emotional investing merely indicates that you are abstaining from it, not that you are liberated from it. Up to this point, I have marinated our discussion with this because this is the spirit of how you should invest. Behavior is everything and in everything. It is not a point among many, it is *the point*. That's because individual investors not only underperform the Rip Van Winkle strategy, on average their extra moves barely earn them more than they could earn in the bank.

Humans are less rational than anyone cares to admit. Let's do a thought experiment. I'll put $1,200 down on the table and you put $1,000 down. We'll flip a coin and the winner takes all. Deal?

Hold on, before you say "no," let me point out that you have the upper hand on me here. You could gain $1,200, while the most I could gain is $1,000. Deal?

Most people would not go for this scenario because the thought of *losing* $1,000 is far more powerful than the possibility of *gaining* $1,200. What if we made it $1,500? $2,000? $100,000? Everyone has a number, but whatever it is, the amount of money you might gain must be *much more* than what you are willing to lose.

This is what's called **asymmetric loss aversion**. How much a **10%** gain feels good doesn't balance out how much a **10%** loss feels bad. Seeing your portfolio go up **10%** feels like getting a nice birthday card in the mail. Seeing it go down feels like your dog died. We fear the downside far more than we enjoy the upside.

I will step up on my trusty soapbox for a moment to alert you that a whole-heck-of-a-lotta sales and marketing in the financial services industry targets this irrational trait. People *really really really* don't want to see their portfolio balances decline. There are many companies and financial professionals who are more than happy to earn a buck letting you shoot yourself in the face with your own asymmetric loss aversion.

The next time you hear or see an advertisement for an investment product (or are being sold one), see if you can spot the appeal to your asymmetric loss aversion. Maybe they are trying to get you to buy a certain portfolio because it is less volatile? An insurance company protects your "downside risk" for a fee? Trading systems brag about having stop-losses and math equations to sell out if it goes down? They are all appealing to your natural asymmetric loss aversion; make a hobby of discerning it.

Thankfully investing in the stock market is not as extreme as our coin flip thought experiment. If you are diversified and investing in normal equities, outside of catastrophic financial collapse you can't lose *all* of your investment.

The flip side to the risk of selling out of the market is to invest in highly aggressive things that are going through a boom. Another large portion of financial services sales are **greed baiting**.

During the real estate boom/bubble I worked at a savings and loan bank. I saw many Depression-era customers cash in their CDs to speculate on real estate. During this same time, I saw people liquidate their IRAs (paying taxes on all of it) to speculate on real estate. When the stock market is skyrocketing, people with minimal investing experience will come out of the woodwork wanting to buy into the most aggressive portfolio available.

People have this innate impulse to suddenly have complete comfort with considerable risk. It's a devil that lives in all our souls. Just as temporary market declines create temporary insanity, so do bubbles. Beware veering off course by fleeting "opportunities." It never feels like greed. It will always feel like "investing," when in reality it is speculating.

Look for a key marker of a price bubble: rates of return that exceed the historical trendline for an extended period of time, for no fundamental reason. When amateurs see these high growth rates, it attracts ignorant money, causing prices to rise beyond reason. Make no mistake, people always justify themselves, for no one ever declares that they are speculating. People can be incredibly articulate and informed about their terrible decisions.

Price bubbles are a highly tangible illustration of humans trying to game the system. But is this system gameable? Is it possible to be the village money manager of Lake Wobegon, where all the returns are above average?

An Ungameable System: The Divining Rod of Outperformance

Let's pivot to portfolio construction. First, let us state the obvious: you have a money manager. This person (or persons) is either going to be (1) someone else, or (2) you. This is an important thing to point out because as I mention "money managers," you need to have a mental image of who this person is and not let it be an aloof reference. If you aren't working with someone, you need to think "me" when I say this—even if I speak with an assumption that this is a professional.

What are the implicit goals of most money managers? This may seem obvious, but normally goals aren't outright declared, but meekly *implied*. I would say that these goals are some mix of:

1. Lower volatility
2. Increase performance

They imply they can handicap the index. This is the noble pursuit of stock-like returns while enjoying less-than-stock-like volatility. Or perhaps even the pursuit of moderate returns with less-than-moderate volatility. They want to beat the system.

If you are managing money yourself, many of your decisions incorporate this presumption. Your methods may or may not be effective, but you are hoping to catch the market on its upswings and get out of the way of downswings. Professionals are no different fundamentally. They may have methods, research teams, or math equations, but the goals are ordinarily the same.

I would like to pose a question: ***can you handicap the stock market? In other words, can you consistently outperform it or somehow maintain the same return and lower your risk?***

American society has a love-hate romance with Wall Street, stock trading, and the capital markets. Studies show over and over again that *on average* traders and money managers *underperform* the general stock market. As we learned with our **9%** vs. **10%** illustration, *any* amount of underperformance is too much. We'll get into these studies in a moment. For now, let's look at the pursuit of these goals.

Goal #1: Lower Volatility

When I asked you the question about handicapping the stock market, I really hope that you caught my red herring: risk. I used the phrase "lower your *risk*." If you caught it, congratulations on riding the bike without training wheels. This is why we spent all that time redefining risk, because the word "risk" is thrown around in varied and misleading ways. If you accept the premise that volatility isn't a risk at all, then why go through the effort of trying to "lower volatility"?

Lower volatility is fine. Heck, who wouldn't want a boring excellent long-term return? The problem is, can you lower volatility without sacrificing return?

I would argue that most efforts to lower volatility lower long-term expected return. If you are using hedging strategies on your stock positions, the cost to set this up will directly cost you returns. If you are using an insurance company (through an annuity) for long-term money you aren't taking withdrawals from, the indelible business reality is that the insurance makes money because on average the amount you pay in fees is going to be less than what you receive in benefits.

The nature of trading—that is, the structure of the stock market *as a market*—means that there is always someone on the other side of your efforts to lower volatility getting your forfeited returns when you are wrong. The stock market is much like a zero sum game, but it's a **11.62%** sum game on average per year. There are going to be some right people, some wrong people, but the sandbox return averages **11.62%**. Think of this as a line in the sand. When you put yourself on the doubting side of that line *by any extent,* I believe that you will always be wrong in the long term and this will lower your return. It's just the reality as a participant in this market.

It should be assumed that any effort to lower volatility simultaneously lowers your return, and inevitably lowers your long-term wealth. Unless you have a short time horizon, effort to lower volatility is self-destructive. It is the near certain forfeiture of future wealth.

A more worthy sacrifice would be to sacrifice your sense of comfort and use your energy resisting self-destructive behavior. Use that extra return money to get yourself a massage, attend a meditation retreat, spend some time at a sweat lodge, or do whatever it takes to stay the course.

To state it unequivocally: I do not think you should even try to lower or avoid volatility. In most cases, certainly in average cases, if a money manager claims lower volatility as a benefit, I don't think you should see it as value—you should see it as a *cost*.

Goal #2: Increase Performance

While it is easy to quantify the financial disadvantage of lowering volatility, any amount of increased performance is *highly* valuable. If you can increase your return above the historical averages *at all*, this multiplies wealth over the long term.

As I said, "money manager" can mean either you or somebody else. More precisely we could split our evaluation between (1) professional money managers and (2) everybody else. Let's then look at how each of these groups have performed.

Professional money managers are people you hire to manage your investments for you. Before this chapter is done I will go over what you need to know in working with a financial advisor. For now, let's look at this logically.

If you are working with a professional, you can assume that you are paying somewhere between 1%–6% per year. Yes, much to my horror, some money managers charge 6% per year. This is the all-in cost, including management fees, expense ratios for the funds themselves, and trading costs. If you are working with a commissioned broker, often your commissions will average out in this range over an extended period of time. To illustrate what these costs mean, let's assume your costs are 2%. Also, for simplicity's sake, let's assume that the portfolio is 100% in the S&P 500.

So if normally you'd average **11.62%**, you should expect to only get **9.62%** after costs. Unfortunately, even though you've given up some return, your volatility will be exactly the same. If the market goes down **10%** over a one-year period, your portfolio, after costs, goes down **12%**. If it goes up **30%**, your portfolio would go up **28%**.

Earlier we talked about how on a longer term basis, annual returns *roughly* follow a bell curve, but don't follow a normal distribution *exactly*. We can appropriately use a bell curve to get a *rough* expectation of return. On a one-year basis, about two thirds of the time you'd expect the return to fall between **-9.59%** and **32.84%**. Subtracting out 2% costs fully *left-shifts* your bell curve as you can see on the next page.

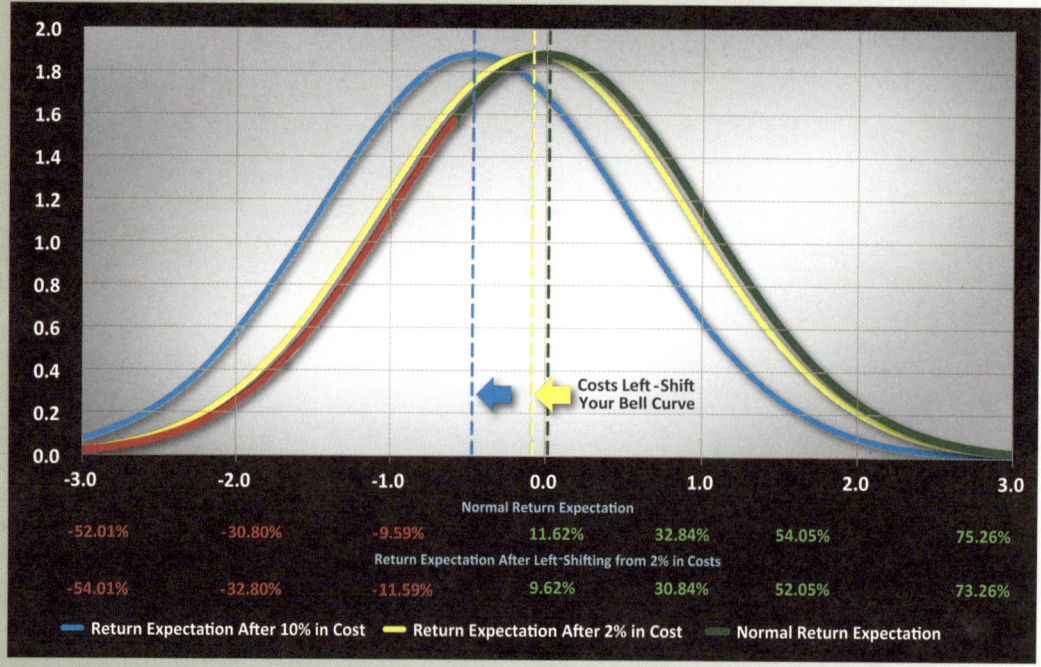

If your personal goal is to beat the index average of **11.62%**, statistically, on any given year, the market has a 50% chance of doing this on its own. If you pay someone 2% and your money is 100% in the S&P 500, two very important things happen:

- Your expected average return drops to **9.62%**
- You need the market to return **13.62%** return in order to get to the **11.62%** average after the 2% cost are taken out

When you combine these two forces, it means that as costs go up, the likelihood of averaging *at least* the S&P 500's return rapidly goes down. You need to get *lucky* to end up *average*. How lucky? You could break it down using 2% in costs:

- Expected return = **9.62%** (this is **11.62%** - 2%)
- Needed return to achieve **11.62%** average = **13.62%**
- *Probability* of a **13.62%** return = **42.520979%**

Again, we are assuming a perfect distribution to make this rough point. This may not sound like such a big deal, but keep in mind that what is "normal" for one-year periods is the very broad range of **-9.59%** to **32.84%** (a 42.43%-wide range with a **11.62%** average). As we move up the time-frame, the width of a "normal" expectation range narrows. For 20-year periods, this range is from **7.89%** to **14.40%** (a 6.51%-wide range with a **11.14%** average). This narrower range makes beating the average by 2% far more unlikely.

This is what these 20-year numbers look like:

- Expected return = **9.14%** (this is **11.14%** - 2%)
- Needed return (20-year average) to achieve **11.14%** average = **13.14%**
- *Probability* of a **13.14%** 20-year average return = **10.950165%**

As portfolio costs go up, expectations should go down. At the bottom of the page is a chart of all of these numbers. Again, the stock market only *sort of* follows a normal distribution, but this is a rough idea. Although these numbers are not fully predictive, your expectations should not wander far from these results.

It should be no surprise then that few fund managers beat the S&P 500 on the short term, but especially not over any length of time. After 30 years, averaging a **11.18%** is very ordinary if you are paying no costs. However, if you are paying 2% in costs, averaging **11.18%** would be an extraordinary result—as in, a 1 in 1,000 rarity of performance. Welcome to life's easiest path to extraordinary: do nothing, and pay as little as possible.

Probability of Above Average Returns

	1 Year			5 Year			10 Year		
Cost	Expected	Needed	Probability	Expected	Needed	Probability	Expected	Needed	Probability
0%	11.62%	11.62%	50.000000%	10.25%	10.25%	50.000000%	10.38%	10.38%	50.000000%
1%	10.62%	12.62%	46.243878%	9.25%	11.25%	40.575766%	9.38%	11.38%	35.972466%
2%	9.62%	13.62%	42.520979%	8.25%	12.25%	31.670126%	8.38%	12.38%	23.625851%
3%	8.62%	14.62%	38.863647%	7.25%	13.25%	23.717635%	7.38%	13.38%	14.060959%
4%	7.62%	15.62%	35.302505%	6.25%	14.25%	17.007054%	6.38%	14.38%	7.539033%
5%	6.62%	16.62%	31.865695%	5.25%	15.25%	11.656042%	5.38%	15.38%	3.624930%
6%	5.62%	17.62%	28.578211%	4.25%	16.25%	7.623950%	4.38%	16.38%	1.557430%
7%	4.62%	18.62%	25.461381%	3.25%	17.25%	4.752883%	3.38%	17.38%	0.596236%
8%	3.62%	19.62%	22.532483%	2.25%	18.25%	2.821028%	2.38%	18.38%	0.202938%
9%	2.62%	20.62%	19.804529%	1.25%	19.25%	1.592673%	1.38%	19.38%	0.061302%
10%	1.62%	21.62%	17.286207%	0.25%	20.25%	0.854615%	0.38%	20.38%	0.016411%

	15 Year			20 Year			30 Year		
Cost	Expected	Needed	Probability	Expected	Needed	Probability	Expected	Needed	Probability
0%	10.77%	10.77%	50.000000%	11.14%	11.14%	50.000000%	11.18%	11.18%	50.000000%
1%	9.77%	11.77%	32.458116%	10.14%	12.14%	26.941231%	10.18%	12.18%	6.086506%
2%	8.77%	12.77%	18.145018%	9.14%	13.14%	10.950165%	9.18%	13.18%	0.098372%
3%	7.77%	13.77%	8.616132%	8.14%	14.14%	3.260803%	8.18%	14.18%	0.000172%
4%	6.77%	14.77%	3.440198%	7.14%	15.14%	0.697855%	7.18%	15.18%	0.000000%
5%	5.77%	15.77%	1.146404%	6.14%	16.14%	0.105975%	6.18%	16.18%	0.000000%
6%	4.77%	16.77%	0.317097%	5.14%	17.14%	0.011321%	5.18%	17.18%	0.000000%
7%	3.77%	17.77%	0.072506%	4.14%	18.14%	0.000846%	4.18%	18.18%	0.000000%
8%	2.77%	18.77%	0.013663%	3.14%	19.14%	0.000044%	3.18%	19.18%	0.000000%
9%	1.77%	19.77%	0.002117%	2.14%	20.14%	0.000002%	2.18%	20.18%	0.000000%
10%	0.77%	20.77%	0.000269%	1.14%	21.14%	0.000000%	1.18%	21.18%	0.000000%

One could expect from this table that 60% of professionally run funds underperform on any one year. The truth is that around 75–90% of fund managers underperform each year on a 12-month basis. There are a lot reasons to explain this gap, but I suspect that this is because despite their reputation, fund managers are humans too. They are susceptible to emotional investing and inopportune market moves just like everyone else.

Naturally you wouldn't pay someone 2% to just buy and hold the S&P 500. No money manager that I'm aware of only passively invests in the S&P 500. Assessments of professional money managers don't enable easy apples to apples comparison. However, 2% is a normal "all in" cost amount and you could easily add another 1% to account for typical underperformance. If a professional is managing your money for you, a realistic expectation is to lag the index by 3%.

Now, before you get too high and mighty, here's the catch: if you are *managing your own* investments the picture is *even worse.* Each year the research company DALBAR creates their Quantitative Analysis of Investor Behavior (QAIB). The 22nd edition of the QAIB takes us up through December 31, 2015—the one-year period is just the performance in 2015, not a rolling average. For the 30 years that ended on that date, they report that the S&P 500 produced an annual return of **10.35%**, while the average equity mutual fund investor got **3.66%**.[6] This is a *6.69% return gap.* The study also confirms that this gap is nearly entirely attributed to the investor's self-destructive behavior. A similar wide performance gap also exists for bond investors.

We can see the results from this study in the table below. A more visually digestible version of this features on the opposite page. The equities are green and fixed income orange with the lighter colors to the right showing the underperformance.

Average Individual Investor Results

| | Inflation | Equity Funds | | | Fixed Income Funds | | |
		S&P 500	Average Investor Returns	Difference to S&P 500	Barclays Aggregate Bond	Average Investor Returns	Difference to Barclays
30 Year	2.60%	10.35%	3.66%	-6.69%	6.73%	0.59%	-6.14%
20 Year	2.20%	8.19%	4.67%	-3.52%	5.34%	0.51%	-4.83%
10 Year	1.88%	7.31%	4.23%	-3.08%	4.51%	0.39%	-4.12%
5 Year	1.58%	12.57%	6.92%	-5.65%	3.25%	0.10%	-3.15%
3 Year	1.07%	15.13%	8.85%	-6.28%	1.44%	-1.76%	-3.20%
1 Year	0.95%	1.38%	-2.28%	-3.66%	0.55%	-3.11%	-3.66%

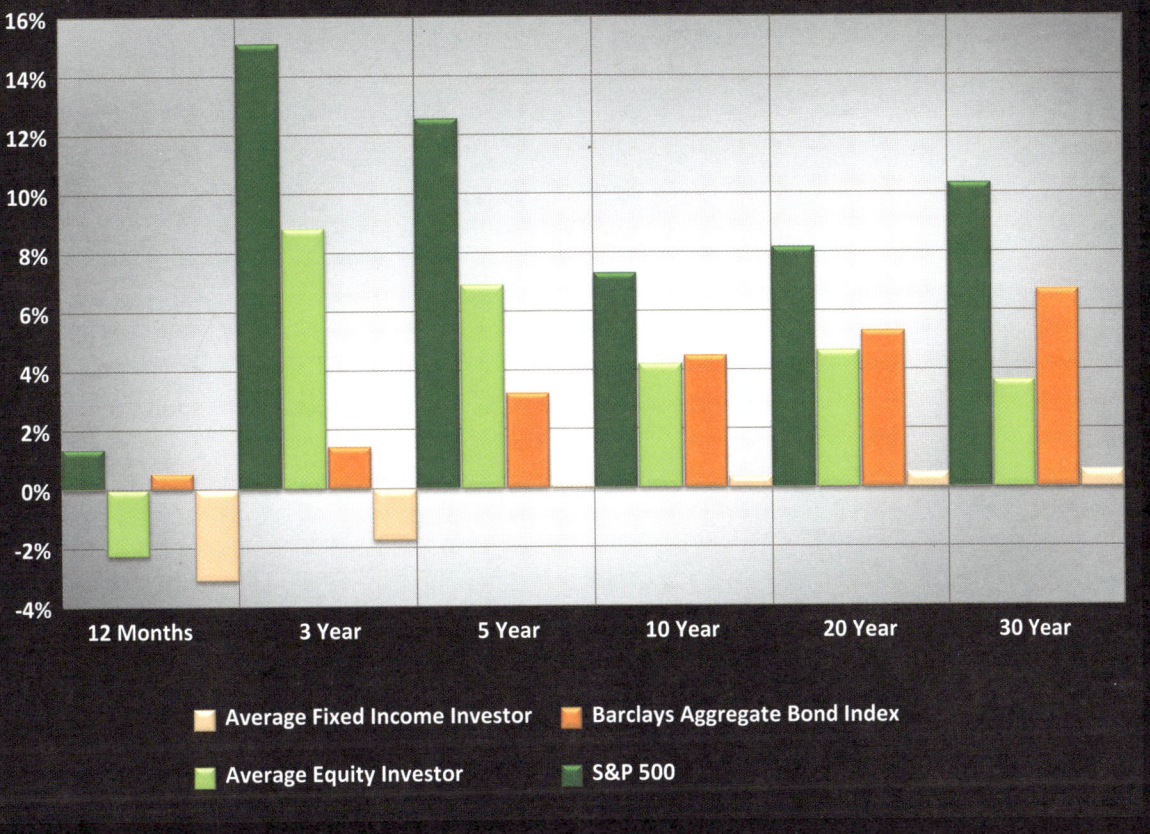

Average Fixed Income Investor		Barclays Aggregate Bond Index
Average Equity Investor		S&P 500

As we saw earlier, while portfolio costs should certainly lower expectations, they don't fully explain this performance gap. The additional underperformance comes when people do what feels right emotionally: they sell when it goes down and buy after it has gone up. This always feels logical and responsible, but never works in the long run. When you try to outsmart the market, you ride to war, but not to victory. Okay, I *may* have taken that from *The Lord of the Rings*.

If we combine the DALBAR study with my probability numbers, we are pretty confident that regardless of what your brother-in-law brags about, over time, hardly anyone beats the index. If we assume the same volatility, but use the DALBAR averages, we can infer that last year roughly 25.61% of individual equity mutual fund investors beat the index. If we go out to 20 years, we can predict that only 2.34% of investors beat it.

At the top of the next page is a table of my estimations.

Beating the Index

	Estimated % of Equity Mutual Fund Investors Beating the Index
1 Year	25.61%
5 Year	34.55%
10 Year	13.47%
20 Year	2.34%
30 Year	0.00000029%

My broad advice is to never sell. If you never sell, you have the lovely assurance that your performance is almost certain to beat out 80% of your neighbors each year and nearly all of them over the long term. You will never beat the market, but you will nearly always have above average returns—if you are looking at the real life average experience of actual people.

I'm not saying the stock market is absolutely ungameable, but you as an individual are better off *on average* assuming that it is. Just simply never sell and you'll do fine. Those who try to beat the index consistently get less than the index. My notion is: why not just be happy with the index knowing that you are beating the average *investor*?

A massive portion of financial journalism is devoted to the vain task of prognostication. Part of the Wall Street mystique is the idea that some magical part of humanity can see the future. No profession has this. At best there are probabilities and we've already gone over all the probabilities you need to know. You don't ask your doctor if you'll break an arm in the next five years. You don't ask your lawyer if you're going to get sued. Professionals should talk in averages and statistics, not prophesies. Run, do not walk, from people offering certainty.

The stock market is a steady moving train that at times erratically stops, goes backwards, and bolts forward just as masses of passengers jump off, declaring the train to be broken. Some people think that by jumping off, they can outrun the train, or at least avoid the "risk" of going backward. The train inevitably takes off without them.

Be a calm passenger. Ignore the movement and enjoy the beautiful scenery out the window. Hum quietly as your fellow passengers lose their minds throughout the journey. You'll travel *much* farther.

The Secret Sauce

Knowing what you now know, portfolio construction becomes fairly automatic. We embrace volatility as normal—the price of admission. Money eventually buys stuff and your job is to make sure that you are giving yourself enough of a time cushion to allow the stock market to go through normal declines and recoveries.

How to Think about Financial Planning

Preventing permanent loss is very much about controlling the timing of the sale. You should not invest unless you are confident that you don't need the money beyond the time it normally takes for the market to recover from a decline. Financial planning means pre-deciding when your money will buy stuff and controlling the timing of exiting of the market around this.

You will often hear people describe both a "short-term" and "long-term" investing horizon, but all I hear is semantics. In the absence of a comprehensive financial plan, it's an artificial distinction. The short term doesn't matter unless you expect to spend that money. Money only counts as income once you are buying stuff with it.

How to View your Portfolio

The first factor you have to come to terms with is when your money will buy stuff. This has nothing to do with your age, retirement status, or even your risk tolerance. What is the magic date when your dollars will be converted into goods and services?

We can then segment your money up into three key categories:

1. Money you need *income* from
2. Money that will buy stuff *soon*
3. Money that will buy stuff a *long time* from now

Think of each of these categories as three separate portfolios. It wouldn't hurt to actually keep these as three separate accounts if you need all three.

Income Money

Income money is money that you are getting regular paychecks from. When you think of money that you are taking income from, it's highly important to know whether or not you are buying stuff with that income. Sometimes I'll have clients tell me that they just want to get income from their money. My first question is if they are going to *spend* that income. If you are taking income from your money and it's just building up in your bank account, this means you have too much money in the income money category.

Determining how much income money you need to fill your *income gap* is fairly simple:

Calculating the Income Gap

Amount of Money Needed to Buy Stuff - **Amount Coming in from Fixed Sources** = **Income Gap**

Let's say you spend $5,000 per month and you get $3,000 from pensions and Social Security. You have a $2,000 income gap.

Calculating the Income Gap

$5,000 - $3,000 = $2,000

To get an annual figure, multiply it by 12 months and you have need $24,000 per year from your investments. Let's say that you are able to reliably get **5%** from an investment. You would need to fund that investment with $480,000. Here's the math:

Filling in the Income Gap

$$\frac{\$24,000}{5\% \ (0.05)} = \$480,000$$

Which investments are suitable for generating this amount of income? They constantly change. Once upon a time, a bank CD would do the trick, but that ship has sailed. At other times, federal government bonds worked great for income, but these days, no dice. Currently, if for some reason I can't use equities, I've used bond ladders (usually municipal or corporate) and lower cost annuities.

Each household has a subjective amount of *income gap sensitivity*. Let's say the person from the example above only has $480,000 and there's *no way* to reduce their $2,000 per month income need. I wouldn't have this person invest in anything that isn't highly reliable with mild volatility. This household has no wiggle room to patiently wait through stock declines. This is unfortunate because they will *probably* be better off in stock, but near term stock market performance is not reliable.

On the other hand, if the household needs $480,000 to fill the income gap, but they have $1,000,000, they have the cushion to invest in a manner that's most likely to last as long as possible and generate the strongest buying power.

At times you'll hear of income methods such as keeping 2 years of income in cash, or even 5 years in cash. You may also hear of the "bucket strategy" where the first 2 years are in a cash "bucket," years 3–7 are in a bond "bucket" and the rest is in the stock "bucket." There are a lot of roads that lead to Rome and we won't analyze them here. As you know by now, I believe that people should have as much in equities as possible.

Just as I mourn when people fail to start saving early and investing in equities, I cringe when they are too conservative in retirement. In the span of a 30-year retirement, being too conservative at the beginning can innocently impoverish you at the end. If you choose to invest in fixed income investments instead of equities, it is likely to result in a balance that is *multiples* lower than what it would have been.

Let's illustrate what would seem like an aggressive retirement income strategy: investing *all* of the money from which you plan to take income in the S&P 500 and never touching the balance. Your income will come to you in the form of dividends and the balance does whatever it does. Since 1928 dividend rates have changed with time like this:

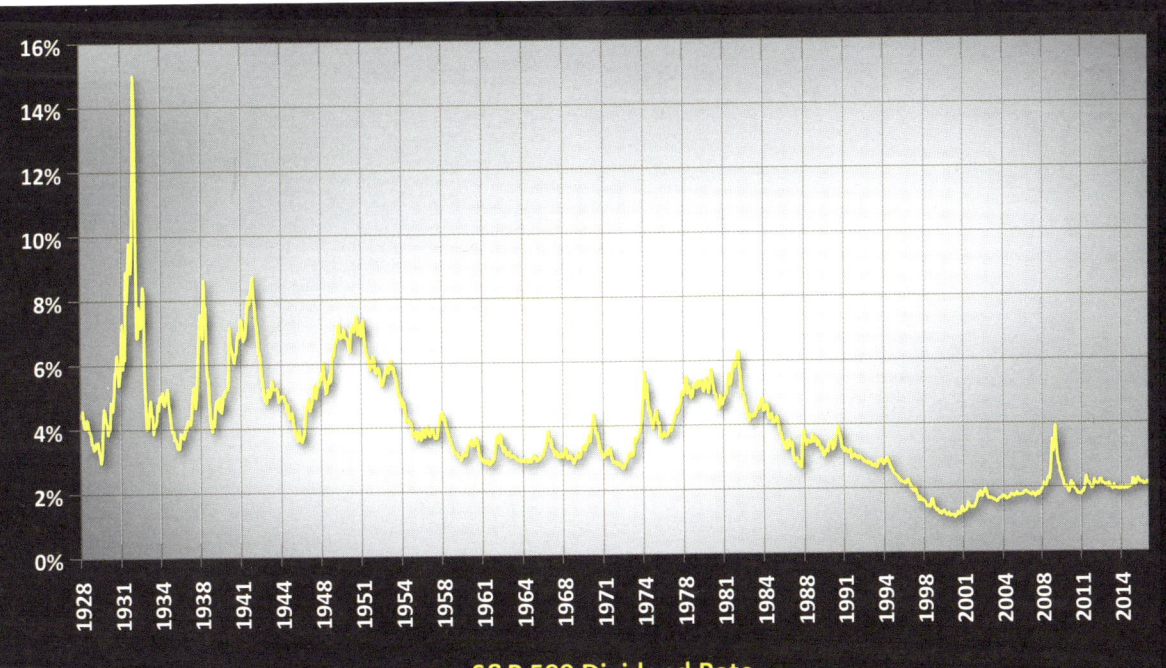

— S&P 500 Dividend Rate

Let's say it's January 1, 1928 and you do the math and find out that your income gap is $1.00. In 1928, the dividend rate on stocks was 4.37%. This tells you that you need $22.88 in order to fill in your $1.00 income gap with the dividends from stocks. To be sure, at first this $22.88 meets 100% of your $1.00 income gap need. Also, as inflation changes your income needs to change along with it—we will adjust your income as prices change.

Shortly after your retirement, the Great Depression begins. This causes three different moving parts to alter how those dividends meet your income needs:

1. Your account balance falls horrifically (a bad thing)
2. Deflation causes the price of stuff to go down (a good thing)
3. Dividend rates go up as high as 15% (a good thing)

While at the beginning of this, the dividends met 100% of your needs, at its worst point, the dividends only met 71.54% of your income gap needs. This is accounting for all of these three moving parts. In real money, you need to figure out how to live on a fourth less money. The plan didn't quite work how it was intended.

This actually wasn't as bad as your younger brother who did the same plan when he retired on January 1, 1931. For him, he funded a stock account where his dividends were meeting 100% of his income need. As the three forces moved around, at one point his dividends were only giving him 52.82% of his income gap needs. A more extreme plan failure.

The good news for the fictional brothers is that they seem to be immortal and are today still collecting dividends. They've never touched the principal and keep collecting their dividends each month. Because of this, their account balance has continued to grow *even as* they received dividends. Not only has the dividend growth handily kept up with inflation, but today they are receiving *3–4 times more* income than what they need. This is even accounting for 89 years of inflation—acknowledging that in most years their "income need" goes up with rising prices. While they had the bad luck of retiring at the onset of the Great Depression, in time the strategy worked out. We could see their dividends meeting their income gap over time:

Dividends meeting Income Gap over Time

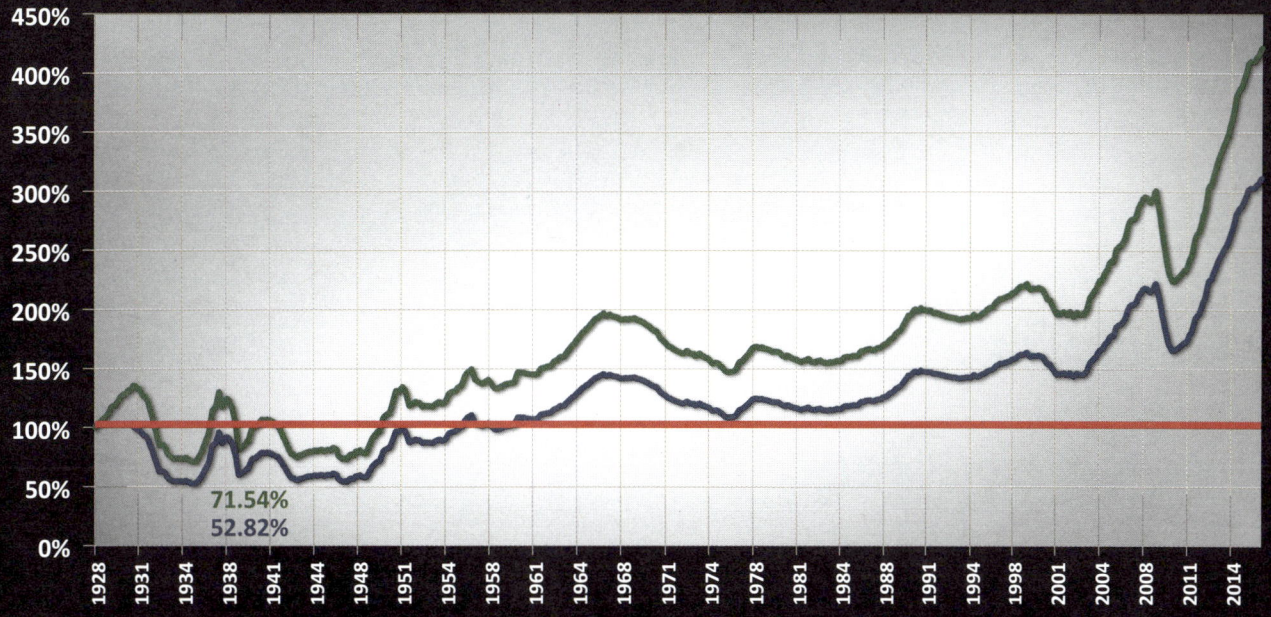

So you now understand the concept here. The most important number is the percentage of their income gap needs met. The best case scenario is that you retire and the dividends meet 100% of your income needs for the rest of your life and you never have to make budget cuts.

Below is a graph of the historic numbers. Each year we are assuming that you retire on January 1 of that year.

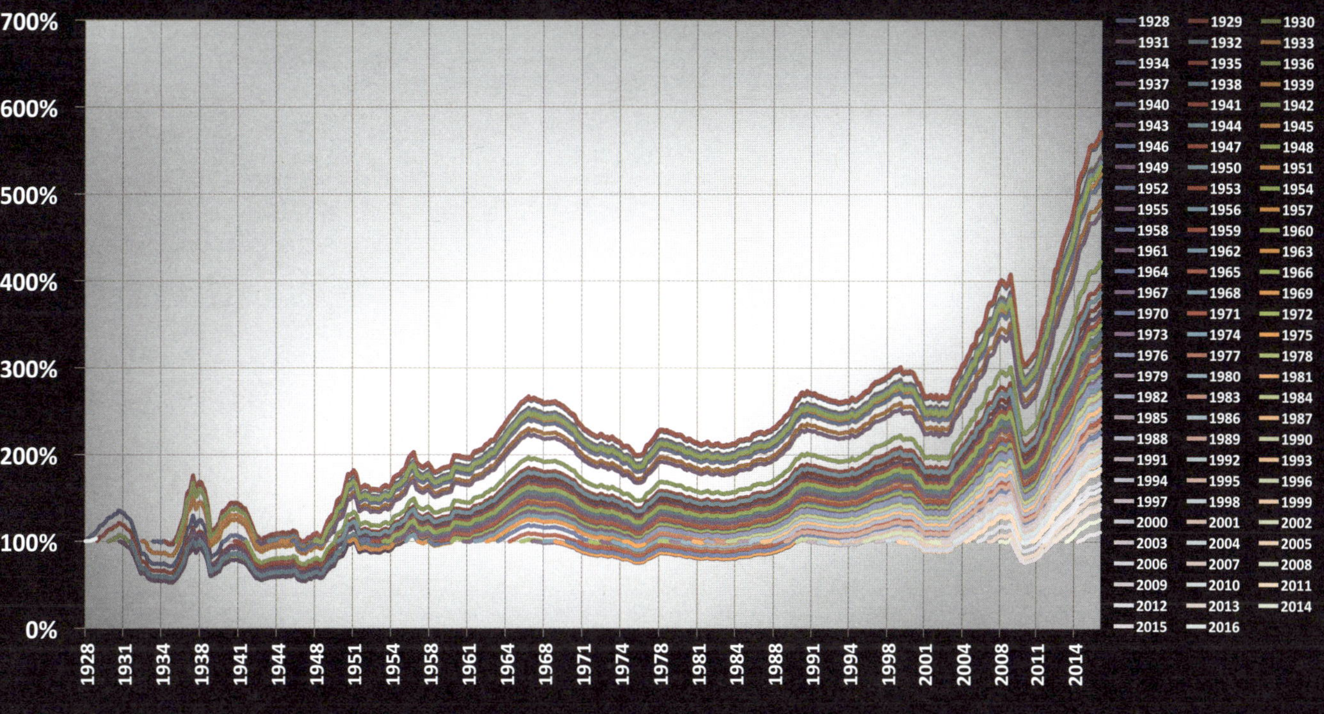

Using Dividends for Income Gap

	Worst	Best		Worst	Best
1928	71.54%	421.61%	1973	89.08%	255.45%
1929	63.86%	376.37%	1974	90.47%	259.43%
1930	56.57%	333.42%	1975	94.92%	272.18%
1931	52.82%	311.33%	1976	99.64%	285.73%
1932	57.89%	341.21%	1977	99.26%	270.30%
1933	83.70%	493.29%	1978	92.18%	251.00%
1934	96.18%	566.83%	1979	92.85%	252.84%
1935	97.06%	572.07%	1980	94.88%	258.36%
1936	94.52%	544.20%	1981	97.54%	265.61%
1937	63.50%	365.61%	1982	98.43%	268.01%
1938	58.85%	338.81%	1983	98.77%	268.94%
1939	89.66%	516.24%	1984	99.93%	270.90%
1940	73.31%	422.10%	1985	100.00%	263.69%
1941	68.85%	396.38%	1986	100.00%	261.28%
1942	73.39%	422.53%	1987	99.68%	253.60%
1943	94.17%	542.20%	1988	100.00%	247.28%
1944	93.27%	537.00%	1989	100.00%	233.59%
1945	90.96%	523.73%	1990	98.43%	216.47%
1946	89.75%	516.75%	1991	95.69%	210.45%
1947	99.09%	570.52%	1992	97.11%	213.57%
1948	98.67%	531.95%	1993	98.87%	217.45%
1949	100.00%	479.88%	1994	100.00%	219.23%
1950	100.00%	386.80%	1995	99.27%	215.86%
1951	90.19%	323.40%	1996	96.95%	210.36%
1952	98.98%	354.91%	1997	92.82%	201.40%
1953	99.59%	357.10%	1998	90.66%	196.71%
1954	99.54%	349.55%	1999	88.02%	190.99%
1955	100.00%	326.76%	2000	88.85%	192.79%
1956	95.73%	303.77%	2001	94.47%	204.97%
1957	94.81%	300.82%	2002	98.18%	213.02%
1958	95.67%	303.57%	2003	99.22%	213.36%
1959	100.00%	312.49%	2004	100.00%	199.18%
1960	100.00%	297.11%	2005	97.44%	183.20%
1961	99.33%	289.76%	2006	89.08%	167.50%
1962	97.71%	280.19%	2007	81.24%	152.75%
1963	93.92%	269.31%	2008	76.11%	143.10%
1964	88.81%	254.67%	2009	75.89%	142.69%
1965	81.84%	234.67%	2010	98.07%	184.40%
1966	76.61%	219.68%	2011	100.00%	181.53%
1967	75.41%	216.23%	2012	100.00%	160.47%
1968	76.82%	220.30%	2013	100.00%	138.22%
1969	76.30%	218.79%	2014	100.00%	125.07%
1970	78.88%	226.19%	2015	100.00%	110.88%
1971	83.94%	240.69%	2016	100.00%	102.97%
1972	88.37%	253.41%			

Of this chart of too many lines, it may be easier to simply look at the numbers on the long table on left side this page. We can see the two brothers in 1928 and 1931, along with how they would have fared retiring in each year.

As aggressive as this method may have sounded, the strategy works better than one might expect. 19% of the time, you never experienced a pay cut and dividends always met your needs. Half the time, the dividend met 95%+ of your income needs. On the opposite page is a summary—"worst case range" meaning how much of your income needs were satisfied with the dividends.

Keep in mind that these worst case scenarios are usually for a season of time early on in the retirement—usually within the first 10 years of retirement. The best news is that in *all* instances, as growth compounded the balance of the equity account, your dividends exceed your needs. Because you are growing in your ability to buy stuff, you are growing in wealth as we've defined it.

If we were to run these scenarios and reinvest extra income, the results would be all the more powerful. As I see these results, while some of the people had to pinch pennies during some years, *all* of them eventually saw their income exceed their needs.

Summary of Worst Case Scenarios

Worst Case Range	Number in Range	% of Instances	% of Instances
100%	17	19%	
95% - 100%	28	31%	
90% - 95%	15	17%	81%
85% - 90%	8	9%	
80% - 85%	4	4%	
70% - 80%	10	11%	
60% - 70%	3	3%	19%
50% - 60%	4	4%	
Total Number of Years			89

This is not foolproof. It favors those with less income gap sensitivity. In the worst case scenario, they would be making some hard decisions during the Great Depression. However, if they had *twice* the money and spent *half* the dividends as income and reinvested the rest, then even at the worst point in history, the plan works comfortably.

If you have more than twice your income gap amount, invest 100% in stock, spend half your dividends as income and reinvest the other half. While it may sound aggressive to have your *income money* in equities, I feel that this focuses your energy on the true enemy: running out of money before you run out of days. When it comes to retirement income, it is not enough to just get the income. The principal must be growing to keep up with rising costs.

Soon Money

The second category of money is money that will be spent "soon." This may be a wedding, car, or down payment on a house. The time-frame for these expenses is within two years. If it's within two years, the money should be 100% in cash. If it's 2–7 years, you can look at some short-term bonds. If it's more than 7 years, I wouldn't call this "soon" money and it should usually be in equities.

These days, attractive short-term rates are hard to come by. It's no fun having your money not earning anything, but it's far less festive permanently losing buying power when you end up in a position where you *must* spend money that has declined in the stock market.

Long-Term Money

If that magic date of when your money will be converted into goods is more than 15 years from now it needs to be 100% in equities. Declines longer than this simply do not have historical precedent in modern times. As you move down the range and you think you probably aren't going to spend the money for 7–15 years, you are *probably* going to be okay being 100% in equities. Even the 2008 Financial Crisis was completely erased in five and a half years. Let's review what we've learned. **Of all the numbers I've thrown at you, on the opposite page are the most important charts.**

It's crucial to be really honest when you imagine when the dollars in your portfolio will buy stuff. It very well may not be in your lifetime, nor your children's lifetime. Many people have investments that are on the indefinite time horizon. There is no tangible time-frame for when that money will buy stuff. In such a case, invest 100% in equities. If your portfolio is intended to serve multi-generational needs, this is especially true.

Of course, there are exceptions to this which include:

1. You truly do have a short-term objective (you need a down payment on a house in two years, or your child is starting college next year)
2. You have absolutely no stomach for volatility and do impulsive things when under stress
3. You don't care and just want something simple that gives you some income and keeps up with inflation, but you don't care about *outpacing* rising prices
4. You have a principled or personal aversion to paying taxes and need a highly tax-efficient strategy

The Meat and Potatoes

Thus far I have avoided the hype of saying *how much* your investments could grow and focused more on the principle that (very nearly) everyone has a long-term investing horizon and because of this (very nearly) everyone should be invested entirely in stocks. This is the moment when I tell you the secret sauce on how I think you should invest.

First of all, I can't pass up the chance to remind you that while the specific equity investment mix certainly matters, it isn't nearly as important as investing in equities and not panicking out when stocks are volatile. Or to put it another way, what matters is not whether or not you chose XYZ or ABC but whether or not you were in equities *at all*. Investment selection matters, but your emotional energy should be on *staying* in equities, not choosing them.

Secondly, let's talk about the ways that people usually invest. Normally it's with a financial advisor, a do-it-yourself online trading platform, or through work. Financial advisors are usually in three places:

Summary of Rolling Total Return Performance of the S&P 500 1928-2016

Period	Worst	Average	Best	% Positive	% of the Time a Positive Return Period Follows a Negative Return Period
1 Year	-68.34%	11.62%	190.73%	73.96%	69.47%
5 Years	-18.42%	10.25%	36.44%	88.79%	90.48%
10 Years	-4.72%	10.38%	21.52%	94.87%	100.00%
15 Years	-0.54%	10.77%	19.80%	99.84%	100.00%
20 Years	1.85%	11.14%	18.51%	100.00%	N/A
30 Years	7.51%	11.18%	14.73%	100.00%	N/A

	Decline Range	Name	Amount of All Declines in Range			PERSPECTIVE OF DECLINE			PERSPECTIVE OF RECOVERY
						Amount of Declines this Bad or Worse	Amount of Declines that Escalate to Next Range	How Often Declines in this Range Happen	Average Length of Declines that Don't Escalate
Normal Declines	1.0 - 2.5%	Routine Declines	58.36%	99.32%		100.00%	41.67%	11.42 days	10.46 days
	2.5 - 5%	Mild Declines	28.40%			41.67%	32.04%	27.42 days	26.36 days
	5 - 10%	Moderate Declines	10.36%			13.35%	21.50%	2.83 months	2.20 months
	10 - 20%	Severe Declines	2.20%			2.87%	23.69%	1.08 years	6.15 months
Bear Markets	20 - 30%	Mild Bear Markets	0.36%	0.68%		0.68%	47.06%	4.62 years	1.96 years
	30 - 40%	Moderate Bear Markets	0.14%			0.32%	56.25%	9.76 years	2.23 years
	40 - 50%	Severe Bear Markets	0.07%			0.18%	61.11%	17.57 years	4.82 years
	50%+	Extreme Bear Markets	0.11%			0.11%	N/A	29.28 years	6.59 years

Asset Class Performance 1928-2016

Asset Class	Return	Beginning Balance	Ending Balance
S&P 500	9.63%	$1.00	$3,269.24
Long-Term Corporate Bonds	5.96%	$1.00	$162.79
Long-Term Government Bonds	5.51%	$1.00	$112.48
Intermediate-Term Government Bonds	5.18%	$1.00	$85.33
U.S. Treasury Bills	3.42%	$1.00	$19.33
Inflation	3.04%	$1.00	$13.69

Asset Class Performance 1928-2016 (Inflation Adjusted)

Asset Class	Return	Beginning Balance	Ending Balance
S&P 500	6.17%	$1.00	$193.53
Long-Term Corporate Bonds	2.71%	$1.00	$10.54
Long-Term Government Bonds	2.27%	$1.00	$7.20
Intermediate-Term Government Bonds	2.00%	$1.00	$5.72
U.S. Treasury Bills	0.29%	$1.00	$1.29
Inflation	0.00%	$1.00	$1.00

1. Wirehouses (think of any classic Wall Street firm)
2. Banking institutions (think of a bank or credit union, odds are they have an investing arm)
3. Independents and Registered Investment Advisors (RIAs) (in most cases, these advisors operate private practices that they brand and own)

It's getting harder to characterize the difference in experience between these venues. I have worked in all three. I found a happy home as an RIA with my own firm, where I can teach the public, write, and manage client accounts according to philosophies that I've personally nurtured. This wouldn't be possible at a big name brand firm or bank.

If you can get a 401(k) through your work, certainly do. If you are reclusive, inherently mistrustful, or feel that you'd rather just go it alone, there are online investing platforms. We've all seen the ads.

Thirdly, investment selection is nearly infinite. For this book we have focused entirely on the S&P 500 as a long-term generalization of "the market," but as I said earlier, I don't advocate investing 100% of your money into it.

I'm not going to advise specific investments, but I'll tell you what *types* of investments to look for. Often they are categorized by where they are invested. The first distinction is where it's invested geographically. This can be:

1. Domestic (meaning it's in the U.S.)
2. International (meaning it's outside of the U.S.)

Simple enough. However, sometimes "international" can mean what I would call "global." It is both U.S. and non-U.S.. This is key because it affects how much you are diversified. If your goal is to be 30% in non-U.S. and you buy an "international" investments that is half in U.S., you end up with only 15% international. So mind your p's and q's.

Because of this, sometimes the title will say "ex-U.S.," meaning it's the whole world *except for* U.S. equities. Other geographies can be:

1. Emerging Markets
2. Latin America
3. BRIC (stands for Brazil, Russia, India, China)
4. China
5. Middle East
6. Africa

So on and so forth. Nearly everything you can think of exists out there as an investment option. Another nuance you'll hear are the terms value, growth, and blend. Generally these will tell you how the companies deal with their profits.

1. Value—These companies tend to be more traditional and are usually priced lower than the broader stock market. They also give you more profits in the form of dividends that you can either take as income or reinvest in the stock.
2. Growth—These companies tend to not pay dividends and use the profit to invest in the company. They also tend to be priced higher than the average stock and usually experience more volatility.

To me, both these terms are misnomers. I think that the term "growth" is misleading. It's easy to imagine people picking their 401(k) investments, seeing the word "growth," and picking it because, of course, they want growth. "Value" can be confusing because the word can also mean the investing approach of looking for undervalued investments rather than solely looking for steady, dividend-paying stocks. You will also hear the word "blend," which is a mix of these two approaches.

The next nuance is the size of the company. Generally there are large, mid, and small. These describe the **capitalization** of the stock, which is the value of the entire company as measured by the current share price multiplied by the total number of shares outstanding. You may see an investment described as Large-Cap, Mid-Cap, Small-Cap. You may also hear of Mega-Cap or Micro-Cap. Think of a big company ... that's probably a Large or Mega-Cap stock. Think of a delicious, local chain restaurant that has a few locations in your state... that might be a Micro-Cap stock if it's publicly traded. The virus protection software on your computer might be a Small-Cap stock. You get the idea.

The final nuance of types of equity investments are **sectors**. Sectors are niche areas of the economy. Sectors include:

1. Biotechnology
2. Financials
3. Internet
4. Commodities
5. Health Care
6. Real Estate
7. Precious Metals
8. Transportation
9. Agriculture
10. Energy

So on and so forth. There are four main ways of categorizing investments: geography, investing style, company size, and sector. These can also be called **asset classes**. This will help you decode something if you see it called:

1. Large-Cap Value (you can assume that unless it says otherwise, it is domestic)
2. Small-cap Growth
3. Israel Small-cap
4. Swiss Financials
5. Columbia Health Care
6. Biotechnology (again, you can usually assume it's mostly domestic unless otherwise stated)

The S&P 500 would be considered a Large-Cap Blend. In a 401(k), the selection will be fairly limited to normal mainstream categories. Unless you have a very clear pre-decided buy/sell discipline that's in writing, I wouldn't suggest veering outside of mainstream categories. If you don't know what a buy/sell discipline is, definitely do not veer from these standard categories. There are also bond categories, which we mentioned earlier.

One final word before my general recommendation for a 100% equity portfolio. The plan here is not individualized advice, just a description of what I would consider a diversified equity portfolio. I will soon talk about financial advisors and financial planning. Perhaps it's unsurprising that as a financial advisor and financial planner, I strongly think the bulk of the population should work with one. When I get new clients, I like to get a sense of where they've come from and how they've invested. Nearly always I find mistakes that have cost them far more than what they would have paid to a financial advisor to prevent.

Anyone can set up a portfolio. I don't want to give you the impression that by providing this portfolio, it satisfies the value you would otherwise get from a good financial advisor. It doesn't, but it's better than nothing.

100% Equity Portfolio

	Asset Class	Percentage	US/International
Domestic	Large Growth	10.00%	
	Large Value	10.00%	
	Mid Growth	11.00%	
	Mid Value	11.00%	70.00%
	Small Growth	14.00%	
	Small Value	14.00%	
International	Non US - Large Growth	5.00%	
	Non US - Large Value	5.00%	
	Non US - Mid Blend	4.00%	30.00%
	Non US - Small Blend	4.00%	
	Emerging Markets	12.00%	
		100.00%	100.00%

A few notes:

1. This portfolio over weights the small-cap equities over companies with a large capitalization. Over the long term, historically these have outpaced larger companies. They also tend to decline in price more during downturns. They are more volatile.

2. On the international side I have split it fairly evenly between emerging economies and more established ones. The emerging economies and smaller non-U.S. companies tend to also be more volatile. Investing in non-U.S. companies adds the possibility of currency fluctuations hurting or helping your portfolio. It's just another moving part to consider.

3. The dividends on a portfolio like this are likely to be less than the S&P 500.

4. Each of these asset classes will grow at different rates, which means that every year you'll need to rebalance it.

5. On a year over year basis the high growth areas will shift around. The United States has outperformed the rest of the world the past 8 years. The 8 years before that, much of the world outperformed the United States. It's just what happens when you diversify.

6. Lastly, there is an American bias with this. 70% is made of United States companies.

Once Upon a Time in America

On this last point, you should know that if I were setting up a portfolio for someone from China or Europe I would recommend the exact same thing. I'll spare you the John Wayne pro-America speech, but my U.S. bias is for a number of reasons:

1. America is very good at capitalism.
2. Our economy is among the most stable in the world.
3. We are one of the few industrialized nations without economically punishing demographics.
4. We are huge and established.

If you're like me, it's easy to lose sight of the productivity within our borders. If you looked at the economic output of each of the 50 states and found a country with a comparable economic output, you could relabel the map by equivalent economic power.[7]

Patriotism ain't got nothin' to do with it. We simply have a lot within our borders, as you can see in the map.

Country GDP over Closest U.S. State GDP Equivalent

Financial Advisors and Leaning on the Virtues of Others

Ahhh, financial advisors, golly gee where do I start? First of all, let's declare some realities:

1. No financial advisor self-identifies as a bad financial advisor. Not even the imprisoned ones. When you work in the industry, I can tell you that there is sporadic talk of "bad financial advisors" as if they are lurking within the walls. Whatever financial advisor you work with, know that there's a 50% chance that they are below average. That's how averages work.

2. Poor ethics in advisors are rarely black and white. Willful blindness is a more common sin than outright deception. This can happen when advisors *want* to believe something that benefits them financially.

3. "Bad" financial advisors are not necessarily evil, but they may be incompetent. It is evil to know the right thing for a client and to advise an alternative that enriches the advisor. However, in my observation, this describes a minority of the bad financial advisors out there. The rest are bad because they don't understand what they are selling, or they haven't been around the block long enough to spot fads, or worse yet, they chase fads and drag clients along with them. In short, they don't have the experience, or they have the experience, but it has taught them nothing. It's never a good idea to volunteer to be one of their guinea pigs.

4. Many advisors who work for a big company get the majority of their ongoing financial education from companies selling products. These companies minimally interact with the people who buy their products. This means that advisors who are on the front lines get their knowledge from people who are not. Because of this, advisors tend to repeat the company doctrine. A company's doctrine is ordinarily driven by revenue. Bad products are mostly sold with the conviction that they are excellent products—which just happen to make the advisor and company a bunch of money. It is remarkably easy to convince yourself of things that you *really* want to believe. This isn't saying *all* companies are bad, nor that *all* individuals in bad companies are also bad. But individuals have a tendency to absorb attitudes from institutions.

5. No financial advisor will ever tell you that they "time the market," yet the subtext of virtually all investing philosophies is market timing. "We use a tactical approach ... when the market goes up, we use strategies to tell us where to overweight ... we use a momentum model ... we use relative strength ... we use technical analysis ... we use moving averages ..." All of these are euphemisms for "time the market." The public has been educated to be skeptical of market timing, so the industry uses different wording. Ask your broker what their buy/sell discipline is and you'll be able to add to this euphemism list. I'm not

judging whether or not any of these methods work, but it *is* market timing and you need to know that this is what you are signing up for.

6. Stock market value is highly abstract. Nobody knows what the value should be any more than they know how the masses will vote to assess that value.

7. Correlation does not imply causation. Keep this logical fallacy in mind when investing.

8. Everyone talks about the great sin of emotional investing. "Emotional investing" goes by many aliases. Feelings take on many rational sounding forms, "My gut tells me ... with that person running the White House ... with that foreign country causing those problems ... with oil at that price ... with that piece of legislation." If you already feel pessimistic, you are just going to mine the news for rationalizations. Emotional investing is never honest enough to tell you, "I'm selling out because I'm scared." Be wary of those who raise their sails to the slightest breeze of pessimistic winds.

9. The financial services business is a relationship-based business. A big reason people select a particular advisor is how that person makes them *feel*. Beware of being charmed into a bad decision. In all relationship-based businesses, there will be an abundance of Eddie Haskells.

10. Fear of litigation has forced the darkest parts of financial services industry into being *transparently deceptive*. We have become desensitized to dense, opaque legal language. We sign contracts without reading them, sign legal waivers for every activity, and tune out litanies of disclosures. Even shampoo and toothpaste have fine print. Don't let this confusing pile of fine print mislead you. Investing can be complicated, but understanding that complication is not a prerequisite to wealth.

11. Nobody can outperform or time all the peaks and troughs of the market. Going to an advisor with this expectation is foolish. Getting mad at your advisor for not selling you out before it went down is foolish. Getting mad at your advisor for not investing your money in some boom area of the market is foolish. Pressuring your advisor to change things around a downturn is foolish. All in all, any expectation that you have for a financial advisor to deliver for you superior returns should be jettisoned. This is *not* what you should expect a financial advisor to bring to the table.

That's my story and I'm sticking to it. Where you go from here is up to you. These are my recommendations:

1. The greatest value a financial advisor can deliver for you is big mistake insurance. The prevention of big mistakes goes straight to your bottom line and *is unequivocally* tantamount to higher performance.

2. No financial advisor knows what interest rates are going to do, where oil prices are going, what gold is doing, or if the current **5%** decline will become a **10%** decline. Nobody knows, so there's no shame in not knowing. If they

say they know, don't believe them—at best, it is a gross misallocation of ego and possibly your nest egg along with it.

3. A financial advisor who can talk you out of your own self-destructive behavior is worth their cost. On average, each and every year the market will drop more than **10%**. That means you have the risk of incurring a 10% fee to your own panic every year. A financial advisor who talks you off the ledge is worth their cost.

4. Because most financial advisors engage in thinly disguised market timing, and because on average people trying to time the market grossly underperform the market, you can expect a higher performance from an advisor who very candidly, openly, and unashamedly does not engage in this practice. In choosing an advisor, you insulate your household with a financial philosophy. Not all philosophies are equal and not all advisors have philosophies.

5. Find an advisor who actively educates you and prioritizes your understanding as a key component of staying the investment course. They should focus on *long-term perspective*. An advisor who inculcates this perspective is giving you something that most people cannot find on their own. A huge critique I have of our industry is that nearly all "education" has a hidden agenda. Everyone is trying to guide people into products. Facts can be manipulated to tell you whatever story they want you to hear.

6. Value an advisor who bolsters that psychological steadfastness with a long-term financial plan. A financial plan may represent a relatively small percentage of your time with your advisor, but it is *the* organizing document showing where to allocate your capital. I once had a pilot tell me, "Anyone can fly a plane." He added, "But I'm paid to *land* planes." Sometimes, all the value you receive compresses into a few short moments and you want the best pilot at the helm of those moments.

7. An advisor should deliver the intangible benefit of minimizing what you need to worry about. They direct your anxiousness away from the things you can't control to the things you can. There should be a sense of calmness and relaxation with the advisor, particularly *when* the capital markets become excitable. If your advisor can't be calm, you won't be calm.

8. One person can't perform all the functions of a financial advisor. These include: research, portfolio management, financial planning, compliance, learning new regulations, preparing for annual regulatory audits, running a business, growing a business, servicing clients, getting new clients, retaining existing clients, processing estates, meeting with attorneys, meeting with tax professionals, and staying up with technology, all the while being heavily solicited by everyone and their mother in the financial services industry. These are far too many hats for one person. Imagine Dick Van Dyke in *Mary Poppins* with his one-man-band. He had a drum kit on his back, a trumpet and harmonica around his neck, concertina in his hands, chimes dangling from his body, and a horn in his face. While this is a mesmerizing circus act, it will never make

excellent music. There are no excellent one-man-bands. Advisors can harm clients by trying to do it all themselves. Work with someone who isn't trying to be the library, but aspires to be the librarian.

9. Lastly, work with someone who will be your legal fiduciary. Earlier I mentioned how the financial services industry can be transparently deceptive. It should be taken for granted that you probably won't *fully* understand what you are investing in. You will hopefully understand it in concept, but probably not in detail. It's just the reality. The safeguard to this is to hire a financial advisor who will sign a contract with you that he or she is your legal fiduciary. This means that he or she is legally *bound* to act in your best interest. To me it seems obvious that all financial advisors should be fiduciaries ... but the sad fact is that only a minority of them are. This is where it can be subtle. Most advisors operate under what's called the "suitability standard" and not the "fiduciary standard." An ethical advisor operating under the lessor "suitability standard" may result in the same advice as one operating as your legal fiduciary. However, as a rule of thumb, don't hire someone who has an inherent, overt, and unmitigated conflict of interest to giving you the best advice. It should be fairly routine for a financial advisor to give clients advice against the advisor's own financial self-interest.

When you work with any professional, you inevitably lean on their virtues. Look for these virtues:

1. Accountability—They don't let you procrastinate doing what you need to do, they hold you to your plans and goals.
2. Discernment—They have the wisdom to see to the heart of situations and intuition as to who you are.
3. Fairness—There is a right price for everything and there is a fair allocation of the advisor's time.
4. Impartiality—There should be a respectful indifference to what you think. They are the professional and there is generally one monolithic way you should be investing. How you feel about it should not change that. An advisor should not bend their advice to get your account. If you disagree, you shouldn't work together.
5. Mutual Loyalty—Excellent advisors often have the luxury of choosing only excellent clients and tactfully declining anyone else. The relationship is bilateral and should have a mutual loyalty and understanding.
6. Mutual Graciousness—Nobody is perfect. This should be mutually acknowledged. Even advisors with decades of experience make mistakes or have lapses in their service. All clients do less than magnanimous things from time to time. We're all humans growing together.

Speaking personally, these virtues are always my highest aspiration, but I never forget my failures. Even though I pride myself in being an advisor/psychologist, every bear market I have clients whom I fail to talk off the panic cliff. The older I get, the less market declines bother me, but I'm still haunted by the look of capitulation on every former client's face. I don't measure myself by performance because I don't see that I have *that* much to contribute to it; I measure myself by how clients behave. Do people invest in equities when they should? Do they stay in equities when they should? I believe that by focusing our energy on behaviors, we will outperform someone focusing on anything else.

When I think about "making money for clients," I think of talking them out of jumping off the cliff of panic. In March 2009 when the stock market was down **57%**, the clients that I talked out of selling at the bottom enjoyed the doubling of the market shortly afterward. This moment alone satisfies a lifetime of costs. As is generally the case, the primary driver of their performance was not what they were invested in, but whether they were patient.

Excellent advice at a fair price is better than bad advice at an excellent price.

My feelings toward my own industry could be likened to a strict father: my love is shown through harsh criticism, sarcasm, and nitpicking, but it is love. I will state my biases on the onset: I believe that a majority of people are going to end up wealthier by working with a good financial advisor. Not everyone needs an advisor. But I would like to draw your attention to one glaring reality: the wealthy, über-wealthy, and dynastically wealthy nearly always work with professionals paid to advise them.

The other advantage of hiring a professional is to have someone in the loop who will force you to do what you need to do. This goes back to the virtue of accountability. They should be your anti-procrastinator. Most people get serious about their money for a season of time, do some sort of positive movement, and then get distracted with life. You may get excited about saving, create a budget, and then never look at it again. You may pay off a car, and reward yourself by buying another one. You may have a passing thought for your legal planning and never call a lawyer.

Your livelihood depends on *finishing*. A financial professional does more than select a portfolio. A good one serves as your accountability partner.

Lastly, as an advisor, I always put myself in a very fireable position; I don't think that it should cost a client any significant sum should they chose to invest elsewhere. I also take clients on for life – meaning, if I take someone on, in my head I plan to advise them to the day they die and then, after they die, their families. My loyalty to my clients extends to multiple generations and I personally know the children and grandchild of nearly every single one of my clients. Many of them are also clients.

The lesson here should be that there are *innumerable* things to look out for and there's no way that you will be aware of them all because one lifetime inevitably limits your experience. Even if you could learn it all in a lifetime, you need all that time to make this work. You need that knowledge and experience as early in your life as possible. Because of this, a realistic alternative is to hire someone who already has it to advise you.

It would be easy to take this "never sell" message and conclude that you don't need an advisor, "Don't sell out, don't let fear rule my decisions, got it. Why pay someone to tell me this?" Before you conclude this and go it alone, I have a homework assignment for you. Find someone who has been in combat, ideally a career military soldier, even more ideally someone who has trained soldiers. Ask them, "Before any shooting starts, before any intense active combat situation, how do you know which soldiers will lose their cool? Which ones will panic in battle?" The answer will likely be that there's no way of knowing. Only years of active combat experience reduce the risk of panic. Panic is certainly not the soldier's fault, it is a perfectly natural and often uncontrolled response.

Because of the uncertainty associated with your innate response to battle, it would be supremely risky to go into war without veteran leadership.

In the course of a 30-year retirement, you are likely to see no less than six bear markets and at least one very severe decline of **40%** or more. What are the odds that you make at least one big mistake and cost yourself far more money than you could have paid to someone to help you through the journey? You go to a financial advisor for the emotional strength that you aren't likely to *always* find on your own.

With an advisor, you should expect them to help you with two key things:

1. Judge the maximum safe amount of money to maintain in equities
2. Keep that money in equities no matter what your emotions may demand of you

You could add two more points which are really just subsets to the first two:

1. Create and maintain a long-term financial plan which tells you how to invest and ensures that your Six Areas of Finance are coordinated
2. Help you maintain a long-term perspective by being an ongoing teacher

You could also add other highly useful services such as interacting with the other professionals you work with, joining in on attorney or tax meetings, being your anti-procrastinator, and helping you make multi-generational financial decisions. These are the things that I think people should value.

The key determining question is to ask the advisor, "What do I get out of the cost I pay?" Zip your lip, and just let them fill the silence for as long as they wish to ramble. Listen for multiple market timing euphemisms. If an advisor's message is that their cost is worth it because of superior portfolio management or some means of lowering volatility, odds are it will cost you considerably more than what they charge you. On the other hand, if the only thing an advisor does for you is help you stay the course in equities under the guidance of a financial plan, statistically they are earning their keep.

Occasionally I am put on the spot and asked, what's the one investment everyone should make right now? I always say invest in a behavior-based financial advisor.

Summary: The Cost of Investing How You Feel

What cutbacks would you have to make if you find yourself living solely on Social Security? To what extent do you want your money to outpace the rising cost of living?

Investing in a way that limits your wealth may not be as dramatic as facing starvation in retirement. But you may have your friends invite you on a trip that you can't afford. You may want to help out a grandchild graduating college or perhaps later when they are buying their first house. You may have a sick family member and not have the money to visit them in hospice or attend their funeral. Or it may be the wedding of someone you've known since they were a child. Your spouse may be diagnosed with a terminal illness and lack the money to really enjoy your remaining time with them by plowing through your mutual bucket list.

Such are the costs of investing in your emotional comfort now instead of physical comfort later. The thought of having to say "no" to things I would have said "yes" to if money were available is a discomfort that I personally fear much more than I fear seeing my investment balance drop temporarily.

So much of this life under the sun is an illusion. The course of most people's lives includes moments of temporary enlightenment. They happen at the death of a spouse, a divorce, a cancer diagnosis, or a tragedy in the community. These are the moments, when in the depth of our sorrow and shock, we are utterly awake and aware. We see the world clearly and we have perception and wisdom. In those moments, we can see that none of this is important. The money and the stuff it's meant to buy, it is all passing and destined for decomposition. In the end, it's just us and the relationships that we've nurtured, the people that we've helped, and the mostly anonymous legacy we've left behind.

When time drifts from these moments and the veils of earthly concern again shroud enlightenment, life continues and we go back to our screens. Our concerns drift back to the petty. If for a moment you can muscle that veil away and hold fast to the vision of something bigger out there, then may it guide your decisions today to equip you for those precious times. In the end, nothing has ever come from borrowing tomorrow's worries. Don't waste your life worrying about things you have no control over.

I have often said that facing the brutal facts is the beginning of wisdom. One of the brutal facts is that the world will have no memory of us 100 years from now. Biologically, you have 8 great-grandparents. How many can you name? Let alone details of their life, just their mere *names*? Maybe you can name a few, but if I were to take it up a generation to your 16 great-great grandparents my guess is that most people couldn't name one.

As you know by now, I look at the past and project to the future. My guess is that my great-great grandchildren aren't going to know my name, let alone anything else about me. When I first realized this, it was a touch depressing. But as I said, facing the brutal facts is the beginning of wisdom.

I feel lucky to have some connection with three people of the generation of my great-grandparents. One of them was my mother's grandfather who I got to meet when he was 100 years old. He was known to the family as Pa. He was born in the wild west of Texas. Pa spent much of his life as an itinerant preacher and tenant farmer. I remember a conversation with my Great Uncle Angus (his son) who said that they were dirt poor. My grandmother challenged him, "We were not!" Uncle Angus justified it in his calm Texas accent, "Yes we were, Willie Belle, the floor of our house was made of dirt, that's where the sayin' comes from." Yes, these were actually their names. Had my great-grandfather not tragically died at the spritely young age of 101, I might have learned direct wisdom from him. Instead, looking at his life, I can't help but infer these lessons:

1. Longevity—You may end up living far longer than anyone imagines.
2. Standard of living—Apart from the breathtaking technological sweep of history experienced, standards of living went up just as surprisingly. When he was born in the 1880s, to have a dirt floor was a fairly normal experience among lower class people outside of cities. By the time he was a young man in the 1920s, this meant abject poverty. By the time of his death, this was virtually nonexistent in America.

You can't assume that what is normal to you will stay normal for long. The other great-grandfather that influenced me is known in the family as Pocky. I never met him. He died six years before I was born. However, to this day, his spirit of love, generosity, and joy resonate throughout our family. He set the long-term tone for our rather large family. Pocky was able to influence his grandchildren (my father's generation) because he had planned well and therefore retired well. It was because of this planning that his grandchildren could spend a month each summer with him at his home on the shores of Lake Michigan. Pocky made a lifetime of sound financial decisions and was able to spend his retirement energy pouring wonderful experiences into the lives of his grandchildren—experiences that they still talk about to this day.

The third person of that generation was a man named Harold Swift. You may know of Swift Meats. This company was started by Harold Swift's father, Gustavus Franklin Swift—the Midwest meat tycoon of the Industrial Age. For a reason lost to history, Uncle Harold (as he has always been referred to by everyone in my family) took Pocky under his wing when Pocky was a young man. He mentored him through college at the University of Chicago, where Pocky was the star running back. This began a college tradition and, as a result, nearly everyone in my family has at least a Bachelor's degree. Some of them have graduated from places like Harvard, Stanford, Yale, and Columbia. Afterwards, Harold and Pocky remained lifelong friends, and it was Uncle Harold who bought him that house on Lake Michigan—thus also filling many minds full of cherished memories. The generosity of Harold Swift 100 years ago changed the lives of 100 people and everyone around them.

It is easy to get caught up in the issues of the day, but our ancestors had it far worse that we do. We cannot get caught up in the temporary. I doubt everyone who benefited from Uncle Harold's generosity knows his name. From what I know of Uncle Harold, it wouldn't necessarily matter to him that we knew, but he'd be happy to see such a solid return on his investment in my family.

The point I am trying to make is that the long view is the wise view. Money in the hands of people with good hearts is a good thing. And if you don't invest in people, at least invest in your future. The choice can be summarized:

Comparison of Choices

Choice:	Probability of running out of money in retirement ...	Probability of gaining wealth as measured by the power to buy stuff ...	When you get to enjoy your sense of security ...
Fixed Income	Greater	Lesser	Now, when you are younger
Equities	Lesser	Greater	Later, when you are older

My view is that "conservative" investments (such as bonds and cash) should only be used for short periods of time. On a lifelong basis, they are highly risky in their inability to keep up with rising prices. By hoarding money in things deemed as "riskless," you are gaining the benefit of a present day sense of security at the cost of the long-term risk of running out of money when you are older and have the least ability to get more of it.

Endnotes

1   With these charts I am *not* going to base my columns off a standard deviation. You will see that the mean is roughly in the middle of a column, but that the ranges are round numbers. This makes the chart far easier to read for those not familiar with these concepts. My aim is Main Street more than ivory towers. If you want to know which category you fit into, I'll give you a hint: one of these groups likes to read endnotes.

2   This is slightly longer than a year because the one-year mark fell on a weekend. As you may remember, June 25, 1932 was a Saturday, and it rained a little in the afternoon.

3   The astute reader may notice that this average is different that the earlier one. This is because it is an average of much less data. This average is only looking at *calendar* year returns, while the other data was using *all* rolling one-year returns. Interestingly, it's not that different for only 89 pieces of data versus 22,953 rolling periods.

4   The 15th fell on a Saturday.

5   Data used from Ibbotson SBBI Classic Yearbook Table 2-3 Basic Series. Used with permission.

6   Source: "Quantitative Analysis of Investor Behavior, 2016," DALBAR, Inc. www.dalbar.com. Used with permission.

7   Sources: The World Bank, GDP Ranking and U.S. Bureau of Economic Analysis. Based on 2014 data.

The only sane
measurement of
"wealth" is the power
to buy stuff.
Getting wealthier only
happens when your
ability to *"buy stuff"* is
growing.
If it is not, then you are
getting poorer.

When I heard the learn'd astronomer,

When the proofs, the figures, were ranged in columns before me,

When I was shown the charts and diagrams, to add, divide, and measure them,

When I sitting heard the astronomer where he lectured with much applause in the lecture-room,

How soon unaccountable I became tired and sick,

Till rising and gliding out I wander'd off by myself,

In the mystical moist night-air, and from time to time,

Look'd up in perfect silence at the stars.

Walt Whitman

Optimism

Some people are incurably pessimistic. They are like Eeyore from Winnie the Pooh.

"Who do you want to be president?"

"They're all crooks!"

"It sure is a beautiful day!"

"I heard it's going to rain Wednesday."

While negativity can be funny, it's also much easier to respect a skeptic. Pessimism somehow feels closer to *realism*.

Folks on the opposite end of the spectrum are far more rare. They are like Disney's Pollyanna. In our society, optimism is unfashionable. It is perceived as naïve, foolish, and unseasoned. Optimism somehow feels *unrealistic*.

When it comes to the pursuit of wealth, the Pollyannas always end up better than the Eeyores. In the long run, *always*. We have looked at the stunning 89 year sweep of stock market performance. Along the way, there were better "moments" than others, but for a long-term optimistic investor, the memory of bad moments is eclipsed by a superior outcome.

The optimistic and patient Pollyanna Investor had to endure the same constant assault of reasons *not* to invest. Eeyores will always have plenty of headlines to rationalize fear. Pessimism is easy.

Doubt is the Root of Panic

During the post-9/11 era the concern was "the next terrorist attack." It was spoken of as a foregone conclusion. During the Iraq War, for many, war with Iran and some would say North Korea were also foregone conclusions. I remember a man telling me very specifically that he wanted to time his investment after the war with Iran had started. Then it was the myriad of dangers surrounding the Financial Crisis and then the risk of a double dip recession—about which, note, all recessions are double dip *eventually*. Then it was European problems, government shutdowns, problems with Russia, war in Syria, multiple terrorist attacks, ISIS, the presidential election, and everything in between.

The market often reacts negatively initially, but eventually skips along with a Pollyannaish indifference. At some point, we must observe the stock market's long-term callousness to our daily worries. Astoundingly, the market always overcomes. The optimists who ignore the headlines are rewarded.

On the next two pages is a list of the past 89 years. I have written down what I think was the best reason *not* to invest money in the stock market for that year. Each would have been a very logical reason not to invest. I have also created a portfolio worth $1.00 at the beginning of 1928. The right column in green shows the balance.

I encourage you to take a moment to slowly read through the list. Try to imagine living in that year and knowing nothing about what would happen beyond that scary moment. No one could have blamed you for lacking faith in the future.

There are always scary things. Historically speaking, no matter how scary they are, the best response for the long-term investor has always been to ignore them. When I survey this history, it's stunning to me what the people of Earth have endured. It is painful to read. Then, oddly, the green column marks the constant jagged climb of equities. All along the way, it would have been easy to hang your hat on any of these events and conclude that it was best to stay on the sidelines. It is human nature to play it safe.

We look backwards for understanding, but life must be lived forward. We can only look out from our own skulls at the world and at our life, a small crack of consciousness bookended by two vast eternities. Our narrow experience always makes us vulnerable to ignoring our resolutions and acting on the moment.

The lesson of history is that optimism *is* realism, even if present reality is very dark. Your return is driven by the one thing that only you have control over: your behavior. Your behavior will be largely driven by what you believe about the world. Faith is discipline's little helper.

When I was in college, I went through a phase where I was obsessed with the writings of the Puritans. Outside of my academic studies, they were the only thing I read. Their lessons in discipline, and particularly how beliefs drive discipline, stuck with me. The Puritans were, as their name implies, obsessed with not sinning. They said that the root of all sin is *doubt*.

The greatest investing "sin" is panic selling.

This sin happens when you doubt what you believe about the world and about the capital markets.

It happens when you doubt the core of your creed, which must forever be ***optimistic.***

What do you *believe* about the world as an investor? I suspect that your lifelong rate of return could be accurately predicted based on where you are located along an optimistic-pessimistic spectrum.

My outright advice is that if your worldview is pessimistic, if you think we have peaked as a species, if you think the next generation will have it worse than yours, if you think the world is going to hell in a hand-basket, if you are the type to think that whoever is elected into office will literally destroy the country, then you have no business investing in the market. You are a ticking time bomb for panic selling and it will wipe out more of your dollars than inflation ever will.

On the other hand, if you have a glimmer of faith, permit me to evangelize the creed of Pollyanna optimism.

89 Years of Scary Headlines

	NEGATIVE HEADLINE	DATE	VALUE
1928	Okeechobee hurricane kills 2,500 in Florida	Sunday, September 16, 1928	$1.22
1929	Black Tuesday stock market crash	Thursday, October 24, 1929	$1.55
1930	Unemployment soars, trade suffers from Smoot-Hawley	Tuesday, June 17, 1930	$1.27
1931	Mukden Incident begins Japanese occupation of China	Friday, September 18, 1931	$0.76
1932	Six million die in Soviet famine	Sunday, August 7, 1932	$0.50
1933	Germany and Japan withdraw from League of Nations	Saturday, October 14, 1933	$0.77
1934	Dust Bowl problem continues, drought plagues 75% of the US	Tuesday, May 1, 1934	$0.84
1935	Nazis repudiate Treaty of Versailles	Saturday, March 16, 1935	$0.69
1936	Spanish civil war begins	Saturday, July 18, 1936	$1.38
1937	Beijing falls to invading Japanese forces	Wednesday, July 7, 1937	$1.51
1938	Hitler annexes Austria	Sunday, March 13, 1938	$1.02
1939	Germany invades Poland	Friday, September 1, 1939	$1.18
1940	France falls under Nazi occupation	Tuesday, June 25, 1940	$1.06
1941	Pearl Harbor attack	Sunday, December 7, 1941	$1.12
1942	Allies invade North Africa	Sunday, November 8, 1942	$1.23
1943	Roosevelt freezes prices and wages to prevent inflation	Thursday, April 8, 1943	$1.53
1944	Battle of the Bulge	Saturday, December 16, 1944	$1.90
1945	Hiroshima and Nagasaki nuclear bombings	Monday, August 6, 1945	$2.17
1946	Worst work stoppages since 1919	Tuesday, January 1, 1946	$2.61
1947	Soviet Union rejects US plan for atomic-energy control	Tuesday, March 4, 1947	$2.43
1948	Soviets begin blockade of Berlin	Thursday, June 24, 1948	$2.84
1949	First Soviet atomic bomb detonated	Monday, August 29, 1949	$2.74
1950	North Korean communists invade South Korea	Sunday, June 25, 1950	$3.66
1951	Seoul falls to Communist forces	Thursday, January 4, 1951	$4.16
1952	US detonates first hydrogen bomb	Saturday, November 1, 1952	$5.47
1953	Russia announces detonation of hydrogen bomb	Thursday, August 20, 1953	$5.67
1954	McCarthy communist hearings	Thursday, April 22, 1954	$6.72
1955	Soviet Union and East Europe sign Warsaw Pact	Saturday, May 14, 1955	$9.55
1956	Egypt takes control of Suez Canal	Thursday, July 26, 1956	$13.19
1957	Asian Flu Pandemic claims two million lives	Tuesday, October 1, 1957	$11.96
1958	The Great Chinese Famine kills 30 million	Tuesday, April 1, 1958	$11.98
1959	Cuban Revolution	Monday, February 16, 1959	$16.04
1960	American U-2 spy plane shot down over Russia	Sunday, May 1, 1960	$16.61
1961	Bay of Pigs	Monday, April 17, 1961	$21.07
1962	Cuban Missile Crisis	Monday, October 22, 1962	$18.19
1963	Kennedy assassination	Thursday, November 22, 1962	$20.19
1964	Gulf of Tonkin incident	Sunday, August 2, 1964	$29.09
1965	State troopers attack peaceful march in Selma, AL	Sunday, March 7, 1965	$30.96
1966	Chairman Mao launches China's Cultural Revolution	Monday, May 16, 1966	$31.19
1967	Communist China announces detonation of hydrogen bomb	Saturday, June 17, 1967	$35.48
1968	Martin Luther King Jr. assassinated	Thursday, April 4, 1968	$36.93
1969	Rising Inflation is a worldwide problem	Wednesday, January 1, 1969	$41.80

Year	Event	Date	Value
1970	Four students shot dead by National Guardsmen at Kent State	Friday, May 1, 1970	$34.26
1971	Anti-war militants disrupt Washington 12,000 arrested	Monday, May 3, 1971	$45.06
1972	Watergate scandal	Saturday, June 17, 1972	$48.85
1973	OPEC oil embargo	Tuesday, October 16, 1973	$51.63
1974	Richard Nixon resignation	Friday, August 9, 1974	$39.09
1975	Vietnam War ends as Communist forces take Saigon	Tuesday, April 29, 1975	$42.79
1976	Khmer Rouge leader Pol Pot becomes dictator of Cambodia	Tuesday, April 13, 1976	$52.57
1977	Four Palestinians hijack Lufthansa airliner	Thursday, October 13, 1977	$51.68
1978	US Senate ratifies Panama Canal neutrality treaty	Thursday, March 16, 1978	$50.57
1979	Iran hostage crisis	Sunday, November 4, 1979	$63.11
1980	US breaks diplomatic ties with Iran	Monday, April 7, 1980	$63.06
1981	Reagan assassination attempt	Monday, March 30, 1981	$88.43
1982	Falklands War	Friday, April 2, 1982	$80.26
1983	Terrorist explosion kills 237 US Marines in Beirut	Sunday, October 23, 1983	$124.72
1984	Indian Prime Minister Indira Gandhi assassinated	Wednesday, October 31, 1984	$130.56
1985	Gunmen capture TWA airliner	Friday, June 14, 1985	$151.38
1986	Iran-contra scandal breaks	Monday, November 3, 1986	$209.50
1987	Black Monday stock market crash	Monday, October 19, 1987	$196.86
1988	US Navy ship shoots down Iranian airliner in Persian Gulf	Sunday, July 3, 1988	$244.27
1989	Exxon Valdez runs aground	Friday, March 24, 1989	$265.87
1990	Iraqi troops invade Kuwait	Thursday, August 2, 1990	$338.56
1991	Persian Gulf War	Saturday, January 26, 1991	$328.76
1992	Rodney King riots	Wednesday, April 29, 1992	$419.21
1993	World Trade Center bombing	Friday, February 26, 1993	$462.20
1994	Rwandan Genocide	Thursday, April 7, 1994	$485.33
1995	Oklahoma City bombing	Wednesday, April 19, 1995	$558.94
1996	British outbreak of mad cow disease	Wednesday, March 20, 1996	$735.23
1997	Asian currency crisis	Tuesday, July 1, 1997	$1,035.46
1998	Russian financial crisis	Monday, August 17, 1998	$1,280.28
1999	NATO begins combat involvement in Kosovo War	Wednesday, March 24, 1999	$1,511.30
2000	Dot-com bubble pops	Monday, March 13, 2000	$1,668.42
2001	September 11 terrorist attacks	Tuesday, September 11, 2001	$1,341.45
2002	North Korea admits to developing nuclear arms	Wednesday, October 16, 2002	$1,073.66
2003	Iraq War begins	Wednesday, March 19, 2003	$1,099.45
2004	Indian Ocean earthquake and tsunami kills 250,000	Sunday, December 26, 2004	$1,567.02
2005	Hurricane Katrina	Monday, August 29, 2005	$1,587.85
2006	North Korea detonates nuclear bomb	Monday, October 9, 2006	$1,806.45
2007	US and Chinese stock market major sell off	Tuesday, February 27, 2007	$1,882.27
2008	Financial Crisis reaches apex	Monday, September 15, 2008	$1,654.67
2009	Greece debt crisis begins	Tuesday, October 20, 2009	$1,562.98
2010	Flash crash	Thursday, May 6, 2010	$1,634.75
2011	S&P downgrades US Credit Rating	Friday, August 5, 2011	$1,779.62
2012	Hurricane Sandy	Monday, October 22, 2012	$2,180.50
2013	Boston Marathon bombing	Monday, April 15, 2013	$2,386.17
2014	Russia annexes Crimea	Sunday, March 16, 2014	$2,882.85
2015	Paris terrorist attack	Friday, November 13, 2015	$3,274.52
2016	The United States presidential election	Tuesday, November 8, 2016	$3,537.52

There Will Be a Future

There will be a future. With your creed you actively decide what you believe about the future. A creed is something you believe regardless of short-term hints or seeming contradictions. Creed is held to because of a faith that abides regardless of emotion.

The evidence of history gives me the following creed: *optimism is realism*. This creed respects the existence of terrible events. It observes that in spite of all the reasons for the world to end, we have endured. The stock market is a long-term agnostic to the horrors that have faced humanity.

It's easy to lose sight of this stock market climb amidst calamity. I like to remind my Baby Boomer clients that on the date their generation started, January 1, 1946, the price of the S&P 500 was 17. Just to make sure you don't think I forgot a zero in there, *seventeen*. If you are more familiar with the Dow Jones, the price on that same first day was 193.

Conceptualizing exponential progress doesn't come naturally to us. I have found that people can imagine a portfolio doubling over a certain amount of time. But it seems ridiculous to imagine it quadrupling over twice the time. Octupling in thrice the time feels like fantasy.

When it comes to the economy, it's easy to focus on the demise of manufacturing jobs over the past 40 years. Politicians constantly focus on this sector that contributes $2.17 trillion dollars to the U.S. economy.[1] However, in the 40 years that manufacturing consolidated and outsourced, the recently nonexistent cell phone industry became a $3.3 trillion part of the global economy—much of it in the U.S. It is easy to focus on the threat that robotics and automation are to the job market and completely miss what new technologies will contribute to economic production.

Until very recently, the notion of having an at-home Rosie the Robot humanoid helper was the stuff of science fiction and Saturday morning cartoons. Now, a majority of people see this as an inevitable component of the not-too-distant future. Imagine the additional human potential that will be unleashed when people no longer have to waste precious hours cleaning their homes, doing their laundry, or cooking. Certainly many will squander the extra time, but to whatever extent people aren't wasteful, it will supplement the economy. Imagine the revenue household robots will generate for the companies that sell these products. It's easy to see them becoming an industry larger than the cell phone industry.

Entire multi-trillion dollar industries exist today only in their infancy. The world is quickly delivering science fiction dreams. Only 10 years ago people scoffed at the possibility of self-driving cars. As I write this, thousands of people are enjoying an automatic ride. In a decade, self-driving capability will be a standard feature on new cars. Imagine how much demand this will give to the automotive industry. Much like cell phones, cars may inch toward being a product that people are eager to update and replace.

There are also industries that have yet to become household names. Take metamaterials, which are new arrangements of atoms that don't occur in nature. Graphene is a two dimensional lattice of carbon atoms with astounding properties of strength and conductivity. It will open up a world of ultra lightweight aircraft powered off of ultra-high capacity batteries. You will eventually have a phone that virtually never runs out of electricity. This will enable electric cars to drive thousands of miles on a charge.

Graphene will be the founding father of metamaterials. Every year new metamaterials give us unthinkable capabilities. All of this eventually translates into revenue for companies.

Medicine is undergoing its own science fiction renaissance. Soon microscopic monitors will be able to travel through your bloodstream diagnosing and eventually fixing threats to your life. Medical technology will add decades to the life expectancy of the human race and stretch productive years of a lifespan. Right now, people see aging and death as inevitable realities of life. Within 15 years, most people will view these as curable and fixable problems. All of this merging of technology and medicine will translate to trillions of dollars of company revenue as the people of the earth clamor to consume these life-enhancing medical products. Your own life experience and life itself is emblematic of this progress. You've likely had multiple maladies that would have killed you if you were born only a few decades earlier.

On that front, we are in the process of the global emerging middle class. Right now there are billions of people who are essentially outside of the world economy. Technology is bringing us together and pulling more people into the consuming class of humans, thus creating more revenue for companies. These are people who now have access to the internet to educate themselves and can see the world outside of their own. Their skills and labor are now easily available online, which enables people to expand their businesses efficiently while creating work for people around the world. As they earn income, they too will be consuming these products creating more revenue for companies, thus driving up stock prices.

This may all sound like pie in the sky Pollyanna thinking, but consider how many of the world's richest made their money in products that didn't exist only a few decades ago. Bill Gates made his money selling operating systems, networking software, and desktop publishing software. In 1980, it may not have seemed plausible that these nonexistent products would make him the world's richest man for a generation. One of the biggest companies in the world right now is Google. Only 20 years ago, even Bill Gates did not see that there was any money to be made in search engines. Another one of the biggest companies is Apple, who gets most of its revenue from iPhones, which have only been around 10 years. I remember people laughing at the rumor of Apple getting into the cell phone business in 2006, "A little late to the game, guys." Jeff Bezos made his wealth from Amazon, which for years was ridiculed as a viable business. 15 years ago, to many people, it was not obvious how a company like Facebook could be profitable. Yet now, the company is worth about ten times more than Ford or about twice as much as Wal-Mart.

It is difficult to imagine how companies will earn money 10, 15, 20, or 30 years from now. Optimism is *blind*. You will never be able to see the future clearly, but you believe in its positive nature. There will be times when you want to lose faith in the human race. But the most probable trajectory for the people of the earth, and their markets, is upward and onward.

Because of this, the most probable way to achieve financial security for you and your family is to have, if nothing else, blind faith in upward trajectory and to simply look the other way when you doubt.

The next time the market drops significantly, I want you to start keeping an ear out for certain phrases, "I've been investing for years, but I've never seen anything like this before." "This time is different." "This is unprecedented." "This is uncharted territory." Now, program your mind to laugh. If a child gets angry at you and yells, "You're not getting any presents from Santa Claus!" What is your reaction? When someone is trying to justify their market fears, no matter how sound the logic, remember that during the long horizon of your investments, it will pass.

As we discussed, investing is about that which is probable, and what *should* be. Yes it's possible that we could slide into an apocalypse, but it's not probable. And if history is our guide (and it's our only guide), the human race habitually overcomes its perpetual apocalypses. Our generation may be the last, but all the other generations were for a while, too. The world seems to have a pesky ability to *not* end. Right now, multiple prophets are predicting an imminent stock market crash. They are the latest in a long line. As far as I know, the star spangled banner still waves.

This doesn't mean it waves over a utopia. Science fiction writers imagined our present year with a mix of technology and terror. Perhaps in time, whether through a robot revolution or nuclear catastrophe, humans will utterly capitulate. If we ever do come to that, your net worth isn't going to translate into wealth as we've defined it.

Investing is not unlike Pascal's Wager. Pascal reasoned that it was better to behave as if God exists, since if he doesn't, you don't lose much in comparison to what you could gain. Call optimism Gordon's Wager. If the future *isn't* bright, if it is nigh onto apocalyptic, pessimists and optimists are going to end up in the same place anyway.

You have to put your flag in the beach of optimism. The near term is unknowable. In the long term, the Pollyannas always win. Stand tall as a Proud Pollyanna. Hindsight is easy, foresight with action takes courage.

I'll leave you with an abstract prediction of the stock market for the future. We are revisiting an earlier graphic. The path is the same, but the interpretations differ. Either way, there will be a future.

Endnotes
1   http://www.nam.org/Newsroom/Top-20-Facts-About-Manufacturing/

Optimism

The Pessimistic View

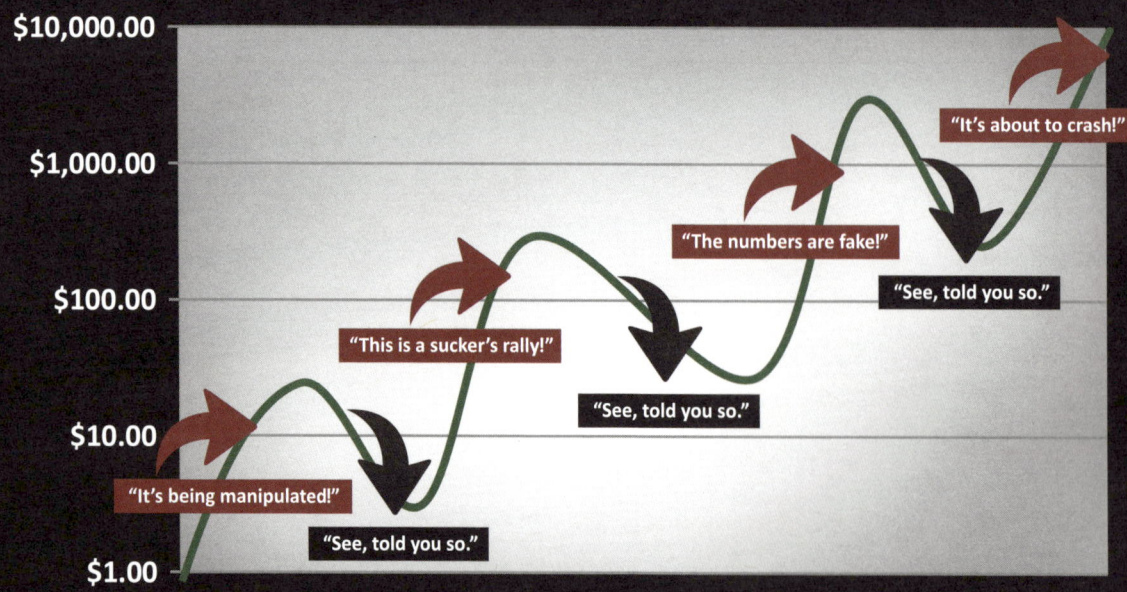

The Optimistic View

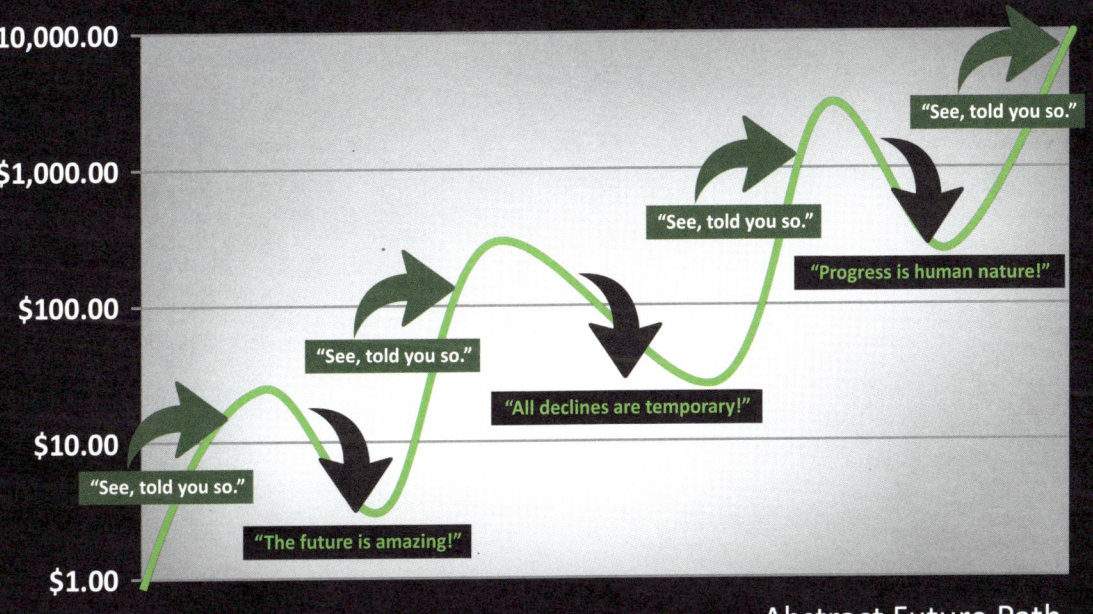

Abstract Future Path

"**Pessimists are always right ... eventually, but only temporarily.**"

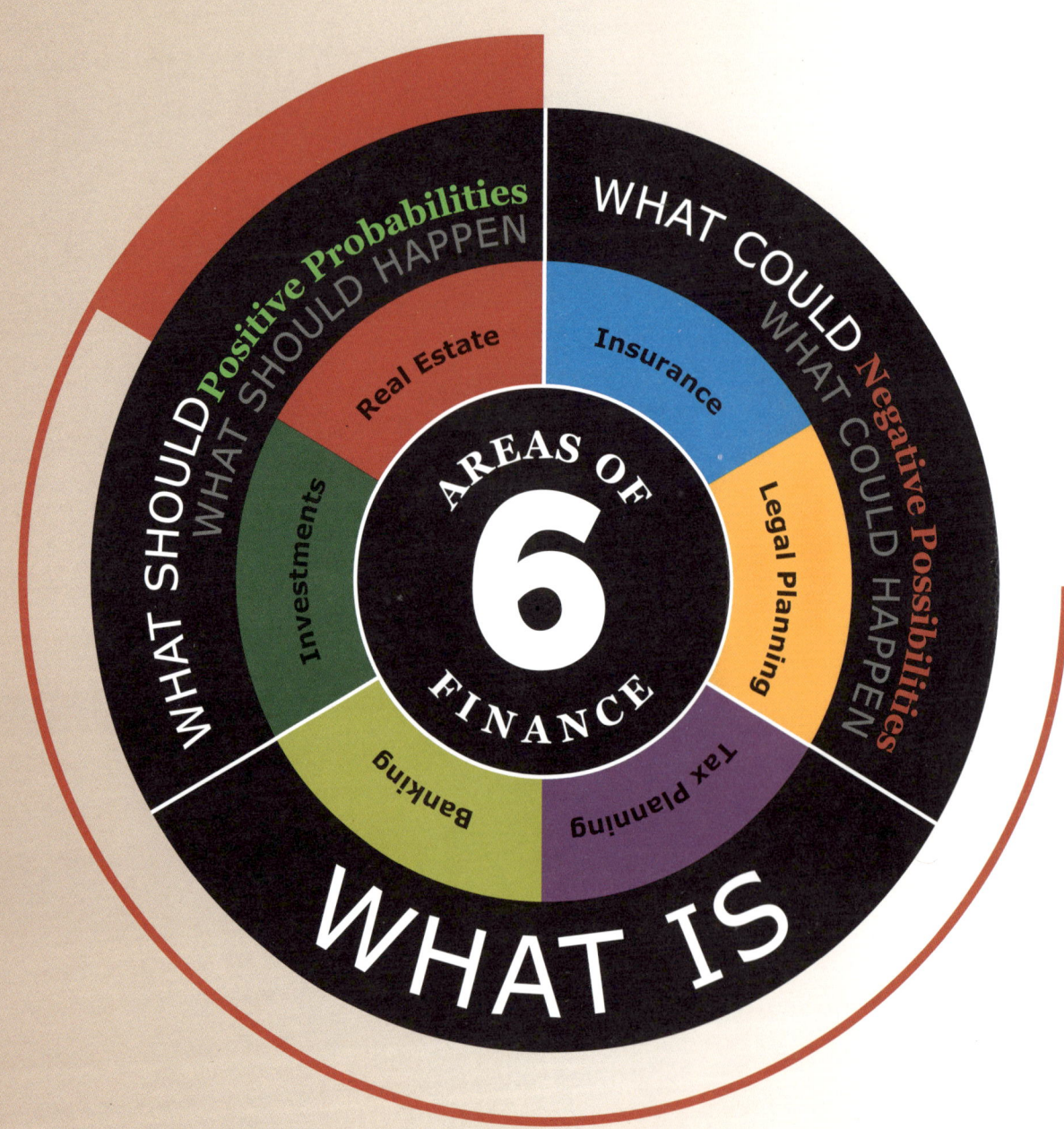

A smooth sea never made a skilled sailor.

Franklin D. Roosevelt

Real Estate

The primary functions of your home are to provide shelter, safety, and memories for you and your family. The secondary function is to create wealth. That's it. Your home is the investment you live in.

Owning a house for an extended period of time nearly always puts you in a stronger financial position relative to not owning a house. The caveat is "nearly always." Losing money is possible, but not probable.

However, owning a home is a solid guard against inflation—the most certain financial risk a person faces over a lifetime.

The Basics

There are a few main parts to the monthly "hard costs" of homeownership:

1. Property tax
2. Homeowner's insurance (mandatory if there is a mortgage)
3. Mortgage payment (the money goes partly toward *interest*, partly toward *principal*, and partly toward the above two **escrowed** items—meaning they gather money from you throughout the year and make these payments for you)

Sometimes you will have mortgage insurance if your home doesn't have much **equity** in it. This is another instance of a word used in two different, but similar ways.

We talked about stocks as *equities* because you own parts of companies. The part of the house value, less the mortgage balance, is your *equity* in the home. The *total* value of the house is the asset value. The liability, or debt, is the mortgage.

Liability (Mortgage)	Equity
Asset (Value of House)	

If you buy a $100,000 house and put $20,000 down on it and get an $80,000 mortgage, this is what it looks like:

$80,000 (Mortgage)	$20,000
$100,000 (Value of House)	

There are also the variable costs of the utilities (water, gas, electricity, sewer) and the cost of owning a building (repairs, damages, and maintenance).

If you rent a home, in a roundabout way you are paying for all its variable and ownership costs. Your landlord, the owner of the home, seeks to maximize cash flow and (should) rent it above their costs—the rent will be whatever the market supports *regardless* of their costs. What drives rental costs upward are basic urban economic reasons, not actual costs *per se*. As the largest element of inflation, the rising cost of housing will be the most important concept of this chapter.

The Anatomy of a Mortgage Payment

Your mortgage payment has three components. The biggest part is the *principal* and *interest* payments—sometimes abbreviated as "P&I." The other two are home-owner's insurance and property tax which (nearly always) go up every year, forever. If you rent a home, the rent will (nearly always) go up each time you renew the lease. Let's assume both payments are $1,200. Let's also add a row for the cost of ownership that we'll call "maintenance." Maintenance is an oft neglected line item in these kinds of comparisons. For now, we are *not* using real numbers, so we'll assign maintenance an arbitrary $200 for owners and nothing for renters—though surely as a for-profit business, the landlord is factoring maintenance costs into rent. Here's a breakdown of the fixed (green) vs. variable costs (red).

Owning		Renting	
Principal and Interest	$800	Rent Payment	$1,200
Insurance	$100		
Taxes	$100		
Maintenance	$200		
TOTAL	$1,200	TOTAL	$1,200

If you look down the road 30 years from now, assuming a 3% inflation rate, this is what you'd expect as your last mortgage payment. It compares it to what you could expect to pay in rent:

Owning		Renting	
Principal and Interest	$800	Rent Payment	$2,913
Insurance	$243		
Taxes	$243		
Maintenance	$485		
TOTAL	$1,771	TOTAL	$2,913

Utilities cost the same whether you own or rent the house. Homeowner's association payments (if applicable) would be factored into your rent payment or paid separately if you own. Again, for now we won't worry about actual numbers, this is just to get on the same page on the moving parts, and notably the non-moving part: the principal and interest. In the above example, after 30 years when the house is paid off (assuming it's a 30-year mortgage), the next day looks like this:

Owning		Renting	
Principal and Interest	$0	Rent Payment	$2,913
Insurance	$243		
Taxes	$243		
Maintenance	$485		
TOTAL	$971	TOTAL	$2,913

Just for grins, 30 years after this date—after being in the home 60 years—this is what your payments would look like:

Owning		Renting	
Principal and Interest	$0	Rent Payment	$7,070
Insurance	$589		
Taxes	$589		
Maintenance	$1,178		
TOTAL	$2,357	TOTAL	$7,070

Leverage

Another consideration is the benefit or detriment of financing a house with a mortgage. Most people can't afford the 100% down mortgage and instead put 20% down and get a mortgage for the rest. This is what's called **leverage**. Leverage *amplifies* the rate of return *on your down payment*, based on the underlying asset price movements.

Let's say you buy a house for $100,000, put $20,000 down, and get a mortgage for $80,000. We'll also pretend for a moment that you can buy and sell without costs and commissions. This is what the rate of return would be on your money if the house price goes down $10,000 in value versus up $10,000 in value:

Leverage

	At Purchase	$10,000 Decline	$10,000 Increase
Equity	$20,000	$10,000	$30,000
Mortgage	$80,000	$80,000	$80,000
House Value	$100,000	$90,000	$110,000
House Value Gain/Loss	0%	-10%	10%
Equity Gain/Loss	0%	-50%	50%

Or for the graphically inclined:

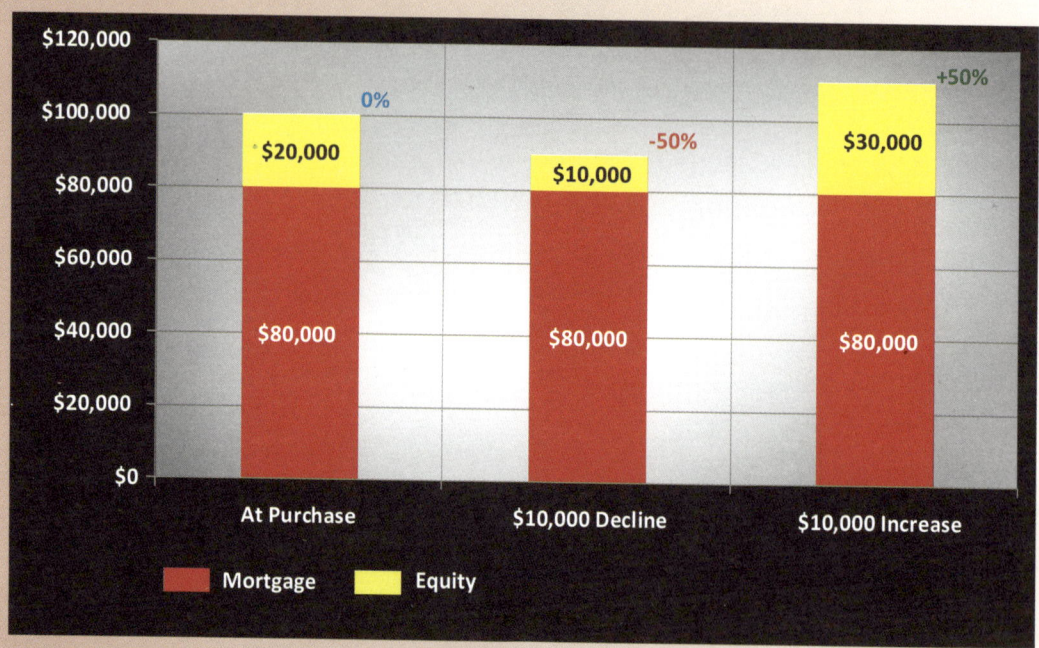

From this, you can see that the big question is *future value*. More specifically, what is the most *probable* direction of future value? As we dig into historical housing prices, I want you to keep those two bugs in your ear:

1. A mortgage *freezes* part of your monthly budget, thus giving you some *protection* from inflation.
2. For better or worse, the rate of return on your *down payment* is amplified through the principles of leverage.

The Probable Future Values of Real Estate

Before we look at the hard numbers of historical real estate prices, let's consider the moving forces. Over time, real estate valuations go up because of simple supply and demand. The *demand* for real estate is inevitable: people *must* have it to live and work, and the world is gaining more people. The *supply* of land is limited. As Mark Twain quipped, "Buy land, they're not making it anymore."

Let's imagine an island with 100 plots of land with houses built on them. If the population is 100 families, you wouldn't expect the prices of the homes to change much. You would expect the price to track with the prices of everything else. But let's imagine that these people are fertile little pups and the families each have a half-dozen kids. Years later, when the kids start their own families, there won't be enough houses to go around. The kids who can afford it will clamor to buy the available homes (causing the prices to go up) and the rest will have to swim somewhere else. If you have *limited* housing supply, so long as a population is growing, an economy productive, and a place desirable, you would normally expect real estate prices to *outpace* general inflation.

There are a few things that cause real estate prices to go up (both rental and purchase prices):

1. General inflation
2. Rising incomes
3. Growing populations (more numbers of people)
4. Urbanization (people moving into cities)
5. Increasing population densities (more people in smaller areas)
6. Demand for a location convenient to commerce and employment

As general prices go up, incomes go up. As incomes go up, spending goes up. As spending goes up, prices go up. That cycle includes housing prices, especially with a limited supply. Growing populations intensify the cycle.

We're taking broad sweeps here in hopes of understanding why urban (and suburban) housing prices tend to outpace inflation. With inflation, all types of prices go up, but urban housing prices tend to rise faster because of limited supply.

Let's take a moment to look at how the inflation number is determined. The technical name for the measure of inflation is the Consumer Price Index (or CPI). Every month the U.S. Bureau of Labor Statistics publishes how much prices went up or down. They weight the number based on a typical household's spending. For example, in December of 2016, the average household spent 8.230% of their annual spending on groceries.

Here are some more items:

- 3.189% is for education
- 3.101% is for clothing
- 6.569% is for medical care services

Each year these allocations of typical spending change a little bit as American spending habits shift. This becomes very important when we observe that historically the cost for shelter is the biggest piece of it, comprising of 30.24–33.20% of the inflation figure over the years 2000–2016. The 17 year average weight of shelter in the inflation number was 32.09%.

This changes the conversation because, as we'll soon see, the prices of housing typically rise *faster* than general prices. But this comparison is redundant by about 32.09%. When we adjust the inflation rate and remove the housing part of it, the difference between how much housing prices go up and how much everything else goes up is even *more extreme*.

Let's put some hypothetical numbers to this. Let's assume housing prices go up by 4% and inflation goes up by 3%. If housing is 32.09% of the inflation number, then this is the math:

Removing Housing from Inflation

	% of Inflation	Rate	Contribution to Inflation
Housing Prices	32.09%	4.00%	1.28%
Implied Inflation without Housing	67.91%	2.53%	1.72%
Inflation	100.00%	3.00%	3.00%

If housing prices go up by 4% and the prices of everything else go up by 2.53%, we would end up with about a 3% inflation rate. When we look at the history of housing prices (as measured by the Housing Price Index or HPI) and adjust inflation to take out housing (assuming that it's 32.09% of the inflation number), on the opposite page is a chart of what we've seen from 1890–2016[1].

The distance between each horizontal line shows a doubling in price. Part of what drove this was America's rapid urbanization and suburbanization. At the end of WWII, roughly half the population lived in cities. Now it's north of 80%. It should be noted that these prices reflect national averages. If we were to isolate urban areas, we would see an even sharper rise in housing prices.

One can also see this and observe the familiar ups and downs that we see in the stock market—though with substantially less volatility. More recently we see a respectable dip in housing prices during The Great Recession of 2008–2009.

You may remember vehement criticism of the bankers who designed mortgages off the flawed observation that housing prices are stable and don't go down. If you were to only look at the era from 1941–2006, it would be easy to make this assumption. In fact, national housing prices went up virtually without interruption.

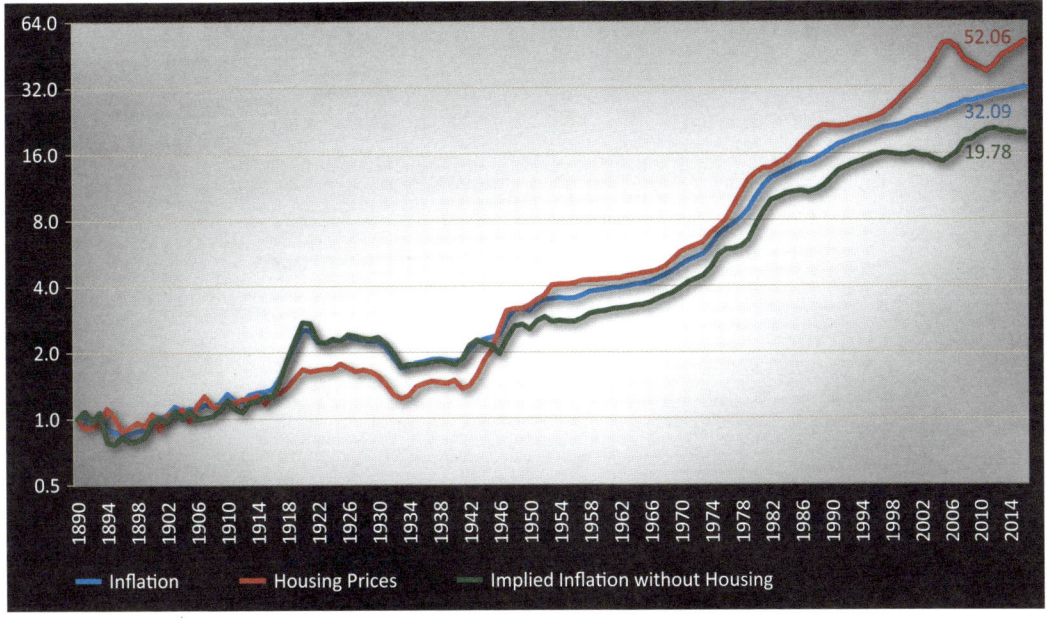

In 2006, it may have seemed unimaginable that the next five years would look like:

2007 ... **-5.39%** | 2008 ... **-11.99%** | 2009 ... **-3.85%**
2010 ... **-4.14%** | 2011 ... **-3.89%**

Clocking in what the media was routinely calling an "unprecedented" **-26.24%**[2] five-year national housing price decline. Yup, unprecedented ... if you ignore those two pesky eras prior to 1941:

1894–1896 ... **-21.35%** | 1925–1932 ... **-30.49%**

In fact, if we zoom in on this chart, we can see that 100 years ago, housing prices, and prices in general were highly volatile:

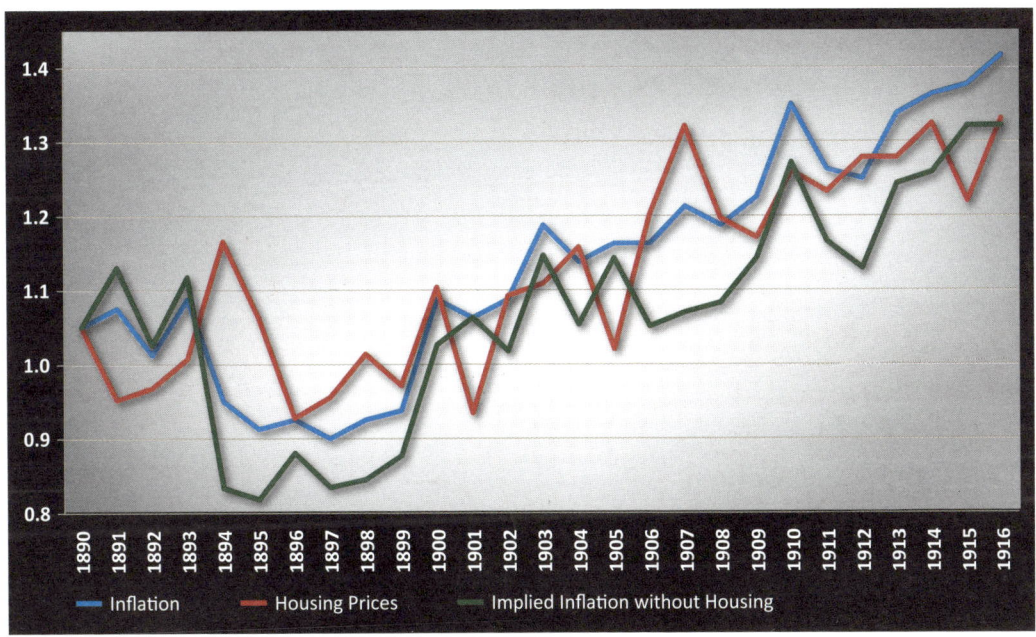

During that generation, in roughly 1 out of 3 years, housing prices were negative. That was one reason for the creation of The Federal Reserve Bank in 1913. As with stocks, in real estate, time prevails over volatility. Values historically increase *at least in accordance with inflation*—and normally more.

Granted, we are looking at all of the United States housing market. We could look at specific cities where this wasn't the case (come on, we're all thinking it: Detroit) or parts of cities that become the rough part of town where considerable patience would not have panned out. In a moment, we'll paint a scenario of buying a house in Detroit before the city declined.

Again, just as with stocks, it's absolutely *possible* that over the course of multiple decades a house did not go up in value. It is not *probable*. Let's look at the "return" of housing values from 1890–2016, as if it were a stock. On the opposite page we can see the one-year and five-year period.

Once you get to five-year eras you have three main periods where houses lost value:

1. The general price volatility from 1890–1916
2. The Great Depression
3. The Great Recession

Once you go to longer eras, the only solidly negative time was the Great Depression. Your worst luck situation would be if you bought a house in 1926. It would have taken until 1944 before you saw your value eclipse your purchase price. Later, we'll see an analog of this experience with the Detroit example.

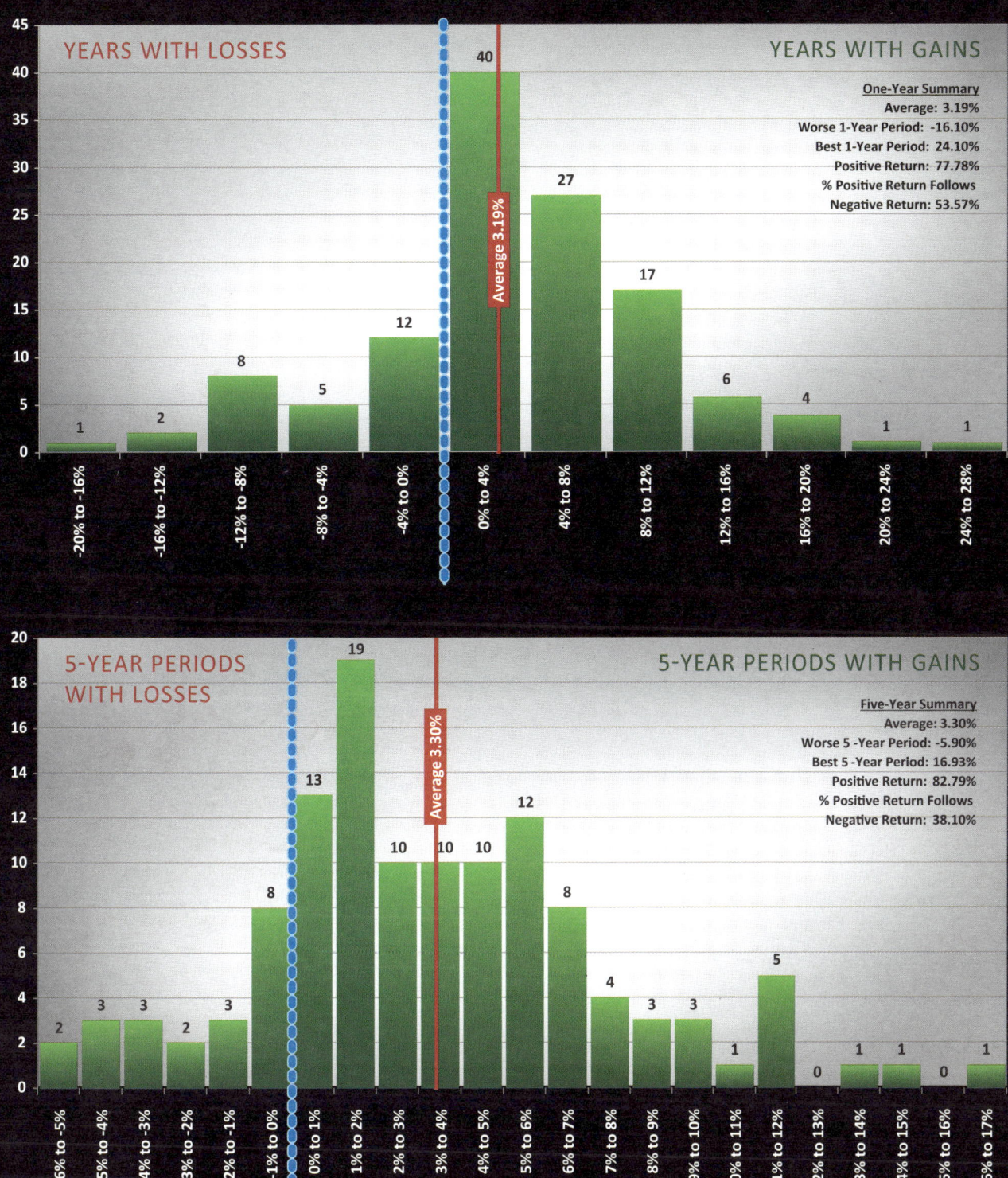

161

From 1890–2016 here were three key rates:

> Inflation without housing prices ... **2.40%**
> Inflation ... **2.79%**
> Housing Prices ... **3.19%**

If you want to evaluate with more recent history, here are some epochs:

	All	Post Federal Reserve	Post WWII	Post High Inflation
Beginning	1890	1914	1946	1983
End	2016	2016	2016	2016
Years in Range	126	102	70	33
Inflation (CPI)	2.79%	3.18%	3.78%	2.81%
Housing Prices (HPI)	3.19%	3.70%	4.41%	3.96%
CPI without HPI	2.40%	2.78%	3.35%	2.05%
Difference	**0.79%**	**0.92%**	**1.06%**	**1.91%**

The "difference" at the bottom is the difference between housing prices and all other prices. In the past 125 years, there have been three giant hinges in the United States economy:

1. The first was the creation of the Federal Reserve which had a very strong stabilizing effect to our economy.
2. The second was WWII which brought us out of isolationism to global economic dominance. Part of the spoils of this war were a global trade network and being the only major industrialized nation to emerge from the war with its infrastructure virtually untouched. Before the war our military was the 17th biggest, afterward we were *the* biggest. Before the war we had 14 overseas bases, afterward we had a vast network of them along our trade network. We became the biggest creditor in the world, controlled 2/3rds of the gold supply, and we produced *half* the world's manufacturing. The wind in our sails from this era is not likely to be replicated.
3. The third hinge was fixing the economic problem of elevated inflation that plagued us from 1968–1982. 1983 was the first year of (more or less) consistently normal inflation rates.

To me, the 1983–2016 is the most relevant one to our experience. Currently we have low inflation—nigh unto *deflation* until recently. At a minimum, the "Post Federal Reserve" era would be more relevant to us because of the Fed's primary objective of keeping inflation stable.

When you look at the numbers you can see that housing prices have historically outpaced inflation by *some* amount. In my opinion, the 1983–2016 era is most relevant to us. I recognize that this period happens to bias the numbers *in favor* of what we will talk about. I feel that this period rightfully excludes influences that don't apply to our economy today. Either way, it doesn't radically change things—using the other numbers only makes our analysis a nudge less powerful, but it doesn't undermine it.

An interesting financial phenomenon is that even if we assume that housing prices only track with inflation, the benefits of homeownership still stand. This will make sense shortly.

The exact number is less important than the relationship between them. We should see inflation without housing prices—adjusted to remove the 32.09% redundancy:

General prices (without housing) ... **2.05%**
Housing Prices ... **3.96%**

Bookmark those two numbers in your brain and let's talking about renting. Do rental rates follow housing prices? In a word: yes. Though with less volatility. In a graph:

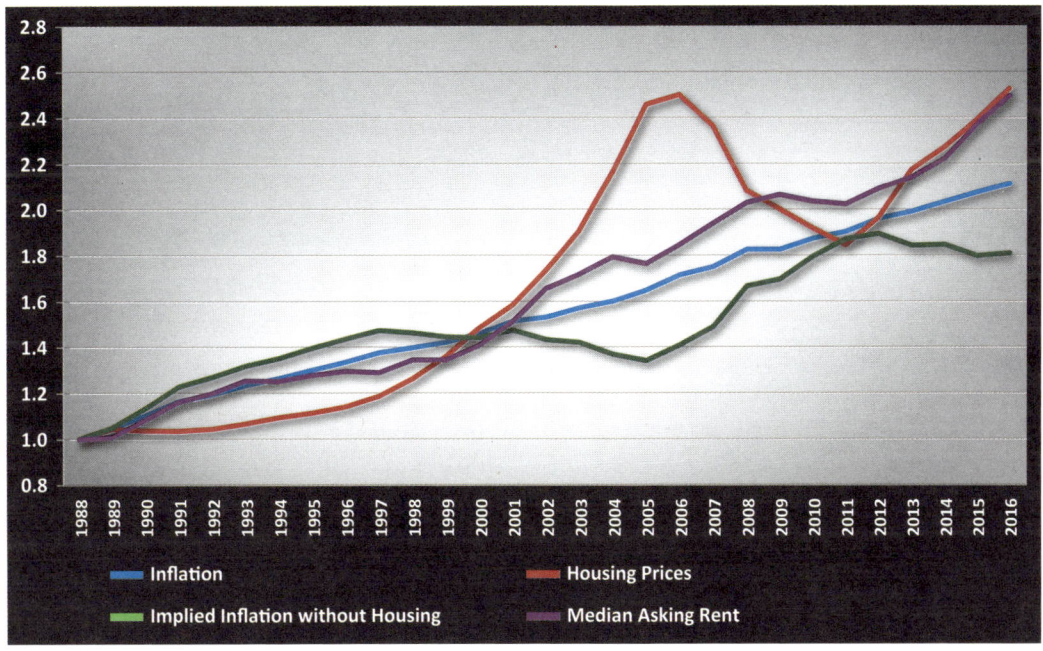

Unfortunately, it's harder to find reliable long-term data on rental rates than on housing prices. In the period that we have data, you can see the statistical do-si-do. This is not terribly surprising, since rents and home prices respond to highly related economics. It's all supply and demand. A poignant example is around 2007 when housing prices were crashing, rents increased sharply. Imagine masses of people getting foreclosed on (demand down = price down on housing) … and needing to rent some other place (demand up = price up on rentals).

Prior to this, among the red flags that suggested a housing bubble was that the rate at which housing prices increased *vastly outpaced* how fast rent rates were going up. Hindsight is 20/20. Things that correlate will *always* revert to the mean. The economics will always cause these two prices to oscillate around one another.

Another interesting thing we see is during the Great Recession era, when economists were crying about the need to fight deflation. If you pull (falling) housing prices out of inflation (the green line), we can see that the Great Recession was actually a period of sharp *inflation* for the prices of everything but housing. The deflation monster had already been in our midst from 1997–2005—an era when nobody was talking about it.

Over this regrettably short period we end up with:

General prices (without housing) … **2.14%**
General prices (with housing) … **2.71%**
Rent Prices … **3.32%**
Housing Prices … **3.37%**

These numbers are different than the earlier ones because we have a different time period. You can see (1) rent prices more or less following housing prices, and (2) both prices outstripping all other general prices. Here's the question, getting back to our core premise of the *actual* creation of wealth in *real dollars*: does homeownership *actually* create wealth?

What makes real estate unique is that you *must* participate in it as either a renter or an owner. Yes, you could be homeless, couch surf, or live in someone's closet, but most people pay for their shelter as either a renter or a buyer. Forced with this decision, let's look at renting versus owning from a financial planning standpoint.

Decreasing Spending *is* Increasing Wealth

For the time being, we are going to set aside the risks of homeownership—namely, the risk of owning a big expensive asset that will inevitably have big expensive problems. We will come back to this after contrasting owning versus renting, and financially optimizing homeownership.

Money is to buy stuff. Wealth is the power to buy stuff. On a monthly basis, having additional income is to experience greater wealth. Also, in the same manner, to have lower expenses is to experience greater wealth.

Imagine twins living in identical houses next door to each other. The first twin buys her house and the other rents his house. They have identical income as well. Starting out, they both make $3,740 a month, which makes their $1,200 per month housing cost exactly 32.09% of their income.

Owning Twin #1		Renting Twin #2	
Income	$3,740	Income	$3,740
Principal and Interest	$800	Rent Payment	$1,200
Insurance	$100		
Taxes	$100		
Maintenance	$200		
TOTAL	$1,200	TOTAL	$1,200
% of Income	32.09%	% of Income	32.09%
Remaining	$2,540	TOTAL	$2,540

After their housing needs are paid for, the two twins experience identical wealth. They both have $2,540 to buy other stuff. However, as we saw earlier, over time the benefits of freezing the principal and interest part of your housing cost make Twin #1 experience greater wealth *even though* their incomes remain identical. We'll assume that their incomes and variable housing costs both rise at *the same 3% rate*. This was where the twins stood just after the home-owning twin paid her last mortgage payment:

Owning Twin #1		Renting Twin #2	
Income	$9,077	Income	$9,077
Principal and Interest	$0	Rent Payment	$2,913
Insurance	$243		
Taxes	$243		
Maintenance	$485		
TOTAL	$971	TOTAL	$2,913
% of Income	10.70%	% of Income	32.09%
Remaining	$8,107	TOTAL	$6,165

Because Twin #1 is spending less, she is wealthier—in *addition to* the net worth bump from owning a home. In terms of income, their $9,077 in monthly income is $108,924 per year. However, because Twin #1 is spending $1,942 less per month,

Twin #2 would have to make $132,228 per year for them to have the same cash flow and to *experience* identical wealth.

Decreasing spending *is* increasing wealth. From a cash flow perspective, it is the same as having an additional source of income. This is true whether or not your house is rising in value or your income tracks with inflation. The opportunity to not spend money is the same as an opportunity for additional income.

The Elusive Goal of Saving up for a House *Without* a Mortgage

You hate banks, hate the idea of them making money off you, hate the idea of having any debt at all. I get it. Much of my career is driven off the same sentiment. Personally, it drives me nuts being dependent on, well, anything. But remember, *how you feel about something ain't got nothin' to do with if it's good for you.*

Let's paint a picture of someone starting out in 1983 who wants to buy a house *without* a mortgage. This is understandable since mortgage rates at the time were in the 13% department, having only two years previously peaked at 18.45%[3].

Let's say this person commits 10% of his gross income to savings. We'll assume he's earning the historical median income of a U.S. Household in that year.[4] His savings will be put into a bank account earning the same interest rate as a one-year U.S. government treasury bill, which you can see in the white column. We start in 1983, as it is the beginning of our "normal" period. He would be saving up $2,089 (the median household income that year was $20,885). As his income increases each year, he also increases how much he saves.

His goal is to buy a typical house. Starting out in 1983, this happens to be $70,915. The problem is that this goal becomes rather elusive because by 1989, the price of an average home rose to $112,066.

The way that he motivates himself is by focusing on what *percent* of the house price he has saved up. In 1983, he saved up $2,089 toward a $70,915 purchase price. So he would be 2.95% toward his goal. Not too bad. At this pace, he'll get to his goal of paying for a house in cash in 34 years (which happens to be early 2016). Fast forward a few years, in 1989, between his account earning interest and each year's savings, he has accumulated $21,661. With the house priced at $112,066, he is now 19.33% toward his goal.

His savings account balance is the entirety of his net worth, which you can see in the yellow column. This is what the numbers would look like (these are all year end numbers):[5]

Year	Average House Price	Median Income	Rent Amount	Savings Amount	1-Year US Treasury Securites Rate	Net Worth (Saving Account Balance)	How Much Price Went Up or Down	House Price Increase as % of Income	Amount Applied Toward Goal	Amount to Chasing a Higher Price	% to Goal
1983	$70,915	$20,885	$6,397	$2,089	9.57%	$2,089	$3,228	15%	$0	($640)	2.95%
1984	$75,189	$22,415	$6,782	$2,242	10.89%	$4,530	$4,273	19%	$0	($678)	6.02%
1985	$80,628	$23,618	$7,273	$2,362	8.43%	$7,385	$5,440	23%	$0	($727)	9.16%
1986	$87,742	$24,897	$7,914	$2,490	6.46%	$10,497	$7,114	29%	$0	($791)	11.96%
1987	$95,656	$26,061	$8,628	$2,606	6.76%	$13,781	$7,914	30%	$0	($863)	14.41%
1988	$103,742	$27,225	$9,358	$2,723	7.65%	$17,436	$8,086	30%	$0	($936)	16.81%
1989	$112,066	$28,906	$10,108	$2,891	8.54%	$21,661	$8,324	29%	$0	($1,011)	19.33%
1990	$117,551	$29,943	$10,603	$2,994	7.88%	$26,504	$5,485	18%	$0	($1,060)	22.55%
1991	$119,970	$30,126	$10,821	$3,013	5.86%	$31,606	$2,419	8%	$594	($488)	26.34%
1992	$122,508	$30,636	$11,050	$3,064	3.89%	$36,521	$2,539	8%	$525	($580)	29.81%
1993	$125,090	$31,241	$11,283	$3,124	3.43%	$41,065	$2,581	8%	$543	($585)	32.83%
1994	$127,901	$32,264	$11,537	$3,226	5.31%	$45,702	$2,812	9%	$415	($739)	35.73%
1995	$131,857	$34,076	$11,893	$3,408	5.95%	$51,536	$3,956	12%	$0	($1,189)	39.09%
1996	$136,691	$35,492	$12,330	$3,549	5.51%	$58,151	$4,834	14%	$0	($1,233)	42.54%
1997	$142,037	$37,005	$12,812	$3,701	5.63%	$65,057	$5,346	14%	$0	($1,281)	45.80%
1998	$148,830	$38,885	$13,424	$3,889	5.05%	$72,608	$6,793	17%	$0	($1,342)	48.79%
1999	$156,710	$40,696	$14,135	$4,070	5.08%	$80,346	$7,880	19%	$0	($1,414)	51.27%
2000	$167,656	$41,990	$15,123	$4,199	6.11%	$88,625	$10,946	26%	$0	($1,512)	52.86%
2001	$180,882	$42,228	$16,316	$4,223	3.48%	$98,261	$13,226	31%	$0	($1,632)	54.32%
2002	$195,423	$42,409	$17,627	$4,241	2.00%	$105,922	$14,541	34%	$0	($1,763)	54.20%
2003	$213,728	$43,318	$19,278	$4,332	1.24%	$112,374	$18,305	42%	$0	($1,928)	52.58%
2004	$240,432	$44,334	$21,687	$4,433	1.89%	$118,206	$26,704	60%	$0	($2,169)	49.16%
2005	$274,468	$46,326	$24,757	$4,633	3.62%	$125,068	$34,037	73%	$0	($2,476)	45.57%
2006	$293,195	$48,201	$26,446	$4,820	4.93%	$134,414	$18,727	39%	$0	($2,645)	45.84%
2007	$287,575	$50,233	$25,939	$5,023	4.52%	$146,067	($5,620)	-11%	$5,023	$2,429	50.79%
2008	$262,244	$50,303	$23,654	$5,030	1.82%	$157,702	($25,331)	-50%	$5,030	$2,665	60.14%
2009	$237,458	$49,777	$21,419	$4,978	0.47%	$165,554	($24,786)	-50%	$4,978	$2,836	69.72%
2010	$231,194	$49,276	$20,854	$4,928	0.32%	$171,261	($6,265)	-13%	$4,928	$2,842	74.08%
2011	$222,556	$50,054	$20,075	$5,005	0.18%	$176,811	($8,638)	-17%	$5,005	$2,998	79.45%
2012	$225,409	$51,017	$20,332	$5,102	0.18%	$182,234	$2,853	6%	$2,248	$215	80.85%
2013	$247,098	$53,585	$22,288	$5,359	0.13%	$187,912	$21,688	40%	$0	($2,229)	76.05%
2014	$263,490	$53,657	$23,767	$5,366	0.12%	$193,525	$16,393	31%	$0	($2,377)	73.45%
2015	$277,934	$56,516	$25,070	$5,652	0.32%	$199,410	$14,444	26%	$0	($2,507)	71.75%
2016	$287,565	$57,647	$25,938	$5,765	0.61%	$205,816	$9,630	17%	$0	($2,594)	71.57%

Let's focus on the key numbers on this table (1) the price of the house he's trying to buy, (2) the amount in savings, and (3) % to goal vs. % left to save. These numbers are laid out in the graph on the next page.

You can see that even though his savings account is growing (the solid yellow part), the housing price keeps on elusively growing too. This is the unpleasant nature of saving up for something that keeps rising in price. One benefit of a mortgage is that it *locks* the price in. Earlier we emphasized locking part of your monthly expenses and protecting a major expense from being subject to inflation. The additional benefit is that you are locking in the purchase price, which stops the elusive task of saving up for something going up in price.

Going forward, this very determined man would set the world record for treading water. In the final year of our data, the house price was $287,565 and his savings addition that year was $5,765. If you divide the annual savings amount into the housing price you get *2.00%*. What this means is that if housing prices were to go up by *more than* 2.00%, then he is literally going nowhere both in achieving his Sisyphean goal, and as a perpetual renter.

His savings account interest rate of **0.61%** helps him *a little bit* and brings the number up to 2.44%, but housing historically goes up in price faster than this rate. After

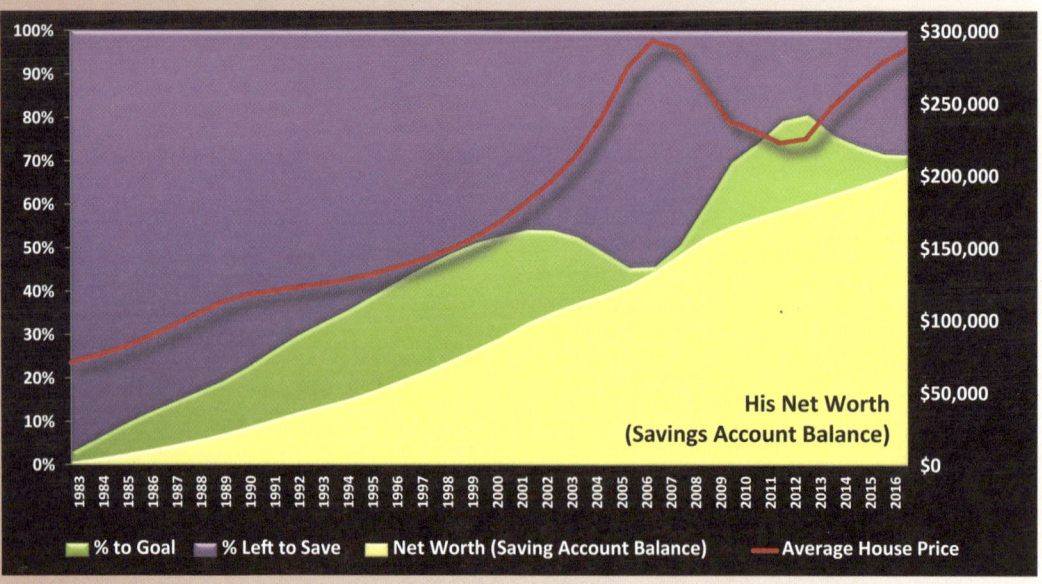

Legend: % to Goal | % Left to Save | Net Worth (Saving Account Balance) | Average House Price

His Net Worth
(Savings Account Balance)

plugging away at this for over 34 years, the man should not expect to realistically reach his goal anytime soon.

The moral of the story is that unless you have all the money now, embrace a mortgage as the only sensible way to homeownership. As we'll learn in a moment, *even if* you do have the money at your disposal, a mortgage is *still* the most sensible way of doing this.

Alas, yet again, we see that the true risk is *rising prices*. Sound familiar? The enemy is inflation and the war is eternal.

An Alternate Path: Eliminating 80% of the Elusiveness

When we talked about this man saving up to buy a house 100% in cash, we briefly mentioned his net worth. Net worth is the total of everything you own after debts are paid off. In the example above, his net worth was his savings account balance (the yellow column). For simplicity's sake we assumed he owned nothing else. His net worth went from $0 at the beginning of 1983 to $205,816 in 2016.

When you own a house, the equity in the house adds to your net worth. If you have $20,000 in savings, and put it as a $20,000 down payment on a $100,000 house, you have just shifted money from one part of your personal balance sheet to another. Your equity is the value minus the outstanding mortgage balance (e.g. $100,000 purchase price - $80,000 mortgage = $20,000 in equity). As the value of the house goes up and as you pay your mortgage down, your equity (and net worth) goes up.

We'll now revisit this same house buying scenario with an alternate path. We'll have this man only save up 20% as a down payment using his same savings plan of 10% of his income. This is still no small task and will take several years. Saving up for 20% of a price that keeps increasing is still an elusive goal, but the finish line is much closer.

Once the man reaches 20%, he'll buy a house at whatever that year's average house price is. For our calculations, he'll also pay "points" (the upfront cost of getting a mortgage) at whatever the average points are that year, pay that year's average 30-year fixed mortgage rate, and keep the mortgage even if rates go down. In other words, he won't refinance into a better rate.

To get a full and fair mortgage payment picture, we must include taxes and insurance. We'll assume 1.25% of the current *house value* in property taxes and 0.5% in insurance—which is about average. These two numbers will go up as the property value goes up, thus making his mortgage payment go up.

We need to factor in another element: rent. We didn't include it in the previous calculation, but we'll add it to see how homeownership changes his cash flow. However, historical rent prices reflect *apartment* rents more than *single family home* rents, so we need to use something equivalent. For a fair and even number for a typical rent for a house, we'll assume that it is 9.08% of the house value (which is the 15-year historical average ratio).[6] As the value of the house goes up, so does his rent. Additionally, as a homeowner, we'll see how protecting most of his house payment from inflation helps him.

Rent matters because once he buys a house, his cash flow changes. When he was saving up, each month he was paying rent and saving up 10% of his income. After he buys a house he instead pays a mortgage payment which may be more, or less than what his rent was. Or, to put it in an image, this is what that "extra cash flow" looks like if his mortgage payment is more than the rent payment:

$1,000 Rent	$500 (10% of Income Savings)
$1,200 Mortgage Payment	$300 Savings
$1,500 Monthly Out of Pocket (the same amount either way)	

That savings amount is no longer needed to save up for a house, so he can apply it somewhere else. To make it a fair comparison we have to decide what to do with that $300 in extra money. We'll give this man two options:

- Option #1—The extra money after paying his mortgage goes into his savings account just as it did before.
- Option #2—The extra money after paying his mortgage goes toward paying down his mortgage balance. If the mortgage costs him more then we will subtract it from his net worth.

The second option would be more in character for this man because he recoils from debt. We'll look at both options. On the opposite page is a table with the numbers from Option #1 along with a graph showing the results.

It took him 9 years to save up that 20% down payment. At the end of 1991 he buys a house and begins 1992 with his new cash flow scenario and mortgage. You see that at first his net worth doesn't change because he's shifting his assets from savings to equity in a home. You'll also notice that at first he saves *less* because at first his mortgage payment is more expensive than his rent payment would have been.

From the moment he gets a house (and mortgage), his net worth (the solid blue part in the graph) begins to go up rapidly *more than* if he were still trying to save up money (the solid yellow part).

At the end of it, his net worth is $349,360 *more by going into debt*, than if he had been trying to save up for the house. Several factors make this happen. The obvious one is that the value of the house is going up, making him wealthier. Additionally, his mortgage payments pay off the liability on the house, increasing his net worth.

The other factor is more subtle. When he bought the house, not only did it freeze the price of the house, but it also froze a bulk of his monthly expenses. Earlier in the chapter, we talked about the hypothetical comparison in which the principal and interest part of a mortgage payment freezes while the taxes and insurance increase.

Now that we have some *actual* numbers to look at, on the opposite page is a breakdown of his monthly expenses in 1992.

Year	Average House Price	Rent Amount	Savings Amount	30 Year Mortgage Rate	Average Mortgage Points Paid	Net Worth (Savings and Equity)	Down Payment	Mortgage Balance	Annual Mortgage Payment	Net Worth as % of House Value
1983	$70,915	$6,397	$2,089	13.24%	2.10%	$2,089				2.95%
1984	$75,189	$6,782	$2,242	13.88%	2.50%	$4,530				6.02%
1985	$80,628	$7,273	$2,362	12.43%	2.50%	$7,385				9.16%
1986	$87,742	$7,914	$2,490	10.19%	2.20%	$10,497				11.96%
1987	$95,656	$8,628	$2,606	10.21%	2.20%	$13,781				14.41%
1988	$103,742	$9,358	$2,723	10.34%	2.10%	$17,436				16.81%
1989	$112,066	$10,108	$2,891	10.32%	2.10%	$21,661				19.33%
1990	$117,551	$10,603	$2,994	10.13%	2.10%	$26,504				22.55%
1991	$119,970	$10,821	$3,013	9.25%	2.00%	$31,606	$23,994	$97,895		26.34%
1992	$122,508	$11,050	$2,306	8.39%	1.70%	$37,068	$0	$97,210	$11,808	30.26%
1993	$125,090	$11,283	$2,554	7.31%	1.60%	$43,409	$0	$96,461	$11,853	34.70%
1994	$127,901	$11,537	$2,860	8.38%	1.80%	$50,407	$0	$95,643	$11,903	39.41%
1995	$131,857	$11,893	$3,329	7.93%	1.80%	$59,549	$0	$94,749	$11,972	45.16%
1996	$136,691	$12,330	$3,822	7.81%	1.70%	$70,517	$0	$93,773	$12,056	51.59%
1997	$142,037	$12,812	$4,362	7.60%	1.70%	$82,813	$0	$92,706	$12,150	58.30%
1998	$148,830	$13,424	$5,044	6.94%	1.10%	$97,701	$0	$91,541	$12,269	65.65%
1999	$156,710	$14,135	$5,798	7.44%	1.00%	$114,693	$0	$90,268	$12,407	73.19%
2000	$167,656	$15,123	$6,723	8.05%	1.00%	$136,204	$0	$88,877	$12,598	81.24%
2001	$180,882	$16,316	$7,709	6.97%	0.90%	$162,166	$0	$87,357	$12,830	89.65%
2002	$195,423	$17,627	$8,784	6.54%	0.60%	$189,540	$0	$85,697	$13,084	96.99%
2003	$213,728	$19,278	$10,206	5.83%	0.60%	$221,462	$0	$83,883	$13,405	103.62%
2004	$240,432	$21,687	$12,248	5.84%	0.70%	$263,535	$0	$81,901	$13,872	109.61%
2005	$274,468	$24,757	$14,922	5.87%	0.60%	$316,640	$0	$79,737	$14,468	115.36%
2006	$293,195	$26,446	$16,471	6.41%	0.50%	$358,614	$0	$77,371	$14,795	122.31%
2007	$287,575	$25,939	$16,266	6.34%	0.40%	$378,886	$0	$74,788	$14,697	131.75%
2008	$262,244	$23,654	$14,431	6.03%	0.60%	$378,320	$0	$71,965	$14,254	144.26%
2009	$237,458	$21,419	$12,577	5.04%	0.70%	$372,622	$0	$68,881	$13,820	156.92%
2010	$231,194	$20,854	$12,071	4.69%	0.70%	$382,758	$0	$65,511	$13,710	165.56%
2011	$222,556	$20,075	$11,521	4.45%	0.70%	$390,013	$0	$61,831	$13,559	175.24%
2012	$225,409	$20,332	$11,825	3.66%	0.70%	$409,129	$0	$57,809	$13,609	181.51%
2013	$247,098	$22,288	$13,658	3.98%	0.70%	$449,292	$0	$53,416	$13,989	181.83%
2014	$263,490	$23,767	$14,857	4.17%	0.60%	$485,678	$0	$48,616	$14,275	184.32%
2015	$277,934	$25,070	$16,193	3.85%	0.60%	$521,886	$0	$43,372	$14,528	187.77%
2016	$287,565	$25,938	$17,006	3.65%	0.50%	$555,176	$0	$37,644	$14,697	193.06%

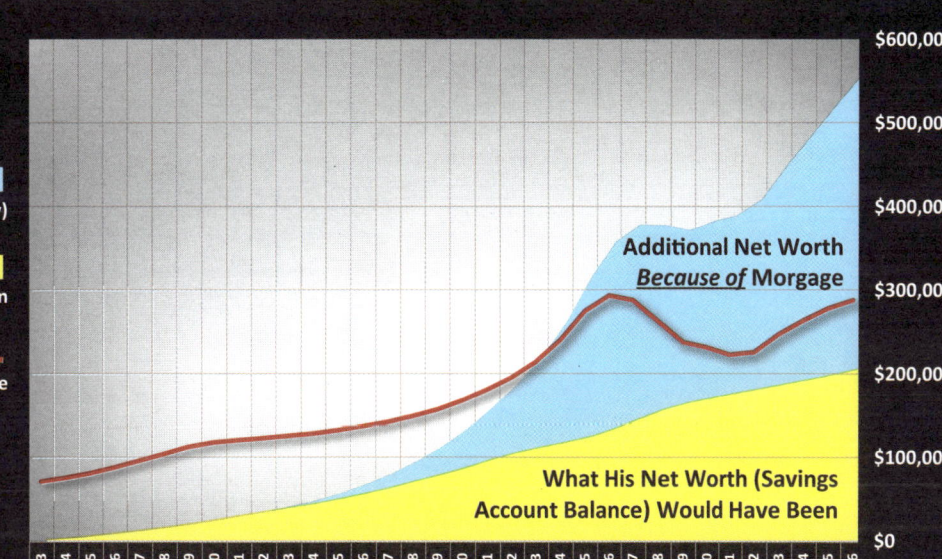

Net Worth (Savings and Equity)

What Savings Account Would Have Been

Average House Price

Additional Net Worth *Because of* Morgage

What His Net Worth (Savings Account Balance) Would Have Been

1992					
Owning			**Renting**		
Principal and Interest		$805	Rent Payment		$7,070
Insurance (0.50% of value)		$51			
Taxes		$128			
TOTAL		$984	TOTAL		$7,070
DIFFERENCE		($63)			$63
Monthly Income Amount		**$2,553**	**Monthly Income Amount**		**$2,553**
Monthly Savings Amount		$192	Monthly Savings Amount		$255
Annual Savings Amount		$2,306	Annual Savings Amount		$3,064
Payment as a % of Income		38.54%	Payment as a % of Income		36.07%
Savings as a % of Income		7.53%	Savings as a % of Income		10.00%
Both as a % of Income		**46.07%**	**Both as a % of Income**		**46.07%**

At first, his mortgage payment was $63 *more than* his rent payment. This meant that he couldn't quite put 10% of his gross income into savings, and could only afford to save 7.53% of his income ($2,306 per year). Over time the rose-colored parts of these payments increased with the house value, while the green principal and interest part froze. This is where he stood in 2016:

2016					
Owning			**Renting**		
Principal and Interest		$805	Rent Payment		$2,162
Insurance (0.50% of value)		$120			
Taxes		$300			
TOTAL		$1,225	TOTAL		$2,162
DIFFERENCE		$937			($937)
Monthly Income Amount		**$4,804**	**Monthly Income Amount**		**$4,804**
Monthly Savings Amount		$1,417	Monthly Savings Amount		$480
Annual Savings Amount		$17,006	Annual Savings Amount		$5,765
Payment as a % of Income		25.49%	Payment as a % of Income		45.00%
Savings as a % of Income		29.50%	Savings as a % of Income		10.00%
Both as a % of Income		**55.00%**	**Both as a % of Income**		**55.00%**

His housing now costs him substantially less as a percent of his income. Because of this, he's able to afford to put aside *much more* money into savings. It's a massive difference: being able to save $937 per month more (or 29.50% of his income) and with the same ease as if he were still renting and putting 10% into savings.

His day-to-day financial outlay is *the same* as the renter, but because of homeownership, he can apply more of this outlay to savings.

Owning an asset that increases in value, while protecting the biggest piece of his cash flow from price increases, creates wealth in every sense of the word. He's better off being in debt, even though it seems like he's losing money paying interest to a bank via the mortgage. Not just any interest, but the historically high interest rate of 9.25%. A modern day rate would favor buying even more.

Let's look at Option #2, where he uses the extra money to pay off his mortgage sooner. On the surface, this makes logical sense. He's paying a mortgage rate of 9.25%, far more than the rate at which the bank rewards his savings. Falling bank interest rates while he owned the home made the discrepancy even more glaring.

Here are the numbers:

Year	Average House Price	Rent Amount	Savings Amount	30-Year Mortgage Rate	Average Mortgage Points Paid	Net Worth (Savings and Equity)	Down Payment	Mortgage Balance	Annual Mortgage Payment	Net Worth as % of House Value
1983	$70,915	$6,397	$2,089	13.24%	2.10%	$2,089				2.95%
1984	$75,189	$6,782	$2,242	13.88%	2.50%	$4,530				6.02%
1985	$80,628	$7,273	$2,362	12.43%	2.50%	$7,385				9.16%
1986	$87,742	$7,914	$2,490	10.19%	2.20%	$10,497				11.96%
1987	$95,656	$8,628	$2,606	10.21%	2.20%	$13,781				14.41%
1988	$103,742	$9,358	$2,723	10.34%	2.10%	$17,436				16.81%
1989	$112,066	$10,108	$2,891	10.32%	2.10%	$21,661				19.33%
1990	$117,551	$10,603	$2,994	10.13%	2.10%	$26,504				22.55%
1991	$119,970	$10,821	$3,013	9.25%	2.00%	$31,606	$23,994	$97,895		26.34%
1992	$122,508	$11,050	$0	8.39%	1.70%	$37,068	$0	$97,210	$11,808	30.26%
1993	$125,090	$11,283	$0	7.31%	1.60%	$40,855	$0	$96,461	$11,853	32.66%
1994	$127,901	$11,537	$0	8.38%	1.80%	$44,905	$0	$95,643	$11,903	35.11%
1995	$131,857	$11,893	$0	7.93%	1.80%	$50,426	$0	$94,749	$11,972	38.24%
1996	$136,691	$12,330	$0	7.81%	1.70%	$57,029	$0	$93,773	$12,056	41.72%
1997	$142,037	$12,812	$0	7.60%	1.70%	$64,219	$0	$92,706	$12,150	45.21%
1998	$148,830	$13,424	$0	6.94%	1.10%	$73,016	$0	$91,541	$12,269	49.06%
1999	$156,710	$14,135	$0	7.44%	1.00%	$82,963	$0	$90,268	$12,407	52.94%
2000	$167,656	$15,123	$0	8.05%	1.00%	$102,862	$0	$82,153	$12,598	61.35%
2001	$180,882	$16,316	$0	6.97%	0.90%	$126,377	$0	$72,925	$12,830	69.87%
2002	$195,423	$17,627	$0	6.54%	0.60%	$152,003	$0	$62,481	$13,084	77.78%
2003	$213,728	$19,278	$0	5.83%	0.60%	$182,709	$0	$50,462	$13,405	85.49%
2004	$240,432	$21,687	$0	5.84%	0.70%	$223,885	$0	$36,232	$13,872	93.12%
2005	$274,468	$24,757	$0	5.87%	0.60%	$275,380	$0	$19,145	$14,468	100.33%
2006	$293,195	$26,446	$25,826	6.41%	0.50%	$339,494	$0	$309	$5,131	115.79%
2007	$287,575	$25,939	$25,930	6.34%	0.40%	$362,412	$0	$0	$5,033	126.02%
2008	$262,244	$23,654	$24,095	6.03%	0.60%	$364,560	$0	$0	$4,589	139.02%
2009	$237,458	$21,419	$22,241	5.04%	0.70%	$363,880	$0	$0	$4,156	153.24%
2010	$231,194	$20,854	$21,735	4.69%	0.70%	$379,946	$0	$0	$4,046	164.34%
2011	$222,556	$20,075	$21,185	4.45%	0.70%	$392,967	$0	$0	$3,895	176.57%
2012	$225,409	$20,332	$21,489	3.66%	0.70%	$417,619	$0	$0	$3,945	185.27%
2013	$247,098	$22,288	$23,322	3.98%	0.70%	$462,966	$0	$0	$4,324	187.36%
2014	$263,490	$23,767	$24,521	4.17%	0.60%	$504,165	$0	$0	$4,611	191.34%
2015	$277,934	$25,070	$25,857	3.85%	0.60%	$544,757	$0	$0	$4,864	196.00%
2016	$287,565	$25,938	$26,671	3.65%	0.50%	$581,916	$0	$0	$5,032	202.36%

By paying down, and ultimately paying *off* his mortgage in early 2006, he has $26,740 more than if he had stored his monthly extra income in savings. The rate of return on his savings is *much less* than the 9.25% he's paying on his mortgage. Let's look at this graphically. We now have the new orange part (just a sliver), which represents his net worth as he's using his cash flow to pay down his mortgage:

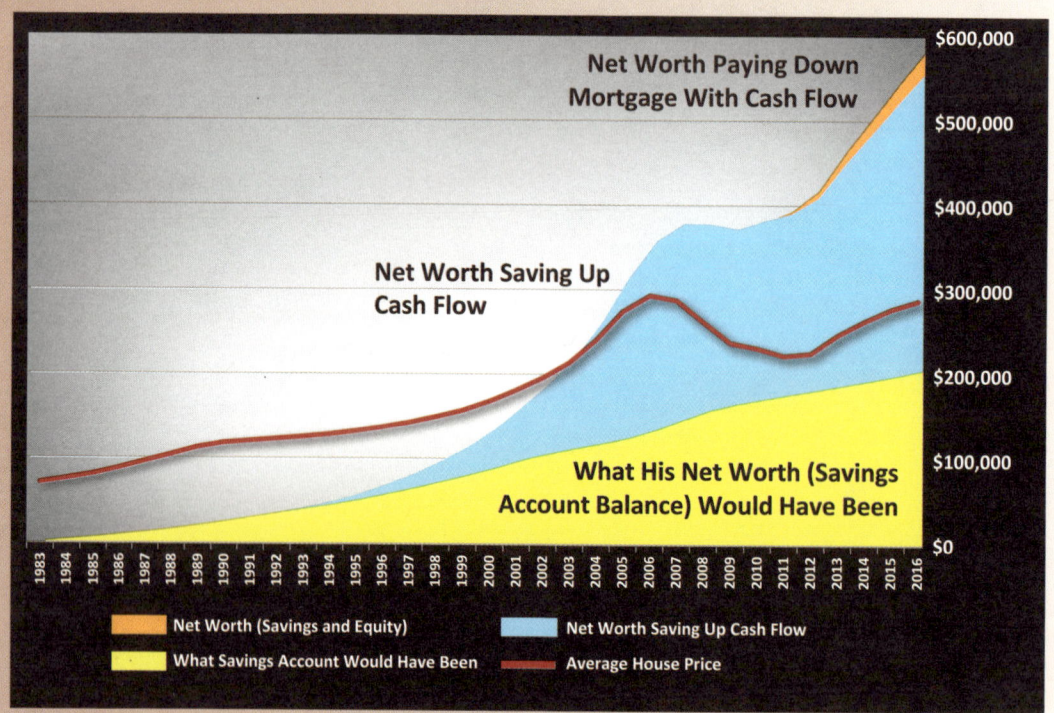

It's not a radical difference, but it is a difference. This infers an Option #3. What if instead of saving his money into a bank (or paying down his mortgage), he put it into the S&P 500? Let's run this using historical stock market returns. On the opposite page is this table along with the graph of the numbers below.

At the end of it, his net worth is $989,446, which is $434,270 more than if he had just kept saving it into his bank. You can see the Financial Crisis taking a much sharper temporary hit on his net worth, but even at its brief worst point, investing would have *still* outperformed just putting it in the bank.

As we beat to a pulp in the investments chapter, his (nearly) million dollar question is if he patiently sat through the downturns. If he panicked out at the bottom, he would have experienced permanent loss. But he didn't panic, and his reward for patience was nearly doubling his net worth.

Year	Average House Price	Rent Amount	Savings Amount	30-Year Mortgage Rate	Average Mortgage Points Paid	Total Return of S&P 500	Net Worth (Investments and Equity)	Down Payment	Mortgage Balance	Annual Mortgage Payment	Net Worth as % of House Value
1983	$70,915	$6,397	$2,089	13.24%	2.10%	24.08%	$2,089				2.95%
1984	$75,189	$6,782	$2,242	13.88%	2.50%	5.72%	$4,833				6.43%
1985	$80,628	$7,273	$2,362	12.43%	2.50%	31.21%	$7,471				9.27%
1986	$87,742	$7,914	$2,490	10.19%	2.20%	18.27%	$12,293				14.01%
1987	$95,656	$8,628	$2,606	10.21%	2.20%	4.85%	$17,145				17.92%
1988	$103,742	$9,358	$2,723	10.34%	2.10%	16.05%	$20,698				19.95%
1989	$112,066	$10,108	$2,891	10.32%	2.10%	31.06%	$26,911				24.01%
1990	$117,551	$10,603	$2,994	10.13%	2.10%	-3.53%	$38,263				32.55%
1991	$119,970	$10,821	$3,013	9.25%	2.00%	30.07%	$39,926	$23,994	$97,895		33.28%
1992	$122,508	$11,050	$2,306	8.39%	1.70%	7.33%	$55,540	$0	$97,210	$11,808	45.34%
1993	$125,090	$11,283	$2,554	7.31%	1.60%	9.79%	$63,642	$0	$96,461	$11,853	50.88%
1994	$127,901	$11,537	$2,860	8.38%	1.80%	1.24%	$73,560	$0	$95,643	$11,903	57.51%
1995	$131,857	$11,893	$3,329	7.93%	1.80%	37.21%	$82,253	$0	$94,749	$11,972	62.38%
1996	$136,691	$12,330	$3,822	7.81%	1.70%	22.65%	$108,686	$0	$93,773	$12,056	79.51%
1997	$142,037	$12,812	$4,362	7.60%	1.70%	33.12%	$134,357	$0	$92,706	$12,150	94.59%
1998	$148,830	$13,424	$5,044	6.94%	1.10%	28.39%	$175,524	$0	$91,541	$12,269	117.94%
1999	$156,710	$14,135	$5,798	7.44%	1.00%	20.89%	$224,039	$0	$90,268	$12,407	142.96%
2000	$167,656	$15,123	$6,723	8.05%	1.00%	-8.32%	$276,025	$0	$88,877	$12,598	164.64%
2001	$180,882	$16,316	$7,709	6.97%	0.90%	-11.98%	$282,075	$0	$87,357	$12,830	155.94%
2002	$195,423	$17,627	$8,784	6.54%	0.60%	-22.23%	$284,475	$0	$85,697	$13,084	145.57%
2003	$213,728	$19,278	$10,206	5.83%	0.60%	28.39%	$275,956	$0	$83,883	$13,405	129.12%
2004	$240,432	$21,687	$12,248	5.84%	0.70%	10.65%	$358,370	$0	$81,901	$13,872	149.05%
2005	$274,468	$24,757	$14,922	5.87%	0.60%	5.51%	$430,777	$0	$79,737	$14,468	156.95%
2006	$293,195	$26,446	$16,471	6.41%	0.50%	13.65%	$481,357	$0	$77,371	$14,795	164.18%
2007	$287,575	$25,939	$16,266	6.34%	0.40%	5.24%	$530,821	$0	$74,788	$14,697	184.59%
2008	$262,244	$23,654	$14,431	6.03%	0.60%	-36.21%	$539,403	$0	$71,965	$14,254	205.69%
2009	$237,458	$21,419	$12,577	5.04%	0.70%	26.61%	$403,876	$0	$68,881	$13,820	170.08%
2010	$231,194	$20,854	$12,071	4.69%	0.70%	14.82%	$475,666	$0	$65,511	$13,710	205.74%
2011	$222,556	$20,075	$11,521	4.45%	0.70%	0.67%	$528,169	$0	$61,831	$13,559	237.32%
2012	$225,409	$20,332	$11,825	3.66%	0.70%	15.59%	$549,339	$0	$57,809	$13,609	243.71%
2013	$247,098	$22,288	$13,658	3.98%	0.70%	32.05%	$648,605	$0	$53,416	$13,989	262.49%
2014	$263,490	$23,767	$14,857	4.17%	0.60%	13.41%	$830,460	$0	$48,616	$14,275	315.18%
2015	$277,934	$25,070	$16,193	3.85%	0.60%	1.14%	$948,915	$0	$43,372	$14,528	341.42%
2016	$287,565	$25,938	$17,006	3.65%	0.50%	13.42%	$989,446	$0	$37,644	$14,697	344.08%

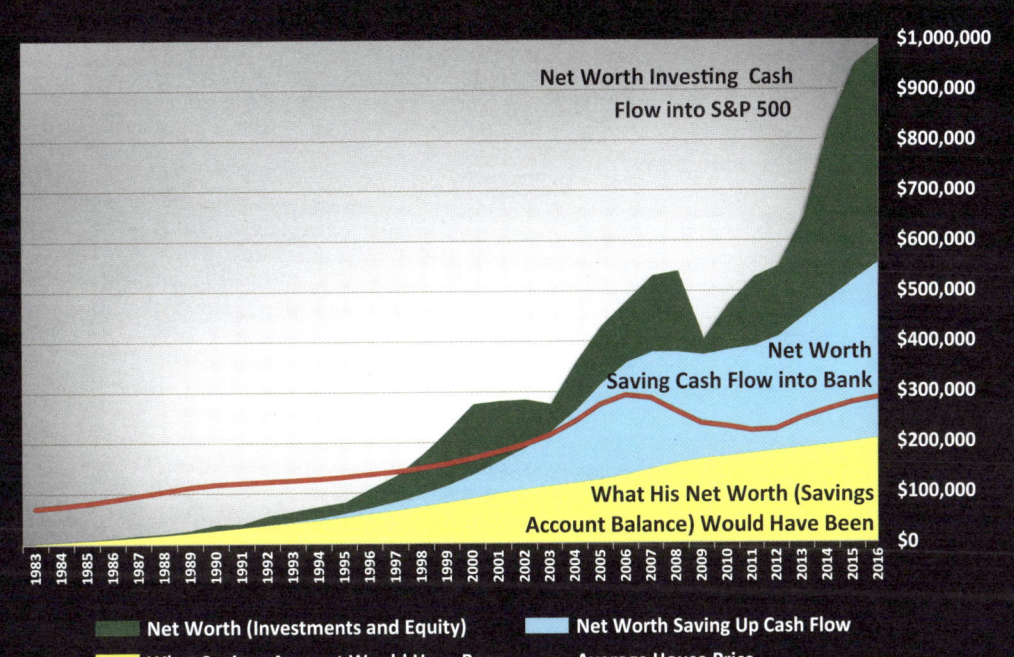

Net Worth Investing Cash Flow into S&P 500

Net Worth Saving Cash Flow into Bank

What His Net Worth (Savings Account Balance) Would Have Been

Net Worth (Investments and Equity)   Net Worth Saving Up Cash Flow
What Savings Account Would Have Been   Average House Price

What if he prioritized paying off his house first and *then* took all that extra cash flow and invested in the market? This is what Option #4 would look like:

Year	Average House Price	Rent Amount	Savings Amount	30-Year Mortgage Rate	Average Mortgage Points Paid	Total Return of S&P 500	Net Worth (Savings and Equity)	Down Payment	Mortgage Balance	Annual Mortgage Payment	Net Worth as % of House Value
1983	$70,915	$6,397	$2,089	13.24%	2.10%	24.08%	$2,089				2.95%
1984	$75,189	$6,782	$2,242	13.88%	2.50%	5.72%	$4,833				6.43%
1985	$80,628	$7,273	$2,362	12.43%	2.50%	31.21%	$7,471				9.27%
1986	$87,742	$7,914	$2,490	10.19%	2.20%	18.27%	$12,293				14.01%
1987	$95,656	$8,628	$2,606	10.21%	2.20%	4.85%	$17,145				17.92%
1988	$103,742	$9,358	$2,723	10.34%	2.10%	16.05%	$20,698				19.95%
1989	$112,066	$10,108	$2,891	10.32%	2.10%	31.06%	$26,911				24.01%
1990	$117,551	$10,603	$2,994	10.13%	2.10%	-3.53%	$38,263				32.55%
1991	$119,970	$10,821	$3,013	9.25%	2.00%	30.07%	$39,926	$23,994	$97,895		33.28%
1992	$122,508	$11,050	$0	8.39%	1.70%	7.33%	$53,235	$0	$97,210	$11,808	43.45%
1993	$125,090	$11,283	$0	7.31%	1.60%	9.79%	$58,613	$0	$96,461	$11,853	46.86%
1994	$127,901	$11,537	$0	8.38%	1.80%	1.24%	$65,179	$0	$95,643	$11,903	50.96%
1995	$131,857	$11,893	$0	7.93%	1.80%	37.21%	$70,438	$0	$94,749	$11,972	53.42%
1996	$136,691	$12,330	$0	7.81%	1.70%	22.65%	$88,652	$0	$93,773	$12,056	64.86%
1997	$142,037	$12,812	$0	7.60%	1.70%	33.12%	$105,423	$0	$92,706	$12,150	74.22%
1998	$148,830	$13,424	$0	6.94%	1.10%	28.39%	$131,961	$0	$91,541	$12,269	88.67%
1999	$156,710	$14,135	$0	7.44%	1.00%	20.89%	$162,312	$0	$90,268	$12,407	103.58%
2000	$167,656	$15,123	$0	8.05%	1.00%	-8.32%	$201,402	$0	$82,153	$12,598	120.13%
2001	$180,882	$16,316	$0	6.97%	0.90%	-11.98%	$214,218	$0	$72,925	$12,830	118.43%
2002	$195,423	$17,627	$0	6.54%	0.60%	-22.23%	$226,474	$0	$62,481	$13,084	115.89%
2003	$213,728	$19,278	$0	5.83%	0.60%	28.39%	$236,008	$0	$50,462	$13,405	110.42%
2004	$240,432	$21,687	$0	5.84%	0.70%	10.65%	$297,593	$0	$36,232	$13,872	123.77%
2005	$274,468	$24,757	$0	5.87%	0.60%	5.51%	$358,663	$0	$19,145	$14,468	130.68%
2006	$293,195	$26,446	$25,826	6.41%	0.50%	13.65%	$427,751	$0	$309	$5,131	145.89%
2007	$287,575	$25,939	$25,930	6.34%	0.40%	5.24%	$466,773	$0	$0	$5,033	162.31%
2008	$262,244	$23,654	$24,095	6.03%	0.60%	-36.21%	$474,924	$0	$0	$4,589	181.10%
2009	$237,458	$21,419	$22,241	5.04%	0.70%	26.61%	$395,378	$0	$0	$4,156	166.50%
2010	$231,194	$20,854	$21,735	4.69%	0.70%	14.82%	$452,872	$0	$0	$4,046	195.88%
2011	$222,556	$20,075	$21,185	4.45%	0.70%	0.67%	$498,271	$0	$0	$3,895	223.89%
2012	$225,409	$20,332	$21,489	3.66%	0.70%	15.59%	$524,467	$0	$0	$3,945	232.67%
2013	$247,098	$22,288	$23,322	3.98%	0.70%	32.05%	$616,112	$0	$0	$4,324	249.34%
2014	$263,490	$23,767	$24,521	4.17%	0.60%	13.41%	$775,297	$0	$0	$4,611	294.24%
2015	$277,934	$25,070	$25,857	3.85%	0.60%	1.14%	$884,252	$0	$0	$4,864	318.15%
2016	$287,565	$25,938	$26,671	3.65%	0.50%	13.42%	$927,484	$0	$0	$5,032	322.53%

Because the S&P 500 outperforms his mortgage interest rate, the choice to pay down his mortgage instead of saving it into the market *cost him* $61,962.

This is similar to our tale of Mary and Terry in the chapter on the Time Value of Money. The choice to pay down a mortgage in the first years of having one means losing the opportunity to have money in the stock market earlier in your life, thus forfeiting the powerful time value of money.

The grand graph of all of this is on the opposite page.

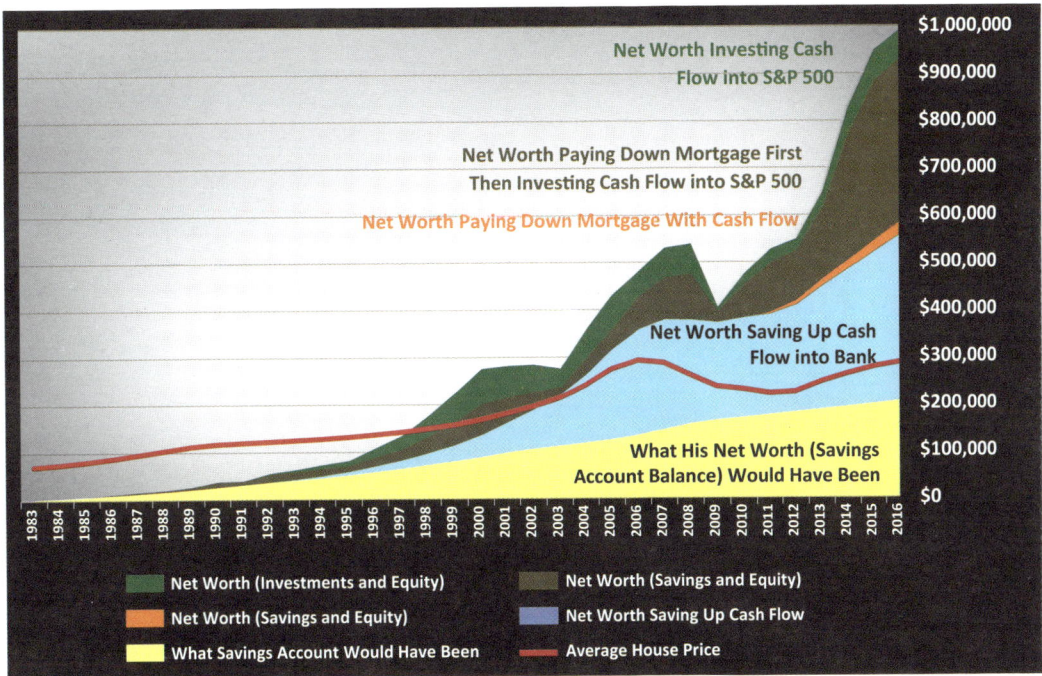

There is also a sixth option, in which he saves up for a house into the S&P 500 (instead of a bank—not necessarily advisable since this is "soon money"). With that option he would reach his goal and buys a house in cash in 1999.

This also makes him rather lucky because 1999 was right at the peak of the dot com stock market bubble. He ends up selling out of the market just before the peak and then continues to buy into the S&P 500 aggressively during the next highly volatile 15 years.

On the next page is a table and graph of his lucky experience. Graphically we now have this final option in solid Calamine lotion pink.

His net worth, between his investment account and house value, is at $1,136,079. This handily beats the others. I must reemphasize that much of this has to do with the luck of his timing and had this luck plopped him 10 years later, in 2009, it would be a very different story.

Year	Average House Price	Median Income	Rent Amount	Savings Amount	Total Return of S&P 500	Net Worth (Investments and House)	How Much Price Went Up or Down	100% Cash Purchase	Annual Tax & Ins. Payment	Net Worth as % of House Value
1983	$70,915	$20,885	$6,397	$2,089	24.08%	$2,089	$3,228			2.95%
1984	$75,189	$22,415	$6,782	$2,242	5.72%	$4,833	$4,273			6.43%
1985	$80,628	$23,618	$7,273	$2,362	31.21%	$7,471	$5,440			9.27%
1986	$87,742	$24,897	$7,914	$2,490	18.27%	$12,293	$7,114			14.01%
1987	$95,656	$26,061	$8,628	$2,606	4.85%	$17,145	$7,914			17.92%
1988	$103,742	$27,225	$9,358	$2,723	16.05%	$20,698	$8,086			19.95%
1989	$112,066	$28,906	$10,108	$2,891	31.06%	$26,911	$8,324			24.01%
1990	$117,551	$29,943	$10,603	$2,994	-3.53%	$38,263	$5,485			32.55%
1991	$119,970	$30,126	$10,821	$3,013	30.07%	$39,926	$2,419			33.28%
1992	$122,508	$30,636	$11,050	$3,064	7.33%	$54,993	$2,539			44.89%
1993	$125,090	$31,241	$11,283	$3,124	9.79%	$62,150	$2,581			49.68%
1994	$127,901	$32,264	$11,537	$3,226	1.24%	$71,462	$2,812			55.87%
1995	$131,857	$34,076	$11,893	$3,408	37.21%	$75,759	$3,956			57.46%
1996	$136,691	$35,492	$12,330	$3,549	22.65%	$107,502	$4,834			78.65%
1997	$142,037	$37,005	$12,812	$3,701	33.12%	$135,550	$5,346			95.43%
1998	$148,830	$38,885	$13,424	$3,889	28.39%	$184,339	$6,793	$148,830		123.86%
1999	$156,710	$40,696		$15,462	20.89%	$226,483	$7,880		$2,742	144.52%
2000	$167,656	$41,990		$16,388	-8.32%	$268,394	$10,946		$2,934	160.09%
2001	$180,882	$42,228		$17,373	-11.98%	$290,615	$13,226		$3,165	160.67%
2002	$195,423	$42,409		$18,448	-22.23%	$310,460	$14,541		$3,420	158.87%
2003	$213,728	$43,318		$19,870	28.39%	$323,065	$18,305		$3,740	151.16%
2004	$240,432	$44,334		$21,913	10.65%	$402,721	$26,704		$4,208	167.50%
2005	$274,468	$46,326		$24,586	5.51%	$478,628	$34,037		$4,803	174.38%
2006	$293,195	$48,201		$26,135	13.65%	$534,749	$18,727		$5,131	182.39%
2007	$287,575	$50,233		$25,930	5.24%	$588,021	($5,620)		$5,033	204.48%
2008	$262,244	$50,303		$24,095	-36.21%	$602,523	($25,331)		$4,589	229.76%
2009	$237,458	$49,777		$22,241	26.61%	$476,779	($24,786)		$4,156	200.78%
2010	$231,194	$49,276		$21,735	14.82%	$555,934	($6,265)		$4,046	240.46%
2011	$222,556	$50,054		$21,185	0.67%	$616,607	($8,638)		$3,895	277.06%
2012	$225,409	$51,017		$21,489	15.59%	$643,599	$2,853		$3,945	285.52%
2013	$247,098	$53,585		$23,322	32.05%	$753,821	$21,688		$4,324	305.07%
2014	$263,490	$53,657		$24,521	13.41%	$957,142	$16,393		$4,611	363.26%
2015	$277,934	$56,516		$25,857	1.14%	$1,090,490	$14,444		$4,864	392.36%
2016	$287,565	$57,647		$26,671	13.42%	$1,136,079	$9,630		$5,032	395.07%

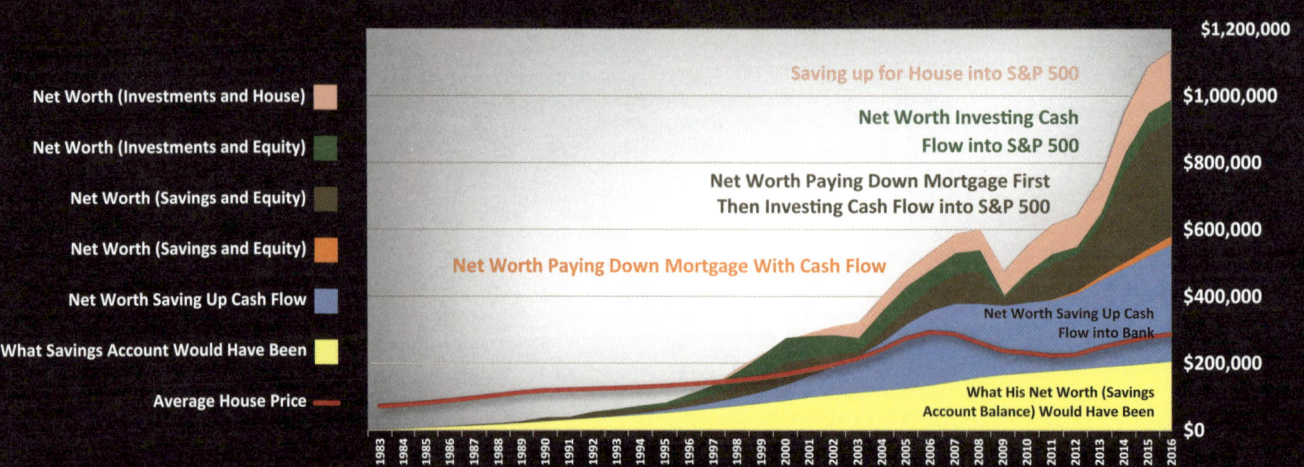

Net Worth (Investments and House)

Net Worth (Investments and Equity)

Net Worth (Savings and Equity)

Net Worth (Savings and Equity)

Net Worth Saving Up Cash Flow

What Savings Account Would Have Been

Average House Price

Saving up for House into S&P 500

Net Worth Investing Cash Flow into S&P 500

Net Worth Paying Down Mortgage First Then Investing Cash Flow into S&P 500

Net Worth Paying Down Mortgage With Cash Flow

Net Worth Saving Up Cash Flow into Bank

What His Net Worth (Savings Account Balance) Would Have Been

This reflects all six options for him. The results would look like:

2016 Year End Net Worth

$205,816	Trying to save money up into a bank for a house
$555,176	Buying a house with 20% down and saving up extra cash flow into a bank
$581,916	Buying a house with 20% down and paying off your mortgage with your extra cash flow
$927,484	Buying a house with 20% down, paying off mortgage first, then investing extra cash flow into the S&P 500
$989,446	Buying a house with 20% down, investing extra cash flow into the S&P 500
$1,136,079	Investing into the S&P 500, buying a house, keep investingv

Beyond anything, what should strike you is that the difference between these outcomes *has nothing to do with how much money he's making or his spending*, but how and where he's applying the money he has. On a month-to-month basis, all six options cost the same amount of money out of pocket.

The Takeaways and Application

It's highly important to separately identify luck from general patterns. A few things were unique to this man's situation:

- Very high mortgage rate. His mortgage was 9.25% when he got it, but by 2016 the going rate was 3.65%. The options where he pays down his mortgage look better than if he had a lower rate.
- Very high bank interest rate. Similarly, when he was getting started bank interest rates were much higher than today. The 2016 rate was **0.61%**. If his rates were less (as they are now), he couldn't have purchased his house as soon as he did.
- In 1983, for a variety of reasons, the S&P 500 was poised for a substantial bull market. This was lucky, particularly where he saved his down payment into the stock market.

It should be noted in all of this that housing prices did not go up an *abnormal* amount. It was slightly higher, but roughly in line with historical averages. This being said, here are the principles that are true for the ages:

- A mortgage accelerates the growth of your net worth, if for nothing else because it freezes part of your monthly spending. Additionally, as a renter, rising prices hurt you, but as an owner, they are wind in your net worth's sails—just as we saw when you own stocks.

- Paying off your mortgage only makes financial sense if you can't reasonably expect to beat that rate elsewhere. If you are weighing paying down a 3.65% mortgage with money earning **0.61%**, you don't need me to tell you what makes better financial sense. However, all long-term average returns of the S&P 500 are well north of 3.65%, which means that we are in an age where it's likely better to *not* pay off your mortgage, but to have a disciplined investment plan instead. The Achilles' heels to this are (1) you must *actually have* an automatic plan of investing or this becomes just a personal license for more spending, and (2) you must have the self-control to *not* panic out of the market. When his net worth was tied to the S&P 500 we saw large swings in his net worth. Panicking blows up this entire strategy.

One could also hesitantly add that if real estate appreciation is high enough, you are effectively living for free. A back of the envelope example: imagine you have a $200,000 house with a $1,000 mortgage payment. Let's say the house goes up in value **6%**. The $12,000 you paid in mortgage payments is offset by your house now being worth $212,000. This wouldn't be a normal appreciation rate. But, if your house goes up a normal **4%** amount, then effectively, of your $1,000 payment, $667 of it is going back into your pocket. What is also normal is that later in the life of the mortgage the house would be worth $300,000 and **4%** appreciation would offset $12,000 in payments. Of course this is an oversimplification, but it's true as a broad stroke.

During the housing boom leading up to the 2008 Financial Crisis, it irritated me when people said you are "throwing away your money renting." This is only partially true. Owning a home exposes you to risk that renting does not. Sometimes those risks don't matriculate and the financial experience resembles our back of the envelope examples. However, one major expense as a homeowner erases years of the early marginal benefit of paying down the principal through normal mortgage payments.

Because of this, I want to state it as clearly as I know how. If you are in a financial position to handle the additional risks of owning a home, and if you can have a decent amount of long-term certainty that you won't be forced to sell the home, then homeownership is the much stronger long-term financial option. While there are short-term risks, time makes this work.

Short-term risks (like broken furnaces) amplify their pain early on (such as the first 5, even 10 years of homeownership). But gradually, your monthly payment eats less of your income and you have more cushion to afford repairs. As with equities, the pain is now, the reward is later. The difference is that with equities, the pain (of short-term temporary price fluctuation) is not a risk. With real estate, the pains often are a real risk. We'll address those risks in a moment.

Your Personal Inflation Rate

As we mentioned, each month, the U.S. Bureau of Labor Statistics publishes inflation statistics. The problem is that the general inflation number is an average, and each person's experience will be different.

Money is to buy stuff and how you *personally spend money* changes what your own inflation rate is. I call this your **Personal Inflation Rate**. Over the past 17 years (back to when they began publishing the detailed information), the average inflation rate has been 2.155%, but yours may be 3.000% or maybe only 0.500%, particularly if the things you spend your money on are going up in price or down in price.

Let's look at three different people who each spend $4,000 per month:

- Example #1—Someone who has their house paid off (which means their "shelter" payment is just the taxes and insurance). Otherwise, their spending is fairly standard.
- Example #2—Someone who is in long-term care. They hardly spend any money other than on the long-term care facility that feeds them, provides shelter, etc. Their inflation rate is nearly entirely based on medical costs (which are going up at a higher rate than most other things).
- Example #3—Someone who is determined to put their child through college. They only have $4,000 per month. Luckily, they too have their house paid off, but otherwise are epically frugal, putting every penny toward education.

The table at the top of the next page shows what each of their personal inflation rates would look like.

The type of your expenses will dramatically alter what you need to plan for. If your spending is tied to something that goes up in price more rapidly, then you will have a higher personal inflation rate. This is relevant to our discussion on real estate because the rising price of real estate generally outpaces the price of everything else. Using numbers from the earlier example of the twins, if your housing payment is 10.67% of your budget as an owner versus 32.09% as a renter, then it's likely your personal inflation rate is lower than the national average rate. Keep in mind that inflation is just an average and your own experience will be above or below it.

Personal Inflation Rate

National Inflation Rate (17-Year Average)		2.155%

	Personal Inflation Rate	Difference
Example #1 - House Paid Off	1.870%	-0.285%
Example #2 - Long-Term Care	3.643%	1.488%
Example #3 - Child in College	4.583%	2.428%

	17-Year Average			Example #1 - House Paid Off			Example #2 - Long-Term Care			Example #3 - Child in College		
	BLS Inflation	BLS Weight	Contribution to Rate	Personal Monthly	Personal Weight	Personal Inflation Rate	Personal Monthly	Personal Weight	Personal Inflation Rate	Personal Monthly	Personal Weight	Personal Inflation Rate
Food and Beverages												
Food at home	2.21%	8.34%	0.18%	$800	20.000%	0.441%	$0	0.000%	0.000%	$140	3.500%	0.077%
Food away from home	2.76%	5.95%	0.16%	$200	5.000%	0.138%	$0	0.000%	0.000%	$100	2.500%	0.069%
Alcoholic beverages	2.06%	1.05%	0.02%									
Housing												
Shelter	2.61%	32.09%	0.83%	$384	9.600%	0.251%	$0	0.000%	0.000%	$384	9.600%	0.251%
Fuels and Utilities	3.53%	5.05%	0.17%	$100	2.500%	0.088%	$0	0.000%	0.000%	$60	1.500%	0.053%
Household furnishings and operations	-0.26%	4.49%	-0.01%	$300	7.500%	-0.019%	$0	0.000%	0.000%	$0	0.000%	0.000%
Apparel	-0.34%	3.81%	-0.02%	$200	5.000%	-0.017%	$100	2.500%	-0.009%	$0	0.000%	0.000%
Transportation												
Private Transportation												
New and Used Motor Vehicles												
New Vehicles	0.16%	4.27%	0.00%	$0	0.000%	0.000%	$0	0.000%	0.000%	$0	0.000%	0.000%
Used cars and trucks	-0.58%	1.89%	-0.01%	$300	7.500%	-0.043%	$0	0.000%	0.000%	$0	0.000%	0.000%
Motor Fuel (all types)	5.91%	4.08%	0.14%	$100	2.500%	0.148%	$0	0.000%	0.000%	$200	5.000%	0.296%
Motor Vehicle Parts and Equipment	2.09%	0.41%	0.01%	$250	6.250%	0.131%	$0	0.000%	0.000%	$0	0.000%	0.000%
Motor Vehicle Maintenance and Repair	2.79%	1.26%	0.04%									
Public Transportation	1.48%	1.17%	0.02%	$100	2.500%	0.037%	$0	0.000%	0.000%	$0	0.000%	0.000%
Other Travel (Airplane, Train, etc.)	3.09%	3.73%	0.11%	$100	2.500%	0.077%	$0	0.000%	0.000%	$0	0.000%	0.000%
Medical Care												
Medical Care Commodities	2.69%	1.63%	0.04%	$200	5.000%	0.135%	$800	20.000%	0.539%	$80	2.000%	0.054%
Medical Care Services	4.05%	4.93%	0.20%	$300	7.500%	0.304%	$3,000	75.000%	3.040%	$20	0.500%	0.020%
Recreation	0.78%	5.89%	0.05%	$150	3.750%	0.029%	$0	0.000%	0.000%	$0	0.000%	0.000%
Education and Communication												
Education	5.02%	3.02%	0.15%	$0	0.000%	0.000%	$0	0.000%	0.000%	$3,000	75.000%	3.768%
Communication	-1.19%	3.23%	-0.04%	$200	5.000%	-0.060%	$0	0.000%	0.000%	$16	0.400%	-0.005%
Other Goods and Services	2.91%	3.70%	0.11%	$316	7.900%	0.230%	$100	2.500%	0.073%	$0	0.000%	0.000%
Inflation Rate			2.155%	$4,000		1.870%	$4,000		3.643%	$4,000		4.583%
Difference to National						-0.285%			1.488%			2.428%

Let's look at the personal inflation rate for someone renting in the face of rising real estate prices. Let's use the numbers from yet another previous example. The man who had saved up down payment money and bought a house in 1992.

1992

Owning		Renting	
Principal and Interest	$805	Rent Payment	$7,070
Insurance (0.50% of value)	$51		
Taxes	$128		
TOTAL	$984	TOTAL	$7,070
DIFFERENCE	($63)		$63

2016

Owning		Renting	
Principal and Interest	$805	Rent Payment	$2,162
Insurance (0.50% of value)	$120		
Taxes	$300		
TOTAL	$1,225	TOTAL	$2,162
DIFFERENCE	$937		($937)

Again, because that principal and interest part is frozen, over time his spending changes and housing becomes less of a portion of his income. If we compare owning to renting, on the next page we can see how this impacts his personal inflation rate in 2016.

The owner's personal inflation rate is only 1.694%, while the renter not only has more in spending, but he has more of a need for more future income because his inflation rate is 2.497%. You would expect a renter to have more inflation and thus face a stronger headwind in gaining wealth.

The takeaway is that apart from the net worth benefit, the long-term cash flow benefit, there is also the benefit of enjoying a generally lower inflation rate as an owner of your shelter. Relative to other things, when you freeze the price of something, by nature it gets cheaper over time.

Personal Inflation Rate (Renting vs. Owning)

National Inflation Rate (17-Year Average)	2.155%

	Personal Inflation Rate	Difference
Renting	2.497%	0.342%
Owning	1.694%	-0.461%

	17-Year Average			Owning			Renting		
	BLS Inflation	BLS Weight	Contri-bution to Rate	Personal Monthly	Personal Weight	Personal Inflation Rate	Personal Monthly	Personal Weight	Personal Inflation Rate
Food and Beverages									
Food at home	2.21%	8.34%	0.18%	$800	14.129%	0.312%	$800	14.129%	0.312%
Food away from home	2.76%	5.95%	0.16%	$200	3.532%	0.098%	$200	3.532%	0.098%
Alcoholic beverages	2.06%	1.05%	0.02%						
Housing									
Shelter	2.61%	32.09%	0.83%	$420	7.418%	0.194%	$2,162	38.184%	0.997%
Principal and Interest (frozen)	0.00%	0.000%	0.000%	$805	14.218%	0.000%			
Fuels and Utilities	3.53%	5.05%	0.17%	$150	2.649%	0.094%	$150	2.649%	0.094%
Household furnishings and operations	-0.26%	4.49%	-0.01%	$100	1.766%	-0.005%	$100	1.766%	-0.005%
Apparel	-0.34%	3.81%	-0.02%	$200	3.532%	-0.012%	$200	3.532%	-0.012%
Transportation									
Private Transportation									
New and Used Motor Vehicles									
New Vehicles	0.16%	4.27%	0.00%	$300	5.298%	0.009%	$300	5.298%	0.009%
Used cars and trucks	-0.58%	1.89%	-0.01%	$0	0.000%	0.000%	$0	0.000%	0.000%
Motor Fuel (all types)	5.91%	4.08%	0.14%	$500	8.831%	0.522%	$500	8.831%	0.522%
Motor Vehicle Parts and Equipment	2.09%	0.41%	0.01%	$100	1.766%	0.037%	$100	1.766%	0.037%
Motor Vehicle Maintenance and Repair	2.79%	1.26%	0.04%						
Public Transportation	1.48%	1.17%	0.02%	$0	0.000%	0.000%	$0	0.000%	0.000%
Other Travel (Airplane, Train, etc.)	3.09%	3.73%	0.11%	$100	1.766%	0.055%	$100	1.766%	0.055%
Medical Care									
Medical Care Commodities*	2.69%	1.63%	0.04%	$200	3.532%	0.095%	$200	3.532%	0.095%
Medical Care Services	4.05%	4.93%	0.20%	$300	5.298%	0.215%	$300	5.298%	0.215%
Recreation	0.78%	5.89%	0.05%	$150	2.649%	0.021%	$150	2.649%	0.021%
Education and Communication									
Education	5.02%	3.02%	0.15%	$0	0.000%	0.000%	$0	0.000%	0.000%
Communication	-1.19%	3.23%	-0.04%	$200	3.532%	-0.042%	$200	3.532%	-0.042%
Other Goods and Services	2.91%	3.70%	0.11%	$200	3.532%	0.103%	$200	3.532%	0.103%
Total			**2.155%**	**$4,725**		**1.694%**	**$5,662**		**2.497%**
Difference				**-$937**		**-0.461%**	**$937**		**0.342%**

The Risks of Owning a Home

Thus far, we have waxed long over the benefits of homeownership. But at times, things hit the fan. Let us revisit risk. What is risk? The *permanent loss* of capital. You could expand the definition by adding that it is the permanent loss of capital from an investment from which there is no realistic expectation of recovery any time soon.

Value Risk

Let's say you buy land in the Alaskan boonies rumored to have gold in them thar hills. You pay more for the property because of this. When you don't find gold, you are in a tough situation. The value will not likely increase significantly in your lifetime—it would be hard to find a buyer for property in the middle of nowhere. This is value risk: the risk of permanent loss of principal. It's the same risk you face with stock in a company that goes bankrupt or for property you expected to be developed into a ski resort that citizens voted to block. These are declines in value that are not likely to be erased in a reasonable amount of time.

Real estate is tough in this regard. It's very difficult to diversify real estate. Most people are going to own one home, in one city, within one economy. That's a great deal of eggs in one basket. If you have a second home or a rental home, it's likely within a three hour drive away and still vulnerable to the same economics of your primary home. So it goes.

Real estate also risks becoming illiquid. Liquidity is a term to describe how easy it is to sell something. Cash in your bank is highly liquid; you can just go get it. Stocks are highly liquid; you can sell any time. Real estate is more of an ordeal to liquidate. Even in the most aggressive real estate market, it would still take around 60 days to sell. However, you might not be able to find a buyer for the price you want. You may have to bring money to the table to even just dispose of it. That Alaskan boonies land without gold would likely become very illiquid—undeveloped land in remote areas is some of the more illiquid real estate you can own. If your real estate is illiquid, embrace a long-term owning horizon.

More than 80% of America lives in urban areas. Because of this, much of what we have talked about with regard to the historical value of real estate assumes an urban setting. If you own real estate in a small town, the value of your house is less certain to follow national averages. It might, but it is less probable. On the other hand, real estate prices in highly desirable areas will tend to favorably respond to demand and the reality of limited supply.

In an urban area, growing population means more buyers in the future and gives your real estate more price security. This is the core reason why small towns can be vulnerable, such generations ago in farming communities. Technology and the corporatization of farming reduced the number of jobs needed for farming. Populations decline, buyers decrease, and so do small town housing prices. The Midwest has seen this too, as manufacturing has been outsourced, automated, and roboticized.

Appreciation is not certain. It is just probability. There will always be exceptions to the rule of appreciating real estate values. A way to mitigate this is to try to buy in an area where you think people will always want to live.

In general, real estate prices rise faster than inflation. This is especially true in desirable areas with limited supply.

My first house was near a university. My thought was that even if the economy softened, there would be a demand for student housing. Worst case scenario if things got *really* tough and I couldn't afford it, I could rent it out. Embrace the long-term possibilities in your personal life.

In owning real estate, just like owning equities, you must embrace the probable long-term future value of the asset. The value is certain to fluctuate over time, and all but certain to increase in the long term. Sound familiar?

Real estate, like equities, is simply another investment with price fluctuation. It is an inherent reality best dealt with by embracing a long time horizon. The good news is that it's much easier to buy and hold real estate because it's your home.

A Tale of Exception

I'm not trying to pick on Detroit, but earlier I promised you that I'd run a scenario where someone had terrible luck. We also used six different options for a prospective home buyer. Let's recycle the familiar numbers from the scenario where an average person saves up for a 20% down payment and then saves their extra cash flow into a bank (this will be like the blue scenario earlier). As he is saving up for the house in Detroit, we'll pretend that the value of the house is tracking the national average—it wasn't, but I want to reflect the assumption of averages, and then the experience of *below* average.

The moment this homebuyer buys the house in Detroit, the price starts trending down, along with Detroit's house values. We'll look at how this bad luck changed his net worth. We have a new column showing "Detroit Average Price" that exactly mirrors how Detroit's housing prices trended from 1992 onward.[7] After 22 years the house still isn't worth as much as what he paid for it, as we can see in the table at the top of the opposite page.

The graph below the table has some familiar data. As we saw before, the blue section reflects what his net worth would be *if his home value rose with the national average*. Also, the yellow one is also the same: it shows the elusive scenario of trying to save up to buy an average house 100% in cash. The new purple part shows what his net worth would be if his home happened to be in Detroit. We also have added a lime green line showing his Detroit house value diverging from the U.S. average house value (the red line).

The lesson here is for those worried that they may buy a house that would go down in value. While improbable, this is a legitimate concern. The Detroit example doesn't

Year	Average House Price	Detroit House Value	Rent Amount	Detroit Rent Amount	Savings Amount	30-Year Mortgage Rate	Average Mortgage Points Paid	Net Worth Owning Detroit Home	Net Worth Renting Detroit Home	Down Payment	Mortgage Balance	Annual Mortgage Payment	Net Worth as % of House Value
1983	$70,915		$6,397		$2,089	13.24%	2.10%	$2,089	$2,089				2.95%
1984	$75,189		$6,782		$2,242	13.88%	2.50%	$4,530	$4,530				6.02%
1985	$80,628		$7,273		$2,362	12.43%	2.50%	$7,385	$7,385				9.16%
1986	$87,742		$7,914		$2,490	10.19%	2.20%	$10,497	$10,497				11.96%
1987	$95,656		$8,628		$2,606	10.21%	2.20%	$13,781	$13,781				14.41%
1988	$103,742		$9,358		$2,723	10.34%	2.10%	$17,436	$17,436				16.81%
1989	$112,066		$10,108		$2,891	10.32%	2.10%	$21,661	$21,661				19.33%
1990	$117,551		$10,603		$2,994	10.13%	2.10%	$26,504	$26,504				22.55%
1991	$119,970		$10,821		$3,013	9.25%	2.00%	$31,606	$31,606	$23,994	$97,895		26.34%
1992	$122,508	$120,564	$11,050	$10,875	$2,306	8.39%	1.70%	$35,123	$36,696	$0	$97,210	$11,808	30.26%
1993	$125,090	$120,585	$11,283	$10,877	$2,554	7.31%	1.60%	$38,904	$41,654	$0	$96,461	$11,853	34.70%
1994	$127,901	$120,011	$11,537	$10,825	$2,860	8.38%	1.80%	$42,516	$47,023	$0	$95,643	$11,903	39.41%
1995	$131,857	$123,536	$11,893	$11,143	$3,329	7.93%	1.80%	$51,228	$53,678	$0	$94,749	$11,972	45.16%
1996	$136,691	$124,232	$12,330	$11,206	$3,822	7.81%	1.70%	$58,058	$61,543	$0	$93,773	$12,056	51.59%
1997	$142,037	$124,888	$12,812	$11,265	$4,362	7.60%	1.70%	$65,664	$70,183	$0	$92,706	$12,150	58.30%
1998	$148,830	$124,355	$13,424	$11,217	$5,044	6.94%	1.10%	$73,226	$80,231	$0	$91,541	$12,269	65.65%
1999	$156,710	$121,302	$14,135	$10,941	$5,798	7.44%	1.00%	$79,285	$91,547	$0	$90,268	$12,407	73.19%
2000	$167,656	$113,617	$15,123	$10,248	$6,723	8.05%	1.00%	$82,164	$105,269	$0	$88,877	$12,598	81.24%
2001	$180,882	$101,505	$16,316	$9,156	$7,709	6.97%	0.90%	$82,789	$123,082	$0	$87,357	$12,830	89.65%
2002	$195,423	$111,198	$17,627	$10,030	$8,784	6.54%	0.60%	$105,315	$139,204	$0	$85,697	$13,084	96.99%
2003	$213,728	$109,477	$19,278	$9,875	$10,206	5.83%	0.60%	$117,211	$155,726	$0	$83,883	$13,405	103.62%
2004	$240,432	$109,211	$21,687	$9,851	$12,248	5.84%	0.70%	$132,314	$173,933	$0	$81,901	$13,872	109.61%
2005	$274,468	$105,604	$24,757	$9,525	$14,922	5.87%	0.60%	$147,776	$197,078	$0	$79,737	$14,468	115.36%
2006	$293,195	$108,432	$26,446	$9,781	$16,471	6.41%	0.50%	$173,851	$225,695	$0	$77,371	$14,795	122.31%
2007	$287,575	$108,063	$25,939	$9,747	$16,266	6.34%	0.40%	$199,375	$258,043	$0	$74,788	$14,697	131.75%
2008	$262,244	$107,653	$23,654	$9,710	$14,431	6.03%	0.60%	$223,729	$288,685	$0	$71,965	$14,254	144.26%
2009	$237,458	$107,243	$21,419	$9,673	$12,577	5.04%	0.70%	$242,407	$310,669	$0	$68,881	$13,820	156.92%
2010	$231,194	$109,313	$20,854	$9,860	$12,071	4.69%	0.70%	$260,878	$328,053	$0	$65,511	$13,710	165.56%
2011	$222,556	$111,239	$20,075	$10,034	$11,521	4.45%	0.70%	$278,697	$344,144	$0	$61,831	$13,559	175.24%
2012	$225,409	$112,920	$20,332	$10,185	$11,825	3.66%	0.70%	$296,640	$360,017	$0	$57,809	$13,609	181.51%
2013	$247,098	$114,457	$22,288	$10,324	$13,658	3.98%	0.70%	$316,651	$377,970	$0	$53,416	$13,989	181.83%
2014	$263,490	$116,035	$23,767	$10,466	$14,857	4.17%	0.60%	$338,223	$397,134	$0	$48,616	$14,275	184.32%
2015	$277,934	$119,990	$25,070	$10,823	$16,193	3.85%	0.60%	$363,942	$417,512	$0	$43,372	$14,528	187.77%
2016	$287,565	$124,355	$25,938	$11,217	$17,006	3.65%	0.50%	$391,966	$439,341	$0	$37,644	$14,697	193.06%

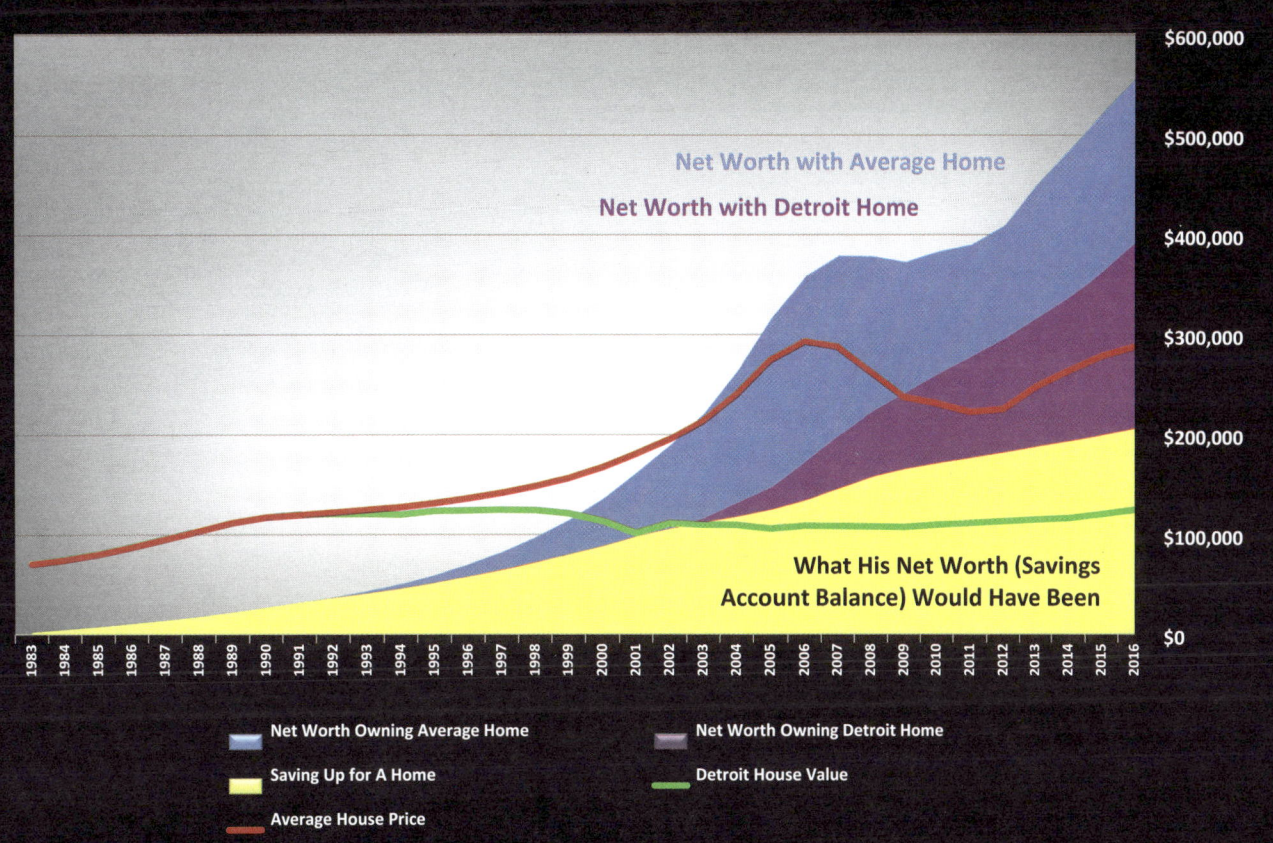

Net Worth with Average Home
Net Worth with Detroit Home
What His Net Worth (Savings Account Balance) Would Have Been

Legend:
- Net Worth Owning Average Home
- Net Worth Owning Detroit Home
- Saving Up for A Home
- Detroit House Value
- Average House Price

prove that it's good to own a house during a significant decline in price. Obviously it's not, we can see this in the table as "Net Worth Renting Detroit Home"—in hindsight, he would have been better to rent a house in Detroit. What this does teach us is that a declining home value was not as destructive to his net worth as one may assume.

What I'm showing here is that even if you had bought into the worst major metropolitan real estate market in America, you would still be better off financially than someone elsewhere in the country trying to save up to buy a house in cash. Detroit is an example of an exception to the rule, an improbability, that even if it was your own improbability, you'd still be better off than an average person who was fearful of declining home values.

More commonly, people don't end up wealthier through homeownership is when they aren't there long enough to benefit from appreciation and amortization. You can control this by thinking long term about your housing choice. However, as with investing in the stock market, you have to embrace that the value will constantly change. In most cases, volatility is less consequential the longer you hold onto the asset. Real estate is no different.

Yes, it is *possible* that the value of your house could drop substantially, even permanently. It is not *probable*. One thing is nearly certain: the value and cost of your "shelter" will increase over time, and this will either be a headwind or a tailwind depending on whether you own or rent.

Leverage Risk

This is a subset of value risk. Thus far we've been speaking in terms of *net worth*, not your specific skin in the game (your down payment). Toward the beginning of the chapter we punctuated the power of leverage in both a positive and negative sense. If we look at average house prices versus Detroit house prices, there is a sharp difference in the rate of return, as we can see in the table on the opposite page.

If we are looking at a tale of two homes here, both people put down the same down payment. For the average house in 2006, this peaked at a **721.95%** total return on this original money. We calculate that by how much the house went up or down after purchase divided by the down payment amount.

Average House Total Return		
Peak Year: 2006		
Growth Amount ($293,195-$119,970)	$173,225	
Down Payment Amount ($23,994) =	$23,994	= 721.95%

Year	Average House Price	Detroit House Value	Rent Amount	Savings Amount	Net Worth Owning Detroit Home	Net Worth Renting Detroit Home	Down Payment	Average House Price Annualized Rate of Return on Down Payment	Average House Price Total Return on Down Payment	Detroit House Price Annualized Rate of Return on Down Payment	Detroit House Price Total Return on Down Payment	Net Worth as % of House Value
1983	$70,915		$6,397	$2,089	$2,089	$2,089						2.95%
1984	$75,189		$6,782	$2,242	$4,530	$4,530						6.02%
1985	$80,628		$7,273	$2,362	$7,385	$7,385						9.16%
1986	$87,742		$7,914	$2,490	$10,497	$10,497						11.96%
1987	$95,656		$8,628	$2,606	$13,781	$13,781						14.41%
1988	$103,742		$9,358	$2,723	$17,436	$17,436						16.81%
1989	$112,066		$10,108	$2,891	$21,661	$21,661						19.33%
1990	$117,551		$10,603	$2,994	$26,504	$26,504						22.55%
1991	$119,970		$10,821	$3,013	$31,606	$31,606	$23,994					26.34%
1992	$122,508	$120,564	$11,050	$2,306	$35,123	$36,696	$0	10.58%	10.58%	2.48%	2.48%	30.26%
1993	$125,090	$120,585	$11,283	$2,554	$38,904	$41,654	$0	10.15%	21.34%	1.27%	2.56%	34.70%
1994	$127,901	$120,011	$11,537	$2,860	$42,516	$47,023	$0	9.99%	33.06%	0.06%	0.17%	39.41%
1995	$131,857	$123,536	$11,893	$3,329	$51,228	$53,678	$0	10.58%	49.54%	3.52%	14.86%	45.16%
1996	$136,691	$124,232	$12,330	$3,822	$58,058	$61,543	$0	11.16%	69.69%	3.32%	17.77%	51.59%
1997	$142,037	$124,888	$12,812	$4,362	$65,664	$70,183	$0	11.48%	91.97%	3.16%	20.50%	58.30%
1998	$148,830	$124,355	$13,424	$5,044	$73,226	$80,231	$0	11.94%	120.28%	2.43%	18.28%	65.65%
1999	$156,710	$121,302	$14,135	$5,798	$79,285	$91,547	$0	12.31%	153.12%	0.68%	5.55%	73.19%
2000	$167,656	$113,617	$15,123	$6,723	$82,164	$105,269	$0	12.93%	198.74%	-3.36%	-26.48%	81.24%
2001	$180,882	$101,505	$16,316	$7,709	$82,789	$123,082	$0	13.47%	253.86%	-13.65%	-76.96%	89.65%
2002	$195,423	$111,198	$17,627	$8,784	$105,315	$139,204	$0	13.80%	314.47%	-4.05%	-36.56%	96.99%
2003	$213,728	$109,477	$19,278	$10,206	$117,211	$155,726	$0	14.18%	390.76%	-4.68%	-43.73%	103.62%
2004	$240,432	$109,211	$21,687	$12,248	$132,314	$173,933	$0	14.81%	502.05%	-4.47%	-44.84%	109.61%
2005	$274,468	$105,604	$24,757	$14,922	$147,776	$197,078	$0	15.41%	643.91%	-6.31%	-59.87%	115.36%
2006	$293,195	$108,432	$26,446	$16,471	$173,851	$225,695	$0	15.08%	721.95%	-4.28%	-48.09%	122.31%
2007	$287,575	$108,063	$25,939	$16,266	$199,375	$258,043	$0	13.87%	698.53%	-4.19%	-49.62%	131.75%
2008	$262,244	$107,653	$23,654	$14,431	$223,729	$288,685	$0	12.06%	592.96%	-4.15%	-51.33%	144.26%
2009	$237,458	$107,243	$21,419	$12,577	$242,407	$310,669	$0	10.36%	489.66%	-4.11%	-53.04%	156.92%
2010	$231,194	$109,313	$20,854	$12,071	$260,878	$328,053	$0	9.53%	463.55%	-3.04%	-44.41%	165.56%
2011	$222,556	$111,239	$20,075	$11,521	$278,697	$344,144	$0	8.67%	427.55%	-2.24%	-36.39%	175.24%
2012	$225,409	$112,920	$20,332	$11,825	$296,640	$360,017	$0	8.36%	439.44%	-1.64%	-29.38%	181.51%
2013	$247,098	$114,457	$22,288	$13,658	$316,651	$377,970	$0	8.72%	529.83%	-1.18%	-22.98%	181.83%
2014	$263,490	$116,035	$23,767	$14,857	$338,223	$397,134	$0	8.82%	598.15%	-0.78%	-16.40%	184.32%
2015	$277,934	$119,990	$25,070	$16,193	$363,942	$417,512	$0	8.81%	658.35%	0.00%	0.09%	187.77%
2016	$287,565	$124,355	$25,938	$17,006	$391,966	$439,341	$0	8.67%	698.49%	0.67%	18.28%	193.06%

This is only looking at the return on their down payment and not on any additional money paid to investments or as principal reduction. This is what it looked like for the Detroit house:

Detroit House Total Return

Low Year: 2001

$$\frac{\text{Growth Amount } (\$101,505 - \$119,970)}{\text{Down Payment Amount } (\$23,994)} = \frac{(\$18,465)}{\$23,994} = -76.96\%$$

Graphically, these two total return paths are the solid pieces after the homes were purchased at the end of 1991:

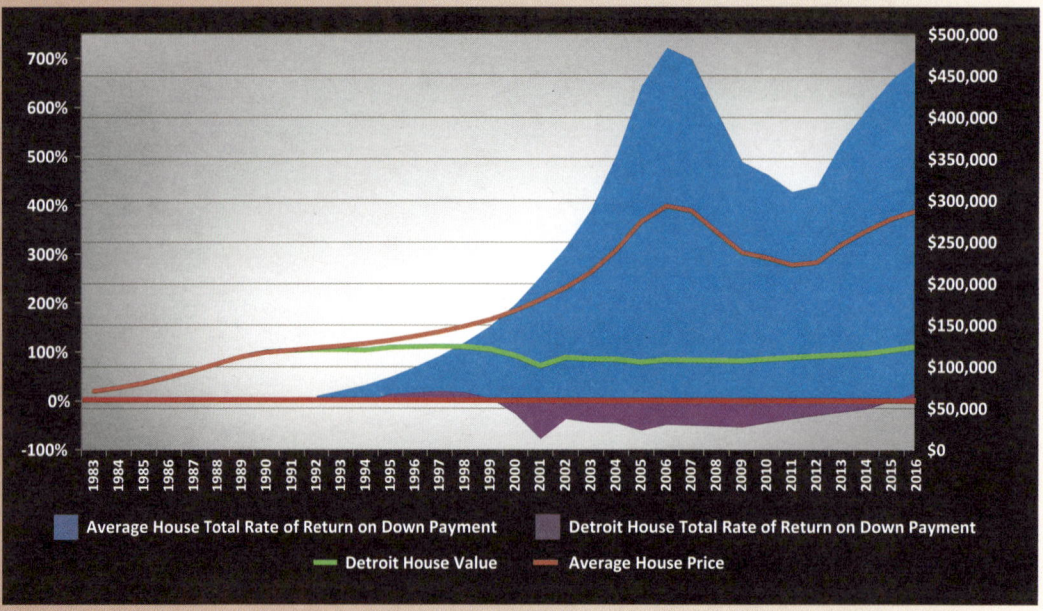

The fact that you are also paying down your mortgage helps minimize the risk of being upside down in the mortgage, but price fluctuations always amplify any kind of leveraged position like this. In most cases, leverage is powerful and helpful to your net worth. However, when prices fall, *if people sell their house*, they can experience *more than* complete loss of the original down payment. If you put 20% down and the house value falls 20% and you sell (ignoring selling costs), the leverage makes this a 100% loss. The Detroit homeowner didn't *quite* see their home value decline in price beyond their mortgage balance.

Naturally, just like stock, real estate value declines only become losses if you sell. All the more reason to embrace the purchase of a house as long-term investment and to fight to keep yourself in a position where you wouldn't be forced to sell your house at a loss.

Collateral Damage Risk

This is also a subset of value risk. If your home gets damaged or destroyed, the value obviously goes down. When you get a mortgage, you are required to carry homeowner's insurance to cover the costs of damage to the home. However, there is also the risk of collateral damage to an entire area. When Hurricane Katrina struck, thousands of people permanently left New Orleans. Before the hurricane, the population was just under 500,000 people. Afterward it was 200,000. Now, more than 10 years after the hurricane, the population is still under 400,000. Your insurance might rebuild a destroyed house, but it may not bring the value back.

Cost of Ownership

For a first-time homebuyer, unexpected costs of ownership are perhaps the greatest risk faced in the first few years. Certainly this is true if you take into account your leveraged position. I bought my first house at the ripe old age of 24. Those were different days. Among the lessons the banks learned during the Financial Crisis was that late pubescent humans pose an elevated credit risk. At that age, I'm not sure I could have told you how much it cost to replace a roof. It was only by pure luck that I never had a major expense on my first house. The second and third house, however, both had repairs within two years of ownership.

The cost of ownership is difficult to predict because it entails voluntary costs, involuntary costs, and everything in between. Your furnace goes out—usually suddenly in the middle of winter—which is an involuntary cost. On the other hand, voluntary upgrades are inevitable, too. Whether it's getting a few buckets of paint or remodeling a kitchen, as a homeowner you will spend money a renter wouldn't. On yet another hand (your third hand), voluntary upgrades may increase the value of the home. As a generalization, voluntary costs are more likely to end up on the asset side of your balance sheet as "sweat" equity, while involuntary costs merely normalize the valuation. But how do you quantify the various moving parts of the cost of ownership?

Insurance coverage makes a massive difference on involuntary costs. Let's say your roof gets hail damage and needs to be replaced for a cost of $15,000. Normally your homeowner's insurance will pick up the tab and you'll just be out of pocket the deductible (often around $1,000). I would certainly count this as a cost of ownership, but only $1,000 would be your cost, not the full $15,000. Sometimes you have large expensive "must do's" that insurance may not cover, such as replacing a broken sewer line, major appliance, or eradicating a massive pest or mold problem.

I would argue that even some of your *voluntary* costs should be factored into the cost of purchasing a home. If you buy a car knowing the transmission clicks, you expect, eventually, a big repair tab. If you buy a house with old avocado-colored carpet or a rose-colored bathtub, for most people's tastes, these are aesthetic financial time bombs. Not every nickel and dime cost to homeownership is a financial risk *per se*, but some expenses your self-respect will force upon you. The fun of upgrading exacerbates this.

My first house was, ummm, we'll say *rustic*. Quickly after moving my family in with small children, the aesthetic time bomb went off pretty much right away. It's just the reality. While, "I hate those curtains" is quite different than, "I think I smell a gas leak," they are both money out of the same pot of gold. The inevitability of involuntary costs can be just as probable as voluntary ones.

Acknowledge that any numerical cost estimate will be fictional. I've heard estimates that the cost of ownership is 1–4% of the house value. A $300,000 house would expect $3,000–12,000 in annual costs to maintain it. My experience has been on the lower end of this, if not below it.

I'll give you this admonition: learn how to fix stuff. Get really cozy with the miracle of YouTube. Any normal mishap with your house will have a "how to fix it" tutorial on YouTube. Laying tile? YouTube. Replacing a doorknob? YouTube. Clogged sink, dripping faucet, running toilet, broken garbage disposal, drywall repair? Everything is learnable.

To put a number on cost-of-ownership risk, we'll use three figures as a percent of the value of the house: 0%, 2%, 4%. We'll revisit our familiar scenario of saving up for a house and buying it in 1992, but adjust the results with the cost of ownership coming out of the savings account. We can see these results on the opposite page.

The moral of the story is that even with the expectation of an extremely high (4%) annual cost of maintaining a house, the wealth creation benefits of owning far outweigh renting. I feel like I should say that personally, not even in a single year, never have I spent anywhere near 4% as my cost of ownership for any of the houses that I have owned. My largest costs have always been voluntary (and still nowhere near this number). When I think of the value of my own house, even the full cost of having our roof and gutters replaced in the summer of 2014 was still only 2.6% of the value. But the roof was damaged in a hailstorm and the replacement was mostly covered by insurance.

Reducing the Risk of Ownership

Mitigate your cost of ownership. Before you buy a house, get the best inspection money can buy. When you own a house, prioritize prevention as an ongoing expense. The inspector will tell you exactly what needs to be maintained. Replacing a $20.00 furnace filter pushes back the $4,000 cost to replace a furnace, which gives you more *time* for your savings to grow in the stock market. Maintaining your house should be thought of as direct reduction of cost of ownership risk.

It is a risk to own a house and desperately need money to maintain it, and not have that money. Being too broke for repairs can be the beginning of financial demise. If your sewer line breaks and it's backing up sewage into the house, this is not something you can reasonably delay. If you don't have the money to fix it. You put it on a credit card. You now have an additional monthly payment and still need to maintain the house, pay the mortgage, etc. You can't afford the house anymore. You are forced to sell it and thus abandon your long-term buying horizon.

Year	Average House Price	Rent Amount	Savings Amount	2% House Cost Maintenance			4% House Cost Maintenance			Net Worth as % of House Value
				Net Worth (Savings and Equity)	2% House Maintenance	Savings Balance	Net Worth (Savings and Equity)	4% House Maintenance	Savings Balance	
1983	$70,915	$6,397	$2,089	$2,089		$2,089	$2,089		$2,089	2.95%
1984	$75,189	$6,782	$2,242	$4,530		$4,530	$4,530		$4,530	6.02%
1985	$80,628	$7,273	$2,362	$7,385		$7,385	$7,385		$7,385	9.16%
1986	$87,742	$7,914	$2,490	$10,497		$10,497	$10,497		$10,497	11.96%
1987	$95,656	$8,628	$2,606	$13,781		$13,781	$13,781		$13,781	14.41%
1988	$103,742	$9,358	$2,723	$17,436		$17,436	$17,436		$17,436	16.81%
1989	$112,066	$10,108	$2,891	$21,661		$21,661	$21,661		$21,661	19.33%
1990	$117,551	$10,603	$2,994	$26,504		$26,504	$26,504		$26,504	22.55%
1991	$119,970	$10,821	$3,013	$31,606		$31,606	$31,606		$31,606	26.34%
1992	$122,508	$11,050	$2,306	$34,617	$2,450	$9,319	$32,167	$4,900	$6,869	28.26%
1993	$125,090	$11,283	$2,554	$38,362	$2,502	$9,733	$29,985	$5,004	$4,686	30.67%
1994	$127,901	$11,537	$2,860	$42,628	$2,558	$10,370	$31,220	$5,116	$2,591	33.33%
1995	$131,857	$11,893	$3,329	$48,720	$2,637	$11,613	$33,042	$5,274	$784	36.95%
1996	$136,691	$12,330	$3,822	$56,310	$2,734	$13,392	$36,293	$5,468	($815)	41.20%
1997	$142,037	$12,812	$4,362	$64,983	$2,841	$15,652	$40,740	$5,681	($2,179)	45.75%
1998	$148,830	$13,424	$5,044	$75,890	$2,977	$18,600	$46,120	$5,953	($3,211)	50.99%
1999	$156,710	$14,135	$5,798	$88,646	$3,134	$22,204	$53,446	$6,268	($3,843)	56.57%
2000	$167,656	$15,123	$6,723	$105,481	$3,353	$26,702	$62,421	$6,706	($4,021)	62.92%
2001	$180,882	$16,316	$7,709	$125,949	$3,618	$32,424	$74,986	$7,235	($3,794)	69.63%
2002	$195,423	$17,627	$8,784	$148,154	$3,908	$38,428	$90,566	$7,817	($2,959)	75.81%
2003	$213,728	$19,278	$10,206	$174,973	$4,275	$45,128	$108,365	$8,549	($1,362)	81.87%
2004	$240,432	$21,687	$12,248	$211,659	$4,809	$53,129	$131,098	$9,617	$1,253	88.03%
2005	$274,468	$24,757	$14,922	$258,296	$5,489	$63,564	$163,750	$10,979	$5,220	94.11%
2006	$293,195	$26,446	$16,471	$292,295	$5,864	$76,471	$204,884	$11,728	$10,152	99.69%
2007	$287,575	$25,939	$16,266	$303,544	$5,751	$90,757	$231,239	$11,503	$15,415	105.55%
2008	$262,244	$23,654	$14,431	$294,326	$5,245	$104,047	$232,841	$10,490	$20,054	112.23%
2009	$237,458	$21,419	$12,577	$282,349	$4,749	$113,771	$213,777	$9,498	$23,497	118.90%
2010	$231,194	$20,854	$12,071	$287,436	$4,624	$121,754	$195,009	$9,248	$26,431	124.33%
2011	$222,556	$20,075	$11,521	$289,936	$4,451	$129,211	$194,816	$8,902	$29,134	130.28%
2012	$225,409	$20,332	$11,825	$304,362	$4,508	$136,762	$192,721	$9,016	$31,995	135.03%
2013	$247,098	$22,288	$13,658	$339,400	$4,942	$145,718	$203,426	$9,884	$35,826	137.35%
2014	$263,490	$23,767	$14,857	$370,371	$5,270	$155,497	$233,872	$10,540	$40,190	140.56%
2015	$277,934	$25,070	$16,193	$400,881	$5,559	$166,319	$260,189	$11,117	$45,315	144.24%
2016	$287,565	$25,938	$17,006	$428,030	$5,751	$178,109	$285,526	$11,503	$50,964	148.85%

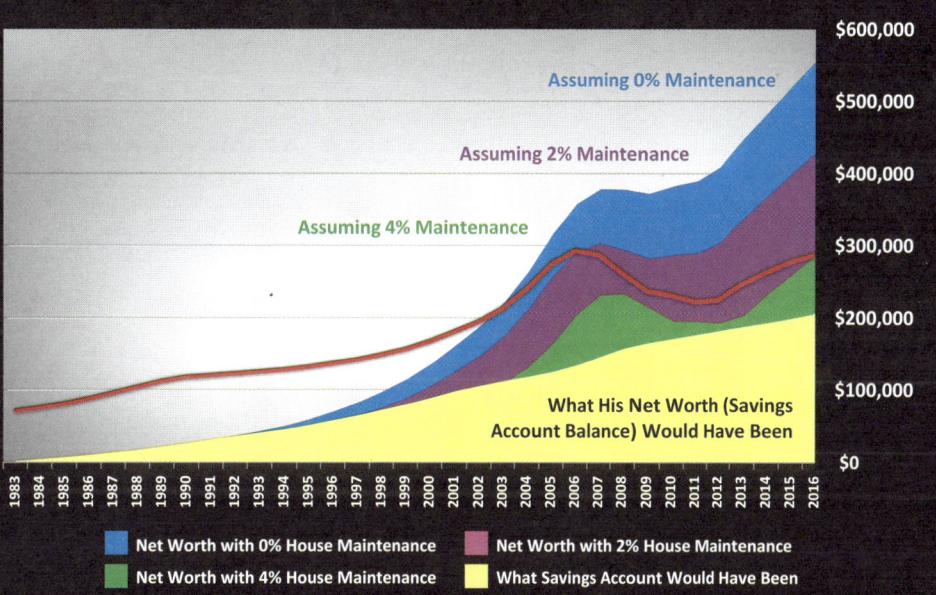

Assuming 0% Maintenance

Assuming 2% Maintenance

Assuming 4% Maintenance

What His Net Worth (Savings Account Balance) Would Have Been

- Net Worth with 0% House Maintenance
- Net Worth with 2% House Maintenance
- Net Worth with 4% House Maintenance
- What Savings Account Would Have Been
- Average House Price

My rule of thumb is this: keep 5% of the value of your house available in cash or at least that much available as a line of credit. An aggressive alternative is to have 10% invested in equities that you can sell without penalty or significant taxation—in other words, not in a retirement account or annuity. Many major home repairs happen over a very long-term horizon (10+ years). Even if the stock market experiences a decline of 50%+ *and* you experience a major home repair, having that money in equities all that time is likely to deliver for you more net worth even in this terribly unlucky coincidence.

Another idea that can heavily mitigate risks associated with the costs of ownership is a home equity line of credit. A home equity line of credit, or HELOC, certainly fits into the category of "dangerous in the wrong hands." You have to be really honest with yourself about your discipline and self-control. A home equity line of credit is like a big credit card (normally minus the actual card) against the value of your home.

A standard banking guideline is that they will open a line up to 80% of the value of the home (your loan-to-value ratio or LTV). Just for easy math, let's say your home is worth $500,000 and you have a $300,000 mortgage. This means you have $200,000 in equity in the home. You could get a home equity line of credit (HELOC) for $100,000. The math is: $500,000 home value x 80% = $400,000 - $300,000 mortgage balance = $100,000 HELOC.

Let's say you needed $10,000 to fix a sewer line. You would open up the $100,000 HELOC and only advance $10,000 and only pay interest on that $10,000. The other $90,000 would still be available to you and count as equity in the home. This is what it would look like:

Loan-to-Value (LTV) Ratio				
20%	40%	60%	80%	100%
$300,000 Mortgage Balance			$200,000 Equity	
$300,000 Mortgage Balance			$100,000 HELOC	$100,000 Equity
			$10,000 Balance / $90,000 HELOC	$100,000 Equity
				$190,000 Equity ($90,000 Available on HELOC + $100,000 Equity)
$500,000 Home Value				

For some people, that $90,000 would burn a hole in their pocket. Be honest with yourself. I also see the HELOC as a foreclosure preventer of last resort. Let's say you are in a really soft market like 2009 and you lose your job. In the above scenario, your house value may have dropped enough to eliminate your equity and you can't realistically sell it and get any money out of it. Facing foreclosure, the HELOC may be able to float you through the tough time or at least delay foreclosure. You could even make HELOC payments from the HELOC itself. If you had $90,000 available and your total mortgage payments were $2,000, it would last you nearly four years. If you could manage to contribute $1,000 each month to the payment, it would last you nearly eight years that would hopefully be enough time to find employment, rent the home out to someone else, or to sell the home in a better market. However, you can see that this takes a lot of discipline. Access to the equity in your home could utterly undermine the power of a long-term position.

Additionally, a HELOC may protect you from a forced sale event or even enable you to keep the home as a rental. Often the reason people need to sell a home is to free up the equity to buy another home. Instead, the remaining $90,000 available on the HELOC could be used as a 20% down payment on a $450,000 home.

The Difficulty of Diversification

As we've mentioned, real estate tends to be a lot of eggs in one basket. For many households, a home is the family's biggest asset. You can buy stocks in different industries and geographies to diversify against value fluctuations; most people can't buy a portfolio of real estate to diversify.

The next best option is to buy real estate in a diversified market. In some cities, a large portion of the economy is tied to a single industry. For Detroit, it's automotive. For Houston, it's oil. For Las Vegas, it's entertainment. While all of these cities are *mostly* diverse, the value of real estate in these communities will be tied to the fluctuations of that sector. When the proverbial coal mine or widget manufacturing plant closes in a small town, economic change may create permanent loss of value in a home. At times you can't help it; you live where you live. You may have family, friends, and community. The ability to buy stuff should never be a priority over these forms of spiritual wealth. But at a minimum, acknowledge when you own real estate in an undiversified market, and then amplify your financial cushion.

If you live in an area where the values have been going up at an abnormally high rate (such as more than **6%**), brace yourself for future years of an abnormally low growth rate. Of course this is always contextual. Sometimes there is a reason for a price boom, but sometimes it is a temporary shift in economics. If your house value has gone up a lot, get a HELOC or if you have one already, expand the available credit amount. I know it may feel like you don't need it, but my advice is that the cushion is well worth the cost of having it open.

It can't be emphasized enough that this is altogether different than "using your home like an ATM." This was a constant pundit sound-bite during the Financial Crisis. Using your HELOC to buy a car, furniture, or to travel is idiotic. Using it to update your house has a *chance* at being a good idea, but I'm not advocating any of these things.

The focus should always be on the long term. People get in trouble with stocks when they sell at the bottom. The most probable way to grow your wealth through a house is by holding onto it for a long period of time. If you run out of money and are forced to either sell it or let it go into foreclosure, this ruins the plan. While the financial cost of the loss is obvious and quantifiable, the loss of time (namely, the time value of money) is always the greater financial tragedy. Your mortgage itself can also be your friend, helping you mitigate risks, as we'll learn with mortgage planning.

Mortgage Planning as an Element of Financial Planning

Thus far, we have gone over many nuances of homeownership, but here are two key takeaways:

1. The benefits of homeownership assume that you have to pay for shelter *somewhere*.
2. The benefits of homeownership are financially marginalized *without* a mortgage.

On the first point: let's consider the approximate environment we are in right now. If you pay a 4% mortgage rate for a home that normally appreciates at **4%**, for a while this doesn't do much of anything to your net worth other than expose you to risky costs of ownership. However, when you assume your monthly dollars have to pay for shelter *somewhere*, then the decision is clearer. Not all cash flows are created equal. Some cash flows create wealth and equity, others don't.

On the second point: if you are paying cash for a home, you are giving up S&P 500 average returns (historically averaging over **11%**) in exchange for housing appreciation returns (historically just under **4%**). The moment you buy a house in cash that would be otherwise invested in equities, you should expect your net worth growth rate to *slow down*. A mortgage leverages you into a home without yielding the opportunity cost of investing elsewhere.

The Household Balance Sheet

All of this speaks to what you can think of as a household balance sheet. Businesses operate by their balance sheet. If you are a member of a religious body, non-profit group, timeshare owner, board member, business owner, partner, stockholder, or bondholder you know that each year the annual report includes a balance sheet.

The simple equation is:

Assets = Equity + Liabilities

Or we could rearrange it:

Assets - Liabilities = Equity

We are already familiar with this, with homeownership. If you buy a $200,000 home (the asset) and have a $160,000 mortgage (the liability), then you have $40,000 in equity. Or,

$200,000 Home Value (Asset) - $160,000 Mortgage (Liability) = $40,000 (Equity)

When talking about a household, we've been using the more common term "net worth" to describe what a balance sheet would call "equity." For nearly all households, these terms are synonymous. If you also have a $10,000 car, $5,000 in your bank, $50,000 in your investments (all assets), and a $20,000 credit card balance (a liability), these expand out to:

Household Balance Sheet			
Assets		**Liabilties**	
Home	$200,000	Mortgage	$160,000
Car	$10,000	Credit Card	$20,000
Bank Account	$5,000		
Investments	$50,000	**Total Liabilities**	**$180,000**
Total Assets	**$265,000**	**Equity (Net Worth)**	**$85,000**

Let's say that this household is a woman who gets a $100,000 financial windfall. Her net worth becomes $185,000. She is considering three options (1) pay down her debt (2) add it to her bank account (3) add it to her investments. Wherever she places the money, all options will result in a $185,000 net worth:

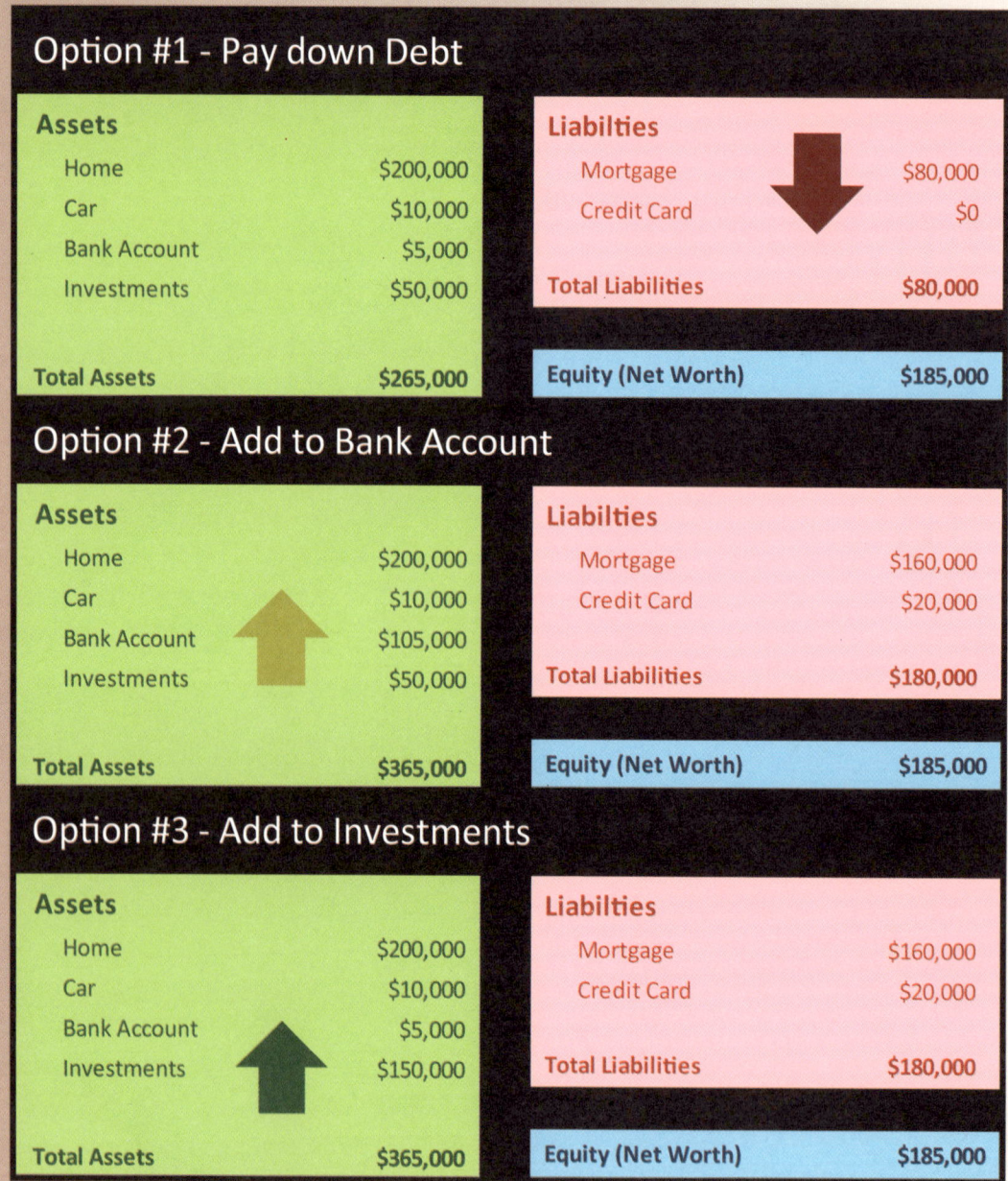

Option #1 - Pay down Debt

Assets		Liabilties	
Home	$200,000	Mortgage	$80,000
Car	$10,000	Credit Card	$0
Bank Account	$5,000		
Investments	$50,000	Total Liabilities	$80,000
Total Assets	$265,000	Equity (Net Worth)	$185,000

Option #2 - Add to Bank Account

Assets		Liabilties	
Home	$200,000	Mortgage	$160,000
Car	$10,000	Credit Card	$20,000
Bank Account	$105,000		
Investments	$50,000	Total Liabilities	$180,000
Total Assets	$365,000	Equity (Net Worth)	$185,000

Option #3 - Add to Investments

Assets		Liabilties	
Home	$200,000	Mortgage	$160,000
Car	$10,000	Credit Card	$20,000
Bank Account	$5,000		
Investments	$150,000	Total Liabilities	$180,000
Total Assets	$365,000	Equity (Net Worth)	$185,000

From a net worth perspective, where she puts the money is *net worth neutral*. However, from a psychological perspective, it will *feel* different. I'll say it again: how you *feel* about it ain't got nothin' to do with what's good for you.

Earlier when we talked of the man who was saving up to buy a house, you could see that once he bought the house, his net worth didn't change at that moment of transaction. The 20% down payment shifted from his savings account over to equity in the home. There are two things that don't create or destroy net worth *at first*:

1. Paying off debt
2. Getting into debt (if it's collateralized with an asset)

The key thing is which asset the debt is used for, and if that asset is creating wealth for you faster than not having it. Using a 12.99% credit card to buy a $1,000 computer that will drop 50% in value the first year is a two front net worth war you always lose. However, at the instant of transaction, you are $1,000 in debt and have a $1,000 asset. One year later, the computer has cost you $1,129.90 and is worth $500. At first, it is net worth neutral, but in time it's a **62.99%** permanent loss.

This is similar—but not as harsh—to a car that depreciates roughly **15%** per year. With a home, the long-term average *appreciation* rate is **3.96%**. Not all debts are created equal, but in the *moment* they are created, they look the same on a balance sheet. The long view is the wise view.

The Household Rate of Return

Let's expand the information in the original balance sheet. If this woman has $5,000 in a bank account earning **0.61%** in interest, this helps her $31 per year. If she is paying 12.99% on her $20,000 credit card balance, this hurts her $2,598 per year. If her $10,000 car is depreciating at **15%** rate per year, then this costs her net worth $1,500 per year. Before the windfall, her household balance sheet would then look like:

Household Balance Sheet

Assets	Rate of Return	Annual Amount		Liabilties	Interest Rate	Annual Amount	
Home	3.96%	$7,920	$200,000	Mortgage	3.65%	$5,840	$160,000
Car	-15.00%	($1,500)	$10,000	Credit Card	12.99%	$2,598	$20,000
Bank Account	0.61%	$31	$5,000				
Investments	11.62%	$5,810	$50,000	Total Liabilities	4.69%	$8,438	$180,000
Total Assets	4.63%	$12,261	$265,000	Equity (Net Worth)	4.50%	$3,823	$85,000

You could observe that on the whole, her $265,000 in assets are growing at a **4.63%** rate. Her $180,000 in liabilities are costing her a weighted average rate of **4.69%**. When you combine these, and weight them by balance and value, her $85,000 net worth has a net growth rate of **4.50%**.

You can see that her home (the full value, not just the equity) is appreciating at the average rate of **3.96%** and her investments are growing at the long-term S&P 500 average of **11.62%**. Note: the home doesn't care whether it has a mortgage or not. The price fluctuates regardless of the debt owed on it. This may seem obvious, but you'll see the importance of this subtle point in a moment.

Let us revisit our $100,000 windfall. Her decision about where to place this money affects the rate of return *on her net worth*. We can see these options in the table on the bottom of the page.

In all scenarios, her net worth ends up at $185,000. Where she places it radically changes her rate of return. Look at the home: whether or not she pays down the mortgage doesn't change the appreciation rate of the asset.

You could look at her decision as an attempt to *optimize the rate of return on her net worth*. Her most optimized route is to pay off her credit card costing her 12.99% and to take the remaining $80,000 and put it in investments. The 12.99% rate is a *certainty*, while the **11.62%** rate on investments is a *probability*. To pay off her credit card means that the rate of return on that $20,000 is certain to be 12.99% better each and every year that she no longer has the debt. The stock market doesn't offer this certainty.

We'll call this Option #4. She pays her $20,000 credit card balance off and invests the remaining $80,000.

Option #1 - Pay down Debt

Assets	Rate of Return	Annual Amount		Liabilties		Interest Rate	Annual Amount	
Home	3.96%	$7,920	$200,000	Mortgage		3.65%	$2,920	$80,000
Car	-15.00%	($1,500)	$10,000	Credit Card	↓	12.99%	$0	$0
Bank Account	0.61%	$31	$5,000					
Investments	11.62%	$5,810	$50,000	Total Liabilities		3.65%	$2,920	$80,000
Total Assets	4.63%	$12,261	$265,000	**Equity (Net Worth)**		5.05%	$9,341	$185,000

Option #2 - Add to Bank Account

Assets	Rate of Return	Annual Amount		Liabilties		Interest Rate	Annual Amount	
Home	3.96%	$7,920	$200,000	Mortgage		3.65%	$5,840	$160,000
Car	-15.00%	($1,500)	$10,000	Credit Card		12.99%	$2,598	$20,000
Bank Account	0.61%	$645	$105,000					
Investments	11.62%	$5,810	$50,000	Total Liabilities		4.69%	$8,438	$180,000
Total Assets	3.53%	$12,875	$365,000	**Equity (Net Worth)**		2.40%	$4,437	$185,000

Option #3 - Add to Investments

Assets	Rate of Return	Annual Amount		Liabilties		Interest Rate	Annual Amount	
Home	3.96%	$7,920	$200,000	Mortgage		3.65%	$5,840	$160,000
Car	-15.00%	($1,500)	$10,000	Credit Card		12.99%	$2,598	$20,000
Bank Account	0.61%	$31	$5,000					
Investments	11.62%	$17,430	$150,000	Total Liabilities		4.69%	$8,438	$180,000
Total Assets	6.54%	$23,881	$365,000	**Equity (Net Worth)**		8.35%	$15,443	$185,000

Option #4 - Pay of Credit Card, Add the Rest to Investments

Assets	Rate of Return	Annual Amount		Liabilties		Interest Rate	Annual Amount	
Home	3.96%	$7,920	$200,000	Mortgage		3.65%	$5,840	$160,000
Car	-15.00%	($1,500)	$10,000	Credit Card	↓	12.99%	$0	$0
Bank Account	0.61%	$31	$5,000					
Investments	11.62%	$15,106	$130,000	Total Liabilities		3.65%	$5,840	$160,000
Total Assets	6.25%	$21,557	$345,000	**Equity (Net Worth)**		8.50%	$15,717	$185,000

The key numbers from that table could be summarized as such:

BEFORE $100,000 WINDFALL			
Household Balance Sheet	Rate of Return	Annual Amount	Net Worth
Equity (Net Worth)	4.50%	$3,823	$85,000
AFTER $100,000 WINDFALL			
Option #1 - Pay down Debt			
Equity (Net Worth)	5.05%	$9,341	$185,000
Option #2 - Add to Bank Account			
Equity (Net Worth)	2.40%	$4,437	$185,000
Option #3 - Add to Investments			
Equity (Net Worth)	8.35%	$15,443	$185,000
Option #4 - Pay of Credit Card, Add the Rest to Investments			
Equity (Net Worth)	8.50%	$15,717	$185,000

Thirty years ago, the average mortgage rate was higher than the average stock market return—in which case, paying off the mortgage would probably produce higher long-term net worth. Nowadays, the decision entails having faith in probabilities. As we learned in investments, there is simply no historical precedent for the stock market to produce less than her mortgage rate of 3.65% over a 30-year period of time.

Asset Allocation and Homeownership

In the chapter on investments, we talked about asset allocation. The takeaway of the chapter *was that for those who can psychologically and behaviorally deal with the volatility*, a 100% equity portfolio makes sense for most households for a majority of their investments. Let us look at how homeownership fits among traditional asset allocations. In common use, the term "asset allocation" falsely refers *only* to your mix of stocks and bonds. This is wrong. You must look at the *whole balance sheet* to get a sense of the diversification. If instead of being 100% in stock, our windfall receiver was 50/50 stocks and bonds. This is what all of her assets would look like:

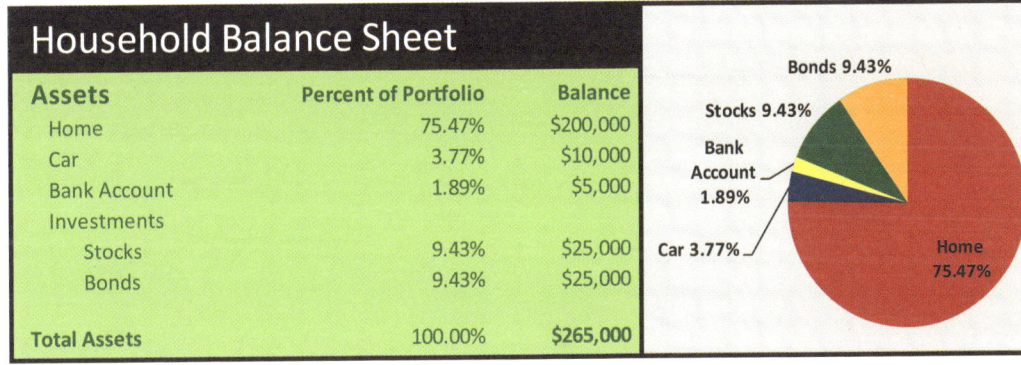

Household Balance Sheet		
Assets	Percent of Portfolio	Balance
Home	75.47%	$200,000
Car	3.77%	$10,000
Bank Account	1.89%	$5,000
Investments		
Stocks	9.43%	$25,000
Bonds	9.43%	$25,000
Total Assets	100.00%	$265,000

What's striking is how 3/4th of her assets are tied up in the home. The value of the home will whipsaw her total asset performance. We'll consolidate the stocks and bonds and call them "investments." This is how her options for the windfall affect her total asset allocation:

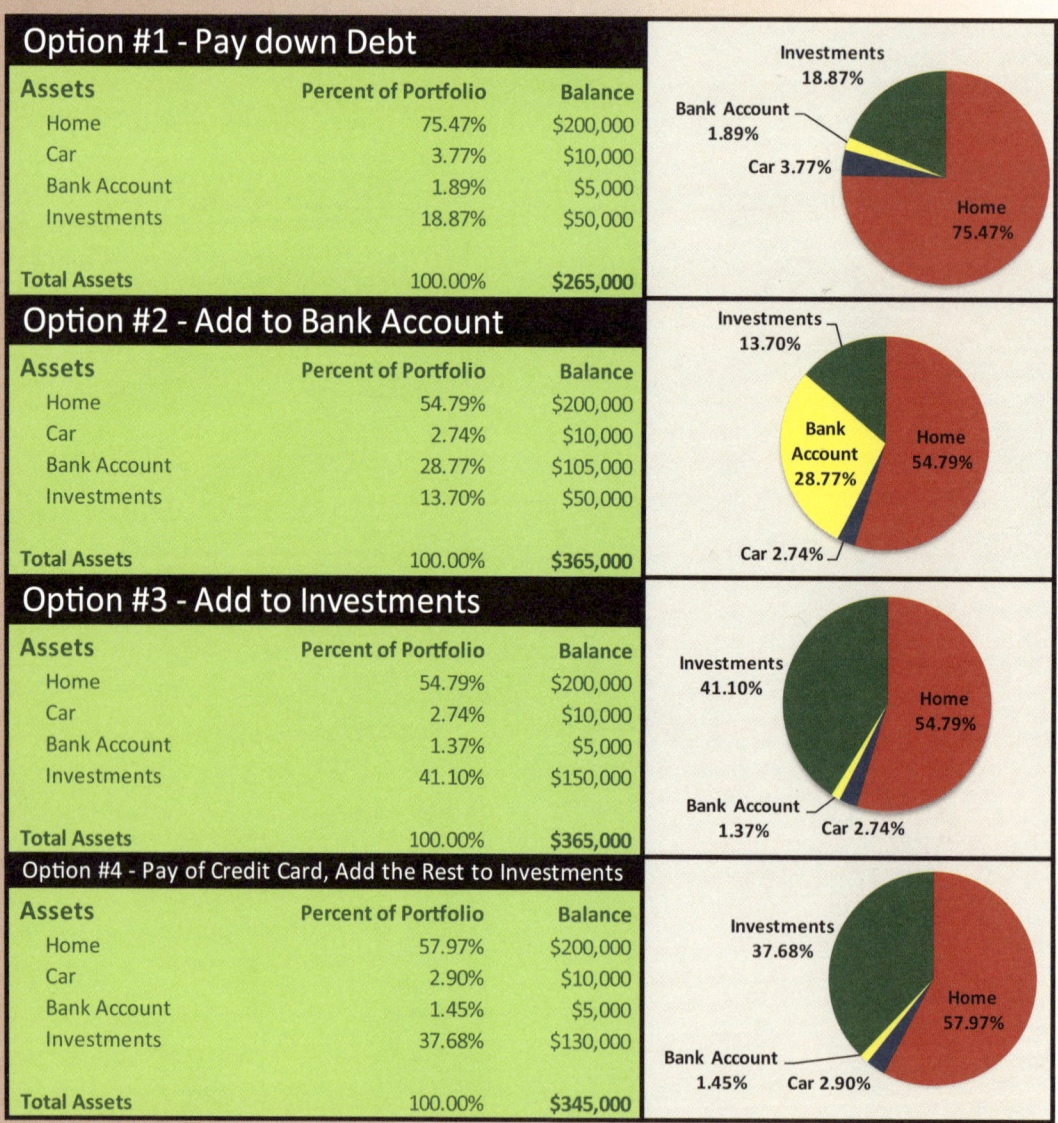

Option #1 - Pay down Debt

Assets	Percent of Portfolio	Balance
Home	75.47%	$200,000
Car	3.77%	$10,000
Bank Account	1.89%	$5,000
Investments	18.87%	$50,000
Total Assets	100.00%	**$265,000**

Option #2 - Add to Bank Account

Assets	Percent of Portfolio	Balance
Home	54.79%	$200,000
Car	2.74%	$10,000
Bank Account	28.77%	$105,000
Investments	13.70%	$50,000
Total Assets	100.00%	**$365,000**

Option #3 - Add to Investments

Assets	Percent of Portfolio	Balance
Home	54.79%	$200,000
Car	2.74%	$10,000
Bank Account	1.37%	$5,000
Investments	41.10%	$150,000
Total Assets	100.00%	**$365,000**

Option #4 - Pay of Credit Card, Add the Rest to Investments

Assets	Percent of Portfolio	Balance
Home	57.97%	$200,000
Car	2.90%	$10,000
Bank Account	1.45%	$5,000
Investments	37.68%	$130,000
Total Assets	100.00%	**$345,000**

In Option #1 when she pays down her debt with the windfall, she does not gain additional assets, nor does she gain additional power for those new assets to appreciate in value. *Her appreciation opportunity is identical to before she received the $100,000.* She merely reduces liabilities. Her mortgage balance is reduced, but most of her eggs remain in one basket.

The balance of her mortgage has no effect on her assets, nor in their ability to appreciate or depreciate in value. Be mindful of the *opportunity cost* of paying down your mortgage. This is not a definitive reason to *not* pay down your mortgage, it's just a reality to be aware of. More importantly, this decision will affect your cash flow.

Cash *Flow* is King, Let it Reign

It is often mused that "cash is king." That is a smidgen oversimplistic. *Cash <u>flow</u>* is king.

Let's revisit the woman who received a $100,000 windfall. Let's say she uses it all to pay down debt. There is now light at the end of the tunnel with her mortgage, with only $80,000 remaining. Here is how her monthly housing payment would change:

Paying Down Mortgage

BEFORE		AFTER	
Asset Value	$200,000	Asset Value	$200,000
Liability Balance (3.65% Mortgage)	$160,000	Liability Balance (3.65% Mortgage)	$80,000
Equity	$40,000	Equity	$120,000
Payment		**Payment**	
Principal and Interest	$732	Principal and Interest	$732
Amount Applied to Principal	*$245*	*Amount Applied to Principal*	*$489*
Amount Applied to Interest	*$487*	*Amount Applied to Interest*	*$243*
Insurance (0.50% of value)	$83	Insurance (0.50% of value)	$83
Taxes (1.25% of value)	$208	Taxes (1.25% of value)	$208
Maintenance (2% of value)	$333	Maintenance (2% of value)	$333
TOTAL	**$1,357**	**TOTAL**	**$1,357**

She then pays exact same payment, but more of it will go toward principal—hastening the pay down. What happens if she pays down her mortgage and then one month later loses her job and can't make the payment? In the words of Aristotle, "Tough noogies."

The mortgage company expects the full mortgage payment each and every month until it is paid off. No exceptions. All cash problems are cash *flow* problems first. Shifting money from the asset side of your balance sheet to pay down a liability can *increase* your exposure to cash flow risk.

The decision to either save money or pay down debt is more than just a question of paying interest versus earning interest. It is also weighing your vulnerability to the risks of homeownership, like paying for that broken furnace.

A notoriously risky feature of real estate is that it can be difficult to sell in tough times. The equity you have in your home is only on paper until you sell it. In fact, until you sell it, in real day-to-day terms, your appreciating house value is actually *hurting* you as taxes and insurance increase. The only way that appreciation may help you is if you give yourself access to it through a home equity line of credit.

Once you own the home, the asset *value* of the home doesn't help you financially *at all.*

Tax Benefits and Mistakes

Those of you already familiar with the tax benefits of mortgages may be wondering why I'm only now talking about this. If you read other material on renting vs. buying, there is normally a lot of hoopla about how if you have a 3.65% interest rate that's tax deductible, and you're in the **25%** tax bracket, then this is really only a 2.74% rate. It's not that simple.

I will fully flesh this out in the chapter on taxes, but it would be helpful in this context. Mortgage interest paid can be deducted from your ordinary income taxes. Let's put nuance aside for a moment. What this means is that comparing a 12.99% credit card rate with a 3.65% mortgage rate is not apples for apples because the 3.65% is effectively paid from your *gross* income and the 12.99% from your *net* income. If you assume a **25%** tax bracket, here is how you could recast these interest rates to get them on the same side:

Net Income Rate		Gross Income Rate	
Credit Card Rate	12.99%	Credit Card Rate	17.32%
Mortgage Rate	2.74%	Mortgage Rate	3.65%

Choose your truth. I've found that when we're *paying* interest, we tend to think of things in post-tax money (i.e. the left side of this table). What this means is that this 3.65% mortgage is effectively less than one would naturally think of it.

However, as I've mentioned before in the chapter on banking, when we're *earning* interest, we tend to think of things in pre-tax money. If you have a **5.00%** CD, you don't think, "It says, **5.00%** ... *but* I have to give up some of it in taxes, so *really* it's **3.75%**." Similarly, if you had an auto loan (not tax deductible) at a 3.50% interest rate, it would be natural to think that this is a lower rate than your 3.65% mortgage, but we could add this line item to our table:

Net Income Rate		Gross Income Rate	
Credit Card Rate	12.99%	Credit Card Rate	17.32%
Mortgage Rate	2.74%	Mortgage Rate	3.65%
Auto Loan Rate	3.50%	Auto Loan Rate	4.67%

So this is good news and it entirely *enhances* everything we've talked about so far. The tax treatment means it's all the more likely that *not* paying off your mortgage makes sense. On top of that, the money you pay in property tax is *also* deductible. A rent payment isn't deductible at any level.

Why didn't I factor this into the examples?

The tax benefits of homeownership are a tad overstated. I don't want to steal the thunder from the tax chapter, but there will be a bit of redundancy here and you know by now that I'm not shy about redundancy. I'm not shy about redundancy.

An honest net income interest rate analog for your mortgage is highly circumstantial. It is not as simple as, "A 3.65% tax deductible mortgage rate for someone paying **25%** in taxes is really 2.74% so anyone earning more than **2.74%** in their investments shouldn't pay off their mortgage." If you pay off your house you still get what's called a "standard deduction" from the IRS—which might be just as much as what you pay in mortgage interest. This is especially true now, since mortgage rates are incredibly low.

In 2016, the average home price was $287,565. If someone put 20% down, their mortgage balance would be $230,052. If they have a 3.65% interest rate, this amounts to $8,397 per year in interest. They will certainly have other write-offs on their taxes to add to this number. But if we're talking about a married couple who can take a $12,700 standard deduction (for 2017), it's perfectly conceivable that they wouldn't bother itemizing anyway since the write-offs may not eclipse the standard deduction.

For this couple, if they pay off the mortgage, they do not *really* "lose their deduction" (that they aren't taking anyway). Also, their true interest rate isn't really 2.74%, but actually the full 3.65%, because you aren't taking the deduction. Because of this, and especially because of the present day reality of very low interest rates, I'm completely ignoring tax deductibility. Just know that if you do itemize, everything I'm saying is all the more powerful. But for the average situation, it would be a gross overstatement to get you worked up about losing your tax write-off.

On the other hand, if you are itemizing, you should know that you only have one shot at keeping the tax deductibility of your mortgage. For it to be fully deductible, it must be the mortgage used to acquire the home (or refinance it). If you cash out on your home, the new mortgage interest is not necessarily tax deductible. The deductible loan amount is capped at $100,000 unless it's used for home improvements. However, let's say you own a house free and clear. If you buy a new house and get a mortgage, because it's a mortgage associated with the acquisition of the property, the new mortgage should be fully deductible. You can do whatever you want to with the money from your old house. This area of real estate and taxes is a treacherous tar pit of big mistakes.

However, this being said, with rates so low currently and the generous standard deduction, you may not write-off the mortgage interest anyway—for you, the $100,000 deductible cap is possibly a moot point.

A Return to the Long View of Return

There is further wisdom in *not* paying off your house. Lost time can never be redeemed. It is said that money comes and money goes. Time only goes. Paying off your house loses the power of continual leverage with disciplined investing. Long-term moves are either programed to create wealth or they're not.

Let's revisit the woman who received a $100,000 windfall. We found that Option #4 optimized the rate of return on her net worth, she should use $20,000 to pay off the credit card and invest the remaining $80,000:

Option #4 - Pay of Credit Card, Add the Rest to Investments				
Assets	Rate of Return	Annual Amount		
Home	3.96%	$7,920	$200,000	
Car	-15.00%	($1,500)	$10,000	
Bank Account	0.61%	$31	$5,000	
Investments	11.62%	$15,106	$130,000	
Total Assets	6.25%	$12,557	**$345,000**	

Liabilties	Interest Rate	Annual Amount		
Mortgage	3.65%	$5,840	$160,000	
Credit Card	12.99%	$0	$0	
Total Liabilities	3.65%	$5,840	$160,000	
Equity (Net Worth)	8.50%	**$15,717**	**$185,000**	

Let's look at the power of making this optimized choice. We'll imagine she *just* bought a house for $200,000 in 1987. She put 20% down, so her mortgage balance is $160,000 at 3.65%. We'll use actual S&P 500 and housing appreciation rates from 1987–2016 to give us a full 30-year sweep. The average return over this era was **11.32%**, which is fairly close to the 89-year average return of **11.62%**. These 30 years enable us to cast out a standard mortgage term. Just after she buys the house, she gets the windfall. Option #1 was to pay down the credit card and apply the rest to the mortgage. This accelerates paying it off down to 10 years, when her mortgage payment drops to just the taxes and insurance. At that point, she uses the monthly savings to invest in the stock market. Option #4, the optimized one, was to methodically keep paying that payment and invest the remaining $80,000 in the S&P 500. On the opposite page is a table of the results along with a graph.

Option #1 - Pay Down House   Option #4 - Invest the Windfall

Year	Total Return of S&P 500	House Value	Year End Mortgage Balance	Annual Housing Payment	Savings Amount	Net Worth (Investments and Equity)	Year End Mortgage Balance	Annual Housing Payment	Savings Amount	Net Worth (Investments and Equity)	Results of #4 over #1
Year 1	4.85%	$200,000	$74,289	$12,283	$0	$125,711	$157,007	$12,283	$80,000	$122,993	97.84%
Year 2	16.05%	$216,907	$68,115	$12,592	$0	$148,792	$153,903	$12,592	$0	$146,881	98.72%
Year 3	31.06%	$234,310	$61,711	$12,936	$0	$172,599	$150,684	$12,936	$0	$180,968	104.85%
Year 4	-3.53%	$245,778	$55,070	$13,287	$0	$190,707	$147,345	$13,287	$0	$226,005	118.51%
Year 5	30.07%	$250,835	$48,183	$13,648	$0	$202,653	$143,882	$13,648	$0	$230,024	113.51%
Year 6	7.33%	$256,143	$41,039	$13,886	$0	$215,104	$140,291	$13,886	$0	$275,926	128.28%
Year 7	9.79%	$261,540	$33,631	$13,991	$0	$227,909	$136,566	$13,991	$0	$296,786	130.22%
Year 8	1.24%	$267,418	$25,947	$14,101	$0	$241,471	$132,703	$14,101	$0	$323,350	133.91%
Year 9	37.21%	$275,689	$17,979	$14,213	$0	$257,711	$128,697	$14,213	$0	$337,974	131.14%
Year 10	22.65%	$285,797	$9,714	$14,335	$0	$276,083	$124,542	$14,335	$0	$423,309	153.33%
Year 11	33.12%	$296,974	$0	$13,043	$3,180	$300,153	$120,233	$14,507	$0	$498,147	165.96%
Year 12	28.39%	$311,177	$0	$5,934	$4,485	$319,895	$115,764	$14,717	$0	$623,285	194.84%
Year 13	20.89%	$327,652	$0	$6,166	$4,649	$343,494	$111,129	$14,949	$0	$765,860	222.96%
Year 14	-8.32%	$350,539	$0	$6,461	$4,819	$374,509	$106,322	$15,244	$0	$908,320	242.54%
Year 15	-11.98%	$378,192	$0	$6,803	$4,995	$405,163	$101,337	$15,586	$0	$885,729	218.61%
Year 16	-22.23%	$408,595	$0	$7,278	$5,177	$437,513	$96,166	$16,061	$0	$848,368	193.91%
Year 17	28.39%	$446,867	$0	$7,852	$5,366	$474,723	$90,804	$16,635	$0	$772,875	162.81%
Year 18	10.65%	$502,700	$0	$8,483	$5,562	$544,025	$85,243	$17,266	$0	$952,600	175.10%
Year 19	5.51%	$573,864	$0	$9,278	$5,765	$625,356	$79,475	$18,061	$0	$1,086,524	173.74%
Year 20	13.65%	$613,018	$0	$10,437	$5,975	$673,325	$73,493	$19,220	$0	$1,164,316	172.92%
Year 21	5.24%	$601,267	$0	$11,914	$6,193	$675,997	$67,289	$20,698	$0	$1,244,027	184.03%
Year 22	-36.21%	$548,305	$0	$12,727	$6,419	$633,368	$60,855	$21,511	$0	$1,234,692	194.94%
Year 23	26.61%	$496,483	$0	$12,483	$6,654	$557,402	$54,182	$21,267	$0	$919,000	164.87%
Year 24	14.82%	$483,384	$0	$11,384	$6,896	$567,411	$47,261	$20,167	$0	$1,039,676	183.23%
Year 25	0.67%	$465,324	$0	$10,308	$7,148	$568,952	$40,084	$19,091	$0	$1,118,238	196.54%
Year 26	15.59%	$471,290	$0	$10,036	$7,409	$583,024	$32,640	$18,819	$0	$1,136,307	194.90%
Year 27	32.05%	$516,637	$0	$9,661	$7,680	$653,473	$24,920	$18,444	$0	$1,298,164	198.66%
Year 28	13.41%	$550,911	$0	$9,785	$7,960	$739,564	$16,913	$18,568	$0	$1,598,914	216.20%
Year 29	1.14%	$581,111	$0	$10,726	$8,250	$803,320	$8,609	$19,509	$0	$1,780,266	221.61%
Year 30	13.42%	$601,246	$0	$11,438	$8,552	$834,546	$0	$20,221	$0	$1,822,815	218.42%

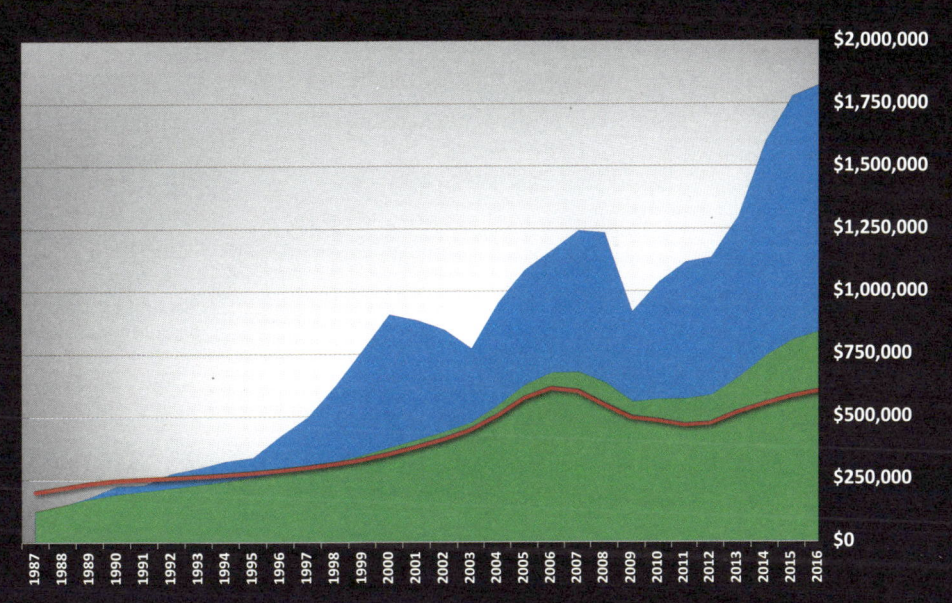

Although it may *feel* like the right thing to do to pay down the mortgage, by the end of 30 years the choice to *not* pay it down put another $988,269 in her pocket.

In choosing Option #4 she kept all the power in her hands. If she lost her job, she still has all that money as a cushion. Toward the end of the 30 years, the investment balance had grown to the point where the dividends alone could have bankrolled the mortgage payment. In Option #1, for those first ten years, her lack of liquidity would have made her vulnerable to losing the house if her income was interrupted. Liquidity empowers you to stay on the long-term path toward wealth.

Many of us will never receive a big windfall like this and we allocate money based on our month-to-month income. So let's say she had an extra $500 per month and was weighing whether to invest it (Door #1) or pay down her mortgage (Door #2):

Year	Total Return of S&P 500	House Value	Door #1 - Invest $500 per Month				Door #2 - Pay Down House, then Invest				Results of #1 over #2
			Year End Mortgage Balance	Annual Housing Payment	Savings Amount	Net Worth (Investments and Equity)	Year End Mortgage Balance	Annual Housing Payment	Savings Amount	Net Worth (Investments and Equity)	
Year 1	4.85%	$200,000	$157,007	$12,283	$6,000	$49,024	$150,976	$12,283	$0	$49,024	100.00%
Year 2	16.05%	$217,646	$153,903	$12,592	$6,000	$77,676	$141,842	$12,592	$0	$75,803	102.47%
Year 3	31.06%	$237,277	$150,684	$12,936	$6,000	$109,090	$132,594	$12,936	$0	$104,683	104.21%
Year 4	-3.53%	$257,335	$147,345	$13,287	$6,000	$139,601	$123,227	$13,287	$0	$134,108	104.10%
Year 5	30.07%	$277,982	$143,882	$13,648	$6,000	$174,473	$113,737	$13,648	$0	$164,245	106.23%
Year 6	7.33%	$291,587	$140,291	$13,886	$6,000	$210,187	$104,120	$13,886	$0	$187,467	112.12%
Year 7	9.79%	$297,587	$136,566	$13,991	$6,000	$223,865	$94,370	$13,991	$0	$203,216	110.16%
Year 8	1.24%	$303,884	$132,703	$14,101	$6,000	$258,885	$84,484	$14,101	$0	$219,400	118.00%
Year 9	37.21%	$310,287	$128,697	$14,213	$6,000	$281,731	$74,456	$14,213	$0	$235,830	119.46%
Year 10	22.65%	$317,261	$124,542	$14,335	$6,000	$308,662	$64,281	$14,335	$0	$252,980	122.01%
Year 11	33.12%	$327,073	$120,233	$14,507	$6,000	$330,241	$53,954	$13,043	$0	$273,119	120.91%
Year 12	28.39%	$339,065	$115,764	$14,717	$6,000	$398,537	$43,468	$5,934	$0	$295,596	134.82%
Year 13	20.89%	$352,325	$111,129	$14,949	$6,000	$462,068	$32,819	$6,166	$0	$319,506	144.62%
Year 14	-8.32%	$369,175	$106,322	$15,244	$6,000	$562,797	$22,001	$6,461	$0	$347,174	162.11%
Year 15	-11.98%	$388,721	$101,337	$15,586	$6,000	$678,395	$11,006	$6,803	$0	$377,715	179.61%
Year 16	-22.23%	$415,874	$96,166	$16,061	$6,000	$798,345	$0	$7,278	$171	$416,045	191.89%
Year 17	28.39%	$448,681	$90,804	$16,635	$6,000	$802,741	$0	$7,852	$11,366	$460,179	174.44%
Year 18	10.65%	$484,750	$85,243	$17,266	$6,000	$797,124	$0	$8,483	$11,562	$511,076	155.97%
Year 19	5.51%	$530,156	$79,475	$18,061	$6,000	$765,989	$0	$9,278	$11,765	$571,050	134.14%
Year 20	13.65%	$596,395	$73,493	$19,220	$6,000	$933,622	$0	$10,437	$11,975	$651,519	143.30%
Year 21	5.24%	$680,824	$67,289	$20,698	$6,000	$1,073,950	$0	$11,914	$12,193	$755,663	142.12%
Year 22	-36.21%	$727,275	$60,855	$21,511	$6,000	$1,158,195	$0	$12,727	$12,419	$818,454	141.51%
Year 23	26.61%	$713,334	$54,182	$21,267	$6,000	$1,223,972	$0	$12,483	$12,654	$784,155	156.09%
Year 24	14.82%	$650,500	$47,261	$20,167	$6,000	$1,203,606	$0	$11,384	$12,896	$753,063	159.83%
Year 25	0.67%	$589,019	$40,084	$19,091	$6,000	$938,002	$0	$10,308	$13,148	$719,930	130.29%
Year 26	15.59%	$573,480	$32,640	$18,819	$6,000	$1,039,343	$0	$10,036	$13,409	$718,680	144.62%
Year 27	32.05%	$552,054	$24,920	$18,444	$6,000	$1,105,444	$0	$9,661	$13,680	$733,575	150.69%
Year 28	13.41%	$559,131	$16,913	$18,568	$6,000	$1,130,369	$0	$9,785	$13,960	$812,791	139.07%
Year 29	1.14%	$612,930	$8,609	$19,509	$6,000	$1,290,114	$0	$10,726	$14,250	$914,866	141.02%
Year 30	13.42%	$653,592	$0	$20,221	$6,000	$1,565,109	$0	$11,438	$14,552	$973,531	160.77%

Again, by *not* choosing to pay down her mortgage, she ends up with more net worth—in this case $$591,578 more. The takeaway is that each of these scenarios have the exact same tool box. The only difference is the choice of where to allocate money *within her balance sheet*.

One aspect of this that I feel a pinch self-conscious about is that when you glance through the S&P 500 return numbers, you can see some serious boom years that bookend the two most horrific declines of our lifetimes. It's never wise to cherry pick rosy numbers from the past. But this 30-year growth rate of **11.32%** is actually fairly close to the historical average of rolling 30-year periods: **11.18%**. Only five of the years were outside of the "normal" **-9.59%** and **32.84%** range—this is about half of what you'd expect. Housing also averaged out to a slightly below normal **3.74%** rate of appreciation.

Being the armchair numbers historian that I am, I can't help but wonder if the last 30 years are normal. Are there any points in the past 89 years of data where this technique of *not* paying down your mortgage *wouldn't* have worked?

The two core long-term assumptions we're operating under are:

1. The S&P 500 will outperform your after-tax mortgage interest rate.
2. Your housing value will be higher at the end versus the beginning.

As far as the mortgage rate is concerned, for reasons I explained earlier, we will set aside the tax benefits. If you have a fixed 30-year rate, historical interest rates are irrelevant to a present day decision. At each point in the past, your decision would be, "Is my current mortgage rate higher or lower than normal 30-year returns of the S&P 500?" In the chapter on investments, when we looked at all rolling 30-year returns from 1928–2016, this is what we found:

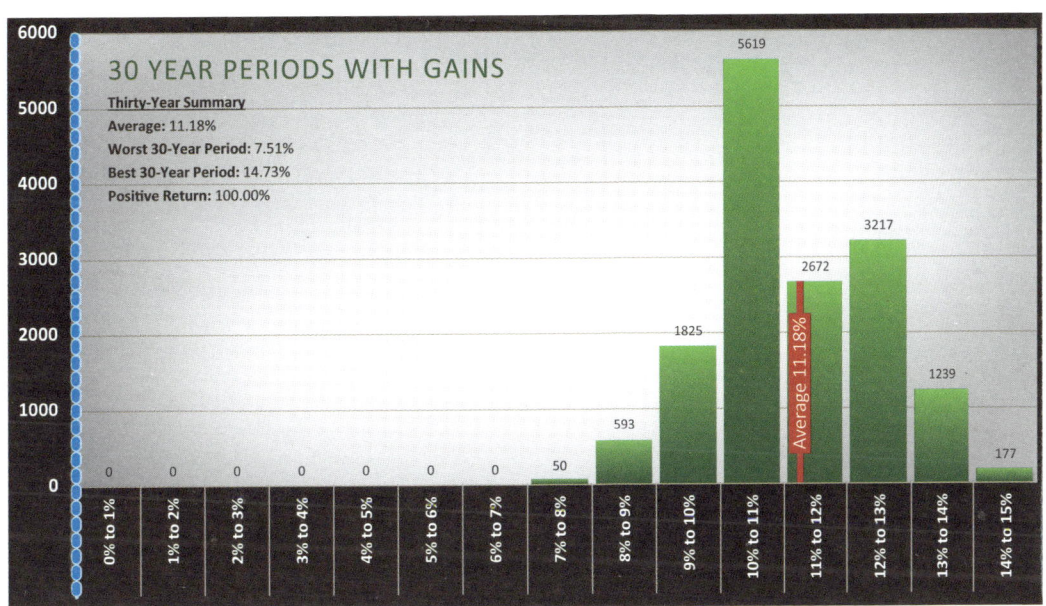

The 30-year return was positive 100% of the time. The worst you would have done was **7.51%**, the best **14.73%**, the average **11.18%**. If your mortgage rate is below **7.51%**, then there is no historical reason to not pay your mortgage and instead invest extra cash flow into investments.

We have good data for historical mortgage rates going back to 1972. This was the beginning of a high interest rate era where mortgage rates were *inside* the range of 30-year rolling averages. To invest (versus pay off) was more of a roll of the dice. By the early 2000s, average mortgage rates dropped below the lowest 30-year return. Since then, we can say that with today's mortgage rates, there simply is no historical precedent for this not working. With rates so low, at no point was it financially better to pay down your mortgage instead of saving your cash flow into the stock market. This is what the past 45 years looked like:

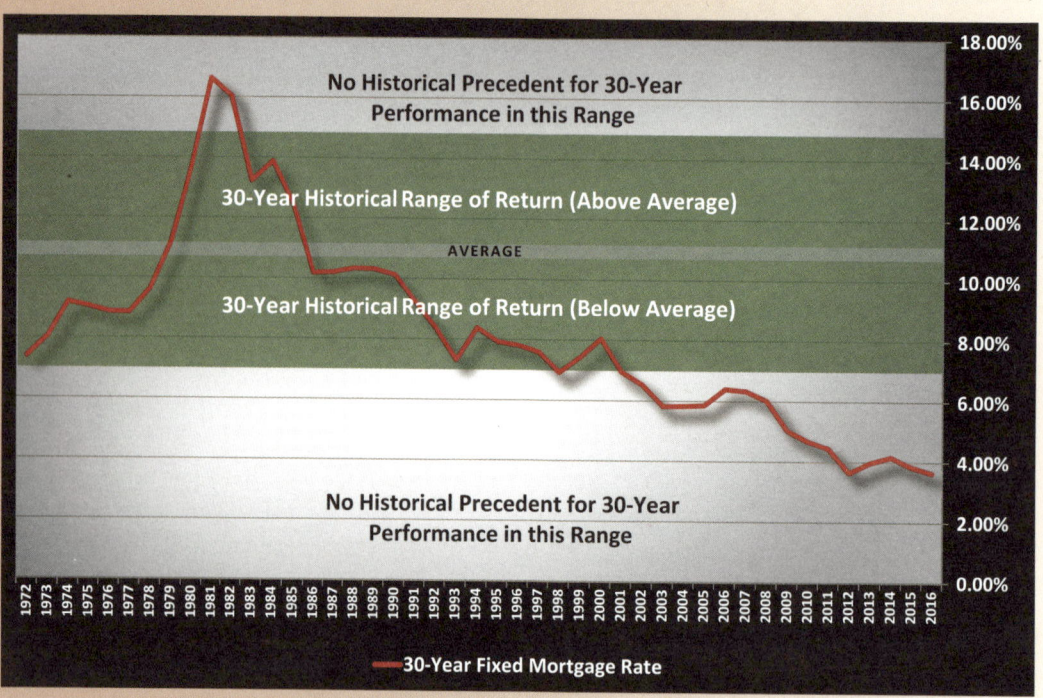

However, if you were sporting a 18.45% mortgage back in 1981, you would have no historical reason to do anything *but* pay your mortgage balance down as fast as possible. Conversely, if you are getting a 3.65% mortgage today, you have no historical reason to pay down your mortgage and expect to beat funneling that spare cash to a diversified equity portfolio.

You can imagine how much my heart bleeds for the mortgage data prior to 1972, but for the most part mortgage rates before then were well below the average return of the S&P 500. Meaning, that yes, in nearly all ages and eras it has been better to *not* pay down your mortgage—the lower the rate, the truer this is. With historically low mortgage rates, this has never been truer.

The appreciation rate on your house is less of an issue because, again, your house's value grows regardless of your mortgage. The moment you buy a house, your net worth 30 years later will depend on three key things:

1. How you allocate your money along the way (i.e. putting extra money to pay down your mortgage or to save it into investments)
2. The appreciation rate of your investments and your house
3. Your ability to be disciplined, stick to an investment plan, and, most of all, *not panic* out of the stock market when things get scary

On that second point, let's look at the history of all available 30-year periods on housing prices and investments. We are looking at it on a calendar year basis.[8] Our first data point covers the 30-year period starting in 1928, meaning if you had bought a house in 1928, the top row of the table below would have been your results. For the right-brained, a graph of these numbers is on the next page.

Undoubtedly there is a measure of luck in what your own 30-year experience may be, but all historical 30-year periods are well into positive territory.

Thirty-Year Rates of Return for Stocks and Housing Prices

Beginning Year	Ending Year	S&P 500 (Ave.)	Housing Prices	Beg.	End.	S&P	Housing	Beg.	End.	S&P	Housing
1928	1958	8.52%	3.11%	1947	1977	10.87%	3.64%	1968	1998	12.33%	5.49%
1929	1959	8.35%	3.15%	1948	1978	10.68%	3.25%	1969	1999	13.06%	5.48%
1930	1960	9.02%	3.24%	1949	1979	10.98%	3.65%	1970	2000	13.86%	5.46%
1931	1961	11.20%	3.40%	1950	1980	10.73%	4.15%	1971	2001	12.46%	5.45%
1932	1962	13.26%	3.72%	1951	1981	10.24%	4.47%	1972	2002	11.32%	5.61%
1933	1963	12.57%	4.14%	1952	1982	9.61%	4.52%	1973	2003	11.23%	5.74%
1934	1964	12.67%	4.28%	1953	1983	10.63%	4.54%	1974	2004	12.77%	5.94%
1935	1965	12.65%	4.26%	1954	1984	9.94%	4.18%	1975	2005	12.73%	5.93%
1936	1966	11.05%	3.98%	1955	1985	9.35%	4.31%	1976	2006	12.32%	6.15%
1937	1967	11.37%	3.92%	1956	1986	9.68%	4.47%	1977	2007	12.82%	6.32%
1938	1968	12.57%	3.88%	1957	1987	10.54%	4.69%	1978	2008	12.03%	5.90%
1939	1969	12.27%	3.99%	1958	1988	10.11%	4.91%	1979	2009	10.77%	5.19%
1940	1970	11.94%	4.17%	1959	1989	10.01%	5.16%	1980	2010	10.85%	4.29%
1941	1971	12.87%	4.30%	1960	1990	10.25%	5.40%	1981	2011	10.84%	3.91%
1942	1972	13.57%	4.88%	1961	1991	10.06%	5.52%	1982	2012	11.29%	3.59%
1943	1973	12.31%	4.91%	1962	1992	10.67%	5.46%	1983	2013	10.73%	3.43%
1944	1974	10.96%	4.63%	1963	1993	10.52%	5.45%	1984	2014	11.24%	3.49%
1945	1975	10.41%	4.21%	1964	1994	10.02%	5.40%	1985	2015	10.83%	3.69%
1946	1976	10.60%	4.16%	1965	1995	10.30%	5.43%	1986	2016	9.96%	3.59%
				1966	1996	11.20%	5.46%				
				1967	1997	11.83%	5.48%				

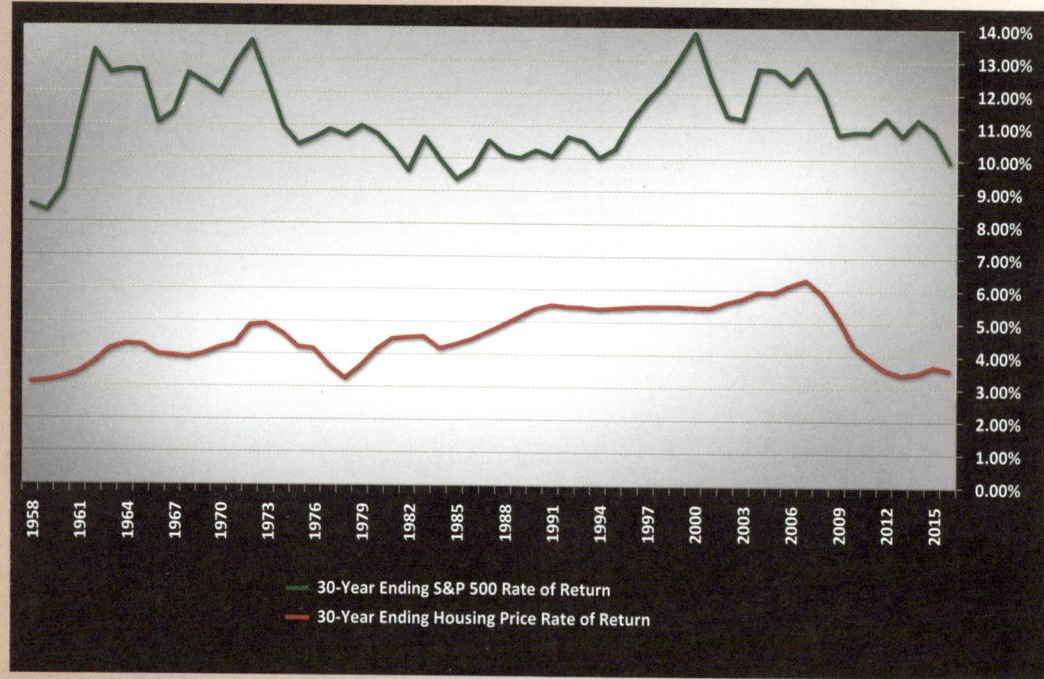

Legend:
— 30-Year Ending S&P 500 Rate of Return
— 30-Year Ending Housing Price Rate of Return

A Return to the Real World

As we close out, let us take a moment to riff on averages. Today, the average person selling their home has lived there nine years.[9] With such a short average time-frame, the level of certainty with this strategy goes down dramatically. This is particularly true considering that nine years is an average, meaning that half of the people selling their homes have lived there less than nine years.

The long view is the right view and all of these examples assume that you are committed to a long (30-year) horizon. It's not that you cannot change homes, but that the risk of this "keeping your mortgage" strategy failing increases with short time-frames. Only by sticking to this long time-frame can you reduce the risk of the strategy failing—at least within the realm of modern historical precedent. Results are never guaranteed, but probabilities are the only basis humans are ever given to help them make future decisions. It is not naïve to observe history and make decisions based on it, knowing full well the future may not follow the past. It is, however, pessimistically naïve to make decisions based on fear. Fear is easy, faith is work.

We will soon talk about working with real estate professionals. Selling a home costs a great deal of money that will back a few miles off your financial plan odometer. Because of this, it is crucial to minimize the number of *selling* transactions in the course of your life. Buy a house as a long-term decision, get a mortgage as a long-term decision, and commit to saving into investments rather than paying down that mortgage.

It is crucial that you don't miss the point. This is not advice to *merely* not pay down your mortgage. The decision to not pay down a mortgage must be actively coupled with a disciplined investing plan with the money you were going to pay down the mortgage with. Naturally, I cannot pass up the opportunity to reiterate that your biggest risk in the stock market is always you, and your proclivity to panic out when the going gets rough.

Applying this Advice

Applying these principles looks more or less the same whether you are buying your first house, moving, buying a second home, or an investment property.

First Time Homebuyers

The core advice I would have is to buy a house as soon as you safely can. If you are single and not a basket case, buy a house with rooms that you can rent out. In a strong market, it's conceivable that you could live there for free as you apply what you would have paid toward your investments. Of all of the financial strategies I know of, this is the most powerful structure that I am aware of that's accessible to typical people. Getting ahead like this would radically jumpstart a young person's finances.

I also don't want to put you off by constantly speaking about a 20% down payment. I mostly chose this to show the moving parts and to be consistent in the examples. There are still many options out there for first time homebuyers to put down as little as 3.5%. Expect higher fees and rates with this route, but almost any amount of fee is going to be worth the benefits. The 2016 average price for a home was $287,565, which would have a down payment of $10,065. A respectable chunk of change, but achievable within a few years by someone consciously deciding to drive an older car instead of financing a new one.

For young people, I realize that it may be very difficult to make a long-term decision of 30 years if you haven't even been alive that long. The odds are that your first house won't exactly be your dream house. Many people openly buy their first homes with the goal to upgrade in 5 or 10 years. The way you can make this a long-term decision is to commit to the idea of converting the home into a rental when you move out. Communicate this objective to your real estate professionals.

The key point is to buy a home as soon as you *safely and responsibly can.*

Second Homes

For many of my clients who have considered getting a second home, they often *could* buy one 100% in cash. This offers one heck of an ego massage. It's fun to imagine showing up at the closing and slamming a briefcase of money on the table, plopping down in the chair, putting your feet up, and twirling your mustache. However, this is not a good financial idea in the present environment.

Everything that we've talked about also applies to buying a second home, *especially* if you have the cash. Let us revisit a familiar scenario. Let's say there's a woman who has enough money to buy a house in cash and was considering whether to (1) put 20% down and get a mortgage at 3.65% or (2) buy the house in cash. To make it fair, for the scenario where she buys it in cash, we'll have her investing the money that she would be paying for the mortgage (just the principal and interest). She would be paying taxes and insurance either way, so these cancel each other out.

Year	Total Return of S&P 500	Average House Price	Option #1 - 20% Down, Invest 80%					Option #2 - Buy in Cash					Results of #1 over #2
			Year End Mortgage Balance	Annual Housing Payment	Investment Amount	Investment Account Balance	Net Worth (Investments and Equity)	Year End Mortgage Balance	Annual Housing Payment	Investment Amount	Investment Account Balance	Net Worth (Investments and Equity)	
Year 1	4.85%	$200,000	$157,007	$12,666	$160,000	$160,000	$202,853	$0	$3,500	$9,166	$9,166	$209,166	96.98%
Year 2	16.05%	$217,646	$153,903	$12,975	$0	$167,753	$237,514	$0	$3,809	$9,166	$18,777	$236,423	100.46%
Year 3	31.06%	$237,277	$150,684	$13,319	$0	$194,683	$287,411	$0	$4,152	$9,166	$30,958	$268,234	107.15%
Year 4	-3.53%	$257,335	$147,345	$13,670	$0	$255,143	$371,401	$0	$4,503	$9,166	$49,738	$307,073	120.95%
Year 5	30.07%	$277,982	$143,882	$14,031	$0	$246,142	$386,656	$0	$4,865	$9,166	$57,150	$335,132	115.37%
Year 6	7.33%	$291,587	$140,291	$14,269	$0	$320,146	$478,019	$0	$5,103	$9,166	$83,498	$375,085	127.44%
Year 7	9.79%	$297,587	$136,566	$14,374	$0	$343,624	$511,401	$0	$5,208	$9,166	$98,788	$396,375	129.02%
Year 8	1.24%	$303,884	$132,703	$14,484	$0	$377,270	$555,406	$0	$5,318	$9,166	$117,628	$421,512	131.77%
Year 9	37.21%	$310,287	$128,697	$14,596	$0	$381,963	$570,724	$0	$5,430	$9,166	$128,257	$438,544	130.14%
Year 10	22.65%	$317,261	$124,542	$14,718	$0	$524,109	$724,236	$0	$5,552	$9,166	$185,154	$502,415	144.15%
Year 11	33.12%	$327,073	$120,233	$14,890	$0	$642,813	$857,320	$0	$5,724	$9,166	$236,255	$563,329	152.19%
Year 12	28.39%	$339,065	$115,764	$15,100	$0	$855,745	$1,086,994	$0	$5,934	$9,166	$323,681	$662,746	164.01%
Year 13	20.89%	$352,325	$111,129	$15,332	$0	$1,098,674	$1,348,123	$0	$6,166	$9,166	$424,734	$777,059	173.49%
Year 14	-8.32%	$369,175	$106,322	$15,627	$0	$1,328,207	$1,599,643	$0	$6,461	$9,166	$522,635	$891,810	179.37%
Year 15	-11.98%	$388,721	$101,337	$15,969	$0	$1,217,749	$1,514,075	$0	$6,803	$9,166	$488,338	$877,059	172.63%
Year 16	-22.23%	$415,874	$96,166	$16,444	$0	$1,071,879	$1,400,914	$0	$7,278	$9,166	$439,008	$854,881	163.87%
Year 17	28.39%	$448,681	$90,804	$17,018	$0	$833,624	$1,201,245	$0	$7,852	$9,166	$350,592	$799,273	150.29%
Year 18	10.65%	$484,750	$85,243	$17,650	$0	$1,070,287	$1,479,988	$0	$8,483	$9,166	$459,290	$944,041	156.77%
Year 19	5.51%	$530,156	$79,475	$18,444	$0	$1,184,270	$1,645,629	$0	$9,278	$9,166	$517,371	$1,047,527	157.10%
Year 20	13.65%	$596,395	$73,493	$19,603	$0	$1,249,582	$1,783,680	$0	$10,437	$9,166	$555,069	$1,151,464	154.91%
Year 21	5.24%	$680,824	$67,289	$21,081	$0	$1,420,099	$2,045,386	$0	$11,914	$9,166	$639,980	$1,320,804	154.86%
Year 22	-36.21%	$727,275	$60,855	$21,894	$0	$1,494,485	$2,173,256	$0	$12,727	$9,166	$682,670	$1,409,945	154.14%
Year 23	26.61%	$713,334	$54,182	$21,650	$0	$953,399	$1,625,541	$0	$12,483	$9,166	$444,672	$1,158,006	140.37%
Year 24	14.82%	$650,500	$47,261	$20,550	$0	$1,207,105	$1,824,019	$0	$11,384	$9,166	$572,169	$1,222,669	149.18%
Year 25	0.67%	$589,019	$40,084	$19,474	$0	$1,385,995	$1,949,337	$0	$10,308	$9,166	$666,129	$1,255,148	155.31%
Year 26	15.59%	$573,480	$32,640	$19,202	$0	$1,395,314	$1,951,342	$0	$10,036	$9,166	$679,774	$1,253,254	155.70%
Year 27	32.05%	$552,054	$24,920	$18,827	$0	$1,612,894	$2,156,051	$0	$9,661	$9,166	$794,942	$1,346,995	160.06%
Year 28	13.41%	$559,131	$16,913	$18,951	$0	$2,129,833	$2,688,964	$0	$9,785	$9,166	$1,058,890	$1,618,021	166.19%
Year 29	1.14%	$612,930	$8,609	$19,893	$0	$2,415,528	$3,028,458	$0	$10,726	$9,166	$1,210,096	$1,823,025	166.12%
Year 30	13.42%	$653,592	$0	$20,604	$0	$2,443,139	$3,096,731	$0	$11,438	$9,166	$1,233,094	$1,886,686	164.14%

After 30 years, *because she got a mortgage*, she has twice the net worth than if she had bought the house in cash. The key reason is that once she buys the house, she owns it. Her asset went up in price, contributing to her net worth, regardless of a mortgage. Graphically:

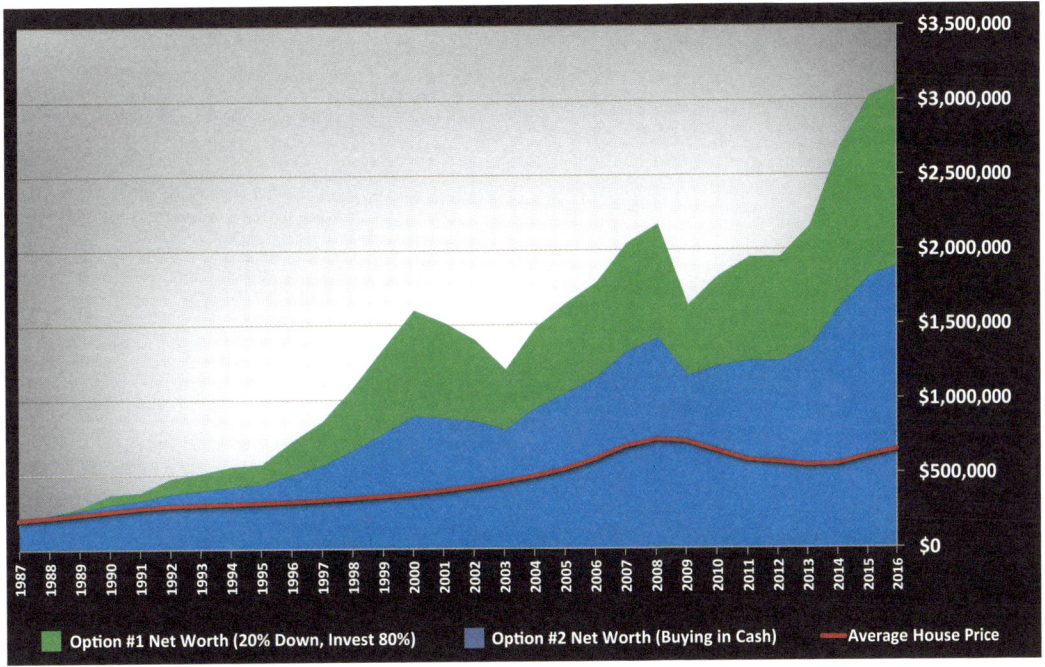

■ Option #1 Net Worth (20% Down, Invest 80%)	■ Option #2 Net Worth (Buying in Cash)	▬ Average House Price

Rental Homes

Unsurprisingly, the same principle applies to rental homes. Some added nuances apply. You collect rental income. On your taxes, you will normally "depreciate" the home as an asset—yet another term used in a different way. This will be fully explained in the chapter on taxes. The practical advice is identical to our example on second homes. You could analyze whether to use extra rental income cash flow to pay down the mortgage, but this would yield the same conclusion: a mortgage frees your money to work for you elsewhere.

Another can of worms that I won't open is life as a landlord. This isn't always a pleasant experience. Laws regarding "squatter's rights" will vary from state to state. This may be one of the few areas in life where anecdotal information can tell you everything you need to know. In short, ask around and get advice from people you know who have rental property.

Other Debts

Maybe as you read this you are starting out, have student loans, or are drowning in debt. Many free resources exist on strategic debt reduction. I have nothing to add to that conversation other than to elaborate on my answer to the question, "Should I invest money or pay down my debt?" First off, if you have a 401(k) at work with a matching contribution, that should always be your first priority. This is an immediate 100% return on your money and nothing will beat that.

Beyond 401(k)s, it is a question of the interest rate. If you pay interest greater than the average **11.62%** of the S&P 500, you should pay off that debt before investing. Commit to getting rid of it with vehement determination. If your interest is in the **7.5–11.62%** range, it's more of a gamble, but my advice would be to prioritize paying it off before investing.

The key thing with either savings or debt reduction is *actually* doing it. I apologize if you are getting lightheaded with how profound that is. Hopefully you were sitting down and not operating heavy machinery. You have to actually do it. These days it is extremely easy to set up automatic financial transactions. If you have a $100 per month student loan payment at 5% and had been considering paying it down by $200, but instead decided to follow my strategy and invest it, set up an automatic monthly investment of $200. I sometimes wake up in a cold sweat thinking about people who only apply half the advice—they don't pay down the debt *and* never set up the automatic contribution to investments.

Extra money tends to vanish into the ether of your daily spending. If you get a raise, after a few months it doesn't feel any different. You have to constantly be proactive and automatically allocate your extra capital. Again, this always goes back to a household balance sheet issue. Your net worth will greatly depend on how you allocate your capital.

As a final note, if you are drowning in debt, I will give you the teaser that in the chapter on legal planning I will go over using bankruptcy as *a financial planning tool*. This sounds crazy, but you will see what I mean when we get there.

On Working with Real Estate Professionals

I have a lot of respect, mixed with frustration, for real estate professionals. By "real estate professionals," in my mind I am thinking of both real estate agents and mortgage brokers. Of all the professionals I've worked with, they are, as a group, the most disciplined at running an efficient business, promoting themselves, and creating a good experience for their clients. This is particularly true with real estate agents. Twenty-four hour availability, particularly evenings and weekends, is par for the course in the life of real estate professionals.

Mortgage brokers have a lot of Financial Crisis reputational baggage to carry around. For the most part I've found that the bad ones have been weeded out by several very difficult years after the crisis, new licensing requirements, and the new highly regulated mortgage environment with somewhat insane underwriting guidelines.

Here are some things to keep in mind when working with real estate professionals—these are the things I find frustrating.

Their world is highly transactional and fast-paced. It's not their fault; it's just the nature of it. The client sees a house, the offer needs to come in *right* away. They need to get the mortgage in place *right* away. All the mortgage documents need to come in *right* away. There isn't enough time to talk about mortgage planning and thinking long term. The tyranny of the urgent drives the relationship.

I feel that all financial decisions should be filtered through a financial plan, in the course of your life and often a house is the biggest asset in that plan. In my observation, real estate agents virtually never go into planning and long-term decisions. They don't consider life after the transaction. Mortgage brokers sometimes do factor in the long-term. I've heard them go into the benefits of having a mortgage and investing the difference. Unfortunately for mortgage brokers, this conversation may inadvertently come across as suspicious because the larger the mortgage balance, the more they get paid. It doesn't mean they're wrong.

The industry is not exactly a planning culture. Enter a potential real estate transaction with your plans written and decisions made. Before you even start the process of buying a home, run the decision through your financial advisor.

I would encourage you to share with your real estate professional your long-term aspirations, but it's possible that some of this stuff will be foreign to them. If it is, there's a really great book you can refer them to. At a minimum, just ask them their thoughts on keeping the home for 30 years or ask them about the renting prospects. Many real estate agents are also landlords and should have some advice on operating a rental. You'll also find, virtually without exception, that they see real estate as a powerful way to get ahead. They may or may not use the words "leverage" or "inflation," but this is the primary reason. You may also find that they may believe this to the utter exclusion of investments *at all*. I've known many real estate professionals who have 100% of their net worth tied up in real estate, without a dime in the stock market.

If you are selling a home, plan on netting about 7% less than the selling price. Roughly 3–7% is paid in commissions to the real estate agents. If the commission is 6.00% then this is split between your agent and the buying agent (who you don't usually meet until the closing). If your agent works for a real estate company or has their own business, this 3.00% goes to their company and they may get anywhere from 25–100% of the commission.

When you sign on to working with a real estate agent to sell your home (normally a six month contract), you will agree on a commission rate. If you negotiate it down, it is only their commissions that you are talking about. If you negotiate it down to 5.5%, then 2.5% would go to your agent and 3.0% to the buying agent. In my opinion, any respectable professional doesn't negotiate their costs down. If a professional is good, they naturally rise to a point where they can command a higher cost. Good service and advice costs money. If you want to pay less, embrace a substandard experience working with sub-par professionals or beginners in the industry. Any amount of commission you pay on a real estate transactions is going to be a substantial amount of money. Often the commission pays for itself in just a single piece of advice or moment of intervention by the agent.

These days, it has become more common for the *buyer* to pay for the costs associated with getting a mortgage, such as points, origination fees, title insurance, appraisals, inspections, etc. In a softer market, these costs can shift to the seller's side. Recent mortgage regulation has limited how much a seller can pay and what costs can be wrapped into a mortgage.

All in all, if you are selling a home, plan on 7% as the cost to liquidate. Let's say you have a $200,000 home with a $160,000 mortgage. $200,000 x 7% = $14,000. After closing costs, you'd end up with $186,000. Then $160,000 goes toward paying off the mortgage and you end up with $26,000.

This brings us full circle to the concept of leverage. Let's say you buy a house and are putting $40,000 down. You see the house go up in value and sell it for $215,000. You are happy because you feel like the magic of leverage worked in your favor. Your $40,000 investment added $15,000 to your net worth, a return of **37.5%**! But you sell it and here's what happens:

Before Selling	
Purchase Price	$200,000
Mortgage	$160,000
Downpayment (Investment)	$40,000
Current Value	$215,000
Current Return on Investment	**37.5%**
After Selling	
Selling Price	$215,000
Closing Costs (7%)	$15,050
Net After Costs	$199,950
Net After Mortgage Payoff	$39,950
Net Return on Investment	**-0.13%**

This further emphasizes the importance of reducing your real estate transactions. Each time you sell your house, you are setting back the clock roughly two years of average appreciation just to liquidate it. You must look at asset values from an after-costs-to-liquidate perspective. This is not unlike taxes, namely tax deferred income, as we'll see in the tax chapter. Often hullabaloo about the benefits of tax deferral totally ignores the selling costs (i.e. taxes) associated with taking possession of the value. You have to look at this from an after-liquidation cost perspective.

Summary: The Mathematical Answer vs. The Real World

One of my favorite things to say to clients and innocent bystanders is, "There is the math answer and there is the real world answer." The real world of real estate can be destructive and devastating. Job loss, divorce, disability, physical health problems, mental health problems, and market specific downturns are all well within everybody's experience. These can all derail the ability to hold onto real estate for the long term. You can also add crazy neighbors, natural disasters, and less conventional disruptions. You can add difficulties in being able to buy a house in an aggressive market or selling one in a soft market—although everyone's situation will be unique, the aspiration should be the same.

The good news is that you only need to worry about the things you can control. With investing, the biggest thing you have control over is the choice to never sell out of the market, especially in a spirit of panic. Using a mortgage to leverage your net worth into a better position only works if you are coupling it with a disciplined investing and homeownership strategy.

At a minimum, homeownership puts you on the path toward independence. This is true even if you can only afford to pay the mortgage. When you buy a house, you are freezing the biggest cost in your budget. As you pay it down, you increase your net worth. When you eventually pay it off, it is a massive boon to your cash flow, and cash *flow* is king.

In the real world there is a lot of peace of mind that comes from having your house paid off. If you could measure it, my guess is that owning a $200,000 house free and clear has a stronger and more secure psychological register than having a mortgage and investments. Psychological security satisfies a deep biological need. But how you feel about it doesn't have anything to do with if it's truly good for you. Sometimes in life you have to override your own emotional programing. This will always be the reality of disciplined investing.

Endnotes

1 Source: Robert Shiller, U.S. Home Prices 1890–Present. http://www.econ.yale.edu/~shiller/data.htm. I've levelized the numbers to both start at 1.

2 If you total these declines up, it would be a sum worse than this number. This is a good example of geometric return.

3 Source: FreddieMac "Monthly Average Commitment Rate and Points On 30-Year Fixed-Rate Mortgages Since 1971" http://www.freddiemac.com/pmms/pmms30.htm

4 Source: United States Census Bureau "Table H-6" https://www.census.gov/hhes/www/income/data/historical/household/

5 The anal and observant may notice that these housing price ups and downs don't match our earlier ones. The reason why is because these are *median* house and rent prices. Earlier when we talked about averages, we were using the *mean* (or average). Mean house prices are skewed to a higher number because of luxury homes driving up the average. During the Financial Crisis, luxury homes declined the most, making the *average* house price decline worse. None of this radically changes our narrative.

6 Source: Fiserv, PPR, Moody's Economy.com http://money.cnn.com/real_estate/storysupplement/price_to_rent/

7 Source: Federal Reserve Bank of St. Louis, "All-Transactions House Price Index for Detroit-Dearborn-Livonia, MI (MSAD). https://research.stlouisfed.org/fred2/series/ATNHPIUS19804Q#

8 As I've soap-boxed before, the investment industry is a little obsessed with calendar year returns. There isn't anything magical about the calendar year, nor is it relevant to most people's buying and selling decisions. Regrettably, housing prices aren't priced on a daily basis like the S&P 500, so it's a bitter pill I have to swallow here. Gulp.

9 National Association of Realtors "2015 Profile of Home Buyers and Sellers" p. 7.

The use of a mortgage to leverage your net worth into a better position *only works* if you are coupling it with a *disciplined* investing and homeownership strategy.

It is not the man who has too little, but the man who craves more, that is poor.

Seneca

Minimalism

Why does wealth have to be so damned expensive? I started working with people's finances straight out of college. I was freshly married and crankin' out babies like the best of 'em. As the sole breadwinner, I couldn't help but feel a tinge of envy when I came across those with substantial money in their bank accounts. In my mind, these financial achievements were emblematic of what I ultimately wanted: peace of mind.

Over those initial years, I saw an endless stream of people. It slowly dawned on me that these people didn't seem any less stressed out about money than I was. I have a mental lineup of multi-millionaires expressing to me with complete sincerity that they were worried about running out of money. They weren't certain if they had enough or if they could safely retire.

I've also had the fortune to see people become millionaires. Each time, they glide past the milestone without any fanfare. I've tried to talk people into being proud of their financial accomplishments, "Mr. Smith, you are a multi-millionaire. You realize that's a big deal, right?" Each time it's met with a shrug of the shoulders. Those shrugs are fueled by something beyond modesty.

I'm often at a loss for words to persuade people into a rightly earned financial peace of mind. The accumulation of money doesn't always buy what it's intended to buy.

What I found in my early 20s is that when you don't have much money, it's easy to envision wealth as "everything above you." But whatever territory you tread, wealth continues to have an inner definition of "everything above you." At some point, this elusiveness must be reined in.

It is *you* that sets the price of what feels like wealth. It is you, influenced by the family you grew up in, your society, your ambition, your spouse, and your friends. The price of wealth is extremely subjective. Wealth doesn't have to be as expensive as we may imagine. Minimalism is about making wealth cheaper.

Our lovely American society has pre-answered our natural biological yearnings with "get more money." We yearn for shelter, stability, food security, and the power to do what we want in life. It is easiest to see wealth as the answer to this yearning *because it does answer* these needs. However, it's not the *only* answer.

I feel that part of stress is not because we have too little, but because we have too much. All objects in our lives occupy some amount of space in our brains. They carry a sense of "need to take care of that thing." The less we have, the less taxing the "wealth yearning" feels. This is counterintuitive to our indoctrination. Minimalism is about freeing up your mind.

Thus far, our focus has been about maximizing your wealth using existing resources. While the expansion of wealth is intended to grow your ability to buy stuff, minimalism is about the deliberate choice to have less, regardless of financial abilities. If you buy less and have less, not only are you wealthier, you are more likely to experience peace in your wealth.

With this book, I have various hopes for readers. The more obvious one is comprehensive financial education. I hope to make what you should do with your money as clear as possible. I hope that these optimized choices increase your wealth. But to me, this implies the question, "Why?"

I don't just want my readers wealthy. Ultimately, I want people to be happy, feel peace, and reduce unnecessary stress. This goal is why I feel minimalism is relevant.

Years ago, I heard about actors Sean Penn and Robin Wright's house burning down in a 1993 Malibu fire. They lost everything except each other and the clothes on their backs. I remember Penn saying that once they got over the shock of the loss, the experience was cathartic. Years later he reflected, "Everything in life burned, except my family, and it was so liberating." He said, "It reinvigorated my interest in a lot of things."

In the past when I've moved houses, I have taken the opportunity to get rid of everything that I didn't need—which was much closer to "everything" than I knew. I have found it oddly invigorating to have cabinets, drawers, and closets that were empty as a drum. That was the surprising liberty of minimalism: the freedom of having nothing.

Minimalism will mean very different things for different people, but wherever you are, I would challenge you to get rid of (give away, sell, or recycle ideally) as much as you can. Start with your closet. Which items in your wardrobe have you actually worn in the past year? After you go through a winter, take an honest look at everything and simply remove anything you didn't wear last winter (the same thing with summer). Pass it along. Things you've kept for sentimental reasons, but don't wear: let them go. Enjoy remembering what an item brought you and let it go.

Do you need all those shovels and landscaping tools? You use the newest and best, get rid of the rest. Do you have a storage unit? Get rid of enough so that you don't need it. Financially consolidate your accounts. Delete the apps off your phone that you don't use. Unsubscribe from email newsletters you don't read. Get rid of books that you won't realistically read again. Get rid of movies you won't watch. Just get rid of it.

Again, minimalism looks different for everyone. To me, it is not that you literally have the minimum that you need, but an attitude of actively removing anything you explicitly don't need. I am not saying this for financial reasons. Granted, if you aren't wasting money on trivialities, it helps your bottom line. But I advocate minimalism as a key component of noise reduction. Much of the trick of investing we've discussed was strategically drowning out the harmful noises that cause stress. Noise in your life tends to cause mental clutter and catatonic indecisiveness. Noise makes it difficult to focus and ultimately take action.

Clear out the physical things you don't need. With fewer mental barriers, look at what you want out of life and what's important to you. Clutter mentally prohibits people from change. It prevents your active movement, and moving is living.

If you have been motivated by this book and are choosing to make major decisions, I encourage you to couple it with big steps toward minimalism. Remember: worry only about what you can control. I believe that simplicity mixed with financial independence is freedom, and to me freedom is the landscape of happiness.

If your outgo exceeds your income, then your upkeep will be your downfall.

Bill Earle

Insurance

We now shift from the "what shoulds" to the next two chapters on the "what coulds." Investments and real estate are about observing the past and having faith in the positive probabilities of our world. With insurance and legal planning, we protect ourselves from the negative and devastating possibilities.

You create a financial plan based on probabilities and use insurance to protect the plan from the possibilities. Create the plan, insure the plan.

Nearly everyone has some sort of insurance policy. Because of this we don't need to dwell *too long* on the basics. Humor me for a moment and let's remind ourselves what it is, but from the perspective of *the insurance company.*

The Basics

Insurance has existed in some form for thousands of years. The key financial planning concept with insurance is your ***insurable need***. Life insurance is a perfect illustration.

In the section on banking, we talked about longevity and I provided a chart showing life expectancies based on age and gender. Let's imagine a crowd of 10,000 thirty-year-old men. Each of them know that if they were to die, their families would be in deep trouble financially. We'll imagine that they each have an insurable need of $1,000,000.

Based on the need, an insurance company gathers a bunch of data from when people normally die and knows that each member of this brigade of gentleman has only a 0.14% chance of dying this year. Which means that out of these 10,000 thirty-year-old males, fourteen will die this year. As an insurance company, this means that if they insure 10,000 thirty-year-old men, they will have to pay out $14,000,000 in insurance claims.

They have to collect *more than* $14,000,000 this year from this group of men or they don't make money. Indeed, never forget that insurance companies are a *for-profit* business. They have competitors trying to do the same thing, so they want to make sure that what they charge these men is competitive. Let's say the company determines that 15% is their acceptable cushion. They then add 15% on top of the claims they expect to pay and calculate that they need to collect $16,100,000 over the year from the 10,000 men. This means that each man needs to pay $1,610 into the pool of money, or what would be a monthly payment of $134. This monthly payment then becomes the premium amount to each of the young men.

This basic example is how all insurance works. Of course it only gets more complicated from here. Yes, on average 0.14% of all thirty-year-old men die each year. But what if we make our pool better and only insure young men who don't smoke, don't have major health problems, aren't overweight, and don't go hang gliding? These cause the death rate to go down along with the premium amount. Part of the hope of the insurance company is to only insure thirty-year-old men who won't die. The insurance companies are very good at this. Because they are good, you as the insured will always lose this game and that's perfectly okay.

When we spoke about investments, we talked about what *should* happen. In nearly all cases, investing money in the stock market for the long term grows your wealth. If you are a thirty-year-old male, in nearly all cases, you will make it to your 31st birthday ... but not for 14 of you. Imagine you and the other 9,999 young men are treading water in the open ocean. This year, sharks will come up from underneath and eat 14 of you.

There is a *negative possibility* that you are one of the 14. You have no personal way to completely mitigate this risk. Exercising willpower can control the risk of panicking out of the equities market, exercising vigilance can reduce the risk of real estate investments needing major repairs. Regrettably, death isn't quite as subservient.

The Types

There are innumerable negative possibilities and plenty of types of insurance to meet them.

Types of Insurance

What Could Happen	Name
What if I die too soon?	Life Insurance
What if I crash my car?	Auto Insurance (also Boat and Airplane)
What if I have a huge expensive medical problem?	Health Insurance (also Dental and Vision)
What if I become disabled and can't work?	Disability Insurance
What if my health declines and I have to go into long-term care?	Long-Term Care Insurance
What if my house burns down?	Property Insurance
What if somebody sues me and takes all my money?	Umbrella Insurance

Those are the common types, but then there are:

What Could Happen	Name
I'm a farmer, what if my crops fail?	Crop Insurance
I'm getting married, what if I've paid my caterer and they don't show up?	Wedding Insurance
What if I'm kidnapped and held for ransom?	Kidnapping Insurance
What if my dog swallows a sewing needle and needs surgery?	Pet Insurance

I'm just scratching the surface. Vampire bites, alien abductions, and zombie attacks are all things you can (and definitely should not) insure against. I'm not making this up. If you have a crazy paranoia about something, there's a company out there more than happy to take your money to protect you from your imagination.

This leads perfectly into the whole point of this chapter: insurable needs.

Insurance According to Insurable Needs

Watch out, here comes my trusty soapbox. In the investment chapter I talked about how financial companies tend to market their services by appealing to your asymmetric loss aversion. Auto insurance companies appeal to the cost of insurance versus the benefits of it. Most ads that I see preach the message that they can lower your premium. The problem with this is that it completely ignores:

1. Your insurable need
2. The risk of being underinsured

Most states require drivers to get auto insurance. This requirement is largely in the spirit of protecting *everyone else* but you. It wouldn't be fair for a driver to hurt someone else or their property and leave them high and dry to pay for it. Because of this, some states allow you to get *liability only* insurance which means that if you crash, the other person is covered, but you'll have to pay to replace your own car. Because of this reduced exposure to the insurance company, the premiums are lower. Any monkey could *lower your premium* simply by under-insuring you.

Lowering your premium ain't the point. The point of insurance is that a statistically unlikely negative possibility may hit you and you don't want it to derail your financial plan. Insurance protects your financial goals and plans. You should only evaluate lower premiums in the apples for apples context of comparing your policy with an essentially identical one. Nobody exchanges their sports car for a minivan and then brags that they lowered their car cost—not without acknowledging that they've also lowered their sex appeal.

When evaluating the cost of any insurance, at some point you have to come to terms with the following: I have a risk and I'm paying money to mitigate it. *Even if* it feels like you're throwing money away every month, and *even knowing* that the insurance company is likely going to beat you at this game, you are paying to mitigate the risk. Peace of mind costs something.

Think of Insurance in the Context of a Financial Plan

You can have a glorious financial plan that in a perfect world would likely create wealth for you and your family. You get on that train track and wealth is virtually inevitable. In a perfect world, without negative possibilities.

Let's say you are young and starting out financially in life. You may be *way* ahead of the game and disciplined in saving up money, buying a house, etc. and have put you and your family in a high probability path for long-term wealth. But if you die suddenly then the choo-choo train of the financial plan derails. So you get life insurance to make sure your train gets to its destination with your family and dependents on board.

What if you are retired, you have your income calculated out and you are taking a safe amount from investments? Then an accident sends you into long-term care and you suddenly pay another $7,000 per month. If you aren't prepared for this, your train may derail and leave your spouse destitute upon your passing. So you get long-term care insurance. The premium is the cost to know that the unexpected won't prevent your train from going where it's supposed to. Insurance buys peace of mind that your financial plan is protected from improbable but devastating possibilities.

Think of it as the cost of luck. Last year, you *weren't* one of the 14 thirty-year-old men that died in your insurance pool. Congratulations, you paid out some money that you'll never see again. You will keep paying it out, enjoying the peace of mind that if you aren't lucky *this* year, your family will be okay financially.

Your Insurable Need and Self Insuring

So, what are your insurable needs? The core *needs* are easy to figure out. Personal decisions will determine how much additional insurance you *want* to get. It's one single question: how much would it cost you if the improbable happens?

If it's auto insurance, the core need is going to be the value of the car and perhaps any loan balance beyond the value. Your state will have a minimum amount you need to have to insure the other driver, but if you hit a luxury car, it may not be enough and you may be stuck with the difference. If it's for your house, the variables are more known. Your insurable need will be no more than the cost it would take to rebuild your house, but there may be decisions about specific coverage for your roof and water damage. With these two types, the coverage amounts always have a minimum as required by your state, auto loan company, or your mortgage company. There are a myriad of bells and whistles available.

Life insurance is tougher to quantify because it's a moving number. An old insurance acronym is D.I.M.E. which stands for Death (as in the cost to celebrate your life and put you in the ground), Income (replacement for 10 years), Mortgage (to pay off your house), and Education (cost of putting dependents through school). Let's imagine we live in a 1950s sitcom with modern prices. We have a traditional household where the father makes $50,000 per year, there's a $300,000 balance on the mortgage, three children (who will go to a lower cost state college), and nothing substantial in savings. Here's what this might look like:

Life Insurance Need

Item	Reason	Need
Death	Typical burial cost	$20,000
Income	$50,000 x 10 years	$500,000
Mortgage	Current balance	$300,000
Education	$60,000 x 3 kids	$180,000
Total Needs		**$1,000,000**
Assets Available		**$0**
Insurable Need		**$1,000,000**

I think this is a good starting point, but a financial plan should be able tell you more precisely. If you have fresh out-of-the-box babies at home, then 10 years of income isn't going to cut it. If you don't have a mortgage, then you can omit it.

What if you are retired and have a fixed income that is guaranteed through your spouse's life? Then you don't need to worry about replacing income. Knowing how your pension and Social Security checks change upon the death of each spouse is a *highly* important detail. On the other hand, you may not have dependents and may not have any insurable need. The root question is: if I kick the bucket, who will suffer financially? The answer may be: nobody.

Whatever your insurable need number is, you may subtract out your assets. If your number came out as $1,000,000, but you have $200,000 in savings, then there is only an $800,000 insurable need. What if you had $1,000,000 in savings? Then there isn't an insurable need and you can *self-insure*. Again, insurance is to give you the peace of mind that the improbable won't financially upset life for your loved ones.

The amount of protection you need is a calculable number and it changes as your finances improve. Imagine a couple whose income is guaranteed for both of their lives, their house is paid off, their kids are grown, and they have $500,000 in savings. This is what their situation would look like:

Life Insurance Need

Item	Reason	Need
Death	Typical burial cost	$40,000
Income	Fixed income	$0
Mortgage	Already paid off	$0
Education	Adult children	$0
Total Needs		**$40,000**
Assets Available		**$500,000**
Insurable Need		**$0**

In other words, not everyone has an insurable need for life insurance. It's the same with long-term care insurance. The cost of long-term care will vary city by city, but just for simplicity's sake, let's assume it's $7,000 per month.

If you already have $2,000 per month coming in from fixed income, then your insurable need is $5,000. If you have $1,000,000, at $5,000 per month, $1,000,000 would last you 200 months or 16.66 years. It would be tough to argue that there is an insurable need there. However, if you have a living spouse who is surviving off savings of only $200,000, three years of long-term care would leave the surviving spouse destitute.

None of this is meant to directly help you come up with your numbers, but to guide the discussion toward how all insurance should be viewed. Because your needs constantly change and the insurance world experiences ongoing changes, it's important to work with insurance agents who think in terms of insurable needs. The landscape is rife with insurance agents who peddle unnecessary and expensive products. Only work with people who guide you through pinning down your insurable needs, and independently shop around for the best price to meet those needs.

Life Insurance

Term, Universal, or Whole?

When we discussed the basics of insurance we described life insurance in its most basic form which is *term insurance*. Term insurance is often quoted as "10 years certain" or "20 years certain." This tells you how long the premium amount stays the same and how long you're covered. A term insurance quote at age 30 may be quoted as "10 years certain, $100 per month, $1,000,000." Please note that I am making up the premium amount. This means that for the next 10 years, as long as you pay $100 per month, if you die then the insurance company will pay your heirs $1,000,000. If you live, the insurance company made $12,000 from you—$100 per month x 120 months.

The quote may also give the option of "20 years certain, $150 per month, $1,000,000." This means that you pay a higher premium for knowing that you can keep the insurance for 20 years. A risk you face in getting a 10 year certain policy is that you may become terminally ill in the 10th year and the policy ends just as you become uninsurable. In which case, you can't get more life insurance, and then you die and your family isn't covered. At a minimum, you should expect that if you want to renew the policy for another 10 years, the premium will go up by quite a lot (because you are older and more likely to die). That's the warm and cozy world of life insurance.

Term insurance is always the cheapest version of life insurance. Back in yesteryear, we can imagine that there were some people who didn't like two aspects of it:

1. Having to make a decision about the "years certain" length, "Can I just get this for the rest of my life?"
2. Having to "lose" money to the insurance company in premiums, "Can I just get *some* of it back?"

This spawned the world of *permanent* life insurance. There are two main types: universal life and whole life. They are both permanent in the sense that they are designed to last your whole life. There isn't a set period such as with term. As long as you keep paying the premiums, the insurance stays in force. If you don't pay the premium, the policy may cancel out—"lapse" is the industry term. Both universal and whole life policies have the ability to build a **cash value** over time, which you may be able to borrow against tax free.

Whole life offers a fixed payment that stays the same the rest of your life. It's pretty straightforward; you pay a higher premium to know that you can have coverage the rest of your life. You also build a cash value that you can borrow against or cash out if you cancel the policy.

Universal life is more flexible. It may give you the ability to adjust how much you pay in premiums each year, by letting premiums be paid from the cash value. Some may also allow you to increase your death benefit. Any growth you have is tax deferred. You don't pay taxes until you take it out. If you die, your heirs normally inherit it tax free. A subset of universal life is variable universal life, which gives you the ability to invest in a wider range of options including things tied to the stock and bond markets.

If you are going the permanent life insurance route, I would urge you to consider:

Question #1: How long will you truly have an insurable need?
Question #2: What does the insurance company know that you don't about Question #1?

If you are good with money, then you may not have an insurable need for life insurance in 20 years. You might, but it's something that you need to determine with a financial plan. Also, the insurance company *does* know this. Of the people getting a "permanent" insurance policy, how many of them do you think really keep the thing to the end of their life? In reality, 20% of permanent policies are canceled in the first three years, 39% in the first 10 years.[1] If this is you, it means that you paid *much* higher premiums to an insurance company that was more than happy to collect them, and even happier when you canceled your policy. The insurance company makes money when they don't have to pay claims. Secretly, they hope you *don't* keep your whole life policy your whole life.

Because of the risk of becoming uninsurable, it makes sense to get an insurance policy guaranteed at least through your the time of your insurable need. However, the insurance company is well-versed in the real world, where people waver from long-term plans.

Insurance that Builds a Cash Value

For some people, living is not enough of a consolation prize to not utilizing their life insurance policy. Insurance plans where you build a cash value comprise a very broad universe and it's not easy to generalize. But as a matter of principle, let's look at this from the insurance company's standpoint for our familiar thirty-year-old man:

1. Whether or not the individual is building up a cash value or not, we (as an insurance company) are still at risk of $1,000,000 if the person dies.

2. Because of this, we still have to collect enough in premiums across an insurance pool to hedge or risk for the 14 people we know will die each year.
3. For the insured to build a cash value, we'll have to collect *more* in premiums than the amount we need to cover our costs.

Simple enough reality of being an insurance company. Again, it's impossible to speak generally, but if you are getting a policy that is building cash value, then you shouldn't expect to experience something magical. The insurance company is simply collecting more money from you and forcing you to save up money into whatever it's invested in. There are no additional forces at play here.

But buyer beware. Since these cash accumulation policies have multiple features of insuring, saving, and borrowing, they are often sold as "the only investment product you'll ever need." That statement alone should set off all the alarms on your BS detector. At best, what you'll experience is:

1. The insurance company collects the normal amount in premiums to pay for the their risk of insuring you.
2. They collect some more money in premiums on top of this, put into an account invested in *something*.

At best, the policy is merely forcing you to save money in something. Not necessarily a bad thing, except:

3. That *something* is often worst performing or more fee intensive than something you could find on your own.

That third point is tough to generalize, but it is absolutely what I've seen firsthand. In my experience with the policies that I've come across, performance is usually closer to **0.00%** than it is to any of the S&P 500 historical averages.

In my opinion, this area of insurance is in an ethical fugue state. To me, the concept of insurance is a good-hearted fair deal where people pool their risks to gain great protection and power. On the other hand, getting people to tie up exorbitant amounts of capital in high fees over a long period of time is the opposite of that. While it certainly accumulates *something*, it is inevitably less than something lower in fees, which means that the policies inherently put people in a long-term place of *less* power and *less* protection.

A Back of the Envelope Comparison

Because I can only speak generally, I'll give you a little trick you can do to help you make a decision. If you get a life insurance quote, get all the different types. For simplicity's sake, let's say you only had two options. One is a plain term policy and the other builds a cash value. Let's say the premiums quoted are:

1. Term = $50/month
2. Some Cash Value Building Type = $150/month

The difference is that you are paying $100 per month extra to build cash value and to be able to borrow against it. The question you should ask is, "What if I set up an automatic monthly investment of $100 *outside* of the insurance policy?"

In the chapter on investments, we learned the historical best, worst, and average return of the S&P 500. We observed this over rolling 5-year, 10-year, 15-year, 20-year, and 30-year periods. For a back of the envelope sense of this, if you saved $100 per month at these rates, this would have been your result:

Disciplined Investing Over Time

	Worst	Average	Best
5 Years	-18.42% $3,939	10.25% $7,795	36.44% $16,527
10 Years	-4.72% $9,580	10.38% $20,936	21.52% $41,485
15 Years	-0.54% $17,294	10.77% $44,505	19.80% $109,244
20 Years	1.85% $29,015	11.14% $88,184	18.51% $248,940
30 Years	7.51% $135,015	11.18% $291,693	14.73% $650,182

Look at the quote you were given for the cash value insurance and see what future accumulation value it projects. If it's lower than the *worst* numbers of investing on your own, the decision should be fairly easy.

Admittedly, this is very simplified, but what I imagine you'll find is that you are going to experience much less growth building up a cash value *inside* of an insurance policy versus building one up *outside* of one. The fees alone will shackle you to sub-par performance.

On the other hand, in saving up money outside of an insurance policy, you are losing the ability to grow tax deferred and the ability to borrow against it, along with possible legal protections. I would argue that tax deferral is often far overstated as a value. Keep in mind, also, that ongoing fees eat up your return. We will see both of these fleshed out in the chapter on taxes. In a nutshell, from what I've personally observed, most insurance policies that build a cash value are tantamount to taking a laxative and sleeping pill at the same time. Whatever your best hopes may be, the results are predictable.

As far as borrowing, I would be interested to know what percent of policy owners ever actually borrow against life insurance. I would guess that it's not very many. It's been my observation that good savers tend not to need big chunks of money. Of my clients who have needed big chunks of money, most have needed it to lend it to someone else in the form of a personal loan (such as their adult children for a down payment on a house). At times, the loans become unintended gifts.

Personal loans are normally a bad idea. If someone you know can't get a loan from a bank or credit union, it means that a highly experienced financial institution believes that they are more likely to lose money than make money on the loan. They're very good at making that determination, and you should assume they are right. Do not get involved in personal loans. I'm sure some policy owners get loans for their own use or for something strategic like buying real estate, but I suspect that loans from cash accumulation balances in insurance policies are uncommon.

Using Life Insurance for Reasons Other Than Having an Insurable Need

Insurable needs should always be the primary consideration when buying life insurance. However, insurance can be used in creative ways because of how it is taxed. What this means is that you may not have an insurable need at all and still benefit from life insurance.

Let's say you have a portion of money that you want to go to your heirs. You won't need it during your lifetime. You can fully fund a universal life policy with a onetime premium (or set it up where you pay the premiums for only five years or ten years). This large premium immediately creates a much larger death benefit, that normally reaches your heirs tax free.

There are some people who will strategically pass their IRAs onto their heirs using such a strategy. When people inherit IRAs, the entire amount is taxable when the heir takes it out of the IRA. Let's say you had a $500,000 IRA and the heir cashed it all out in one year, depending on their income and the state they live in, it's likely that around **40%** of it would be taxed away. If they took it out more slowly it wouldn't be as harsh—taxes would most certainly be paid, only at a lower rate. If it is **40%**, $500,000 becomes $300,000 after taxes.

Another option is to slowly take your IRA out over a 10 year period and have it fully fund a life insurance policy which will go to your heirs tax free. The downsides are that you pay taxes now and in a sense are getting the taxes over with *for the family*;

often, retired parents are in a lower tax bracket than working children. However, in doing this, you lose control over the money, along with the possibility for it to grow more than the death benefit through the stock market. Many insurance policies have a borrowing feature that could be used in case of an emergency. In a sense, this strategy gives you a set dollar growth amount. It will tell you exactly how much your heirs will inherit tax free.

Sometimes I've set this strategy up to kill two birds with one stone by making the insurance policy a hybrid of both life and long-term care insurance. Some life insurance policies have a feature called a **long-term care accelerated death benefit**. This is a mouthy way of saying that you can use the death benefit *while you're alive* for the purposes of funding your long-term care needs.

This strategy can effectively give your heirs more money without causing them tax burdens, while also giving you access to the funds for long-term care. Whether or not it works for you depends on your age, income, and insurability. Run it by all relevant advisors before implementation.

Long-term Care Insurance

Long-term care insurance covers you in case you need ... long-term care. There are a few definitions to keep in mind when you are shopping for it.

Unique Terms within Long-term Care

Elimination Period (also called the deductible period, or benefit waiting period)—With auto insurance, when you crash your car you normally pay a deductible of around $500 (i.e. the first $500 of your repair costs come out of your pocket). This is also the same experience with health insurance. With long-term care, your deductible isn't money, it is time before the insurance company starts paying.

When you are in long-term care, the term for this is your "elimination period"—which sounds more fatal than it is. This is the waiting period before benefits start. If the elimination period is 90 days, the insurance company doesn't pay out benefits until you've been there for 90 days. In other words, the elimination period is on your nickel (it's your deductible so to speak). Just as we've said, think about it from the insurance company's standpoint: the more you personally have to pay out of your pocket, the less likely you are to go into long-term care. Also, if your elimination period is shorter (such as 30 days), it means that the insurance company has to pay more in benefits. The longer the elimination period, the lower the cost of the premium. Sometimes the elimination period can be six months or even a year.

Activities of Daily Living—It can be assumed on an existential level that *qualifying* for claims in the insurance world is a bad thing. If you qualify for the life insurance claims, you are dead. In long-term care, it's a smidgen less cut and dry, so the insurance company has to draw a line to determine if you qualify for the benefits of the policy. The way it's determined is if you can't perform *some* activities of daily living. These are:

- Eating
- Bathing
- Dressing
- Transferring (such as moving yourself to and from bed)
- Toileting
- Continence (not the seven found on a map)

A policy may say you are qualified for long-term care benefits if you can't perform 2 out of 6 activities of daily living.

Instrumental Activities of Daily Living—These are secondary to the core activities of daily living. They are the beginning of the need for long-term care. The key difference is that there is less of a need for medical care professionals. Some of these are:

- Shopping for groceries and clothes
- Using the phone or other communication devices
- Taking care of pets
- Managing money
- Cleaning and doing light housework
- Cooking meals and cleaning up
- Taking medication
- Driving or getting around community
- Responding to emergencies (such as fire alarms)

Policies will sometimes allow coverage if the insured (you) can't do one out of six activities of daily living and four instrumental activities of daily living. Every policy is different.

At Home Coverage Versus in a Facility Coverage—This is not so much of a term, but something to pay attention to when buying a policy. Some policies (especially older ones) only provide coverage if you are physically in a long-term care facility. Some policies allow at-home coverage, where caretakers come to your home. When buying a policy, I think the decision is simple. When you have the flu, where do you want to be? In your own home, in your own bed. When my grandmother was passing away, she had only one request: to die in her own home. My parents had to fight tooth and nail to take her by ambulance back to her home of more than half a century. Ideally, this was where she should have stayed during her ailing.

Naturally there has to always be an assessment of insurable need, but this is a good example of an insurable want. Decisions are not always all about pragmatism. I feel very good about the clients that I've set up with long-term care policies that have at-home coverage. In most cases, aging is a slow process, especially when it is a memory-related illness. Normally it isn't overnight that you have to go into long-term care. It is the slow multi-year progress of, "Dad seems to be having more and more senior moments ... Dad has really gone downhill ... I can't believe he's still driving ... he accidentally set the dock and boat on fire ... my sister is moving in with him ... he greets her every morning surprised she came for a visit ... he can't be left alone ... long-term care." Every phrase in this was the exact path of my grandfather as he slowly succumbed to dementia over a 15-year period. I've seen the same path with many clients.

Some people decline much faster than my grandfather, but normally the need for long-term care is on a gradient. You might at first need someone to clean your house for you, which then progresses to help with shopping, then perhaps it's food preparation, then taking medication, then activities of daily living. I'm not a fan of policies that make seniors feel they need to wait until it gets really bad before they get help from insurance. The best policies are the ones that mirror the aging process and give you help along the way.

On a side note, the long-term care insurance industry has been in decline since about 2002, and especially since the Financial Crisis. The reasons for this are:

1. The current low interest rate environment which reduces profits for insurance companies
2. Increasing longevity, which means that insurance companies are paying claims longer than they had planned
3. Mispriced premiums—in short, the insurance companies thought fewer people would use it and the companies collected less than they needed in premiums

These combined factors have drastically shrunk the industry and resulted in more expensive products. If you are thinking of doing this, in the words of television ads, "Act now while supplies last."

Medicaid, Medicare, Medigap

This is a whole can of worms, so let us open the lid a little and let two worms out. When you turn 65 you can get Medicare benefits. Worm #1 is to give you a rough idea of that decision and what to expect. Worm #2 is to circle back around to long-term care and determine if you are covered.

Worm #1—Government Health Care

Medi<u>care</u> provides health coverage for anyone who is 65 or older or if you have a disability. Medi<u>caid</u> provides health coverage for low income families; often covering disabled adults and children as well. If both of these are applicable, you can have both.

When you are 65, you can enroll in Medicare. More specifically, enrollment begins three months before you turn 65 and continues for 7 months. If you are already collecting Social Security, you don't need to do anything because you'll be automatically enrolled.

Getting health care services and products can mean a lot of different things. Are you in a hospital or at a doctor's office? Is it a short stay or a long stay? Is it a routine exam? Do you need prescription drugs? Do you need an oxygen tank? All of these different services are split up by type and assigned a letter. Some of those letters (types) are covered by Medicare and you can buy additional insurance to *fill in the gaps* of coverage called Medigap. The core parts of Medicare are A and B.

Medicare	
Part A	**Hospital Stays**
Part B	**Physician Fees**

These two can be thought of as basic coverage. Roughly, they only pay for about half of your health care cost, which is why you should buy a supplemental insurance policy. This is called a Medigap Insurance Policy. The Medigap policy pays for some of the remaining cost that Parts A and B didn't cover. It also opens you up to Parts C and D which are:

Part C (also called Medicare Advantage)	Allows you to receive medical care from different delivery options (such as vision, dental, and hearing)
Part D	**Prescription Medications**

A key thing with Part C is that it is more commonly known as Medicare Advantage—this is where the costs for your Part A and Part B coverage are paid by a private insurance company instead of directly from Medicare.

When you get a supplemental plan, they call the plan by letter—such as Medigap <u>Plan</u> A (not to be confused with the letters of Medicare <u>Part</u> A). The plans are: A, B, C, D, F, G, K, L, M, N. I won't compare them here, but Plan F is the most popular one, as it includes all 9 of the Medicare supplements. That's as much of Worm #1 that we'll examine. One more before we'll close the lid.

Worm #2—In Bed with Uncle Sam for Long-term Care

Will Medicare pay for my long-term care? If it's for medical (non-aging) reasons, possibly, otherwise probably not. If it's for medical reasons, Medicare does cover care in a long-term care hospital stays, skilled nursing care, eligible home health services, and hospice care.

But most long-term care isn't what would be called medical care. If long-term care is needed for activities of daily living unrelated to a specific medical reason, then it's usually not covered.

What about Medicaid? Again, who is Medicaid for? Low income folks. You may have heard things about spending down your assets, putting your money in a trust, etc. in order to qualify for long-term care coverage. This is done in an attempt to qualify for Medicaid to cover the costs. Before we go into this, I should say that this probably doesn't apply to many (if any) of the people who would read a book like this. But it's a question that people keep asking me even if they have a lot of money. Let us then shoot this bird out of the sky. Loopholes to qualify for Medicaid have gotten far more scarce, if not entirely eliminated. Here's what that would look like and a few things you should know.

Financial Eligibility—Because Medicaid is intended for the poor, there is a line drawn about how much money you can have, and what of your own assets you can keep. Think of it as a financial limbo bar that you have to fit under. This limbo bar varies from state to state, but it's around $24,000 per year in income and no more than $2,000 in assets. If there is a spouse still at home, the healthy spouse is allowed to keep up to half the assets but not more than $119,220 (for 2016). However, if the assets are less than $23,844 the healthy spouse can keep it all. Real estate is treated differently state by state. Generally if a spouse is still living there they won't be forced into a sale. If the property is vacant or if it has a lot of equity in it, the spouse might be forced to sell. Because of these rules, some people enter a rather unsettling period of spending down their assets to qualify for Medicaid.

Countable Assets—What does the government count as assets? Cars, boats, or planes that aren't used primarily for transportation. Life insurance with a cash value, bank accounts, investments, and trusts. They look at your house or any other real estate that your spouse or child isn't living in (if the equity is greater than

$500,000). They don't count personal items such as clothing, furniture, jewelry, one car, and life insurance with a face value under $1,500. What's the term they use for assets they don't count? Non-countable assets. When was the War of 1812? It was from 1812–1815.

Estate Recovery—I know what you're thinking, "What, the government is going to recoup from my estate what they paid in long-term care costs? Over my dead body!" Exactly. They only recoup what they spent. If you own a house (that they didn't make you sell) worth $100,000 and they paid for $30,000 in benefits, they collect it from the sale of the house and the rest goes to heirs. This may not sit well with you, but keep in mind that we're talking about Medicaid here. It is something designed for those who cannot pay for medical care. If you have assets, you can pay for it. At least that's how they see it.

Transfer of Assets—Some people have the idea of giving away all their money so they can qualify. Or sell their homes and cars for $1.00 to get them out of their name. Not so fast. When you apply for Medicaid there is a look back period that may disqualify you for a period of time.

Look Back Period—The government can look back through your financial records for up to five years prior to your application for Medicaid. They are looking for any transfers of assets during that period.

So, will Uncle Sam pay for your long-term care? Probably not, but now you have a sense of what qualifying would entail. There are, however, some legal planning tactics that may be available, but in general, loopholes are closing. In fairness, Medicaid is really for those who can't afford it, rather than those who are determined to not pay for long-term care out of their own pocket. And thus, we put the lid back on the can of worms.

As a closing thought, actively planning to be declared poor by the U.S. government is not the best way to use your financial planning energy. Just sayin'.

Statistics

In determining whether or not you want to hedge your risk of long-term care costs eating up your livelihood, let's look at some statistics. I'll organize these by questions that you may be asking yourself.[2]

Do I need it?

- 40% of people who reach age 65 will live in a nursing home at some point during their lifetimes.
- The average age of admittance to a nursing home is 79.
- 78% of the elderly in need of long-term care receive it from family members and friends.
- 68% of people over age 65 will become cognitively impaired or unable to complete at least two activities of daily living in their lifetime.

When my kids act up, I tell them that my one goal in life is to live long enough to be a burden on them. I'm joking, of course. Even though I did many tours of duty changing diapers, I hate the thought of them having to return the favor because I didn't plan properly for my inevitable demise.

Should I get a 90 day elimination period or save money and get a longer one?

- The average length of stay is 892 days (2.44 years).
- 10% of people who enter a nursing home will stay there five or more years.
- 65% of people who enter a nursing home die within one year of admission.
- Of those who die in a nursing home, the average length of stay is five months between admission and death.
- The average length of stay for discharged nursing-home residents is 272 days (8.94 months).

If your long-term care situation is temporary (meaning you aren't going out to pasture and moving there) then the average stay is 272 days. This is the average so if you have an average length of stay of 272 days and your policy's elimination period is 365 days, it is less likely to help you.

Also, the combination of these statistics should encourage you to look at a hybrid policy. If a great deal of people die before benefits begin, at least there's a death benefit going to heirs, particularly for a spouse who's still at home and perhaps has been depleting assets waiting to fulfill an elimination period.

INSURANCE

Should I get a 90 day elimination period or save money and get a longer one?

How much coverage is enough?

When I create financial plans, I project today's current cost of long-term care into the future by increasing the cost at the national inflation rate *for health care services*. I also take my clients' fixed income and project that forward. I also look at how much they will have in investments. I take these numbers and look to fill that future gap, *not the whole amount*. The gap is the insurable need. Here's a simple way to look at it.

- $73,000: Median rate for one year of nursing-home care in the U.S.
- $162,425: Annual cost of nursing home care, Manhattan, New York (the most expensive).
- $60,773: Annual cost of nursing home care, Des Moines, Iowa (the least expensive).
- $86,140: Annual cost of nursing home care, Tampa, Florida (the stereotype).

We'll use the $73,000 rate. If it's monthly, then it would be $6,083 per month. The average age for someone to go into long-term care is 79. If it's just you (no spouse), subtract out your Social Security or any other sources of fixed income. Let's say you have $3,000 per month coming in. Your insurable need is $3,083. If you have $300,000 in assets, then this will last you about eight years. However, if you have a spouse at home then you may have $3,000 per month coming in but your spouse needs $2,000 per month to live on, so your insurable need is $5,083. If you have $300,000 in assets, this will last five years and leave your spouse without any money. If you are significantly younger than 79, you need to adjust all these numbers up for inflation.

You can do your own back of the envelope math with real numbers, but a good financial plan should tell you what your insurable need is.

When should I get it and how much will it cost?

- The average age for someone who purchases long-term care insurance is 59 years old.
- Let's use an actual quote that I just ran (and won't be valid by the time you read this). The policy has a daily benefit of $150 (around $4,500 per month), five years of coverage, with at-home and institutional coverage with a 90 day waiting period and inflation protection. The cost per year is:
  - $1,831—If issued at age 55 or younger
  - $3,421—If issued between age 70–74

Insurance (ditto getting a line of credit from the bank) should be purchased when you can qualify for it. When you need it the most is usually when you can't get it (again, it's the same with getting a loan). Let me tell you a tale of two people. One is my friend's grandmother, Trudy, and the other is a former client of mine named Norma.

What I've found is that typically in a marriage, in the same way that one spouse does the majority of the cooking, one spouse does the majority of the finances. Trudy's husband was the household CFO and he prided himself in taking care of his lifelong bride. I never met her husband, but I imagine that I would have had a lot in common with him. From what I gathered, he was a believer in the philosophies I advocate. Unbeknownst to Trudy, he really set her up before he died. He had all their legal work together, the investments were exactly where they should be, and best of all to Trudy, he set her up with the crème de la crème of long-term care insurance policies. Years after her husband died, she began a slow slide into dementia. As she needed help, the policy paid for it. In time, Trudy's mental and physical health declined to where she needed 24 hour care. Instead of going into a home, her long-term care insurance policy fully paid for around the clock care *in her home*. A constant rotation of three nurses were with her all the time, making her comfortable *in her home*. I think this is marvelous. Again, when you have the flu, where do you want to be? In your own bed, in your own home. Quickly these caretakers became like family to her. At her funeral, several of them gave brief eulogies and wept at her passing.

I spoke of Norma in the blueprint chapter as one of the "Horror Stories to Read Under the Sheets." I will repeat the story here because it makes the point better than any other experience I have. Norma was a client I worked with early in my career. I noticed that she had $100,000 sitting in a savings account not earning much. At the time, there was an insurance policy where you could put $100,000 into it and immediately it would become a $250,000 fund that you could use for long-term care and if you died with it, then the $250,000 (or whatever you didn't use for long-term care) would go to your heirs as a death benefit. Also, you could close it down any time and get the whole $100,000 back. What you give up is earning interest on the $100,000—which wasn't much to write home about. The key thing is that you have to qualify for it with good health.

Norma liked this idea, but eventually decided against it because, as she said, "I'm a nurse, I'm around medicine all the time, I'm healthy and plan to work to the day I die." Six months later Norma called me crying. I immediately thought her husband John had died. I said, "Norma, what's going on? Is John okay?" She said that he was fine, then, "I just found out that I have a tumor wrapped around my spinal cord. It's malignant and so they have to operate and there's a 50% chance I'll be paralyzed. Is it too late to get that insurance policy?" She was facing both death and being in a long-term care situation. She desperately needed insurance and was now uninsurable. The moral of the story is to get the policy if you can't self-insure, *especially* when you are healthy.

Self-Insuring and the Aspiration for Self-Insurance

Buying insurance should always be considered in the mental context of hedging against financial risks that you and your family can't afford to (or don't want to) experience.

Think of long-term care as insuring yourself against the risk of draining down your assets to pay for care. The other risk is leaving your spouse destitute after a prolonged financially draining time in long-term care. Some people have the assets and this isn't a risk for them. They can self-insure.

There are also those who can *semi-self-insure*. They can't afford $6,083 per month, but they can afford $4,000 per month, so they insure themselves for the remaining $2,083. You can also reduce the premium by making the long-term care insurance more stingy. Or, make the elimination period 360 days and tell yourself that you are self-insuring for the first year (and have a full year of cost set aside to pay for it). Understand that whatever the elimination period is, you are self-insuring for that time.

Property and Casualty Insurance

I'm grouping these together because often they are part of the same policy, which normally saves you money.

Auto Insurance

This has got to be the most advertised industry out there. I constantly hear and see ads pleading with me to get a quote from them. From a financial planning perspective, most retired people who've saved well, probably won't derail their finances with an auto accident. However for some people, especially those starting out in life, this is a big deal. Let's diverge slightly from insurance itself.

Among the advice I tell people starting out in life is to be very pragmatic about cars. Buy a used car of a very reliable brand. A reliable car with 100,000 miles on it is very often better than a poorly made car with 30,000 miles on it.

Let's say you buy a new car and have an auto loan payment of $380 for seven years. However, since it's a new car, the auto insurance is also $100 more than a used one. So you are paying $480 more per month than someone with a used car, no loan, and cheaper insurance. After seven years you would have spent $40,320 in car and insurance payments. If instead you invested $480 per month for seven years in the stock market averaging an **11.62%** year over year return, that money would have accumulated to $62,018. If you *didn't touch it* for the next thirty years (neither adding to it or subtracting from it) and it continued to compound at **11.62%**, it would grow to $2,045,494. It's easy to draw out the numbers and see the folly. Similar to The Smoker's Challenge, in a perfectly equitable world, the implication of your neighbor (with identical income and expenses) paying a car loan when you don't is that you can afford to *save* $480 per month. Again, we see our theme of forgoing the comforts of today for the fortunes of tomorrow.

Insurance comes back into play when people, particularly young people, don't get adequate insurance. On average, cars depreciate **19%** in the first year. If you buy a $40,000 car, one year later it's worth $32,400. If you crash the car early on, you might not collect enough money from the insurance company to even pay off your car loan. This means that you will still be making the full monthly car payment on a car you don't have, without a way to get to work. You can get something called gap insurance which will pay for any gap between what you owe and what the car is worth, but the very existence of this insurable need suggests a poor decision.

In your state you might be able to save money by getting liability only insurance (if you crash your car and it's your fault, the policy covers the cost to repair the other car, but not yours). I would encourage you to add up how much you would be saving in cost to see if it adds up to how much you'd have to pay in getting a new car. Also take into consideration your medical costs and civil liability to the other driver. Again, view insurance as hedging against risks that you and your family can't afford to (or don't want to) experience. Contrary to insurance advertising, you highest consideration *is not* the monthly price of the premium. It is your insurable need and acceptable risk.

A final consideration is liability coverage. Some policies only cover the other car up to $25,000. So what happens if you run into a $100,000 car? You're on the hook for the difference. Is that risk on your mind worth it to save a few bucks per month? For me, it's not.

Homeowner's Insurance

Similar to auto insurance, homeowner's insurance is also focused around the cost of the premium. Insurance companies know that most people tend to weigh monthly cost rather than consider how much money they need in an emergency. Keep in mind how the insurance company makes money. They make money when they collect more in premiums than what they pay in claims. Reducing claims increases their profitability. However, they must pay all legitimate claims. The insurance companies microscopically tweak policies to reduce legitimate claims. Here are some things to look out for:

How is roof damage covered?

Your roof will age. Does the policy cover the *actual* value of the roof or the *replacement* value? If you have hail damage, it may cost $20,000 to replace the roof. But if your roof is 20 years old, it may only be "worth" $7,000. If your policy is only for the true value of the roof, the insurance company gives you $7,000 and you have to come up with the other $13,000.

You can reduce your monthly homeowner's insurance premium if your policy is only for the actual value of the roof, rather than the replacement value. However, I'd encourage you to take this monthly savings and see how long it would take to add up to $13,000 (or whatever your real number is). As a committed long-term owner of real estate, you should expect to replace the roof at some point in the course of your 30-year mortgage. Most real estate agents and home inspectors can approximate the age of the roof if the previous owner doesn't know.

How are floods covered?

I don't mean just the floods when the levee breaks and your house gets destroyed. I mean things like basement flooding, plumbing breaking, or if the hose on your washing machine busts a line. If you have a crawlspace, some policies may allow you to reduce your premium amount by not covering flood clean up.

It's up to you what risks you are comfortable with, but keep in mind that the insurance company is very well aware of the things that drive up their claims. If they are trying to give you an incentive to not insure yourself for something, it's probably because you are at a greater risk of experiencing it.

How is catastrophic damage covered?

If your house burns to the ground or otherwise experiences unscheduled destruction, your policy will state how much they will pay to rebuild it. If your house is worth $300,000 the policy normally pays $200,000 because there's an acknowledgment that the land is worth something and they are insuring just the building. It's expensive to build a new house and what the insurance company states as the value of the house may not be enough to build a new house, or a house of the same quality. Often, policies have different options in this regard.

Umbrella Insurance

Umbrella insurance protects you from litigation. It's usually something that you can add onto your property and casualty insurance policy rather than as a separate piece of insurance. For years I've urged people to get this. I always explain it as, "We can project out a beautiful financial plan, but if you get sued and someone takes all your savings from you just before your retirement, then all bets are off."

I have a client named Terry I took on about a year before his retirement. My standard practice when I take on a client is to do a comprehensive financial plan for them before I move any money or change anything. Once I present a plan, I make specific recommendations across the Six Areas of Finance, even if those recommendations are outside of my investment world (and there are always things that need to be addressed in several areas). Among my recommendations to Terry was that he talk to his insurance agent about getting umbrella insurance.

Each winter Terry takes a week off to ski with a group of friends. A few months after we had done his plan, he was on a ski trip and had a collision with another skier. Later that evening, Terry was approached by someone asking for the contact information for Terry's attorney because of the collision. About six weeks prior to this, he had listened to me and gotten umbrella insurance. That's the good news, but the great news is that the attorney request was a joke on him. One very understandable accident could have undermined his entire retirement plans only one year before he reached the finish line.

The amount you need should be at least the value of your net worth. Umbrella insurance doesn't normally cost much and it's nice to have one less legitimate vulnerability. The reason is that *you* are someone else's retirement plan. What? Yes, responsible ol' *you* who have saved up money. Your efforts and hard work are someone else's retirement plan. Over the years, surveys have been done asking people how they plan to fund their retirement. Among the surprisingly common answers are:

1. Lottery
2. Lawsuit
3. Inheritance

Somehow my core message of "withholding the comforts of today for the comforts of tomorrow" didn't make the list. There are people out there lurking for a reason to sue someone. It's just the reality. My fellow Americans, protect yourself from your fellow Americans.

Working with Insurance Agents

When we look at the Six Areas of Finance and the professionals you work with, some may be legal fiduciaries on your behalf, others may be accountable to an ethics board. In my opinion, the front lines of the insurance industry have the least ethical safeguards compared with other areas of finance. My guess is that people within the industry will disagree with this.

The insurance industry has *some* of these safeguards, but when it comes down to it, the suitability of an agent's advice leans more on the character of the agent than it does for other areas of finance. Within the industry, even the word "agent" itself typically implies working for a commission (versus a fee or salary). The silver lining of this is that people who have the character to earn their money from commissions while giving advice against their self-interest are saints to be highly valued.

My key advice is that the commissioned nature of insurance makes the public vulnerable to over-insurance, buying unnecessary insurance, or being sold terrible insurance. Insuring clients according to their needs is a far less lucrative route.

Multiple times per year, I come across insurance products that are *horrific*. I've seen elderly people who have put their money into contracts that they *cannot* close down. About a month ago, an 84-year-old client of mine showed me a product he was talked into 14 years ago that he would have to pay a *25% penalty* to exit. It astounds me that these products are legal at all.

People get talked into terrible ideas by persuasive people claiming to be acting in their best interest. It is essential that you run all major decisions through the *other* professionals that advise you—namely your financial advisor or your tax accountant. These two types are likely to have familiarity with these products. On more than a few occasions I have put the brakes on some disastrous decisions.

Summary

I don't love insurance companies any more than I love my proctologist. Both are necessary, but I use them as little as I can safely get away with. Assume that when you get insurance, on average, you lose. My bias is to give the insurance companies as little in premiums as I can safely get away with, without personally risking my livelihood or those I'm responsible for.

I personally don't want to risk getting in a car wreck with a luxury car and wake up from a coma six months later with $500,000 in medical bills. I don't like paying my insurance premiums. Just like stock market volatility, I don't have to like it. But *I really like* not having to worry about this risk. I suggest you view insurance the same way. Peace of mind and hedging devastating risks cost money. It's worth it to know that your train will keep charging down the tracks.

Remember: insurance is about controlling the uncontrollable (or at least the difficult to control). With both of these, here's the question you need to be asking is: what is my insurable need? You will have a rough idea, but two factors will narrow down your decision:

1. A financial plan that calculates insurable need
2. The advice of a competent insurance professional(s)

Look for someone who issues you insurance according to your insurable needs and isn't trying to sell a product to you for a commission.

The professionals I've worked with are not always people I'd normally be friends with or personally enjoyed being around, but they know their trade and they care about doing it with honor and ethics. Hollywood movies are hardly ever accurate. But in movies about corruption, there is a whistleblower who simply can't be bought. Often this is the guy or gal that is so principled about what is right that they are hard to be around and have few friends. That seems to accurate in my experience. God bless the nerds, and hire them to advise you.

Make your financial plan. Then insure it.

Endnotes

1 Source: http://www.wsj.com/articles/SB10001424052702303296604577450313299530278

2 Source: http://news.morningstar.com/articlenet/article.aspx?id=564139#cpage=1

You create a financial plan based on probabilities and use *insurance* to *protect* the plan from the possibilities.
Create the plan, insure the plan.

Life is mostly froth and bubble,
Two things stand like stone.
Kindness in another's trouble,
Courage in your own.

Adam Lindsay Gordon

Finding Purpose in Life

The purpose of life is to convert food into feces, and make babies who do the same. Everything else is just to keep us distracted while this happens. Indeed we are but highly evolved compost machines and in the end, regardless of what we've done in life, we are consumed by the flora and fauna, just as we consumed them. From this rather nihilistic starting point, all of us fill up this blank canvas with *something*.

All goals need a reason. That reason may be fueled by a core survival instinct, it may be altruistic, or it may be fictional. Heck, who's to say that the goal can't be outright delusional? Whatever financial ambition you have *must* be fueled by a compelling reason.

Let's take stock in a brutal fact here: getting wealthy is not all that important. When I think of my career and the effort I've poured into it, the reality is that it's not very important to make people money. My largest client is a millionaire many times over. My smallest client has a few hundred dollars in her account. On the peace and happiness scale, the wealthy and the broke are indistinguishable. To me, the wealthy seem just as stressed out about losing their money as the poor are about not having it.

For some, religion answers this question. Others prioritize relationships. Still others dedicate themselves to a cause or influencing the world in their own unique way. It is human nature to have purpose, and many people feel off-center when they aren't pursuing a purpose. There are things we love and things we feel strongly about. Everyone has an answer to the one-question-quiz:

1. I exist on this planet because the mission of my life is_____.

Let us then consciously answer it. Before you fill in the blank, I want to remind you of the privacy of your mind. America is a generous society and I think our culture sometimes expects saintly selflessness as our highest ambition. It is easy to feel that life is not purposeful unless it is altruistic. Again, allowing you the privacy of your mind, what naturally fills in that blank for you?

If you fumble through an answer, please know that this is entirely normal. If you float through life and it doesn't feel right, I encourage you to do whatever you can to fill in the blank. Find your own personal compelling mission in life. Getting a bunch of money isn't all that difficult … if all you want to do is get a bunch of money. It's also a goal that's usually achieved with a stunning anti-climactic question, "That's it?" Without a substantive undergirding reason, wealth buys *nothing*. Here is my advice:

1. Write down or print out your goals in physical form. Career, health, relationships, travel … just write it down. As you write it, continuously answer for yourself, "What do I want?" Think of "want" with many nuances. You *want* a vacation, but you also *want* to feel like you are helping people in a measurable and observable way. Enjoy the privacy of your thoughts. There's no shame in what you want, just write it down. Trust your heart. Most people's wants are naturally balanced and diverse.

2. Revisit your list of goals weekly. Read over it with a red pen in hand. Over time, your wants will change—let them. Feel free to add more abstract things that will make you a better person. If your motivation for wealth is actually peace of mind, an easier more expedient route is to pursue peace of mind directly, *regardless of wealth.*

3. Dig up the core of who you are. Life often causes us to get away from our passions. Our careers, families, and relationships can pull us away from the core of who we are. Sometimes this is good and natural. Sometimes we end up losing ourselves. To dig up the core of who you are, think back to what you loved when you were young and first expressed your individualism. Music, art, writing, and many other creative passions easily take the back-burner in our over-pragmatic world. What do you love at your core?

4. Re-engage the passions of your childhood. Take music lessons, an art class, try out for a play, or get back into horseback riding. Perhaps you somehow got on the wrong career path and found success in the wrong occupation. You

don't need to wait for a second career. Just do something to plug back into what you love.

5. Serve people. Just serve people. Be creative. You are surrounded by needs. Do you have a neighbor with young children? Pay $100 to have their house cleaned. Host a potluck for your neighbors. Be a listener. It's amazing how much people just want to have someone to talk to. We live in a densely populated, lonely world. Serving others is only selfless on the face of it. You will likely benefit from service even more than the people you serve. Nobody's going to starve because you aren't standing behind the counter at a soup kitchen, but a soul that doesn't serve goes gangrene. By serving you find yourself, and you get mental clarity.

6. Grow your relationships. Growing your wealth is fine, but building deep relationships is far more likely to create for you a positive return of happiness. The next time you meet someone who spent time overseas in a foreign community, ask them what their favorite thing was. My guess is that they will say, "The people." Be the creator and facilitator of your community. In time the community becomes your curation of wonderful people. It doesn't have to be fancy. Just bring people together.

Again, I can't emphasize it enough, write down what you want and revisit it every week. Time flies and life's too rare and amazing to let it drift. It's okay if what you want is selfish, at least it's purposeful. You'll find that accomplishing your more personal goals will give you strength to pursue altruistic ones. But there's no shame if it doesn't. Just be true to yourself.

What's a conscience! I'll tell ya! A conscience is that still small voice that people won't listen to. That's just the trouble with the world today.

Jiminy Cricket

Legal Planning

Legal planning is the suited, briefcase-toting cousin of insurance. Strictly speaking, not all legal planning covers a mere *possibility*: someday, you will die. Unless you want to bank on unrealized technology giving you an indefinite lifespan, you must plan for this inevitability. Everything else is a *possibility* at various levels of likelihood:

- Possibility of being incapacitated and unable to make financial decisions
- Possibility of ending up in a vegetative state
- Possibility of divorce and custody battles
- Possibility of your heirs battling over your estate
- Possibility of litigation

Legal planning reduces the financial impact of such events. It's often about personal relationships and making sure that your death doesn't fracture your family. Sometimes it's about making decisions for them—to neutralize their ability to fight over your estate after you are gone. Multiple times I have had clients pass away and have seen their children sue each other over inheritance. Ahh, how money brings out the best in us.

The words "legal planning" can inspire visions of hemorrhaging money to expensive lawyers. It's important to note that you have a need in these areas whether or not you hire an attorney to professionally address them. After we address possible legal needs, we'll wrap it up with some advice on working with attorneys and keeping costs under your control. First, let's see how legal planning mitigates your risks.

Shielding Medical Risks

Serious medical issues put your finances at risk, and they can challenge your end of life wishes. Legal planning empowers the people you trust to make decisions on your behalf if you are unable to. To me, legal planning is largely about addressing the "what ifs" of life as a mortal human.

Every attorney I've worked with offers an estate planning package with all of these documents. It's also possible to do these à la carte. Either way, this should help you understand what the documents do and how you should structure them.

Some of you may remember the Terri Schiavo case from 1990–2005 in Florida. Terri suffered a heart attack in 1990. Even though she was resuscitated, she had massive brain damage and fell into a persistent vegetative state. After eight years of artificial life support and unresponsiveness, her husband petitioned to remove her feeding tubes. Her parents insisted she could recover. Over the next seven years, through 14 court appeals, the case went back and forth about whether she would be allowed to die. It involved people as high up as the President, the Supreme Court, and members of Congress. In time, her husband prevailed and she passed away in 2005.

But it didn't end there. After she died, her husband and parents continued to argue about what to do with Terri's remains. Her parents wanted her body to be buried in Florida and her husband wanted her cremated and ashes buried in her home state of Pennsylvania. A compromise was made and she was cremated with ashes buried in Florida, but her parents were angered about the epitaph on her tombstone. But it didn't end there. They parted ways and continued on in activism for each of their causes. Her parents started a foundation in her name, but her husband charged improper use of her name as recently as 2010. Most of this could have been prevented with a few simple documents.

Living Will

This can also be called a Health Care Directive. This specifies whether or not you would like to be kept on artificial life support if you are in a persistent vegetative state. It may also be specific about your health care wishes if you are unable to communicate those wishes consciously.

Do Not Resuscitate Order (DNR)

This is an order written up by a doctor based on a living will. It orders that resuscitation should not be attempted if the patient goes into cardiac or respiratory arrest. Doctors obviously avoid putting themselves in the position of interpreting legal documents. DNRs are more common when people have a terminal illness and wish to let death takes its natural course without invasive medical procedures.

HIPAA Release

The Health Insurance Portability and Accountability Act (HIPAA, pronounced like, "I broke my *hip-a*" or what you'd call a female hippo) was put into law in 1996 in an effort to protect the privacy of your health information. By default, nobody can see your medical information but you and the medical professionals caring for you.

There is a big fat grey area dealing with health care privacy when the patient is unconscious. Various doctors and nurses interpret it differently. The rule states that they are to use "professional judgment" when discussing your health care with your family and friends. Let's say you have a stroke and are in a coma. Your family rushes to the hospital and desperately wants to know, "How serious is it? Will she live? Can I have her Cadillac?" Without a HIPAA Release, they may be in the dark depending on a stranger's professional judgment.

Power of Attorney (POA)

Powers of Attorney give someone the ability to make decisions on your behalf. They are acting as you. Even though the word "attorney" is in there, this person is not normally your lawyer. There are a few different types that give power in specified areas:

- General Power of Attorney
- Power of Attorney for Real Estate
- Power of Attorney for Finance
- Power of Attorney for Health Care

Power of Attorney documents are often described as "durable" or "non-durable" (e.g. "Durable Power of Attorney"). Sometimes they use the word "limited" instead of "non-durable" (e.g. "Limited Power of Attorney"), but it is the same thing. These tell you when they go into effect. Non-durable is often for a single task. If you are selling a house and can't be there for the closing, you can grant your real estate agent a "Non-durable Power of Attorney for Real Estate," which means that once the transaction is done, the powers go away. Also, it's common with real estate transactions to grant a limited power of attorney to fix small errors (like missing dates). If you are incapacitated, non-durable POAs have no power. All POAs lose the power if the person dies.

Durable POAs have power whether or not you are incapacitated and grant nonspecific, ongoing power. One form of Durable POA goes into effect *only if* the person is incapacitated. This is sometimes called a *Springing Power of Attorney,* because the specific event springs the POA to life. It is *highly important* to be specific about what incapacity means and what standards must be met.

Without a *Durable Power of Attorney*, nobody can represent your interest if you are incapacitated. That is, unless they go to the court and get a conservatorship or guardianship over you.

This is an area where *not* having proper legal documents could harm your finances. Let's say you are still in that coma from the stroke, and mortgage payments are coming in. If someone had a Durable Power of Attorney for Finances, they could go down to the bank, present their POA documents and pay bills for you. Or, you could be sailing around the world and they could present the same documents and drain your bank account. So indeed, do be judicious. It's not unheard of that people grant POA to their future embezzlers. Or they, quite logically, grant POA to their spouse, years later forget that it's still in force whilst going through a divorce, and bad things happen.

Ask your lawyer about the safeguards that are available. The title of the person you appoint the powers to is your *Attorney-In-Fact*.

Conservatorship

If you don't have a power of attorney, then the only way that someone can (legally) make decisions on your behalf is by getting a conservatorship. This is a lengthy process that culminates with a judge granting conservatorship over your affairs. This gives someone a tremendous amount of power and discretion, so needless to say, this is not an easy to thing to do—and it shouldn't be.

The other risk is that whoever the court appoints as conservator *may not be the person* that *you* would want to be your conservator. You may find it unsettling to wake up from your coma and find out that Bob, the neighbor who has been "borrowing" your leaf blower and extension cords the past seven years, is now in charge of your financial affairs.

Sound crazy? Let me tell you a story. Many years ago I had an older couple named Jerry and Rosemary as clients. I'm not aware of any other octogenarian pair who I've met who were more in love than these two. They fell in love at first sight when he was an Olympic diver in the 1952 games. They would often come in just to chat, holding hands through the entire meeting.

In time, Rosemary's mental health declined and she slowly slipped into advanced dementia and had to go into an assisted living home. I would take Jerry to go visit Rosemary. It still haunts me to remember those visits. I can still hear Jerry next to me in my car. His still-imposing Olympic physique made charismatic gestures as he explained how Rosemary was going to get better—believing that she would get out this week, perhaps that day. He asked me to help him convince the doctors to let her go home and that she'd do better if she was just with him. Each time we visited, her rapid decline was notably worse.

Within a month, she didn't recognize her husband and in time she didn't speak. I'll never forget the way that Jerry would force Rosemary to stand up and get her to walk around, "Come on Rosemary, you're okay, let's get you moving." He'd keep kissing her on the cheek and he fully supported her limp body, promenading among the other patients who were also experiencing their demise. Even though Jerry was well over 50 years older than me, I felt as though I was watching a little boy, moving the legs of his deceased puppy to convince himself that it was still alive.

Within weeks, Rosemary passed away. Jerry went into inconsolable depression. Up to this point I hadn't met their children, who lived out of town. When Rosemary was still in good health, I always got the sense that they didn't want to talk about their kids. So we didn't, and I then found out why. The children of this loving couple were not people I would have cared to know. They seized this opportunity of having a deceased mother and a catatonically depressed father to gain conservatorship over their assets. During this process, I pleaded with Jerry that he needed to get up and fight or his kids were going to have complete control over everything. He just couldn't muster himself to stop it. His kids won and the assets were promptly gone. It was completely illegal for his kids to abuse their rights of conservatorship, but with Jerry so deflated I couldn't persuade him to care about it.

Jerry and Rosemary had a massive legal planning need that should have been addressed long before any of this happened. I'm not sure what their wishes would have been with regard to their estate. Again, they never wanted to talk about their kids. My hunch is that they would have rather seen their money go to a charity, or at least someone who wasn't going to screw them over upon their death and incapacitation.

Additional Legal Planning Terms

Legal planning uses intimidating terms that sound like *Star Wars* characters. Here are some to know:

Executor/Executrix—This is the same role. A male is an "executor" and a female is an "executrix." Personally I've hardly heard anyone use the term "executrix" other than at cocktail parties with some alcohol-infused knowledge displays. The executor is the person in charge of settling an estate. If there is a will, then normally the deceased has chosen this person: "I appoint my brother John." If there isn't a will, then a judge will appoint this person when the estate goes to probate.

Probate—Is there life after death? Yes, it's called probate court. Don't confuse this with the thing that makes older men get up several times a night. Probate is the legal process following a person's death. In probate, a will is verified, property is inventoried and appraised, debts and taxes are paid from the estate, and whatever is left gets distributed to heirs according to the will. If there isn't a will, probate includes additional steps of determining next of kin. Because probate is a legal process, it involves hearings, judges, and attorneys (normally paid from the estate). Also, because it is a legal process, everything that goes through a probate court becomes public record. More on that in a minute, when we discuss the pros and cons of trusts and wills. Every now and then I will hear someone talk about "avoiding probate" as though it were a terrible thing. This is going to be different from state to state, but generally states are moving toward an efficient probate process that makes it easier for executors and successor trustees. I only say this to note that avoiding probate shouldn't be the central motivation for estate planning.

Trustor (or Grantor) and Trustee—It's all in the suffix: "or" or "ee." The "or" does it, the "ee" receives it. A trustor creates a trust and funds it with their own assets and/ or property. A trustee, appointed by the trustor, manages the trust. If it's a living trust, the trustor and trustee are often the same person. There is also the successor trustee who takes over management if the trustee dies. A successor trustee can be analogous to the executor of a will. To help keep the "or" and "ee" thing straight, think of employment. The employer does the employing and the employee does the jobbin'. Can you learn grammar from a sentence that ends in bad grammar?

Estate Planning

We are grownups here. We are talking specifically about "death planning." "Estate planning" is a euphemism for getting what you want after you die. It is about extending your power and wishes beyond the grave. This is done through one of two documents:

1. Will
2. Trust

Here's the non-good news. If you haven't established either of these documents, one will be set up for you. If you die, a probate court will decide where your money goes.

Trusts vs. Wills

If you ask an attorney which is better, or really any question for that matter, the attorney will say, "It depends." Though frustrating, this is really the best answer. That's why you should discuss estate planning with a professional. The best attorneys can help you narrow down "it depends" to reflect your circumstances.

However, I will give you my two bits. A will puts your estate through a probate court where a judge rules on the validity of your will. Because of this there are three key downsides to it:

1. It can be contested by literally anyone who cares to
2. A will can be overruled
3. This whole process is public record, which means that the details of your estate are public record

Sound strange? Google: "wills of the famous" and you will soon enjoy the odd experience of peering into highly personal details of a famous stranger's life. You may learn that:

- Joe DiMaggio left nothing to his estranged son.
- Jerry Garcia left his guitars to Doug Irwin (whose name he spelled wrong in his will).
- Sammy Davis Jr. died with his debts outweighing his assets.
- Doris Duke named her butler as the executor of her billion dollar estate.
- Jack Benny left a florist a large sum of money so that his wife would get one long stemmed rose every day for the rest of her life.
- Leona Helmsley left her dog $12,000,000.

Personally I think it's really weird that we know these private details. The truth is that we probably wouldn't know them if these famous people had set up a trust instead of a will. To some, privacy, particularly postmortem privacy, isn't a concern. The event of one's death does bring on a certain amount of indifference. But perhaps contestability is a concern.

While Jerry Garcia's will clearly states that he wanted Doug Irwin to have his guitars, his bandmates disagreed. They contested it in probate court. The judge ruled that Mr. Irwin only receive two of the guitars. Also, while Leona Helmsley clearly wanted $12,000,000 to go to her dog, the judge over-ruled this and granted the pooch a more modest $2,000,000. Again, wills can be overruled at the discretion of the probate judge. While these things may be trivial to us, they were important enough to the deceased to write down into a legal document and *still* the deceased didn't get what they wanted.

Trusts have the benefit of (usually) being harder to contest, private, and bypassing probate court. This isn't to say that they are non-contestable, but contesting a trust is not part of the normal process of settling an estate. The act of contesting a trust involves litigation and is generally more costly than contesting a will. Because of this, it tends to deter people from challenging them. There can also be some tax efficiencies using trusts. Trusts also have the ability to be hyper-specific. For example,

"To my son Junior, I give $50,000 upon my death and the remainder of the estate on his 30th birthday or 10th anniversary of my death, whichever is later. If Junior goes to college, his cost can be paid for by the estate with a bonus of $30,000 upon his graduation. If he graduates from my alma mater then it will be $50,000."

You can be as creative as you want. I've had clients use trusts to prevent a drug-addicted son from inheriting a bunch of money—they worded the document so that their son could use the estate only for drug rehabilitation until he had been clean at least two years. I've had a client use a trust to protect her son from his controlling wife leeching all the money away. With a will, just as we learned with Jerry Garcia's guitars, there is simply no way to know that what you write in the will actually gets carried out.

If you have a complicated Brady Bunch-style family, then consider a trust. In the "Horror Stories" at the beginning of the book, I mentioned a client who I advised until the day of his death. I had a certain affection for him because he reminded me of Warren Buffett. He loved to talk about stocks and the economy. I never met his wife or kids or knew much about his personal life. On his investment account, his wife was listed as 100% the primary beneficiary. His kids were the contingent beneficiaries, splitting the money evenly. Pretty standard practice. When he died, I met his wife for the first time. We put the account in her name and she tells me that she wants to take *his kids* off as beneficiaries and put *her kids* on instead. I said something along the lines of, "What?" I come to find that his wife is a second marriage and that *his kids* hate her. I urged her that it was obviously his intention that they receive that money upon her death. She glares at me coldly, "No way. They aren't getting a dime." And there was nothing that could be done. Had he set up a trust, his true wishes would have been honored.

I am obviously biased toward trusts based on what's important to me and what I've witnessed with clients. However, trusts are typically more expensive. A good attorney can advise you which is better for your needs and wants.

Terrible Mistakes in Estate Planning

Oh boy. I've seen a lot and it's not even the central part of my line of work. Here are some more common ones:

1. An unfunded trust—Let's say you go to an attorney, pay a bunch of money and set up your trust. It's beautiful and detailed and has put every contingency into consideration. You sign it and rest easy at the assurance that your family will be taken care of upon your inevitable demise. However, that's only half the battle. You must *fund the trust*, meaning you have to retitle your property into the name of it (e.g. The John and Jane Doe Revocable Trust). You have to change your investment accounts into the name of the trust or make the trust itself the beneficiary. Otherwise you have an unfunded trust that ain't worth a hill of beans. The trust will only exercise power over things that it "owns." Anything outside of it will likely go through the probate process. Crazy as it may sound, on more than one occasion I have come across people who spent

several thousand dollars on a trust and didn't fund it with a single buck. Fund your trust.

2. <u>Putting the estate or the trust as the beneficiary of a retirement account</u>— Many times I've come across accounts where there either isn't a beneficiary of an IRA or 401(k) or it simply says, "Estate." There are some non-probate assets which can go directly to heirs. If a house, financial account, or car is held jointly then the surviving person (not necessarily a spouse) becomes the sole owner. Retirement accounts, such as IRAs, are also a non-probate asset. If there is a beneficiary on file then the account inherits directly and they assume ownership of the IRA as a Beneficiary IRA. If you name "Estate" as the beneficiary of an IRA (or any other retirement account such as a 401(k)s, 403(b)s, etc.) then the entire balance is counted as income *to the estate*. Let's say the IRA is worth $500,000, that means the Estate just got a $500,000 paycheck and the entire balance is subject to taxation. Taxwise, this is much *worse* than if you got a paycheck for $500,000. Using 2016 numbers for a married couple filing jointly, the highest income tax bracket of **39.6%** starts at $464,850. For estates, the **39.6%** tax bracket starts at *$12,500* (for 2017). On $500,000, you end up immediately paying about $196,309 in taxes. On behalf of your fellow Americans, we'd like to thank you for your very generous mistake. The same goes for naming "John and Jane Doe Revocable Trust" as the beneficiary. A trust can't own an IRA, so if it is the beneficiary of one then the whole thing is liquidated and—you guessed it—hideously taxed.

3. <u>Trying to use "joint" to prevent an asset from being counted as part of an estate</u>—Maybe you read my remark about how the surviving *person* of jointly held assets receives it directly and thought, "Why not just make the children joint owners of the house?" As I've said before, my value as an advisor often comes in the phrase, "You *really* don't want to do that." We'll go into this at greater length in the next chapter on taxes, but for now, a quick teaser. Let's say your parents bought their Palo Alto, CA home on the GI Bill back in 1950 for the princely sum of $10,000. Your mother, now in her mid-90s is still living in the home that would easily sell for $1,000,000. This means that the house has experienced a $990,000 capital gain ($10,000 is the "cost basis"). There's more. Your father worked for Hewlett-Packard and in the spirit of his Depression Era frugality consistently bought (and was granted) HP stock, which is now valued at $5,000,000 with a cost basis of $500,000. This means that the stock is sitting on a $4,500,000 capital gain. If your mother passes away, these two assets get a *step-up in cost basis*. These capital gains go away along with the taxes that would otherwise need to be paid. If you and your mother were on the deed as joint owners, then the cost basis *stays intact*. This means that you inherited the capital gain along with the tax burden. Oops. I've seen this firsthand many times.

4. <u>Not retitling assets after the death of one spouse</u>—Over the years, I've had the fortunate experience of saying my superhero catchphrase, "you *really*

don't want to do that" in time to save people money. However, sometimes I'm not involved early enough to prevent big mistakes. Let's expand out another "Horror Story." I have a client named Steven whose mother lived into her early 90s and passed away in 2013. Years previously, Steven's father had built up a respectable real estate portfolio. By the time of his death in 1990, he had accumulated a few apartment buildings and homes which were titled solely in the father's name. When her husband died, Steven's mom was eligible for a step-up in cost basis. But her intention was to just keep the rentals going, so she never bothered retitling the properties in her name. By the time of her death in 2013, they were still in her late husband's name. When it went through probate, the courts saw the buildings as inheriting directly to the kids *from the father* which meant that their step-up in cost basis happened in 1990, *not* 2013. All the appreciation from 1990–2013 was subject to taxation and it cost the estate more than $500,000 in taxes. An attorney could have fixed this for a few hundred dollars, or they could have filed the form themselves for about $6.00 per property. Some states have made this even easier by creating Beneficiary Deeds, which is like having a beneficiary on real estate.

I want to scare the snot out of you. Pure and simple. This list is far from comprehensive. I encourage you to seek a professional who will look over your shoulder and guide you through these labyrinthine details.

It is not a matter of intelligence or ability, it's a matter of experience. *Maybe* in the course of your life, you will process one estate. Maybe two. Rarely three. That's the extent of your experience. Some of the older attorneys I've worked with have thousands of clients. There is so substitution for this experience.

Six Takeaway Tips for Estate Planning

1. Around 55% of people die without a will or a trust (many of them smart, educated, rich, and famous). The next time you're at a dinner party, look around the room. Half of them haven't done estate planning. The first tip is to actively put yourself in the prepared 45%. I pride myself on being the anti-procrastinator financial advisor. I make my clients do estate planning. I introduce them to attorneys and sit in on the first meeting with them. However, as a general rule of thumb, unless you make yourself do it, nobody will.

2. Make sure the heirs are at least somewhat involved and know the name of your attorney and where your estate planning documents are. My dad was a great proponent of this. He always had a certain folder in a hidden location. Before he and my mom went on vacation, he'd show the three of us boys the secret location and remind us, "If anything happens ..." This is a good practice. On the far end of this, I've had clients have me run a full multi-generational family meeting where I walk everyone through the assets, give them contact

information for all the professionals, and walk them through the process of what would happen if their parents were to pass away.

3. Destroy old documents. Wills and trusts have language about how this document supersedes any previous document. I know it's hard to destroy a will or a trust that you remember paying a bunch of money for. I have come across clients who are excellent record keepers who keep every version of their will. You *really* don't want to do this. Siblings often have a falling out with one another. You might have one particularly nefarious one who goes through the wills and finds the one that is more favorable to him and destroys the more recent ones. It happens.

4. Review all your beneficiaries, especially for retirement accounts. We just learned about the problems of having non-humans inheriting retirement accounts. It is also terribly common that people don't have beneficiaries on retirement accounts *at all*. You can go years assuming you have them on there. When I travel, it's amazing to me how easy it is to simply remember a detail incorrectly. I may book a flight months in advance and *have it in my head* that it leaves at 9:00 at night and find out a few days before that it leaves at 9:00 in the morning. I doubt I'm the only one that's done this. You may not remember putting "Estate" on your trust as the beneficiary of your IRA or other retirement account, but it's a good idea just to take a look to avoid a forced distribution. 42% of assets pass onto the heirs through a beneficiary form, while 32% of accounts don't have a form on file. Just the facts ma'am.

5. If your estate documents are five years or older, they're likely out of date. Keep in mind that documents can become out of date because *your life changes* and because *laws change*. Getting your documents reviewed doesn't necessarily mean going through the whole process again. It's sometimes as simple as adding an amendment. Another advantage of a trust is that the core can stay the same and amendments can be added. Wills generally need to be totally redone.

6. Don't DIY this. It's far too important. Lawyer jokes aside, there are some really good people in this profession who care about getting things rights. I know that you hear or know about websites that will do this stuff for you for a lower cost. They exist, but I wouldn't put a discount pacemaker in my chest. A good attorney will cause you to think of things that you hadn't considered and will spot things that a computer program won't. At times there are free resources through the state, but if you have an estate worth protecting, then do it right. Attorneys have seen everything; the boilerplate documents see nothing.

Death and Taxes

We have already talked about taking advantage of the more conventional benefits of dying and taxes. The primary one is the automatic step-up in cost basis. There isn't anything you need to do to enjoy this, simply don't make the mistakes we discussed earlier. Here are some less automatic ideas:

Gifting to Charities from your IRA

"Gifting" the legal term for what Earthlings call "giving." Let's say you have $500,000 and want to give $100,000 to a specific charity and the remaining $400,000 to your children. If you have a $250,000 IRA and a $250,000 ordinary taxable account, be sure to gift the money from your IRA. Charities normally don't pay taxes. If a charity inherits money from an IRA, the money entirely skips taxation. If a person inherits money from an IRA, that money is fully taxable. We will go over this again with specific numbers when we talk about taxes.

Gifting Money Prior to Death

Things have changed a great deal. During the 2000–2010 era there was constant speculation about what Congress was going to do with the Estate Tax (shrewdly re-branded as the Death Tax). At one point, estates had a $1,000,000 exemption and anything above it was taxable. As of 2017, the exemption (called your Estate Tax Exclusion amount) is $5,490,000 per person (couples get twice this) and anything above this is taxed at **40%**.

If your estate is less than this amount, then this doesn't apply to you. If you think it *might* climb above it, then you can gift $14,000 each year to anyone and it won't be taxed. This is also per person. A couple could give their child $28,000 as two separate gifts of $14,000. They can give it to whoever they want. They could give it to their garbage man, but that's how rumors get started.

In the chapter on taxes, I will show you how you can use a strategy called Present Value Gifting to effectively increase your Estate Tax Exclusion amount. If your estate is near or above the limit (don't forget to add in real estate, life insurance, and the Renoir painting), then you really need to work with professionals to give strategically.

Note: estate tax is different than *estate income tax*. Earlier I mentioned that the **39.6%** estate income tax bracket starts at $12,500 (for 2017). This is speaking of income for *estates*.

ly as assets get liquidated the money pools into an estate banking account. The interest income from this account is counted as estate income and subject to estate income tax. For retirement accounts that have "Estate" as the beneficiary, this tax deferred account is liquidated. Essentially the estate gets a massive retirement paycheck and it is taxed in arguably the most hostile area of the U.S. tax code.

Charitable Remainder Trust

If you want to give a sizable amount to a charity, and *you are really* certain that nothing will happen to make you change your mind, an estate tax efficient option is a Charitable Remainder Trust. This is a tax-exempt *irrevocable* trust. Once set up, you can transfer cash or assets into the trust and may receive some income from it for life (or a specific amount of years, but not more than 20 years). The income payment to you must be at least 5% and not more than 50%. At your death, the remaining amount in the trust goes to the charity that you designated as part of the trust arrangement.

And now, a story about a Charitable Remainder Trust. Those of you who weren't hermits during the '80s will remember the infamous televangelist era. "I hear the Lord, he's speaking to me now ... hold on everybody ... yes, yes, okay Lord ... folks, get your checkbooks." These new American deities of the '80s sure seemed to need some heavy financing. And while the profits, oops, I mean *prophets* of these deities worked tirelessly to do their Lord's bidding, the U.S. government interpreted these tax-exempt actions with less praise. Two years ago, I got a random call from a woman (not a client) who asked me to help her close down her IRA because she heard that President Obama was going to seize all IRAs.

Okay, so in these situations, it's my habit to be polite, listen attentively, and ultimately try to talk the person off their cliff of paranoia. I don't have a very good track record. I gently assured her this wasn't legal, sensible, and at a minimum it would be logistically very very difficult for the President to do that. But no dice. No matter what I said, she wanted me to help her close her IRA. Just to note: no-way-in-hell was this a transaction or client I was going to put my name on.

As the conversation progressed, I ended up reviewing her documents and noticed that the beneficiary of her account was one of these old TV evangelists. I came to find that she had put nearly all her money into a Charitable Remainder Trust that would *irrevocably* give all of her money to a televangelist who, from what I could tell was, ummm, out of the business. I probed further. It turned out that she had done this back in the '80s and that the "ministry" had very generously done her the favor of *free* estate planning and set up a *free* trust to ensure that the Lord's work continue on after she was gone. Wow, whatta guy.

Insanely, even after unpacking the situation, there wasn't a lot I could do *even if* I could have persuaded her chronic gullibility away. That one still haunts me.

Shielding from Litigation

As with all legal planning, do not DIY this. Hostile lawyers are excellent at finding missteps, exploiting them, and splitting you open to full personal financial exposure. As with insurance, if you feel that you might face litigation, set up your legal protections *before* you need it. Here are some basic ways you can protect yourself using the law:

1. If you are married, have your accounts and property strategically titled separately. I know a couple in which the Mrs. doesn't work and isn't normally in a position that would expose her to a lawsuit. The Mr. has a job with an elevated exposure to litigation. Their million plus dollar house is titled in just her name. If push came to shove and he got sued, the house wouldn't get wrapped up into it, at least in most states. Keep in mind that any money you hold jointly is subject to any problems the other person has. If your child is on your bank account and they have a tax lien, the joint bank account could be seized.

2. If you have rental property, protect yourself from litigation by creating a separate business entity (such as an LLC or corporation). If a renter sues, they can attack the assets the entity holds, but not your personal assets. Note: plan on getting separate liability insurance *for the business* (a personal umbrella insurance policy only covers you).

3. Make sure that businesses and business partnerships are very (ahem, very very) clearly delineated. If you have a partnership that isn't formally established, your personal assets could get sucked into a litigation against your business partner. Generally speaking, avoid partnerships.

4. If you have a business, don't operate as a sole proprietorship. Set up a specific business entity.

5. If litigation is possible, preemptively plan for bankruptcy to minimize long-term damage. This is a new can of worms.

Bankruptcy as a Financial Planning Tool

People can end up in bankruptcy for a variety of reasons and at various degrees of personal fault. Sometimes people are careless and mismanage their money. Sometimes people go bankrupt from medical problems or because of a divorce. Whatever the reasons, let's explore bankruptcy as a financial planning tool.

First of all, any kind of commingled finances needs to be kept at a minimum. For a married couple, consider building your credit as separately as possible. Don't have joint credit if you can avoid it. Sometimes this isn't possible, particularly when buying a house. The advantage of this is that if you run into financial problems, you can bankrupt just one person without affecting the other person's credit.

Although in the investment section I strongly advocated for an optimistic Pollyannaish disposition, when it comes to financial partnerships, go ahead and be an Eeyore. Consider the worst that could happen. Years ago I had a friend who had nearly paid off a lovely home. His father-in-law was in construction, lost the business, and moved into his basement. Years later the father-in-law found success again during the real estate boom and convinced my friend to sell his home as a down payment on a big house they would all move into. The father-in-law ran into financial problems again and they lost the house and all the equity he built up.

My friend wasn't exactly an innocent victim, but keep the financial ball in your own court if you can. It would have been better to keep his old house as a rental and when they lost the big house, return to the old one.

If you are a homeowner facing foreclosure, consider this: rent out the house you can't afford and move somewhere you can. In time, your renter will pay down your mortgage. When facing severe financial damage, the biggest mistake is to do nothing. If there is a storm on the horizon, face the brutal facts and make some tough decisions. If you are able to rent the house out for more than your mortgage payment, living elsewhere may actually *accelerate* your financial plan. Decide before you don't have choices.

This will be the most personal part of the book. It might get messy. To me, it's only fair. Through this book I have been rather brazen in holding up the mistakes of people I've come across through my profession, but now it's my turn to tie myself to the whipping post. I tried to tell stories with sympathy rather than judgment. Mistakes are mistakes, and misinformation is very difficult to roll off the odometer. The next best thing to life experience is borrowing it from others. I offer to you lessons from the school of hard knocks—a place where, although the tuition is expensive, the education is excellent.

As you've been reading, you heard me mention my roots and my family. Legacy and relationships are highly important to me. I remember being in first grade, day-dreaming about being a grandfather someday. I come from a big family and I always loved the patriarchal sense that my grandfather conveyed. This was always on my mind as a focus of my life. When I came of dating age, I never really casually dated. I would only date girls that I could see myself marrying. Thankfully for my middle school romantic counterparts, I kept this to myself.

With this sober-minded stance toward romance, it is no wonder that I married at 21. Not only this, I married a single mother of a seven-year-old. We had our first child when I was 23, the second at 25, and the third at 26.

My ambition to propagate the species was met with my ambition for financial establishment. We bought our first house when I was 24 and a rental house when I was 26. At this time, I also decided to focus my career entirely on financial advising.

I was born in 1980, so the math is easy. When I was 27, it was the year 2007. The Financial Crisis was just beginning. I should note that despite how recklessly aggressive my financial situation may sound, I was actually fairly cautious. When we bought those houses, we put money down. We bought good homes in attractive neighborhoods.

Denver was a market that wasn't as caught up in rapidly rising prices in the way that Phoenix, Las Vegas, and parts of Florida were. I also wasn't stupid when it came to the mortgage. I was working inside of banks at the time and, in proverbial water cooler chats, I would hear of these incredibly lenient mortgages they were giving to anyone who could fog a mirror. As I listened, the oneupmanship of the conversation seemed to drift toward amazing stories of unqualified borrowers to whom the bank was lending hundreds of thousands of dollars. When we got our homes, we vehemently decided to go a more conventional route and get a traditional mortgage. When we bought our first house, the mortgage broker told us we could qualify for twice what we were buying—we opted for a more modest sum and normal mortgage.

Then, the 2008–2009 financial crisis drifted into our lives. For me, it began with my ex-wife's family. Forgive my disguising of identities here, but one of them was a mortgage broker. His income plummeted, he lost his house and declared bankruptcy. Another worked for a real estate title insurance company. He was laid off, the family lost their house, and declared bankruptcy. In January 2008 another called to say that she had been laid off from her job and she was going to lose her house as well, 10 years from her retirement. She asked if we could help until she found another job. So we put all of our stuff in storage, put our house up for rent, moved in with her and paid her mortgage to keep her from foreclosure—her house was bigger than ours and so was her mortgage.

And then there was me. I was still getting established as a financial advisor. My income was largely tied to what the stock market did, but more specifically with the public's appetite to invest in the stock market. One year into helping this relative keep her house, the market was down by about half, and so was my income. Then one of my rental tenants lost his job and stopped paying rent. That meant I was entirely eating a mortgage payment on that property while I went through the prolonged eviction process—a horrible thing to have to do to someone.

It is a point of pride for me that even with all of this, up to May 2009, I had never been a dollar short or a day late on any of these payments. Yes, my financial cushion was razor thin, but I somehow kept it going. That is, until the bombshell of my life.

In the background, my ex-wife was rapidly changing. Out of respect for my children who may someday read this, I won't go into details. I'll leave it to you to read between the lines. After our last child was born, she took it upon herself to reclaim her youth with abandon. She was gone quite a bit. She often took trips with her friends for the weekend. In May of 2009, she came back from one of these trips. I picked her up from the airport and, in what was to me entirely out of the blue, she requested a divorce. The possibility of divorce had literally never even crossed my mind.

Knowing what you know about me and my childhood patriarchal aspirations, you can imagine how this cut me to my core. Our children were still very young: 14, 5, 3, and 2 years old. I was horrified by how divorce would affect them and their marriages down the road. I was crushed to not be able to be with them every possible second. I'll spare you the emotional devastation and jump to the financial.

On top of the many financial things that I was juggling, in the divorce I also had to pay my ex-wife a monthly sum that was greater than any of the mortgages. By this point the Great Recession had hit rock bottom. Both houses were under water and banks had largely frozen credit, which made it impossible to refinance them just in my name or even sell them in a depressed market. One of the homes stayed listed for 18 months. The car that my ex-wife kept had an auto loan (in my name) that she wasn't paying and was eventually repossessed. I knew banking. I knew mortgages. I knew that the bank sells the repossessed car for a fire sale price, maximizes their tax write-off, and files suit against you for the balance of the loan (which of course keeps growing from double digit penalized interest). This would also be the fate of the homes. I also knew that it would take me years to recover from this, even if I didn't let it all go.

Meanwhile, the backdrop to this personal financial razing was the heartbreaking impact this was having on the children. There were things they had to go through that I never could have imagined.

In the spirit of my own advice, I faced the brutal facts that I was in a terrible position and I had to choose the least worst option. I used bankruptcy laws to wipe my slate clean, in order to focus my energy on the trauma that my kids were going through.

As I write this, it has been a long time since this bombshell. When I look back on it, so much of this era went against everything that was part of my inner narrative of where I fit in the world. In my family, divorce is very rare. Nearly everyone stays married for life. My family also embodies Scottish frugality. Bankruptcy and two foreclosures were very bitter pills to swallow—particularly as a financial advisor. I felt a deep sense of hypocrisy and it still haunts me to some extent.

I have mixed feelings about my decision to file for bankruptcy, and there's a side of me that thinks it was a mistake and that I could have muscled through it. However, knowing only what I knew at each stage of this, I don't know that I could put my finger on any one mistake.

The one key thing that I failed to factor into my risk assessment was something that literally hadn't even crossed my mind until it was thrown in my face: divorce. Without that, I'm certain that even though it was so financially tight, I was making it work. The divorce happened at the very bottom of the recession and bottom of my income. Things would have gotten easier from then on out.

In the moment of decision, I was pressed against a wall with the choice of either letting my finances go or not paying my ex-wife. The thought of not providing for my family was utterly detestable. But as a subject of the laws of the state of Colorado, if I didn't pay I would face jail and potentially losing my kids. I, of course, opted to pay my ex-wife. Up until the separation, I wasn't a dollar short or a day late on my obligations. After it, I've never been a day late or a dollar short on any payment.

The moral of the story is that you can't make chicken soup out of chicken poop. At times, *bankruptcy itself can be an excellent financial planning tool.* Bankruptcy should be used responsibly, but it is an available life raft. Sometimes, it is the least worst option.

Dwelling on failures is perhaps financially macabre, so let's shift to the hypothetical. Pretend we have someone who has $30,000 in debt and needs to maximize their resources to retire optimally. They have average income and in their career, massive income increases are not likely. We'll assume that each month they must pay 12.99% in interest.

Door #1: Pay off the $30,000 debt balance. Initially, they pay the interest payment on the debt, which is $325 per month, along with an extra $250 to pay down the balance for a total payment of $575. As they pay down the debt, their interest payment reduces and they apply this extra money toward aggressively paying down the debt—which happens after six and a half years. Once it is paid off, they continue to apply this $575 per month toward their investments, that we'll assume grow at a straight 11.62% (assuming no stock market volatility).

Door #2: Declare bankruptcy, wipe out the debt, and immediately save up $575 each month into the stock market. In both scenarios, it is the same amount out of pocket. Where would they be 5, 10, 20, 30 years from now? I'm glad you asked.

These are the results:

Bankruptcy as a Financial Planning Tool

		Door #1 Pay off Debt	Door #2 Bankruptcy	Difference
Year 0	Debt Balance	($30,000)	$0	$30,000
	Savings Balance	$0	$0	
Year 5	Debt Balance	($9,504)	$0	$55,969
	Savings Balance	$0	$46,465	
Year 10	Debt Balance	$0	$0	$99,101
	Savings Balance	$30,203	$129,304	
Year 15	Debt Balance	$0	$0	$176,682
	Savings Balance	$100,311	$276,993	
Year 20	Debt Balance	$0	$0	$314,994
	Savings Balance	$225,303	$540,297	
Year 25	Debt Balance	$0	$0	$561,583
	Savings Balance	$448,143	$1,009,726	
Year 30	Debt Balance	$0	$0	$1,001,210
	Savings Balance	$845,430	$1,846,640	

Capitulation to bankruptcy creates the most wealth long-term. Specifically, the choice to declare bankruptcy on $30,000 created more than $1,000,000 in additional net worth 30 years later.

Either way you slice it, declaring bankruptcy and implementing Door #2 puts you in a better long-term position. The Achilles heel of this plan remains actually saving the money each month into the stock market. We can see these options graphically:

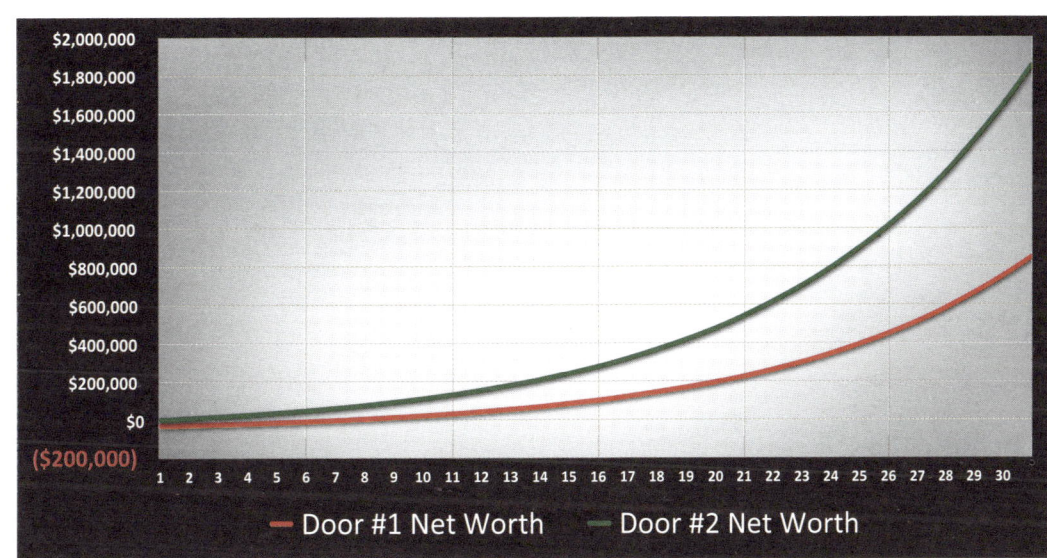

Another highly important point: not all situations with $30,000 in debt are equal. If you are perpetually late, if your credit is destroyed, if you are constantly being charged late fees, and all of these things have caused the credit card company to charge you the maximum legal interest rate, then declaring bankruptcy will almost certainly make you wealthier in both the short-term and long-term. If the debt is split among multiple maxed out credit cards, medical bills, and/or payday loans, then this is all the more true. If you can't reasonably dig yourself out from under this within five years, declaring bankruptcy may be a more expedient path toward better long-term wealth ... *if* you take advantage of that respite in the form of disciplined investing. On the other hand, if a simple shift in discipline (i.e. not spending money) can wipe out the debt within a reasonable amount of time, then declaring bankruptcy may not be worth the enormous credit setback.

Believe me, I know the tough situations people can find themselves in. It is also wrong not to repay people. Some people even consider bankruptcy laws amoral. I have at least a toe in this camp. My other toe also observes that many lending and banking laws are amoral, even immoral in their predatory nature. It should not be legal to prey upon the poor. Loan sharkery has been formalized into legally operating businesses that you can find in strip malls across America. While these two amoral, yet legal, realities don't cancel each other out, bankruptcy and high-interest lending are the rules of the game in our society.

Long-term Effects of Bankruptcy

In Door #1's aggressive scenario, it took 6 ½ years to pay off the debt. Bankruptcy can stay on your credit for up to 10 years, but the actual discharged debts generally drop off at seven years. If you are trying to buy a house, there will be some amount of time that must pass before you can get a mortgage. For me, that was three and a half years from when my bankruptcy was discharged, but this amount of time constantly changes and will differ depending on the mortgage. The indebted family in the earlier scenario may not have a shot at buying a house in the next few years anyway. In our hypothetical example, after five years they could have saved up a 20% down payment on a home. By that point, their credit could feasibly be repaired enough to get a mortgage. Bankruptcy is like all financial planning: you take the long view and face unpleasant realities with valor today.

I had the advantage of knowing how credit scores worked and doing what I needed to repair mine. Within about a year of my bankruptcy being discharged, my score was already into the "B range." After about three and a half years I was able to buy a house again. After six years, my scores were back in the "A range." At seven years, my scored entered "A+ range." Three years after that is the 10 year bankruptcy-versary and it drops off my credit. C'est la vie. Life moves on.

While bankruptcy negatively affects your credit, so does not paying creditors. Your scores seem to treat early bankruptcy as the beginning of a credit healing process. Because of this, some people's scores actually go *up* after declaring bankruptcy. You immediately become less of a credit risk because all of your obligations are wiped out. But the method for determining credit scores changes endlessly.

Another downside is having limited access to credit. For some people, a credit card is their emergency fund. You likely won't be able to get unsecured debt at first, and lacking access to money may feel unsettling. But, as always, how you feel about something doesn't have anything to do with whether it's good for you. Alas, not being allowed to get into debt for a few years may help financial habits.

Financially, my biggest setback was losing my modest real estate portfolio. I would have loved to have those two houses today and collect rent while paying down a modest mortgage. It bugs me, but I know that I couldn't have realistically kept them in those times and in that economy.

It may just be my grinding optimism, but there is nothing in life I ultimately regret. I've undoubtedly made mistakes and experienced tragedies and troubles, but I wouldn't back any of the miles off my odometer. Having gone through divorce has enabled me to comfort people who are in troubled marriages. It has granted me a perspective that, while I didn't want it in the first place, I certainly wouldn't give up now that I have it. My view on bankruptcy is similar. However much a setback it has been financially it has been absolutely worth the counsel I'm *only* able to give from personal experience.

Additional Benefits of Bankruptcy and a Case Study

Declaring bankruptcy doesn't necessarily wipe you out. Your retirement account balances (IRA, 401(k), etc.) are normally exempt assets. If you own your primary residence, it may also be exempt. Also, usually annuities and insurance contracts are also exempt. Laws vary from state to state, so don't assume this is true for you—talk to a professional in your state. There are many options to explore, but each has their flaws.

I once met a man on an airplane who was about 12 years from retirement. He said he lived in the house he grew up in and it was falling into disrepair. In particular, the roof was old and needed to be replaced. He asked me if I thought it was a good idea if he took out a loan from his 401(k) to replace the roof.

After doing some probing, I found out the rest of the story. He said that he and his wife had $50,000 in credit card debt, paying 24% in interest with a $1,500 monthly payment. More poignantly, as he put it, their "credit was shot" so they couldn't get a loan to fix the roof. At one point in time, their house was free and clear, but they took out a mortgage for an addition. Because of the mortgage, the house didn't have much equity in it.

This was a rough spot to be a mere 12 years from retirement. Their one saving grace was that he had saved up $150,000 into his 401(k). I asked him if he thought he and his wife were going to move or buy another house in the next seven years? In his words, "I was born in that house, I will die in that house." I confirmed, "Your credit is shot anyway, right?" "Yes."

My advice was to talk to a bankruptcy attorney. If they decided to declare bankruptcy, he would likely be able to keep his house and the full balance of his retirement account. Since their credit was shot, they're not giving up anything by limiting their access to credit. They could wipe out the $50,000 in debt, and instead to save up that $1,500 monthly payment that would go away. One year later, they would have enough saved up to replace the roof. Then they could use the next 11 years saving that $1,500 into their retirement savings.

Let's plug these real world numbers in to our Door #1 and Door #2 scenario. Door #1 is to keep paying $1,500 per month to pay down the credit card and then build up savings. Door #2 is slightly different this time: save up the money and then replace their roof in one year for $15,000. They then continue to save up the $1,500 each month. Once they retire after these 12 years (in Year 13), they take their savings and draw a 5% income rate from the money.

Not only does Door #1 have no realistic near-term plan for fixing the roof, it also leaves them with roughly half the retirement income at the end of the plan. While psychologically, declaring bankruptcy 12 years from retirement may feel like abject failure, from a financial planning perspective I'm not aware of any other way that is so certain to put them in the optimal retirement position. As with any plan, it's about facing the brutal facts, coming to a decision, and sticking with the plan.

Bankruptcy as a Financial Planning Tool

		Door #1 Pay off Debt	Door #2 Bankruptcy	Difference
Year 0	Debt Balance	($50,000)	$0	$50,000
	Savings Balance	$0	$0	
Year 1	Debt Balance	($43,294)	$0	$63,968
	Savings Balance	$0	$20,674	
			-$15,000 for roof	
			$5,674	
Year 3	Debt Balance	($24,003)	$0	$71,643
	Savings Balance	$0	$47,641	
Year 5	Debt Balance	$0	$0	$91,867
	Savings Balance	$8,479	$100,346	
Year 10	Debt Balance	$0	$0	$163,784
	Savings Balance	$136,382	$300,166	
Year 12	Debt Balance	$0	$0	$206,402
	Savings Balance	$212,179	$418,582	

Using End Savings Balance as 5% Income

Door #1 = $884

Door #2 = $1,744

Difference = $860

Summary

Whatever your situation, talk to a professional. The value for their fee often occurs outside the problem you diagnosed. You may have set the appointment to design a trust, but your situation may raise unrelated red flags, or even green flags, to which you yourself are colorblind.

I hope that exploring these dark days in my life will somehow help you, and that at a minimum, you see how bankruptcy can be the least terrible option during a terrible time.

For me, after all of this settled, life turned a happy page. Shortly after my divorce, I started my financial advising private practice. It was something I wanted to do and with so much wiped clean financially, it felt like a now or never moment. Much to my delight, the business was a success.

Financially, I immediately worked hard to make myself "Door #2" and aggressively saved up money both in the stock market, with the goal of buying a house as soon as I was allowed. Within a few months of my divorce, my freedom-inclined ex-wife said that she only wanted to have the kids every other weekend. I love being with my children and this was a delight to me. In time, I came to peace with my patriarch visions. Sometimes you have to re-write the dreams of your youth according to the chaos of your adulthood. Life has a better narrative than your imagination.

Just as the kids and I were getting settled into our new life, I met the woman who would become the love of my life. I found with her a more perfect union than I thought was possible. We bought a house together and got married.

I'll spare you the gushiness and leave you with this. My divorce and the cyclone of excrement that accompanied it was by far the hardest thing I've ever endured. I survived by focusing on my children, and in the absence of light, imagining it. Like the stock market, life is volatile, but we dream uphill.

Planning for Divorce

There's nothing more romantic than a prenuptial agreement.

Prenuptial (and Postnuptial) Agreement (the Financial Risk of Divorce)

A prenup is a touchy subject. I was lucky in that I never had to talk my second wife into a prenuptial agreement. She had a house and a business she wanted to protect just as I had assets and a business to protect.

Take it back to our principles. Embrace the things you can't control ... and insure against them. You have no (reasonable) control over whether or not your house gets leveled by an earthquake. Insure the risk. You don't have total control over whether or not your spouse has a mid-life crisis. You always lose some control by joining your life to another person. Get a prenuptial agreement. It's not romantic, it's not sexy, it's because when someone decides to leave you ... it's just you.

This is especially true *even if* you are getting married without any assets to lose. It's common to get married early in life without a significant net worth, but years later (especially if you take notes from this book), you will have assets and a livelihood that requires those assets.

I would say that in most marriages, one person tends to be the financial person who is more frugal than the other spouse. I've seen a couple's finances sailing against the headwinds of one spouse's terrible spending habits. The frugal spouse goes without and the spender gets double the toys. Then, they divorce and the spender ends up with half the money. To me that's colossally unfair. I have seen the frugal person come from money, or inherit money, and then their spouse burns through it, divorces and takes half. A prenuptial agreement is perfectly fair and reasonable.

It may be helpful to share how my wife and I viewed it. My divorce was by far the most painful thing I've ever gone through emotionally. It was also financially devastating. Needless to say, I had reservations about tying up myself with another person on just the financial front. The way my wife and I look at the prenup is that we want our desire to stay married to be because we *want* to stay married, not because we are worried about the financial consequences of being apart. It has been wonderful to help each other toward our financial goals. I have also found it more liberating to enjoy things because I don't feel like I am spending "our" money. She earns hers, I earn mine, and we collaborate on household expenses.

If you are already married, the document is called a postnuptial agreement. Ummm … it's no surprise that these are harder to get a spouse to sign. Usually one person has more to lose and the document puts the spouse in a more financially vulnerable position. Not to mention how suspicious it may sound. All I can say is good luck with that conversation.

If you are going into business with someone, I would encourage you to write a requirement into your operating agreement that each partner has their spouse sign a postnuptial or prenuptial that excludes the business as a marital asset. You don't want to find yourself in a situation where your business is booming, the money is flowing in, your partner ends up divorcing, and half of your partner's votes and shares are in the hands of an indignant and bitter ex-spouse awkwardly sitting in on all board meetings with control over the company. It happens, folks.

Also, if you have a sizable estate, consider writing something into your trust that protects your hard-earned legacy from ending up in the hands of your heirs' ex-spouses. There are various ways to do this, but one of them is to put a clause into your trust that says that heirs can't take possession of their inheritance without either a prenuptial or postnuptial agreement in place that excludes the inheritance as a marital asset. Let's be real here. Half of marriages ending in divorce means that half of your heirs may go through a divorce. You are doing your heirs a favor by making yourself the bad guy/gal and forcing them to protect their assets. It's a lot easier to have a conversation with your spouse about a nuptial agreement if it sounds like, "Sorry honey, you know how crazy Grandma was. We legally can't inherit this money unless we both sign a postnuptial agreement. Should we just let go of all this money in honor of our love?" The spouse will sign it.

Tips on Working with Attorneys

There's a saying in law that either you can pay a lawyer a bunch of money upfront or pay the lawyer ten times that in a trial. I think that's true. I view attorneys as insurance. Hopefully you never use it, but it's worth knowing your family is protected.

In my early days, I never talked to attorneys. I was intimidated by them. Even as a financial advisor when I inevitably had to talk to my client's estate planning attorneys, I was intimidated. I think I was worried I'd get some bill in the mail or get sucked into some legal situation. Or I would slip up and the lawyer would take advantage of my stupidity and sue me.

I've found that nearly all of our fears are (almost) completely without warrant. We're told wolves (as in real wolves, not metaphorical) are fierce and scary, but there are very few recent records of wolves killing humans.

As I began to work with attorneys, I found that they weren't scary and many of them are very cost conscious. The first time I ever paid an attorney, I was 28 years old, going through my very painful and unexpected divorce. In hindsight, her legal advice was the difference between me having a lot of time with my children or very little at all. My kids would be very different people without my lawyer—you don't hear *this* very often.

Money and Attorneys

If you are getting estate planning documents, generally you will be quoted a flat fee for all of the work no matter how long it takes the attorney to draft them. Bankruptcy attorneys often work the same way.

Most other attorneys work on an hourly basis. When you pay them by the hour, they will usually ask you for a large upfront "retainer." Let's say you give them $5,000 as a retainer and they charge $300 per hour. You'll see a month-end statement that subtracts $150 for a 30 minute phone call, $30 for a 6 minute email response, and $75 for a 15 phone call to the opposing attorney. If the retainer runs out, they will ask for more. When an attorney asks for a retainer, they will explain that they bill themselves from it and whatever is left will go back to you. This is true in theory, but don't expect to see it back unless you prematurely terminate your relationship.

In my experience, retainer money seems to go quicker than it should. The person with the control over your money has all the incentive to *not* be frugal. That's just the reality. It's the same with brokers and commissions. It doesn't mean that the people compensated this way are unethical, but that their ethics are most of the barrier preventing you from hemorrhaging money.

I happily paid my attorney a few retainers during my divorce, and she was wonderful. Since then, I've avoided retainers. When I need an attorney I'll ask them their hourly rate and then ask them for *one hour* of their time to pick their brain. I come to the meeting highly prepared, questions ready, and get considerable value in a short time. Not all attorneys will do this. In my experience the most valuable time has always been in the first hour of engagement ... so I just pay for that one hour. I don't know if this is normal. I've never heard of anyone else doing this, but I have on multiple occasions called attorneys with my issue and asked them what their hourly rate is—$150, $200, $250, $299, and $499 are all rates I've paid. It's key to come prepared (including having the check already written out). I manage the pace of the meeting to make sure we go over what I need them to go over. When the hour hits, I slide the check across the table, thank them for their time, and ask them another question—sometimes you can get a freebie. I've learned that attorneys love to talk and share what they know, and by golly it's valuable stuff.

If it's estate planning, you could draft boilerplate documents and ask an attorney to review them—however, expect them to tell you that they need to be totally redone. Again, not all attorneys will agree to do this, particularly the better ones. Just like anything in life, the best professionals are too good to bother with clients who will nickel and dime them.

Lastly, be open to working with at-home professionals. Personally I've had great luck with these. The first divorce attorney I talked to worked at a big high power law firm downtown. If you go to a big firm, you are paying for a lot of layers. You are paying for your attorney, their boss, their boss's boss, the beautiful office you stand in, the coffee they offered you, the partners of the firm, and whatever advertising they do. If you pay the attorney $499, you can assume that they are only pocketing $150–300 of it. Attorneys who work out of their homes can sometimes do the same work with the same quality if you (yes, you) can get over the residential setting and the cocker spaniel sniffing around and cats jumping on your lap during the meeting. I can.

Summary

We live in a world inundated with free information. Terrible mistakes cost more than attorney fees.

Excellent advice at a fair price is always better than terrible advice at an excellent price.

There was a boy and on his 12th birthday he got a horse. Everyone in the boy's village says, *"How wonderful! The boy got a horse. What a lucky boy!"*

And the Zen Master said, ***"We'll see."***

Three years later the boy falls off his horse and everyone in the village says, *"How terrible! That boy will never be able to run again. This is awful!"*

The Zen Master said, ***"We'll see."***

Three years later there's a war and all the young men in the country have to go off to war, but the boy doesn't have to go because his leg is withered. Everyone in the village says, *"How wonderful!"*

And the Zen Master said, ***"We'll see."***

Buddhist Parable

Philanthropy and Altruism

I've worked with many people over the years. It seems that nearly everyone wants to do something good with their money, while providing for their own needs. Many calls for giving away money stem from an implied sense of obligation, guilting people into philanthropy. It is my belief that anyone with money has all the guilt-free right in the world to do whatever they want with it.

This is not a call to give away money. I am only addressing those who wish to do so, and to somewhat reconcile this yearning with the contradictory fear of running out of money. In addition to this, I hope to direct your philanthropic engagement with a mind toward *maximum impact* for your hard-earned money.

Personally, when I see or hear of a dire need, my heart has a monk-like reaction. I immediately want to sell everything, live a minimalist lifestyle, and give everything to the poor. Instead ... I do nothing at all, and life goes on and I forget about it. I doubt I'm alone with this experience.

I want to make a connection between philanthropy and investing. In the spirit of this book, my perspective on altruism involves using your money for maximum good. It is the aspiration for philanthropic leverage. There are a lot of parallels between giving money away and saving money. The two key ones are:

1. Return on investment—Return on gift
2. Regular and ongoing investments—Regular and ongoing gifts

We invest money with the assumed objective of seeking the best and most certain return on the dollar. We don't always think of philanthropy this way. We should. Your *assumed* objective should be to gain the best and most certain return on your gift.

I've observed that giving and charity aren't always driven by this *assumption* of seeking a maximum return on a gift. For example, a co-worker does a charity run, so you give a little money. Local firefighters are raising money for a new truck, so you put a little money in a boot. Your nephew is doing a mission trip, so you give. Your public radio station is doing a fund drive, so you give. None of this is bad, but it's often driven by the moment and not by a long-term perspective. It is excellent giving, but not necessarily with a specific goal.

To begin this process of dislodging traditional thinking, let's look at uses of money from *only* an altruistic standpoint. We are not, for the moment, concerned about your needs. We are only thinking of this in terms of what uses of the money would help others the most. I think that if you were to order the uses of money by *most altruistic* to *least altruistic* it would be:

1. Give it
2. Spend it
3. Save it

Each of these categories contains a considerable amount of nuance. If you don't plan for your own needs, then in time your needs become someone else's philanthropy.

To be clear, yes, I believe that much of what we've talked about is geared toward the *least* altruistic thing you can do: simply having more money. Increasing your net worth to retire is *necessary*. However, if in retirement you need $50,000 in income and have $10,000,000 in the bank, *at least* $8,000,000 of this is *unnecessary net worth*. It mostly satisfies an overzealous sense of financial insecurity.

I'm not saying that hoarding wealth does *nothing* for your fellow humans. It may be helping prop up stock prices, thus keeping someone out there employed. Maybe you own bonds and it's helping a company stay in business. Maybe it's helping a bank maintain liquidity. However, most of the ways that you would store your net worth don't do much altruistically.

The next major category is spending it. Spending is a very broad category and some spending helps people more than other spending. In the week after 9/11 you may remember Mayor Rudy Giuliani asking people to come to New York, go to their restaurants, go to their plays, and stay in their hotels. It was a call to spend money to help them in a natural capitalistic manner. Let's say you wanted to help New York City. If you had $100, you could either:

1. Give the full $100
2. Spend the $100 (knowing that roughly half, or $50, ends up in the merchant's pocket)
3. Keep the $100 (i.e. do none of the above)

The key nuance in spending is *what* you spend it on. The basic premise of economics is that my spending is your income and vice versa. If you buy a product from someone who will use your spending as their income, and that person then hoards the money in a savings account for 50 years, this is altruistically barely different than you hoarding it. However, if you were in a developing country and bought a product from someone who uses that income (roughly half of what you paid for the product) to buy medicine to save their ill child, the impact is rather different.

The third major category for how money can be used altruistically is the more obvious one: giving it away. Much like spending, not all giving is created equal. If you give money to someone who just saves the money in a bank, it is different than giving directly to someone who is starving and marginalized.

All three categories have tremendous overlap, which leads us into the concept of looking at the rate of return on your giving.

Philanthropic Return on Investment

As we closed out the chapter on investments, I shared with you my own personal story about Uncle Harold the man, who showed kindness to my great-grandfather, who I never met. My family has benefited from this generosity for over 100 years; this was a positive return on investment.

When you invest money, it's clear what you want back: more money than what you started with. With philanthropy big and small, "return" can be very tough to measure. If you give to a large non-profit, sometimes overhead costs erode away your return on investment. On the other hand, sometimes overhead creates more return—particularly if the overhead raises more money for the cause than not having it. Some charities are by necessity inefficient, such as disaster relief—much goes into preparation and readiness, which is not an obvious return on investment until disaster strikes and that preparation saves lives. Some philanthropy has far more tangible, direct, and immediate benefits, such as food programs or educational grants.

On the absolute darkest end of the spectrum, some charities are merely tax shelters or criminally bogged down with administrative fees. Others are more gifted at fundraising than problem solving. However, backing off immoral extremes, the depressing truth is that there are a scope of charities that, while good intentioned and run by good people, have no measurable philanthropic impact. While measurement can be nebulous, fewer than 100% actually move the needle for their cause. Because of this, it is upon the discernment of givers to make the best measurement they can.

To me, philanthropy should expect results. As a giver, what do you want to see change?

This isn't meant to be rhetorical. I'm literally asking, "What do you want?" When you look at the needs of the world, what problem would you *really* like to see go away? For the moment, don't worry about how it may be solved or whether it is the most important existentially. It might be helping the extremely poor, preventing fatal diseases in developing countries, fighting human trafficking, protecting or restoring the environment, a political cause, a religious cause, an awareness cause, animal rescue, disaster relief, medical research, funding artistic expression, cultural preservation, or youth foreign exchange programs. The world's needs are vast and various.

When we talked about finding purpose in life, I encouraged you to find candor in the privacy of your mind and think about what's important *to you* without judgment. If your passion is abused animals, don't feel like you *should* care about humans. Speaking as one myself, I can say that we're a little overrated. Just care about what you care about.

Now, I want you to imagine that you are the last person on earth with $100,000. All the other money has evaporated and you must spend every penny to try to solve this problem. Once you utilize it, you can't get it back, but are left with results (i.e. your return on investment). To put it visually, although your $100,000 may not mean scoring a touchdown, what would move the football down the field *as many yards as possible*? How would you approach this decision?

Effectiveness

For starters, you would ideally optimize the effectiveness. Let's say you have two charities with two solutions to a problem. One solution costs $200,000, and the other costs $100,000. This may seem obvious, but using our football analogy, if the more expensive solution moves the ball seven yards and the cheaper one (at half the cost) only moves it two yards, then it means the more expensive one is better. We could analyze these like this:

Solution #1		Solution #2	
Total Cost	$200,000	Total Cost	$100,000
Effectiveness (in "yards")	7.0	Effectiveness (in "yards")	2.0
Yards per $100,000	3.5	Yards per $100,000	2.0
More Effective Solution			

The costs aren't everything in the decision. They must be looked at from a perspective of *effectiveness*. Of course in the real world, "yards" are much harder to quantify, but measurement should always be the aspiration. Also, sometimes philanthropic problems exist because money won't directly fix them, or they are very difficult to measure.

If possible, consider the following factors of measurement:

1. Overhead costs and financial efficiency
2. The probability that a solution works

I strongly encourage you to question your giving and to run it through your effectiveness filter. Organizations raising money to solve a problem don't necessarily have *any* impact on the problem. As the steward of your passion and your money, it's crucial to be mindful of your yardage effectiveness.

Some Love to Higher Overhead

To illustrate how overhead costs *alone* do not necessarily tell you the cost effectiveness of a charity, let's do a thought experiment. There are many organizations who spend a lot of money fundraising. In the past, I've heard much criticism toward these organizations because of their "high overhead cost." This is a perfectly valid concern.

The case is stated that if you have two charities and one has lower overhead costs then more of your money is going to "the cause." We could contrast two charities this way:

Charity Overhead Comparison

	Your Donation	Overhead	Amount for Overhead	Amount to Cause
Charity #1	$100,000	50%	$50,000	$50,000
Charity #2	$100,000	10%	$10,000	$90,000

Let's say both charities were implementing the exact same solution. On the face of it, it would seem like your money was far more effective going to Charity #2. However, let's say that with Charity #1, while half is going toward "the cause," the other half will be used to attract more donations through *highly effective fundraising*. Because this fundraising itself is effective, they are able to convert your $50,000 into another $300,000 in donations. Yes, technically your money is being spent schmoozing at cocktail parties, but this attracts another $300,000 in donations. That $300,000 is then again split, and $150,000 goes to "the cause." As a result, it meant that ultimately, your $100,000 turned into a $200,000 contribution to "the cause." Of course, these are all made up numbers and the real world is always more cloudy, but the point is to look at the whole picture.

Regular Giving

If you've committed to helping solve a problem, and you've determined the most effective way of solving it, you should immediately engage in regular monthly giving. I think the Biblical concept of tithing 10% of your income is a noble practice to emulate, but anything is better than nothing. Regimented giving puts ongoing mindfulness to your cause, as an expectation of specific results and accountability.

In the same way that regular saving gradually moves you closer to your financial goals, regimented monthly giving moves an organization closer to its altruistic goals. I'll show you how I personally approach this.

A Personal Example of Altruistic Global Triage

When I think of the problems of the world, I'm overwhelmed. I don't know how to prioritize whether I should give money to help free sex slaves, prevent malaria, feed the hungry, or to aid efforts to lower infant mortality. I also care about helping abused animals, as well as protecting the environment and promoting the arts. I have no surefire method to triage the needs that are important *to me*. Also, I'm not trying to evangelize you to any cause, but I invite you to eavesdrop on my thoughts on helping "my cause" and my approach.

The extremely poor in the world have always had an emotional pull for me. I think that on a per capita basis, they have the most vital needs in terms of problems that lead to death and suffering. I also feel that many of these needs can be tangibly reduced by small amounts of money. From a philanthropic return on investment perspective, there is a lot of bang for the buck.

In giving, my worry is that the money just ends up in the wasteful ether, or even makes the problem *worse*. I also struggle with abstract giving. I've given to medical foundations, abuse shelters, disaster relief, the arts, and with micro-lending organizations. I have no certainty my gifts did anything positive at all.

If I'm going to give, I want to know exactly what I'm getting—or more specifically, what the needy are getting. I also want to know that what I'm giving them will tangibly help. When I think of the extremely poor, my training as a financial advisor and financial planner intuitively comes into the picture. There are short-term, medium-term, and long-term needs.

Short Term

When I think of the short-term needs of the extremely poor, my priority is to prevent someone from dying today, someone who will die if resources are not provided. One of the areas where I feel like I can make a tangible life or death difference is malaria prevention. It is a highly efficient way to save a life.

As you know, malaria is transmitted through mosquitoes. Half a million people die from it every year, 70% of whom are children under the age of five. In addition to this, 400 million get sick from it. The short-term organization I donate to is called the Against Malaria Foundation. The money to goes to developing countries and distributes long-lasting insecticide treated mosquito nets. The cost to produce and deliver a net to a vulnerable family is about $4.85.[1] To me, my money buys something very specific that will do good for an extended period of time and possibly enjoy other uses once it wears out. The organization itself is highly rated across multiple spectrums by multiple charity rating agencies for its efficiency and effectiveness in actually solving a problem. The organization is also impressively transparent. All of its financial information is public and easily accessible online. Every single net distribution is documented by photographs and videos and this documentation is accessible to you as a donor.

It's impossible to know for certain if somebody would have died from malaria if they didn't have a net. Certainly it's not as though every single net is protecting someone who would have otherwise died. We currently don't know if there are adverse effects to sleeping under an insecticide treated net. However, looking at malaria rates in communities who have nets and those who don't, independent studies have estimated that $2,838 in donations saves one life. If you wanted to save a life annually, it would cost only $236.50 per month. For what's important to me, this is the highest return on investment that I am aware of.

In addition to saving one life per year, you can also know that you are preventing hundreds of people from getting sick from malaria. Because these people aren't sick, they are able to work and provide for their families—which helps them and the economies they live in.

Medium Term

Providing a $4.85 net for a family is a good thing. For that family to earn extra money and buy that net themselves is even better. Increasing the permanent economic well-being of the extremely poor is a surprisingly difficult and complicated task. Again, I like to avoid uncertainties and stick to the basics. I believe that if you reduce diseases, not only is this an altruistically good thing to do for people, economically it frees up time and resources that could build wealth. If you look at how industrialized nations increased their standard of living the past few centuries, part of what helped the progress was that people's time was freed up by new products. Instead of having to grow and preserve your own food, you could buy it. Instead of having to make your own clothes, you could buy them. Instead of having to write checks, we have automatic bill pay. You can add dishwashers, washing machines, internal plumbing, hot water, furnaces, public education, and automobiles to the list. These are all things that greatly freed up time. This edges toward the abstract, but I believe in the power of additional time in the hands of self-interested people. Time itself is a massive resource for fighting poverty.

A common problem with living in extreme poverty is an intestinal parasitic flatworm disease called schistosomiasis. The worms prevent your body from absorbing nutrients. It affects over 200 million people worldwide and causes tens of thousands of deaths per year. While less deadly than malaria, the disease has considerable health, education, and financial impacts. Research has shown that deworming children boosts school attendance and nutrition. It's hard to quantify the medium and long-term benefits of this, but these are indisputably good things. Even if at a minimum, suffering is reduced, I'm happy with this result. From a purely selfish point, the thought of children not suffering because of money I donated makes me very happy and grateful I had that money to give to a charity called The Schistosomiasis Control Initiative.

Deworming is very inexpensive. Schistosomiasis is treated through annual treatment. It cost about $0.80 to deworm one child. If you were wanting to balance out a donation toward mosquito nets and match with one toward deworming, your same $2,838 would deworm 3,547 children. This is a huge number—you can visualize it as half a dozen of your local elementary schools. I'd feel nervous standing in front of this many people. How do you balance out the value of saving one life versus reducing the suffering of several thousand? I don't know.

Long Term

The further you zoom out from very tangible needs and to long-term needs, it is exponentially riskier for the hubris of our experience to cause more harm than good. A very basic example is to imagine a country suffering from famine. It would be easy to see the starvation and organize a massive food drive and give away free food. In practice though, giving away free food could put considerable amounts of farmers, ranchers, and merchants out of business—the community then loses these skillsets, causing new long-term problems. Even in a famine, there are usually still *some* crop yields, and *some* people who have food to sell.

It's important to be humble and recognize that it is not realistic to make a long distance diagnosis through a pinhole. With extreme poverty in an undeveloped country, you are inconceivably far removed from the problem. This is where a little empathy and imagination can help.

I want you to imagine your current standard of living happens to be extreme poverty on a global scale and there are not many people in the world poorer than you. For whatever reason, some extremely wealthy stranger from far away has the goal to help you move closer to their own standard of living. They have decided to spend what you make in a year to help your life get better. They are weighing whether to give you health care, education, food, or clean water.

Objectively, your wealthy random patron is probably the *least* qualified person to make that determination. For some people, the best use of that money will be to pay off debt and get out from under the grip of a loan shark. Others may save it. Others may use it to pay for health care needs. Others may squander it. For some, it may be to pass it along to their brother whose family is suffering from his unemployment. Whatever the exact need is, the wealthy patron doesn't know your needs, nor could they relate to your problems.

The poor know their own needs better than the rich do. Some charities facilitate giving money directly to extremely poor people. The one that I give money to is called GiveDirectly. Roughly 85% of whatever you give goes directly into the hands of extremely poor people as an unconditional gift. How they use it is completely up to them. Some may buy their own mosquito nets or deworming medication, but ultimately they will make the decision. Inevitably, some will squander it, waste it, or possibly invest it in something nefarious. Of course this concerns me, but not any more than any other charity's chance of misusing funds. If you assume that *half* of the people you give money to squander it, this is still far more financially effective than an ineffective charity. Humans seem like pretty good people to me and I doubt half would squander it. Besides if squandering it means spending it on *something* then it means additional money passing around a poor community.

A Princeton University study[2] surveyed the results of households 4.3 months on average after receiving an unconditional gift of money. It found that people chose to spend this money mostly on food, medicine, and education. Another study by the World Bank showed zero impact on what they charmingly labeled "temptation goods," such as alcohol and tobacco. About 39% of the transfer went toward increasing their assets (giving the average household a 58% boost in their assets). Business and agricultural income were up 33%. Studies have also shown that on average, five years after the gift, income amounts are up 64–96% of the transfer amount.[3]

With this direct giving, the tangible benefits edge toward the abstract. You will never know what your money ended up purchasing. All humans are more or less the same and our relative goodness and badness spans across the same spectrum of shades of grey. If 100 random people in your community were to receive one year of their annual income, I suspect a majority would use it in a positive or neutral way. The random humans in extreme poverty would likely do the same.

Once again using our same dollar amount to save a life, $2,838 would put $2,412.30 directly in the hands of extremely poor people. If this was targeted among those earning $2.00 a day or less, this donation represents the annual income of 3.3 households. At a minimum, you would be able to create a life changing event for some random family nearly every turning of the season. You are welcome to let your imagination fill out what joy this must be for these extremely poor families and how they may be using this colossal windfall.

None of these short, medium, and long-term solutions are flawless. Inevitably each will carry unintended consequences. But on the whole, for the problem that I want to help with, it is a well-rounded way to tangibly improve many people's lives. I believe everyone can approach their passion causes the same way.

The 10% Challenge

Ladies and gentlemen, you are a 1%er. In December 2015, Median U.S. Household income was $57,153[4]. How much do you need to make in order to be in the top 1% of *global* income earners?[5]

$32,400

If your income topped that, you're a 1%er. At least globally speaking. If you are looking at only the income swimming pool of the United States, this number is $434,682, but globally being a 1%er doesn't sound like such an exclusive club to us.

Let's say your income is the median number of $57,153 and you donated 10% of your income. First of all, you would still be well into the 1%er club, but that annual donation of $5,715.30 could provide either of:

1. 1,076 mosquito nets saving two lives per year
2. Deworming of 7,144 children
3. The annual incomes of 6.65 people earning $2.00 per day

There's a coin toss's chance that if you are reading this in America, you make more than this. 10% is a significant portion of any person's household income, but impoverished people throughout the world regularly engage in the 10% tithing practice. If you had a 10% pay cut, you'd likely just figure it out.

I think that sometimes people experience a mental slippery slope of giving. You may feel that if you cut back to save two lives per year, you are going to feel guilty and cut back more to save more lives. It feels like a slippery slope to minimalism, where you feel like you can't enjoy the fruit of your labor because of the guilt you feel. Giving will always force you to confront certain existential realities. It's important to sell yourself on giving based on the amazing *opportunity* rather than as an obligation.

I don't think there's any shame in getting excited about what giving does for you personally, emotionally, or psychologically. You are going to feel *amazing* knowing that you are saving people from dying, preventing thousands of children from being sick, or enabling families to win the lotto—or, whatever your cause happens to be. It's not about guilt, it's about the opportunity to have an amazing experience for a bargain price.

Even if it's for purely selfish reasons, I'm convinced that nearly everyone would experience far more satisfaction and joy from altruism than they would from whatever else they may buy with that same amount of money.

The extremely poor are those who are on my conscience. Everybody has their own perfectly valid and worthy causes. As you aid your cause, I would advise three things:

1. Trust and follow your heart. If your passion is something that has a more abstract and intangible benefit to the world, there's no shame in this. Giving money with vague charitable benefits is much better than hoarding unnecessary wealth in a way that only bankrolls fund managers and/or massages an overactive yearning for financial security.
2. Try to compare them. While there is nobility in loyalty, be brave if you need to change your giving. Sometimes, how you feel ain't got nothing to do with it. If by donating to one cause you will prevent people from dying, and donating to another cause merely keeps a wasteful operation limping along ... well, it's your money, but you aren't doing the world any favors enabling inefficiency.
3. Question everything. Applicable with everything in life, most especially here because the helpless depend on your questions, and, even more importantly, on your answers and actions.

As with your financial plan, stick to your giving plan. Organizations change over time. It's normal. The best case scenario is that the problem goes away, or maybe the funding needed for the project maxes out.

Endnotes

1   Source: http://www.givewell.org/charities/against-malaria-foundation#Costperlife-saved

2   Source: http://www.princeton.edu/~joha/publications/Haushofer_Shapiro_UCT_2013.pdf

3   Source: https://www.givedirectly.org/research-on-cash-transfers

4   Source: U.S. Census Bureau, *Current Population Survey (CPS)*

5   Source: http://www.investopedia.com/articles/personal-finance/050615/are-you-top-one-percent-world.asp

Your goal should always be to *maximize* the *return* on your investment, even if the *return is intangible.*

Why should I play the Roman fool and die
On mine own sword? Whiles I see lives, the gashes
Do better upon them.

William Shakespeare
Macbeth, Act V, Scene 8

Tax Planning

With taxes we come full circle and return to "what is." Why have I saved taxes for last? Because nobody likes taxes. Also, because tax planning looks back on everything we've discussed so far. It touches on all five of its financial cousins.

The goal of financial planning is to maximize wealth as we've defined it—to maximize the ability to buy stuff and to *grow* in your ability to buy stuff. From a financial planning perspective, the sole objective of tax planning is to minimize how much you and your heirs pay in taxes, within the parameters of U.S., state, and local tax laws.

As always, this directs you back to a professional who will individually advise you. We're not going into the minutiae of tax preparation. This is a superficial treatment to give you ideas that you can ask a professional to implement. No book or anything you read on your own will ever substitute personal and comprehensive advice. The goal we have is threefold:

1. To give you some ideas to bring back to your tax advisor
2. To put taxes in the context of a broader investment picture
3. To illustrate, in an apples for apples manner, the net result of tax saving methods

Bored already? Hang in there, I wouldn't go into this if I didn't love you.

A Brief Explanation of Taxes

For individuals, the majority of their taxes will fall into two categories:

1. Ordinary Income
2. Capital Gains

If you earn income, then it is taxed as ordinary income. If you have an investment that goes up in value and you sell it, this is a capital gain which is also taxed. Capital gains can be broken down as either a short-term or long-term capital gain. A gain that happens in less than one year is short term, anything one year or more is long term. One year is the magical IRS line in the sand.

Ordinary income is what most people think of as their tax rate, "I'm in the **28%** tax bracket." This is referencing a table of tax brackets based on your income. The truth is that, except for a math fluke, nobody pays exactly **28%** in taxes—it's always some weird number like **20.98%**. Let's say you have a single woman making $100,000 per year. She would be a "single filer."

This is her 2017 tax table:

Single Filers		
Marginal Tax Rate	**TAX BRACKETS**	
	Over	But Not Over
10.0%	$0	$9,325
15.0%	$9,326	$37,950
25.0%	$37,951	$91,900
28.0%	**$91,901**	**$191,650**
33.0%	$191,651	$416,700
35.0%	$416,701	$418,400
39.6%	$418,401	

You can see how her income falls on the lower range of the **28%** tax bracket. But this doesn't mean she pays $28,000 in taxes. From the table you can see how she pays **10%** on the first $9,325 of her income ($933) and **15%** on the next range of income (i.e. $37,950 - $9,326 = $28,624 x **15%** = $4,294), etc. on up. This is what she would be paying in taxes:

Single Filers

Marginal Tax Rate	TAX BRACKETS		Income Earned in Range	Taxes Paid from Range
	Over	But Not Over		
10.0%	$0	$9,325	$9,325	$933
15.0%	$9,326	$37,950	$28,624	$4,294
25.0%	$37,951	$91,900	$53,949	$13,487
28.0%	**$91,901**	**$191,650**	$8,099	$2,268
33.0%	$191,651	$416,700	$0	$0
35.0%	$416,701	$418,400	$0	$0
39.6%	$418,401		$0	$0
			Ordinary Taxes	$20,981
			Effective Rate	20.98%

Before you accuse the IRS of taking every penny they can from you, it should be noted that they take every *dollar* they can from you, as taxes are always rounded to the nearest dollar.

So this is for a single filer. People can also file as:

1. Married filing jointly (or surviving spouse)
2. Married filing separately
3. Head of household

Let's say our single $100,000-in-income-per-year woman gets married to someone who does not work outside the home. The key point is that there is no additional income with the marriage and their *joint* income is $100,000. They now fall into a different table "Married Filing Jointly."

Married Filing Jointly

Marginal Tax Rate	TAX BRACKETS		Income Earned in Range	Taxes Paid from Range
	Over	But Not Over		
10.0%	$0	$18,650	$18,650	$1,865
15.0%	$18,651	$75,900	$57,249	$8,587
25.0%	**$75,901**	**$153,100**	$24,099	$6,025
28.0%	$153,101	$233,350	$0	$0
33.0%	$233,351	$416,700	$0	$0
35.0%	$416,701	$470,700	$0	$0
39.6%	$470,701		$0	$0
			Ordinary Taxes	$16,477
			Effective Rate	16.48%

She (and her spouse) are now in the **25%** tax bracket and effectively pay **16.48%** in taxes. This is a simplified way of looking at it and truly the most ordinary of ordinary income.

So, what types of income will tally up what is counted as ordinary income? Pretty much everything but *long-term* capital gains and qualified dividends. Examples of ordinary income: wages, salaries, tips, commissions, bonuses, retirement account distributions, bank interest, rent, royalties, and even gambling winnings. Jerks. *Short-term* capital gains are taxed as ordinary income as well.

Capital gains are simple. You are taxed on how much an investment goes up. How much you are taxed depends on *how long* you held it. If you buy a stock for $10,000 and when it goes up to $11,000 you sell it, that is a $1,000 capital gain. If the time between buying and selling was *less than a year*, then that gain is considered a short-term gain and taxed as ordinary income. If you held it for *more than a year*, then it is a long-term capital gain. The tax rate on long-term capital gains is either **0%, 15%,** or **20%** depending on what tax bracket you fell in. Let's say that this couple experienced a $1,000 long-term capital gain, this is how it would fit into their total income of $101,000.

Married Filing Jointly

Marginal Tax Rate	TAX BRACKETS		Income Earned in Range	Taxes Paid from Range	Tax Rate on Qualified Dividends and Long-Term Capital Gains	Amount of Dividends and Long-Term Capital Gains	Taxes Paid
	Over	But Not Over					
10.0%	$0	$18,650	$18,650	$1,865	0%		
15.0%	$18,651	$75,900	$57,249	$8,587	0%		
25.0%	$75,901	$153,100	$24,099	$6,025	15%	$1,000	$150
28.0%	$153,101	$233,350	$0	$0	15%		
33.0%	$233,351	$416,700	$0	$0	15%		
35.0%	$416,701	$470,700	$0	$0	15%		
39.6%	$470,701		$0	$0	20%		
			Ordinary Taxes	$16,477		**Total Taxes**	$16,627
			Effective Rate	16.48%		**Total Rate**	16.46%

Those of you wearing scanning electron reading glasses may have noticed that the new tax rate column is labeled, "Tax Rate on Qualified Dividends and Long-term Capital Gains." Generally any dividend paid for a domestic stock, mutual fund, or other regulated investment company is considered a "qualified dividend." Dividends from foreign investments, partnerships, and real estate investment trusts are typically considered "ordinary dividends" and taxed as ordinary income. Have you ever heard the complaint that the über-wealthy pay only **15–20%** in taxes? That's because their income mostly comes as a qualified dividend. It is hardly tax gymnastics to accomplish this.

As of 2013, for higher income earners, there is also a new Net Income Investment Tax of **3.8%** that applies to income from investments. Net investment income includes: interest, dividends, capital gains, rental income, royalty income, and non-qualified annuities. The IRS regulations governing this one specific tax is 400 pages long. I'm not making this up. Broadly, whether or not you pay it is based on your Modified Adjusted Gross Income. You are likely to have to pay it if your income is above $200,000 for single people and $250,000 for married people.

Naturally there are nuances to all of this. In addition, state taxes will be unique for each state. I'll use my home state of Colorado as an example because it's very simple. Here we have a flat tax of **4.63%**. Other states have higher property taxes instead of a state income tax, or they may have tax brackets like at the federal level. Sales taxes fund different levels of government (state, the county, and the city). There are also Federal Insurance Contributions Act (FICA) taxes—more conventionally known as "payroll taxes"—that fund entitlement programs such as Social Security, Medicare, Medicaid, unemployment insurance, worker's compensation, and food stamps. These are partly paid by you and partly by your employer—because of this we'll exclude them from this explanation.

Here is a hypothetical total effective tax rate for a couple earning $100,000:

Married Filing Jointly	
Net Federal Taxes	$16,627
Colorado State Taxes	$4,630
Property Taxes	$2,000
Sales Taxes	$1,000
Local Sales Tax	$500
TOTAL Taxes	$24,757
TOTAL Effective Tax Rate	24.76%

This entirely ignores deductions to reduce your ordinary income down to an *adjusted gross income*. For this couple, at a minimum they are eligible to a $12,700 *standard deduction*. Their $100,000 ordinary income would be adjusted down to $87,300, which is the actual income number they'd use to determine their tax bracket. They could also choose to *itemize deductions* if they could produce *more than* $12,700 in write-offs. Common things you can itemize are mortgage interest, medical expenses, car registration fees, charitable donations, fees to prepare taxes, and financial advisory fees (but not commissions).

Also, long-term capital gains can be offset by long-term capital loss. If you have a capital loss in a previous year, you can carry it forward to offset a gain in this year. More on that in a minute.

Taxes on Social Security Income

Social Security income is taxed depending on your *combined income*. It's unique in that at least *some* portion of it is always tax free. Your combined income is a different calculation:

> Your adjusted gross income
> + Nontaxable interest
> + Half of your Social Security Benefits
> = **Combined Income**

The most common form of nontaxable interest is municipal bond interest. We will go over municipal bonds shortly. If you are filing jointly, this is a chart of how much of your Social Security is taxable. To clarify, if 50% o*f your Social Security* is taxable, then the other 50% is tax free. If 0% is taxable, then you don't pay taxes on your Social Security:

Taxes on Social Security Benefits

% of Social Security that's Taxable	Single Filers Combined Income		Married Filing Jointly Combined Income	
	Over	But Not Over	Over	But Not Over
0%	$0	$25,000	$0	$32,000
50%	$25,001	$34,000	$32,001	$44,000
85%	$34,001		$44,001	

US Federal Discretionary Spending of $100

Health Care	$26.56
Social Security	$25.16
Defense (Military, Homeland Security, Veterans)	$18.60
Welfare (Unemployment, Housing, Worker's Comp, Food Stamps)	$9.21
Education	$3.14
Transportation	$2.42
Protection (Police, Fire, Courts, Prisons)	$1.38
Other Spending (NASA, Agriculture, Forestry, Science)	$3.30
General Government	$0.63
Interest on Federal Debt	$9.59
TOTAL	**$100.00**

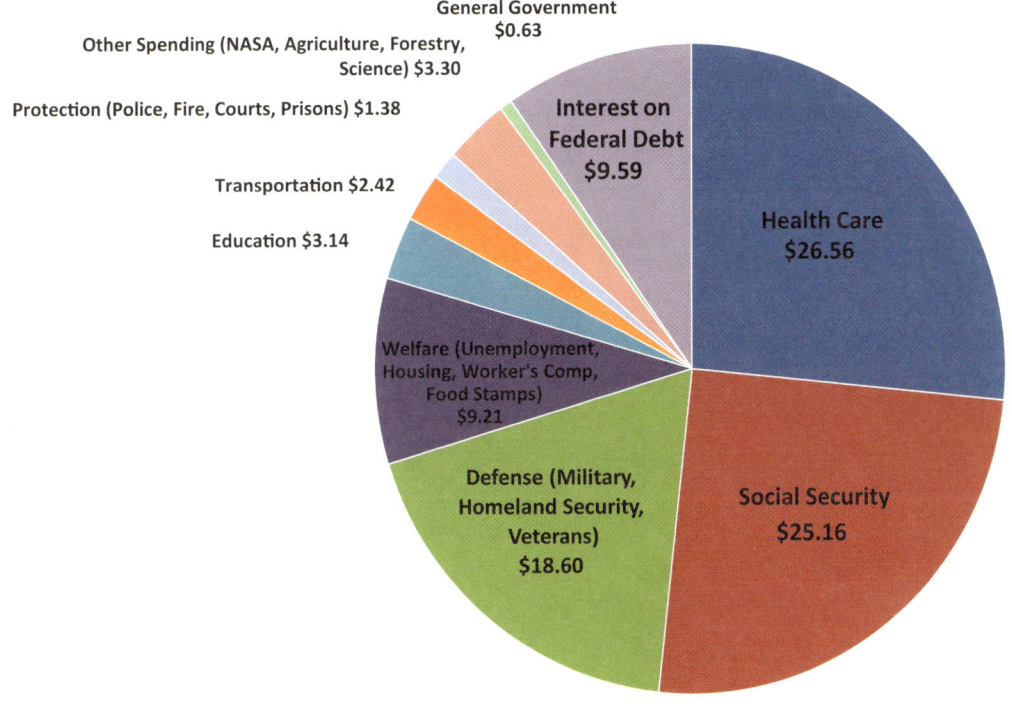

Pie chart labels:

- General Government $0.63
- Other Spending (NASA, Agriculture, Forestry, Science) $3.30
- Protection (Police, Fire, Courts, Prisons) $1.38
- Transportation $2.42
- Education $3.14
- Interest on Federal Debt $9.59
- Health Care $26.56
- Welfare (Unemployment, Housing, Worker's Comp, Food Stamps) $9.21
- Defense (Military, Homeland Security, Veterans) $18.60
- Social Security $25.16

Where does it go?

We'll only look at federal taxes. For easy math, let's say you paid $100 in 2017 federal taxes. We'll ignore whether it came from payroll taxes or through your tax return. Here's are the 2018 planned outlays:

I'll pass on the temptation for commentary. Let's shift gears to using the tax code for maximizing wealth over a lifetime.

Banking and Investments

Broadly speaking, banking and investment accounts are divided between retirement and non-retirement accounts. The less obvious IRS terms are:

1. Qualified = Retirement Accounts
2. Non-Qualified = Non-Retirement Accounts

"Qualified" suggests that the account *qualifies* for special tax treatment. "Non-qualified" accounts are taxed normally, like interest, dividends, and capital gains. I never liked this way of saying it. For clarity, I'm going to distinguish accounts as either "retirement" or "non-retirement" and shelve the confusing "qualified" term.

Taxes on Non-Retirement Accounts

Money that you gain in non-retirement accounts is going to be taxed as ordinary income or as a capital gain.

Interest Income

Money in a bank earning interest is considered interest income. It is taxed as ordinary income. Credit Unions sometimes call interest "dividends" to punctuate the membership aspect of their organizations, but the IRS still counts it as interest.

When you have a brokerage account with investments, a cash portion of it usually earns interest. I've found that this can confuse clients, so let's look at the anatomy of a brokerage account. Think of the cash portion as a *transition zone* for money going in and out of the account and investments.

If you deposit money into a brokerage account, it first goes into that cash portion and then "buys" whatever investment you get. If you sell something, the money goes back to the cash portion. This cash portion is what is (normally) earning interest. Brokerage firms often have multiple options in which to invest your "cash" money. Most people keep nearly all of it in "the investments," but there's usually at least *some* small amount of cash balance.

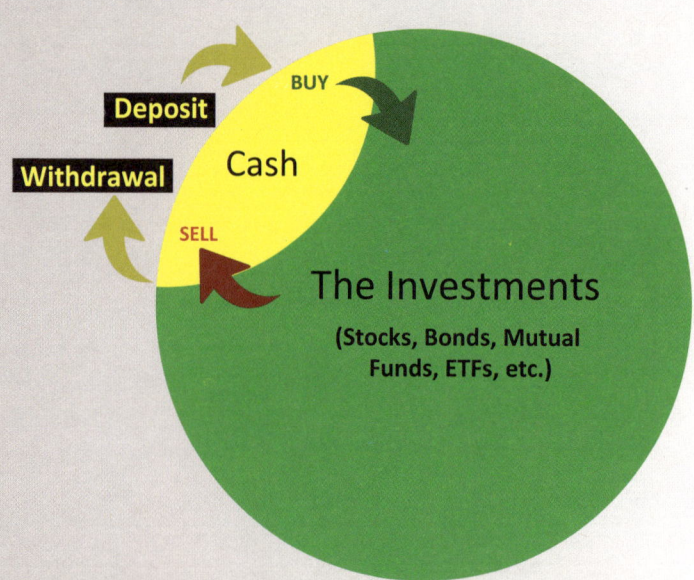

Additional investments that earn interest income are treasury bonds, notes, and bills, as well as savings bond interest. Sometimes when you have a mix of assets in a brokerage account, these terms will be used in confusing ways. You can own a money market *mutual fund* or even a publicly traded CD, but your brokerage account may call it a "dividend."

Sometimes these conflated terms have little significance, but other times missing the nuance can lead you on a dangerous path. Again, the industry uses various words interchangeably. If you sit still and behave, after we talk about dividends, I'll share with you a bedtime story from yesterday that illustrates how the public can, very understandably, be confused by terminology.

Dividends and Capital Gains

As we learned in the chapter on investments, a dividend is a little bit of profit paid to the shareholders of a stock. If you have stock worth $10,000, they may give you $200 in dividends over the course of a year (this would be a 2% ***dividend yield***). If the company is in the U.S., those dividends are taxed the same way as long-term capital gain and not as ordinary income.

Let's rehash our previous example. You have $10,000 in stock that goes up to $11,000 in value, which is a $1,000 gain. If that stock has a 2% dividend yield then technically you have $200 in dividends and $800 in capital gains, but both are taxed the same way. Here's a 30,000 foot view of it:

$10,000 Starting Value	$200 Dividends	$800 Capital Gain
$11,000 Ending Value		

When you bought the stock, you already paid taxes on the $10,000—since it is after tax money. It obviously wouldn't be fair to make you pay taxes on it again, so the $10,000 number becomes your ***cost basis*** and any growth above that is a capital gain.

So if dividends and long-term capital gains are taxed the same way, why does the IRS make a distinction? Because you pay tax on dividends every year, in the year you receive them, *even if the dividends stay inside the investment account*. On the other hand, you only pay capital gains *when you sell the investment*. After you've paid taxes on the dividends, you get an *adjustment in your cost basis*. If you sold the stock the next year, your cost basis is $10,200, not the $10,000 you started with, because you already paid taxes on $200 of it. So then we could amend our chart to add this tax information:

$10,000 Starting Value	$200 Dividends	$800 Capital Gain
$10,200 Year End Adjusted Cost Basis		$800 Capital Gain
$11,000 Ending Value		

If there's a decline in the account and the year end value is $9,000, it *still* earned the $200 in dividends, but it now sits at a capital loss. Yes, this means that you pay taxes on an account that went down in value. Here's a graphic of what it would look like:

$10,000 Starting Value	$200 Dividends
$10,200 Year End Adjusted Cost Basis	$-1,200 Capital Loss
$9,000 Ending Value	

So, while it feels unfair to pay taxes on the dividends of an investment that has gone down in value, if you sell it at a loss, you can recoup taxes you paid.

One more really important feature with how the IRS measures cost basis is death. When a person dies, all capital gains go away and the cost basis "steps up" to the value on the date of death. In the above example, if they died and the value was $11,000 on their date of death, the cost basis immediately jumps up from $10,200 to $11,000. That $800 in gain then becomes tax free, skipping taxation entirely. Conversely capital losses also go away, which is why they should continuously be harvested each year. This point is going to be very important soon when we talk about annuities. This is what the picture looks like at death:

$10,000 Starting Value	$200 Dividends	$800 Capital Gain
$10,200 "Stepped Up" Cost Basis at Death		$800 Capital Gain
$11,000 Ending Value		

Here's a point of confusion. If you own a bond, then you are earning interest. Think of having a mortgage. You pay interest on your loan, the mortgage company gets that interest. Often in the investment world they will call bond interest "dividends," particularly when talking about mutual fund yields. Even though the IRS may call the interest "dividends," they consider it "interest income" and tax it as ordinary income. I'll wait here while you reread that. An unhelpful mixing of terms.

If the bond goes up in value then it will experience a capital gain and if you hold it for more than a year it is a long-term capital gain. This is true for all types of bonds: government, corporate, or municipal. Municipal bonds have special tax treatment that may be of *interest* to you if you pay a lot in taxes. Did you see how I did that? Just after I whined about using terms differently, I threw a pun in there. We'll talk about municipal bonds next, but first I owe you a story.

Whether it is technically a dividend or interest, and regardless of how it is taxed, investment statements normally generalize these regular payments as "income." I've found that this can be confusing to clients as it seems to imply that it's value doesn't go up and down. Hot off the press is an example from *yesterday*.

BAM!!! Our coffee cups rattle as the eighty-year-old man in front of me slams his fist on the table. We are at my favorite coffee shop near my first home, full of college kids on laptops. At the loud sound, the clickety-clack of their typing stops and I feel dozens of sideways eyes assuming this elderly man's anger was directed at me, that young business man in front of him. **BAM!!!** He hits the table again, breathing short panicked breaths, and says, "I feel like I'm going to have a heart attack." I believe him. He rubs his chest to calm himself. I feel a roomful of eyes on me. I say to him, in an awkwardly elevated volume loud enough to divert the accusing eyes, "Don't shoot the messenger. We'll fix this."

In the short time that I've known Tom, I've found him to be one of the most intelligent octogenarians I've ever met. He understands investments better than probably 95% of my clients and 70% of my fellow financial advisors. Oh how I wish I was making this up.

Several weeks ago when he called to set up the meeting, I could immediately sense his deep knowledge and lifelong experience investing. I bluntly told him that based on the questions he was asking me, he knew more than most advisors and suggested he consider doing it on his own. Tom is by no means a poster-child of the vulnerable elderly.

Yesterday morning was the first time we reviewed his existing accounts at another firm. He told me that his accounts were earning 9% in *income* on an annual basis. The investment company he works with (a very big one you would know) takes out 1.5% in management fees, and he was taking the remaining 7.5% as his personal *income*. Hopefully you're picking up on how I'm using the term "income" in two different ways.

There were a lot of red flags in what he was saying. As it turned out, technically, yes, his investments were giving him 9% in "income" (in the form of dividends) but his account was down about **11.5%** in *value* in the past 12 months … and he was charged 1.5% in management fees (and it wasn't disclosed to him that his investments themselves also had internal nontransparent expenses that added another 1.7% or so in fees).

His 12 month math looked something like this:

+9% in income
-1.5% in management fees
-7.5% in his withdrawals (what he was taking out as literal income to supplement his retirement)
<u>**-11.5%** as account performance (-1.7% from hidden fees)</u>

Net result … -11.5%

Was he lied to? Well, it *is* true that he was getting 9% in *income*, right? ... Right? It got worse. I recognized the investments they put him in and knew that they were likely self-liquidating, and that some of his "income" was actually getting his own money back as what they enigmatically called a "managed distribution." While the investments paid 9%, the fine print said that if the underlying holdings don't generate enough income, they sell off some of the assets and give the money to you as "income." For the worst holding, 93% of the "income" was his own money going back to him. That detail gave the illusion that it was performing as advertised.

On average over half his "income" was merely his own money being returned to him. The 9% income was actually less than 4.5% and he was being charged another 3.2% in total fees (a real return of 1.3%). Plus the investments were highly volatile. You can see why Tom was pounding on the table in anger. This may seem tangential, but in a moment it will make sense why I'm going into this. For now, the point is that income ain't the whole picture. Where the income comes from matters a great deal.

Municipal Bonds

I have a special place in my heart for municipal bonds. As you know, my belief is that people should generally be invested almost entirely in equities and that bonds don't have a sustaining place in a long-term portfolio, at all. And to hell with what you feel comfortable with. However, being a financial advisor in the real world, I have a limited ability to overcome people's psychology. In a nutshell, investing in stocks worries them regardless of how much I try to educate them to feel otherwise.

Over the years, I've generally found municipal bonds a happy home for people who can't stomach full-on stock market volatility. A municipal bond (the cool kids call them "muni bonds") is a bond that lends money to local municipalities like a state, county, public transportation district, airport, etc. The interest that you earn from them is federally tax free. Tax free forever, not tax deferred. Also, the interest you earn steps up your cost basis as well—which lends itself to some excellent tax harvesting opportunities. If you live in the city or state where the municipal bond is issued, then it is also state and city tax free (or "triple tax exempt"). Bonds issued from U.S. territories (such as Puerto Rico and Guam) are also triple tax exempt.

You have to be careful if you are drawing out Social Security. Social Security is taxed based on your "combined income." You may remember how "nontaxable interest" adds directly to your "combined income" and makes your Social Security more vulnerable to taxation.

Let's say your adjusted gross income is $18,000. You get $24,000 from Social Security and aren't earning nontaxable interest:

Social Security Taxation without Municipal Bond Interest	
Your adjusted gross income	$18,000
+ Nontaxable interest	+ $0
+ Half of your Social Security benefits	+ $12,000 (half of $24,000)
= Combined Income	= $30,000 ... none of your Social Security is taxed

Let's say you have $1,000,000 in the bank earning **0%** interest. You put it into municipal bonds earning **5%** in interest and now have $50,000 in nontaxable interest. Now this is your combined income:

Social Security Taxation without Municipal Bond Interest	
Your adjusted gross income	$18,000
+ Nontaxable interest	+ $50,000
+ Half of your Social Security benefits	+ $12,000 (half of $24,000)
= Combined Income	= $80,000 ... 85% of your Social Security is taxed

In this example, since 85% of $24,000 becomes taxed, if you pay **25%** in taxes, then this amounts to $5,100. In a sense, you could subtract this from the municipal bond interest and say that—net of all taxation—your bonds are delivering for you $44,900 more money (or **4.49%** versus what seems like **5%**).

The moral of the story goes back to one of the main thrusts of this book: all financial decisions must take the full financial picture into consideration. On the face of it, it might sound like a no-brainer to put a bunch of money in municipal bonds, but there is a bigger picture to consider. If you are on the edge of the Social Security tax brackets, a little bit of nontaxable interest could actually be financially worse than not earning interest at all.

If we are trying to compare taxable interest with tax free interest, we have to do a little math to get an apples for apples number. If you have a taxable bond paying you **5%** and you pay **20%** in taxes, then you end up with **4%** after taxes. This is the same money in your pocket as having a **4%** tax free bond.

This is important to keep in mind when you look at municipal yields because we are all accustomed to seeing pre-tax interest rate. If you see a CD quoted at **2%**, most people don't think, "But I'm paying **27.4%** in taxes so this is *actually* **1.452%**." Because our familiarity is with pre-tax interest when you earn it, the way that you convert a municipal yield into a "if it were pre-tax yield" is with this equation:

Municipal Bond Yield ÷ (1 - your effective *federal* tax rate)

If it is double or triple tax exempt then you need to also subtract your state, and possibly local, taxes as well.

Municipal Bond Yield ÷ (1 - your effective federal tax bracket - state tax rate - local tax rate)

For example, if you had a municipal bond from *another state* yielding **4.88%** and you pay **27.4%** in federal taxes, this would be the math:

4.88% ÷ (1 - 27.4%) = 6.72%

If the bond was in your state and you pay **5%** in state taxes and **1%** local taxes, this would be the math:

4.88% ÷ (1 - 27.4% - 5% - 1%) = 7.33%

In other words, a taxable bond or CD paying you **7.33%** will net you the same as a triple tax exempt bond paying you **4.88%**. But that's not the end of the story. Bond prices are subject to price fluctuation. Over the years I've sometimes had clients who want to be 100% in municipal bonds, which is utterly undiversified. Unfortunately, the only way to get tax free yield is from municipal bonds, so there's nothing to diversify with that is also tax free. Every couple of years the municipal bond market experiences something that upsets it and values drop across the board.

In any given year, you may get *income* of **4.88%** (or whatever yield), but the value of your portfolio may go down by more than this. On the other hand, it may go up by more than this. This fluctuation is treated just as any other capital gain or loss. In practice, you can choose less volatile (and lower yielding) or more volatile (and higher yielding) bonds.

To be clear, let's pretend the stock numbers from earlier were a municipal bond. The bond is earning **2%** tax free and experienced an additional **8%** capital gain—which to note, is not a normal thing, but I want to keep the numbers the same for simplicity. This would be your chart:

$10,000 Starting Value	$200 Tax Free Dividends	$800 Capital Gain
$10,200 Year End Adjusted Cost Basis		$800 Capital Gain
$11,000 Ending Value		

The yellow indicates money you don't have to pay taxes on (the money you paid into it and the tax free dividends). If the value went down, this is what it looks like:

$10,000 Starting Value	$200 Tax Free Dividends
$10,200 Year End Adjusted Cost Basis	$-1,200 Capital Loss
$9,000 Ending Value	

You actually get an inflated capital loss because of how the IRS steps up your cost basis with tax free dividends. A key thing to keep in mind is that yield ain't everything, and you have to look at the whole picture.

Mutual Funds

For the most part, mutual funds are taxed similarly to stock, but they can get funky. Mutual funds normally have a dividend, which is taxed like a dividend. If it goes up in value, it's taxed when you sell it as either a long or short-term capital gain. This is the normal part.

The weird thing with mutual funds is when they incur *internal* short and long-term capital gains that are passed along to the shareholders. Think of a mutual fund as if it were a person holding a bunch of stocks. Inevitably, those stocks go up and down in value and are sold with gains or losses. But it's a fund, not an person, so those taxes are passed along to the shareholders.

What this means is that mutual funds have two layers of taxation. The personalized one that you experience in the form of dividends and capital gains tax, along with an *internalized* layer for *the fund's* capital gains that it spreads among shareholders. If a mutual fund holds a stock for a really long time and sells it at a capital gain, this gain is divided up and passed along to shareholders *regardless of when you entered the fund*.

Here's an extreme example. Let's say there's a mutual fund that you invested in one year ago. The mutual fund has a large variety of stocks. Among them is one stock that has done really well that the fund has owned for 50 years. When it sold this year, the stock incurred a huge long-term capital gain. It's a mutual fund, so this capital gain is passed along to the shareholders. Let's say the fund experienced a **5%** capital gain. If you have $10,000, then you have to pay taxes on a $500 capital gain, even though you personally didn't enjoy the growth of that stock. No, this isn't fair. That's part of why mutual funds can have bad surprises.

Most of the time capital gains are not as extreme as my example, but over the years I have seen some doozies. I once saw an entire mutual fund company get bought out and merge with another one. The new company saw it fit to liquidate the entire portfolio of stocks before they came over and investors had massive capital gains even if they were new to the fund. Each year, mutual funds will declare their internal short and long-term capital gains. These inevitably incur as the fund buys and sells the investments they manage.

This can get really ugly when the stock market substantially goes down and people are panicking out and selling their mutual funds. The mutual fund has to sell off stock in its portfolio to get money to meet redemptions. Sometimes funds have no choice but to incur capital gains. This means that in a year like 2008, some mutual fund investors saw their portfolio go down 50% or more *and got a big tax bill* on top of it—even though they didn't sell anything personally.

ETFs

ETF stands for Exchange Traded Fund. This is an area that has seen rapid growth and it wouldn't surprise me if in time they outsized mutual funds in assets. This won't happen any time soon though—society is far too embedded with mutual funds. Pound for pound, I think ETFs are better than mutual funds. ETFs offer constant liquidity (you can buy and sell them throughout the day). Best of all, a well-managed ETF won't usually have those pesky internal capital gains that mutual funds have—it is easier to predict taxation and avoid bad tax surprises.

If you had two identical portfolios: one made of mutual funds and one made of ETFs, the ETF one is almost always more tax efficient. With my clients, when I can, I primarily use ETFs in managing their money. Taxwise, if the ETF incurs a dividend or a capital gain, it's treated just like a stock. They also marry well with my philosophies. ETFs are far more efficient when you are going to hold onto an investment during a down market.

Annuities

Annuities can be taxed in a variety of ways depending mostly on whether or not you annuitize them. If you *don't* annuitize them and simply take a withdrawal from them, then they are taxed LIFO (Last In First Out)—the other method is FIFO (First In First Out).

To explain the difference, when you take $1.00 out of an account, does the IRS consider that dollar as coming from the money you started with that was "first in" or is the dollar from the growth that was "last in"? If we say the dollar is from the money you started with, we are treating it as FIFO. If we are saying that dollar is growth or interest, or the *last* dollar to go into it, we are treating the $1.00 withdrawal as LIFO.

Annuities are taxed LIFO. If you start with $10,000 and it grows to $11,000, you have a $1,000 gain. If you take out $1,000, it's 100% taxable as a withdrawal and counted as *ordinary income*. Assuming no growth, any additional money withdrawn is not taxed, because you're just taking your original principal back.

A benefit of annuities is that the growth occurs on a *tax deferred* basis. You don't have to pay taxes on the dividends or internal gains *until you make a withdrawal*. The money you would have paid in taxes gets to hang out in the account for as long as you'd like—you are earning interest on money that you would have given up to Uncle Sam. Sounds like a great deal right?

Not so fast. In my opinion, the benefits of tax deferral are *way* overstated. That's because of how the gains are taxed. When you take the money out of an annuity, you pay *ordinary income* taxes on the growth. This income is normally *on top of* your current income, which means that it is effectively being taxed at your top tax bracket and possibly beyond. This can be especially ugly if the annuity has a big gain on it. Closing it out would be like giving yourself a massive paycheck—and taxed accordingly.

You may find this news bitter after years of people trumpeting the assumed benefits of tax deferral. Let's look at two identical accounts with identical starting balances, identical growth, and taxes that stay the same. Just to make sure we're on the same page:

1. In the Taxable Account, dividends and capital gains are taxed at the long-term capital gains rate.
2. In the Annuity Account, no taxes are paid until you take it out when all growth is taxed as ordinary income.

We'll assume these accounts are starting with $10,000 and they are in the **25%** tax bracket, which means that they would pay **15%** in taxes. I am also assuming that all taxes are paid from the accounts themselves. Here is what the next thirty years looks like:

Taxable Account | Annuity Account

	Beginning Value	Dividend	Ending Value (before taxes)	Ending Value (after taxes)	Cost Basis	Capital Gain	After Tax Closeout Amount	Beginning Value	Deferred Value	Capital Gain	After Tax Closeout Amount	Value Difference (before taxes)	Value Difference (after taxes)
Year 1	$10,000	$200	$11,000	$10,970	$10,200	$770	$10,855	$10,000	$11,000	$1,000	$10,750	$30	($105)
Year 2	$10,970	$219	$12,067	$12,034	$10,419	$1,615	$11,792	$11,000	$12,100	$2,100	$11,575	$66	($217)
Year 3	$12,034	$241	$13,237	$13,201	$10,660	$2,541	$12,820	$12,100	$13,310	$3,310	$12,483	$109	($338)
Year 4	$13,201	$264	$14,522	$14,482	$10,924	$3,558	$13,948	$13,310	$14,641	$4,641	$13,481	$159	($468)
Year 5	$14,482	$290	$15,930	$15,887	$11,214	$4,673	$15,186	$14,641	$16,105	$6,105	$14,579	$218	($607)
Year 6	$15,887	$318	$17,475	$17,428	$11,531	$5,896	$16,543	$16,105	$17,716	$7,716	$15,787	$288	($757)
Year 7	$17,428	$349	$19,170	$19,118	$11,880	$7,238	$18,032	$17,716	$19,487	$9,487	$17,115	$369	($917)
Year 8	$19,118	$382	$21,030	$20,973	$12,262	$8,710	$19,666	$19,487	$21,436	$11,436	$18,577	$463	($1,089)
Year 9	$20,973	$419	$23,070	$23,007	$12,682	$10,325	$21,458	$21,436	$23,579	$13,579	$20,185	$572	($1,274)
Year 10	$23,007	$460	$25,308	$25,239	$13,142	$12,097	$23,424	$23,579	$25,937	$15,937	$21,953	$699	($1,471)
Year 11	$25,239	$505	$27,763	$27,687	$13,647	$14,040	$25,581	$25,937	$28,531	$18,531	$23,898	$844	($1,682)
Year 12	$27,687	$554	$30,455	$30,372	$14,201	$16,172	$27,947	$28,531	$31,384	$21,384	$26,038	$1,012	($1,908)
Year 13	$30,372	$607	$33,410	$33,319	$14,808	$18,511	$30,542	$31,384	$34,523	$24,523	$28,392	$1,204	($2,150)
Year 14	$33,319	$666	$36,650	$36,550	$15,474	$21,076	$33,389	$34,523	$37,975	$27,975	$30,981	$1,425	($2,408)
Year 15	$36,550	$731	$40,206	$40,096	$16,205	$23,891	$36,512	$37,975	$41,772	$31,772	$33,829	$1,677	($2,683)
Year 16	$40,096	$802	$44,105	$43,985	$17,007	$26,978	$39,938	$41,772	$45,950	$35,950	$36,962	$1,965	($2,976)
Year 17	$43,985	$880	$48,384	$48,252	$17,887	$30,365	$43,697	$45,950	$50,545	$40,545	$40,409	$2,293	($3,288)
Year 18	$48,252	$965	$53,077	$52,932	$18,852	$34,080	$47,820	$50,545	$55,599	$45,599	$44,199	$2,667	($3,621)
Year 19	$52,932	$1,059	$58,225	$58,067	$19,911	$38,156	$52,343	$55,599	$61,159	$51,159	$48,369	$3,093	($3,974)
Year 20	$58,067	$1,161	$63,873	$63,699	$21,072	$42,627	$57,305	$61,159	$67,275	$57,275	$52,956	$3,576	($4,349)
Year 21	$63,699	$1,274	$70,069	$69,878	$22,346	$47,532	$62,748	$67,275	$74,002	$64,002	$58,002	$4,125	($4,746)
Year 22	$69,878	$1,398	$76,866	$76,656	$23,743	$52,912	$68,719	$74,002	$81,403	$71,403	$63,552	$4,747	($5,167)
Year 23	$76,656	$1,533	$84,322	$84,092	$25,277	$58,815	$75,269	$81,403	$89,543	$79,543	$69,657	$5,451	($5,612)
Year 24	$84,092	$1,682	$92,501	$92,248	$26,958	$65,290	$82,455	$89,543	$98,497	$88,497	$76,373	$6,249	($6,082)
Year 25	$92,248	$1,845	$101,473	$101,197	$28,803	$72,393	$90,338	$98,497	$108,347	$98,347	$83,760	$7,151	($6,577)
Year 26	$101,197	$2,024	$111,316	$111,013	$30,827	$80,185	$98,985	$108,347	$119,182	$109,182	$91,886	$8,169	($7,098)
Year 27	$111,013	$2,220	$122,114	$121,781	$33,048	$88,733	$108,471	$119,182	$131,100	$121,100	$100,825	$9,319	($7,646)
Year 28	$121,781	$2,436	$133,959	$133,594	$35,483	$98,110	$118,877	$131,100	$144,210	$134,210	$110,657	$10,616	($8,220)
Year 29	$133,594	$2,672	$146,953	$146,552	$38,155	$108,397	$130,293	$144,210	$158,631	$148,631	$121,473	$12,079	($8,819)
Year 30	$146,552	$2,931	$161,207	$160,768	$41,086	$119,682	$142,815	$158,631	$174,494	$164,494	$133,371	$13,726	($9,445)

Let's focus on the numbers in the 30th year. On the face of it, it would seem like it's much better to have a tax deferred annuity account. At the end, here are the balances:

1. Taxable Account: $160,768
2. Annuity Account: $174,494

   Difference = **$13,726**

It looks like the annuity is much better, but this ignores the large capital gain that each account is sitting on and how that annuity gain is taxed as ordinary income. If you were to close each account and pay taxes, here is what you'd end up with:

1. Taxable Account: $142,815
2. Annuity Account: $133,371

   Difference = **-$9,445**

The tax deferred annuity ends up with $9,445 *less* money than the taxable account. In the words of Paul Harvey, "And now you know … the rest of the story." I should note the power of compounding eventually makes tax deferral better, but this wouldn't happen until the 58th year. 58 years may not sound like a long time for a young whippersnapper such as yourself, but people rarely get annuities before age 50. Namely because if you take money out of an annuity before the age of 59 ½ there is a 10% penalty. This is separate from, but similar to, the penalty on Traditional IRAs.

This example also ignores the near-certain reality that the fees in annuities are normally higher than an ordinary account. On the other hand, it also ignores the various guarantees available through annuities that no brokerage or advisory account can make. For the moment, our focus is on taxes.

With such a long perspective, it's safe to say that outside of miraculous life-extending technology, the benefits of tax deferral probably won't happen within your lifetime. Speaking of kicking the bucket, there is one final negative tax kicker with annuities. You may remember how I said that taxable accounts get a "step-up" in cost basis at death. As a visual refresher:

$10,000 Starting Value		$200 Dividends	$800 Capital Gain
$10,200 "Stepped Up" Cost Basis at Death			$800 Capital Gain
$11,000 Ending Value			

To use our taxable account example above, after 30 years the value of the account was $160,768, but of this amount, $119,682 was a capital gain. Of this gain, **15%** of it was due in taxes once the investments were sold ($119,682 x **15%** = $17,952). Which means that after taxes, you end up with $142,815. Let's say at the end of these 30 years, the person dies. The day before they die, this is the situation:

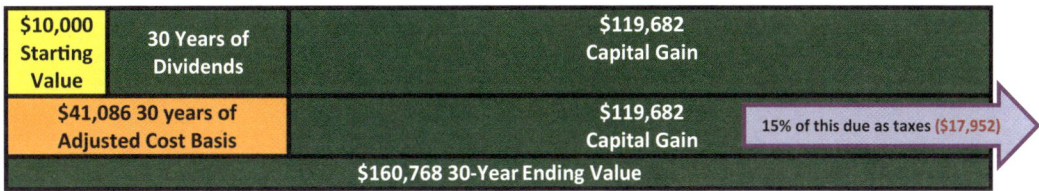

The day after they die, this is their situation:

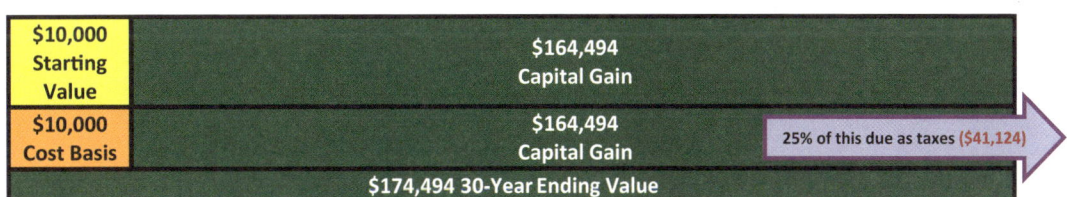

That $17,952 due in taxes simply goes away upon death *for the heirs*. For annuities, it's a vastly different picture because you don't get that step-up in cost basis. The heirs have to pay the capital gain (at the higher ordinary income tax rate) whenever the money is taken from the annuity. Again, looking at that 30th year, the day before they die, this is the situation:

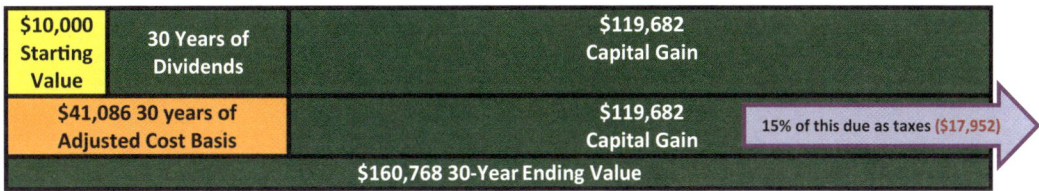

The day after they die, this is their situation:

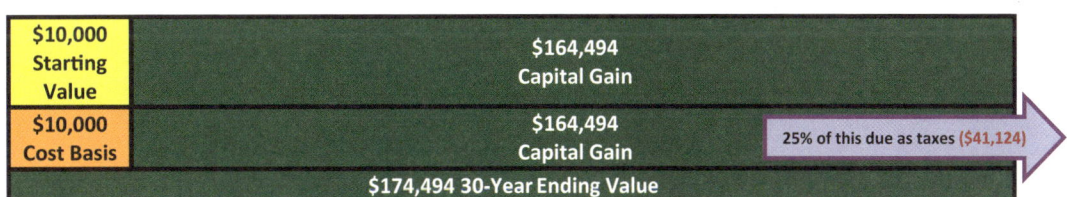

Before you hurt yourself straining to see the difference, you should probably know that there isn't one. So while the benefits of tax deferral *may* happen after 58 years, you'll likely die by that time. When you do, the taxable account gets a step-up in cost basis and wins the race. In time, compounding eventually makes tax deferral *actually* become beneficial ... after 106 years. I'll spare you the table showing this. After a *century*, on an after-tax basis, tax deferral eventually finds its value.

Personally, I would never ask anyone to commit to anything where the visible benefits are that long term. Particularly considering my notion that it's unlikely that our own descendants will even know our names 106 years from now. Keep in mind that any amount of fee that you pay for the right of tax deferral only pushes these years even more into the distant and anonymous future.

The moral of the story is that there are benefits to annuities, but tax deferral ain't one of them. When considering an annuity, focus primarily on the guarantees as a value in exchange for fees and more favorable taxation. I feel that I should point out that we are still in the non-retirement account section. If a Traditional IRA is in an annuity, it is money that has never been taxed, that will be taxed upon withdrawal and taxed entirely as ordinary income regardless of how much you put into it and whether it grew or not.

Taxes on Annuitized Annuities

Just as a reminder, so far we've discussed normal withdrawals from an annuity. An annuity may have a guarantee on it called a Guaranteed Minimum <u>Withdrawal</u> Benefit (or GMWB). An insurance company may guarantee that you will be able to get a percent of the value for the rest of your life, even if the annuity runs out of money. It should be noted that this is really the key benefit of an annuity—when you can get a guarantee on income or growth from an insurance company. Nothing else that an individual can get does this. A *withdrawal* benefit means that as you get those payments, if the account is sitting on a gain, then the entire payment is counted as ordinary income. Again, annuities are taxed LIFO as ordinary income.

However, if you annuitize your annuity contract then it is taxed differently. An annuity may have a guarantee on it called a Guaranteed Minimum <u>Income</u> Benefit (GMIB), which is taxed according to a special IRS equation spreading out the capital gains over many years based on your life expectancy. The IRS sees each payment partly as a return of your original deposit (tax free) and partly as growth (taxable).

It should be noted that the theme of this book is taking in the whole picture when you make financial decisions. Solely looking at the taxation aspect of it, one may be tempted to annuitize their annuity contract. But doing so may cause problems in other areas, as well as causing you to lose control of the assets.

Tax Loss Harvesting—A Little Taste of Death

Inevitably the stock market goes down (on average, barely less than half of all trading days are negative). Similarly, the stock market is frequently down for an entire year or will experience deep intra-year declines. Tax loss harvesting from temporary capital losses is a strategy to lower your tax bill. Let's say you have a stock that goes down in value this year:

$300,000 Starting Value	$6,000 Dividends
$306,000 Year End Adjusted Cost Basis	$-25,000 Capital Loss
$281,000 Ending Value	

If you sold it, you'd have a $25,000 capital loss that you could still write off on your *ordinary income* taxes (you can write off up to $3,000 per year). To be clear, long-term capital *gains* are taxed at the *lower* capital gains tax rate. Capital *losses* are written off against the *higher* ordinary income tax rate. Also, any amount that you are unable to write off (because of the cap) can be carried forward to the next year.

The term for this is a capital loss carryover (or synonymously as "carryforward loss") that you can tap into in future years. Here is what the next nine years would look like:

Capital Loss: $25,000		
	Ordinary Income Write Off	Capital Loss Carryover
2017	$3,000	$22,000
2018	$3,000	$19,000
2019	$3,000	$16,000
2020	$3,000	$13,000
2021	$3,000	$10,000
2022	$3,000	$7,000
2023	$3,000	$4,000
2024	$3,000	$1,000
2025	$1,000	$0
TOTAL	$25,000	

I once took on a client who was 75 years old and had a $180,000 carryover loss (ahem, from a previous broker). It would take him 60 years to write this off. If he were to pass away, this carryover loss goes away and all his accounts get a step-up in cost basis (his family would lose out on the potential tax write-off). What we did instead was to let his investments go up about $150,000 in gain and then sell them. We let the $150,000 capital gain be offset by $150,000 of the capital loss carryover, leaving him $30,000 to write off over the next 10 years. Upon death, one final carryover loss can be used on the final tax return.

In the investment section, the overarching point was that you should generally sell investments never, like never ever. Does this contradict it? The short answer is no. There is a big difference between selling in panic and strategic selling. Besides, selling doesn't necessarily mean selling and going to cash (which is characteristic of panic-selling). Generally those wanting to harvest their capital losses are wise enough to know that they also risk being on the sidelines of the stock market and seeing it rebound while they are trying to carve out tax savings. So let's go a little deeper into the strategy.

The IRS knows about this tax avoidance strategy. They block it *a little* with the Wash-Sale Rule. The rule makes sure that you are not simply selling and then re-buying the same stock or security to establish a loss. There is a waiting period of 30 days before or after the date of the sale (a total of 61 days). In other words, you can't sell the stock and buy it back right away. Nor can you buy up the same amount of money in the stock with other money and then sell your existing holding as a loss.

Methods More Likely to Get Around the Rule

The rule states that you can't write off a loss if you buy a "substantially identical" security within the 30-day before and after window. If the goal is to minimize your down time in the market—which our philosophy says should nearly always be your objective—the big question is, "What counts as *substantially identical*?" Obviously, exchanging common stock of the same company is identical. But so is exchanging common stock for preferred stock. They are "substantially identical." However exchanging a company's stock for their bonds is not "substantially identical." If the stocks are two separate companies, they are also not substantially identical, even if they are of the same industry. You could sell the stock of ABC Airline and buy the stock of XYZ Airline and then after 30 days reverse the money back to ABC Airline.

Another strategy is to proportionally allocate funds away from a holding with a loss. Take the money and spread it among your other holdings, wait 30 days, and then put it all back to the original holding. This doesn't spare you if the original holding pops up in price and the others don't. However, this approach is a more diversified way of doing it than the ABC Airline/XYZ Airline switch.

Another method is to switch an indexed fund with a managed fund or vice versa. This would likely hold up in an IRS audit—the managed fund would get their feathers ruffled being accused of being "substantially identical" to an indexed fund. If you are an indexed investor you can do a *slight* shift in where it is. Switch out a large cap for either a mid-cap or a mega cap. Or, switch a value fund for a growth fund. You should be fine moving from one managed fund to another.

Generally these strategies should hold up in an IRS audit. From an investing standpoint, it should be enough to mostly guard you from having money on the sidelines in cash for a month. If you want to be a little more daring and are okay with the risk of the IRS raining down on your tax loss harvesting parade, here are some more iffy methods that may not pass the "substantially identical" test.

Methods That are Less Likely to Get Around the Rule

XYZ S&P 500 Index Fund is not going to be *radically* different than ABC S&P 500 Index Fund except that they are at different companies and have slightly different expense ratios. They are technically different, but virtually the same. Swapping those gets as close as I think you can get to establishing a loss without changing your portfolio. But this may not pass the test to an IRS auditor. Could you switch out an Indexed ETF for an Indexed Mutual Fund? Is that *more* different? Yes, but is it different enough? More importantly, do you want your tax strategy to force an IRS auditor to make a judgment call?

Methods That Won't Get Around the Rule

Those of you familiar with stock options may be thinking, "Can't I just buy an option that would lock in a sideways buyback price?" Nope. The rule states that you can't have an option or contract to acquire shares when you establish a capital loss. The same is true for put options because the cost basis gets added onto the new shares. If what I'm talking about doesn't sound vaguely familiar, don't worry about it because it doesn't work anyway.

Summary

It should also be noted that short-term losses throw a (albeit small) wrench in the gears of this, and the rules are a little different. All the more reason to have a professional advise you before you do this. Tax loss harvest season is usually the same time as citrus season (December), though far more sour if you do it wrong. With large tax loss harvesting, such as with that seventy-five-year-old client of mine, if you do it right, it's like you get a free cost basis step-up without the nuisance of dying. It's important to remember that although capital gains go away upon death, so do capital losses along with the opportunity to harvest them.

Taxes on Retirement Accounts

Taxation on retirement accounts is much more simple. The IRS doesn't care how it grows, if the growth is a dividend or a capital gain, or even whether it grows. The only thing they care about is:

1. What kind of account it is (as in whether it is a 401(k), Traditional IRA, Roth IRA, etc.)
2. When you take it out (specifically, your age when you take it out)

The names of retirement accounts can seem intimidating and confusing, but we can simplify them into two types:

1. Accounts you contribute *pre-tax dollars* to that grow *tax deferred* and that you pay *ordinary income tax* on when you withdraw the money. These are: Traditional IRAs, 401(k)s, 403(b)s, 457s, 409(a)s, Solo 401(k)s, SIMPLE IRAs, SEP IRAs, ESOPs, and a few other rare ones.
2. Accounts you contribute *post-tax* dollars to that you pay *no taxes* on when you withdraw the money. These are: Roth IRAs, Roth 401(k)s, and the new myRA.

Each of these plans have their own nuances. For the sake of discussion, we're going to simplify it. Ignore all of those names and we'll generalize them as either Traditional or Roth. These options are really just an agreement with the IRS on how they will tax you. As you are building up money in a Traditional account, you are writing off the contribution on your taxes. However when you take it out, all withdrawals are taxed as ordinary income. With Roth accounts, you don't take the tax write-off, but you don't pay taxes on withdrawals—in essence, Roths enable you to skip out on taxes normally paid on dividends and capital gains.

These accounts have a few restrictions. One is that there is a limit on how much you can contribute each year. With a Traditional account, once you contribute to it, you can't take it out before age 59 ½ or there is a **10%** penalty *and* you are also fully taxed on it. Roth accounts have these penalties, but only on the growth amount.

After age 59 ½ Traditional account withdrawals are taxed as ordinary income, Roth withdrawals are tax free. Traditional accounts also have a ***Required Minimum Distribution (RMD)*** that starts at age 70 ½. Roth accounts don't have this. When RMDs hit, you are forced to take withdrawals whether you want to or not. We'll come back to RMDs shortly.

Let's get a full view of the long-term effects of each one. Spoiler alert: generally Roth accounts are going to be better than Traditional accounts or taxable accounts. Here's another spoiler on something many people will find shocking: it is debatable whether Traditional accounts actually benefit you *at all* except for their protection in the case of bankruptcy and litigation—all retirement accounts enjoy the same protection.

On the opposite page is a familiar looking table. It compares the net result of having a taxable account versus Traditional account versus Roth account. This example shows a person starting with $10,000 in each of the three accounts and never adding money to it. They pay **25%** in ordinary taxes and **15%** on long-term gains and qualified dividends. Also, it assumes **10%** growth as **2%** in dividends and **8%** as a capital gain.

	Taxable Account							Traditional Account			Roth Account	
	Beginning Value	Dividend	Ending Value (before taxes)	Ending Value (after taxes)	Cost Basis	Capital Gain	After Tax Closeout Amount	Beginning Value	Tax Deferred Value	After Tax Closeout Amount	Beginning Value	After Tax Closeout Amount
ar 1	$10,000	$200	$11,000	$10,970	$10,200	$770	**$10,855**	$10,000	$11,000	**$8,250**	$10,000	**$11,000**
ar 2	$10,970	$219	$12,067	$12,034	$10,419	$1,615	**$11,792**	$11,000	$12,100	**$9,075**	$11,000	**$12,100**
ar 3	$12,034	$241	$13,237	$13,201	$10,660	$2,541	**$12,820**	$12,100	$13,310	**$9,983**	$12,100	**$13,310**
ar 4	$13,201	$264	$14,522	$14,482	$10,924	$3,558	**$13,948**	$13,310	$14,641	**$10,981**	$13,310	**$14,641**
ar 5	$14,482	$290	$15,930	$15,887	$11,214	$4,673	**$15,186**	$14,641	$16,105	**$12,079**	$14,641	**$16,105**
ar 6	$15,887	$318	$17,475	$17,428	$11,531	$5,896	**$16,543**	$16,105	$17,716	**$13,287**	$16,105	**$17,716**
ar 7	$17,428	$349	$19,170	$19,118	$11,880	$7,238	**$18,032**	$17,716	$19,487	**$14,615**	$17,716	**$19,487**
ar 8	$19,118	$382	$21,030	$20,973	$12,262	$8,710	**$19,666**	$19,487	$21,436	**$16,077**	$19,487	**$21,436**
ar 9	$20,973	$419	$23,070	$23,007	$12,682	$10,325	**$21,458**	$21,436	$23,579	**$17,685**	$21,436	**$23,579**
ar 10	$23,007	$460	$25,308	$25,239	$13,142	$12,097	**$23,424**	$23,579	$25,937	**$19,453**	$23,579	**$25,937**
ar 11	$25,239	$505	$27,763	$27,687	$13,647	$14,040	**$25,581**	$25,937	$28,531	**$21,398**	$25,937	**$28,531**
ar 12	$27,687	$554	$30,455	$30,372	$14,201	$16,172	**$27,947**	$28,531	$31,384	**$23,538**	$28,531	**$31,384**
ar 13	$30,372	$607	$33,410	$33,319	$14,808	$18,511	**$30,542**	$31,384	$34,523	**$25,892**	$31,384	**$34,523**
ar 14	$33,319	$666	$36,650	$36,550	$15,474	$21,076	**$33,389**	$34,523	$37,975	**$28,481**	$34,523	**$37,975**
ar 15	$36,550	$731	$40,206	$40,096	$16,205	$23,891	**$36,512**	$37,975	$41,772	**$31,329**	$37,975	**$41,772**
ar 16	$40,096	$802	$44,105	$43,985	$17,007	$26,978	**$39,938**	$41,772	$45,950	**$34,462**	$41,772	**$45,950**
ar 17	$43,985	$880	$48,384	$48,252	$17,887	$30,365	**$43,697**	$45,950	$50,545	**$37,909**	$45,950	**$50,545**
ar 18	$48,252	$965	$53,077	$52,932	$18,852	$34,080	**$47,820**	$50,545	$55,599	**$41,699**	$50,545	**$55,599**
ar 19	$52,932	$1,059	$58,225	$58,067	$19,911	$38,156	**$52,343**	$55,599	$61,159	**$45,869**	$55,599	**$61,159**
ar 20	$58,067	$1,161	$63,873	$63,699	$21,072	$42,627	**$57,305**	$61,159	$67,275	**$50,456**	$61,159	**$67,275**
ar 21	$63,699	$1,274	$70,069	$69,878	$22,346	$47,532	**$62,748**	$67,275	$74,002	**$55,502**	$67,275	**$74,002**
ar 22	$69,878	$1,398	$76,866	$76,656	$23,743	$52,912	**$68,719**	$74,002	$81,403	**$61,052**	$74,002	**$81,403**
ar 23	$76,656	$1,533	$84,322	$84,092	$25,277	$58,815	**$75,269**	$81,403	$89,543	**$67,157**	$81,403	**$89,543**
ar 24	$84,092	$1,682	$92,501	$92,248	$26,958	$65,290	**$82,455**	$89,543	$98,497	**$73,873**	$89,543	**$98,497**
ar 25	$92,248	$1,845	$101,473	$101,197	$28,803	$72,393	**$90,338**	$98,497	$108,347	**$81,260**	$98,497	**$108,347**
ar 26	$101,197	$2,024	$111,316	$111,013	$30,827	$80,185	**$98,985**	$108,347	$119,182	**$89,386**	$108,347	**$119,182**
ar 27	$111,013	$2,220	$122,114	$121,781	$33,048	$88,733	**$108,471**	$119,182	$131,100	**$98,325**	$119,182	**$131,100**
ar 28	$121,781	$2,436	$133,959	$133,594	$35,483	$98,110	**$118,877**	$131,100	$144,210	**$108,157**	$131,100	**$144,210**
ar 29	$133,594	$2,672	$146,953	$146,552	$38,155	$108,397	**$130,293**	$144,210	$158,631	**$118,973**	$144,210	**$158,631**
ar 30	$146,552	$2,931	$161,207	$160,768	$41,086	$119,682	**$142,815**	$158,631	$174,494	**$130,871**	$158,631	**$174,494**

If they closed down the accounts and take the money out at these same tax rates, then the *after tax* apples for apples result would be:

1. Roth Account—$174,494
2. Taxable Account—$142,815
3. Traditional Account—$130,871

Yes, when you look at the balances in *after tax* money, the Traditional account ends up with *less money* than even an ordinary taxable account. I imagine many people finding this surprising, if not angering.

This example is oversimplistic. Let's take this a few steps closer to reality. Here's what we'll add:

1. We'll use historical IRA maximum contribution amounts.
2. We'll use actual stock market year-by-year performance.
3. We'll use actual historical dividend yields (which affects the taxation on taxable accounts).
4. We'll also create a *fair* "total out of pocket" contribution amount based on the maximum allowed contribution to an IRA.

This fourth point takes a little bit of mental gymnastics. In a sense, someone contributing to a Roth account is contributing more than someone contributing to a Traditional account because they don't enjoy the tax write-off. It is more of a financial stretch for someone to contribute the same amount of money to a Roth. This bias helps the Roth and taxable accounts. To equalize it, we'll give the Traditional account an ancillary taxable account in which to contribute their tax savings. Here's how we'll make it fair:

Traditional Account	Roth and Taxable Account
$1,500 Contribution	$1,500 Contribution
$500 in Tax Savings Added to Taxable Account	$500 Paid to IRS in Taxes (25%)
Total out of Pocket: $2,000	Total out of Pocket: $2,000

Another detail is that Traditional IRAs started in 1974, which is when we'll start our analysis. Roth IRAs didn't exist until 1998. Thus far, the maximum IRA contribution in either account has been the same. For the sake of our analysis, we'll pretend that the Roth IRA existed between 1974–1997 and that the maximum allowed contribution was the same. It doesn't matter that it didn't exist because we are just trying to evaluate the net difference in a lifelike scenario. On the opposite page is the first account with a combination of a Traditional account and a small taxable account where the tax savings go.

	Contribution Limit	Total Return of S&P 500	Dividend Yield of S&P 500	Taxable Account								Traditional Account			Total at Closeout
				Beginning Value	Contribution	Dividend	Ending Value (before taxes)	Ending Value (after taxes)	Cost Basis	Capital Gain	After Tax Closeout Amount	Beginning Value	Tax Deferred Value	After Tax Closeout Amount	
1974	$1,500	-26.85%	4.35%	$500	$500	$22	$366	$363	$522	($159)	$386	$1,500	$1,097	$823	$1,209
1975	$1,500	36.78%	4.29%	$863	$500	$37	$1,180	$1,174	$559	$615	$1,082	$2,597	$3,553	$2,664	$3,746
1976	$1,500	23.30%	3.73%	$1,674	$500	$62	$2,064	$2,055	$621	$1,434	$1,840	$5,053	$6,230	$4,672	$6,512
1977	$1,500	-7.39%	4.47%	$2,555	$500	$114	$2,366	$2,349	$735	$1,614	$2,107	$7,730	$7,159	$5,369	$7,476
1978	$1,500	5.91%	5.13%	$2,849	$500	$146	$3,017	$2,995	$882	$2,114	$2,678	$8,659	$9,170	$6,878	$9,556
1979	$1,500	17.84%	5.22%	$3,495	$500	$182	$4,119	$4,092	$1,064	$3,028	$3,637	$10,670	$12,574	$9,430	$13,068
1980	$1,500	31.78%	5.04%	$4,592	$500	$231	$6,051	$6,016	$1,295	$4,721	$5,308	$14,074	$18,546	$13,910	$19,218
1981	$2,000	-5.48%	5.02%	$6,683	$667	$336	$6,316	$6,266	$1,631	$4,635	$5,571	$20,546	$19,420	$14,565	$20,136
1982	$2,000	20.96%	5.71%	$6,933	$667	$396	$8,386	$8,326	$2,027	$6,299	$7,382	$21,420	$25,910	$19,433	$26,814
1983	$2,000	24.08%	4.35%	$8,993	$667	$391	$11,159	$11,100	$2,419	$8,681	$9,798	$27,910	$34,630	$25,973	$35,771
1984	$2,000	5.72%	4.56%	$11,767	$667	$537	$12,440	$12,359	$2,955	$9,404	$10,949	$36,630	$38,726	$29,045	$39,993
1985	$2,000	31.21%	4.16%	$13,026	$667	$541	$17,092	$17,011	$3,497	$13,514	$14,983	$40,726	$53,438	$40,079	$55,062
1986	$2,000	18.27%	3.44%	$17,677	$667	$609	$20,907	$20,815	$4,106	$16,710	$18,309	$55,438	$65,566	$49,175	$67,484
1987	$2,000	4.85%	3.00%	$21,482	$667	$645	$22,523	$22,426	$4,751	$17,675	$19,775	$67,566	$70,840	$53,130	$72,905
1988	$2,000	16.05%	3.49%	$23,093	$667	$805	$26,800	$26,679	$5,556	$21,123	$23,511	$72,840	$84,533	$63,400	$86,911
1989	$2,000	31.06%	3.23%	$27,346	$667	$882	$35,838	$35,706	$6,439	$29,267	$31,316	$86,533	$113,407	$85,055	$116,371
1990	$2,000	-3.53%	3.49%	$36,373	$667	$1,270	$35,089	$34,899	$7,708	$27,191	$30,820	$115,407	$111,336	$83,502	$114,322
1991	$2,000	30.07%	3.24%	$35,566	$667	$1,154	$46,259	$46,086	$8,862	$37,224	$40,502	$113,336	$147,411	$110,558	$151,060
1992	$2,000	7.33%	2.97%	$46,752	$667	$1,388	$50,181	$49,973	$10,250	$39,723	$44,014	$149,411	$160,368	$120,276	$164,290
1993	$2,000	9.79%	2.77%	$50,639	$667	$1,404	$55,598	$55,387	$11,654	$43,734	$48,827	$162,368	$178,266	$133,700	$182,527
1994	$2,000	1.24%	2.80%	$56,054	$667	$1,567	$56,751	$56,516	$13,221	$43,295	$50,022	$180,266	$182,509	$136,881	$186,903
1995	$2,000	37.21%	2.49%	$57,183	$667	$1,426	$78,463	$78,249	$14,647	$63,602	$68,709	$184,509	$253,173	$189,879	$258,588
1996	$2,000	22.65%	2.15%	$78,916	$667	$1,696	$96,789	$96,535	$16,343	$80,192	$84,506	$255,173	$312,966	$234,724	$319,230
1997	$2,000	33.12%	1.75%	$97,201	$667	$1,705	$129,399	$129,144	$18,048	$111,095	$112,479	$314,966	$419,298	$314,474	$426,953
1998	$2,000	28.39%	1.47%	$129,810	$667	$1,913	$166,661	$166,374	$19,961	$146,413	$144,412	$421,298	$540,896	$405,672	$550,084
1999	$2,000	20.89%	1.24%	$167,041	$667	$2,066	$201,938	$201,628	$22,027	$179,601	$174,688	$542,896	$656,318	$492,238	$666,926
2000	$2,000	-8.32%	1.16%	$202,295	$667	$2,346	$185,472	$185,120	$24,373	$160,747	$161,008	$658,318	$603,570	$452,677	$613,685
2001	$2,000	-11.98%	1.33%	$185,786	$667	$2,478	$163,532	$163,160	$26,851	$136,309	$142,714	$605,570	$533,030	$399,773	$542,486
2002	$3,000	-22.23%	1.61%	$164,160	$1,000	$2,651	$127,671	$127,273	$29,502	$97,771	$112,607	$536,030	$416,883	$312,662	$425,269
2003	$3,000	28.39%	1.72%	$128,273	$1,000	$2,205	$164,689	$164,359	$31,707	$132,651	$144,461	$419,883	$539,086	$404,314	$548,775
2004	$3,000	10.65%	1.65%	$165,359	$1,000	$2,727	$182,969	$182,560	$34,434	$148,126	$160,341	$542,086	$599,817	$449,863	$610,204
2005	$4,000	5.51%	1.74%	$183,893	$1,333	$3,196	$194,035	$193,555	$37,631	$155,925	$170,167	$603,817	$637,117	$477,838	$648,005
2006	$4,000	13.65%	1.80%	$194,889	$1,333	$3,508	$221,483	$220,957	$41,139	$179,818	$193,984	$641,117	$728,603	$546,453	$740,437
2007	$4,000	5.24%	1.79%	$222,290	$1,333	$3,968	$233,934	$233,339	$45,107	$188,232	$205,104	$732,603	$770,978	$578,234	$783,338
2008	$5,000	-36.21%	2.40%	$235,006	$1,667	$5,647	$149,920	$149,073	$50,754	$98,320	$134,325	$775,978	$495,031	$371,273	$505,599
2009	$5,000	26.61%	2.73%	$150,740	$1,667	$4,117	$190,853	$190,236	$54,871	$135,365	$169,931	$500,031	$633,093	$474,820	$644,751
2010	$5,000	14.82%	1.95%	$191,902	$1,667	$3,751	$220,342	$219,779	$58,622	$161,157	$195,605	$638,093	$732,656	$549,492	$745,098
2011	$5,000	0.67%	1.94%	$221,446	$1,667	$4,296	$222,935	$222,290	$62,919	$159,372	$198,384	$737,656	$742,616	$556,962	$755,347
2012	$5,000	15.59%	2.08%	$223,957	$1,667	$4,663	$258,880	$258,180	$67,581	$190,599	$229,590	$747,616	$864,197	$648,148	$877,738
2013	$5,500	32.05%	2.04%	$260,014	$1,833	$5,292	$343,349	$342,555	$72,874	$269,682	$302,103	$869,697	$1,148,438	$861,329	$1,163,432
2014	$5,500	13.41%	1.94%	$344,389	$1,833	$6,694	$390,585	$389,581	$79,567	$310,013	$343,079	$1,153,938	$1,308,727	$981,546	$1,324,624
2015	$5,500	1.14%	2.03%	$391,414	$1,833	$7,939	$395,888	$394,697	$87,507	$307,190	$348,619	$1,314,227	$1,329,250	$996,937	$1,345,556
2016	$5,500	13.42%	2.13%	$396,531	$1,833	$8,463	$449,762	$448,492	$95,970	$352,522	$395,614	$1,334,750	$1,513,930	$1,135,448	$1,531,062

The total after tax value is $1,531,062.

If you don't have that ancillary taxable account then it would be $1,135,448.

On the next page is a chart of the same thing if it were just a taxable account or just a Roth account.

	Contribution Limit	Total Return of S&P 500	Dividend Yield of S&P 500	Taxable Account Beginning Value	Dividend	Ending Value (before taxes)	Ending Value (after taxes)	Cost Basis	Capital Gain	After Tax Closeout Amount	Roth Account Beginning Value	After Tax Closeout Amount
1974	$1,500	-26.85%	4.35%	$1,500	$65	$1,097	$1,088	$1,565	($478)	$1,159	$1,500	$1,097
1975	$1,500	36.78%	4.29%	$2,588	$111	$3,539	$3,522	$1,676	$1,846	$3,246	$2,597	$3,553
1976	$1,500	23.30%	3.73%	$5,022	$187	$6,193	$6,164	$1,864	$4,301	$5,519	$5,053	$6,230
1977	$1,500	-7.39%	4.47%	$7,664	$342	$7,098	$7,047	$2,206	$4,841	$6,321	$7,730	$7,159
1978	$1,500	5.91%	5.13%	$8,547	$438	$9,052	$8,986	$2,645	$6,341	$8,035	$8,659	$9,170
1979	$1,500	17.84%	5.22%	$10,486	$547	$12,357	$12,275	$3,192	$9,083	$10,912	$10,670	$12,574
1980	$1,500	31.78%	5.04%	$13,775	$694	$18,152	$18,048	$3,886	$14,162	$15,924	$14,074	$18,546
1981	$2,000	-5.48%	5.02%	$20,048	$1,007	$18,949	$18,798	$4,893	$13,905	$16,712	$20,546	$19,420
1982	$2,000	20.96%	5.71%	$20,798	$1,188	$25,158	$24,979	$6,081	$18,898	$22,145	$21,420	$25,910
1983	$2,000	24.08%	4.35%	$26,979	$1,174	$33,476	$33,300	$7,256	$26,044	$29,393	$27,910	$34,630
1984	$2,000	5.72%	4.56%	$35,300	$1,610	$37,319	$37,078	$8,866	$28,212	$32,846	$36,630	$38,726
1985	$2,000	31.21%	4.16%	$39,078	$1,624	$51,275	$51,032	$10,490	$40,541	$44,950	$40,726	$53,438
1986	$2,000	18.27%	3.44%	$53,032	$1,827	$62,720	$62,446	$12,317	$50,129	$54,927	$55,438	$65,566
1987	$2,000	4.85%	3.00%	$64,446	$1,936	$67,569	$67,279	$14,253	$53,026	$59,325	$67,566	$70,840
1988	$2,000	16.05%	3.49%	$69,279	$2,416	$80,400	$80,037	$16,668	$63,369	$70,532	$72,840	$84,533
1989	$2,000	31.06%	3.23%	$82,037	$2,647	$107,515	$107,118	$19,316	$87,802	$93,948	$86,533	$113,407
1990	$2,000	-3.53%	3.49%	$109,118	$3,809	$105,268	$104,697	$23,124	$81,573	$92,461	$115,407	$111,336
1991	$2,000	30.07%	3.24%	$106,697	$3,462	$138,776	$138,257	$26,586	$111,671	$121,506	$113,336	$147,411
1992	$2,000	7.33%	2.97%	$140,257	$4,163	$150,542	$149,918	$30,750	$119,168	$132,043	$149,411	$160,368
1993	$2,000	9.79%	2.77%	$151,918	$4,211	$166,793	$166,161	$34,961	$131,201	$146,481	$162,368	$178,266
1994	$2,000	1.24%	2.80%	$168,161	$4,701	$170,253	$169,548	$39,662	$129,886	$150,065	$180,266	$182,509
1995	$2,000	37.21%	2.49%	$171,548	$4,279	$235,389	$234,747	$43,941	$190,806	$206,126	$184,509	$253,173
1996	$2,000	22.65%	2.15%	$236,747	$5,088	$290,367	$289,604	$49,028	$240,576	$253,518	$255,173	$312,966
1997	$2,000	33.12%	1.75%	$291,604	$5,116	$388,198	$387,431	$54,145	$333,286	$337,438	$314,966	$419,298
1998	$2,000	28.39%	1.47%	$389,431	$5,738	$499,982	$499,122	$59,883	$439,239	$433,236	$421,298	$540,896
1999	$2,000	20.89%	1.24%	$501,122	$6,198	$605,815	$604,885	$66,081	$538,804	$524,065	$542,896	$656,318
2000	$2,000	-8.32%	1.16%	$606,885	$7,038	$556,415	$555,359	$73,119	$482,240	$483,023	$658,318	$603,570
2001	$2,000	-11.98%	1.33%	$557,359	$7,435	$490,595	$489,480	$80,554	$408,926	$428,141	$605,570	$533,030
2002	$3,000	-22.23%	1.61%	$492,480	$7,953	$383,012	$381,819	$88,507	$293,313	$337,822	$536,030	$416,883
2003	$3,000	28.39%	1.72%	$384,819	$6,616	$494,068	$493,076	$95,122	$397,954	$433,383	$419,883	$539,086
2004	$3,000	10.65%	1.65%	$496,076	$8,180	$548,907	$547,680	$103,302	$444,377	$481,023	$542,086	$599,817
2005	$4,000	5.51%	1.74%	$551,680	$9,589	$582,105	$580,666	$112,892	$467,775	$510,500	$603,817	$637,117
2006	$4,000	13.65%	1.80%	$584,666	$10,524	$664,449	$662,871	$123,416	$539,455	$581,952	$641,117	$728,603
2007	$4,000	5.24%	1.79%	$666,871	$11,904	$701,802	$700,017	$135,320	$564,697	$615,312	$732,603	$770,978
2008	$5,000	-36.21%	2.40%	$705,017	$16,941	$449,761	$447,220	$152,261	$294,959	$402,976	$775,978	$495,031
2009	$5,000	26.61%	2.73%	$452,220	$12,351	$572,560	$570,707	$164,612	$406,095	$509,793	$500,031	$633,093
2010	$5,000	14.82%	1.95%	$575,707	$11,254	$661,025	$659,337	$175,866	$483,470	$586,816	$638,093	$732,656
2011	$5,000	0.67%	1.94%	$664,337	$12,889	$668,804	$666,870	$188,756	$478,115	$595,153	$737,656	$742,616
2012	$5,000	15.59%	2.08%	$671,870	$13,988	$776,639	$774,541	$202,744	$571,797	$688,771	$747,616	$864,197
2013	$5,500	32.05%	2.04%	$780,041	$15,877	$1,030,047	$1,027,666	$218,621	$809,045	$906,309	$869,697	$1,148,438
2014	$5,500	13.41%	1.94%	$1,033,166	$20,081	$1,171,754	$1,168,742	$238,702	$930,040	$1,029,236	$1,153,938	$1,308,727
2015	$5,500	1.14%	2.03%	$1,174,242	$23,818	$1,187,664	$1,184,092	$262,520	$921,571	$1,045,856	$1,314,227	$1,329,250
2016	$5,500	13.42%	2.13%	$1,189,592	$25,390	$1,349,286	$1,345,477	$287,911	$1,057,567	$1,186,842	$1,334,750	$1,513,930

The total after tax value of the taxable account is $1,186,842 and the Roth account is $1,513,930. Here's a list of the results:

1. Traditional + Ancillary Taxable Account $1,531,062
2. Roth $1,513,930
3. Taxable $1,186,842
4. Traditional $1,135,448

Keep in mind that these are the results of the **25%** tax bracket where you also pay **15%** tax on dividends and long-term gains. These are the results of all the tax brackets:

After Tax Comparison of the Different Types of Accounts

	10.0%	15.0%	25.0%	28.0%	33.0%	35.0%	39.6%
Orinarary Income Rate	10.0%	15.0%	25.0%	28.0%	33.0%	35.0%	39.6%
LT Gains/Dividend Rate	0.0%	0.0%	15.0%	15.0%	15.0%	15.0%	20.0%
Traditional + Ancillary Taxable Account	$1,530,752	$1,554,005	$1,531,062	$1,551,580	$1,598,898	$1,623,124	$1,629,756
Roth Account	$1,513,930	$1,513,930	$1,513,930	$1,513,930	$1,513,930	$1,513,930	$1,513,930
Taxable Account	$1,513,930	$1,513,930	$1,186,842	$1,186,842	$1,186,842	$1,186,842	$1,091,077
Traditional Account	$1,362,537	$1,286,841	$1,135,448	$1,090,030	$1,014,333	$984,055	$914,414

There are a few surprising things:

1. If you look at *just* the three bottom options, in every instance the Traditional is the worst long-term option ... *even worse* than just doing an ordinary taxable account. That's because of how gains are taxed. The benefits of tax deferral don't outweigh the benefits of paying the lesser long-term gains and qualified dividend tax rate.
2. The results of the Roth account are the same in all tax brackets. This may not be surprising after thinking through it a little. If you are contributing money to something that you already paid taxes on, the results will be the same no matter what tax bracket you're in.
3. The Traditional account *only outperforms* if you actively use your tax savings to save into the stock market in a different account. If you do this, it outperforms everything. If you don't, it underperforms everything.

All things considered, I suggest getting a Roth account. Bite the bullet and pay the taxes—you'll thank me when you're older. For extra credit, push yourself to also do a normal taxable account. Maximizing out your IRA contribution should be the first priority in saving for retirement. Unless you have a 401(k) with a matching contribution—then maximize that first. If your 401(k) has a Roth 401(k) option, do that.

One could easily critique this by saying that people don't normally stay in the same tax bracket their whole lives. It really wouldn't change it. You can see that in every scenario the accounts stay in the same order of best to worst.

Historically speaking, our taxes right now are on the low side. This should edge you toward the wisdom in putting money in a Roth account. If taxes are higher in your retirement (either because taxes increase or because you have a lot of income to tax), then this all the more makes sense. Just get them over with.

These examples show a 43 year sweep of saving up money. If we imagine a household with a few cute little tax exemptions running around, on average your taxes are going to be less than **25%**. Keep in mind what we said before about how a family may be in the **25%** tax bracket, but they only pay **16.48%** in taxes (or whatever the actual lower number is). The lower your taxes, the more you should bite the bullet, pay the minimal taxes, and get a Roth versus a Traditional.

Please note that I added the ancillary taxable account to make the annual out-of-pocket amount the same. In reality, I've personally *never* seen anyone do this. People just seem to contribute to their Traditional account and enjoy the tax savings and spend the money. If you don't actually save up your tax savings into a separate investment account, it is actually better to *not* do a Traditional account and instead do a taxable account. This feels crazy even writing it, but the math doesn't lie. It's really interesting how much society seems to emphasize the importance of opening a Traditional IRA to get the tax write-off, when in reality it just causes you to have really ugly taxes in retirement and less flexibility in your spending. It is also said that the more you pay in taxes, the more suitable it is to do a Traditional IRA. This is sort of true. It's only true if you actually use your tax savings to additionally save up money. Otherwise Roth the night away.

Protection of Investments Accounts from Bankruptcy and Litigation

Retirement accounts enjoy a special protection from creditors, even in the case of bankruptcy and litigation: creditors can't go after your retirement funds. Two exceptions to this are tax liens and if you embezzled money from a retirement plan. In the case of bankruptcy, up to $1,283,025 is protected—in my experience, you don't come across a heck of a lot of IRAs over a million dollars. Litigation protection is similar, but varies depending on the state where the lawsuit is filed. However, before you skip down the street and file bankruptcy, know that every state is different and any such drastic decision must be met with a heap of professional advice.

High Income Situations

It should also be noted that Roth IRAs have an income limit. For 2017, if you filed a joint return and your modified adjusted gross income is over $196,000 then you can't contribute to a Roth IRA ($133,000 if you are single). There is, however, a work-around using a Roth conversion—more on that in a minute.

Traditional IRAs don't have a contribution income limit, but once your income is above a certain amount then you can't deduct the contribution off your taxes. If you can't take the deduction, you aren't taxed on that money when you take it out, but only taxed on the capital gains at the ordinary tax rate instead of the *lower* capital gains rate. I can't see why anyone would do this unless they are purposely paying more in taxes to shield money from litigation and bankruptcy.

If your income is above the Roth limit, there is also a way to do a back-door Roth IRA contribution. Make a nondeductible Traditional IRA contribution and immediately do a Roth conversion on the funds. If you do this right away, you won't have any earnings and no taxes to pay on those earnings. Effectively it's the same thing as just contributing to a Roth in the first place. Best of all, there is no income limit for a Roth conversion.

Roth Conversion

Those of you who have been persuaded by the relative merits of a Roth IRA may have also heard of a Roth conversion and wonder if this makes sense. Let's go over how this works. Any retirement funds that you convert into a Roth are fully taxed as ordinary income *when you convert them*. As soon as the funds are in Roth world, they grow tax free and can be withdrawn tax free as long as it's in accordance with the Roth IRA withdrawal rules.

First of all, if you're younger than 59 ½, you need to be able to pay the taxes from money other than the IRA itself (otherwise it will have a 10% early withdrawal penalty). Secondly, if you have a big IRA and do it all at once, keep in mind that this may move you into a higher tax bracket.

Let's go back to our single filer earning $100,000, who is in the **28%** tax bracket:

Single Filers				
Marginal Tax Rate	**TAX BRACKETS**		**Income Earned in Range**	**Taxes Paid from Range**
	Over	**But Not Over**		
10.0%	$0	$9,325	$9,325	$933
15.0%	$9,326	$37,950	$28,624	$4,294
25.0%	$37,951	$91,900	$53,949	$13,487
28.0%	**$91,901**	**$191,650**	$8,099	$2,268
33.0%	$191,651	$416,700	$0	$0
35.0%	$416,701	$418,400	$0	$0
39.6%	$418,401		$0	$0
			Ordinary Taxes	**$20,981**
			Effective Rate	**20.98%**

If you converted an entire $500,000 Traditional IRA into a Roth IRA, it would be as though you made $600,000 that year. This is what your taxes would look like:

Single Filers

Marginal Tax Rate	TAX BRACKETS		Income Earned in Range	Taxes Paid from Range
	Over	But Not Over		
10.0%	$0	$9,325	$9,325	$933
15.0%	$9,326	$37,950	$28,624	$4,294
25.0%	$37,951	$91,900	$53,949	$13,487
28.0%	$91,901	$191,650	$9,249 + $89,300	$2,590 + $18,345
33.0%	$191,651	$416,700	$222,199	$73,326
35.0%	$416,701	$418,400	$1,699	$595
39.6%	$418,401		$186,802	$73,974

Total Income	$600,000
Ordinary Taxes	$187,542
Effective Rate	31.26%

Although our imaginary person is in the **28%** tax bracket, they only pay **20.98%** in taxes. But any amount you convert will be taxed at your *top* tax bracket, and possibly higher if the conversion amount pushes you into the next bracket. I chose an extreme number to show you how converting the whole thing could make part of it taxed at **39.6%**.

There are ways to strategically do this:

1. One of the more obvious ways is to convert it over a number of years. In this example, before the conversion there is still room for $89,300 to be taxed at only **28%**. You could pace the conversion over a six year period and eventually have it all converted.
2. Do the conversion when you are have a low income year. If you are between jobs, traveling the world, on sabbatical, going back to school, unemployed, or starting a business then there could be an opportunity to convert your IRA at a lower tax rate.
3. If the stock market drops deep into bear market territory, convert it. However much the market is down should be viewed as a direct tax discount opportunity.
4. Another way is one that applies to small business owners. If you have a Sole Proprietorship, LLC, S Corporation or pretty much *anything but* a C Corporation that has a net operating loss (an unused loss), then you might be able to do an *unlimited* tax free Roth Conversion up to the loss amount. This would make the funds entirely tax free. This is perfectly legal, but plan to experience some IRS scrutiny if you do this.

If you know people with small businesses, you may want to grab some scissors and cut that paragraph out for them. You'll earn a new best friend. If they are really struggling and facing bankruptcy, you may also want to cut out that other paragraph about IRA assets (usually) bypassing bankruptcy. Yes, so this means that someone may have a $1,000,000 Traditional IRA and a business with a $1,000,000 net operating loss. They could pay no taxes while converting the Traditional IRA to a Roth IRA as they zero out the loss. Then they could declare bankruptcy and wipe all their debt out, while keeping their primary residence (so long as they keep paying the mortgage and it's under the equity maximum). If they are over 59 ½ they could take out the (now) Roth IRA money tax free, pay off their house with the taxes they would have paid, and retire off the rest. Now, if you need help getting the stink off your soul, I can't help you much. This is however a very good example of the considerable benefit of professional advice. There is a vast difference between having a tax preparer and a tax *planner*.

To close out, let's look at a real(ish) world example of a Roth conversion. We'll assume a straight **10%** growth (**2%** dividend + **8%** capital gain) and a person in the **33%** tax bracket (higher because of the conversion) who pays **15%** in long-term capital gains and qualified dividends. In the spirit of apples for apples, we're going to compare two different scenarios for $100,000.

Door #1 is to convert the Traditional IRA to a Roth and pay the $33,000 in taxes out of pocket. Door #2 is to leave the Traditional IRA alone and to keep that $33,000 aside in an ancillary ordinary taxable account. It's crucial to take this $33,000 "opportunity" cost into effect. Here are the results:

	Door #1		Door #2							
	Convert Traditional IRA to Roth, Taxes Paid Out of Pocket		Leave Traditional Alone, Use the Money You Would Have Paid in Taxes to Invest in the Market							
	Roth IRA		**Traditional IRA**		**Taxable Account**					
Year	Balance	Out of Pocket Cost	Balance	After Tax	Before Tax	After Tax	Before Tax Total	After Tax Total	Before Tax Difference	After Tax Difference
Year 0	$100,000	$33,000	$100,000	$67,000	$33,000	$33,000	$133,000	$100,000	($33,000)	$0
Year 1	$110,000		$110,000	$73,700	$36,201	$35,820	$146,201	$109,520	($36,201)	$480
Year 2	$121,000		$121,000	$81,070	$39,712	$38,913	$160,712	$119,983	($39,712)	$1,017
Year 3	$133,100		$133,100	$89,177	$43,565	$42,307	$176,665	$131,484	($43,565)	$1,616
Year 4	$146,410		$146,410	$98,095	$47,790	$46,029	$194,200	$144,124	($47,790)	$2,286
Year 5	$161,051		$161,051	$107,904	$52,426	$50,113	$213,477	$158,017	($52,426)	$3,034
Year 6	$177,156		$177,156	$118,695	$57,511	$54,593	$234,667	$173,287	($57,511)	$3,869
Year 7	$194,872		$194,872	$130,564	$63,090	$59,507	$257,962	$190,071	($63,090)	$4,801
Year 8	$214,359		$214,359	$143,620	$69,210	$64,898	$283,569	$208,519	($69,210)	$5,840
Year 9	$235,795		$235,795	$157,982	$75,923	$70,812	$311,718	$228,795	($75,923)	$7,000
Year 10	$259,374		$259,374	$173,781	$83,288	$77,300	$342,662	$251,080	($83,288)	$8,294
Year 11	$285,312		$285,312	$191,159	$91,366	$84,417	$376,678	$275,575	($91,366)	$9,736
Year 12	$313,843		$313,843	$210,275	$100,229	$92,224	$414,072	$302,499	($100,229)	$11,344
Year 13	$345,227		$345,227	$231,302	$109,951	$100,788	$455,178	$332,091	($109,951)	$13,136
Year 14	$379,750		$379,750	$254,432	$120,617	$110,184	$500,366	$364,616	($120,617)	$15,134
Year 15	$417,725		$417,725	$279,876	$132,316	$120,490	$550,041	$400,366	($132,316)	$17,359
Year 16	$459,497		$459,497	$307,863	$145,151	$131,797	$604,648	$439,660	($145,151)	$19,837
Year 17	$505,447		$505,447	$338,650	$159,231	$144,200	$664,678	$482,850	($159,231)	$22,597
Year 18	$555,992		$555,992	$372,514	$174,676	$157,806	$730,668	$530,321	($174,676)	$25,671
Year 19	$611,591		$611,591	$409,766	$191,620	$172,732	$803,210	$582,498	($191,620)	$29,093
Year 20	$672,750		$672,750	$450,742	$210,207	$189,106	$882,957	$639,849	($210,207)	$32,901
Year 21	$740,025		$740,025	$495,817	$230,597	$207,068	$970,622	$702,885	($230,597)	$37,140
Year 22	$814,027		$814,027	$545,398	$252,965	$226,773	$1,066,992	$772,171	($252,965)	$41,856
Year 23	$895,430		$895,430	$599,938	$277,502	$248,389	$1,172,932	$848,327	($277,502)	$47,103
Year 24	$984,973		$984,973	$659,932	$304,420	$272,101	$1,289,393	$932,033	($304,420)	$52,940
Year 25	$1,083,471		$1,083,471	$725,925	$333,949	$298,114	$1,417,419	$1,024,039	($333,949)	$59,431
Year 26	$1,191,818		$1,191,818	$798,518	$366,342	$326,650	$1,558,159	$1,125,168	($366,342)	$66,650
Year 27	$1,310,999		$1,310,999	$878,370	$401,877	$357,954	$1,712,876	$1,236,323	($401,877)	$74,676
Year 28	$1,442,099		$1,442,099	$966,207	$440,859	$392,294	$1,882,958	$1,358,501	($440,859)	$83,599
Year 29	$1,586,309		$1,586,309	$1,062,827	$483,622	$429,966	$2,069,931	$1,492,793	($483,622)	$93,517
Year 30	$1,744,940		$1,744,940	$1,169,110	$530,533	$471,291	$2,275,474	$1,640,401	($530,533)	$104,539

The before tax and after tax difference is key. The Traditional and taxable account are taxation ticking time bombs. The benefits of conversion *in after tax* dollars are found almost immediately.

In this 30-year sweep, converting the Traditional IRA puts $104,539 more in your pocket *in after tax dollars*. The more you pay in taxes, the truer this is. Here's a chart of results for the current tax brackets:

	10.0%	15.0%	25.0%	28.0%	33.0%	35.0%	39.6%
Orinarary Income Rate	10.0%	15.0%	25.0%	28.0%	33.0%	35.0%	39.6%
LT Gains/Dividend Rate	0.0%	0.0%	15.0%	15.0%	15.0%	15.0%	20.0%
Roth Conversion Account	$1,744,940	$1,744,940	$1,744,940	$1,744,940	$1,744,940	$1,744,940	$1,744,940
Traditional + Ancillary Taxable Account	$1,744,940	$1,744,940	$1,665,744	$1,656,240	$1,640,401	$1,634,065	$1,619,493
Difference After Taxes	$0	$0	$79,196	$88,700	$104,539	$110,875	$125,447

We have assumed a **10%** growth rate. The greater the growth, the more it makes sense to convert it. Any kind of positive growth still shows a benefit of conversion. Where this *really* doesn't make sense is if you are in a high tax bracket when you convert the IRA and a lower tax bracket when you would have drawn money out of the Traditional IRA—which is easily an imaginable retirement scenario.

The verdict: convert it. Or at least convert parts of it. A middle of the road approach would be to "fill up" the remainder of your tax bracket with a Roth Conversion. It may take a very long time to convert it depending on which bracket you're in. My bias is to get your taxes as low as possible in retirement. In my observation, many of the nickel and dime "gotcha" taxes have to do with how they count modified adjusted gross income. When you are 70 ½, you are forced to take withdrawals which will push your income higher. A Roth IRA puts the power in your hands, since there is no required distribution.

The other exception to keep in mind is that if you are planning to give your Traditional IRA to charity (either while you are living or whilst turning up daisies), don't convert that portion of it. If you have a $100,000 Traditional IRA and want to gift $25,000 to charity when you die, then only convert $75,000 of it and make the charity the sole beneficiary of the $25,000 Traditional IRA, because nobody will ever be taxed doing it this way. Keep in mind that if you don't gift it before you turn 70 ½ then you'll still have to take your Required Minimum Distributions, which we'll talk about next.

It's important to re-emphasize that the benefits of tax deferral are *way* overblown unless you are *absolutely* going to be in a lower tax bracket in retirement *and* taxes don't go up. It's hard to know this and it's impossible to know tax rates for the future. The truth is that if you pay the same amount in taxes as you do in retirement, all tax deferral is doing is building up money *for the government*.

Required Minimum Distributions (RMDs)

While working with clients, I've found that RMDs are perhaps a slightly over-dreaded event. The deadline for taking your first Required Minimum Distribution from your Traditional IRA is the April 1st after you turn 70 ½. Yes, "the April 1st after you turn 70 ½" is really the rule. I would give anything to have been at the IRS meeting that came up with that. I don't want to take the fun away from you in figuring out your RMD date. Going forward after this first distribution, your deadline is then December 31st of each year. This means that if you wait until April 1st for your first distribution, then you'll end up taking two RMDs in one year.

As far as how much they require you to take out, it is (shocker) a weird IRS equation. I'm going to put it in plain English. Think of the distribution as a percent of the balance. The balance is, of course, a moving target, so they use the balance on December 31st of the previous year. In terms of how much they require you to take out, this percentage goes up as you get older.

Note the purple "RMD (%)" column. Your first distribution is 3.65% of the balance, the next year it goes up to 3.77%, then 3.91%, 4.05%, 4.20%, etc. Below is a table, and on the next page, you can see graphically what it would look like over the course of a very long life.

Required Minimum Distributions (RMD)

Age	Balance	RMD (%)	RMD ($)	Monthly Amount	Age	Balance	RMD (%)	RMD ($)	Monthly Amount
70	$100,000	3.65%	$3,650	$304	95	$148,747	11.63%	$17,296	$1,441
71	$104,350	3.77%	$3,938	$328	96	$143,350	12.35%	$17,698	$1,475
72	$108,761	3.91%	$4,248	$354	97	$137,121	13.16%	$18,042	$1,504
73	$113,213	4.05%	$4,584	$382	98	$130,048	14.08%	$18,317	$1,526
74	$117,687	4.20%	$4,945	$412	99	$122,135	14.93%	$18,229	$1,519
75	$122,157	4.37%	$5,334	$445	100	$113,677	15.87%	$18,044	$1,504
76	$126,595	4.55%	$5,754	$480	101	$104,727	16.95%	$17,750	$1,479
77	$130,968	4.72%	$6,178	$515	102	$95,355	18.18%	$17,337	$1,445
78	$135,268	4.93%	$6,663	$555	103	$85,646	19.23%	$16,470	$1,373
79	$139,426	5.13%	$7,150	$596	104	$76,027	20.41%	$15,516	$1,293
80	$143,430	5.35%	$7,670	$639	105	$66,594	22.22%	$14,799	$1,233
81	$147,234	5.59%	$8,225	$685	106	$57,123	23.81%	$13,601	$1,133
82	$150,788	5.85%	$8,818	$735	107	$48,092	25.64%	$12,331	$1,028
83	$154,033	6.13%	$9,450	$787	108	$39,608	27.03%	$10,705	$892
84	$156,905	6.45%	$10,123	$844	109	$32,072	29.41%	$9,433	$786
85	$159,335	6.76%	$10,766	$897	110	$25,205	32.26%	$8,131	$678
86	$161,316	7.09%	$11,441	$953	111	$19,090	34.48%	$6,583	$549
87	$162,780	7.46%	$12,148	$1,012	112	$14,035	38.46%	$5,398	$450
88	$163,655	7.87%	$12,886	$1,074	113	$9,760	41.67%	$4,066	$339
89	$163,861	8.33%	$13,655	$1,138	114	$6,474	47.62%	$3,083	$257
90	$163,315	8.77%	$14,326	$1,194	115	$3,909	52.63%	$2,057	$171
91	$162,054	9.26%	$15,005	$1,250	116	$2,164	52.63%	$1,139	$95
92	$160,013	9.80%	$15,688	$1,307	117	$1,198	52.63%	$631	$53
93	$157,127	10.42%	$16,367	$1,364	118	$664	52.63%	$349	$29
94	$153,330	10.99%	$16,849	$1,404	119	$367	52.63%	$193	$16

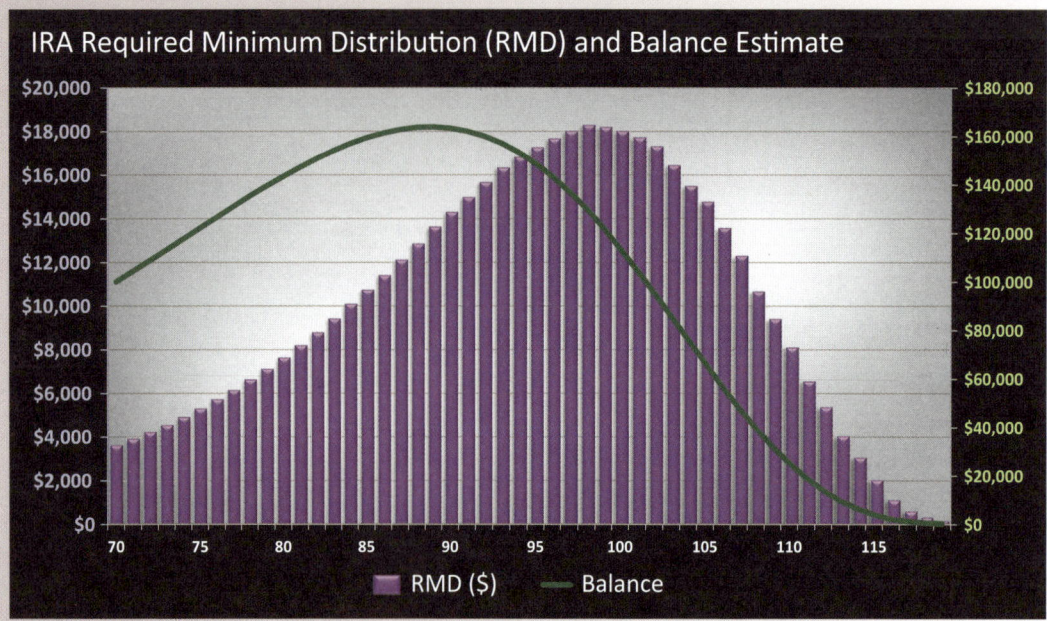

IRA Required Minimum Distribution (RMD) and Balance Estimate

In this graph, we are assuming they start with $100,000 balance earning a straight **8%** per year. If that balance was $100,000 and your RMD is 5% of that balance, then they require you to take out $5,000 from your IRA. They do this because they want to get the tax money. If your tax rate is **25%**, then you pony up $1,250 in taxes and keep the $3,750. You can do whatever you want with it. I have some clients who put that money right back into the market in an ordinary taxable account. I have others who have their account automatically send the RMD to them in November and this becomes their holiday spending money.

You can see that under ordinary growth circumstances, the IRA balance keeps growing up into their late 80s and the RMD amount doesn't peak until the owner is in their late 90s. Naturally, if you are in the market, the growth rate shifts this around. If you robbed the cradle and your spouse is more than 10 years younger than you, your RMD is slightly less. Once again, Roth IRAs are exempt from RMDs.

Taxes on Educational Savings Accounts

There are a few options when it comes to saving up money for education. The two main ones are:

1. Coverdell Education Savings Account (ESA)
2. 529 Plans

Taxwise, both ESAs and 529s work similar to a Roth IRA. Contributions are not deductible, but withdrawals and gains come out tax free when they are used for education. When you open it up, you declare one specific "beneficiary" (the child) per account.

Coverdell Education Savings Account (ESA)

Formerly called an Education IRA, the named changed because "IRA" stands for … Individual *Retirement* Account. With ESAs, you are eligible to contribute $2,000 per year to them if your joint modified adjust gross income is less than $220,000 (or $110,000 for an individual). You can't add money to it once the beneficiary is 18. The entire account must be withdrawn and closed out by the time the beneficiary reaches age 30.

The beneficiary doesn't have to be your dependent. Anybody can contribute to any minor's ESA. You are eligible to use the account for some K–12 expenses, but it is generally geared toward college. When you pull money out, the withdrawals are tax free if they are used for education.

You can change the beneficiary, so long as the new beneficiary is a qualified family member (or spouse) of the original beneficiary. A qualified family member of the beneficiary may be: the *beneficiary's* sibling, half-sibling, step-sibling, child, grand-child, parent, niece, nephew, aunt, uncle, first cousin or the spouse of any of these people and if any of these are by adoption or marriage. Yes, you could transfer it to your adopted nephew-in-law.

Withdrawals for non-education reasons are taxed on the gains at the ordinary income rate *for the beneficiary* and they are also hit with a 10% penalty on the gains.

529 Plans

Taxwise, 529 Plans are similar to an ESA. A big difference is the contribution amount. Most plans have a lifetime contribution maximum of $300,000 and there are no income limits. This becomes particularly opportunistic for those who embrace the time value of money coupled with investing in stocks with education money. We'll talk about this in a minute with regard to how to invest the funds.

529s also don't have the eighteen-year-old contribution age limit, nor the requirement to withdraw by 30 years of age. Like an ESA, you must name a beneficiary and can change it to a qualified family member of the previous beneficiary. Also, funds can stay in a 529 plan as long as you'd like. Considering the broad definition of a family member combined with the lack of age restrictions, a 529 plan could become a family's multi-generation source for college funding. We'll talk about that in moment as well.

Withdrawals for non-education reasons are taxed on the gains at the ordinary income rate *for the owner* (not the beneficiary) and they (the owner) are also hit with a 10% penalty on the gains.

Effects on Financial Aid

For financial aid purposes, ESAs and 529s are treated the same way. The account is considered an asset of the owner. This is potentially much better than if it was considered the student's personal assets. If the owner is not the parent or guardian, then the account is potentially "off the radar" for qualifying for aid—or, at least it wouldn't be rocket science to take it off the radar.

How to Invest the Money

Investing 529 plans is perhaps a discussion that belonged in the investment chapter. However, I felt it would be good to put it here to serve as a nice refresher on the time value of money.

Often I come across 529s and ESAs with small balances. This is also true of minor investment accounts and small IRAs. Normally, investment firms charge annual fees for small accounts ($50 is normal). It's important to do the math of what this is as a *percentage basis*. If I were to tell you that I'd open an account for you, but charge you 10% of your assets *every year*, you probably wouldn't be too keen on it. But that's exactly what a $50 is to a $500 account. When an account is small, *any* kind of annual fee can be a substantial headwind to growth.

The wincingly named "myRA" was created in 2014 to help young people battle this. It is an IRA account held with the U.S. Treasury Department. It's similar to a Roth IRA, but is designed for small balances and young people trying to build up their accounts to the point where they won't have an annual fee. You can start with as little as $25 and once it reaches $15,000, or when the owner reaches age 30, it rolls to a private institution.

In the chapter on investments, the key point is that you usually have a very long investment time horizon and should therefore be (nearly) entirely in equities. Education is an exception. It is one of the few things that has a very specific time horizon and possibly dollar amount. According to the U.S. Department of Education[1], for the 2012–2013 school year, this was the average cost for one year of education (tuition, fees, room, and board):

- Public four-year College $17,474
- Private four-year College $35,074

These numbers are increasing at a rate *greater* than inflation. Therefore, in real money, college is becoming a greater expense. From 2003–2013, the cost of college went up by 65% (*even in* inflation adjusted dollars, the cost went up by 30%). Over that decade, this represents an education inflation rate of 5.16%.

If we use this 5.16% college education inflation rate number, we can project the costs. Let's say we have a little baby born today named Natalie. Once she's 18 she will go to a public four-year college. We'll take the 2012/2013 academic school year's cost of college and project forward her cost 19–22 years from now when she enters an undergraduate program. Here are the costs:

Pre-College				College			
Preschool	Elementary School	Middle School	High School	Freshman	Sophomore	Junior	Senior
Years 1-18				$45,421	$47,763	$50,226	$52,816

The total is $196,227. The big question is: what is the time horizon? Starting out, my recommendation would be to invest 100% in equities. Yes, I mean it. Historically, bear markets of **20–30%** declines happen every five years and last on average a little under two years. Bear markets of **30–40%** declines happened every ten years and lasted a little over two years. Extreme bear markets of **40–50%** declines happened every 17.5 years and last about five years.

The chief concern is that when Natalie graduates high school, and her college funds are down **50%** and must effectively withdraw half of the account to pay for only one year of the education. To account for this risk, I would back off equities and go into low volatility investments when *the money will be spent* within three years. Because of this, you can imagine the account balance as being in four different chunks of money for four different spending events:

Pre-College				College			
	High School			Freshman	Sophomore	Junior	Senior
Freshman	Sophomore	Junior	Senior				
$45,421 in Equities	$45,421 for Freshman Year in Cash			$45,421			
$47,763 in Equities		$47,763 for Sophomore Year in Cash			$47,763		
$50,226 in Equities			$50,226 for Junior Year in Cash			$50,226	
$52,816 in Equities				$52,816 for Senior Year in Cash			$52,816
Years 1-18				$45,421	$47,763	$50,226	$52,816

This method of strategic selling is not flawless, but under normal circumstances this will enable you to stay in the market as long as you responsibly can. It also has the added psychological benefit of being entirely in cash when Natalie graduates high school. If this is too aggressive for you, shift the planned selling to earlier dates. If we assume a **10%** interest rate that goes until the money goes to cash, this is how much you need to fund it on the day Natalie was born:

Pre-College				College			
	High School			Freshman	Sophomore	Junior	Senior
Freshman	Sophomore	Junior	Senior				
$9,885 at Birth	$45,421 for Freshman Year in Cash			$45,421			
$9,450 at Birth	$47,763 for Sophomore Year in Cash				$47,763		
$9,034 at Birth	$50,226 for Junior Year in Cash					$50,226	
$8,636 at Birth	$52,816 for Senior Year in Cash						$52,816
Total Investment at Birth: $37,005				Total College Cost: $196,227			
Years 1-18				$45,421	$47,763	$50,226	$52,816

If someone invested $37,005 in equities at birth, it should get you pretty close to the full 4-year cost of college. A 529 would enable you to put all this money into it the day Natalie is born. On the other hand, the ESA would force you to do it in chunks and weaken the power of time on the account's growth.

Some may say it is nuts to invest college money in equities. I would argue that at an education inflation rate of 5.16%, it's nuts not to. Know that in the 22 year sweep of Natalie's pre-career you should expect to see around five bear markets. It's likely that at least one of them will happen while Natalie is in high school. Just be prepared for how this psychological event may tempt you. The whole point behind this plan is to keep the foot on the gas, but guard you from being forced to take out money in the pits of a bear market. If the stock market is down considerably, and you are scheduled to pull money out, talk to your advisor about waiting for a little recovery. You have a three year time cushion, which would be an above average time for recovery.

Now I know what you're thinking, "But Chad, if I fund Natalie's 529 plan with $37,005, then won't this trigger a gift tax on the amount that is over $14,000?" Good job. Luckily, 529s have a special gifting feature where you can gift up to $70,000 ($140,000 for a married couple). Contributions beyond this need to be spread out to avoid the gift tax.

My Two Bits

My bias is strongly in favor of 529 plans. I love the thought of fully funding one of these with $300,000 and it getting passed around a family for multiple generations. In Natalie's example, let's say a 529 plan was funded with $300,000 at her birth. Assuming a straight **8%** growth (we'll tame expectations), by the time she was 18, the balance would be $1,198,806 (plenty to choose whatever school she wanted). After four years of the above college expenses along with additional growth, the balance would still be $1,410,973.

Let's say that at age 25, Natalie has triplets who 18 years later go to college. Still using that 5.16% college inflation rate, the four year cost would be $689,665—note, this inflation rate is not economically sustainable for a society to be broadly educated. When the triplets are 18 and Natalie is 43, the account would have grown to $7,102,601. Even after four years of college, the balance would still be $7,343,466.

Let's say that when those triplets reach age 25, the each have sextuplets (a total of 18 babies). 18 years later they go to college. Natalie is now age 68, the triplets 43, and the 18 babies are 18 years old. Still using a 5.16% education inflation rate, the four year cost would be $2,423,916 *per person*. But the account has now grown to $36,965,787 and is ready to bankroll the education of 18 kids. Even after four years, the balance is still $1,377,552. Natalie is now 72, her triplets are 47 and the proud parents of eighteen twenty-two-year-old college grads. In a perfect world ...

The reality is that using *one* 529 plan account to fund 18 simultaneous college students would be tricky because you'd have to change the beneficiary multiple times each year. The other pesky thing about reality is that little Natalie may decide college isn't for her and she'd rather tour with the Stones for a few years, who will of course still be rockin' 18 years hence. While Natalie may have other qualified family members you *could* transfer it to, there may not be anyone you would *want* to transfer it to.

The tax savings are indisputable, but the restrictions may cramp your style. There is no certainty as to what the rules on 529 plans will be 72 years from now.

I also think the world is changing and Bachelor's degrees are simultaneously becoming a dime a dozen and colossally expensive. The children of today's Millennial generation will be raised by parents who spent the first decade or two of their adulthood battling down massive student debt for a degree that had questionable benefits to them. I can't help but think that this chicken may come home to roost in unfortunate ways.

Real Estate Revisited

As with anything, notably here with taxes, this is a very wide and highly detailed area. We continue onto real estate, addressing the key tax issues on a superficial level. We'll start with the easy and familiar before moving onto the particulars.

Real estate is taxed similarly to stock capital gains. Long and short-term capital gains are also split at the one year mark. Long-term gains use the purchase price as the cost basis and the capital gain is determined by the selling price. In a moment I'll go over what can adjust this, along with the difference between your primary, secondary, and investment properties. But here's a rough look:

$225,000 Purchase Price	$75,000 Capital Gain
$225,000 Cost Basis	$75,000 Capital Gain
$300,000 Selling Price	

Unlike with stock, we obviously don't get dividends each year that we pay taxes on and increase our cost basis. However, other things can either step your cost basis up or *down*. With stocks, your cost basis never adjusts down. Here's what can adjust the cost basis:

Things that *increase* basis when you purchase the home:

- Real estate commissions
- Real estate taxes owed by the seller
- Settlement fees
- Title insurance

Things that *increase* basis while you own it:

- Improvements or additions (this may include streets and sidewalks if you pay for or help pay them)
- Tax credits for home energy improvements
- Amount spent to restore home after damages

Things that *reduce* basis while you own it:

- Depreciation
- Any gain you rolled into the home as a 1031 exchange
- Deductible casualty loss not covered by insurance
- Insurance settlement amounts

This is what your capital gain situation could look like after adjustments:

$225,000 Purchase Price	$10,000 Purchase Adjustments	$65,000 Capital Gain
	$20,000 Decreased Basis Adjustments	$65,000 Capital Gain
	$50,000 Increased Basis Adjustments	$35,000 Capital Gain
$265,000 Final Cost Basis		$35,000 Final Capital Gain
$300,000 Selling Price		

So think about this in your record keeping. Don't just hoard a disorganized credenza of receipts. Your house should have a folder labeled "Cost Basis Adjustments" where you store records specifically related to this. You need to keep cost records for every improvement, such as bathroom remodels, roof replacements, additions, fencing, landscaping, driveways, upgrading electrical, etc.

Before you get worried about that $35,000 capital gain, if the home is your primary residence then you get a $250,000 capital gain exemption. If you are married, it is twice this. If the previous example is someone's primary residence, the capital gain is tax free.

In the legal planning chapter, when we talked about terrible mistakes people can make with their estate, I gave you a hypothetical example. The example was of a couple who bought a house in 1950 in Palo Alto, CA for $10,000. The house is now worth $1,000,000. Ignoring any adjustments, this means that the house has experienced a $990,000 capital gain ($10,000 is the "cost basis"). But the couple gets a $500,000 exemption, so this is what it would look like:

$10,000 Purchase Price	$500,000 Exemption	$490,000 Capital Gain
$510,000 Cost Basis		$490,000 Capital Gain
$1,000,000 Selling Price		

That capital gain is taxed at the long-term capital gain rate. Death, with the automatic step-up in cost basis, works the same way. The above chart shows their situation when either are alive. After they have both passed away, this is what happens:

$10,000 Purchase Price	$500,000 Exemption	$490,000 Capital Gain
$1,000,000 "Stepped Up" Cost Basis at Death		
$1,000,000 Selling Price		

The cost basis steps up to the value of the home on the date of death of the last owner. What about losses on real estate? You can't deduct them and therefore there are no carryover losses as with investments.

You can deduct some of the expenses of owning a home off your *ordinary income* tax. Some of these are:

1. Mortgage interest
2. The interest on a second mortgage up to a $100,000 loan amount
3. Origination fees and points you paid when you got the mortgage
4. Property tax
5. Home improvements for medical care (again this is deducting it off your *ordinary income*, as most other kinds of home improvements will adjust your *cost basis*)

Currently there are also a slew of "green" improvements (such as solar panels) for which you can receive tax credit for. My guess is that these will go away soon. The momentum toward green is marching toward a critical mass and will soon be at price parity. Tax credit is different (and much better) than a tax deduction. A tax credit directly subtracts from how much taxes are owed, while a tax deduction reduces how much income they are taxing you on.

Losing Your write-off

We touched on this briefly in the chapter on real estate, but society tends to overstate "losing their write-off" when they pay off their house. There are reasons to *not* pay off your house, but worrying about losing the write-off from their mortgage interest isn't the primary reason for this. It's an issue certainly, but it is secondary to the other reasons.

Right now 30-year mortgages are clocking in at under 4.00%. If you had a $300,000 mortgage, this means you would pay about $12,000 in mortgage interest per year. As you make your payments, your loan balance drops and so does the amount that you are paying in mortgage interest. For a married couple in 2017, the standard (when you don't itemize) deduction is $12,700, which means that you would need to have at least $700 in additional tax write-offs to even bother itemizing your deductions.

Let's go over this to show how, for most people, losing their mortgage interest deduction is no big deal. Paying $12,000 in mortgage interest costs you $12,000 out of pocket (of your gross income). Since most of our spending comes from post-tax money, you could think of it as effectively a post-tax cost of $9,000 (assuming you're in the **25%** tax bracket.) However you want to dice it, the mortgage interest you pay costs you real money. When you itemize deductions, it means that you have real money coming out of your pocket. The deduction means that some of the money you would have spent on taxes, helps (by **25%**) pay for the things you are deducting ... but you still spent the money.

When you take the standard deduction, the difference between what you actually spend and the standard deduction amount is "free" money in your pocket. It also means that you are in a comparatively better place because you managed to save money by not spending it. There are a lot of moving parts with this. Let's look at a side-by-side comparison from both a net and gross income perspective.

Itemized			Standard Deduction		
	Net	**Gross**		**Net**	**Gross**
Mortgage Interest	$9,000	$12,000	Mortgage Interest	$0	$0
Property Tax	$2,250	$3,000	Property Tax	$3,000	$4,000
Charitable Donations	$750	$1,000	Charitable Donations	$1,000	$1,333
TOTAL AMOUNT OUT OF POCKET	$12,000	$16,000	**TOTAL AMOUNT OUT OF POCKET**	$4,000	$5,333
Deductible Amount		$16,000	Standard Deduction		$12,700
25% Tax Savings (Applied to the Cost of Deductions)		$4,000	25% Tax Savings (Direct Tax Savings)		$3,175
Final Amount Out of Pocket		$16,000	**Final Amount Out of Pocket**		$825
"Free" Tax Savings		$0	**"Free" Tax Savings**		$1,842

In the itemized world, you spent $16,000. By spending it on these things, you don't have to pay $4,000 in taxes that you would have otherwise. In the standard deduction world, you are giving up the deductions in exchange for the higher standard deduction of $12,700 (for a married couple), which means that you have $3,175 less in taxes to pay. This means that effectively, the things you would have otherwise itemized are out of your net income. In this example, you spent $4,000 of money but received back $3,175, making your actual out-of-pocket cost $825.

In this scenario, you didn't have to actually spend all of the $12,700 that you are deducting, which means that $1,842 is actually "free" tax saving. You had nothing out-of-pocket, but got back $1,842—which **25%** of the difference between what you spent in gross dollars and the standard deduction. This is in contrast to the itemized example where you spent $16,000 and simply avoided $4,000 in taxes (not actually "free" tax savings).

In the real estate chapter, you may remember my objection to declaring that a 4.00% mortgage is really a 3.00% mortgage after tax. The truth is not as cut and dry because the standard deduction waiting for you with open arms. If the entire universe were just the above two scenarios, then for the itemized person, the 4.00% rate is effectively about 3.79%. Better, but *not* **25%** better as it would seem.

Hopefully this makes the thought of "losing your tax write-off" seem a little less loathsome. Many things can shift how true this may be for you, namely your tax rate or if you are a single filer and have a smaller standard deduction (only $6,350).

Second Homes

If it's a secondary home (such as a vacation home), you can similarly deduct many of these same things. If you rent out the home, the rental income must be declared and will be taxed as ordinary income. However, if you rent it out for only 14 days, the income is tax free and you don't need to declare it. Even if you are renting it out for a million dollars a day, the IRS doesn't care. You can also deduct rental expenses, which can sometimes complicate a tax return.

One thing to be aware of with second homes is that they are not eligible for the free $250,000 of cost basis ($500,000 if you are married). Thankfully that exemption can be used an unlimited amount of times, so a plausible workaround is to declare your second home your primary when you sell it. Then declare your (real) primary home your official primary home again before you sell it. These transactions need to be spaced by a period of two years. As always, talk to a tax professional before doing any of this—paying one a few hundred dollars to pick their brain for an hour could save you a very painful mistake.

Rental Homes

As far as write-offs, rentals are similar to the previous write-offs we've discussed:

1. Upkeep and maintenance
2. Costs to manage the property (including groundskeeping, property management, maintenance workers)
3. Some property improvements and repairs
4. Utilities
5. Any travel associated with managing the property

If you have rented the home for three out of the past five years, then the capital gain is taxable (there is no exemption). The one really unique thing with rental homes is depreciation. Depreciation is a very long-term process in which you simultaneously write off part of your purchase cost each year (a good thing) while reducing your cost basis (not a good thing). Let's go back to our basic example. You buy a rental house for $225,000, rent it for a number of years and then sell it for $300,000:

$225,000 Purchase Price	$75,000 Capital Gain
$225,000 Cost Basis	$75,000 Capital Gain
$300,000 Selling Price	

The normal method is to write off the depreciation annually. It is calculated as if the building becomes worthless after 27.5 years. Why that number? It was probably the same sadistic rascals who came up with the 59 ½ and 70 ½ year rules for IRAs. You can keep depreciating it until your cost basis is fully recovered. If you've done nothing to the home to *increase* your cost basis, then the math is simple: $225,000 divided by 27.5 years = $8,182 per year. Let's say you are 10 years (and $81,818) into your depreciation, this is what it would look like:

$225,000 Purchase Price		$75,000 Capital Gain
$143,182 Cost Basis	$81,818 Depreciation	$75,000 Capital Gain
$300,000 Selling Price		

When you came to sell it, you'd pay **depreciation recapture** taxes on the amount you depreciated ($81,818) and the normal capital gains from the property going up in value ($75,000) for a total of $156,818. The tax rate on the $81,818 from depreciation is taxed at **25%** and the $75,000 is at the long-term capital gains rate.

For those scratching your heads, yes the IRS entices you to write it off over a long time so they can take it all back in taxes later as a large lump of money regardless of your tax rate along the way—to note, the average person pays much less than **25%** as their actual tax rate. Now, golly, I would *never* imply that the IRS would create a rule that seems great along the way because they get more money at the end ... but that is what tends to happen.

With our house example here, if you keep the house over 27.5 years and it's fully depreciated when you sell it, you effectively just gave yourself a $225,000 paycheck which is going to send you up through the tax bracket stratosphere. So while you may have only written it off at **25%**, you end up paying it back to the IRS at the **25%**, **28%**, **33%**, etc. tax bracket.

Again, as with much of this, broad strokes. Technically the IRS doesn't allow you to depreciate the land (just the building), so even though you bought it for $225,000, the depreciable amount of the building may only be $150,000, but you get the idea.

Rental properties also enjoy an automatic step-up in cost basis after death. You may remember when we talked about estate planning how my client's parents missed out on a step-up in cost basis. As a refresher, his father built up several rental properties that were titled only in his name. He died in 1990 and his mother never put the properties in her name. When she died in 2013, the probate courts considered the properties as part of *his* estate and the step-up in cost basis was based upon the date of his death in 1990—thus missing out on the free cost basis step-up from 1990–2013.

It's worth rehashing this to make the point: be highly mindful of who technically owns the property. I can nearly promise you that at some point in your life you'll hear a friend say that they've put themselves onto their parent's property as joint owners because, "When Mom dies I get the house anyway, may as well make it simple." Hopefully, knowing what you now know about cost basis, you are invited to steal my line, "Ummm ... you *really* don't want to do that." With real estate, little mistakes = big costs.

Estate Taxes

I can hear it. Your wheels are turning. You wonder if you can transfer a property (a house or stock) into your (ahem, really old) parent's name, pining for that imminent cost basis step-up? Could you have the parent set up a trust to make it certain that it goes back to you? It seems like there are constantly new tactics and loopholes. The laws constantly change and this will always necessitate the involvement of professionals.

In the course of my career, estate laws have shifted considerably. Early on, the notion was to get assets into the hands of the younger generation through gifting and put the rest into a trust to bypass probate. Now, as we've discussed, this can be highly inefficient. It's getting less and less common for estates to pay taxes. Most will pay at least a little bit of estate *income* taxes, but not estate tax. The most recent data available shows that in 2011, only 0.13% of all estates were subject to estate tax and those that were paid 14.69% of the estate in taxes.[2] On the opposite page is what the estate tax history has been.

The blue line is tied to the left axis showing that in 1934 around 1% of all estates were subject to estate taxes. This peaked in 1976 at 7.65% before winding downward. The right axis shows the effective estate tax rate peaking in 2004 at 21.77% of the estate.

The oddball year in this was 2010, when there wasn't an estate tax. The new estate laws passed in 2013 instituted a very large exclusion that goes up with inflation. This ensures that most households will not be subject to an estate tax for the foreseeable future. For 2017, this exclusion amount is $5,490,000, or $10,980,000 for a married couple. If one spouse predeceases another, then their unused exclusion can be passed along to the second person's estate.

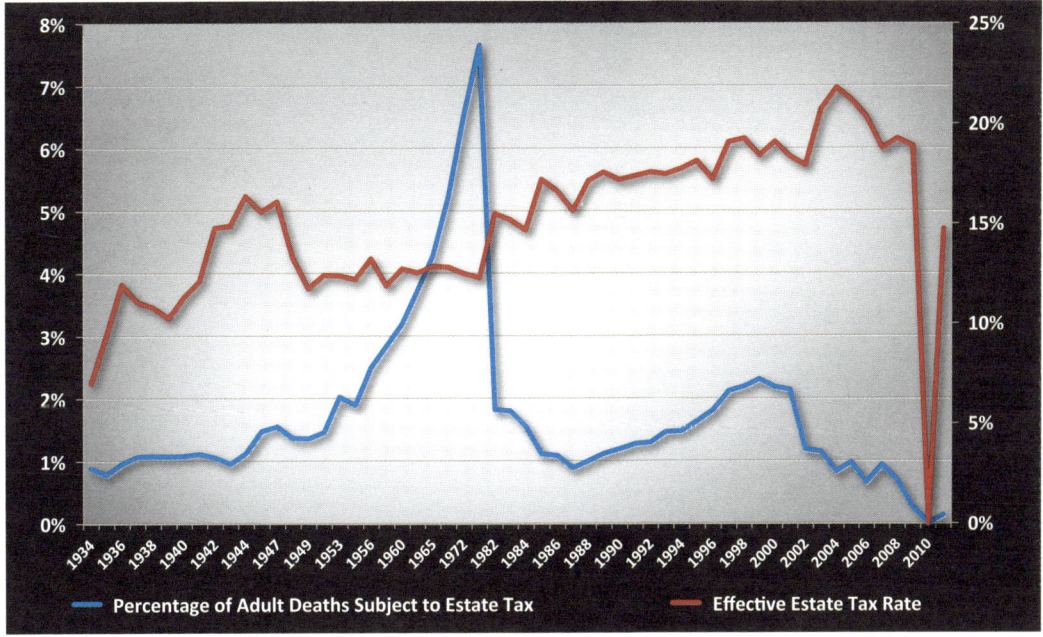

		Percentage of Adult Deaths Subject to Estate Tax	Effective Estate Tax Rate

Let's keep it simple and assume we have a single person with a $20,000,000 estate. That exclusion amount works like a free coupon, effectively reducing the amount of the estate. Any amount above that exclusion amount is taxed at **40%**. Here is a basic view of the estate:

$5,490,000 Estate Exclusion Amount	$14,510,000 Taxable Part of Estate	
$14,196,000 Inherited Amount		$5,804,000 40% Estate Taxes
$20,000,000 Estate Size		

Now what about the step-up in cost basis at death? You still get that as an *individual*, but the estate tax is an umbrella tax over everything. Without the step-up in cost basis, you would have been taxed even more as an individual when you sold the assets.

Gifting

We went over this briefly in the legal section and now we'll add some numbers. When you give larger assets (more than $14,000 in 2017) then the person *receiving* the assets also gets the cost basis. This also works for capital losses. The gift is also possibly subject to a gift tax on the part of the *donor*—not the receiver, which would make more sense.

Estate Tax Exclusion

	Year	Amount	Increase
Actual	2011	**$5,000,000**	
	2012	**$5,120,000**	2.40%
	2013	**$5,250,000**	2.54%
	2014	**$5,340,000**	1.71%
	2015	**$5,430,000**	1.69%
	2016	**$5,450,000**	0.37%
	2017	**$5,490,000**	0.73%
Projected	2018	**$5,599,800**	2.00%
	2019	**$5,711,796**	2.00%
	2020	**$5,826,032**	2.00%
	2021	**$5,942,553**	2.00%
	2022	**$6,061,404**	2.00%
	2023	**$6,182,632**	2.00%
	2024	**$6,306,284**	2.00%
	2025	**$6,432,410**	2.00%
	2026	**$6,561,058**	2.00%
	2027	**$6,692,279**	2.00%
	2028	**$6,826,125**	2.00%
	2029	**$6,962,647**	2.00%
	2030	**$7,101,900**	2.00%

If you want to gift more than the $14,000, you can subtract the additional amount out of your estate exclusion amount *before you die*. If you gift $1,014,000, the $14,000 is free of taxes, and you can also make the $1,000,000 free by reducing your future Estate Tax Exclusion amount when you die. However, keep in mind that the receiver still receives the cost basis. Earlier I mentioned that for 2017, this exclusion amount was $5,490,000. If you gave $1,000,000 away in 2012 as an exclusion and then died in 2017, your exclusion amount is $4,490,000.

Starting in 2011, the exclusion amount was set at $5,000,000 and changes every year as it increases with inflation. To the left is a chart of the real Estate Tax Exclusion (in purple) along with a *projected* amount (in blue) assuming a 2% inflation rate—which is more than what we've seen recently, but less than the historical average.

In 2017, you could give away your full exclusion amount of $5,490,000. Years later when you die, you will still have *more* Estate Tax Exclusion available as it increased over time.

Another nuance of gifting against your exclusion amount is that the *value* of your gift is determined on the day you gift it *regardless of its appreciation*. This is a strategy called **Present Value Gifting**.

Let's say in 2017 that you gift $5,490,000 in a stock that grows at **10%** until you pass away in 2030. By the time you passed away, the stock is worth $18,952,969 and you still have another $1,671,900 of your Estate Tax Exclusion. We can see this projected out on the opposite page.

Estate Tax Exclusion

	Year	Amount	Increase
Actual	2011	$5,000,000	
	2012	$5,120,000	2.40%
	2013	$5,250,000	2.54%
	2014	$5,340,000	1.71%
	2015	$5,430,000	1.69%
	2016	$5,450,000	0.37%
	2017	$5,490,000	0.73%
Projected	2018	$5,599,800	2.00%
	2019	$5,711,796	2.00%
	2020	$5,826,032	2.00%
	2021	$5,942,553	2.00%
	2022	$6,061,404	2.00%
	2023	$6,182,632	2.00%
	2024	$6,306,284	2.00%
	2025	$6,432,410	2.00%
	2026	$6,561,058	2.00%
	2027	$6,692,279	2.00%
	2028	$6,826,125	2.00%
	2029	$6,962,647	2.00%
	2030	$7,101,900	2.00%

Present Value Gifting

Stock Value	Bonus Exclusion	More Available	Total Excluded
$5,490,000	$0	$0	$5,490,000
$6,039,000	$439,200	$169,800	$6,208,800
$6,642,900	$931,104	$281,796	$6,924,696
$7,307,190	$1,481,158	$396,032	$7,703,222
$8,037,909	$2,095,356	$512,553	$8,550,462
$8,841,700	$2,780,296	$631,404	$9,473,104
$9,725,870	$3,543,238	$752,632	$10,478,502
$10,698,457	$4,392,173	$876,284	$11,574,741
$11,768,303	$5,335,893	$1,002,410	$12,770,713
$12,945,133	$6,384,075	$1,131,058	$14,076,191
$14,239,646	$7,547,367	$1,262,279	$15,501,925
$15,663,611	$8,837,486	$1,396,125	$17,059,736
$17,229,972	$10,267,324	$1,532,647	$18,762,619
$18,952,969	$11,851,069	$1,671,900	$20,624,869

Of course, inflation reality is going to dictate the exclusion target in 2030 and laws can change. Astute readers may be tying a few things together here, "If I gift that $5,490,000 away, doesn't the recipient also receive the cost basis?" Yes they do. So it's not all peaches and cream. By the time you bite the dust in 2030, the recipient would have a *large* capital gain. In reality, most people aren't going to give away a single stock holding, but instead a portfolio of stocks. As that stock portfolio grows, the dividends bring up the cost basis and hopefully they are harvesting capital losses along the way.

Even if there are no dividends, paying a **20%** capital gain on the growth amount is better than paying the **40%** estate tax on the appreciation of the money that would otherwise be above the exclusion amount. If we assume that the money was gifted without existing capital gains, this is the story:

A Tale of Two Taxes

Options	Taxable Amount	Tax Rate	Taxes
Amount Over Exclusion	$11,851,069	40%	$4,740,427
Capital Gain	$13,462,969	20%	$2,692,594
Tax Savings			**$2,047,834**

In this case, the strategy saved the person a *minimum* of $2,047,834 in taxes, but likely more if they used any amount of tax strategies. Here's the flip-side of all of this: if you don't gift the money, the stock market growth would *balloon* your estate well past the exclusion amount. Keep in mind that most of your assets count toward the value of your estate, such as your house and the lock of Elvis' hair you bought on eBay. In this hypothetical example, the inflation-increased exclusion amount would open up another $1,671,900 to exclude from estate taxes. Hopefully enough room to exclude all your other assets.

It should be said that if your estate is not going to be more than the exclusion amount, there is no reason to do this. In fact, doing this is likely *worse* for your heirs, who would miss the step-up in cost basis.

If you chose *not* to do present value gifting, and don't declare it as a gift against your exclusion amount, the person *giving* the money owes taxes on that $1,000,000 at the ordinary income tax rate. Yes, I too think this is weird. Again, the receiver also receives the cost basis. Let's say it's that Palo Alto home we talked about earlier. The elderly mother has to pay taxes on the value of the home (minus the $14,000 gift exclusion) *and* the son would have only a $10,000 cost basis on the house. So, what I'm saying is: don't do that.

Using the Present Value Gifting method opens up a lot of ancillary strategies. While it may seem natural to gift your kids your home, on average real estate appreciates much less than equities. Because of this, it would be wiser to gift assets with greater growth appreciation.

One item I would especially encourage you *never* to gift is an investment property for which you've already fully depreciated the purchasing cost. If it's fully depreciated, it means you are sitting on a capital gain along with the depreciation recapture tax. If you were to gift the property, you also gift these tax unpleasantnesses. Death erases all of this with a step-up in cost basis.

Cash doesn't have a cost basis and annuities do not get the step-up in cost basis upon death, so there is less to dodge when gifting cash. However, annuities are contracts on a person's life (not the Don Corleone type) and you are generally not able to transfer them over to someone without writing a new contract.

Charities don't pay taxes. If you want to give money to a charity, consider gifting your Traditional IRA or 401(k) money. You can (sometimes) do this when you're still alive through an **IRA Charitable Rollover**. This is an option that over the years has come and gone, so if it's available when you want to do it, don't assume you will always be able to. The rule also has caps. If you are older than 70 ½ and in your Required Minimum Distribution period, up to $100,000 of the charitable rollover can count toward your RMD. To note, your RMD is almost certainly going to be less than $100,000.

This works with any charity, but we'll paint a scenario. Let's say you are a regular churchgoer and tithe 10% of your income. I would consider tithing each year from your IRA as a charitable rollover. We can imagine someone older than 70 ½ who must take their RMDs each year. Because this is a hypothetical world, let's conveniently imagine that this RMD is exactly how much they want to tithe to their church.

Their RMD amount is $1,000 and they pay **25%** in taxes. Effectively, the amount of money that would have gone to the government goes to the charity of their choice. This is what it looks like:

Normal Distribution		Charitable Rollover	
RMD Amount	$1,000	RMD Amount	$1,000
Net Amount to Church	$750	Net Amount to Church	$1,000
Net Amount in Taxes	$250	Net Amount in Taxes	$0

In any year when people are taking distributions from a Traditional IRA and giving to a charity, they should do the distribution as a charitable rollover. It's all money from the same pot of gold and doing it this way gives your charity the money that you would have paid in taxes.

This is especially true for RMDs. Do the charitable rollover for their RMD amount. Since this is less than $100,000, all of it will count as their RMD. Since they are donating it, they won't have to pay taxes on what's effectively their RMD.

Many of my older clients no longer have many deductions. Even though they donate money, they effectively don't write it off on their taxes because it is better to take the standard deduction as we discussed before. If that's the case, your RMD is fully taxable and the donation nondeductible. By donating the RMD, you remove the income for yourself and this helps you benefit even more from the standard deduction. From an out-of-pocket perspective, it means that the "free money" via the standard deduction is all the freer. A lot of moving parts here.

If your (human) heirs inherit your *Traditional* IRA, they have to pay ordinary income taxes on it just as you did. We'll return to our example in the legal planning chapter. Let's say you have $500,000 and you want to give $100,000 to a specific charity and the remaining $400,000 to your children. If you have a $250,000 IRA and a $250,000 ordinary taxable account, gift the money from your IRA to the charity. The easiest surefire way is to make the charity a direct beneficiary on your

IRA through the account itself, but double check with your estate planning attorney. This is what it would look like assuming your heirs pay **25%** in taxes:

Doing It Correctly

Children's Inheritance		Charity Gift	
From IRA	$150,000	From IRA	$100,000
Taxes Owed	*$37,500*	*Taxes Owed*	*$0*
From Taxable	$250,000		
Taxes Owed (step up)	*$0*		
TOTAL	**$362,500**	**TOTAL**	**$100,000**

TOTAL PASSED ON: $462,500

Doing It Incorrectly

Children's Inheritance		Charity Gift	
From IRA	$250,000		
Taxes Owed	*$62,500*		
From Taxable	$150,000	From Taxable	$100,000
Taxes Owed (step up)	*$0*	*Taxes Owed*	*$0*
TOTAL	**$337,500**	**TOTAL**	**$100,000**

TOTAL PASSED ON: $437,500

This slight shift saves your kids a $25,000 tax burden. And still, they never call, they never write.

There is also a closely-related tactic of giving appreciated stock to a charity. Before you give a large donation to a charity, consider gifting stock that is sitting on a large capital gain. The taxation completely goes away once the charity takes possession of the funds.

As a closing thought on estate taxes, I have told you how early in my career, dodging estate taxes was a major theme in the industry. With the 2013 law, most of that discussion has gone away.

Because there was so much uncertainty around "what Congress will do with the estate tax" leading up to 2013, many trusts have very strong language and are oriented about doing complicated things in an attempt to avoid estate taxes. If you have a trust that was written prior to 2013, there's a pretty good chance that it is out of date and needs to be reviewed.

Contributions Taxed	Distributions Taxed
Roth IRA	Traditional IRAs and Similar
Life Insurance	
Municipal Bonds	401(k)s and Similar
529 Plan	
Both Taxed	
Taxable	
Non-IRA Annuity (growth is tax deferred)	

I bring this up because in the years since, I've heard several people in the insurance world say the same thing. You can't call anything tax free. If you ever hear of anyone tell you this, blow the whistle and throw the BS penalty flag.

The proceeds from life insurance are generally tax free, but the premiums are not. Some policies that build a cash value enable you to take loans from the cash value, but often at an interest rate paid to the insurance company. Not to mention that these policies often have many and complicated fees associated with them which likely make the remote possibility of needing a loan from it not financially sensible.

It should also be noted that life insurance proceeds add to the estate total and could push it over the exemption amount. Additionally, based on your age and income, long-term care insurance premiums can be deductible (but hybrid insurance premiums usually aren't). The policy must have specified coverages in it to be tax deductible.

Health Care and Taxes

Health care has been the biggest legislative drama of the decade up to this point. The Patient Protection and Affordable Care Act of 2010, more commonly called The Affordable Care Act or Obamacare, was both loathed and loved before anyone understood it. I'll spare you my musings. In practice, the Act seems to nudge people, who *can* afford the risk, toward buying major medical insurance along with a ***Health Care Savings Account (HSA)***. In practice, it makes middle income people who can afford it, self-insure *some* of their health care risk. At the same time, if you cannot afford to self-insure, it pushes you into Medicaid and subsidized HMO plans.

One impetus for HSAs is that costs have been driven up in part because the patient doesn't have a reason to care about cost. We've all gotten those "This is not a Bill" statements that explains what was billed to the insurance company, "Whoa, they billed $10,000 to the insurance company for that night in the hospital? The poor sods, I guess I got my premium's worth." If you knew you had to pay for the bill, then you are going to at least hesitate before using medical care. Again, I'm going to pass on editorializing whether or not this is the best approach.

If we can help it, my wife and I don't let our family drift into a situation we don't like. In 2015, we bit the bullet and changed our insurance to a major medical plan coupled with an HSA. If you aren't eligible for Medicare yet, this may be something to consider.

For us, having a major medical policy was about $300 cheaper per month while only exposing us to a maximum cost of $500 per month (i.e. $6,000 per year in financial exposure). At the same time we also opened an HSA and maxed out the contributions. We felt that this risk and opportunity to save up more money was worth it. In 2017, a family is allowed to contribute pre-tax dollars (similar taxation as a Traditional IRA) up to $6,650. An individual can contribute up to $3,350. Once the account has built up enough, you can invest the money in the stock market. Obviously my cup of tea.

In theory, if we didn't have any medical expenses, in one year of maxing out contributions to the HSA we'd have enough in the account to meet our worst case annual out-of-pocket deductible—which is $6,000 for our whole family.

If you continue to have good health and don't need the HSA money, then it would keep growing and eventually you could roll it into a retirement account. If your family on average used only $1,000 per year of the account and the other $5,650 keeps supplementing it, the account could conceivably grow to more than $1,000,000 at retirement.

It's important to note that before funding your HSA, you need to have at least your full deductible in cash in case you have a medical problem before you build up the HSA balance.

I feel that I should also note that generally my wife and I have been using more of the HSA than I originally estimated—partly because we are able to use it for more medical services that would otherwise not be deductible at all. If you are thinking of doing this, I would encourage you to look at the list of eligible medical expenses. It is surprisingly loose.

Getting, Ummm, A Little *Too* Creative with your Taxes

The American tax system is a strange beast. It makes everyone accountants at some level, while largely relying on the honor system. This system is occasionally checked through IRS audits, but these are relatively rare.

Inevitably, this cultivates citizens who sometimes get a little too creative with their taxes. In helping people with their money, I've seen many things. My stance has always been to maintain 100% confidentiality and be entirely free of judgment. I will however give some insight on what I have seen other people experience.

The Difference Between Tax Write-Offs and "Aggressive" Tax Write-Offs

The IRS makes a very specific list of what you can write-off. There is *much less* grey area than anyone would care to admit. I've heard people use the word "aggressive" to talk about their write-offs. This is a euphemism.

Earlier in my career I was a business banker and did loans to small business owners. I once did a loan for a guy who was living in a half million dollar house, driving a luxury car, and his taxes said that he only received $22,000 in annual income. His income was less than the sum of his mortgage payments.

Truth be told, those taking aggressive write-offs are rolling the dice that they won't be audited. My guess is that it's highly unlikely that anything being called "aggressive" would pass an IRS audit. I once had another small business owner confide that they'd be out of business if they ever got audited. My guess is that this is pretty widespread. The IRS's guess is 17%.

What to Expect When You're Expecting an Audit

Be brave and face the brutal facts. Here's what to expect in IRS audits. 2014 audits (on 2013 taxes) is the most current year that we have complete data on the subject. Out of the 190,0000,000 tax returns filed, the IRS audited 1,400,000 of them (or 0.7%). They also audited 1.3% of business tax returns. Of those 1,400,000 audits, only 400,000 were field audits (where they come to your house). This is a near-term low point in audit rates. This is mostly because of budget cuts at the IRS. I can't imagine it would keep going that way. At some point, some intelligent person will see the irony of (1) the government not having funds or (2) cutting funds from the agency that raises funds.

What to expect:

1. Roughly 70% of audits are through the mail or by phone. Some of my clients have brought these letters in to me. Sometimes they've keyed in the wrong number on their 1099. Sometimes they sold a security with a missing cost basis. They simply ask for documentation showing that your number is right or to amend your return. Amendments will result in either a refund or additional tax payment.

2. They can audit you up to seven years back, but generally it will be the most recent return. However, if that audit throws up a bunch of red flags, expect them to dig.

3. Just because you're audited doesn't mean you did something wrong or that there was an error. Sometimes it's just random. The three ways that you're likely to get audited are:
   a. Random
   b. Mismatched documents
   c. A related tax return gets called into an audit (such as your business or a partnership)

4. The IRS is much nicer than their fearsome reputation. If you are audited, they are instructed to treat you with respect and confidentiality. They will explain everything to you. You have the right to appeal, and the right to bring representation with you.

Things that reduce the chances of an audit:

1. Have your return prepared by a CPA or tax professional (not signed off on by you personally).

2. Double check your numbers. When you have a brokerage account, bank account, real estate transaction, income from nearly anything, you get a 1099, 1098, K-1, or W2. What you see on the form is exactly what gets reported to the IRS electronically. Keying in the wrong number sends up red flags.

3. Report the real numbers. Sounds crazy, I know. The IRS has algorithms to flag what is a realistic amount of deductions, income, etc. If you report $22,000 in income and deducted a $10,000 charitable contribution, this turns on the flashing sirens at the IRS headquarters. I like to imagine the headquarters as the last scene of Raiders of the Lost Ark with endless boxes and crates.

4. E-File. This is how they want you to file. It's much easier to avoid errors, yet about 33% of returns are still filed in physical form. The IRS reports that 21% of physical tax returns have errors, versus only 0.5% of electronically filed returns.

5. Don't use round numbers when you estimate deductions. $1,012 and $987 look more real than $1,000.

6. File on time and pay what you owe.

Also beware that if you are reporting a net operating loss for a business, your odds of an audit go way up. If you have been truthful and kept good records, an audit is nothing to fear.

I should say that there is a lot of fraud done in the name of the IRS—as in people posing as the IRS. Everyone has some fear of this powerful agency. If you get a call from someone saying they're from the IRS, barking at you to pay taxes, don't. A phone call from the IRS will nearly always be preceded by a letter in the mail. Warnings from the IRS arrive *long* before they start getting grumpy with you. Things can be pretty sluggish at the IRS and there's usually a pretty good lag time between an audit and a bill. Also, the IRS will *never* contact you by email.

The Proverbial Swiss Bank Account

Come on, you've seen too many cheesy '80s movies about white collar crime. This is a real thing that people do, but I'm not going to encourage it here. Switzerland (and the Cayman Islands) have ironclad privacy laws that create a barrier against subpoenas and searches. This attracts a lot of foreign assets, some of them nefarious, some of them people trying to protect their money from their unstable government back home. These protections do not hold up in the case of crimes. It ain't the '80s anymore, so stop asking me about these things or I'll have to send you to bed without your cocaine.

Working with a Tax Advisor

As I wrote this chapter, and even this entire book, I constantly refrained from elaborating. My goal is understanding, not comprehensive knowledge. I'm horrified at the thought of someone trying to do any of this without getting quality professional help. There are so many moving parts and the IRS gets rather cantankerous if you do it wrong.

As I've said over and over again, the greatest value I've provided to clients is usually when I say, "You *really* don't want to do that." My guess is that tax advisors say the same thing. This is why there is a massive difference between someone who is *advising* you on your taxes versus someone who is merely *preparing* your taxes. Besides, keep in mind that the payments you make to tax and investment advisors (including managed money fees) are tax deductible.

Just like hiring an investment advisor, a tax professional is big-mistake insurance.

When you hire any professional, there's a very wide range in what you get. With no fear of redundancy here: always work with people who *actively advise* you. Don't work with an order taker, work with an order *giver*. You are hiring your boss.

Summary

I'm not shy to say it: I don't like our tax system. I think it's weird and inefficient that we all have to be accountants (or pay someone to be) once per year. I think there has to be a better, more efficient way for us to do this as a society. But we must embrace "what is." From a financial planning standpoint, taxes are about maximizing the benefits of the system you are in—and minimizing your taxation.

Those of you familiar with these tax methods will know that there are exceptions to nearly everything we've talked about. There also many more details and nuances that I've chosen to skip over. It is my assumption and certainly my advice that you get professional tax help.

Endnotes

1   Source: U.S. Department of Education, National Center for Education Statistics. (2015). Digest of Education Statistics, 2013 (NCES 2015-011), Chapter 3.

2   Source: Tax Policy Center, Taxable Estate Tax Returns as a Percentage of Adult Deaths, Selected Years of Death 1934–2011. http://www.taxpolicycenter.org/taxfacts/content/pdf/deaths.pdf

No book can give you
personalized advice,
so run your situation by
someone who will.

The whole is greater than the sum of its parts.

Aristotle

Benediction

People ask me what "Wealth by Virtue" means. I have always taken it to mean two things. First, I believe that the most probable path to wealth is virtuous. Obviously, plenty of people collect ill-gotten gains, but I believe that the virtues of patience, steadfastness, humility, moderation, perseverance, faith, and optimism, applied to finances, make wealth almost inevitable. They certainly grow wealth relative to the resources at hand.

The second meaning of wealth by virtue is the need to maintain a virtuous perspective. Globally speaking, if you own a toilet, you are wealthy. Ever since I was a child, I've felt that I won the lottery to be born an American. As I've aged and traveled, although my childlike awe has matured, I still believe this. A global perspective helps me recognize that I've been given a massive leg up in life. I know that if you took my same brain and abilities and put them in the body of someone in a remote village in a developing country, there's no way I would reach where I reached in America. The wealth and success we achieve in life owes the majority of credit to the society and community in which we were born. There is no such thing as self-made wealth, and it is unforgivable arrogance to think otherwise. An enormous portion of success in America stems from a societal boost that simply isn't afforded to all people in the world. This realization should breed a virtuous perspective, and a sense of gratitude. Recognizing your good fortune creates empathy for those without it. It costs nothing to regard your wealth from a global vantage point.

This virtuous perspective of wealth must also reach our families and relationships. My mind goes back to Mr. Tonlin, the man with four million dollars in the bank where I used to work. I can still see the look of sorrow of a man who, though he hadn't lost a penny, lost all the value of his fortune the moment he lost his wife. I assume that his virtues of discipline and frugality enabled him to build his millions, but the virtue of perspective came to him at the end of his journey.

The mistakes we make in the pursuit of wealth can sometimes be quantified in currency and numbers. The most painful ones have nothing to do with our balances.

Although I've repeatedly said not to worry about the things you can't control, I know that it's hard. For me, I worry that the advice I've given you will only be applied in pieces and not as a comprehensive whole. I worry that in my advocating of a 100% equity portfolio or to invest, instead of paying down your mortgage, you set up the system and then forget to stay steadfastly in the market, despite your panic, when it drops horrifically. There are so many moving parts where investing can go wrong.

I believe that because of these complications, people need advisors. That is also why I believe that everyone who takes their financial security seriously must have a financial plan. The Six Areas of Finance have internal and inter-connected parts that must work in compliment. A plan is the only thing that will tie together an unquantifiable real life and a complicated financial system. A plan raises the red flags. It tells you how your finances are missing or uncoordinated.

I believe that there is an upper limit for "do it yourself" financial planning. Financial planning is much more than goals and money. As a financial author, I will always be the first to say that the best real world answers are not found in books. A book won't notice destructive portfolio holdings. Financial planning software is abundant and sometimes free, but software will never have a conversation with you about your fears. Software may tell you that you need legal planning, but it isn't going to hold you accountable to re-titling the deed of your house so that your family doesn't miss out on a huge step up in cost basis. We are accelerating our reliance on artificial intelligence, but for the time being, it takes a human to tell a human to suppress unhealthy biological instincts. In my experience, people who create their own financial plans look at them for a season and eventually never again.

There is always the math answer and the real world answer. Right now, I hope you are at an apex of financial motivation. You may recognize a lot of financial matters you need to address, perhaps even urgently. However, if you are like me, as you finish this, you probably already know which book you will read next. Before you move on, I want you to take a moment and consider where you are right now. Ask yourself, "What specific areas do I need to improve, develop, change, or explore?"

We've learned that a typical retirement lasts around 30 years. We've also learned that over the course of a 30-year retirement, prices typically rise 2–3 times. We all share the central fear that at one point we will desperately need money and not have it. In retirement, this comes down to the monolithic question, "Will your money outlive you, or will you outlive your money?" In my experience, most people don't know the answer.

My mission is to help people not only answer this question, but to answer it with a wealth-optimized outcome.

My goal in writing this book was to paint a comprehensive picture that, as far as I could tell, has never been painted before. Selflessly, I wrote the book because I felt that it needed to exist. Selfishly, I wrote the book as a beacon to those who want to work with someone like me.

Please consider this your invitation. I don't know what level of exposure this book will have, nor what level of attention this open invitation will get. I will say that it is my goal to serve anyone who wants help and accountability. At times, we've had to wait-list people while we created capacity, but my professional goal is to always provide a home for this style of comprehensive advice.

As I write this, the stock market has enjoyed a bizarrely long bull run. Secretly, I had hoped the market would experience a significant drop just in time for this book to come to print so that it could serve as a voice of calm and reason amidst the storm. Instead, I'm in the regrettable position of publishing a bullish book, possibly on the cusp of a long overdue bearish market—that, to be clear, is not a prognostication, just a statistical inevitability. I also write this in the context of a myriad of political scandals and what feels like a growing global ideological conflict. While I have a hobby of mocking the overuse of terms like "unprecedented" and "literally," when you read the headlines it feels like we are literally living in unprecedented times. But, there is, as always, a strong echo of the past. While the turmoil of our nation feels new, it's just a remake of movies we've all seen before. As I look at the present, just like anyone, it is easy to lose sight of humanity's long-term optimistic narrative. It is easy to tell yourself that this time is different and that the future may not follow the past.

There's no shame in feeling this way. Fear is part of living. Humans have gotten to where we are because of our attentiveness to our fears and present day discomforts. However, your most probable path to wealth is to utterly ignore the headlines of the present. You will never have any difficulty convincing yourself to not have faith in the future. Your greatest challenge will be to override your fears and behave as though the future is bright, regardless of how the present feels.

The core of my message is to withhold the comforts of today, both emotional and financial, to increase the probability of greater comforts tomorrow. Volatility, frugality, and scary headlines may never be comfortable, but enduring them is much more comfortable than running out of money in old age. When you subscribe to optimism, outsiders see naiveté. However, long-term optimism is what history teaches us. If wisdom is built on experience, the wisest choice is an applied faith in the future.

Thank You

To the University of Colorado, thank you for generously letting me use your vast research facility. Thank you for your hospitality, helpfulness, and for paying for expensive data subscriptions that enabled me to give such a long-term perspective of the capital markets.

To my favorite government organizations, it is without irony that I would like to thank the Bureau of Labor Statistics, Census Bureau, Federal Deposit Insurance Corporation, Bureau of Economic Analysis, U.S. Department of Commerce, National Oceanic & Atmospheric Association, Federal Reserve Board, and Internal Revenue Service. I would not have tried writing this book if your raw data wasn't so easily and publicly available, at my favorite price: free. To these precious public servants, I would like to say that the next time your eyes glaze over staring at data, please know that there's one man out there who thinks you're a rock star.

To my editor Christopher Benz, the book's greatest cheerleader and advocate. The readers have you to thank for making this digestible and not a jumble of verbal hieroglyphics. Thank you for humoring my unusual, if not stubborn, approach to publishing and for seeing the vision along with me. I hope you are proud of the work we've created.

Ron Carson, Nick Murray, Rahn Anderson, Kit Culver, Jonathan Hammond, Joe Medrano, Kati Standefer, Jules Ohman, Gabi Hill, and Juan Fuentes. Your mark is all over this book.

To my childhood friends Ryan Lewis, Christopher Belitz, Kelly Heaney-Romero, and Roxanne Anderson. What a lottery it is to have four of the smartest, most talented people I know also be people that I've known longer than my memories.

I particularly need to thank Ryan, one of the country's leading mathematicians. You left me in the intellectual dust long ago. As I wrote this book, all along the way you have been my ballast for making my analysis fair and truthful. You are the most honest human I know, which combined with your superhero mathematical abilities made you invaluable, both as a resource and a conscience.

To my extended family, thank you for defining me, reminding me who I am, and being the collective embodiment of my highest aspirations. You are my greatest treasure.

To my dear cousin Katie Gordon-Motwani, the first person to whom I mused this idea for a book. Thank you for urging me to write it.

To my brothers Edwin and Todd, there is nothing like being the youngest of three boys to help you maintain perspective on where you are in the universe. You were generous to me and always treated me as your equal—even if I wasn't.

To my parents Pete and Suzanne Gordon, who taught me never to be afraid, to work hard, and to always tell the truth. I think the older you get, the more you realize how much your parents have done for you and how impossible it would be to express your thanks.

To my four children Grae, Finneas, Fyetka, and Archimedes, in times when I've found the world unreasonable, you are always my reasons. I'm so proud of the virtuous people you are and it is the thrill of my life to see you blossom. When you have children of your own, you will enjoy the unusual experience of seeing someone at all ages, all at once. When I look at you, I see the sweep of your lives—as cooing babies and as young adults. Grae, you amaze me. I appreciate how you've always valued family and relationships. I admire your wisdom, determination, and the passion you've always had to be your own person and to write your own story. Finneas, my curious boy, you are a brilliant person and have a unique talent for looking to the future. You have a brilliant and dilligent mind that will discover and understand great things. Fyetka, I often tell you that the moment you were born, the nurse cried because she had never seen such a beautiful baby. You are a beautiful soul who creates beautiful things. I love how you approach the world with patience and with vision. You are an observer and an artist. It is your character that will lead others to see the world in new ways through your art. Archimedes, you have a smile bigger than your name. You have always been perceptive beyond your years. You have an emotional intelligence that I've never seen in a child. I admire your hard work, steadfastness, and focus to meet your goals. I love you, my four sweet muffins.

And to my wife Makendra, you understand me more than I ever intended to be understood. Thank you for putting up with my eccentricities and obsessive pursuits. You amaze me in your ability to create harmony. You show love to strangers and are sensitive and serving when those around you need love and care. The kids are immensely fortunate to have you as their Maky. You make everything beautiful and pour love into the precious details of life. It doesn't hurt that you are quite easy on the eye. Thank you for your encouragement as I wrote this, believing in the importance of the work, and your compassion for my sleepless nights and mindless days. I love you.